DATE DUE

AP 7 '97			

DEMCO 38-296

Also by Felipe Fernández-Armesto

The Canary Islands After the Conquest
Before Columbus
The Spanish Armada
Barcelona: A Thousand Years of the City's Past
Columbus
General Editor, The Times Atlas of World Exploration
Columbus on Himself
Edward Gibbon's Atlas of the World
Editor, The Times Guide to the Peoples of Europe
Editor, The European Opportunity
Editor, The Global Opportunity

MILLENNIUM

A History of the Last Thousand Years

FELIPE FERNÁNDEZ-ARMESTO

SCRIBNER

NEW YORK   LONDON   TORONTO   SYDNEY   TOKYO   SINGAPORE

CHARLES SCRIBNER'S SONS
Simon & Schuster Inc.
Rockefeller Center
1230 Avenue of the Americas
New York, NY 10020

First Charles Scribner's Sons Edition 1995
Published by arrangement with Transworld Publishers Limited

SCRIBNER and design are
trademarks of Simon & Schuster Inc.

Designed by Irving Perkins Associates

Manufactured in the United States of America

10 9 8 7 6 5 4 3 2 1

Library of Congress Cataloging-in-Publication Data

Fernández-Armesto, Felipe.
    Millennium : a history of the last thousand years / Felipe Fernández-Armesto.
        p.   cm.
    Includes bibliographical references and index.
    1. World history.   I. Title.
    D20.F36   1995
    909—dc20   95-18899   CIP
    ISBN 0-684-80361-5

It is the dead who govern. Look you, man, how they work their will upon us! Who have made the laws? The dead! Who have made the customs that we obey and that form and shape our lives? The dead! And the titles to our lands? Have not the dead devised them? If a surveyor runs a line he begins at some corner the dead set up; and if one goes to law upon a question the judge looks backward through his books until he finds how the dead have settled it—and he follows that. And all the writers, when they would give weight and authority to their opinions, quote the dead; and the orators who preach and lecture—are not their mouths filled with words that the dead have spoken? Why, man, our lives follow grooves that the dead have run out with their thumbnails!

M. Davisson Post, *Uncle Abner*

– El Aleph?, repití.
– Sí, el lugar donde están, sin confundirse, todos los lugares del orbe, vistos desde todos los ángulos . . .
Traté de razonar.
– Pero . . . no es muy oscuro el sótano?
– La verdad no penetra en un entendimiento rebelde. Si todos los lugares de la tierra están en el Aleph, ahí estarán todos los luminarios, todas las lámparas, todos los veneros de luz.
– Iré a verlo inmediatamente.

J. L. Borges, *El Aleph*

"The Aleph?" I echoed.
"Yes, the place where all the places of the world meet without mingling, beheld from every possible angle at once. . . ."
I tried to make sense of it.
"But isn't the cellar very dark?"
"Truth never penetrates an unwilling mind. If all the places of the earth are in the Aleph, then all sources of illumination, all lamps, all veins of light are there."
"I shall go and look at once."

CONTENTS

NOTE ON NAMES

In the English-language editions of this book, names are given in the forms thought most likely to be recognizable to most readers. Those transliterated from non-Roman alphabets are not therefore treated consistently, and the diacritical marks demanded by rigorous systems are omitted unless necessary to avoid ambiguity.

PREFACE

I have a vision of some galactic museum of the distant future in which diet Coke cans will share with coats of chain mail a single small vitrine marked "Planet Earth, 1000–2000, Christian Era." The last decade of our millennium may be under-represented, because so much of our significant trash will have biodegraded into oblivion; but material from every period and every part of the world, over the last thousand years, will be seen by visitors as evidence of the same quaint, remote culture: totem poles and Tompion clocks, Netsuke ivories and Nayarit clays, bankers' plastic and Benin bronzes. The distinctions apparent to us, as we look back on the history of our thousand years from just inside it, will be obliterated by the perspective of long time and vast distance. Chronology will fuse like crystals in a crucible, and our assumptions about the relative importance of events will be clouded or clarified by a terrible length of hindsight.

This problem of perspective seems painful to me as, from my vantage point in Oxford, I contemplate the past. In the University of Oxford, for instance, Cambridge is beheld as a strange and alien place where people leave their napkins behind them when they adjourn for dessert and where colleges are run by small all-purpose committees called "councils," instead of by their governing bodies. Yet such differences, of absorbing interest to members of the two universities, seem negligible to those outside. In a fairly recent survey of Japanese businessmen's opinions about world centres of learning, Oxford and Cambridge counted as one. Distinctions diminish with emotional, as with physical, distance. To take another Oxford example, Marx, Engels, and Lenin were formerly treated as "one" option by detached examiners in political thought, whereas to their adherents the subtle shading of their works is a matter of passionate concern and of dogmatic squabbles.

In this book I want to try to combine at least two uneasily compatible points of view: to see the millennium from an imaginary distance, with detachment, as a future age might see it, "in the round," with unifying themes and an overarching character; and also to exploit the advantages of an in-

11

sider, to detect the diverse and monitor the mercurial—to savour the differences from place to place and the changes over time. The result, I hope, will be to suggest that this really has been "our" millennium and that the societies in which we live, and what little common culture we possess, as we enter the third millennium of our era have been the products of the last thousand years of experience. Although our way of counting time is conventional, dates divisible by ten do, in practice, command enormous power to arrest attention and stimulate the imagination. Though the British National Heritage Secretary has announced that the next millennium will begin on 1 January 2001, both the Royal Albert Hall in London and the Rainbow Room, on top of Rockefeller Center's flagship building in New York, were engaged for New Year's Eve, 1999, twenty-five years in advance; as I write in 1993, most of London's top hotels are already fully booked for the same evening and "the Millenium [sic] Society of London and New York," the *Daily Mail* reports, "is planning a party at the Pyramids."

The habit of thinking in terms of decades and centuries induces a self-fulfilling delusion, and the way people behave—or, at least, perceive their behaviour—really does tend to change accordingly. Decades and centuries are like the clock cases inside which the pendulum of history swings. Strictly speaking, a new millennium begins every day and every moment of every day; yet the approach of the year 2000 makes the present a peculiarly—indeed, an uniquely—good time for taking stock of our last thousand years of history, asking where they have led us and wondering where we go from here. We ought to take the opportunity to look closely at this millennium of ours and to characterize it for ourselves, before the initiative passes to the galactic museum-keepers of the future—stowing, perhaps, with unimpassioned discretion, artefacts unearthed, through mind-boggling technology, by humanoid archaeologists with queer-shaped heads.

The subject of this book is the fate of civilizations, defined (in some prominent cases) by seas: the shifts of initiative from the China Seas and the Mediterranean, the hegemony of the Atlantic, the cultural counter-invasion from the Pacific. Almost daily, while I was doing some work on the book in London, I walked past the starting-point of the Prologue—a site symbolic of the reversal of fortunes, where Madame Prunier's restaurant once stood on a conspicuous corner of a grand London street, dispensing without alloy the great tradition of French food, civilizing the barbarians from the palate downwards. Today a Japanese restaurant has colonized the spot. The tide of empire has been rolled back by a wave of Pacific seaweed and raw fish. "The Rise of the Pacific" has become a cliché, and no one wants another book about it; but it has to be included here, as a final example of the shifting initiatives of our millennium.

In the background of this enormous story, I have tried to speckle the broad canvas with a pointillist technique, picturing the past in significant details rather than bold strokes or heavy impasto. Western world dominance, which books on world history usually try to describe or "explain," is seen in what follows as neither foreordained nor enduring; I argue that it was later, feebler, and briefer than is commonly supposed. Therefore, more space is given to the rest of the world.

The depth of coverage is not meant to be even: the landscape of this book is of snowdrifts and thin ice. If the world cannot be comprehensively covered, the material is—I hope—justly distributed, according to a novel bias in favour of the unusual, which helps to even the score. The principles of selection and presentation are explained and justified in the Prologue, after which:

PART ONE: THE SPRINGS OF INITIATIVE starts with a conspectus of some of the discrete worlds of a thousand years ago. Chapters Two to Five look in turn at each of four major civilizations between the eleventh and fifteenth centuries—centuries of crises and survival for China, of total refashioning for Islam, of forged consciousness and fitful growth for western Christendom, and of eclipse and revival for eastern Christendom. By a variety of dates in the fifteenth century, all these civilizations can be characterized as coiled for long-range expansion.

In PART TWO: THE SPRINGS UNCOILED, the "age of European expansion" is seen to have been launched not into a vacuum but into an emulous world already full of aggressive competitors. Chapter Six deals with dynamic states in Africa and the Americas in what we think of as the late middle ages. Chapters Seven to Ten return to the expansion of the civilizations identified in Part One: in conquest, colonization, evangelization, and trade, contenders from all over the world were numerous, and Europeans, it is argued, got only slightly ahead of the rest.

PART THREE: THE ATLANTIC CRISIS tries to show that the "Atlantic civilization" gradually created by European expansion from the sixteenth century, despite its enormous potential, was extremely brittle for its first three hundred years; but over the same period of time a shift of resources helped to ensure that when the crisis of Atlantic civilization was over, the world faced a brief, uneasy spell of western supremacy. Chapter Eleven charts the creation and crisis of the Atlantic world; Chapter Twelve describes changes in the world distribution of resources, especially in terms of population, technology, and the natural environment. Chapter Thirteen traces the reestablishment of Atlantic unity in the nineteenth and early twentieth centuries by mass migration, trade, and military alliances. Chapter Fourteen is about the political and cultural consequences of Atlantic supremacy, the reach and limitations of the world empires of western states.

In PART FOUR: THE TWIST OF INITIATIVE, Chapter Fifteen, on the ideological undermining of western supremacy, is followed, in Chapter Sixteen, by an exploration of some "local difficulties" which have weakened the hold of the west in the twentieth century, including the world wars and the breakup of the Soviet Union—seen here as enfeebling the west, potentially, by removing a common enemy. After a review of some casebook failures of Atlantic societies in Chapter Seventeen, Chapter Eighteen is about decolonization and what I call "counter-colonization" by the former victims of western imperialism. The endurance and resurgence of Islam is the subject of Chapter Nineteen.

In PART FIVE: THE PACIFIC CHALLENGE, we are seen to be heading back to a world balance similar to that of a thousand years ago, when the initiative in human affairs belonged on Pacific coasts. Meanwhile, a process of cultural colonization-in-reverse—accumulated over the last two hundred years— is challenging the dominance of Atlantic tradition. Chapters Twenty to Twenty-two cover modernizing societies in east Asia and the developed "White Pacific." Chapter Twenty-three traces the oriental influences on western thought and science up to our own time. I have succumbed to a deplorably obvious temptation and added, in an epilogue, a short sketch of a possible future.

Particular debts for information and guidance are recorded in some of the endnotes. But this has been a work of resolute self-isolation, written without research assistants or specialist readers. Only Jim Cochrane and Bill Rosen, generous editors, have seen the whole of it. And no one else except my wife, Lesley, has been asked to respond to more than small patches. Some fundamental ideas were tried out in discussion at the Conference of Anglo-American Historians at the Institute of Historical Research and at an NEH Institute on Maritime History at the John Carter Brown Library, Brown University, both in 1992; I presented some points more formally in talks given or papers read in Oxford during 1993 to the St. John's College History Society, the Past and Present Historical Society, and a Colloquium on Historical Ecology at the Maison Française. I am grateful to those who were my guests or hosts or who contributed comments and suggestions on those occasions, especially David Abulafia, Pascal Acot, Rob Bartlett, Roland Bechmann, Alexandra Bollen, Alistair Crombie, James Seay Dean, Norman Fiering, Robert Finlay, Robin Grove-White, Robert Hall, John Hattendorf, George Holmes, Barry Ife, Martin Jones, Maurice Lévy, Ross McKibbin, Patrick O'Brien, Carla and William Phillips, Seymour Phillips, David Quinn, Jeremy Robinson, Joan-Pau Rubiés, Peter Russell, Haskell Springer, Joachim Steiber, Zacharias Thundy, Christopher Tyerman, Charles Verlinden, and George Winius. None of these had any chance to correct the errors of fact, formulation, or judgement which I am bound to have made and which I hope readers will help me to put right.

F.F.A.

Oxford—Providence, Rhode Island—Oxford, 1991–93

Prologue
PRUNIER'S REVISITED

*Micro-historians who atomise the larger problems out of existence con-
demn themselves forever to the status of mini-historians.*

J. H. ELLIOTT, *NATIONAL AND COMPARATIVE
HISTORY*

The little things are infinitely the most important.

A. CONAN DOYLE, *THE ADVENTURES OF
SHERLOCK HOLMES*

I had been here before. Memories recorded by children's eyes are usually
surprised by the way places seem to shrink, but this corner restaurant, in
the elegant London street that joins Piccadilly to Saint James's Palace,
seemed, if anything, to have got bigger. Curiosity dispersed the inhibitions
appropriate to middle age as I squashed my nose against the smoked glass
to peer inside, with the reawakened shamelessness of a nine-year-old. The
room I remembered had been tall, narrow, and opulent, hung with crystal
chandeliers. The walls had been padded with richly brocaded banquettes in
elusive, creamy colours. On tables fat with billowing napery, heavy cutlery,
lavishly moulded, sat like lines of silver braid on soldiers' shoulders. My
chubby little fingertips had tingled and twitched but, abashed by so much
unaccustomed luxury, had touched nothing until reassured by the lulling
murmur of the waiter's French.

The site was still the same, with the entrance still bobbed at an odd angle
to the street, as if the restaurant were backing deferentially away from the
presence of the palace. Inside, too, there were undercurrents of continuity:
the place still seemed hushed, comfortable, restrained, expensive. But noth-

ing visible was unchanged. The room had become low and broad, the tables angular, the napery thin and almost bare, the colours austere, uncompromising. And the staff, who darted about nervously with crisp, jerky movements, were now Japanese.

The menu still seemed to favour fish. Madame Prunier, who in her day had made the restaurant at this address a revered temple of *haute cuisine,* had liked the refined flavours and textures as a canvas for her art; she would surely have been willing to taste the intriguing delicacies of the new menu, like *sushi* and *sashimi* or octopus with lobster stuffing. Her speciality was *bouillabaisse,* which for most gourmets has a hearty and provincial renown, but Madame Prunier's version of this dish was a jewel case of the treasures of the oceans of the world, in which rare crustacea of coral and pearl spilled from one's spoon into the casket's creamy, silky lining. For the rest, she served food in the tradition of Escoffier with ingredients gathered by grand gestures, swept into her kitchens with the imperial reach of the steamship era. Today you can order, on the same spot, a dish called Imperial tepanyaki, which combines raw fish with steak and shrimps, but it represents an imperialism of a different kind. The cuisine of Japan developed in an island empire, entire of itself, supplied in abundance only with fish and rice and, formerly, with the soy beans which the Japanese now import from the United States. Madame Prunier's cooking was nominally French but actually global—concocted with far-flung resources at the command of a world-hegemonic western élite.

In a daring coup of counter-colonization, her Japanese successor restaurant has occupied part of the home territory of a sometime white masterclass. The brown-brick, wrinkled brow of Saint James's Palace sags over a street dedicated to the home comforts of the rulers of a worldwide empire; here, in shops which survive, in some cases, from the imperial age, tourists bent on the re-creation of an historical experience can still fill their cellars and their humidors. Here they can be measured for handmade footwear, club blazers, and old school ties. Much of the rest of the street is lined with gentlemen's clubs, designed to make *realpolitik* seem civilized.

The Carlton Club, the presbytery of nineteenth-century conservatism, has exuded decorum since its foundation in 1832 by opponents of constitutional reform; but there are also survivals from Britain's pre-imperial period in the eighteenth century, when Saint James's Street was a raffish area for louche aristocrats to gamble or whore in. White's and Brooks's were only gradually sobered by nineteenth-century respectability, and Boodle's, with its "proverbial serenity," occupies the site of a disreputably sybaritic earlier club. Today, the frontier of gutter pleasures has been pushed north and east over Piccadilly Circus, where a thrown stone will hit another phenomenon of counter-colonization from the east.

Gerrard Street has become Tong Yahn Gai—even the street sign in Cantonese proclaims it Chinese People's Street—marked off by dragons' wing gates. London had an earlier Chinatown, much further east, formed, like the bigger examples in New York and San Francisco, in the nineteenth century, when white imperialism shunted labour across the globe; old Limehouse was a menacing wen where victims in Victorian crime novels vanished into the darkness down slimy stairways. At its most respectable, in the 1930s, it was the world of George Formby's voyeuristic laundryman, Mr. Wu. Gerrard Street, however, is evidence from a new era—a come-lately Chinese colony created since the mid-1960s by Chinese initiative alone. Its restaurants provide a huge and dispersed expatriate community with the amenities of southern Chinese teashops: aspiring entrepreneurs and ambitious workers do the rounds on Saturday mornings, exchanging potentially profitable news; from as far away as Manchester, waiters and cooks spend their days off here. The local cinemas, grocers, barbers, bookshops, cabbies, and solicitors supply the supplementary services which Cantonese speakers need to feel at home. Though the restaurants have all relaxed their unwelcoming attitude to non-Chinese, the gambling dens remain as extraterritorial paddies of ethnic purity, with bouncers as their frontier police.

Embedded in London with incongruity, the expensive seclusion of the Japanese restaurant and the demotic bustle of the Chinese street are evidence of how the world has changed in the last few decades of our millennium. The Japanese restaurant serves agents of business imperialism from the world's largest creditor nation and feeds European clients with tastes of a culture suddenly elevated to worldwide prestige. The Chinese street is an embodiment of popular colonialism, reversing the general direction of the imperial flow of recent history. In the 1980s, Hong Kong—the former home of many denizens of Gerrard Street—became the first colonial territory in the world to overturn the usual economic relationship with the occupying power: more investment flowed, by 1990, from Hong Kong to Britain than the other way round. As the end of our millennium approaches, the initiative is returning to where it lay a thousand years ago, on the shores of the Pacific.

By "initiative" I mean the capacity of some groups decisively to influence others—and, in particular, the ability of some peoples decisively to influence the rest of mankind—by generating and communicating ideas, creating or adapting technology, and undertaking exploration, colonization, or aggression. The increasing importance of initiative in shaping the world is a distinctive feature of the last thousand years of world history. So is the increasing momentum of its shifts from one culture to another. In the first millennium of our era, in a world riven into sundered cultures, initiative was hard to transmit. Pop archaeologists who propose far-fetched theories of cultural cross-fertilization by transoceanic migrants are figures of fun. We are practically certain about ascribing to China the source of many well-travelled technical innovations, but they were communicated slowly, by routes we can—in most cases—no longer reconstruct. Even the most frenzied aggression of that millennium—the Huns' in the fifth century and the Arabs' in the seventh—ran out of steam. The fate of the world did not depend on, say, the relative technical prowess of China, India, and Rome, as it does today on the relative potential of Atlantic and Pacific economies. Initiative has come to matter in our millennium in a way it never did before.

One way of characterizing a period is by comparing it with equivalent periods before and after. A history of the millennium before ours ought, by rights, to concentrate on China, which then contained—contrary to Gibbon's famous assertion—"the fairest part of the earth and the most civilised portion of mankind." The bulk of the world's population was found there, and from there radiated the effects of the most far-reaching conflicts and the most spectacular technical innovations. A thousand years ago, the balance of the world's resources was still weighted heavily—among prospectively competitive powers—in favour of China. The potential decisively to influence the rest of the world lay with the Chinese.

Yet in the course of our millennium the balance shifted, and that world-influencing role has been played by the also-rans of a thousand years ago. The first half of our millennium was characterized by the slow and fitful formation, consolidation, and expansion of cultures and civilizations which, at about the mid-point, came into contact or conflict. The second half started with a period of competition in expanding arenas. This seems to me to have lasted longer and to have been more keenly contested, among more competitors, than is generally acknowledged; but it gradually gave way to what now looks like a brief interval of domination by a western civilization, grouped around the Atlantic and reaching out from there to control, exploit, and shape the rest of the world.

In this book, "western supremacy" is presented as imperfect, precarious, and short-lived. As the end of the millennium draws on, it is already apparent that the preponderance of Atlantic civilization is over and that the initiative has shifted again, this time to some highly "developed," technically proficient communities of the Pacific seaboard, typified by California and Japan. They live under threat of extinction from war, ecological catastrophe, economic hypertrophy, or seismic upheaval, but, for the time being at least, the future lies with them. The sixteenth-century Spanish historian who argued that "imperium"—the capacity to command the world—had passed westward by divine decree throughout human history, through successive empires, before attaining its final resting place in Spain, failed to notice that there was more space down the line.

At one level, this book is an attempt to describe and explain these shifts of initiative. The rest of this introduction is about how I have gone about it: readers uninterested in conceptual problems or in the agonies of historical

methodology can skip the next few pages. Cosmic explanation—attractive
but glib—is eschewed here. In a lifetime largely spent in reading history
books, I have never met a determinist scheme which arises from the evidence or a model of change which does not sit on the subject like an ill-
fitting hat. In the chapters which follow, I propose that shifts of initiative
cannot be understood wholly or primarily in terms of the movement of resources, of quantifiable data, of cyclical conflicts, of patterns or laws, or of
the grinding structures of economic change. Mega-explanations, though
they may be interesting or culturally significant, are inherently unlikely to
be right. Except for occasional irony, I try to avoid historicist, deterministic,
and teleological language, which turns history into a theme park patrolled,
for example, by "the Rise of Capitalism" or "the Modern World," smilingly
welcoming readers to footling illusions like a giant Mickey Mouse. History
ought to be a zoo full of real creatures with the mythical beasts excluded;
in this book, merchants, industrialists, and financiers appear, but "Capitalism" is unmentioned, except in one or two straitly defined contexts with
strictly limited meaning. There are knights and peasants but no "Feudalism."

Each case has to be examined on its merits and each shift of initiative
understood in its own way. On the other hand, there is a thread in the
labyrinth: the relative performance of rival cultures depends on the self-
perceptions and mutual perceptions of the peoples concerned. History is
scattered with the debris of empires whose peoples talked themselves into
decline and of victories won by superior morale. The course of history is
influenced less by events as they happen than by the constructions—often
fanciful, often false—which people put on them. A shift of initiative ac-
quires force and substance, like the tree in Berkeley's quad, only when registered mentally. In writing this book I have tried consistently to ask myself
not, "Why did this or that change happen?" but "Why did people convince
themselves of the reality of this or that alleged change?"

When I confessed, with shuffled feet and downcast eyes, that I was trying to write a history of the world, a colleague I admire told me there was
no such thing—"only the histories of parts of it." Despite some brilliant attempts in recent years, world history remains a discipline in search of a
method. The world historian really needs the gift of the dervish in the
Thousand and One Nights who conferred the power of seeing all the world
at once, or the magic of Borges's Aleph, which the protagonist of the story
found in a cellar. The diameter "was only two or three centimetres, but the
whole of space was in it, without sacrifice of scale. Each thing was infinite
things because I could see it clearly from every perspective in the universe." Perhaps if one attained it, such omniscience would soon pall, but I
have assumed in writing this book that it is worth trying to imagine from
time to time what it would be like. Therefore, at intervals I climb the rig-

ging of the cosmic crow's nest and try to share with the reader the perspective of what I call the galactic museum-keepers of the future, seeing a planet entire, undifferentiated, and contemptibly small. I ought to admit at once that since the museum-keepers are my own invention, I have taken the liberty of ascribing to them rather more interest in our doings than they would probably have if they ever became enfleshed.

Unswamped by the illusion that we can see the world whole, we can also try to write world history in terms of the interaction between the units of study we call cultures and civilizations. This technique has behind it a long and respectable tradition, which almost all its practitioners have continued in reluctance or abandoned in disgust. I have followed it myself—in which I hope readers will recognize as a heavily modified form—in painful awareness of its limitations. Most attempts founder on the rocks of definition: there is no agreement about what a civilization is. In this book the term is used without connotations of value to mean a group of groups—or set of sets—who think of themselves as a civilization. Even this usage leaves unsolved problems of translation—identifying, that is, equivalent terms in different languages—and of scale. In practice, when I select a group of people for particular scrutiny, I rely on the guidance of what I think is common sense. History resembles a mosaic made by a monkey, but even this simian Clio can sometimes be caught working on the composition one patch at a time. When I stand back to distinguish the patches, I acknowledge implicitly that, looked at differently, they blend and blur and form other patterns. To use a distinguished historian's metaphor, in the "set of sets" of world history, the Venn diagrams overlap, shift, and continually expand and contract. Whenever I highlight some groups of people and some areas of the world for discrete treatment in this book—while dealing with others only comparatively or cursorily, or omitting them altogether—my criteria are of convenience, not of value.

If cultures and civilizations are the tectonic plates of world history, frontiers are the places where they scrape against each other and cause convulsive change. The reader of this book—if kind enough to get so far—will therefore find more, for instance, on the thirteenth century in Tunis than Paris, more on the sixteenth in Siberia than Moscow, more on the eighteenth in Sinkiang than Peking. The familiar landscapes, the smart city skylines of national histories, slip out of focus; instead we join settlers struggling to adapt in unexperienced environments, evangelists crossing barriers of communication, traders scrounging new markets, conquerors victimizing strange subjects. For purposes of world history, the margins sometimes demand more attention than the metropolis. Part of the mission of this book is to rehabilitate the overlooked, including places often ignored as peripheral, peoples marginalized as inferior, and individuals relegated to bit parts and footnotes. Indirectly, this is another way of piling up yet more metropolitan history because, in a sense, peripheries have little history of their own: what gets recorded and transmitted is usually selected according to the centres' criteria of importance. The Hsiung-nu are known only from Chinese annals. We would know little about the Ranquele Indians were it not for Colonel Mansilla's interest in them. Children, women, the socially underprivileged, the sick, the mad, and the ethnic minorities have had to wait for élite perceptions to change before getting historians of their own. This book is not meant to be a history of the unimportant but an attempt to approach what has been conventionally identified as important from fresh directions. Because importance is a relative term, this is also an opportunity to anticipate the importance that may be ascribed in future to hitherto neglected areas. It is impossible to be sure about what the galactic museum-keepers will pick out, but it will surely be a different selection from those made earlier.

In partial consequence, no canon of important events is respected in the pages which follow. To the galactic museum-keepers, events commonly invested with world-shattering importance—such as the English and American civil wars, the European wars of religion, the French and Russian revolutions—will look parochial. As the trends of our millennium are reassessed and the picture modified by the chance survivals and suppressions of evidence, encounters at Runnymede or Canossa will be eclipsed by hitherto undervalued happenings in Makassar or Timbuktu. In this book—where there seems little point in tiring the reader with what is conventionally important and therefore necessarily well known—I pull the unfamiliar into the front window while returning some favourite historical stock-in-trade to storage. There is little in what follows, for instance, on the Investiture Contest or the Hundred Years' War. The Renaissance is contemplated more from the perspective of Hungary than Tuscany, socialism from that of the United States rather than Russia. There is more about the Morocco of al-Mansur than the England of Elizabeth I. Louis XIV appears only to beg to be excused. This is the only mention of Frederick the Great. Bismarck's claims to inclusion have been urged on me by a friend but represent a Eurocentric temptation. I dwell instead on Okubo Toshimichi, who did a similar job and seems, in some ways, a comparable figure. I give no summary of the thought of Descartes, pay no tribute to the achievement of Goethe, say, or—rather more to my regret—of Mozart or Michelangelo. Omissions like these in favour of more obscure examples are not made for reasons of political correctness, and I had better say at once that I am a committed advocate of the traditional humanist curriculum for teaching history in schools and universities. But there is no place for "core content" here, where basic knowledge is assumed and where I aim to delight the reader with surprises.

I make a few simple but critical assumptions which have to be avowed: readers are entitled to examine in advance the ropes by which I propose to haul them across the vast and broken terrain of the last thousand years. First, history is like *Rashomon,* the well-known story by Akutagawa Ryunosuke in which seven witnesses describe a husband's murder from their respective standpoints. Mutually contradictory confessions are made by the wife in the case and the robber who raped her, while the ghost of the dead man, who perhaps speaks with the traditional authority of the ghost in the oriental detective story tradition, recalls the episode as suicide. The objective truth—though there is a sense in which it certainly exists—is indistinguishable, and the evidence is evidence only of the witnesses' states of mind. All historical sources are rays from equally glistening prisms. Even statistics are infected by the priorities of the compiler, and the only securely verifiable statements we can make are statements about the sources. Just as speed and time shrink or expand relative to the speed of the observer, so historical truth seems to twist itself into different shapes and guises according to the angle of approach. I admire (but do not endorse) Immanuel Wallerstein's maxim: "The past can only be told as it truly *is,* not *was.*"

It ought to be reckoned a virtue in an historian to relish, wallowingly, the beguiling contradictions of the evidence and to dodge and slip, as I try to do in this book, between multiple vantage points: the perspectives, for instance, of those who experienced the past as it happened; those who look back on it, revising and re-evaluating to suit the needs or justify the prejudices of their own time; and those like my galactic museum-keepers who will revise it again from a distance inaccessible to us or our predecessors. The aesthetic effect—if the technique could be skilfully applied—would be like a painting by Uccello in which objects vanish or bulk, foreshortened or looming, in unexpected patterns.

Second, history is chaotic—a turbulence which happens at random or in which the causes are often in practice impossible to trace. It happens fast, like a snake darting between stones, tracked in glimpses and coiling unpredictably. Even over a period of a thousand years, most genuine phenomena of long-term change, like topography and climate and biological evolution, are effectively almost static—with exceptions to be confronted in their place. History is a state of near-equilibrium, punctuated—like evolution, according to a current theory—by spasmodic change. Most of the long-term trends and long-term causes conventionally identified by historians turn out, on close examination, to be composed of brittle links or strung together by conjecture between the gaps. Perhaps the most conspicuous trend of historiography in the last generation has been the squashing by revisionists of what were previously thought to be long-drawn-out processes into ever shorter spells. The English Civil War, for instance—long held, by a faith compounded of partisanship and hindsight, to be the culmination of centuries of "progress" towards a teleological end—is now thought by most specialists to be best understood in the context of the two or three years immediately preceding its outbreak. The origins of the French Revolution and the First World War have been chopped short by similar blades. Economic historians tend to be committed to gradualism, but even the Industrial Revolution is now seen as shuddering to a start, or series of starts, rather than accumulating smoothly. The experience of changes—bewilderingly fast, barely predicted—in our own time has helped curtail the hunt for long-term trends: empires have vanished like snow in the river; industrialization has leaped to unlikely places with the speed of a computer virus; and ideological fashions have emulated the readiness with which hemlines rise and fall.

Third, history is a creative art, best produced with an imagination disciplined by knowledge of and respect for the sources. To me—though other standards, equally valid, may appeal more to other tastes—the test of a good history book is not so much whether the past is verifiably reconstructed and cogently expounded as whether it is convincingly imagined and vividly evoked. Better than by many professional practitioners, the enchantment of the subject was expressed by Doreen Grainger, a fourteen-year-old Black girl interviewed by a sociologist some sixteen years ago as I write. "What's important about history," she said, "is that you can sort of be alive when you weren't really alive." Adhering to that insight I try to provide not just a history of what happened but also of what it felt like and how it looked. This book is an attempt to write world history with more intimacy of detail, more intricacy of vision, and more vividness of imagery than is usually attempted in work of comparable scale and scope. I comb the beaches of the present for flotsam and jetsam from the past. I try to use antiquarian bric-à-brac—physical, sometimes friable remnants and fragments—and, where they survive, written sources which seem to me to capture real experience, rather as a geneticist might use fragments of DNA to clone the past or, at least, to evoke its semblance.

The history of early Ming China, for instance, is approached through a look at animals in the imperial menagerie; that of the eighteenth-century Spanish empire through the plants of the Madrid Botanical Garden. I enter late medieval Byzantium under the gates of the Church of Chora and the world of the Maya in the same period by plunging with the Diving God of Tulúm into the plasterwork waves that decorate a temple façade. Responding to the visible, palpable survivals from the past which still surround us releases—for those with appropriate sensibilities—delicious secretions of intellectual pleasure. It can also contribute to our sense of belonging in the hewn and fashioned spaces we have inherited, in ways of life and traditions of thought we feel we can understand. World history can therefore bring comfort as well as inspire awe, and help us face, with resignation or even relish, our cramped coexistence in the next millennium and our place in a shared vitrine of the galactic museum.

PART ONE

THE SPRINGS OF INITIATIVE

It was the last day of the 1999th year of our era. The pattering of the rain had long ago announced nightfall; and I was sitting in the company of my wife, musing on the events of the past and the prospects of the coming year, the coming century, the coming Millennium. . . . When I say "sitting," I do not of course mean any change of attitude such as you in Spaceland signify by that word; for as we have no feet, we can no more "sit" or "stand" (in your sense of the word) than one of your soles or flounders.

"A Square" [EDWIN A. ABBOTT], *FLAT-LAND: A ROMANCE OF MANY DIMENSIONS*

Chapter 1

DISCRETE WORLDS: SOME CIVILIZATIONS A THOUSAND YEARS AGO

The Empire of Sensibility—The Garden of Islam—The Divided Heaven—The Civilization of the Barbarians

THE EMPIRE OF SENSIBILITY

Like the palace cats', the eyes of the Lady Murasaki Shikibu were accustomed to the dark. The gloomy corridors of the vast complex of imperial buildings at Heian, where a wanderer could get waylaid or lost, were her home territory. The half-light in which Japanese court life was lived in the late tenth and early eleventh centuries concealed nothing from her stare, though the obscurity was deep enough to make stories of mistaken identity among lovers credible.

Her powers of observation produced *The Tale of Genji*, which has some claim to be the world's first novel: *Genji's* intricate realism, recorded with the restraint of a Jane Austen and the depth of reflection of a Proust, gave it in its day a popularity which it has never lost. It also makes it, as novels go, a work of unexcelled usefulness to historians, recalling faithfully the customs and values of a long-vanished world. Appearing like a modern serial, bit by bit, over many years, *Genji* became a part of the culture it described, titillating and tantalizing readers who vied for manuscripts of unread chapters, stimulating gossip, and reinforcing the peculiar ideals of Heian, ideals which elevated poetry above prowess, beauty above brawn, and which esteemed a sensitive failure more highly than a coarse success.

Genji was read by women together in the intimate seclusion of a palace full of secret recesses, as in this early twelfth-century illustration of a scene from Chapter Fifty (Azumaya, "The Eastern Cottage"). Hiding in her half-sister's apartments, Ukifune is having her hair dressed while amusing herself with illustrations of the tale which a servant reads her. The landscape-screens were magic windows on distant scenes, which the inmates of the court were condemned never to see at first hand by the sedentary conventions of their way of life. Earlier sequences of illustrations to *Genji* certainly existed but have not survived.

Murasaki was only one of a drawerful of courtly bluestockings. Fiction writing, poetry, diaries, and "pillow books" were all common forms of divertissement for rich and intelligent women, who were free of economic constraints yet barred from public life. Without ever describing herself, she noted what she claimed was others' perception of her: "pretty, yet shy; shrinking from sight; so wrapped up in poetry that other people hardly exist; spitefully looking down on the whole world." The assessment was only partly right. Murasaki's literary proclivities seem to have enhanced rather than displaced her interest in her fellow-courtiers; but her acuity could have been miscast as spite and her detachment mistaken for condescension. That *Genji* is virtually a *roman à clef* is hinted at by one of the characters, who confides how readers are inspired by "things both good and bad, which they have seen and heard happening to men and women and which they cannot keep all to themselves."

Murasaki made her observations from a privileged vantage point. In 1002 a plague left her a young widow at court. By 1005 she was in the household of the emperor's favourite consort, Shoshi. There she was courted, if her diary can be trusted, by the most powerful man in Japan, Shoshi's father, Fujiwara no Michinaga, "with his tap-tap-tap upon the shutters like the cry of the *kuina* bird." Though excluded by her sex from the political stage, Murasaki had a grand view from the balcony.

Her suitor, whom she despised as a drunken lecher, was brother-in-law to two emperors, uncle and father-in-law to another, uncle to one more, and grandfather to two. Puppeteer of emperors' womenfolk, informal arbiter of the succession, he was a classic mayor-of-the-palace or grand vizir figure who arrogated executive power to himself. Encumbered by ceremonial, emperors had to bid for real power by taking early retirement, usually in their twenties or early thirties. The household servants of the Fujiwara clan provided the empire with a working bureaucracy while the nominal officers of state were trapped in the trammels of ritual. Launched to power by an emperor's affection for his niece, Fujiwara secured his position when his main rival was disgraced in a brawl with an ex-emperor over a lady's favours. After the early and rapid deaths of three emperors in factional struggles, Fujiwara ruled through his grandson, Go-Ichijo (986–1022), elevated to the throne at the age of eight. The minister was borne up on a spiral of self-enrichment and enhanced power and left, according to one embittered voice, "not a speck of earth for the public domain."

With a small purse and a large seraglio, emperors were embarrassingly philoprogenitive. Imperial princelings demoted for reasons of economy were accommodated in the Minamoto clan, known as the Gen-ji, and this is the predicament of the hero in Murasaki's tale. Prince Genji is pre-eminent in every quality, but as a seducer he is nothing short of perfect; thus, though excluded from the throne that ought to have been his by merit, he is able to sire a race of emperors. His changing political fortunes form the backdrop of the book; yet it is not primarily a political novel but a chronicle of the loves and friendships of Genji and of the next generation of his family, a prefiguration of the soap opera in medieval Japan. The ruling irony lies not in Genji's reversal of the injustice of the succession but in the fact that his own heir turns out to be a product of cuckoldry.

Still, it is impossible to see Murasaki, with her contempt for Fujiwara's sexual overtures and her sympathy for the victims of dynastic manipulation, as other than the spokeswoman for the excluded brethren of a small but competitively riven political élite. This made her novel something of a *succès de scandale;* for its avid female readers it had a dorm-culture thrill, an anti-establishment tang. The "outs" of politics were consoled, in her world, by a system of values reminiscent of the British cult of the underdog and a sort of "Dunkirk spirit" that made a virtue of defeat. "The nobility of failure" was admired and sometimes deified in Murasaki's Japan.

An earlier loser in an anti-Fujiwara power struggle, whose example may have helped to inform the character of the fictional Genji, was Sugawara no Michizane, a scholar whom the ambitious emperor Uda selected to try to

In life, Sugawara no Michizane was the ideal hero for Heian, who used his exile to make a cult of contemplative leisure, extolled in Chinese verse of painstakingly refined wistfulness—reminiscent, for western readers, of Ovid's *Tristia*. After his death he haunted the court. On the occasion depicted here, he terrorized his enemies with thunder and lightning until a minister of the Fujiwara clan drove him off with a drawn sword.

break the Fujiwara monopoly of authority; but a Fujiwara *coup d'état* in the year 901 sent him into provincial exile—a fate quite as bad as death in the intensely urban world of the Japanese metropolitan élite—and reduced him to "mere scum that floats upon the water's face." For years he was supposed to wreak vengeance on the ruling clan from beyond the grave and was only appeased by the formal proclamation of his apotheosis by a Fujiwara government ninety years later. Against this sort of background, a gutless and anaemic hero like Genji could have romantic appeal, as if the character of Hamlet could have the connotations of James Bond.

Another element of Sugawara's story—the theme of supernatural blight and vengeful haunting—also pervades the atmosphere of *Genji*. The Japanese imagination in the tenth and eleventh centuries was alive with ghosts and demons: crude hobgoblins in lesser tales, personifications, in more sophisticated literature, of powerful emotions. In *The Demon of Rasho Gate* of 974, the authorities are baffled by the mysterious disappearance of several citizens of Heian, until a daring young man vows to patrol the danger zone. He is lulled by the beauty of a young girl who transforms herself into a hideous succubus. Escaping just in time, he severs her arm, which he keeps as a souvenir until it is carried off into the sky by the demon, who returns in disguise. In *Genji* the theme is more subtly handled but at least as strong. Genji's jealous mistress, the Lady Rokujo, projects a hatred so intense that it envenoms Genji's affairs with other women and, undiminished by the lady's death, withers and kills his best-loved girl, like the worm in the bud.

Murasaki's skill is such that she can interweave this sinister strand—crude warp of some primitive, rustic yarn—with the silken thread of her courtly tale, the soft stuff of a delicate comedy of manners. For Genji and his fellow-courtiers move with balletic grace, guided by a yearning for beauty, regulated by a hierarchy of rank, informed by refined sensibilities. Their ruling passion is Weltschmerz, and they are at their most admirable—their inventor admires them most—when they are saddened by fragile beauty or touched by the mutability of nature. The rules of rank in Heian make the Versailles of Saint-Simon seem like a free-for-all. Genji's son's dream was of the day when he would be able to discard the "hateful green robe" that signified his derogation to the sixth rank of the nobility. The emperor's cat was favoured with the status and adorned with the coiffure of a lady of middle rank. A nurse could tell by the timbre of a visitor's cough to what level of noblesse he belonged. Far more tension arises in the tale from the interplay of different levels of hierarchy than from the malign influence of Rokujo's ghost. "Sometimes," Genji observes, "people of high rank sink to the most abject positions; while others of common birth rise to be high officers, wear self-important faces, redecorate the insides of their houses, and think themselves as good as anyone." Genji's origins and misfortunes alike stemmed from what the court condemned as a *mésalliance* between an emperor and the daughter of a provincial official. The perils of courtship in the provinces dominate the prolongation of the tale into the generation after Genji's. Parvenues could inspire fear or mirth—the provincial clod patchily adjusted to court life is a stock comic character—while cases of decayed gentility could chill delicately nurtured palace spines: the chancellor's son who, out of favour in the capital, is a ragged laughing-stock; the "barefoot wandering minstrel the townspeople call The Justice's Miss," whose father was "a high official." In Murasaki's work, struggles for precedence could be deliciously derided: she satirized the emulous vice of "carriage quarrels" in which ladies' conveyances jostled one another in streets cluttered with status symbols at times of public spectacle. She makes fun of the palace dwellers banging their heads together and chipping their combs as they bounce over the sleeping policeman at the gate. This sort of humour thrilled precisely because it touched quarrels and contests of deadly earnest.

Even more than by their rank, Murasaki's characters establish their places in her world by expressions of sensitivity. Her male heroes are excited to love by exquisite calligraphy, a girl by the "careless dexterity" of a folded note. In the opinion of Sei Shonagon, the court's most accomplished expert on love, "a woman's attachment to a man depends largely on the elegance of his leave-taking." It was possible to buy or bludgeon one's way to power, but social acceptability depended on one's ability to extemporize verses, preferably in classical Chinese. The exchange of poems, couched in subtle, sometimes cryptic imagery, was the only way for social intercourse to escape the restraints of the formal and ritual conventions that proscribed explicit utterance and obscured the expression of feeling. One of Murasaki's most heartfelt self-reproaches was at her failure to respond with a suitably aloof verse to one of Fujiwara's passes.

Daiitoku, King of Wisdom, was often an intimidating, even terrifying deity in earlier representations, but eleventh-century sculptors invested him with the characteristic virtues of the culture of Heian: sedate, inert, reflective.

The beauty and sensibility cultivated in the poems—and, in their written versions, the way they were formed and folded—was the object of every form of public display. Only in an archery contest do Genji and his friends approach the practical world of values of their European counterparts and contemporaries; their usual competitions are in painting, dancing, and mixing perfumes and incense. The cult of delicacy of feeling is illustrated in *Genji* by the hero's unwillingness to abandon the courtship of a princess who turns out—when seen close up—to be red-nosed and gawky, in a sort of pre-incarnation of the Code of the Woosters or of the bloodless refinement that restrained Newland Archer in *The Age of Innocence* or the chivalry that obliged Wellington to marry Kitty Pakenham after she had grown "damn ugly." In a different context, the same ideal explains the story of how Emperor Ichijo retired out of earshot when playing on his flute a pop pasquinade aimed at a low-born minister. In order to demonstrate sensitivity to the beauties of nature without venturing into the odious provinces, court officials built gardens in simulation of the "scenic wonders" praised by poets. Trees were trained into fantastic shapes to imitate the wind-bent pines of Amanohashidate.

In Christendom at the time, aristocratic thuggery had to be restrained or at least channelled by the church. Noble hoodlums would be at best slowly and fitfully civilized over a long period by a cult of chivalry which always remained as much a training in arms as an education in values of gentility. From this perspective the existence on the other side of the world of a culture in which delicacy of feeling and the arts of peace were spontaneously celebrated by a secular élite seems astonishing. So little work has been done, and so few sources are available, on the lower levels of society in the Japan of the Fujiwara that it is hard to say how oppressively this empire of sensibility ruled its subjects. Genji's is a world of hard-paste porcelain in which no earthenware appears. No lower orders intrude to uglify; peasants are so unfamiliar as to loom only as "phantoms." Heian was isolated not only from the rest of the world but also from its own hinterland, and the provinces saw paragons like Sugawara and Genji only in times of exile. Most of the time they were ruled by the badly powdered men whose faces reminded Sei Shonagon of "dark earth over which snow has melted in patches." The rice revenues which sustained the court aristocracy were extorted from a peasantry periodically winnowed by famine and plague. Though the imperial army was fit only for ceremonial and officered by sinecurists, the countryside was cowed by the retinues of provincial administrators—gangs of toughs and bravos licensed by authority, like the *rurales* of pre-revolutionary Mexico—which would evolve into the private armies of provincial aristocrats. In the next century they would challenge and eventually overthrow the central power.

Still, what is remarkable is not that the values of the court should have remained unreflected in the country but that they should have existed at all in so refined a form. Even in *Genji*, some characters evince impatience with the conventions of courtly behaviour. In an appeal to "the spirit of Japan" or a rejection of traditional "Chinesified" art as "simpering," it is tempting to suppose some sort of prefiguration of the practical, martial Japan familiar from a later era. Yet hindsight is a highly refractive lens, and all that survives of the art and literature of the late tenth and early eleventh centuries is remarkably consistent in sustaining the impression of a collective project of self-restraint. The art of Heian, like that of the Italian Renaissance, seems actively to reject the emotional self-indulgence and strenuous asperities of preceding eras in favour of moderation and *sprezzatura*. The style was defined for traditional critics by the sculptor Jocho, who decorated the palace of Hojoji for Fujiwara no Michinaga. His divine and heroic images, human, realistic, and placid, set the tone for the rest of the century. The effects of this taste can be admired, for instance, in the Daiitoku of Boston Museum, with his human head and limbs and calculated renunciation of horror, or in the wood carving of Prince Shotoku, made by the sculptor Enkai in 1069, unstamped by passion. Genji might have been at home in Gonzaga Mantua, or Castiglione welcome in Heian.

THE GARDEN OF ISLAM

One might expect Fujiwara Japan to be an unrepresentative corner of the world of a thousand years ago. Isolated by introspection and xenophobia, Japan kept all her sons at home, like one of the jealously possessive mothers popular in Japanese fiction. Marginal members of society might be attracted to travel: India was a suitable destination for a rare hermit or magus. But not even the most committed Sinologist of the tenth century could bear to face a voyage as ambassador to the land which inspired his poetry and set his standards of culture. The Chinese, who might have been flattered by imitation, reciprocated the distaste of "a country which is rude and out of the way." The hero of *The Tale of the Hollow Tree* defied his readers' credulity by being shipwrecked in Persia.

Yet, judged alongside some other eleventh-century court cultures, the values of Heian were not as bizarre as they seemed by the standards of Christendom. A Japanese shipwreck victim in the world of Islam—had there really been one—would have encountered echoes of home. Genji's competitions among princely perfumers are reminiscent of nothing so much, in the world of the time, as the recipes for aromatic vinegars and toiletries expounded by the gardener of al-Mu'tamid, ruler of Seville. With Genji, too, al-Mu'tamid shared an epicene appearance, a love of gardening, a talent for poetry, and a homoerotic appetite. The parallels, of course, break down if pressed too far. The rooms of Heian, with their frail partitions and sparse furnishings, provided austere spaces for living in, as far removed as possible from the cluttered sybaritism of an Islamic interior.

The most conspicuous difference was one of scale. Like all long, thin countries, Japan encompasses a great diversity of climes but occupies a relatively small area. Islam was the biggest—that is, the most widely dispersed—civilization the world had ever seen until it was overtaken by the expansion of Latin Christendom in the sixteenth century. In about 1000, Muslims occupied villas in the Algarve and oases in the Sahara. They congregated in large and settled merchant communities, thousands strong, in Daylub and Malabar, Canton and the Malay archipelago. A continuous band of territory under Muslim rule stretched from the Duero and the Atlantic, across North Africa and the western Mediterranean, to the Indus, the Jaxartes, and the Arabian Sea. The Syrian geographer al-Muqaddasi, who died at the turn of the millennium, surveyed this world in detail, from Syria to Khurasan, with an easy conviction of its cultural unity and a courtier's prejudices about its essential urbanity. The Islam he beheld was spread like a pavilion under the tent of the sky, erected as if for some great ceremonial occasion, arrayed with great cities in the role of princes; these were attended by chamberlains, lords, and foot soldiers, whose parts were played by provincial capitals, towns, and villages respectively.

The cities were linked not only by the obvious elements of a common culture—the veneration of the Prophet, adhesion to the Koran, the use or knowledge of Arabic, the unifying force of the pilgrimage to Mecca—but also by commerce and in many cases by reciprocal political obligations. The strict political unity which had once characterized Islam had been shattered in the tenth century by a form of political schism: the proclamation in Spain and Egypt of rival caliphates by dynasties which arrogated to themselves the spiritual authority, handed down from the Prophet himself, which had formerly been located uniquely in Baghdad. In most of Iran and Kurdistan, usurpation or enforced devolution of power to "minor dynasties" made the caliph's rule nominal. The commander of the faithful became "a venerable phantom." Yet a sense of comity survived, and travellers could feel at home throughout the Dar al-Islam or anywhere—to use an image popular with poets—in a garden of Islam, cultivated, walled against the world, yielding, for its privileged occupants, shades and tastes of paradise. Changes in the agronomy of the Muslim world made the garden image fit particularly well at the time, as growing yields of hard wheat, rice, and sugar all demanded cooling draughts of summer irrigation.

In a civilization which thought of itself as a garden, gardening was naturally an esteemed art. The literature which describes it is prolific from eleventh- and early twelfth-century Muslim Spain, where a veritable school of court gardeners flourished, unparalleled elsewhere in the medieval west.

They knew each other and read each other's works. They dealt with practical agriculture but were more concerned with the high-cost, low-yield delicacies that conferred prestige on princely taste. The dry farming and

Enclosed from the world, enraptured by music, scented by trees, cooled by drinks, and enlightened by conversation, the inmates of the garden of Islam inhabit an earthly paradise, in an illustration to a courtly romance of amorous intrigue comparable, in tone and values, to *Genji*. This is a version from the western caliphate; Mahmud of Ghazni was also a collector of lavish manuscripts of amorous tales.

pastoralism which sustained most of Moorish Spain were ignored in their works. Their common background was in royal patronage, their common formation in the lush experimental gardens of powerful sybarites in Toledo and Seville, where they were employed on every project that might enhance luxury, from concocting compost to inventing recipes for foie gras. They were learned men steeped in the esoteric and even in the occult. They were keen practical gardeners. Ibn Bassal, who was gardening in Toledo when it fell to Christian conquerors in 1085, wrote almost exclusively from his own direct experience, but any discoloration beneath his fingernails is more likely to have been ink than mould.

Gardening is an ephemeral form of monumental art, and only the faintest inkling of the environments they created for their patrons can be got from surviving Moorish gardens of a later age in Granada and Seville. The way of life of which the gardens formed part, however, can be envisaged readily enough in an imagination stimulated by Moorish art, which in the late tenth century assumed its most delicate forms and most opulent aspect. Worldly and ostentatious, the ruins of a caliph's palace outside Cordova exude a sense of pathos and mutability reminiscent of Heian, despite the manicured

In a photograph taken at an early stage of the restoration of the palace of Madinat al-Zahra, the sometime glory and subsequent decay can be viewed simultaneously. This, the most splendid of all the apartments, was added by 'Abd al-Rahman III in the mid-950s as a sumptuous audience chamber. It reflected secular magnificence—aisles of swagged arches rested on columns of contrasting marble and were lined with a "skin" of richly carved stone, applied over the building-blocks—while evoking the caliph's sacred role by including a mihrab as the focal point of the composition.

feel of the current restoration. The palace was in a tradition established by vanished predecessors. Every mutation in the Moorish state was sumptuously and solemnly commemorated. Rulers' prestige demanded that palaces inherited be demolished and excelled. When in 929 the amir of Cordova, 'Abd-al-Rahman III, decided to assume the title of caliph, he conceived a palace that would embody the transformed nature of his authority: formerly pragmatic, active, and personal, his monarchy became withdrawn, sacral, and unseen. Once mobile—a peripatetic prince relying on his physical presence and military clout to exact obedience in distant provinces—he now retired behind a capacious veil beyond which only privileged servants could penetrate. He ruled henceforth by projecting images of "magnificence" and "fear." The new palace was begun in 936 on a vast site a few miles north-west of Cordova, which was then easily the biggest and richest city in the western world. Ten thousand workmen set up four thousand columns to build it. It accommodated a slave family, four thousand strong and growing, and a harem of reputedly sixty-three hundred women; for its sustenance, daily caravans brought thirteen thousand pounds of meat. It was both a pleasure dome and a powerhouse. The caliph's catamite con-

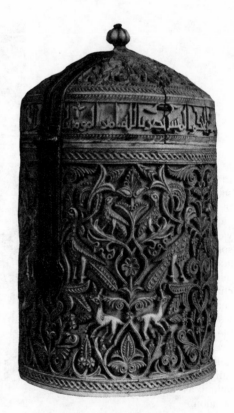

Domed ivory caskets decorated with virtuoso carving were marks of caliphal favour in tenth- and eleventh-century Cordova, usually bestowed—stuffed with precious unguent—to commemorate an achievement worthy of the highest notice. This one was given in about 960 by the caliph al-Hakam II to Subh, his Basque concubine of proverbial beauty, who became the mother of his heir and the patroness—perhaps the mistress—of Almanzor.

tributed verses, engraved on a column base, under his sobriquet of Little Earring. A qadi reproved the ruler for covering a roof with silver and gold. Yet despite every contrivance for self-indulgence, 'Abd al-Rahman declared that he had known only fourteen days' peace in his life.

His palace enjoyed remarkable longevity and was uneclipsed until 979 when a new political revolution was echoed in architecture. The vizier Ibn Abi 'Amir, like Fujiwara no Michinaga in Heian, had effectively usurped the authority of a fainéant figurehead ruler. Like his Japanese counterpart, he owed his rise in part to mastery of seraglio politics: scandal linked him to the caliphal concubine Subh, who ran the harem and whose beauty is celebrated in verses adorning several surviving perfume casks and cosmetics boxes of the previous reign—rather, perhaps, as modern beauty products carry the endorsements of screen goddesses. His other decisive qualities combined ruthlessness, which made him strong man and executioner of successive palace coups, with martial prowess that brought him the prestige of successful raids against the unbelievers to the north. He earned his cognomen of Almanzor, the conqueror. His palace was a calculated snub against the dynasty he nominally served. He called it Madinat al-Zahira—Shining City—as a play on the obscure name of 'Abd al-Rahman's monument, which was said to have been coined in honour of a concubine. It was built on an even larger scale than its predecessor in only two years. Its defiant extravagance and its gaudy lustre are suggested by an illumination in an early eleventh-century Spanish commentary on the Book of Revelation, which shows the city of Antichrist glowing in apocalyptic flames. The sort of luxury it enclosed can be glimpsed in the carved shards of ivory caskets which once contained the yellow unguents for catamites' buttocks, and which display realistic graven images, even portraits, that broke a sacred prohibition.

Almanzor died in 1002. His younger son's inexpert attempted putsch in 1008 enfeebled the state at its centre, while usurpations eroded its edges. In 1009, Madinat al-Zahira was sacked by Berber mutineers in one of those orgies of destruction that Moorish chroniclers handled so well: "in savagery after civility, ugliness after beauty, wolves howled and devils played in the haunts of ghosts, the dens of beasts, that had once been spaces full of luxury and melody. Men like swords, damsels like dolls, overspilling with jewels under vaults so splendid as to conjure heaven—all were scattered when times changed. Those elegant apartments became playgrounds of a destroying force—wilder now than maws of lions, bellowing of the end of the world." An astrologer who had foretold the downfall had, it was said, been tortured and crucified by Almanzor, who viewed all the occult arts with affected abhorrence and obvious unease.

The collapse of the empire of Cordova meant that Islam's defence in the west would be shared among more and weaker hands. At the opposite end

In 1047, a Christian illuminator of the eighth-century *Commentaries on the Apocalypse* by Beatus of Liébana, succumbing perhaps to wishful thinking, depicted Cordova as Babylon burning at the approach of the Day of Judgement. Babylon was an image of wealth as well as of heathendom: the text illustrated here (Rev. 18) reads in part, "Mourn, mourn for this great city; for all the linen and purple and scarlet that you wore, for all your finery of gold and jewels and pearls; your huge riches are all destroyed within a single hour."

of the Islamic world, in Transoxania and Afghanistan, security was threatened in the same period by changes in the fortunes and leadership of the sentinel states centred on Bukhara and Ghazni. Though Transoxania lay on the rim of the civilized—or, rather, of the sedentary—world, it had every qualification to be an ornament of Islam. Its people, according to the greatest geographer of tenth-century Iran, "possessed everything in abundance and were dependent for nothing on the produce of other lands." Though nomads and townsmen were said to "rage against each other in the depths of the heart," the hearts of the merchants of Bukhara and Samarkand were housed under enough fat to keep the rage from showing, and the economies of the steppes and the towns seem to have been complementary. Al-Muqaddasi's list of the region's exports is calculated to excite every sense and includes soap and sulphur, silks and sables and silver cloth, elaborate leatherware, ornamental arms, and prized sweetmeats. "There is nothing to equal the meats of Bukhara, and a kind of melon they have . . . nor the bows of Khorezmia, the porcelain of Shash, and the paper of Samarkand." Khorezmian watermelons were sent to Baghdad packed in lead and snow. Paper from Samarkand became, in the tenth century, the preferred writing medium of the whole Islamic world.

For most of the tenth century the region was dominated by the Iranian (or largely Iranian) dynasty of the Samanids, who, like the other minor dynasties which ruled Iran and the Muslim east, acknowledged without personal inconvenience the supremacy of the caliph and cultivated, without sacrifice of Islamic identity, the traditional arts and verse of Persia. In the mid-century, according to an account based on the childhood recollections of a palace official's son, their capital at Bukhara was "the focus of splendour, the shrine of empire, the meeting-place of the most unique intellects of the age, the horizon of the literary stars of the world, and the fair of the great scholars of the period."

In 976 the Samanids lost control of their mines on the upper Zarafshan River, source of the silver coinage prized as far afield as Poland and Scandinavia. Power began to slip into the hands of generals and nomad chiefs. One disgruntled poet, seeking patronage at "the horizon of the stars of literature," found it had declined to "a sewer, unfit for human life." Yet its royal library, with its suite of rooms, each devoted to a different discipline, was still good enough for Avicenna until 997, only a few years before the final extinction of Samanid power and the dynasty's retirement into private life.

The splendour of Bukhara did not disappear but only departed to a new princely court on the edge of the Samanid world at Ghazni in eastern Afghanistan, in a state founded by one of the Samanids' Turkic generals. Though not as obviously favoured of nature as Transoxania, the environ-

Mahmud of Ghazni relied on Islam for his ideological armoury but his models of king-ship were Persian and the *Shah-Nameh* of Fardosi was composed under his patronage. The earliest surviving illuminations are of the late thirteenth century. This scene, in which the dying hero, Rustam, takes his last vengeance on his treacherous brother, Shaghad, is from the most original of the many early fourteenth-century versions, the Demotte MS in the British Museum. Most of the characters are giants with superhuman powers but, like the western Roland, Rustam is a model of guileless nobility, whose in-nocence exposes him to conquest by hostile cunning. Caught in his death-trap, how-ever, he outwits and slaughters his own murderer. He represents the combination of qualities to which Mahmud aspired—human prowess allied to divine favour—as well as a warning to potential traitors in the ruler's entourage.

ment of Afghanistan could provide civilized amenities as well as strong de-fences. Herat's orchards extended for a day's march to the south of the town, and its brick bridge had twenty-six arches. Ghazni, a little to the north of the modern site, was already an important halting place between the valleys of the Oxus and the Indus before it became a princely court. The founder of its strength was the Samanids' unruly client, Subuktigin (reigned 977–997), but the founder of its splendour was his son, Mahmud (reigned 998–1030). Stepping to the throne over the corpse of a murdered brother, Mahmud wrenched territory from the ruined Samanids and milked vulnerable Indian temples for liquid wealth. He had four hundred resident poets at his court, and one laureate's mouth was thrice filled with pearls in acknowledgement of a well-extemporized eulogy. His palace was deco-rated with wall paintings in a pre-Islamic tradition, with scenes of hunts and banquets, sampled by figures in pointed hats and Sogdian silk coats. The poet Asjadi celebrated the ethos of Ghazni—"lip-repentance and a lustful heart"—in verses as drunken and lubricious as the Archpoet's on Pavia. Though reputedly offended by his own ugliness, Mahmud had an eye for every kind of beauty. Not every scholar and poet, however, was happy with his exacting and self-interested patronage. Fardosi, the writer of Iran's national epic, the *Shah-Nameh,* fled from him. Avicenna refused his invitation. Al-Biruni, the most learned man of the age, who anticipated the science of palaeontology and the theory of heliocentrism, had to be brought to the court as a prisoner.

If the Samanids' was an empire of silver, Mahmud's was an empire of loot; its riches were plundered abroad, not grown or mined at home. His raid into India in 1019 gathered so many captives that prices in the slave marts of Afghanistan fell to two or three dirhams a head. The story of the jewels he struck, like the jackpot out of a giant fruit machine, from the belly of the idol of Somnath, is no doubt a fiction—but it expresses well enough the objectives and triumphs of his Indian campaigns, although a tradition originally of his own making has hailed them as holy wars.

Eventually, Mahmud's war elephants were overwhelmed by nomad cavalry, his realm submerged by the weight of numbers of Turkish tribes. The states of tenth-century Iran and eastern Islam were, in a sense, victims of their own success. So profound was the Samanid peace in Transoxania that thousands of ghazis—the professional paladins on whose strength the state relied—departed in the 960s for the more turbulent frontiers of India or Byzantium. Mahmud's Indian gold at first appeased but increasingly excited the envy of nomad clients. The region's future was foreshadowed, in the early years of the eleventh century, in a dream attributed to the Turkish dynast Seljük, in which fire spurted from his penis and its sparks flew over the world.

Trampled by Turkish hooves, the garden of Islam was also fertilized by the passage of nomad cavalry. The Turks destroyed the old polities and transformed the delicate ecology of Iran and, later, Anatolia. Yet the accession of strength they brought, in manpower and military effectiveness, more than made up for their depredations. Similarly, in the Islamic west, Spain received a new infusion of morale and a new army of defenders, two generations after the fall of the Cordovan Empire, from invasions of warrior ascetics from the depths of the Sahara. In the east, the newcomers' commitment to Islam was hardly less intense. Many Turkish tribes were converted, or at least courted for conversion, for generations before their settlement within the garden. Some of the tenth-century missionaries were hermits and dervishes of dubious orthodoxy, outcasts from the Muslim mainstream, like the Arian bishops who converted barbarian invaders of the Roman Empire. Once inside the fold, most of them submitted meekly to orthodox direction, and in Baghdad the Seljuks were welcomed as Sunni liberators from the yoke of a Shiite regime (see Chapter 3).

Considered as a whole, the tenth and eleventh centuries were an epoch of climacteric for Islam, of political fissures and of enfeebling shifts of power. Losses of territory near the end of the period—to Christian adventurers in Spain, to crusaders in the Levant—were temporary but bitter effects of the dislocations caused by these changes. But the losses were offset by gains on other fronts, and Islam emerged revitalized and equipped for further, sustained expansion.

THE DIVIDED HEAVEN

Compared with the way it looks to us today, the history of no part of our world will seem so different, from the perspective of the galactic museum-keepers of ten thousand years hence, as that of China. From our point of view, China appears as the home of an uniquely successful imperial experiment, which has now endured for over two thousand years with no very conspicuous discontinuities. Since China's first "great revolution"—the formation of a centralized state and the establishment of a lasting dynasty by the peasant-born Liu Pang in 202 BCE—no fundamental mutation, it is commonly said, altered the nature of the empire until another peasant's son brought Red China into being in 1949. On the map—allowing for growth at the edges—the empire of the Han Dynasty, which lasted from 202 BCE to 189 CE, appears to prefigure the China of all subsequent eras, occupying most of the valleys of the Yangtse, Huai, Yellow, and West rivers, and stretching from the Great Wall in the north to Annam in the south and towards Tibet in the west.

This essential continuity survived eras of dislocation and dissolution such as commonly occupied the times of transition from one dynasty to the next: the foreign conquests which brought non-Chinese dynasties to power in the thirteenth and seventeenth centuries CE; the political transformations which, for example, bureaucratized the state in the twelfth century and abolished the monarchy early in the twentieth; the economic and demographic changes which have shifted the centre of gravity of the empire from north to south and back again; the epochs of growth which have incorporated distinct peoples into the empire and added some unassimilable identities to the slowly amalgamating bundle of peoples who have come to think of themselves as Chinese.

Yet, from a point sufficiently far in the future, Chinese history will probably not appear so very different from that of other parts of the world where imperial experiments have flourished at intervals and where a basis of political unity has been laid in the course of a long and uneven historical experience. The unity of China may come to seem different only in degree from that of, say, western Europe or India or central Asia or the Arab world, in which periods of crisis and recovery, fission and fusion, consolidation and dissolution have alternated. A thousand years ago China was falteringly emerging from a period of prostration in which the empire had shrunk and crumbled, and in which unity was compromised by the coexistence of two self-styled and mutually acknowledged "empires" under a divided heaven.

The rival empire was the more remarkable—and the more galling to Chinese sensibilities—because it occupied almost none of the historic lands of China and because it was ruled by a dynasty of formerly despised barbarians from the wastes of northern Asia. The Khitans impinged on Chinese history in 405–6—victims, perhaps, of the same steppeland catastrophe that drove the Huns west and sent the greatest-ever wave of Germanic invaders across the frontier of the Roman Empire. Without sacrificing their nomadic heritage as mounted warriors, they settled, as herders of steeds and growers of millet, into the Shara Muren valley and the north-west basin of the River Liao, where contiguity with China gradually influenced their ideas. Admiring, resenting, and needing, they beheld China with envy. For half a millennium they were held at bay, but by the early tenth century they were emulous as well as imitative. Barbarian habits persisted, of course. Even after intensive Sinification under the visionary Khan Ye-lü A-pao-chi (d. 926), the dowager khatun piled up human sacrifices at the tomb of her husband. Yet in the tenth century, at a time of Chinese weakness, the Khitans had absorbed enough Chinese political philosophy and had retained sufficient traditional barbarian strength to challenge the empire in its own territory and on its own moral ground.

The mandate of heaven was as indivisible as the sky itself. The identity of China depended on it. External relations were normally governed by the convenient fiction that China constituted all the world that counted, and the rest of mankind were barbarians clinging to its rim. This principle could be compromised from time to time, and barbarian kingdoms ranked in greater or lesser proximity to China's unique perfection. At intervals, powerful barbarian rulers had been able to attract titles of equal resonance or exact treaties on equal terms from the Chinese. Tributes due to patrons of equal or even superior status could often be extorted from a court willing to purchase security, though the Chinese rarely admitted that such remittances were more than acts of condescension.

The notion of the uniqueness of the imperial dignity was so successfully communicated to China's neighbours that when the Khitans first aspired to it, they proposed not to share it but to take it over altogether. In 907 the last princes of the Tang were massacred and the dynasty extinguished after nearly three centuries on the heavenly throne. The state established by the usurper collapsed in its turn in 923. None of the fragmentary successor kingdoms among which the former empire was divided could claim the legitimacy conferred by long duration, superior culture, or overwhelming strength. The Khitan khan, A-pao-chi, based his own claims on all three of these criteria. In 924 he declared that the mandate of heaven had been

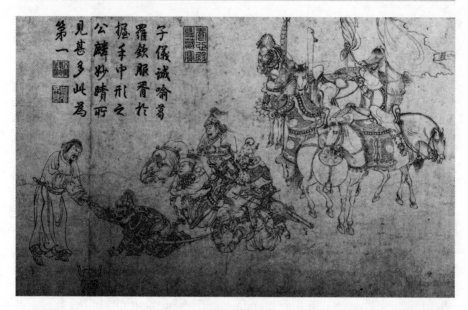

子儀誠喻蒼
羅欽服膚於
握手中形之
公麟妙睛而
見甚多此為
第一

In the Confucian scale of values, superior sagacity outweighed superior strength. The cringing figures with their caps, furs, pelt banners, and armoured horses are Uighurs, Turkic steppe nomads, whom General Kuo Tzu-i, unarmed and simply attired, graciously enlists in Chinese service. The scene depicted was supposed to be an eighth-century episode of the wars against Tibet. For the Sung artist in the eleventh century it represented emotions invested in the programme for harnessing the barbarian world advocated by political theorists such as Ou-yang Hsiu.

transferred to him. He cultivated the traditional rites of emperorship; he made the worship of Confucius and the study of the sage's tradition the defining feature of the culture of his court; he was hailed as the "heavenly emperor" who "inherited a hundred years' line of legitimate succession." From 936 the Khitans had a foothold within traditional imperial territory, between the Great Wall and Peking; and from 946, A-pao-chi's claims were upheld continuously, for in that year a khan captured the imperial regalia from the so-called dynasty of Tsin, founded by an usurping Turkic general. The Khitans had moved to fill a vacuum abhorred by nature in the continuity of the imperial line. There is an irresistible parallel with Charlemagne's arrogation to himself of the title of Roman emperor in 800, at a moment when the squalid politics of Byzantium appeared to violate the rules of succession by elevating a woman to the imperial throne. What Charlemagne was to Rome, A-pao-chi was to China: a lightly civilized barbarian, *plus romain que les romains* or *plus chinois que les chinois* in his exaggerated reverence for imperial traditions.

Imperial status was taken seriously at the Khitan court of the tenth and eleventh centuries. The Khitan state of Liao had its own civil service which, selected by examination on Confucian principles, defended the legitimacy of Khitan emperors in Confucian rhetoric. In the mid-eleventh century, one of the essay questions in the civil service examination demanded a development of the argument that "the state which possesses the imperial regalia assumes the line of legitimate succession." The Sung Dynasty, labouring to

Chao K'uang-yin, transformed from a usurping general to the Tai-tsu emperor, the "great ancestor" of the Sung dynasty. The capacious throne of vermilion bamboo, gold-mounted with dragon finials, declares his status—but its simplicity of framework is of a piece with the rest of the image: essentially, it is a plain campaign stool. The leader is legitimated by his natural command of Confucian virtues: stately gravity, modest simplicity, incorruptible austerity.

reconstruct the old China from bases in the Yellow River valley in the same period, were obliged to reply in kind. A famous essay by their most elegant apologist, Ou-yang Hsiu (1007–72), argued that legitimacy belonged to those Chinese who righted wrongs and reunited China, baubles apart. Because Liao was generally more effective militarily than Sung, the barbarian tribute which flattered imperial courts was more easily accessible to the Khitans, who in 1031 proclaimed the "reunification of the universe." Korea was their tributary for almost the whole of the eleventh century. In 1024, when Mahmud of Ghazni received demands for tribute, the initiative came from Liao.

Faced with irreversible claims and unconquerable might, the Sung were obliged to concede equality to Liao and to acknowledge the new bipolarity of the political universe. The founder of the dynasty, Chao K'uang-yin, the T'ai-tsu emperor, was a general proclaimed by his mutinous soldiers in 960, on his way to undertake a campaign against the Khitans. Once on the throne, he bent his policy to the conciliation of his northern neighbours, partly out of an obsessive fear of the army, which he knew from experience found it all too easy to make and unmake emperors. His desire for disarmament—or, at least, for the disbanding of mutinous units and the superannuation of over-mighty generals—was also inspired by an awareness that the former imperial territories were sated with strife and anarchy, and willing to rally to a focus of hopes for peace and concord. Underlying his methods was the Confucian doctrine that enemies could be pacified by example and reduced by benignity more effectively than by force of arms. On a more practical level, he professed that the reunification of China had to begin in the south, where the task was easiest, before turning to the northern front, which demanded greater strength. In 974, two years before his death, Liao and Sung were mutually proclaimed "eternal allies."

The prudence of this policy was proved by the successors who repudiated it and provoked the Khitans to wars which ranged from the fruitless to the disastrous; in 1005 the Sung were obliged to return to the founder's principles after a Khitan invasion demonstrated the hopelessness of a military solution. The "sworn letters" of Shan-yüan were that rare thing, a treaty equally satisfactory to both sides. The Khitans retained their lands within the curtilage of the Great Wall, and therefore their access by cavalry to all the cities of the northern plain. They received annual payments of silk and silver, which they regarded as tribute but which the Sung could redefine in face-saving language. The two dynasties were united by a fictitious kinship in which, for example, the Liao dowager empress became the Sung emperor's "junior aunt."

The treaty radically modified—or at least signified a change in—the mutual perceptions of the two self-styled empires. All pejorative connotations such as *jung* (barbarian) and *lu* (vile scoundrel) which had formerly been attached to Khitan place disappeared from Chinese usage, although con-temptuous language remained current at court in everyday speech. The terms "northern dynasty" and "southern dynasty" became the normal signi-fiers for Liao and Sung respectively at both courts, and—with some fluctua-tions—the Sung honoured the presumed family connection with their northern neighbours for the rest of the century by exchanging the appropri-ate courtesies on ceremonial occasions. The emperor's yellow robe seemed to have split along a central seam. Even when the treaty of Shan-yüan broke down and hostilities were resumed, policymakers at the Sung court were aware that the Khitans could not be classified with the rest of the bar-barian world but were qualified by their strength and sophistication for a special category of their own.

Chao K'uang-yin was right: the threat to China came, as ever, from the north, but her opportunities lay, as always, in the south. His advice to his brother and successor, Chao Kuang-i, was that the recovery of Szechuan was the key to the renewal of China's greatness. The vast region of Szechuan was Sung China's wild west, a colonial frontier to be Sinified and exploited in a movement which vastly increased the empire's resources and helped permanently to shift its centre of gravity—a change comparable in its effects on China as a whole with the colonization of Sinkiang and the annexation of Tibet in our own times. The millennium opened with an aus-picious rush of settlers to the south-east, lured by the salt-wells, the "springs of avarice" of Szechuan.

Even had the Sung not been ambitious to extend their effective authority in the region, competition to control the sources of salt—against the rich tea and salt magnates of the plains and against the nomad chiefs of the forests of bamboo and fir—would have involved the dynasty in growing political commitments. The regional feudatories were challenged but not ousted by the central bureaucracy. In the early 990s the intractability of the magnates was perceived in the Sung capital in distant Kaifeng as an attempt to repudiate imperial authority. In 996 the government's attempt to bureau-cratize the militias had to be "put to sleep"; in 1005 garrison commanders were forbidden to interfere with local jurisdiction. Meanwhile, however, the accelerating pace of settlement and the quickening interest of the govern-ment were demonstrated by the administrative reforms of 1001, which sub-divided the two provinces of Szechuan into smaller units known as routes.

The magic which transformed Szechuan into an obedient part of the em-pire was worked, *malgré soi,* by the tribal chiefs who threatened the regime's stability. They already had a magical, or at least a demonic, repu-tation, playing in local legend the role of the Welsh demons who tormented Saint Guthlac in the East Anglian fens. The Chinese classified the tribes as "raw" or "cooked" according to their levels of imputed savagery. The wildest were the Black tribes, whose ruling caste, the Black Bone Yi, were led by a chief known as the Demon Master. Their menace enlivened the magnates' sleepy sense of allegiance to the Sung court. In 1008 and 1013 their depredations reached the frontier town of Yujing—the Dawson City of Szechuan's salt rush, a dangerous township of salt miners and convicts. The pacification campaign mounted by Sung armies in 1014 welded a political haft to the economic spearhead which the settlers had represented. Symbolically of the new order in Szechuan, the forbidden hills became denuded of forests in the interests of road building and construction of dwellings. The two moieties of Szechuan—the romantic wastelands of streams and grottoes in the mountainous east and the enviable heavenly storehouse in the rich west—became inalienably Chinese. In 1036 the Demon Master became an official of the state.

Checked in the north, spreading in the south, China in the eleventh century was to be reformed in the centre by a revival of ancient ethics and letters—a "renaissance" after the chaos of the tenth century comparable in scale and tone to the Ottonian Renaissance in values and learning which accompanied Latin Europe's recovery from the age of the Vikings and Magyars (see Chapter 5). In Christendom such revivals depended on the influence of the clergy—a class linked to the ruling élite by ties of blood and of ritually encoded respect, whose independence and altruism were, however, guaranteed by an essentially non-hereditary character and the accessibility of the ranks to new blood. In China the nearest equivalent was the official class: the vast civilian army which made the state work and which, like the church in Christendom, was the guardian of literary traditions, with their messages about purity in style and probity in morals. Although the Chinese civil service had for centuries been recruited by examination, in practice families with established scholarly and official traditions controlled access to about 80 per cent of the posts. This in itself would not necessarily have compromised the integrity of the class as a whole, nor even have eroded its quality: official nominations often favoured promising poor relations rather than the sons of incumbents. High ethical and educational standards can be passed on with other inherited benefits from generation to generation of a closed élite. Yet it is an indication of the high value which rulers and their greater servants placed on the quality of the administration that the trend under the early Sung was towards a more competitive system and a more widely recruited officialdom.

This trend was accompanied in the writings of members of the administrative class by a new emphasis on a code of service—a doctrine of the responsibility of the rulers' representatives to benefit society as a whole. Towards the middle of the eleventh century an attempt was made to write this doctrine into the recruitment process. In 1043 the threat of a Khitan invasion scared entrenched elements at court, who had a vested interest in the existing examination curriculum, into flight to their provincial estates.

Tun-huang was a vital station on the silk route, surrounded by bleak desert, where caves sheltered travellers from the heat. It was also a centre for the diffusion of Buddhism across central Asia and into China: nearly five hundred caves are adorned with Buddhist paintings. The Chinese merchant convert shown here brought his family values with him from Confucianism. The whole of his family is displayed united in prayer at the feet of the Bodhisattva Avalokitesvara.

Among the temporarily promoted cadres was an official of exceptional vigour and vision, Fan Chung-yen (989–1052). He came from a family with a long history of imperial service which had been uprooted and impoverished in a time of troubles in the late ninth century. Members of the clan found official employment after the breakup of the Tang empire in the relatively stable coastal kingdom of Wu-yüeh in southern China but without recovering wealth or social prominence. When Fan's father died in 990, he was raised by the clan into which his mother remarried without knowledge of his true roots. He rediscovered his true identity in his youth, impelled by awareness that his adoptive brothers were unable to accept him without reserve. The clan of Fan was, at first, equally inhospitable to him, and he was allowed to petition the emperor for leave to resume his paternal surname only on condition that he made no claims on his newly discovered relations. Fan purged himself of the bitterness of this history of rejection by immersing himself in the Confucian ethic of the clan. When his success in examinations brought him high office and considerable wealth, he used his power of patronage to benefit members of his paternal and adoptive clans alike and spent his money in the support of his poor relatives. "Virtue," he explained, "has been accumulating from our ancestors for more than a century but has for the first time brought forth its fruits in myself. Now that I have achieved high office, if I should alone enjoy my riches and honourable position without thought for my fellow clansmen, how shall I in future days be able to face our ancestors in the next life, and how should I be able to enter the ancestral temple?"

With the same intensity of personal commitment, Fan embraced the entire Confucian tradition of duty. His proposed reform of the examinations for the civil service was designed to test candidates' social responsibility as well as their textual mastery of the classics and was accompanied by a programme of public education in the provinces. The old examination tested only skill in composition, especially in verse, and in memorizing texts. The new test emphasized the intellectual quality of the prose essay and included questions about ethical standards and moral conduct. Fan's proposals were never implemented, but their principles were influential. Provincial schools grew at public expense, and under the guidance of Ou-yang Hsiu, who presided over the imperial administration in the late 1050s, the examinations were conducted on Fan's lines. Ou-yang Hsiu's essays make it plain that the movement in which he and Fan were joined was a conscious renaissance aimed at reviving utopian models from a remote past, in the writings of Confucius and the supposed practices of early imperial China. Ou-yang Hsiu sought to restore the perfection of "ancient times, when the founders of the Three Dynasties governed the world," an ideal age "when rites and music reached everywhere." His personal culture aligned him with a type familiar in almost every great courtly society: urbane, world-weary, with well-manicured sensibilities. His ennui would have been in place in Heian. His most famous essay, written in exile in 1046, celebrates "the joy of mountains and waters" from "the old tippler's pavilion."

The court that glowed and shone for Fan Chung-yen and Ou-yang Hsiu was daringly sited in the midst of the north China plain. Kaifeng, in Honan, near the middle reaches of the Yellow River, was lucky to be a neglected backwater during the recent convulsions of Chinese history in the era of Mao and his successors (see Chapter 21). By large it escaped the uglification inflicted elsewhere by headlong progress and chaotic macroeconomic lurches. It still has an antiquated charm, conveyed by old houses, cobbled streets, and thatched roofs. In the tourist boom years of the 1980s, the town's old-fashioned artisans did a lucrative trade in craft pottery and reproductions of Sung paintings.

In the eleventh century, Kaifeng was almost certainly the greatest city in the world. Enfolded within a double curtain of defensive walls, compressed into the square shape in which the Chinese detected an image of cosmic

Not much remains of the Sung capital, but the rust-tiled pagoda of 1049, raised on the site of a shrine that once housed relics of Buddha, helps to suggest what it was like: self-confidently monumental, ostentatiously colourful, unselfconsciously cosmopolitan. The designs which can be seen stamped on the tiles in the photograph are Buddhas, dragons, musicians, and the apsarases of the Vedic myth.

order, it housed the court of China's rulers from the 940s, when it was elevated to the status of a capital by the choice of a Turkic general, who realized that he could defend the plain from there—despite the exposed position—on interior lines. Until the 1120s when the Jürchen nomads sacked and burned it, it combined the functions of court and emporium. Later development has obliterated most of the monuments of a thousand years ago, but the eastern corners of the old town are guarded to the south by the Fanta Pagoda of 977, near the railway station, and at the northern end by the celebrated Iron Pagoda of 1049, which stands nearly fifty-six metres high, smothered in rust-coloured tiles, on the site of a shrine which

In deservedly the most famous of Sung scroll-paintings, Chang Tse-tuan captures the vibrancy of life on the Yellow River at Kaifeng in the early twelfth century and the wonderful commercial opportunities brought by the approach of the Spring Festival. Groaning grain ships bring the extra food the city will need and restaurants, just beginning to fill up with visitors, are given great prominence. Hundreds of other wares arrive by cart, mule, or camel train or on poles slung across pedlars' backs.

once housed relics of Buddha. Kaifeng was not just a seat of government but a thriving place of manufacture and exchange, capable of attracting from the Near East a community of Jewish settlers whose descendants retained some distinct identity until the Cultural Revolution of 1964 (see Chapter 21).

Its business is depicted in one of the paintings most frequently reproduced for tourists—the early twelfth-century scene *On the River at Ch'ing-ming* by Chang Tse-tuan. On a roll twenty-five metres long, Chang crowds all the life of Kaifeng at festival time—the craftsmen, merchants, peddlers, entertainers, shoppers, and gawking crowds. The criss-cross framework of the town is scored by a river thick with traffic, intersected by neat streets and crowned by thatch. No image better reflects the mood of *enrichissez-vous* in which, under the lately elevated Sung Dynasty, the Chinese began our millennium.

It looks, in retrospect, like an inauspicious beginning. The Sung were a fledgling dynasty; political stability was an unconvincing novelty; the mandate of heaven was cleft by Liao; the means of imperial defence remained inadequate to the task ahead; there was no prospect of easily recovering the effortless superiority of China in the world of the previous millennium. And yet it was a time of promise. China's advantages are—have always been—a compact shape and concentrated manpower. The reunification of the two densely populated valleys of the Yangtze and Yellow rivers regrouped the basic parts of Chinese power and identity. The beginnings of expansion in the south and west showed what Sung China might do with recovered unity. The Confucian revival re-equipped the rulers with values of an imperial master-class at least as urbane as those of Heian or Cordova and perhaps—because they encouraged flexibility of recruitment at the margins—more serviceable.

The threat which contained and reversed the Sung renaissance came not from a great rival civilization but from the cold, nomad storms that blew across the northern plain. The Jürchen, who would overthrow Kaifeng in the 1120s, had none of the Khitans' sophisticated veneer. They were "sheer barbarians," envoys reported, "worse than wolves or tigers," whose khan's tent was pitched among grazing herds and thronged with wild, painted mime. According to Ou-yang Hsiu—and he had a long Confucian tradition behind him—civilization would always win encounters with savagery; the barbarian would be shamed into submission, where he could not be coerced; influenced by example when he could not be controlled by might; deflected by fingertips when he could not be pummelled by fists; subjected by benevolence when he could not be won by war. The experience of the dynasty the writer served showed the limitations of this optimistic doctrine. Over our millennium as a whole, reputedly the most successful of the civilizations which have contended for world supremacy was also, a thousand years ago, by the standards of Heian, Cordova, or Kaifeng, the most rough-hewn.

THE CIVILIZATION OF THE BARBARIANS

At about the time Almanzor died in Cordova or the Lady Murasaki was widowed in Heian, an aristocrat approaching middle age joined a religious community in the mountains of Catalonia. From one point of view it was not surprising that Oliba Cabreta of Cerdanya, Count of Besalú, Lord of Berguedà and Ripollès, should forsake the world for the cloister. His family had always invested in religion. The monks and hermits patronized by the counts had repaid them by absolving their sins and praying for their wars. Churches and houses of religion had provided jobs for their underemployed scions and berths for their unmarriageable womenfolk. Among Oliba's formative childhood experiences had been the consecrations, which he witnessed at the age of twelve or thirteen, of his parents' monastic foundations, sacred to Spanish saints, in the heart of the Pyrenees and in the Vall del Prat.

His father, in the intervals of a violent secular career, had been the devotee of a hermit of the old abbey of Cuixà, called Romuald, with whom he undertook a sort of religious elopement. Secretly, without informing the count's vassals or advisers, the pair left Catalonia together in 988 on a pilgrimage to the spiritual centre of western monasticism at Monte Cassino. The count never returned. Two years later he died, having swapped his helm for a tonsure, as a professed monk.

Still, Oliba's vocation was a remarkable event. He was in the vigour of his age, with a political role before him. Though third in a family of four brothers, he shared lordship, at least in name, and his attestations of charters show him in the active role of a counsellor. He had lands of his own which he divided, on entering the monastery, between a brother and the church. He did not enter religion for want of prospects outside it, nor was his calling a political career move. Monasteries were engines of power and influence which sometimes commanded great wealth, controlled extensive jurisdiction, and conferred valuable patronage. Oliba, however, was consciously exchanging secular for spiritual values. For instance, a few years later, when King Sancho the Great of Navarre asked his advice on a princess's potential marriage, within prohibited degrees of consanguinity, Oliba refused to give the advice the king wanted. Though it was claimed that the proposed marriage would guarantee peace, promote the church, and speed the "extirpation of pagans," Oliba replied that no end justified abominable means. "We beseech you," he said, "command us in some way wherein we may lawfully oblige you."

On the other hand, though monks always claimed to want to leave the cares of the world behind them, the cloister was a most ineffective form of insulation from politics. Courts and cloisters were too thoroughly interpenetrated—shared too many of the same interests—for the distinction to be kept pure. The wisdom and learning of monks had to be at the disposal of the state, just as governments today demand useful research from universities. Oliba's espousal of religion was not the end of his political career but the start of a new one. The born-again statesman quickly became abbot of his monastery and bishop of his diocese. Demand for his services as a diplomat and adviser in worldly conflicts increased meanwhile. He repeatedly found himself abstracted from the setting he had chosen, restored to that he had abjured. His hardest—but in general highly characteristic—job was to make peace between obsessive enemies, the Archbishop and Count of Narbonne. When the archbishop "launched himself like a devil against the count and made cruel war upon him," Oliba proceeded by degrees, imposing truces little by little, first on Sundays and holy days, then for more extended periods. Ultimately, after Oliba's death, the peace broke down and the antagonists reverted to their common tactics of mutual terror, vio-

The friezes of the west front of the abbey church of Ripoll spread political lessons before royal patrons who came to visit. The carvings are worn but the key to interpreting them survives in a Bible illuminated at Ripoll in the eleventh century and now in the Vatican Library. Moses—divinely appointed judge—displays credentials of sanctity accessible to other holders of high political office. He appears, facing the accusations of the Israelites: a Catalan ruler had to be responsible to the community. His prayers are shown delivering victory—the most precious gift of the medieval Church to kings: Solomon responds in kind, administering justice under the influence of divine grace. David is shown in piety—bringing the ark to Jerusalem and dancing before the Lord— and in sin, inflicting plague on his city, humbling himself in penance. Nathan intervenes in the choice and legitimation of his successor. The message is plain: the ruler is on his best behaviour, to be guided and judged by the Church.

lating sanctuary to murder each other's followers, diverting funds from charity to war. More than a thousand men were said to have died on each side.

Peacemaker and counsellor to the world, Oliba was father and friend to his spiritual brethren. Images of fatherhood dominate his monks' writings about him, and the tone of their obituary circular about him exceeds conventional pieties: "He made our hearts melt," they say. True son of a father who had sought the tradition of Saint Benedict in the birthplace of the monks' rule of life, he was an effective reformer. He turned corrupt nuns out of the socially select convent of Sant Joan de les Abadesses when they had been duly condemned as "wickedest harlots of Venus." He was a patron of learning who doubled the already substantial library holdings which he found on becoming Abbot of Ripoll. These fragments of his life represent the elements of a monk's vocation: charity, discipline, and learning. Oliba the abbot and bishop had to cultivate them as a base both for salvation in the next world and effectiveness in this. Only a holy man could hope to negotiate away some of the savageries of a war like that of Narbonne. Only an exemplary Christian could reprove a king or impose practically unremunerative standards of virtue on Sancho the Great.

The face his monastery presented to the world can still be seen in the worn remains of the west doorway of the monastic church—a work of about a century after Oliba's time but probably following a design adumbrated in his day. On one side of the portal, David dances before the Ark of the Lord and does penance before the prophet Gad. This was a suitable image to adorn a church that humbled kings and kept emperors kneeling contritely in the snow. Above, Solomon is crowned, anointed, and adorned with wisdom; his power and the qualifications he needs for it come alike from God or his intermediary—in this case the prophet Nathan but, by extension and implication, also the Abbot of Ripoll. On the opposite side, amid a bloody battle scene, Moses prays for victory, delivering what was perhaps the church's most precious gift for a ruler of this world.

In trying to bend the secular world to spiritual values, Oliba had examples like these but few effective sanctions. In a typical story of the time from Metz, a monk confronted a count who had stolen church lands. The thief was unafraid: "The king? I don't think much of him. The Duke of Lorraine? Why, he is as my lowest servant to me." When the monk adjured him with the threat of punishment from on high, he merely lost his temper and had to be restrained from violence by his wife. Only a miraculous subsequent illness alerted him to his duty. In practice, Oliba and his fellow-labourers in this often thankless field could hardly hope for such a consummation. They could only triumph by being needed.

Impious counts and bloody-minded archbishops made the Latin west perhaps the least civilized civilization of a thousand years ago; in comparison, that is, with China, Japan, Islam, and perhaps with India, south-east Asia, and eastern Christendom, western Europe had an élite with the most need of the civilizing influence of men like Oliba. It was also a relatively young civilization. The Sung were heirs to a concept of China that was already far more than a thousand years old by the strictest count. The notion of Japan as a single discrete culture had been formulated by the fifth century CE. Islam was born self-conscious and self-differentiated from the rest of the world. The corner of the planet between the Atlantic and the Elbe was of so little account elsewhere that when the great Islamic cosmographer al-Ishtaqri made his world map in the mid-tenth century, with his native Persia properly in the middle, western Europe was barely discernible, ousted to the remotest edge. The margin is sometimes a good place in which to foster an identity, but a Latin Christian identity, providing fellow-feeling among Christians whose common language was Latin and whose spiritual capital was Rome, was only just beginning to take shape. This emerging western European consciousness belonged to four contexts: resistance to invaders; revival of antique values; severance from eastern Christendom; and enhanced communications across the west.

The kingdoms of this part of the world had been founded by barbarian invaders of the Roman Empire. All had begun in varying degrees with the dilemma of Athawulf—the Visigothic chief who vowed to "extirpate the Roman name" but married a Roman princess and founded a sub-Roman state. They had grown up between the fifth and eighth centuries, resolving a love-hate relationship with Rome, civilizing themselves in the vanished empire's spectral shadow. An Anglo-Saxon poet, contemplating Roman ruins, imagined them peopled by giants. Charlemagne, the most successful western barbarian king ever, tackled self-civilization with relish, listening to the *City of God,* since he was not quite literate enough to read it himself, and imitating what he thought was the Emperor Augustus's fashion in legwear. But no sooner had he proclaimed the Renovation of the Empire than the annals of his kingdom started to record Viking incursions. Charlemagne had carried the frontier of Christendom in one direction beyond that of the Roman Empire at its peak, massacring or forcibly converting Saxons; he had smashed the last unassimilated barbarians on the edge of the west—the Avars—and made himself incomparably rich with their stolen treasure. Yet for a century and a half after his death in 814, western Christendom was to be under siege from new barbarians who threatened its life and character as deeply as Charlemagne's ancestors had threatened old Rome. The Vikings from the north, the Moors from the south, and the Magyars in the east had to be resisted, assimilated, or defeated if Latin Christendom was to avoid strangulation at birth.

In the first years of the new millennium it became apparent that the threat had not only been contained but even reversed. In 1000, King

First incorporated into Christendom by Carolingian expansion in the late eighth and early ninth centuries, Magdeburg became in the tenth century an opulent city, where Ottonian power was concentrated and expressed in lavish works of art. This panel from the ivory frontal of the cathedral altar reveals a vital moment in the transformation. Christ blesses the church humbly presented by Otto I, which—beginning in 937, until his death in 974—the emperor raised "of wonderful magnitude" and filled with imported relics and marble columns. Otto's patron saint, Maurice, with St. Innocent—who was the co-dedicatee of the church, supports Otto's figure, tiny under his crown, as he approaches the cosmic throne, while St. Peter and other denizens of heaven look on with features animated by interest.

Stephen of Hungary was crowned; henceforth there would be no more Magyar chiefs, only Christian kings. In 1010, Christian knights sacked Cordova. In about 1013 the conversion of Saint Olaf marked the beginnings of the absorption of the Vikings' northern homelands into Christendom. In the year Oliba entered religion, the historian Radulf Glaber reported churches in Gaul and Italy being built and rebuilt "like new white clothes for the whole world." He imagined—even expected—the Latin church to be extended all over the world "as Christ and Peter trod the sea." This was a bold hope for the formerly beleaguered Christendom but a remarkably accurate prediction of the history of the rest of the millennium.

Like other periods of security in the history of the medieval west, the late tenth and early eleventh centuries produced a renaissance—a revival of ancient Roman learning and letters. Oliba's brethren could commemorate the death of a count with a parody of Virgil, while an abbess in a Saxon convent could write improbable dramas in praise of chastity in the style of Plautus and Terence. We can still get glimpses of scholars at work to tease this revival out of the past. Gerbert of Aurillac, before he became pope, risked denunciation as a magician to seek classical texts in Spain. He found mathematics "very hard indeed . . . almost impossible," and when his own logic teacher settled to the study of arithmetic with him, he was "defeated by the difficulty of the art and utterly humbled by music." When a fellow-pupil remembered their lessons together, sweat appeared on his brow at the recollection of "how we perspired at mathematics." However hard the task and modest the achievements, the effects of this renaissance on the self-perception and self-confidence of rulers could be spectacular. A war leader from the edge of Christendom, like Otto the Great, Gerbert's patron, could fancy himself as another Charlemagne—even another Constantine or Augustus, although he could barely read and spoke no Latin. Sancho the Great also called himself an emperor, though it is not clear what he meant by it. The Holy Empire proclaimed by Otto the Great's grandson, however, was unmistakable in its message and uncompromising in its claims: in one of the sumptuous manuscripts the emperor commissioned in celebration of his majesty, crowned figures of Gaul, Germany, and the Slav world bear tribute to his throne, but they are led by Rome.

Compared even with the "real" Roman Empire of the first half of the previous millennium, Latin Christendom was emerging as an expanding world, stretched between remote horizons. Hands in marriage could be exchanged between Scotland and Hungary. Gerbert of Aurillac travelled from Barcelona to Magdeburg. In Merseburg in eastern Saxony, the historian Thietmar was well informed about Anglo-Saxon England, Burgundy, and the lower Rhine; he incorporated snippets about France and could animadvert knowingly on the Italian national character. Relative peace and security opened pilgrim roads to new, far destinations. Santiago de Compostela,

Ottonian images of kingship represent an ideal of universal monarchy, conferred by divine grace, reminiscent of the Chinese concept of the "mandate of heaven" or of the Islamic notion of the caliphate. The relationship of the monarch to Church and community contrasts with the humbling message of the façade of Ripoll. This self-image of Otto III was reflected back at him from a page of his own gospel-book. Lustrously bejewelled, staring hierarchically, he towers above coadjutors who have eyes only for him. The bishop at his right hand, armed with books, leans on his throne and clasps his garment, like an acolyte at the altar assisting the priest. On his left hand the lay nobility are armed with sword and spear, tentatively reaching to help prop up the weight of his orb, but not quite venturing a profane touch.

tucked into one of the four corners of the world supposedly penetrated by the apostles, had become a numinous shrine in the early ninth century but really began to glow as the cynosure of an international travel industry in the mid-tenth. At the other end of Christendom, Jerusalem began to attract land-borne pilgrims after the pacification of the Magyars at the Lechfeld in 955. Rather like a modern traveller between undifferentiated airport lounges or an eighteenth-century gentleman passing from salon to salon between Saint Petersburg and Sans-Souci, an eleventh-century pilgrim could cross Europe from hostel to hostel or monastery to monastery without a sense of dislocation.

One major trend ran counter to this gentle growth and increasing integration. Although Otto III had a Greek mother and may have dreamed of reuniting the eastern and western moieties of the old Roman Empire, eastern Christendom—overwhelmingly Greek, Slavonic, and Constantinopolitan in inspiration—was drifting away from the predominantly Latin, German, Roman west. Like China, Christendom started the millennium under a divided heaven. In the long run it was a severance that brought strength. Each of the two Christendoms proved to be more cohesive, and therefore perhaps more dynamic, without the other. Their attempts at collaboration in the course of our millennium—in the crusades, in resistance against the Ottomans, in the "romantic repression" of liberal revolution in the nineteenth century—have generally been disastrous. As I write, a new spasm of cooperation is regenerating rhetoric about the creation of a "Europe to the Urals" out of the rubble of communism. The precedents, as we shall see, are not comforting.

Chapter 2

THE COCKPIT OF ORTHODOXY: MEDIEVAL EASTERN CHRISTENDOM

The Perfect Barbarians—The Clash of Two Christendoms—The Business of the Turks—The Rise of the Third Rome—The Mad Planet

THE PERFECT BARBARIANS

The men of the Latin west were still barbarians to those who called themselves Romans. Even in the closing years of the eleventh century, when the First Crusade took large numbers of westerners to Constantinople for the first time, they were regarded by the urbane inhabitants of the "second Rome" with awe inspired by savagery. The emperor's daughter, Anna Comnena, wrote in her father's praise a self-consciously bluestocking history of her own times, full of classical conceits and echoes of Homer. She beheld the uncouth, warlike Latin priests with loathing. The tall, fair, muscular heroes of the Norman contingent she described with obvious attraction and feigned contempt. Robert Guiscard, for instance, "a braggart famed for his tyrannical soul," was "well proportioned from the top of his head to his feet," with a battle-shout like a Homeric hero's. "He was of course a slave to no man . . . for such are great natures, men say, even if they are of humble rank."

For his son, Bohemund, who accompanied the First Crusade and conquered Antioch from the Saracens, Anna seems genuinely to have mingled love and hate. She found him a typical barbarian—crafty, venal, arrogant, deceitful, faithless. Escapades such as his feigned death, nailed into a coffin with a malodorous dead cockerel to escape Byzantine justice in 1104, filled her with indignation and disgust. Yet she described his physical beauty in lingering detail and frank admiration. For he was "a marvel to the eyes . . . such that no one has been seen like him, neither barbarian nor Hellene." She commended his bodily proportions, his stomach, flanks, shoulders, arms, hands, feet, neck, skin, face, hair, eyes, nose, nostrils ("passages for the breath that surged up from his heart") and chin "smoother than any chalk"). Only his back—somewhat misshapen in her exacting eyes—was short of perfection. "Now in this man something sweet appeared but it was impaired by alarming qualities on all sides. . . . In soul and body he was such that anger and love raised their heads in him, and both looked towards war." Crusaders like him, who went to Byzantium to help in what was conceived as a common crusade against the Turks, were perceived in the traditional role of barbarian hordes inflicted on the Romans for their sins, as a scourge of God, "an incurable disease, brought down by Fate or—to speak more piously—by Providence." Even in the face of a common enemy, the Byzantines and crusaders would be driven apart by recriminations over the conduct of the war and squabbles over the spoils.

The parties to this encounter shared important elements of their self-perception and certain convictions of common interest. They all thought of themselves as heirs of Rome, though they saw the legacy differently. They were all Christians, but they belonged to different and increasingly divergent Christian traditions. They were committed together to what would later be called a crusade—an armed pilgrimage to restore to Christian lordship lands sanctified by the presence of Christ but now usurped by Muslim rulers; yet they were unable to agree about strategy or spoils, even under the constraint of the most terrible oaths, sworn on the holiest relics. Underlying these points of contact and conflict were the cultural incompatibilities that could be sensed in Anna Comnena's lines. Even at the height of Roman power, the eastern moiety of the empire had been predominantly Greek-speaking. By the time of the crusades the use of Latin had died out even for the ceremonial and legal purposes for which it had once been favoured. The Byzantine Empire—as historians call the eastern empire in its later phases—was therefore cut off from the basis of western Christendom's unity: the use of Latin as the language of learning, liturgy, and international communication. Moreover, while the west had become an "empire of barbarians," the east had absorbed its invaders or kept them at bay. When envoys presented credentials from the "august Emperor" Otto I at Constantinople in 968, the Byzantine officials were scandalized at "the audacity of it! To style a poor barbarian creature 'Emperor of the Romans'!"

Nothing divided the two Christendoms of east and west like religion. Again, this was in part a matter of language, for Greek tongues could utter theological subtleties inexpressible in Latin. Untranslatability was at the basis of mutual misunderstanding. Dogmas which started the same in east and west turned out differently in Latin and Greek. But religion is more a matter of practice than of dogma, and of behaviour than belief. The differences between the Roman Catholic and Orthodox traditions accumulated over centuries of relative mutual isolation. The process began, or became continuous, as early as the mid-sixth century, when the eastern churches resisted or rejected the universal primacy of the pope. Allegiance to Rome gave the west a basis of common doctrine and common liturgical practice, which gradually took shape until, by the time of the crusades, Rome had established itself as the arbiter of doctrinal questions, the fount of patronage, and the source of liturgical usage from the Atlantic to the Bug and the Carpathians. The western church still enclosed tremendous diversity, but it was recognizably a single communion. Meanwhile, particular doctrinal differences had driven wedges of controversy between east and west; some dogmatic squabbles had come and gone or had been amicably resolved. In 794, however, for reasons that probably had less to do with Christianity than with the political relationship between the empire of Byzantium and the kingdom of the Franks, a western synod had arbitrarily altered the wording of the creed. To this day the western churches—including those now re-formed and without allegiance to Rome—profess their belief that "the Holy Spirit proceeds from the Father and the Son" while the easterners omit mention of the Son and limit to the Father the explicit source of this heavenly emanation. No one knows quite what either formula means or what precisely is the difference between them, yet that difference, impossible to define, has been deadly in effect. During the twelve hundred years since the formula of 794 was accepted in the west, every attempt to effect a rapprochement between the eastern and western churches has foundered on these profound shallows. The westerners acted with unchristian arrogance in presuming to modify the creed without the consensus of their brethren, just as the Church of England errs today in seeking to legitimate the ordination of women without the agreement of the Roman and Orthodox communions. But such errors are always easier to make than unmake.

The split between the eastern and western churches became definitive in 1054, yet not since the fall of the Roman Empire in the west had the need for collaboration between Rome and Constantinople been more obviously in the interests of both. In the upper arm of a Byzantine cross of the period, in the Dumbarton Oaks Museum, an image of the emperor's namesake, Constantine the Great, makes the point by bowing before an icon of Saints Peter and Paul, proffered or brandished by a pope. Pope and emperor both wanted to draw or drive Norman invaders from Italy: the emperor, in order to retain his remaining lands in the peninsula; the pope, to preserve his political independence. Their military alliance had been enthusiastically contracted but inefficiently applied. On 17 June 1053 a Norman army cut the pope's German guard to pieces and, imploring his forgiveness on bended knees, carried the holy father off as a captive. In the long run, the papacy

On a fragment of the upper arm of a Byzantine silver cross, the Emperor Constantine the Great bows before an icon of the saints of Rome, Peter and Paul, displayed by Pope Sylvester. The scene has been interpreted as an allusion to the introduction of the Emperor Isaac I Comnenus into Constantinople by the Patriarch Michael Cerularius on 1 September 1057, but the obvious context is that of the disastrous efforts made in the 1050s to establish entente between Rome and Constantinople.

would win over the Normans and turn them into the pontiff's swordbearers. The captive pope's immediate policy, however, was "to remain faithful to our mission to deliver Christendom" and to maintain the Byzantine alliance until "this enemy nation is expelled from the church of Christ and Christendom avenged."

In Constantinople the patriarch Michael Cerularius was equally determined that the alliance should founder, not for the Normans' sake but for his own and that of his see. Rome's claim to universal primacy threatened the authority of other patriarchs. Rome's increasing fastidiousness in matters of doctrinal formulation and liturgical practice threatened the traditions of the eastern churches. If the emperor became dependent on a western military alliance, the church of Constantinople would be compelled to conform to the dictates of Rome—as indeed would happen later in the middle ages, when, under the influence of the Turkish peril, the Orthodox were driven to submission by despair. The patriarch forestalled any such development by initiating a vulgar exchange of abuse with Latin prelates. In a letter from his mouthpiece, the primate of Bulgaria, Latin practice was denounced as tainted by Jewish influence. He wrote to the pope, urging goodwill but omitting some of the usual titles of courtesy; and when papal legates arrived in Constantinople, he refused to receive them or even to acknowledge their presence. He accompanied this campaign of provocation by forcibly closing the Latin churches in Constantinople.

Pope Leo, teaching himself Greek in the grip of a mortal sickness, was, like most of his line, too confident to barter the rights—as he conceived them—of the church for a worldly advantage. He was resolved to face death standing crutchless on his principles. He responded to the patriarch's insults in kind and sent to Constantinople a mission that did not intend to compromise. Its leader, Cardinal Humbert, was renowned for his theological subtlety, diplomatic skills, and noble principles. All these qualities seemed to desert him in Constantinople. His strategy was to appeal to the emperor over the patriarch's head; but although the emperor enjoyed greater influence over the church in his realms than any ruler in the west, he could not coerce the patriarch, and the legate's policy was doomed. Humbert offended the politicians by his indifference and the churchmen by his arrogance. He denounced a disputatious but moderate monk as a "pestiferous pimp" better suited to a brothel than a monastery. He put the emperor, who was anxious to be conciliatory, into an impossible position by raising the irresolvable question of the procession of the Holy Spirit. After three months of waiting in vain for a dialogue with the patriarch, he lost his temper and slapped a bull of excommunication on the high altar of Hagia Sophia, "upon Michael, neophyte and false patriarch, now for his abominable crimes notorious." It was too late. Death had overtaken Humbert's master, comforted by heavenly visions, in Rome. The legation to Constantinople had therefore outlived the source of its authority. Humbert's bull, moreover, was flawed. Many of the charges it levelled against the Greeks—practising castration, rebaptizing Latins, marrying priests, infringing the commandments, excommunicating the beardless, and distorting the creed—were either false or wrongly formulated. At the time, it was generally supposed that it would soon be rescinded or forgotten. In fact, relations between the eastern and western churches never recovered, and intercommunion has never been fully or enduringly re-established.

The Clash of Two Christendoms

Eastern Christendom was willing to snub and defy the west perhaps because the millennium had opened so brilliantly for Byzantium, and by the mid-century the effects had not yet worn off. The emperor who presided at the turn of the millennium, Basil II, can still be seen in a contemporary effigy, flaking off the page of his own book of hours in the Marciana Library. He appears true to life: a savage and sacral figure, bearded and mailed, attended by angels and heavily armed, towering over cringing barbarian vic-

Except for the defacing effects of time, this is how Basil II liked to see himself when he turned in prayer to his Book of Hours. Barbarian supplicants crawl at his feet. Unlike Otto III he needs no human helpers. He leans on his own sword while angels crown him and invest him with a sceptre. Isolated above the earth, insulated against profanation, he is censed and adorned with a halo. Icons guard him on either hand. The emphasis on divine legitimation is understandable when one recalls his peasant origins: its proof was his victories.

The magnetism of Constantinople exerted its pull beyond the reach of orthodoxy. The Kings of Hungary in the eleventh century derived their legitimacy from the Church of Rome, but were still próud to wear a crown bestowed by Byzantium on King Géza in the 1070s. In the inset enamels the Byzantine monarchs appear in central eminence, with the Hungarian king as a relatively humble petitioner, turning awestruck eyes on them from below.

tims. Grandson of peasants, he became known to posterity as the Bulgar-slayer because of the outcome of his victory over the Bulgars at Kleidion in 1014; all the defeated survivors—fourteen thousand of them, reputedly—were blinded at his command, save one man in every hundred, spared one eye with which to lead home the rest. The Bulgar tsar, Samuel, who had sought to seize or control the empire, was said to have collapsed and died at the sight of the marchers struggling back. Meanwhile, in Constantinople, ladies leaned from elegant bow windows to watch the victor's procession of triumph.

Byzantium's incorporation of Bulgaria and Basil's peace with the Arabs on the southern front gave the empire virtually ideal configurations, with frontiers on the Danube and the Euphrates, beyond which direct rule was considered neither practicable nor desirable. Basil bound the outlying provinces tightly to his crown: in Bulgaria by conciliation, cooperating with an indigenous élite, appointing a native archbishop, and in Greece by repression, forcing acculturation on the immigrant Slavs, imposing the Greek liturgy. The empire he bequeathed exerted influence and drew deference from much farther afield. The emperor's name was blessed in prayer in Kiev and Vladimir and in the sumptuous but schismatic churches at Ani in Armenia. Though Hungary conformed to the rites of the Latin church, her kings felt the pull of Byzantium; as late as the 1070s, Hungary received a crown on which her king is depicted, turning his eyes towards his Byzantine suzerains. When Basil II died in 1025, Byzantium was the cynosure of eastern Europe. The treasury was full. The power and potential of the empire, if not at their peak, were very near it. The high culture of the metropolis, too, was experiencing a glorious age, a sort of renaissance of humanist scholarship and classical art forms. Byzantine ivory workers, who usually avoided pagan and lubricious subjects, were able in a brief dawn to make such delicate confections as the Veroli casket on which Europa cavorts prettily on her bull's back, pouting at her pursuers and archly waving her flimsy stole.

Neither the glamour nor the glory lasted. From inside, the empire was weakened by an aristocracy which had accumulated wealth and privilege in the tenth century and thereafter used them increasingly to impoverish and manipulate the throne. From without, the frontiers were menaced by new barbarians: the Turks in the east and the Normans in the west—the sons of Seljük, who pissed fire in his dreams, and of Guiscard, "whom Normandy produced but whom evil of every sort nurtured and fostered." Emperors of the vigour and virility of Basil II might have coped, but no more were forthcoming. The chequered dynastic history of the eleventh century can be followed in the album of imperial mosaics that line the upper gallery of Hagia Sophia, decorating a space that served as a private devotional enclosure for the imperial family within the cathedral. The botched family portrait of the Empress Zoë reflects her sordid story; the likeness of her third husband is overlaid on that of her second, who murdered her first for her before being forced into a monastery. Her last spouse, Constantine Monomachus, was acquired to recapture the throne from which she had been deposed. She called herself sovereign empress, but she was a frivolous martinette who could not manage without a man.

Her sister, Theodora, who ruled after her in 1055–56, was altruistic and

The uninhibited paganism with which the bone and ivory overlay of the Veroli casket is carved captures the spirit of the eleventh-century Byzantine "renaissance" in humanist scholarship and classical art forms. The themes are all of savagery tamed by art, love, and beauty. Europa, seductively poised on the bull's back, defies pursuers. Hercules settles to play the lyre, attended by cavorting putti. Centaurs play for the Maenads' dance.

The gallery of Hagia Sophia functioned as a private enclosure for members of the imperial family and was decorated with portraits of rulers and their spouses in pious attitudes. The mosaic dedicated to the Empress Zoë betrays the questionable complexities of her sex life. The face of Constantine IX Monomachus, the husband presenting a bag of gold to Christ, was remodelled to replace the likeness of her second spouse, Michael IV, whom she had first employed in the murder of his predecessor, then banished to a monastery when she tired of him. The squashed lettering above his nimbus to the left is clear evidence of a bodged job.

unflighty, but her reign, distinguished by the seventy-year-old's refusal to associate a man with her as emperor, was loudly resented as unnatural. It was shameful, according to the patriarch Cerularius, that a woman should rule the empire. Theodora was tough and characterful but too pious to undertake the dirty work inseparable from successful statesmanship in medieval Byzantium. In 1057 a rich landowner usurped the throne, confirming the trend of the drift of power from state to aristocracy. The tradition of *noblesse oblige* was abandoned by an increasingly self-interested élite. The elderly general Cecaumenus typically advocated an evasive and reclusive response to troubled times: "Lock up your daughters as if they were criminals. Avoid parties. If not on the emperor's business, stay at home with your trusted servants; stockpile supplies and look after the interests of your own family."

This was the era of Byzantine history that evoked Gibbon's memorable scorn for "a degenerate race of princes" and generated a legend of decadence which has distorted Byzantium's popular image ever since. In reality, Gibbon was an enthusiastic Byzantinist. Evident relish underlay his affected distaste. *The History of the Decline and Fall of the Roman Empire* genuinely pioneered Byzantine studies and included the most comprehensive history of the empire then available. While the intrigues, crimes, and vices of the court made good caricaturist's copy, the story emerged, even from his pages, as more like tragedy than satire, enlivened with characters as often deserving of admiration as of contempt. The emperor who presided over and who was blamed for the worst crisis of the eleventh century was a man of exceptional energy and courage; his downfall was the effect of two forms of hubris: rashness and overconfidence, accumulated in success.

The fortifications of Bari—biggest and most splendid of the coastal castles of Apulia— were extended by Frederick II in the early thirteenth century and restored after an explosion in 1524. Under these changes, it remains essentially a Norman castello, built after the conquest from Byzantium in 1071. Though Goths, Lombards, Moors, Carolingians, and Ottonians had captured it in the past, this western outpost had always returned to Byzantine allegiance—but never again.

In 1069, Romanus Diogenes, then a Byzantine general, was awaiting execution for planning a coup d'état when he was chosen by an emperor's widow to command the empire and its armies at a crucial moment: the Normans were investing Bari—Byzantium's western sub-capital—while the Turks threatened the threshold-kingdom of Armenia. Suddenly removed from the condemned cell to the throne room, Romanus embraced the widow and the war with an equal sense of duty. His well-run campaigns seemed to turn the tables on the Turks; his energetic measures promised relief from the Normans. But Robert Guiscard, alerted by the defenders' mood, scattered or sank the task force on its way to Bari. On the eastern front, Romanus was tempted to overextend his forces in pursuing the Turks, whose leader, doused in funerary unguents, turned in triumph and made the captive emperor kiss the ground before his feet.

The twin defeats of 1071 left the empire topped and tailed. Romanus could raise only a fifth of his ransom. It suited the barbarians on both flanks, however, to leave the empire largely intact, to milk for future payola and protection money, and it is doubtful whether the Byzantines really felt obliged to appeal to the western barbarians to save them from those of the east. When it eventually arrived, the help from the west came in a most unwelcome form. The crusading hosts who appeared in 1097 were partly a popular rabble, whom the Byzantines admired for their piety but resented for their poverty, and partly a formidable army, which was welcomed for its usefulness but feared for its lack of discipline. According to Anna Comnena they were "a race under the spells of Dionysos and Eros," among whom those who "undertook this journey only to worship at the Holy Sepulchre" were outnumbered by predatory enemies whose "object was to dethrone the emperor and capture the capital." In the very long run, her words proved prophetic. The tense cooperation between Byzantines and crusaders, which characterized the First Crusade, broke down completely in the Second and Third. The crusaders blamed "Greek treachery" for their failures; the Byzantines emerged fortified in their conviction of superiority over barbarian impiety and greed. The Fourth Crusade, launched in 1202 as a pilgrimage under arms for the recapture of Jerusalem, ended shedding Christian blood on the ramparts and streets of Constantinople.

The reasons for the diversion of this expedition remain mysterious to this day. "Who killed Constantinople?" has become the theme of a sort of historical whodunnit in which conspiracy theorists have paraded the leaders, advocates, patrons, and exploiters of the crusade as suspects. The long-term consequences can be sampled on the outside of Saint Mark's Cathedral in Venice, which is studded and dotted with the spoils of Byzantium and adorned with the riches of an empire acquired at Byzantium's expense. The great bronze horses above the west doors stamp and snort in victory. Below, a Hercules looted from Constantinople carries off, in his turn, the Ery-

"Always harnessed to the bloodstained chariot of victory," the horses of San Marco must originally have formed a team of the sort often illustrated in scenes of Roman triumphs, before they were carried off by the Venetian raiders of Constantinople in 1204. As a fitting mark of Venice's elevation to imperial status at Byzantine expense they were re-erected over the west portal of St. Mark's Cathedral, where, according to Petrarch, "they stand as if alive, seeming to neigh from on high and to paw with their feet." An inspiration to the Venetians and a temptation to their enemies, they were also influential models for artists—"stupendous, marvellous, and perhaps," in Jacopo Sansovino's words, "the finest work in Europe." See p. 175.

manthean boar. On the south side, Roman emperors, carved in porphyry, guard the treasury, while pillars, wrought by a Syrian hand fifteen hundred years ago, lead into the baptistery. The issue of the siege that brought these exotica to Venice is well known, stamped in many readers' minds by Gibbon's famous description of the sack of Hagia Sophia in which self-styled crusaders drank from the holy chalices, trampled the icons, and installed a prostitute on the patriarch's throne, while "their mules and horses were laden with the wrought silver and gilt carvings which they tore down from the doors and pulpit; and if the beasts stumbled under the burden, they were stabbed by their impatient drivers, and the holy pavement streamed with their impure blood." Yet this was the terrible consummation of an expedition begun in piety and altruism "for the succour of the land over the sea" and the redemption of the warrior pilgrims' souls.

The crusade was first preached by a disinterested evangelist in 1198, urging a new effort to recapture Jerusalem, which the Third Crusade had left in Saracen hands. The enthusiastic popular response made the pope, the Cis-

St. Mark's Square and Cathedral were the *Kunstkammer* of the medieval Venetian state, where the choicest spoils of empire were displayed to fill the citizens with pride and visitors with fear. Among the loot of the eastern Roman empire which still stands outside the doors of the treasury of San Marco are Diocletian and his fellow tetrarchs, clasping each other's shoulders in solidarity: the gesture perhaps betrays late third-century anxiety about an empire threatened with dissolution. These carvings in porphyry were already nearly a thousand years old when Venice acquired them.

tercian order, and the barons of north-east France take up the call. Moved to tears at a meeting in San Marco, the Venetians agreed to provide the shipping at what was to prove an unaffordable price. When the designated leader died, after having urged his followers to complete their vows, a successor was found in the person of a paragon of chivalry, Boniface of Montferrat, a Lombard marquis of whose house many promising youths had already been sacrificed to the lure of the Levant, either on previous crusades or in Byzantine service. While the army was assembling at Venice, envoys from the Byzantine pretender, Alexius IV, proposed a detour to Constantinople to install an ally on the imperial throne. Gradually, under the influence of the crusaders' evident inability to pay for their passage by any other means, and, eventually, under pressure of hunger as well as poverty, the party in favour of a diversion came to prevail. When the crusading fleet was languishing at Corfu in May 1203, a majority of the pilgrims agreed to turn their prows towards the Byzantine capital.

The blame for the diversion has been widely apportioned. The Venetian doge Dandolo, wily, old, and blind, behaved like a pre-incarnation of Machiavelli, relishing opportunities to manipulate and exploit the crusade.

He imposed a secret clause in his original contract with the crusaders' envoys, specifying Egypt as the expedition's destination; his grounds, that "nothing could be accomplished by attempting a direct attack towards Jerusalem," were reasonable, but his intention was almost certainly dishonest. Venetians had nothing to gain from an assault on Egypt, their lucrative trading partner. Dandolo induced the crusade to undertake a preliminary diversion to help Venice in her war against the innocent Christians of Zara in Hungary; he set and sustained terms of payment which kept the crusaders under a permanent and unmanageable burden of debt to him. When the conquest of Constantinople was accomplished, he collared the greatest prize: "one quarter and one half of one quarter of all the empire of Romania," turning Venice at a stroke from a commercial polis into an imperial capital. He and his people nourished a long grudge against Byzantium for the suspension of Venetian trading privileges in 1171 and the massacre of the denizens of the Venetian quarter in 1184.

Boniface of Montferrat also had cause for resentment of Byzantium, where one of his brothers had been slighted and another murdered by an emperor's command. Once Constantinople was in the crusaders' hands, he revealed his desire to get the imperial throne for himself—or, at least, the fief of Thessaloníki. Inviting suspicion, he spent Christmas 1201 at the German imperial court along with the pretender Alexius, whose presence is suppressed in all the sources Boniface was able to influence. The host at the Christmas party was Alexius's brother-in-law, Philip of Swabia. He did not take part in the crusade but has been accused as an off-stage puppeteer. His correspondence with the pope showed that he had dreams of acquiring the Byzantine empire for himself through marriage. Realizing, however, that his brother-in-law made a more promising candidate, he sent him to Rome and begged the pope to support him. The pope himself, though he maintained an attitude of lofty rectitude throughout the shabby history of the crusade, was not entirely blameless. He was not above diverting crusades for his own ends; indeed, he sent some dissident crusaders who refused to sail from Venice on bloody business of his own in Apulia. His injunctions to spare Christians, though emphatic, therefore lacked moral authority, especially as he allowed the crusaders to appropriate Christians' resources if necessary. When the crusade was over, he was willing enough to mop up the treasures and patronage of the Byzantine church. Even the Cistercian order is tainted with connivance in the crusaders' crime. The Cistercians took over the popular preaching campaign and all its funds; they made a fortune from the trusteeships of crusaders' estates. They had no particular interest in a diversion to Constantinople; yet it was vital for them to keep the crusade united as a going concern, and Abbot Samson of Loos was perhaps the most eloquent advocate of an accommodation in the crusaders' camp. Most of the rank and file of the crusaders were blameless. Even in Corfu, under the constraints of isolation, penury, and starvation, the majority refused to divert until moved to tears "by the sight of their lords, their relations, and their friends on their knees before them."

They had to attack Constantinople twice: first to install the pretender Alexius, then—before a coup pre-empted them—to dethrone him and impose a Latin emperor and church. The myth of the city's invulnerability was destroyed, and, indeed, the Latin occupation lasted only fifty-seven years before one of the surviving Byzantine rump states mustered enough strength to retake it. Meanwhile, the court of the lawful Emperor of the Romans withdrew to a house in Nicaea, built of rubble under a wooden roof and faced with alternate bands of brick and ashlar. With three large-windowed rooms on the first floor and a monumental external stairway, it made a pleasant residence for a provincial gentleman, but it was a mighty comedown from the marble halls of the Blachernae Palace. Back in Constantinople, meanwhile, the Latin "emperors" found the Blachernae too expensive to keep up and moved to a gloomy, cavernous residence in the quarter of the prison gate.

THE BUSINESS OF THE TURKS

Today, this is a neglected, seedy suburb, cut off from the antique glories of Istanbul by the relentless traffic of the Atatürk Boulevard. The wooden houses are shuttered and rickety, the streets filthy, unfrequented except by raucous children and a despondent fruit vendor. The huge monument which dominates the district is grimy and bare. Its dull pink outer walls sag with great age and vast weight. The surrounding streets are built over parts of its ruins. It must once have been unimaginably big. The central core which survives today, the Church of the Pantocrator, looks ill at ease not only because it is woebegone but also because it is so out of scale with its environs.

It was built in the 1120s by the Byzantine emperor John II Comnenos and his wife, Eirene, a Hungarian princess whom her subjects revered as a saint. The faces of the couple gleam from a mosaic in the cathedral of Hagia Sophia, Eirene framed by her burning red hair, John enveloped by his golden robes. Serene and sublime, the emperor exudes wealth and confidence as he extends towards the figure of Christ a bulging bag of gold. The Church of the Pantocrator was intended as the most generous of their gifts to Christ and, since it was also to be a mausoleum and memorial for their house, the most ostentatiously self-interested. The decayed wreck that can be seen today has vestiges of the grandeur with which the founders endowed it. The marble remains in the apse of the most southerly of the three

The surroundings of a sarcophagus, vulgarly supposed to be that of the foundress of the Church of the Pantocrator, suggest the neglect into which this suburb has fallen since its grand days in the twelfth century, when it housed the imperial pantheon of the Comnenoi.

linked naves; the lavish marble mouldings of the door-frames of the narthex are intact; restorers have exposed the grand geometrical mosaic on the floor. The classical sarcophagus in which Eirene was buried in 1124 survives, removed to Hagia Sophia.

The history of the rise and fall of the foundation reflects the greatness, crisis, and collapse of the Byzantine Empire from the early twelfth century to the mid-fifteenth. As well as housing the dead of two dynasties, it included an enormous monastery, which provided Constantinople with its main retirement home, hospital, and lunatic asylum. It was a centre of social welfare, a powerhouse of the imperial cult, and a school of Byzantine identity from where, in the fifteenth century, the priest Gennadius defied imperial plans to defer to the primacy of Rome. In the thirteenth century, when the Greek Empire was forced out of its own capital by the conquering "pilgrims" of the Fourth Crusade, the Pantocrator became the palace of the usurping Latin rulers. When the Byzantines recaptured the city in 1261, their Genoese allies burned most of the buildings to the ground. The returning monks nourished an aversion for everything Latin. When the last dynasty of Byzantium, the Paleologoi, restored the foundation to its original place of influence by adopting it as their own family mausoleum, it became a rock of orthodox purity in a church increasingly willing, in the face of the menace of the apparently invincible Turkish conquerors, to compromise with potential allies in western Christendom. Gennadius's legendary preference for the sultan over the pope was widely shared by his fellow-citizens—which helps to explain why Istanbul is a Turkish, Islamic capital and neither Greek nor Christian today. The answer to the old song's question, "Why did Constantinople get the works?" is—correctly and according to the same lyricist—"It's nobody's business but the Turks'."

The death of the Greek Empire, however, was a lingering one; its symptoms were various, and it would be naïve to suppose that western medicine would have saved it. The severity of the empire's problems and the deep reach of its identity can be sensed in Istanbul's most beautiful former church, Saint Saviour in Chora, between the walls of Constantine and Theodosius. Like the Pantocrator, it was a foundation of the Comnenoi, but its period of glory, in which it was redecorated with the wall and vault paintings and mosaics that make it famous today, occurred in the second and third decades of the fourteenth century. By then the empire's future conquerors had been established in its former territory for more than a generation. Within five years of the dedication of the church, the nearby city of Bursa became the Ottoman capital; Constantinople was becoming engulfed.

The patron who so lavishly endowed the church of Chora in such unpromising times was, except in the unique scale of his munificence, a representative Byzantine gentleman of his times. Theodore Metochites combined the tastes of a scholar with the vocation of a statesman. His career in imperial service culminated in 1321, the year of the unveiling of his redecorations at the Chora, in his appointment as Grand Logothete—chief executive, in effect, of the imperial government. His writings—on devotion, theology, astronomy, and literary criticism—suffered perhaps from official claims on his time. Yet they were notable for sheer copious output and, in his early years, for a restless striving after originality and an eschewal of

"A work of noble love for things good and beautiful." The rippling domes of the church of the monastery of Chora—the heavenly dwelling-place—are modestly massed and sited under the Sixth Hill, toward the land walls of Constantinople. The roofscape seen here was modified by eighteenth-century alterations, when the present upper dome of wood was hoisted on the original drum and a minaret added, just visible at the right of this photograph. Much of the fabric, however, dates from the foundation of the Comnenoi in the late eleventh and early twelfth centuries. The outer narthex which fills the foreground of the photograph, and the parecclesion, under a fourth dome not visible here, were part of the programme of embellishments of Theodore Metochites, who commissioned the matchless mosaics and wall paintings.

subjects exhausted by the ancients. The aim of Metochites's scholarship, he claimed, was "to behave independently, like the seven planets, and not merely observe their movements." He came to deplore as "slavery" the life he led as a politician, "swept along by ambition." He escaped its sordid confines in his early career through literary work, which gave him the hope of immortality on earth; later, he shifted his efforts to devotion and his sight to heaven. When a coup ousted him in 1328, he sought the consolations of religion. In 1330 he became a monk of his own foundation; the Chora, however, had already been his mental and spiritual refuge long before that. "This monastery," he declared, "has meant more than anything in the world to me. It was a work of noble love for things good and beautiful. . . . The thought of this monastery was alone capable of putting my mind into a more easy disposition, lifting it above all preoccupations, making it feel unburdened and peaceful, and enabling it to function well."

His love for the Chora was peculiarly intense, but his sentiments were widely paralleled and his vocation thoroughly typical. His friend and contemporary, Michael Tornikes, shared the trajectory of his life from worldly glory to cloistered retirement after a successful military career in the 1320s. The old soldier's tomb is in the paraecclesion of the Chora, amid a programme of paintings which celebrate the texts read at feasts of the Virgin, and "portraits" of saints whose feasts shared her festivals. "However many applauses one may collect upon earth," the inscription says, "when they are all dead, Tornikes, a man of myriad victories, Grand Constable, who lies buried here, will put them all to shame as, good friend, a lion shames mimicking apes." This apparently proud boast is followed by an awestruck account of the dead man's virtues, including his royal blood and princely marriage, but the inscription ends, "And leaving his life as a splendid example, he lies, a poor monk among bones."

In the opinion of most of the citizens of Constantinople, the empire depended on the patronage of the Blessed Virgin. She had repelled invaders—Arabs, Rus, and Bulgars—from beneath the capital's walls and could be relied on to deflect, if not to defeat, the Tatars and Turks who, by divine permission, had wrought havoc on other sinful peoples. The Byzantine Empire was not exempt from punishment by the scourge of God but had escaped through the intercession of the most powerful of heavenly protectresses. The name of the Chora, which means heavenly dwelling place, probably alluded to the Virgin's womb—"the container of the uncontainable," as it is called in a mosaic in the narthex. Metochites's scheme of decoration assembled the most comprehensive array of Marian imagery in the world: nineteen distinct scenes in her life precede the story of Christ's birth in the cycle devoted to her. Her birth is preceded by an annunciation, like that of the Saviour himself. On the bays of the inner narthex she learns to walk and is blessed by priests, caressed by her parents, fed by angels, and equipped by divine election with purple wool to make a veil for the temple. After her commendation to Joseph, she is left alone in his house. "Behold," reads the inscription, "I am leaving thee in my house while I go away to build." On his return, Joseph grapples with a human predicament:

Mary presented for enrolment in the census in the unusually extensive cycle devoted to her in the narthex of the Chora. The scriptural authority for the scene is given in the inscription, which is punctiliously illustrated: Joseph went "to be taxed with Mary, his espoused wife, being great with child." As Grand Logothete in a complex bureaucracy, Metochites would have been a good judge of the technicalities of the census. The seated official, perhaps intended for "Quirinius, Governor of Syria," wears a curved cap of office which should be compared with Metochites's skiadion on p. 85. Joseph, with his sons by a former marriage who have a big role in this cycle, seems to thrust Mary forward to bear the burden of the encounter.

"Mary, what is this thy deed?" The painting and mosaics are executed by the artists with unsurpassed brilliance and are informed by the patron with unequalled humanity and drama.

Metochites himself appears in one of the pictures, prostrate at the feet of God, half-raising an abashed and awestruck face. Yet he was not so humble as to appear hatless in the presence. He wears his skiadion or headgear of office—a billowingly exotic affair in white that makes him look, to an innocent eye, just like a Turk. Despite the huge cultural gap that separated the Byzantines from the Ottomans—Christian consciousness from Islamic identity, imperial experience from nomadic tradition, worship of womanhood from values of virility—these hostile neighbours were becoming more and more like each other in the late middle ages, exchanging influence like Don Quixote and Sancho Panza or like the Chinese and the Khitans. Even as they enveloped the shrinking territory of the empire, the Turks forbore for a long time to destroy it altogether. It flattered Ottoman vanity to keep emperors of universal pretensions as clients dependent on their mercy. John V, who suffered the ultimate indignity of being arrested for debt in Venice in 1379 on his way home from a temporizing conversion to the Roman faith, had to get Turkish help to recover his throne.

Metochites offers the Church of Chora at the throne of Christ. In this mosaic, which surmounts the west door of the church, the building is shown without the outer narthex added by the donor: compare the photograph above, p. 82.

In 1403 a visiting Castilian ambassador was given, at his own request, a conducted tour of Constantinople "to visit and view the city, churches, and relics." His first impression was of wealth, induced by the columns and wall-claddings of marble and jasper, the hangings of silk, the richly wrought mosaics, the relics mounted in gem-spangled gold, and the sheer scale of the church of Hagia Sophia, such that "even though the visitor should day by day return, seeing all he could, yet on the morrow there would always be new sights to view." His next impression was of the defensive strength of the site, enclosed "within a stout and lofty wall, defended by many strong towers." As the tour proceeded, however, he spotted signs of decline: the depopulated quarters, abandoned to cornfields and orchards, the many monumental buildings—the greater part, indeed—now ruined. "It is however plain," he concluded, "that in former times when Constantinople was in its pristine state it was one of the noblest capitals of the world." The ambassador was bound for the court of the Tatar chief Timur, who had relieved the pressure of the Turkish menace on Byzantium by defeating the Ottomans and caging the sultan. The relief was only temporary, and the shadow of the Turk still seemed to hang over the city. The ambassador particularly admired the enormous bronze of Justinian—four times life-size—which stood before the cathedral on a tall plinth. The emperor, he was told, was thus splendidly commemorated because "he performed many mighty deeds in his day fighting against the Turks." In reality the campaigns of his reign had been against the Persians, Vandals, and Ostrogoths, and no people whom the Greeks called Turks appeared for two hundred years after his day.

When the Turks finally lost patience with Constantinople, the blow came quickly and inevitably. The accession as sultan of Mehmet II in 1451, at the age of nineteen, marked the end of counsels of prudence. He resented foreign control of a stronghold that dominated a strait vital for the communications of his empire. He fancied himself a Roman emperor. The fall of the city was prepared by every contrivance of the siege engineer's craft. Huge forts—known respectively as the Castles of Europe and Asia—were erected on either shore to command access to the Bosphorus. The heaviest artillery ever founded was used to batter the walls. Ships were transported overland in kit form to outflank the defenders' boom. In the end it was sheer weight of numbers that proved decisive. The attackers climbed the breaches over the bodies of dead comrades. The corpse of the last Constantine was identified only by the eagle devices on his foot-armour.

The Rise of the Third Rome

Now here is a paradox: the period of the decline or eclipse of Byzantium in the fourteenth and fifteenth centuries was also a period of unprecedented expansion for eastern Christendom. To our galactic museum-keepers of the remote future, the fall of Constantinople, if it is noticed at all, will appear as a little local difficulty for one of the fastest-growing civilizations of the late middle ages. The shrinkage and disappearance of the Byzantine Empire was more than made up for by the phenomenon of Muscovy, building a Russian Empire more dynamic and—in its way—more enduring than any of the western European empires which, from today's perspective, seem to have dominated the second half of our millennium. In the hundred years from 1362, Muscovy developed from a poor, despised, small, and upstart principality, under the tutelage of Tatar masters, into a substantial state covering a swath of territory from Solvychegodsk on the northern Dvina to Tula near the source of the Don, dominating the upper and middle reaches of the Volga. In 1478 the conquest of Novgorod—a northern polis with a tradition of independence and a landward empire in the Venetian style—secured frontiers on the Pechora and Lake Ladoga. In 1480, Tatar sovereignty was repudiated and Moscow was proclaimed the "Third Rome," recovering

The walls of the Kremlin are the biggest contribution of Italian Renaissance engineering to the appearance of Moscow. The first vector of the Renaissance was perhaps the Roman-educated empress Zoë Palaeologus who arrived in 1472. When Fioravanti, who had previously worked for Matthais Corvinus (see p. 173), followed from Bologna in 1475 he immediately went on a provincial tour to study Russian architectural traditions. His greatest work within the Kremlin, the Cathedral of the Assumption, where Ivan the Terrible "saw heaven," is remarkably faithful to the native vernacular; and the outline of the towers which crown the red-brick walls are reminiscent of wooden river-forts. In places, fragments of the old white walls emerge. But details like the pedimented dormers and the quotations from the western romanesque betray the designer's origins.

the baton, and perhaps the sceptre, dropped from the dead hand of Byzantium. In the 1490s architects from Italy were adorning the Kremlin with classical motifs, fragments of which can still be seen today.

Moscow's Roman self-consciousness derived from a relationship with Byzantium which began before the millennium, long before the foundation of Moscow itself, during the early history of pre-Muscovite Russian or proto-Russian states. A letter from Novgorod reached a Viking prince in 862. "Our land," it read, "is great and rich. But there is no order in it. Come and rule over us." In response he founded the first of the states which eventually became Russia. The story may have got oversimplified in the record, but it shows how territorial statehood was exported beyond the limits of the old Roman Empire to relatively immature political worlds in northern and eastern Europe. Some of the cultural legacy of the Romans was carried along with it. Its most important vectors were Christian missionaries. Tribal hegemonies could only be turned into territorial states by communications and administration. Because the church monopolized literacy or even—in the case of the Cyrillic alphabet—actually invented it, the range of statehood spread with Christianity. By legitimating strong-arm rule or sanctifying weak authority, the church could also make enormous contributions to political stability. An amazing generation of evangelization around the turn of the millennium equipped an array of emergent states on the eastern and northern frontiers of Europe with these resources. From the point of view of the future of eastern Christendom, the most important of the royal converts was Volodomir, ruler of Kiev.

The blood of this prince, like the culture of his country, was a mixture of Viking and Slav, pagan on both sides. In 1988, to commemorate a thousand years of Russian Christianity, statues and plaques in Volodomir's honour, erected by subscriptions of Orthodox congregations, appeared all over the western world, confirming the honorand's image as a Christian and his status as a saint. But like many great saints he sinned with gusto in his life, reputedly keeping a seraglio of eight hundred girls, coining proverbs in praise of drunkenness, and leaving a reputation in German annals as *"fornicator immensus et crudelis."* His conversion was, in effect, the bride-price of the Byzantine princess whose hand in marriage he extorted from Constantinople by threat of force. The faith he opportunistically espoused he then rigorously enforced. Its reception was oiled by the use of the vernacular Slavonic liturgy, created by the missions of Saints Cyril and Methodius to Moravia—a remote frontier from which Byzantine influence was gradually extended—and disseminated by a numerous native Slav clergy. His wife was an unique prize—a princess "born in the purple," such as Byzantine law and custom forbade to barbarian suitors. Only a short while before the emperor Constantine Porphyrogenitus had banned "monstrous demands" for a marriage alliance with "shifty and dishonourable tribes of the north. . . . For just as each animal mates with its own species so it is right that each nation also should marry and cohabit not with those of other race and tongue but of the same tribe and speech." The marriage proposals brought from the court of Otto I had been rejected as "a thing unheard of."

For Volodomir, elevation by affinity to the imperial house was therefore a prize well worth the sacrifice of his pagan gods. When his reluctant bride arrived, under the inducement of bloody threats, he solemnly dethroned the occupants of his sacred grove of idols. The thunder-god Perun, with his golden, silver-moustached head, was lashed to a horse's tail and beaten with sticks on his calvary to a river-bed grave. It was a measure of the importance of the newly won link with Byzantium that it justified this affront to a supposedly powerful divine protector.

The link endured. An abiding sense of belonging to a community of eastern Christendom, with its head and heart in Constantinople, remained strong in Russia for most of the middle ages and, despite loss of territory at the edges—to the Latin church in central Europe and to Islam in Asia—spread, in net terms, as Russia expanded and as new areas succumbed to Russian arms or Orthodox missions. While a common sense of identity in western Christendom took shape slowly, fitfully, and sometimes painfully, that of the Orthodox community was sprung fully armed. Relations, like those in any family, were sometimes turbulent but were always governed by a sense of fellow-feeling. Thus Russian armies attacked Constantinople in 1043, but twenty-five years later, when Prince Izyaslav marched on Kiev with a Polish army, part pagan, part Catholic, the citizens threatened to burn their city and "flee to the land of the Greeks." Even at Byzantium's last gasp, in 1452, when the Russian church reluctantly transgressed its tradition of deference to the see of Constantinople—defying the Byzantine rapprochement with the Latin communion by electing a patriarch of its own—the tsar felt obliged to apologize to the emperor: "We beseech your Sacred Majesty not to blame us for not writing to your Sovereignty beforehand; we did this from dire necessity, not from pride or arrogance."

For the tradition of eastern Christendom to be transmitted with success from Constantinople to Moscow, and for the civilization to survive, a profound abyss in the thirteenth century, which threatened to engulf the political framework of the Orthodox community, had to be bridged. It was a double crisis. While Constantinople was in the hands of the Latin conquerors—as it was, with much of the rest of the empire, from 1204 to 1261—the northern lands of the Orthodox commonwealth were cut off and almost obliterated by one of the most terrible and transforming invasions Europe had ever received from Asia: that of the Tatars. For eight centuries the broad corridor of the Eurasian steppe had admitted hordes of nomad-warriors into Europe. Between the fifth and tenth centuries the Huns, Avars, Magyars, and Bulgars had all penetrated the west to varying depths but had all ultimately been defeated and settled or destroyed. More recently, and with more persistence, the Pechenegs, Cumans, and Turks had battered and eroded the defences of Byzantium. Despite this long experience, when the Tatars descended, their victims did not know what to make of them.

The first Latins who heard of them—crusaders in their camp at Damietia in 1221—assumed, because of their depredations against Muslims, that they must be Christians, even perhaps the long-awaited legendary people of Prester John. Information from those with direct experience might have disabused them, but the warnings of Queen Russudan of Armenia, who reported them as "evil folk" who "inflict many disasters," mouldered unheeded in the papal archives. Guiragos, an Armenian monk who had lately grown to manhood at the time of the Tatars' first appearance, had little time for Russudan, whom he condemned as "an amorous and shameful woman, like Semiramis." Her recognized agents of a vengeful Providence in "precursors of Antichrist . . . of hideous aspect and without pity in their bowels . . . who rush with joy to carnage as if to a wedding feast or orgy."

When the Tatars struck Russia two years later, the blow was entirely unanticipated; no man knew from whence they came or whither they departed. They were treated by the annalists almost as if they were a natural phenomenon, like a briefly destructive bout of freak weather or flood or a visitation of plague. Some Russian rulers even rejoiced at the greater destruction visited on their hated Cuman neighbours. But the first Tatar invasion of Russia proved to be no more than a reconnaissance. When the nomads returned in earnest in 1237, their campaign lasted three years. They devastated and depopulated much of the land of south and north-east Russia and ransomed or looted the towns. Refugees spread horror stories across Europe, gathered by an incredulous annalist in Cologne. "No little fear," he wrote, "of that barbarous race invaded even very distant lands—not only France but even Burgundy and Spain, where the name of the Tatars was previously unknown. Of the origins, habits, and way of life of the aforesaid barbarian race, we hear many things which are incredible and which we forbear to write down here, because we are not altogether sure about them, until the unadorned truth of them reaches us." When westerners did encounter the Tatars face to face, however, they shared the Russians' wonder. The missionary William of Rubruck found them in 1253, and "when we entered among them," he reported, "it seemed to me at once that we had entered a kind of other world."

Yet although the Tatars were able to establish a lasting steppeland state, which tyrannized and taxed the Russian principalities for two centuries, the permanent effects of their irruptions seem to have been no greater than the impact of the Latin occupation of Constantinople. When the tides of invasion receded from both lands, they left Orthodox civilization unchanged by the experience of temporary submersion. According to one chronicler, the Tatars spared the peasants to preserve continuity of production. Ryazany (a principality on the Volga, south-east of Moscow) seems to have borne the brunt of the invasion and suffered the least discriminating pillage; yet there, if the local chronicle can be believed, "the pious Grand Prince Ingvary Ingvarevitch sat on his father's throne and renewed the land and built churches and monasteries and consoled newcomers and gathered together the people. And there was joy among the Christians whom God saved from the godless impious Khan." Many cities escaped lightly by surrendering soon, and Novgorod, which might have been a coveted prize, was bypassed altogether. The rumours which reached western travellers—like the pope's envoy, John of Piano Carpini, who heard that in Kiev only two hundred houses were left standing and that the fields were strewn "with countless heads and bones of the dead," seem to have been exaggerated by sensationalism, like much wartime reportage.

Deftly handled, Tatar hegemony could be exploited to the advantage of Russian princes. By acknowledging Tatar overlordship, Alexander Nevsky, prince of Novgorod, was able to establish an undying legend as a Russian national hero: submission to the Tatars enabled him to fight off German and Swedish invasions. His dynasty gained from Tatar protection at the expense of the rulers of other Christian states. His son Daniel was the effective founder of Muscovy, proclaiming Moscow's independence of the centres which had formerly ruled it. His grandson became known as Ivan the Moneybag from the wealth he accumulated as a farmer of Tatar taxes. With the title of Grand Prince and the possession of the metropolitan see, Moscow from his time (reigned 1329–53) was able to bid for imperial pre-eminence over other Christian states. Despite a premature challenge to Tatar supremacy in 1378–82, Moscow's privileged relationship with the overlords survived more or less unbroken until 1480 when Ivan the Great, having engorged most of Russia's other surviving Christian principalities,

"The sun of the Land of Suzdaly." One hero of Slav identity painted by another: Alexander Nevsky (r. 1252-63) by Semen Ushakov, 1666. Alexander cannot be said to have earned his reputation as a defender of Russian nationhood: his policy was to appease the Tatars, impose their taxes on his people, and suppress the resistance to them of princes and cities. His victories on the western front against Swedes, Lithuanians and Germans deflected raiders rather than would-be conquerors. The sainthood represented by this icon-like version of him is, however, easily understood: his policy helped to keep the Church immune from Tatar taxation and, at the time of the painting, Swedish irredentism (see p. 224–56) enhanced Alexander's memory.

was ready to repudiate it. He married a Byzantine princess, incorporated a double-headed eagle into his arms, forged a genealogy which traced the house of Alexander Nevsky back to the Roman Caesars, and contemptuously dismissed the Habsburg emperor's offer to invest him as king. "We have been sovereign in our land from our earliest forefathers," he replied, "and we hold our sovereignty from God."

There were—or might have been—other contenders for the role of Third Rome. In the middle of the fourteenth century, the Serbian monarch Stephen Dusan dreamed of beating the Turks to the conquest of Constantinople and described himself with pride—if a little exaggeration—as "lord of almost the whole of the Roman Empire." His younger contemporary, the Bulgar tsar John Alexander, claimed lordship over "all the Bulgarians and Greeks" and had himself painted in scarlet boots with a golden halo. Where a Byzantine chronicler had hailed Constantinople as the New Rome, a translator at John Alexander's court substituted the name of the Bulgar capital of Trnovo and called it "the new Constantinople." But these bids were premature: the proto-empires of the Serbs and Bulgarians were themselves

Byzantine weakness in the fourteenth century excited imperial ambitions among neighbours. The Russians, Serbs and Turks all aspired, in different ways, to deprive Byzantium of its status as the universal empire, as did the Bulgarian Tsar, John Alexander, shown here, elected by the hand of God, combining imperial attire and native coiffure. The picture is a leaf of his gospel-book, translated into Slavonic. His heir also wears an imperial crown and boots and the same sash and cuff as his father.

to be swallowed up by the same Turkish expansion that expunged Byzantium.

THE MAD PLANET

Eastern Europe's geography is hostile to political continuity. Cut into and crossed by invaders' corridors, its open, flat expanses and its good communications and dispersed populations contribute to an environment in which states can form with ease, survive with struggle, and thrive with rarity. It favours vast and fragile empires, vulnerable to external attack and internal rebellion. In our millennium they have come and gone with bewildering rapidity: in the first generation or so of the period, Greater Poland briefly had frontiers on the North Sea and the Danube, the Pripet Marshes and the Bohemian Forest. Similar, volatile hegemonies were established by the Mongols in the thirteenth century, Poland-Lithuania in the fourteenth, and, on either side of the Dnieper, Poland and Muscovy in the fifteenth. After a period of relative stability for most of the modern era, when the area was disputed between the Habsburg, Ottoman, and Russian empires, the region has reverted to its former habits in the present century with the sudden rise and demise of the Third Reich and the Soviet Empire. The galactic museum-keepers of the future might be expected to liken the cockpit of eastern Europe to a mad planet convulsed by wild fluctuations of climate, cosmic storms, and seismic upheaval.

This history of empires made and unmade makes the cultural continuities of the region more conspicuous by contrast. Slav identity and communist ideology have been common influences over much of the region in recent times, but no feature of shared culture has ever matched the range or durability of the Orthodox church. In much of the greater part of the Europe ruled in the middle ages from Constantinople or Moscow, orthodoxy has survived and continues to make a major contribution to the sense of identity of its adherents. The community of eastern Christendom in the first half of the millennium may seem, by comparison with China or Islam or even western Christendom, to have been loosely bound together; but it possessed, in the Orthodox faith and church, a cultural and ideological resource of exceptional power—power and beauty such as seduced the emissaries of Saint Volodomir in their probably apocryphal quest for the perfect religion:

> The Bulgars bow down and sit, and look hither and thither, like men possessed; but there is no joy among them, but only sorrow and a dreadful stench. Their religion is not good. Then we went to the Germans, and we saw them celebrating many services in their churches, but we saw no

beauty there. Then we went to the Greeks, and they led us to the place where they worship their God; and we knew not whether we were in heaven or on earth: for on earth there is no such vision or beauty and we do not know how to describe it. We only know that there God dwells among men.

The strength of orthodoxy's allure can be sensed in remote shrines like Saint Sava's at Mileševa, where after burying the saint in the tomb intended for the monarch, King Vladislav—an eyewitness reported—"leapt high before the holy shrine, as did once the prophet David, dancing and making merry." Sava was a saint whom Christendom could not contain; after the Turkish conquest, Muslims who came to kiss his hand gave the monastery more alms than the Christians, until in 1595 the Turks burned his relics in a useless attempt to extirpate his cult. To the south-east, in the Serbian royal pantheon of Sopoćani, the most purely classical wall-paintings of the middle ages lasted intact until Turkish ravages in 1689. The painter achieved a stunning luminescence inspired by mysticism—a light, according to the priest Domentian who saw them in the mid-thirteenth century, "which may be seen only with the help of angels."

Contrary to appearance and to modern reputations, eastern Christendom was, by one standard of measurement, a more powerful civilization than that of the west. Not only did Muscovy's rate of expansion in the fifteenth century exceed that of any western state: during Europe's "great age of expansion" in the early modern era, while westerners were founding their conspicuous, remote, and ultimately doomed maritime empires all over the globe, the Russians created, as we shall see (Chapter 7), one of the largest and incomparably the longest-lived of all the Europeans' extra-European empires, in Siberia. The story of how this was possible, against a background of dispersed resources, must wait until we have seen how the rest of the world fared in the first half of our millennium.

"Mother, behold thy son." St. John and the Virgin comfort each other at the foot of the cross in the frescos of Sopoćani, commissioned by King Stefan Uroš I in the late 1250s from an anonymous painter who was one of the greatest masters of the humane, classicizing style favoured by the Serbian court. Its hallmarks are fidelity to the scriptural texts, the dramatic postures, the real but restrained emotions, the variety of expression and gesture and the accent on human relationships—the anxiously exchanged glances of the Marys, the decorous intimacy of the embrace in the foreground.

Chapter 3

THE TOWER OF DARKNESS: ISLAM IN THE FIRST HALF OF OUR MILLENNIUM

The Stones of Iconium—The Serpent in the Garden—The Zengid Empire—The Fingers of the Khan—The Auspicious Amir—Frontiers of Islam—The View from the Mimbar

THE STONES OF ICONIUM

An Oghuz Turkish woman in need of a scratch casually exposed her pudenda to Ibn Fadlan, the Caliph's ambassador, during his journey to the court of the Volga Bulgars in 921. Shamefaced, the envoys "veiled our sight and begged God's pardon." The woman's husband chucklingly explained, however, that the display was contrived to teach them a lesson. "Tell them," he said to the interpreter, "that we uncover this part in your presence so that you may see it and be abashed; but it remains unattainable. This is better than covering it up while keeping it available, as you do." Though he felt suitably reproved, Ibn Fadlan continued to evince traditional distaste for the nomads' ways. He was disgusted, for instance, that "the Oghuz do not wash after defecation, nor after urination, neither do they bathe after ejaculation." Even their chief wore a shirt disintegrating from filth, like the rotting silk under Prince Yakimov's armpits.

The ambassador's attitude was characteristic of the ambivalence with which the tillers in Islam's garden beheld the world beyond their hedge. The Turks had their place in the divine order: they were exemplars of infidel virtue for the admonition of Muslims' vice. More than a reproof, they were also a punishment: "the army of God, which I have installed in the east" (according to an apocryphal saying of the Prophet) unleashed to punish offenders. Yet a scourge too freely plied can mar as well as mend. The Turks inspired fear and loathing along with respect. In the first half of our millennium, Islam confronted with similarly divided feelings a series of comparable threats: from heretics within, from the crusaders, from the Mongols, and from the Black Death. All were overcome, with damage limited in varying degrees. Islam—dangerously vulnerable, as we shall see, to a rat-borne bacillus—proved particularly resilient to human enemies.

In the tenth and eleventh centuries, successive waves of Turkic invaders might have shattered Islam as Sasanian Iran had been destroyed by the Arabs, or Rome by the western barbarians. Instead, assimilated, domesticated, they became the great strength and shield of Islam. Having tamed the Turks within her territories and on her borders, the imams of the Muslim way were to repeat the trick with other barbarian peoples further afield. As receivers of the Koran and transmitters of the jihad, Asiatic and North African nomads made Islam the most dynamic world civilization of the late middle ages. The vital difference made by its appeal for such peoples can be gauged by comparing Islam's fate with that of other victims of the same invaders. Byzantium, which had absorbed or deflected so many barbarians, was extinguished by the Turks. China succeeded in seducing her Mongol conquerors into Chinese ways but was unable or unwilling to retrieve the dynamism of expansion. In India and Europe the bounds of the dominant cultures—Hindu and Christian, respectively—were driven back as Turkic invaders intruded new élites.

Islam's attraction for the Turks is easier to express than to explain. The memories they conserved of the time of their paganism stressed their indomitable values and their intractable ways. Boys were not named until they had "lopped off heads in battle." A hero was judged by the number of times he could plait his moustache behind his head. Even women were war-trained and "made the enemy vomit blood." The effect of conversion on the Turks' traditions is made palpable, for instance, in the ruins and remains of the mosques and palaces of the Seljuk Turks' capital at Konya, the ancient Iconium. Towards the end of the twelfth century it was a sizeable and splendid city "of the size of Cologne," according to western visitors. Laid out in the form of a rectangle with rounded corners, it was enclosed by 108 great stone towers. Evidence of growth and bustle can still be read in surviving charters of charitable endowments: a new market-place with shops of all kinds. The pentagonal citadel was built around the hill which still bears the Alaeddin Mosque. Within, the bones of eight sultans dignify an austere space, built in the second half of the twelfth century, when the simplicity of Seljuk taste was uncorrupted by ease. The chief adornment of

In the second half of the thirteenth century, the art of Seljukid Konya developed a "baroque" phase marked by exuberant outward adornment. The most favoured architect of the period was Keluk bin Abdulla and his most esteemed work the "Ince Minare Medrese," shown here before the restoration of the minaret to the height and elegance which gives it its name. The dome, originally covered with glazed tiles, was a victim of a lightning-bolt but the bulky lantern opened into it is typical of Ottoman adaptations. The big, florid portico is characteristic of Keluk's era.

the work of that period was the conquered beauty of columns cannibalized from antique monuments. Dependencies added in the thirteenth century were more glamorous. A palace kiosk, now represented only by fragments in the museum, rivalled the glazed honeycomb-vaulted interior of the Capella Palatina at Palermo; the inside of the cupola of the Büyük Karatay Medrese, decorated in the mid-thirteenth century, still glimmers in blue and gold on triangular pendentives.

As well as for courtly life, worship, death, and burial, this was a city built for trade, where Greek and Armenian carpet merchants continued to gather for centuries after its greatness was past. The caravanserais, built like basilicas, had high-arched aisles to accommodate the camels. The mint was unafraid to coin representational images of the rulers as horsemen, with bared scimitars and stars and haloes around their heads. The vast market-gardens which stretched below the walls into the Anatolian plain were devised to supply a large transient population. Although an aggressively Muslim identity was proclaimed from every slender minaret, the conical mausoleums in which the warriors chose to be buried, and which still dot the city, show that, even at its most urbane, the culture kept in touch with its nomadic past. The tombs are fashioned to resemble tents.

THE SERPENT IN THE GARDEN

The soil of Islam, which absorbed the heavy showers of Oghuz and Seljuk Turks, was turned by worms. Heretics burrowed and bred under the foundations of Islamic unity. Doctrinal and political differences nourished each other so that Islam might easily have been divided permanently, like Christendom, into rival blocks. The differences which separated Islamic orthodoxy, as gradually defined, from the main alternative tradition of Shiism, were in some ways more glaring and more fundamental than those which divided the eastern and western families of Christendom. Like Christian heresies, Shiism has tended to spawn political schisms and to breed increasingly radical sects. Odium and violence have followed, and as in Christianity, some of the splits and much of the hatred have survived into our own day.

At one level the issue between Shiism and Sunni orthodoxy was, like that of Catholics and easterners, a question of authority. In Christendom the problem could be formulated as, "Who, if anyone, is the particular vicar of Christ?" In Islam the corresponding question was, "To whom does the Prophet's mantle as Commander of the Faithful descend?" For Sunnis the caliphal dignity is elective; for Shiites it passes by heredity among the generation of Muhammad's daughter, Fatima, and her husband, Muhammad's cousin, Ali. In addition—as between Protestants and Catholics—Sunnis and

Shiites differ on the nature of man's relationship to God. In Sunni, as in Protestantism, a written revelation, a Book, is a sufficient channel of communication. In Shiah, as in Catholicism, a human agent is interposed: the Imam, "specially chosen by Allah as bearer of a part of the divine being." Yet, whereas in Christendom the Book-venerators have splintered uncontrollably into innumerable sects, while the priest-venerators have stuck together, in Islam Sunni has remained a well-disciplined and homogeneous

"Nowhere have I beheld such prosperity" (see p. 103). The luxury of court life in Fatimid Cairo is evoked by a ewer, carved from rock crystal with motifs suggesting refreshment. Vine tendrils coil round the bowl. A gazelle or water-buffalo rests by a water-hole. A duck swoops after an escaping fish. The delicacy of the object and the fragility of the spindly handle make it seem designed for ornament rather than use but the thumb-guard is evidently intended to assist pouring.

faith, while Shiah has been fissile, riven by charismatic claimants, messianic movements, and subversive secessions. The essential unity of Islam in the last thousand years has survived largely because, outside Iran, Shiite political experiments tend to have been small-scale or short-lived.

When the millennium opened, however, the biggest and most threatening Shiite state ever formed had expanded to occupy almost half the extent of the Islamic world. The Fatimid Caliphate, which had arisen in what is now Tunisia early in the tenth century, had its capital in Cairo while its western rim rested on the Atlantic. In the opinion of the Orthodox geographer al-Muquaddasi, Cairo had displaced Orthodox Baghdad as the greatest city of Islam. The danger of further Fatimid territorial expansion at Sunnite expense was increased by the political jealousy, economic rivalry, and theological odium with which each community beheld the other.

The volatile menace of the Fatimid power was embodied in the ruler, the Caliph al-Hakim, whose reputation for madness was fed by the capricious and arbitrary turns of his policy. He had succeeded to his role at the age of eleven; in adolescence, therefore, his appetite was undisciplined, his whim unchecked, and his self-esteem bloated by exposure to uniform, abject deference. The moods of tyranny which he began to indulge at the expense of his ministers soon extended to victims of every class. Bloodily enforced taboos proscribed common foods and beverages, evening trade, canal traffic, dogs, churches, and women's shoes. Acts of extortion alternated with gestures of generosity. He remitted fines and forfeits with baffling unpredictability and scattered alms with a lavish hand. Perhaps—already feeling his way towards a messianic self-perception—in fulfilment of an apocryphal prophecy of Muhammad's, recorded later, that "in the last days there will be a caliph who will scatter money without counting it." Though he loved ostentation in his youth, he later espoused austerity with the peculiar enthusiasm of the man who has everything, appearing plainly attired and outlawing extravagant salutations. There were elements of consistency: sumptuary regulation, moral rearmament, and persecution of infidels were unfailing features of his rule. But he was justly notorious for contradictions—now enjoining, now prohibiting nocturnal audiences; now abolishing, now reinstating particular taxes; now severing a qadi's hands, now heaping him with gold coins and garments.

In no area was he more indecisive than in his attitude to his Sunnite neighbours. As the Nile rose and fell and the grain-stores filled and emptied, he altered course as if trying to propitiate God or manipulate nature. At various times the traditional Shiite curses against the early caliphs were enforced or forbidden with equal rigour. Orthodox ritual practices—such as determining by observation the hours of the fast in Ramadan—were alternately tolerated or persecuted. His last act of defiance of expectation, on a winter's morning in 1021, was to climb to the observatory where he habitu-

The legacy of the Caliph al-Hakim includes the political intractability of the Lebanese Druze, who continue—nearly a thousand years after his mysterious disappearance—to venerate him, while defying all comers in arms, in the mountains of Chouf to the southeast of Beirut. In the photograph, a sheikh briefs members of Kemal Jumblatt's Druze militia at Moukhtara.

ally retired in private for the astrological computations he made with the aid of his gigantic copper astrolabe, and disappear for ever. Today the Druzes of the Lebanon, who take the Shiite tradition to one of its wilder extremes, worship him as an incarnation of God. To his contemporaries his virtues and vices were typically human. He was remembered as "generous, but a shedder of blood," whose "actions were without reason and whose dreams without interpretation."

Though the state he bequeathed continued to suffer from the bizarre behaviour of boy-caliphs, it was secure in its wealth. Food supplies were still at the mercy of the delicate ecological balance of the Nile. The prosperity of al-Hakim's time could not allay famine in 1008 or shortages in 1012. The richest of all the Fatimid caliphs was al-Mustansir (1035–1094), who rode under a parasol encrusted with jewels and supported on a gold stick, but in 1070 he had to send his womenfolk to Baghdad to escape starvation. The problems were of supply: assets were ample but ill organized for times of need. The development of Red Sea trade routes in the late tenth and eleventh centuries enriched Egypt at the expense of the Levantine coasts, and a Persian envoy of the late 1040s was dazzled by Cairo: "I could see no limit to its wealth, and nowhere have I beheld such prosperity as I saw there."

Though Muslims were tempted to violence by the presence of the serpent of heresy in the garden of Islam, conflict between the rival caliphates of Cairo and Baghdad was limited by three influences. First, there was an abiding sense of a common identity—the garden-arch, as it were, of Islam protecting the faithful of both traditions—in the face of hostile pagan and Christian worlds near at hand. Second, the Fatimid state, though prone to attempt conquests in Asia from time to time, had reached the practical limits of its viability by the end of the tenth century, and in the second half of the eleventh suffered from erosion at the edges. Finally, the main problem of the eleventh century in eastern Islam was the absorption of the Seljuk Turks.

Though it ultimately brought an accession of strength, the process was traumatic. It caused political fragmentation and internal strife, and led to brief, nominal Fatimid suzerainty over Baghdad itself. When restored, the Orthodox caliph was "a parrot in a cage" under Seljuk control. The mutual balance and the simultaneous immobilization of both Islamic traditions towards the end of the eleventh century let a new enemy into the garden. In Syria in the 1090s, Fatimid invaders by sea were confronting Seljuk assailants from the landward side. In 1098, Jerusalem changed hands for the second time in a generation. Meanwhile, the First Crusade had been launched, and when Jerusalem next fell, in 1099, the conquerors were Christians.

THE ZENGID EMPIRE

The galactic museum-keepers will hardly bother with the crusades. A movement which summoned its participants to heroic efforts and inspired its heirs with romantic stories still appears conspicuous at the end of our millennium. To historians who scour the past for evidence of the vitality of medieval Christendom, the crusades seem to offer a clue to the mystery of Europe's later preponderance. From sufficiently far off in time, however, the states founded in the Latin Levant will look like a flea-bite on the hide of Islam. Most of the crusaders were quickly gone; most of their territory was soon recaptured. Except for the ruins of their castles, few of their effects lingered very long. But they were genuinely, profoundly important in one respect: by provoking a form of irredentism deeply dyed in religious self-awareness, the crusades did play their part—less as a threat to Islam than as a stimulus to its resurgence and survival.

The great instrument of this Sunnite revanche was the short-lived empire founded by a Turkish chief called Zengi. Its culmination was the reign of the Zengids' self-elected heir, who remains the most famous figure worldwide of medieval Islam: the Kurdish strong-man Yusuf ibn Ayyub, traditionally known as Saladin, who in his lifetime achieved unique status as a figure of universal respect. Muslims upheld him as a model of piety, Christians as an epitome of chivalry. The invincible warrior was equally at home in "a gathering of scholars, discussing various sciences" or among the workmen making trenches at the siege of Jerusalem, where "he carried stones on his own shoulders to set a good example," strong enough even to shame the scribes into helping with the work. His achievement and that of the Zengids is all the more remarkable in the context of the climate, unpropitious for state-building, in which it was attained. The hostile circumstances are revealed in countless scenes of conflict and rule in the twelfth-century middle east, and in none more graphically than that of Saladin's deathbed.

In February 1193, when Saladin lay dying, his son and successor, al-Malik al-Afdal, drew together the amirs of Syria who were present at the bedside and asked for their oaths of allegiance. Most of them did not feel sufficiently bound to al-Afdal by traditional loyalties to forbear demands on his patronage. Some—Saladin's secretary tells us—made their fidelity contingent on their being confirmed in their jurisdictions or offices, others upon receiving satisfactory additional grants. Still others stipulated that they would answer the sultan's call to arms only in causes they endorsed or in defence of their own rights and possessions—a condition that made a mockery of the oath, which was essentially a promise of military service. Others omitted portions of the oath at their own whim.

This scene is suggestive of a pattern familiar to students of European history: a monarchy bound by ties of lordship and clientage, dependent on dissolving loyalties, threatened at a moment when the suzerain of subordinate lords is weak. Twelfth-century Syria displayed these features as surely as late Carolingian France or the England of Æthelred Unræd. Recently, in an area traditionally unstable and hard to organize politically, revolts in leaders' entourages, political murders, and dynastic uncertainty had become characteristics of the public scene. Heretics and unbelievers had multiplied and grown bolder in defiance of leaders who associated religious uniformity with political unity. The sect of Assassins—a divinely inspired leader with drug-crazed followers—had achieved territorial independence in an enclave in Syria as well as in their traditional mountain fastnesses in

Persia: practising political murder as a ritual obligation, they exacerbated the instability of the region while adding to many modern languages a term derived from the hashish which steeled their nerves or dulled their decency. Commerce, which in the distant past had balanced the region's centripetal tendencies by creating widespread interests in long-range communications, was disrupted or deflected to new routes to the north and west. Trade was still adjusting to the rise of the crusader states along the Mediterranean littoral.

In conditions similar to these, three heroes, Zengi, Nur ad-Din, and Saladin, established, against the odds, states of great size, unity, and cohesion. Saladin's own career makes a good case-study of how it was done. At the death of his own master, Nur ad-Din, Saladin had risen from a captain of bodyguards to be governor of Egypt, which had been won for the Zengids in 1169. Conditions for the salvage or reconstruction of the monarchy seemed, if anything, even less propitious than those bequeathed by Saladin in his turn. No potential heir had time or opportunity to rekindle the fire of empire before the coals slipped from the grate or were seized from the embers by usurpers' tongs. Indeed, Saladin, considered from one point of view, was only the most successful usurper of them all; he used his military prowess, his loyal force of professional guards, and his power base in Egypt to deprive and destroy Nur ad-Din's natural heir and all the other surviving descendants of Zengi.

These objectives imposed a formidable programme: the conquest of the sub-capitals of the Zengid empire in Mosul, Aleppo, and—most important of all—Damascus, where Nur ad-Din had his court. At the same time, Saladin had to overtrump the legitimacy of Zengi's blood heirs by claiming the moral heritage of Nur ad-Din. Marrying the great atabeg's widow may have helped; but it was only by continuing and exceeding Nur ad-Din's policies of ruthless persecution of Shiism and resolute resistance against Christendom that Saladin could vaunt his moral authority. He was therefore committed to war on three fronts—or against three enemies. Nor was his own initial position secure. His turbulent relationship with his master had exposed the fragility of his hold over his own province of Egypt, when Nur ad-Din threatened to replace him. His Black guards had rebelled in 1169, and the very year of Nur ad-Din's death saw Saladin imperilled by a palace conspiracy while the temporary seizure of Alexandria by a crusading task force served as a reminder of the imminence of another source of threat. Saladin was short of allies among his future subjects east of Suez. The large merchant class in a place like Damascus viewed war with abhorrence and would have been happy to exploit profitable coexistence with their Christian neighbours. An observant traveller from the Maghrib in Saladin's time noticed how "the Muslims lived comfortably with the Franks." The sophisticated, town-dwelling amirs of Syria would have been happy on the whole to support the sons, while abjuring the schemes, of Nur ad-Din. The Turks, used to an overlord of their own race, were probably reluctant to submit to a despised Kurd.

It took Saladin twelve years to reunite Zengi's dominions by conquest. He grubbed for the support of any lords who could be bought by mobilizing the resources of Egypt and pledging lands to investors in the momentum of his conquests. His great rival, Imad ad-Din, was unable to keep simultaneous control of Mosul and Aleppo because of the importunate appetites for patronage of the power brokers of those cities. Saladin was able to control them both. Of all the virtues ascribed to Saladin by his own propaganda, generosity was the most remunerative. According to his secretary, he emptied his treasury by acts of largesse. He prepared for campaigns by scattering "benefits and boons." And occasionally he used the obverse of generosity—periodic suspensions of favour, abasing some great lord and inspiring fear in the rest.

By sincere preference and calculated self-interest, Saladin also used spiritual weapons. He began his campaign to reconstruct the realm of Zengi on what seems to have been a cynically phoney basis, pretending to serve the interests of Nur ad-Din's heir, whose youth made him "unequal to the cares of sovereignty and the task of driving the enemies of God from the land." From the mid-1170s he rested his own claims to legitimacy increasingly on the approval of the Caliph, who was lavish in delegating the authority he was powerless to exercise in person. Saladin took the title of king—though his chancery stuck to the old style of sultan—and procured the Caliph's endorsement of it. But the constant feature of his struggle to legitimate his ambitions and justify his wars was his self-identification with the Koranic call to Holy War.

The rhetoric of jihad, used convincingly, made his actions hard for Orthodox Muslims to oppose. He could represent his attacks against co-religionists as pre-emptive strikes to preserve their lands from infidels or heretics. He could exploit the goodwill of the clergy and of the Caliph and, like Nur ad-Din, draw on the literate orders of Sufis, as well as on the jurists who traditionally served secular rulers, for administrators and propagandists. Proclamation of the Holy War was not universally popular. It was an inconvenience to merchants and a menace to religious minorities; and, once proclaimed, it had to be fought. But its advantages, especially for a leader like Saladin who had the example of Nur ad-Din before his eyes, immeasurably outweighed these drawbacks. The depth of his devotion to jihad, his sense of its sanctity, can never be calibrated; by comparison, say, with crusader adhesion to the principles of pilgrimage, which conferred a similar legitimacy and sanctity on their own violence, he seems to have been a rigorous devotee. He tried to practise Holy War with uncompromising purity, fastidious in the extreme when compelled by necessity to make accommodations with heretics or unbelievers. The most eloquent evidence of his sincerity is in the eulogies of his secretary, who claimed credit for the policy. Originally employed by Saladin's enemies, the secretary felt "moved in his heart" by God to change allegiance and presented his prospective new master with his own treatise on the jihad, "which the sultan made his frequent study." Saladin's "zeal in the Holy War" became proverbial.

Jihad worked. Nur ad-Din checked the crusaders. Saladin reversed their progress. When he overthrew the kingdom of Jerusalem in 1187, the Third Crusade was contained, and Latin Asia, though it lasted another century, was confined to Acre and to conquests made at Byzantine expense. Yet that was not Saladin's greatest achievement. He sought to be remembered above all as the "reviver of the empire of the Commander of the Faithful," a restorer of Islamic unity, a torch of Islamic orthodoxy in the Zengid tradition. A eulogist declared with pardonable exaggeration that "no Muslim lord was not subject to him." European imperialism did not return to the middle east until the nineteenth century, but the extinction of the Fatimid caliphate represented, in a sense, a more important as well as a more enduring triumph. Though Islamic uniformity continued to be dappled by heresy, Islamic solidarity—the unity of fellow-feeling—was never again to be challenged by such a large or menacing Shiite empire outside the Shiite heartland of Iran. The other legacy of the era of Saladin and the Zengids was the militancy of Islamic legitimism: jihad remained a way of authenticating the credentials of upstart dynasties and parvenue regimes. Saladin foretold the breakup of his empire after his death, and indeed the laborious story of his work only made the long-term political fragmentation of Islam seem irreversible. The territories he ruled were not lastingly reunited until the sixteenth century. But he made a permanent difference, because his example survived and because the threats he met stayed buried.

THE FINGERS OF THE KHAN

In a famous incident in 1254 the supreme khan of the Mongols, Mongka, grandson of Genghis Khan, summoned to his presence the Franciscan missionary William of Rubruck, who had ridden to Karakorum—deeper into Mongol territory than any previously recorded explorer—in the hope of making converts. William was such a good observer and such a meticulous reporter that the scene can be pictured with some fidelity. The friar approached the long, barnlike audience chamber past the elaborate fountain cast by the Khan's Parisian goldsmith: a trumpeting angel topped a silver tree, entwined by a gilded serpent and guarded by silver lions; mare's milk bubbled from their maws while from the branches poured the several liquors—made from rice or milk or honey—that were served at the Khan's drinking-bouts.

At one end of the palace nave Mongka lolled drunkenly—short, flat-nosed, and clad in "a speckled and shiny fur like a seal." Even when sober, Mongka was the kind of interviewee journalists dread: determined always to be in the right and willing to exploit his claim to deference or to abuse the courtesy of his interlocutor in order to win every argument. Whatever William said in explanation or defence of Christianity, the Khan re-expressed to suit his own purposes; whatever could not be adapted, he dismissed, before substituting a formula of his own choosing.

"Do you find it in your scripture that one man should reprove another?" Mongka asked.

"No, my lord," replied William. "I desire to quarrel with none."

A couple of generations after William of Rubruck met Mongka Khan, this Mongol painting depicted a ruler drinking on his throne, with wine flasks in the foreground. The squatting position and Persian court dress contrast with William's description—though paintings of earlier rulers collected in the same album show the "speckled and shiny fur like a seal" and informal posture noted by the friar. The goblet was obviously part of a royal ritual recorded in this painting with balletic precision and William's contempt for Mongka's "drunkenness" may have owed something to the cultural distance which separated them.

"I am not speaking of you," was the answer. "In the same way you do not find it in your scripture that a man may do injustice for money?"

"No, my lord, and I certainly did not come to this land to get money."

"I am not speaking of that. Thus God gave you Holy Scripture, and you do not follow it. He has given us soothsayers, and we on our part do what they tell us and live in peace."

And despite William's insistence that he was merely a humble missionary, Mongka refused to accept this self-description, assigning him the status, and demanding the performance, of an ambassador of the King of France. Despite his frustration, the friar recorded with candour the Khan's sophisticated philosophy of religion, expressed with the sort of simile that seems to have been Mongka's characteristic rhetorical device. The Khan likened the reach of his sway to the rays of the sun, and the relationship of religions to the fingers of his hand. "We Mongols believe," he said, "that there is but one God, in Whom we live and in Whom we die, and towards him we have an upright heart." Spreading his hand he added, "But just as God has given different digits to the palm, so He has given different religions to men."

The story captures the atmosphere of competition in which missionaries of rival faiths preached at Tatar courts and camps. William was obliged, for the Khan's edification—or, more convincingly, the Khan's amusement—to debate with Buddhists, and Nestorian Christians, who, in the widely scattered enclaves of their sect, maintained the ancient heresy that Christ had two persons as well as two natures. Dalliance with these traditions was not regarded at Karakorum as incompatible with the high-level theism to which Mongka alluded—the reverence of Tengri, usually translated as "Heaven." Nor did it displace the traditional shamanism which populated the earth and atmosphere with gods and demons and invoked the spirits of ancestors—represented by small figures suspended in felt bags from the hides of the nomads' tents—in the ritual trances of an ineradicable priestly élite. Except in the entrenched position of the shamans—never marginalized as thoroughly as the folk healers and wise women of Europe—the tenacity of this popular religion resembled the persistence of folksy magic and pre-Christian rituals in pre-industrial Christendom. Like its European counterpart it was a religion of survival in this world, not salvation in the next. Its aim was the propitiation of a natural universe dense with an invisible cluster of hostile demons. An "ancient text from olden days," garnered in oral performance by an eighteenth-century Lamaist missionary, takes us close, perhaps, to the everyday religion of most Mongols in their imperial era:

We adore deities and dragons, the protectors and tutelary spirits who perfectly accomplish our desires when we make prayers and offerings.

Through the strength of this submission of ours, this worship and praise, we beseech you constantly to be our companions and friends, you sacrificers and those on whose behalf sacrifice is made, at home or in the steppe or wherever we may be. Allay illnesses and the hindrance of the sky-demons and the demons of the dead. . . . Banish all the tormenting, inimical demons of another sort. Banish plague and epidemic and ills of day, month, and year. Avert such evils as wolves attacking the flocks, thieves and brigands stirring abroad, hail, drought, or cattle-pest.

The malleability of this Mongol religion made it both attractive and resistant to missionaries from potentially universal faiths. The Christian mission was launched with particular fervour, since Christendom's first notices about the Tatars in the 1220s raised the hope that they might already be Christians or, at least, pagan allies against Islam who could take the crusaders' foes in the rear. It was not an entirely irrational hope. The Wang Khan, chief of one Mongol people and sometime master of Genghis Khan, was indeed a Nestorian in some sense or at least under strong Nestorian influence. For most of the thirteenth century the Mongol hordes chastized parts of the Muslim world as effectively as any former scourge of God. Mongka Khan was said to favour Nestorianism, but the Buddhists at his court also thought he favoured them. His favour was as elastic as his faith was inclusive, as long as it cost him nothing.

William of Rubruck was convinced that he could have made converts if only he had found a good interpreter or—what might have been easier— the grace to work miracles, like Moses. Mongol conquest brought a brief Christian revival to Persia in the 1230s, and it was said that the Khan Chormagan—before he was inexplicably struck dumb in 1241—had contemplated conversion. Hulägu, conqueror of Baghdad, was under the influence of Christian womenfolk and was hailed as "a new Constantine" by an Armenian monk. In 1287, Arghun Khan sent a Nestorian ambassador to Rome and Paris, ostensibly to negotiate an anti-Muslim alliance. Even in the fifteenth century, westerners were hoping that Mongol rulers would revive their supposed ancient interest in Christianity, and Columbus sailed west in the professed belief that he would find heirs of the khans still eagerly waiting to hear the gospel. In reality, however, there never seems to have been much prospect of spreading Christianity widely among the Tatars. The familiarity of Nestorianism bred contempt; the heartlands of Catholic Christendom were far away; and it was the religions of powerful neighbours which proved to have most appeal in the long run.

In China, for instance, though Kublai Khan kept shamans in residence at his court, the Mongol conquerors blended into the religious environment of Buddhism, Taoism, and Confucianism. Chinese writers ascribed the fall of the Mongol dynasty in 1368 to the corrupting influence of the Tantric orgies, enjoyed to excess by members of an élite who imperfectly understood the spiritual import of the intercourse of Lamaist deities. In what became the Mongol homeland, missionaries from Tibet made Buddhism the national religion—without eradicating shamanism—in the sixteenth and seventeenth centuries (see Chapter 9). In the late middle ages, however, while the Mongols were still a dynamic force capable of moulding and remoulding the world by war, incomparably the most successful of the competing faiths, in winning their allegiance and harnessing their power, was Islam.

Islam's first experience with the Mongols was their terrible destructive force. In 1256 the Assassins were wiped out. In 1258, Baghdad was sacked and the last caliph trampled to death. According to Rashid ad-Din, who was a boy at the time, "The inhabitants, disarmed, came in groups to give themselves up to the Mongols, who massacred them on the spot." The death of Mongka Khan in 1259 and a repulse from Egypt the following year halted

Hulägu's siege of Baghdad is generally represented as a cataclysm—a "turning-point" in world history which destroyed Islam's last symbol of unity. Contemporary moralists did not always see it that way: the illustrator whose work is shown here—produced in Persia under Mongol patronage—was interested in the technical details of the siege operations in the foreground and the dramatic meeting of Hulägu and the caliph, who is improbably shown on horseback, in the background. But he shows the life of the city still going on, birds singing on the battlements and the palace officials and women going about their business. See p. 110.

the destruction. The legacy of Mongka in the west was divided into three huge states that were inefficiently exploited by a still partially nomadic élite: the khanate of the Golden Horde, occupying the steppelands from the Black Sea roughly to the Yenisei River; the Il-khanate in Persia; and, stretching from the Amu Darya to the Altai Mountains, the khanate of Jagatai, named from Genghis Khan's second son, who had been his father's regent in the area and had established its separate character.

In all three the progress of Islam towards final triumph was fitful or gradual. Like that of the Turks, the culture of the Mongols was not obviously suited to the reception of a bookish clergy, rigid monotheism, or Koranic disciplines—especially in diet, drink, and sex. The faith gained converts as formerly nomadic chiefs "went native," marrying into the indigenous populations and adopting customs and practices from their new environments, or when khans fell under the influence of the administrators they relied on to transform nomad masteries into sedentary empires. In the case of the Golden Horde, the call to jihad may have had some special allure, for, uniquely, that khanate had a long frontier with part of Christendom and extensive Christian vassal states. The rulers looked to Islamic madrasas or colleges in their rear to supply their bureaucracies from the 1260s. Pagan lords

The oddities of the Islam of the Mongols, depicted, probably by Ahmad Musa, "the master who lifts the veil from painting," in the Saray album of the early fourteenth century. The Prophet is depicted frankly, without the usual Muslim inhibitions, in the bottom right. The white cockerel which he admires and which angels acclaim seems to stand in a mimbar and perhaps therefore to represent the summons to prayer. Yet the picture has a suspiciously idolatrous air—especially as the Jagatai Khans ruled lands where Zoroastrians made a cult of dawn.

were said to have attempted to frustrate the succession to the throne of a tedious Muslim propagandist in 1312, exclaiming, "Why should we forsake the laws of Genghis Khan for the religion of the Arabs?" But the pretender's triumph and the massacre of his enemies decisively shifted the orientation of the state towards an increasingly fanatical Islamic self-consciousness.

Meanwhile, the Jagatai and Persian khanates lurched uncertainly in the same direction. In the Jagatai state, pagan rebellions and reactions persisted until 1338, though a couple of years later the massacre of a Franciscan mission seems to have been inspired by militant Islamic revanche. The Mongol rulers of Persia wavered between Buddhism, Islam, and Christianity—even, at times, showing interest in Shiism and Zoroastrianism—until 1295, when the pretender Ghazan won decisive Sunnite support in his campaign for the throne by a timely conversion. He burned the temples of other faiths and, in an excessive revulsion from idolatry, erased his father's portrait from the palace walls.

The Islam practised among the Mongols was idiosyncratic. Its peculiarities mark a collection of religious paintings, preserved in Istanbul in a fourteenth-century album, where they are attributed to Ahmad Musa, "the master who lifted the veil from painting" in Persia during the troubled reign of the boy-khan Abu Sa'id, between 1317 and 1335. The novelty of the style for which this master was praised came partly from his realism—especially in the depiction of emotion and the capture, in figure-drawing, of natural postures. Like most ascribed "revolutions" in art, it was not the work of a single genius but the gradual effect of a long process of cross-fertilization, which transformed the rendering of sacred subjects by importing Christian, Zoroastrian, and, perhaps, Mongol conventions into Islamic tradition. Representational taboos were shattered. Muhammad appeared, borne above the mountains on an angel's back, or ascended to heaven on the back of an anthropomorphic horse, or conversing with gigantic angels. In the most curious of the images, while angels acclaim an enormous cockerel enthroned on a mimbar or pulpit, gleaming against a background of darkened silver, the Prophet looks on dispassionately with hands held crosswise on his breast. Presumably the cock is a zoomorph of the muezzin, crowing the hour of prayer, but he inevitably suggests the Zoroastrian cult of dawn.

In other surviving paintings of the Mongol period, among scenes of steppeland life, the demon-dances and shamans' trances of traditional nomad religion recur in the time of Islam. The desert described by Marco Polo comes to life, where "even by day you can hear the demons chatter and . . . still more commonly the beat of drums." Practitioners of horse sacrifices whirl the bloody limbs of dismembered steeds around in savage ecstasy, while demons steal living mounts or appropriate the bones of sacrifice victims as weapons. By rival co-religionists, the Jagatai khans at their best were regarded as imperfectly Islamized and fit victims, in their turn, of the jihad proclaimed in 1386 by the last aspirant world conqueror in the Mongol tradition.

THE AUSPICIOUS AMIR

In Elizabethan England, Christopher Marlowe imagined the hero he called Tamburlaine the Great as an inspired shepherd who drew followers to his standard as much by the commanding beauty of his poetic utterances as by his invincible prowess in war. Romanticization has always occluded the image of the historical Timur. Western writers have seen him as the embodiment of a pastoral ideal-cum-idyll, evidence of the superior virtue which accrues from a bucolic background. His court historian proclaimed him "the being nearest to perfection," and his successful self-projection as a devout practitioner of Holy War—despite the fact that most of the victims of his conquests were fellow-Muslims—has ensured him an enthusiastic press from co-religionists. In reality he was a high-born townsman. His real role models were the pagans Alexander and Genghis Khan. Despite his self-election as "the Auspicious Amir," his victories were, in most of their effects, destructive or short-lived. And though he claimed descent from Genghis Khan and married into his dynasty, all his real forbears seem to have been Turks.

Travellers on the silk routes around the Taklamakan desert frequently complained of the torments of the dancing demon-musicians depicted in the Saray album. Mongols recommended smearing your horse's neck with blood to ward them off. William of Rubruck chanted the creed for the same purpose. Mongol rites of horse-sacrifice and shamanistic dances were designed to appease and—to judge from the treatment of all these subjects in the album—to imitate demonic behaviour.

He was born in 1336, a cadet of the line of lords of Kesh in Transoxania. Service to the Jagatai khanate brought him promotion, over the heads of relatives better qualified by blood, to control of the family domains; he then turned against his masters in a collaborative independence movement by the Turkic nobility of the region. By deftly eliminating his allies as his victories accumulated, Timur was left, by 1370, sole ruler of Transoxania. He placed a royal diadem on his own head and "girded himself with the imperial belt," but his legitimacy was always doubtful, even at the height of his conquests. On the one hand, he appealed to the Mongol tradition, invoking the name and upholding the law-code of Genghis Khan; on the other, he exploited his Islamic credentials, quoting the Koran—especially on the subject of Holy War—and denouncing his enemies as outright pagans or lukewarm Muslims. His empire was an adventure and his strategy was opportunism. The state he created by conquest was a personal monarchy, which could not survive him; even in his lifetime it was held together only by the momentum of expansion, which continually renewed the fisc from which warrior-followers could be rewarded.

When he died at the age of seventy-four, he had conquered Iran, wrecked the khanate of the Golden Horde, reduced the Jagataite state to a rump, halted the growth of the Ottoman Empire and caged its sultan, invaded Syria and India, and projected the conquest of China. The marks of his passing, wherever he went, were the devastated lands of lords and peasants slow to submit and the heaped-up skulls of citizens injudicious enough to attempt to withstand his sieges. His success was by no means uniform, but it was so impressive in total effect as to seem "decreed by God" or by "the hand of fate." His admonitions to potential victims echoed the arrogance of traditional Mongol rhetoric: "Almighty God has subjugated the world to our domination, and the will of the Creator has entrusted the countries of the earth to our power." The day after his death, as the legatees of his divided inheritance turned on one another, his ambitions seemed hollow and his achievements ephemeral. For Islam, Timur's impact is usually seen as unrelievedly negative. But for him, the strength of Islam could have been directed concertedly, it is said, against external enemies; his success against the Ottomans gave Byzantium a reprieve; by humbling the Golden Horde, he encouraged the Christians of Russia; by ravaging the sultanate of Delhi, he delivered millions of Hindus from the threat of Muslim rule. These criticisms, however, ignore what might be called Timur's psychological legacy as a champion of Islamic orthodoxy and an exemplar of the power of Holy War. Turkish by birth, Mongol by self-adoption, he was the last great conqueror in the nomadic tradition and represented the consummation—powerful and terrible—of the process by which the nomads had been converted from the scourge of Islam to the spearhead of the jihad.

The ruins of Timur's mausoleum in Samarkand on a site formerly shared with a vanished madrasa and Sufi hospice, endowed by Timur's grandson and heir, Muhammad Sultan. Timur erected the pantheon when his grandson died at the age of twenty-nine in 1403 and joined him in the main chamber under the soaring dome in 1405. This eminently respectable burial amid the charitable works of his dynasty might be held to symbolize the domestication of the tradition of the great nomad-conquerors, "converted from the scourge of Islam to the spear-head of the jihad."

In 1260 an ambassador from the Mamelukes—slave warriors who had recently seized Egypt in a rebellion—taunted the Mongols in Hulägu's camp with having "kings like donkeys." For "the kings of the Muslims, when they used to drink wine, ordered pistachio nuts, citrus juice, slices of lemon in china cups, ewers of rosewater, basil, violets, myrtle, cloves, narcissus, and other such fine things. You Mongols drink your wine with charcoal, cottonseed, dried grapes, wood shavings, and similar ugly objects." The implied contrast was not only between Muslims and pagans, but also between civilization and savagery—between the sedentary and urban worlds within the garden of Islam and the nomadic barbarism of their excluded neighbours. In 1377, when Ibn Khaldun, in a village in Oran, sat down "with ideas pouring into my head like cream into a churn" to write the most admired work on history and political philosophy of the Islamic middle ages, he made the counterpoint of "Bedouin" and settler the motive force of history.

Everywhere in the late middle ages the survival and success of Islam depended on the civilization's capacity to tame the alien forces which challenged it from the deserts and the steppes.

Except for the Magyars and (on a small scale) the Bulgars, no fully nomadic people had been successfully absorbed by Christendom; India was a victim of Turkic invaders whom it could never convert; China assimilated Mongol conquerors but emasculated them in the process instead of adapting their energies—as Islam did—in the service of the host civilization. Islam's unique achievement in this respect was one of the great formative influences in the late medieval world. The transformation of the Turks and Mongols guaranteed that Central Asia would stay Muslim, while helping to ensure that the Indian Ocean would link mainly Muslim shores, that the ancient trade routes which crossed both spaces would be controlled by Muslim hands and that Islam's manpower would be renewed with battlefield fodder for an expanding frontier.

FRONTIERS OF ISLAM

Only on its north-western edge did Islam's frontier in the late middle ages shrink. Traditional historiography represents the extrusion of Islam from the Iberian peninsula as a continuous process, begun almost at the moment of the Berber invasion of 711 and sustained, with checks and interruptions, of course, but without essential mutation of spirit, until the fall of Granada in 1492. In fact, the Christian Reconquest was the work of widely interspersed bouts of phrenesis in the tenth, eleventh, thirteenth, and fifteenth centuries. The thirteenth-century losses to Islam were decisive, extensive, and never reversed.

At the time, Moorish Spain formed a continuous political world with the Maghrib. In the history of the rich Mediterranean outposts of Islam, the Sahara played a part similar to that of the steppelands in the near and middle east. Impressive but short-lived unity had been imposed on the region in the eleventh and twelfth centuries by two movements of frenzied ascetics from the desert, known respectively as the Almoravids (*al-Murabitun*, garrison folk, a name signifying ascetic withdrawal as well as holy warfare) and Almohads (*al-Muwahhidun,* followers of the oneness of God). But millenarian movements run out of steam, charismatic leaders die, and desert warriors get corrupted by the soft life of the civilizations they conquer. All political authority in western Islam had tended to be displaced in the past by one of three means: conquest from outside, usurpation from the extremities, and putsch from within. After almost a century of dominance, the Almohad state succumbed to a combination of all three. In Spain, Christian opportunists, the kings of Portugal, Castile, and Aragon—animated by a

The minaret of the mosque of Hassan at Rabat, begun in commemoration of the victory over a coalition of Christian Spanish kingdoms at Alarco, in 1195. From earlier generations whose softness and impiety the Almohads despised, Almohad architecture borrowed motifs—especially the scalloped arcading which is so prominent here—and blended them into a new and terrible beauty. The look of austerity and strength is close to their ideology of self-denial and dedication to the jihad.

mixture of crusading fervour and secular, chivalric love of "deeds"—redistributed Majorca and most of the Islamic mainland to aristocratic patrons of colonization and exploitation. In the eastern Maghrib, power was seized by the Hafsids, the family of the local governor; in the centre by the Banu 'Abd al-Wad, a tribe the Almohads had employed to keep control; in the west, by a predator tribe from the south, the Banu Marin.

In the 1330s and 1340s, Ibn Khaldun served as an *haut fonctionnaire* in the courts of each of these three Maghribi states at Tunis, Fez, and Tlemcen. His theory of history as the interplay of tension between sedentary civilization and the savagery beyond reflected the actual experience of his lifetime. Marinid Morocco, for instance, was founded in an act of nomadic aggression, but by the time of their extirpation of the last Almohad strongholds in 1269, the Banu Marin had already begun to absorb the culture of their reluctant hosts. The sultan Abu Yusuf built himself a pleasure palace outside Fez to celebrate his victory and dabbled in connoisseurship and bibliophilia.

Yet before the sandstorm of Berber militancy lost its fury, it spattered and almost buried an important state on the farther rim of the Sahara, where the Almoravids coveted the gold of the Black African realm of Ghana. This pagan kingdom had been admired or desired by Muslim writers since the eighth century and was credited with a much older history, originating, it was said, with the arrival of a white culture hero from the north. In reality there is no reason to suppose that it was ever anything other than a purely indigenous development among the Soninke of the Upper Niger who were able to exploit their dominant position athwart the gold routes which led north to Maghribi markets. The desert constituted a vast frontier, almost impenetrable to invaders; across it they defied Almoravid armies with some success until 1076 when their capital at Kumbi, with its stone palace, fell—presumably after a defiant siege, if the tradition of the massacre of the citizens is true. The political hold of the northerners did not last, but Islam was firmly implanted. By the middle of the next century Ghana was regarded as a model of Islamic propriety whose king revered the true caliph and dispensed justice with exemplary accessibility. His well-built palace; its objects of art and windows of glass; the huge natural ingot of gold which was the symbol of his authority; the gold ring by which he tethered his horse; his silk apparel; his elephants and giraffes: all projected for the rest of the Islamic world an image of outlandish magnificence, alongside Muslim fellow-sentiment. It did not last. After a long period of stagnation or decline, the Soninke state was overrun and Kumbi definitively destroyed by pagan invaders; but Islam was sufficiently widely diffused by then among the warriors and traders of the Sahel to retain its foothold south of the Sahara for the rest of the middle ages.

On Islam's eastern frontier, the breakthrough made in the west across the barrier of the Sahara was paralleled about a century later by the establishment of a lasting Muslim state—or at least a state with a ruling Muslim élite—inside the Indian subcontinent. India has been the Cinderella civilization of our millennium: beautiful, gifted, destined for greatness, but relegated to the backstairs by those domineering sisters from Islam and Christendom. A history of the first millennium of our era would have to give India enormous weight: the subcontinent housed a single civilization characterized by elements of common culture, conterminous with its geographical limits; the achievements it produced in art, science, literature, and philosophy were exported, with a moulding impact, to China and Islam; and it was a civilization in expansion, creating its own colonial New World in south-east Asia. With bewildering suddenness, at about the turn of the millennium, the inspiration seemed to dry up, the vision to turn inward, and the coherence to dissolve. Whereas earlier generations of Muslim scholars had looked to India with eager reverence, al-Biruni, turning in the 1020s to glean further learning from the same source, was disappointed by

The monsoon helped to make the Arabian Sea a Muslim lake. The Indian pilgrim ship depicted in this Iraqi manuscript of the Maqamaat of al-Hariri of 1238 is equipped with square sails to make the most of the following wind both ways. The aedicule on deck was a feature of south Asian ships; see p. 138. Notice the bailers below and the elaborate mechanism of the stern-post rudder, which evidently baffled the artist. The small pillar in front of the skipper at the tiller may be a binnacle.

what he saw. Hindu science, he found, "presumed on the ignorance of the people." Political dissolution accompanied the cultural decline. The large states which had filled most of the subcontinent in uneasy equilibrium since the early ninth century collapsed under the strain of mutual emulation and the impact of invaders and insurgents. The rich temples of northern India became the prey of opportunistic raiders from Afghanistan.

Muslim adventurism was at first of the smash-and-grab variety; systematic

The last written records were said to have been flung into the sea to protect them from German colonial officials in 1886—but the ravaged grandeur of Kilwa is evoked by the ruins of the mosque, probably one of many monuments originally erected in the late twelfth century. Handy for the gold, ivory, and salt traffic from the east African interior (see p. 122), Kilwa was a great emporium of the Indian Ocean trade, with a Muslim community well established by the beginning of the millennium. Towards the end of the middle ages the dome of its mosque was lined with blue-and-white porcelain bowls from China. The decline which left it in ruins started with Portuguese competition and became irreversible after Zimba raiders massacred the remaining citizens in 1587.

conquest was not attempted until late in the twelfth century. The first
enduring Muslim state, the Sultanate of Delhi, was not founded until 1206—
in the time-honoured tradition of a Turkic general repudiating his master
to turn his conquests into a state of his own. In the thirteenth century the
sultanate was confined to the Punjab and the Ganges valley. Even when
Alauddin Khalji (reigned 1296–1316) conquered Malwa and threatened
briefly to impose his rule or hegemony throughout the subcontinent, he left
many Hindu states in his rear. His tempestuous life was a metaphor of the
volatile fortunes of the state he ruled. He was a usurper who eliminated
surviving members of the founding dynasty, styled himself "the new Alexander," aped the Prophet of Islam, and devised a new religion. When his
dreams collapsed and his conquests were lost, "he bit his own flesh in his
fury." A similar but more disciplined attempt to unite India from Delhi was
made by Muhammad Ibn Tughluq in the 1330s, but his achievement lasted
little longer. The next effort, in the early sixteenth century, had to be
launched across the mountains, starting virtually from scratch (see Chapter 7).

Islamization of conquered populations was also a slow business, often
retarded by rulers who were anxious to delay the conversion of taxpaying
infidels into immune Muslims. In India, conversion barely happened at all,
though interesting attempts to synthesize Hindu and Muslim teachings were
produced at intervals in the fifteenth and sixteenth centuries. Yet without
impulsion by conquest, Islam seemed, for most of the first half of the millennium, almost incapable of expanding at all. By a curious symmetry the
sand-frontier of the Sahara was echoed by the sea-frontier of the Indian
Ocean which bordered the lands of Islam to the east. Both were empty regions scored by ancient trade routes, across which Muslims had trafficked
and migrated for centuries without extending the limits of Islam. At the turn
of the millennium there were mosques in Dayub and Canton, Kumbi and
Kilwa, but they were intended for visiting merchants and crew or for immigrant craftsmen and professionals rather than for local converts. The failure
of Islam to penetrate far into south-east Asia, for instance, before the fourteenth century, is conspicuous by comparison with the progress of Hindu
and Buddhist communities in the region. This lack of missionary vocations
and evangelical experience was one of only two conspicuous deficiencies
in Islam's equipment for retaining a world-shaping initiative, ahead of competing civilizations, in the first half of the millennium. The other flaw was a
negative demographic trend relative to Christendom.

THE VIEW FROM THE MIMBAR

Of all the enemies Islam absorbed or contained, only plague was invincible. Like the Mongols, it was an invader from the steppeland, where "a

permanent reservoir of infection" still exists among the wild rodents. Its transmission was sordid, its effects relentless, its treatment unknown. Fleas regurgitated the bacillus, ingested from rats' blood, into the bloodstream of human victims, or communicated infection by defecating into their bites. In cases of septicæmic plague, one of the first symptoms was generally death. Otherwise it might be deferred by the appearance of ugly swellings—small and bulbous like brazil nuts or big and carunculated like grapefruit—over the neck and groin or behind the ears. Jitters, retching, dizziness, and pain might follow, often accompanied by aversion to light, before fainting and prostration. In Cairo when the Black Death broke out in 1347, they smeared the buboes with Armenian clay. In Andalusia, Ibn Khatib advised abstention from corn, cheese, mushrooms, and garlic. Decoctions of barley water and syrup of basil were widely prescribed. The Turks sliced off the heads of the boils and extracted green glands. As devastating as the physical affliction was the psychological ruin wrought by a mysterious visitation, rationally inexplicable, which wrecked morale. It seemed to an Egyptian observer that "everything died, even the year itself." Ibn Khaldun's description is famous but bears repeating:

> Civilisation shrank with the decrease of mankind. Cities and buildings were bared, roads and signposts were abandoned, villages and palaces were deserted; tribes and dynasties were expunged. It was as if the voice of existence in the world had called out for oblivion, and the world had responded to the call.

In most of western Christendom, the plague was probably no less virulent than in Islam. In both civilizations recurrences became commonplace for the rest of the middle ages and into the late seventeenth century. In Islam, however, it does seem that the effects were more persistent, more enduring, and more often lethal. Europe recovered faster and in the long term resisted better. The slow shift of the balance of the world's resources and means, in favour of Christendom, may have begun with the Black Death.

Nevertheless, from the perspective of the galactic museum-keepers of the future, our millennium is more likely to appear as the millennium of Islam than the millennium of the west. The shift of initiative—though it may have started, in some respects, in the late middle ages—took a long time. Islam remained the fastest-growing world civilization into the second half of the era; the whole of what is conventionally called the early modern period, from the sixteenth century to the eighteenth, was really an age of transition. If the present resurgence of Islam (see Chapter 19) continues into the next millennium, the intervening centuries of unchallenged western supremacy will disappear from view at a sufficient distance or be diminished to the dimensions of a curious but ultimately unimportant blip.

The world as seen from Persia in the mid-tenth century by al-Istakhri. Despite its schematic form, this map was the work of a geographer who believed in supplementing theoretical knowledge by travel. He was a pivotal figure in the transmission of the tradition of the school of geography of Balkh in Persia. The notes he supplied to Ibn Hawkal formed the basis of the most influential Arabic geographical compendium at the beginning of the present millennium. Europe is the small triangle visible at bottom right.

In the first half of our millennium, Islam's preponderance was in part a matter of perspective. Its heartlands were in the centre of the island-earth, the land mass of the "known world," from where traders could travel, conquerors reach out and grasp, or savants survey the whole *oikoumene*. Al-Ishtaqri's world map of the tenth century is an important document for understanding the history of the millennium because it demonstrates the range of vision of a world view from Fars or Balkh over the limited perspective available to civilizations such as China and Latin Christendom which had their centres of gravity close to ocean rims. Islam was well informed about both extremities of the accessible world. The Latins and the

Chinese only just knew of each other's existence. In the second half of the millennium, Islam lost that privilege of vision as new oceanic perspectives were opened up, extending the range visible from vantage points on the Atlantic and Pacific shores. From the crow's nest the lookout could see more of the world than the muezzin from the Tower of Darkness.

Chapter 4

THE WORLD BEHIND THE WIND: CHINA AND HER NEIGHBOURS FROM THE SUNG TO THE MING

The Modest Pavilion—The Yaks' Tail-bearers—The Lands of Many Parasols—The Ming Menagerie—The Bright Dynasty

THE MODEST PAVILION

The farewell dinner was a protracted affair. Final leave was not taken until dawn, at the foot of a new pontoon bridge a few miles north-west of Shan-yin, on 4 July 1170. Lu Yu was on his leisurely way to take up a prefecture in Szechuan, on the far side of the Chinese Empire. It was an honourable, remunerative post but a long, challenging journey, and the health of the prefect-elect had been poor. His brothers and friends accompanied him on the first stage of his route, overland towards the Ch'ien Tang River, to see him off in celebration tinged with apprehension.

He left a diary of what was virtually a transnavigation of the empire, toted by sailing barge along nearly a thousand miles of the Yangtze River, like a small corpuscle pumped along China's main vein. His impressions of the country brim with satisfaction: at the newness of that first pontoon, at the flourishing commerce, at the boats crowded together "like the teeth of a comb." He was excited by the war-readiness of seven hundred great river-galleons, with their "speed like flight, breaking through huge waves" to the noise of battle drums and the display of bright pennants. He celebrated the copious signs of growing prosperity, like the Eastern Park at I-cheng, "formerly vast and magnificent, then brambled and desolate," now "after only forty years or so, rebuilt as a garden" by the industry of the citizens. He travelled between respectful halts at hospitable monasteries, walks in parks, and pauses for the contemplation of ancient cypress trees. At every stop he accepted invitations "to wine and dinner," amid plates decorated with pyramids of alum, in rooms cooled with piles of ice. His hosts were cultured provincial officials like his distant relative, Lu Chung-Kao, who had been exiled from the capital in an episode of factional strife but whose initial bitterness had been dispelled by enlightenment. With indifference befitting a scholar, Lu Yu does not divulge the menus. The exotica of Hangchow restaurants—pig cooked in ashes, scented shellfish, lotus-seed soup— would have been out of place, though the ideal Confucian diet of rice with fresh or pickled vegetables would have been supplemented by fish and meat to show respect for the diners' rank.

Everywhere, Lu Yu recorded the beauties of nature, the blessings of peace, and the evidence of the longevity of Chinese civilization. He looked around, with a sense of contentment, and back, with a sense of history, surveying more than a thousand years of the past through the monuments he stopped to visit. Southern Dynasty tombs recalled the tears of a penitent rebel of the fifth century. The stone on which a third-century putsch was planned drew travellers' sighs but sniggers from the earthy attendants. As he travelled east, into newer country with a less distinguished and less accessible past, his admiration turned increasingly to the mountains and

Lu Yu's staid and decorous entertainment by provincial officials—the elaborately laid and decorated tables, the ritual toasts, the literary chat—mirrored the scenes of court social life painted in the tenth century by Ku Hung-chung. This dinner-party from the *Night Revels of Han Hsi-Tsai* may have been rather raffish for Lu Yu's taste, with porcelain ware set out on lacquered tables, and the risqué luxury of a girl musician.

grottoes. As he approached Tzu-kuei he was impressed by Yellow Ox Mountain, proverbially changeless, with its population of wild apes, and marvelled at the Jade Void Grotto, where the sparkling interior was formed by nature into "a thousand immortals, dragons, tigers, birds, and beasts." Nature, however, was there to be enjoyed from a superior distance. Civilization seemed always able to outwit the environment: the Open Grotto Rapids, for instance, with rocks patterned "like writing on a magician's charm," could be bypassed in a sedan chair. Even in the wildest and poorest reaches of the country, Lu Yu's sense of belonging to his surroundings was never impaired. A China he recognized was always around him. The modesty of the outpost he visited in Pa-tung was offset by a sub-prefectural residence of incomparable beauty, where an unambitious official, willing to make a reality of the literary cult of rural bliss, "could sleep and eat in the pavilion and his pleasure would be boundless."

One type of change which was apparent to Lu Yu was in the economic productiveness of the country. In Kweichou province, for instance, an entire prefecture might levy in wheat, millet, and non-glutinous rice only the value of a single household's production in wealthy Kiangsu. The province for which he was destined, despite its remoteness, possessed enviable wealth in salt, forest products, tea, and grain. Szechuan's prefectures of Ch'eng tu-Fu and Tzu-Chou had between them twenty-two centres of population producing annual tax revenues of between ten and fifty thousand strings of cash—more than any other prefecture of the Sung Empire outside the lower Yangtze. The frontier described in Chapter One had been drawn into the empire both culturally and economically. All over the Chinese cultural area—especially in the north but also probably in the empire of the Sung—population growth seems to have halted, from a high point recorded in the census of 1124, when twenty million households were claimed, and to have begun to decline. Officials were not yet alarmed, however, and the empire remained incomparably the world's strongest state in revenues and manpower resources.

Yet Lu Yu's complacency was not unclouded. The Jürchen wars which had devastated his admired Eastern Park had severed the former territory of the empire. The northern plain and the best part of the Yellow River basin were in Jürchen hands, while the mandate of heaven was again divided between Sung and Chin as it had been between Sung and Liao. China had survived many such divisions in the past; since 1161, when the northerners despaired of creating a river-navy capable of conquering the south, the twin empires had settled into a habit of mutual passivity and shared values of *enrichissez-vous*. Paradoxically, however, a greater threat would mature in the following century from a force which would restore—at terrible cost to Lu Yu's world—a measure of political unity unknown to China since the Tang Dynasty. At about the time of Lu Yu's journey up the Yangtze, the infant Temujin—the future Genghis Khan—was being initiated on the banks of the Onon, in the harsh, wild country of what is now Outer Mongolia, into a programme of martial exercises that would equip him for one of the most ambitious schemes of conquest ever conceived.

THE YAKS' TAIL-BEARERS

Sung China was so scored by rivers, so soaked by paddies, so spread with cities, and so ill-provided with pasture that it was almost inviolable to purely nomad armies. By contrast, the Jürchen Empire of the Chin Dynasty, straddling the Great Wall in the north, lay open to invaders. The ossified, Sinicized ex-barbarians became the prey of Genghis Khan, just as the Khitans had succumbed, in their turn, to the Jürchen. China had begun to work its charm on these latest recruits as soon as they had arrived in the 1120s. The founder of the Chin Empire, Wu-ch'i-mai, bathed in the river with his warrior-tribesmen like any nomad chief, but he favoured Chinese administrators and admired Chinese arts. The Jürchen father-statesman Hsi-yin was an ex-shaman who made a collection of Chinese literary classics when his people captured the city that became Peking. From the seventh to the ninth decades of the century, old nomad virtues of simplicity and austerity fought a rearguard action under an emperor who was himself steeped in Confucian lore and whose admiration for an ideal type of barbarian life—a pure model of pastoral virtue—was itself evidence of his personal immersion in a Chinese mentality. In 1191 the abrogation of an old law—never observed—against mixed marriages signalled a decisive return of Jürchen policy in favour of Chinese ways.

The nomad values abandoned by the Jürchen were personified by Genghis Khan. The fascination he exerted on admirers of uncorrupted barbarism is nicely illustrated by the story of Ch'ang Chun, a Taoist wise man summoned to his presence in 1219. "Long years in the caverns of the rocks" had brought the sage a reputation for unexcelled sanctity; yet at the age of seventy-one he declared himself "ready at the first call of the Dragon Court" to undertake an arduous three-year journey to an encounter with the Khan at Perwali, at the foot of the Hindu Kush. There were some sacrifices of principle he refused to make even for Genghis Khan's sake: he declined, for instance, to travel in the company of recruits for the Khan's harem and, at Samarkand, he refused to go farther "into a land where vegetables were unavailable." Yet, with twenty Mongol guards and nineteen disciples, he travelled through some of the most arduous country in the world—across the Gobi Desert, through "mountains of huge cold" and into Dzungaria, where the company smeared their horses' heads with blood to discourage demonic assailants. The Taoist man of peace might have been uncomfortable in the presence of a barbarian chief whose greatest joy was reputedly "to shed my enemies' blood and wring tears from their womenfolk." The tone of the meeting at the journey's end, however, was highly amicable, to judge from the language of a stela composed by one of the sage's disciples in honour of the Khan: "Heaven is weary of the inordinate luxury of China. I remain in the wild region of the north. I return to simplicity and seek moderation once more. As for the garments that I wear and the meals that I eat, I have the same rags and the same food as cowherds and grooms, and I treat the soldiers as my brothers."

As a propaganda image it was successful; as a formula for military victory it was invincible. Although Genghis Khan himself spent most of his time on other fronts, and although the Jürchen resisted with a valour he admired, yielding territory in patches over a total of twenty-three years, the Chin Empire was no more capable than any of his other victims of reversing his fortunes or convincingly challenging his claim to have been divinely elected as a universal conqueror. By the time the last Jürchen rump state was finally extinguished, in 1234, seven years after Genghis Khan's death, the Mongols had developed most of the techniques they needed to confront the Sung: impressing huge forces of foot; mobilizing complex logistical support; organizing siege trains; and exploiting the fiscal potential of conquered lands for war.

The conquest of China turned the Mongols into masters of positional warfare. In the early fourteenth century, illustrators of Rashid al-Din's *World History* were obviously impressed by the technical expertise of Mongol forces in laying sieges. The new kind of ballista praised by Marco Polo and capable of flinging a 300-pound stone was frequently illustrated—attended here by an Arab engineer. The Mongols were adept at harnessing a foreign *savoir-faire*: a thousand Chinese engineers accompanied Hulägu's western campaign in 1253. See p. 110.

Repeatedly deferred and interrupted, the Mongol conquest of Sung China was not complete for another forty-odd years: only in 1276 could the Mongol general Bayan announce that south and north had "become one family." The experience transformed conquered and conquerors alike. For the Mongols, the century that opened under the doughty Genghis Khan drew towards its close under the gouty Kublai. Genghis Khan fought under the shadow of a yak's tail-banner and Kublai fattened beneath a parasol's shade. Where the founder of the dynasty had got about on a pony's back, his grandson needed four elephants to transport him, and whereas a simple tent was good enough to house his ancestors, Kublai Khan decreed a stately pleasure-dome in Shan-tung, built of gilded canes.

Even here there was abundant evidence of the Khan's abiding Mongol taste: in the white mares grazing the grounds, whose milk was reserved for his exclusive use; in the libations of koumiss with which he honoured his ancestral gods; in the unvarying diet of meat served at his banquets; in the freedom with which he chose high servants from outside the traditional Confucian élite—indeed, from outside China; and in the religious eclecticism of his court, which made him repeat to Marco Polo, in a continuator's version, views on the equivalence of different religions very similar to those of his predecessor, the ostentatiously tolerant Mongka Khan (see Chapter

Seen from the air in 1938 Peking still conveyed the character of an armed camp, given to it by Kublai Khan when he established his court there.

3). But Kublai was also, emphatically, a Chinese emperor, who performed the due rites, dressed in the Chinese manner, learned the language, patronized the arts, protected the traditions, and promoted the interests of his Chinese subjects.

The imprint of his passage through Chinese history is most marked today, perhaps, in Peking. He wrenched the centre of gravity of government northward and inland, towards his inherited power-base in Mongolia, in the dusty, windy city, difficult to provision, that has remained the capital—with interruptions—ever since. No building of Kublai's day survives, but the rectangular shape of the old town is as his immigrant Muslim architect designed it. The layout of the streets, in geometrical regularity, with avenues wide enough for nine galloping horsemen abreast, reflects his choice. The rampart of rammed earth has disappeared, but the circumvallatory subway follows its course, marked for all the world by the ring of fifteen-storey apartment blocks above it. The former imperial palace is still where Kublai put it, though the structures he erected have gone and the park is bereft of the tents with which he dotted it in nostalgia for the Mongols' nomadic past.

Kublai's rule also wrenched Chinese eyes towards previously ignored horizons. By Chinese standards, the Sung had been an outward-looking dynasty, who founded a capital by the seashore and promoted trade as a better means of raising revenue—according to an emperor's famous apophthegm of 1145—"than taxing the people." Yet the Mongol tradition of world conquest was far more dynamic than the Chinese concept of the mandate of heaven, which equated China with the world and despised the barbarian rim as unworthy of the benefits and unrewarding of the bother of conquest by Chinese. The legacy of Genghis Khan demanded that his heirs reach out to the world with a heavy hand. Not all Confucian traditionalists in southern China were prepared to collaborate with Kublai's regime, but those who were had to modify their views. To Chou Ta-kuan, for example, who took part in a Chinese embassy to Cambodia in 1296, the mandate of heaven involved the obligation "to spread out over the four seas." Kublai's conquest of Burma and his campaigns against Vietnam, Java, and Japan helped to enlarge the Chinese world-view, to encourage the accumulation of geographical and ethnographic data from far afield, and to inaugurate an era—which lasted until well into the fifteenth century—in which expansionist values were nicely balanced with traditional Chinese isolationism.

THE LANDS OF MANY PARASOLS

Chou Ta-kuan's account of Cambodia opens a direct window from China into the emulous world of rival cultures and states that competed in late

medieval south-east Asia. This was a world of many highly civilized communities but without a dominant state or a unifying culture or a consciousness of shared identity. From the thirteenth century to the sixteenth, the
region was to be transformed by the collapse of a Sanskritic culture inherited from the era of "Indianization" in the previous millennium; by the cultural conquests of Singhalese Buddhism; by the incursions of Islam; by the
collapse of old empires; and by the rise of new states founded by peoples
with distinctive identities, Burmese and Thai.

Chou captured the appearance of Cambodia in a still-brilliant era, when
the "single white parasol" of King Srindravarman was being spread over a
country where many parasols of contending pretenders had been rapidly
opened and closed in a period of disputed succession. Chou found that
"although this is a land of barbarians, they know how to treat a king."
Srindravarman rode in a gold palanquin, behind curtains which girls parted
at the sound of conches, to reveal the king on his lion-skin throne. The
people all knocked their heads on the ground until the conches ceased and
the theatre was over.

Chou's disgust was aroused by some barbaric habits. He deplored the
open display of their preferences by homosexuals, who seemed, curiously,
to have been particularly importunate in soliciting Chinese. He condemned
the inconstancy of Khmer wives, whose fidelity could not outlast a fort-
night's separation. He was fascinated by reports of the ritual deflowering of
virgins by the intrusive fingers of specially hired monks—though monastic
frolics were a topos of Confucian literature and Chou's information may not
have been true. His appreciation of everything was marred by the insuffer-
able heat—which, he thought, encouraged excessive bathing with a consequent increase in disease. The savage tribes of the forests and mountains,
who spent their time killing each other with bows, spears, and poisons,
filled him with alarm. On the other hand, his admiration for the essential
urbanity of the Khmer shines through his account of a city easily identifiable as Angkor.

"It is such monuments, we think, which from the first inspired Chinese
merchants to praise Cambodia as a land rich and noble," he wrote, as he
described the seven-mile wall and the five gates. On the east side golden lions flanked a bridge of gold, resting on gigantic piles covered with Buddhas. A golden tower at the centre of the city was exceeded by another of
copper. In the royal palace, the sleeping chamber was at the top of a third
tower, again of gold, where political stability was reputedly secured by the
king's nightly copulation with a nine-headed serpent. The gold all testified
to the value of Cambodia's exports, for none was produced locally.

Much of the recent history of Cambodia could be read in Chou's observations. Most of the monuments he admired dated from the reign of the
great king Jayavarman VII, who had died about three-quarters of a century

The Bayon at Angkor Thom was built by Jayavarman VII to house a Buddha in the very late twelfth or very early thirteenth century, when the Hindu character of court tradition was being eroded by Buddhist influence. The intricately carved mound-like chambers surrounded the "tower of gold" which so impressed Chou Tai-kuan.

before. The walls, moats, south gateway, and towers of Angkor Thom were only the centrepiece of a great building campaign which surrounded the capital with shrines and palaces, way stations, and—it was said—more than a hundred hospitals, decorated with gigantic human faces. No other people in the world, except perhaps the Maya of Mesoamerica, had ever built on such a scale, with such limited technology, in so humid an environment. The Bayon—Chou's "tower of gold"—had a solid central mass to echo the central mounds of the ancient capitals; its inner chamber, however, contained not the Hindu Devaraja-image of previous reigns but a Buddha, intended to symbolize the apotheosis of the founder-king whose images

Though Indian "cultural colonization" in south-east Asia waned after the turn of the millennium, Sanskritic inscriptions were still made: this example from Angkor, with its praise of Jayavarman's bravery, knowledge, skill and other virtues, is of the twelfth century, when Cambodia was still "full of experts on the Veda." Others survive from as late as the 1330s.

"stared in all directions" from the outer friezes. The transition to a predominantly Buddhist court culture, initiated by Jayavarman, was still going on, though Hindu roots went deep. In Jayavarman's reign a Brahman scholar from Burma could still travel to Cambodia because it was full "of eminent experts on the Veda." Sanskritic inscriptions, which disappeared from the neighbouring kingdom of Champa in 1253, continued to be made in Cambodia until the 1330s.

At terrible expense, Kublai Khan registered only ephemeral successes in south-east Asia: in Java, one native prince was made to replace another, with no permanent gains for the Chinese. In Champa and Vietnam, tribute was levied at a rate insufficient to reimburse the cost of the campaigns. In all these destinations, the Chinese experience was similar: initial military success was undone by the impossibility of maintaining control at a distance over hostile populations. Java—which might have become, if more accessible, the first colony of the world's first long-range seaborne empire—was protected by the monsoons. On China's other main maritime front, to the north-east, expansion was impeded by tougher and less predictable obstacles of climate and navigation. Japan, which Kublai worked hardest to conquer—creating and re-creating an invasion fleet and levying doomed tribute-armies from Korea and the Jürchen—proved invincible, not because of Japanese resistance, which was enfeebled by lack of practice against invaders, but because of the treacherous, capricious weather of the sea that had to be crossed. Both of Kublai's invasion forces were scattered or stranded by typhoons, the *kamikaze* "divine winds" which make lee shores a summer death-trap.

In two respects, however, the ambitious reach of Kublai's imperialism had lasting effects. First, it confirmed the way things were already going in some neighbouring states: fierce nationalism, based on self-differentiation from a perceived Chinese enemy in Korea and Vietnam; isolationism and self-confidence in Japan; cultural transition and political dissolution in southeast Asia. In Sarawak, for instance, where the great island-wide empire of Srivijaya or San fo-Chi had formerly held sway, the homeward-bound Marco Polo reported only an ill-assorted rabble of chiefdoms: one of cannibals, one of tailed men, one regulated by "the law of brute beasts," one

Both of Kublai's invasions of Japan were frustrated—the first deflected and the second destroyed by "divine winds." The encounters with the Japanese were brief and fought mainly with arrows: in the engagement fought by the first task force, the Chinese had already run out of arrows when the wind turned. In the Japanese commemorative scroll, much emphasis is put on the harrying actions of the heroic archer Takezaki, here leading a boarding party onto a war-junk.

with an economy based on camphor, and one—the only one he knew at first hand—where Muslim influence had taken hold on the coast, while the interior was abandoned to "bestial mountain-folk." The Japanese complacently rejected the Chinese world-view. When the next Chinese dynasty tried to resume traditional relations with Japan, demands for tribute were rejected with conviction and threats of invasion with contempt. Instead, the Japanese offered a vision of a politically plural cosmos and a concept of territorial sovereignty: "Heaven and earth are vast; they are not monopolized by one ruler. The universe is great and wide, and the various countries are created each to have a share in its rule."

Second, in China itself, Kublai's campaigns stimulated scientific curiosity and commercial cupidity. The Java expedition brought back a map of the island—an early example, perhaps, of what was to become a great cartographical school, all of whose output has been lost: the mid-fourteenth-century Javanese king Hayan Wuruk commissioned a comprehensive

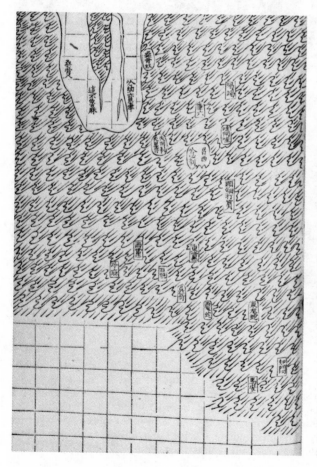

Into the Indian Ocean, in the early fourteenth-century world atlas of Chu Ssu-pen, the southern tip of Africa projects—with its recognizable shape, the attendant islands of Zanzibar, Madagascar, and the Mascarenes and a hint of knowledge of the interior in the form of a vast lake. Because the original has not survived, and is known only from this engraving of the mid-sixteenth century, the reliability of this evidence of Chinese knowledge of Africa has often been doubted; but the scale and frequency of contacts across the Indian Ocean in the middle ages make it seem thoroughly convincing.

survey of his island; when the Portuguese arrived in the early sixteenth century, their explorations in the east Indies seem to have relied on Javanese maps. China's native cartography was stimulated to new achievements, gathering information about the wider world from seamen's reports. The world map of Chu Ssu-Pen (1273–1337) includes most of the islands of the Indian Ocean and a strikingly realistic notion of Africa, with its southward-tapering shape, southern cape, and inland lakes. The invasion of Java, demonstrating Chinese naval and military might beyond the China Sea, must have been a help to Chinese merchants operating in distant waters. Where conquests failed, diplomatic missions sought to promote trade. Chou ta-Kuan, for instance, compiled lists of Chinese products wanted in Cambodia and Cambodian products saleable in China.

To judge from the surviving temple reliefs, the Java of Hayan Wuruk did

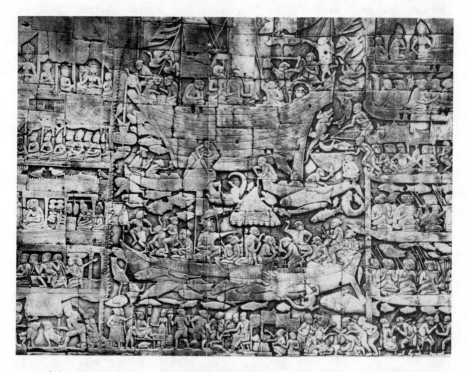

One of the Bayon reliefs captures the maritime background of south-east Asian civilization in the late middle ages. Javanese ships—though they feature on few temple reliefs and on none from the time of Hayan Wuruk—no doubt belonged in the tradition represented by this Cambodian scene of the thirteenth century, which should be compared with the Indian ship of roughly the same period on p. 120. Notice here, on the large merchant ship, the square matting sails, the out-built stern—also a feature of Chinese junks—the aedicule on deck, and the sounding mechanism at the prow. The sea is filled with fish and fishing vessels and a pleasure craft is also shown.

not look to its inhabitants like a great maritime power. The scenes depicted are of neat hamlets of wooden houses perched on pillars over stone terraces. Peasants plough inundated rice fields or tease water buffalo over them to break and fertilize the ground. Women harvest and cook the rice. Orchestras beat gongs with sticks to inspire masked dancers. These details compose a portrait of an agrarian society and an autarchic economy, settled in long-established rhythms and rituals. The island's growing trade must have been attuned to the needs of an élite titillated by foreign luxuries, rather than to the opportunities of a commercial revolution.

When the revolution happened, at the end of the fourteenth century CE, Java should have been well placed to profit from it. The northern ports of the island probably already had the shipyards that dominated Indonesian waters when the first European intruders arrived. In Latin Christendom, the island already had a reputation as the origin or emporium of all the spices of the east. To a cosmic observer, it might have appeared as Java's moment: far more than the remote, backward and contracting states of western Europe, the island looked like a potential starting-place for an empire of long-range trade and conquest.

Hayan Wuruk himself seems to have had dazzling imperial ambitions. His mental world is captured in a poem by his childhood playmate, Winada-Prapañca, a Buddhist scholar of the royal chancery. The *Nagara-Kertagama* of the year 1365 is a panegyric in praise of the ruler, an exercise in the intimidation of neighbours and a manifesto of dynamic and aggressive policy. It lovingly describes the wonders of the royal compound at Majapahit with its gates of iron and its "diamond-plastered" watch-tower. While Majapahit is said to be like the moon and sun, the rest of the towns of the kingdom "in great numbers" are "of the aspect of stars." Hayan Wuruk travels about the country on his royal progresses in numberless carts or is borne through the capital, attired in gold, on his lion-throne palanquin, to the music of tambours and battle-drums, conches and trumpets and singers, to receive tribute in Sanskrit verse from foreign courts. He is both "Buddha in the body" and "Shiwa incarnate." His realm, which according to the poet is incomparable for renown in all the world, except with India, actually occupied little more than half the island of Java. But Hayan Wuruk aimed to make it bigger. The poet's list of tributaries is scattered through Sumatra, Borneo, southern Malaya, Celebes, and the eastern islands as far south as Timur and Sumba, and as far north as the Talaud Islands. Protectorates are claimed in northern Malaya, Siam, Cambodia, and Annam; the poet even makes China and India subservient to his lord. "Already the other continents," he boasts, "are getting ready to show obedience to the Illustrious Prince." Commercial rival-realms in Sumatra indeed seem to have been annihilated by Majapahit. Trade is, on the whole, good for peace; but sudden expansion of trade whets territorial appetites. South-east Asia's late medieval boom set indigenous states at one another's throats as well as drawing Chinese conquistadores and colonists.

THE MING MENAGERIE

On a summer's day in 1415, the Emperor of China, accompanied by a vast retinue of courtiers, hurried, with as much speed as was consistent with the dignity of the occasion, to the Feng-tien gate of Peking to welcome a distinguished foreign arrival, brought by a Chinese fleet all the way from Malindi, on the far shore of the Indian Ocean. The court gathered in repressed curiosity, for only one such visitor had ever been received before, and on that occasion—the previous year—the appropriate state ceremony had not been arranged. Had the welcome been intended for a merely human guest, the occasion would not have been nearly so auspicious, but this time the newcomer was a creature of reputedly divine provenance. According to an eyewitness it had "the body of a deer and the tail of an ox and a fleshy

Shen Tu's drawing of the ch'i-lin or unicorn from Bengal was copied by Ch'en T'ing-pi, among others, and the exotic creatures of the imperial menagerie generally became artists' favourites. Enthusiasm for reading about strange countries and admiring pictures of their fauna survived the demise of Chinese ambition to extend the reach of trade and the range of tribute.

boneless horn, with luminous spots like a red or purple mist. It walks in stately fashion and in its every motion it observes a rhythm." Carried away by confusion with the mythical ch'i-lin, or unicorn, the same observer declared, "Its harmonious voice sounds like a bell or musical tube." But not even that flight of fancy could conceal the true identity of what was actually a giraffe.

The giraffe brought an assurance of divine benevolence made explicit, for instance, in the lines addressed to the emperor by the artist Shen Tu, who had made a drawing from life of the first giraffe to appear at the Ming court:

The ministers and the people all gathered to gaze at it and their joy knows no end. I, your servant, have heard that when a sage possesses the virtue of the utmost benevolence, so that he illuminates the darkest places, then a ch'i-lin appears. This shows that your Majesty's virtue equals that of heaven. Its merciful blessings have spread far and wide so that its harmonious vapours have emanated a ch'i-lin as an endless blessing to the state for myriad myriad years.

Even so, the Emperor was reluctant to display excessive eagerness. When the first giraffe arrived, he declined his ministers' congratulations on the grounds that "even without a giraffe there is nothing to hinder good government." When the second came, he said he would rather have a copy of the Five Classics. Still, he turned out in state to meet it.

The giraffes were only two among a host of strange new creatures that enriched the imperial menagerie in the early fifteenth century. The animals were kept in a part of the imperial park where, despite its inhibiting name of Forbidden Forest, admirers were welcome to come and gape, as in a modern zoo. In 1419 a fleet returning from Ormuz brought "strange birds." An inscription recorded, "All of them craning their necks looked on with pleasure and, stamping their feet, they were scared and startled"—and that was the courtiers, not the birds. The menagerie acquired lions, leopards, ostriches, dromedaries, zebras, rhinoceroses, and antelopes, as well as the giraffes, and the baffling fulfilment of a mythical beast, the Touou-yü. Drawings made this last creature resemble a white tiger with black spots, while written descriptions present "a righteous beast" who would not tread on growing grass, was strictly vegetarian, and appeared "only under a prince of perfect benevolence and sincerity." Truly, it seemed to Shen Tu, "all the creatures that spell good fortune arrive."

The denizens of the zoo and the countries of their provenance—Bengal, Arabia, East Africa—demonstrated the survival, from the time of Kublai Khan, of Chinese interest in the panorama of the world. Chinese trade had crossed the Indian Ocean for centuries: it had smothered the interior of the dome of the mosque of Kilwa in porcelain; "the buried history of Tanganyika" in the first half of the millennium had been unearthed in thousands of blue-and-white and jade-green shards. Just before the Mongol invasions, a high-ranking official had published the *Chu Fan Chih,* a detailed account of the South China Sea and of countries in south-east Asia and India, as a practical handbook for commercial travellers. Yet even by these standards the policies of the early fifteenth century represented a new departure: it was a time of unprecedented official naval expeditions towards the remotest regions of the world known to Chinese geography.

The need for the imperial government to take an interest in oceanlike exploration and perhaps in oceanic expansion was unusually acute. Timur's central Asian empire had revived the threat of conquest from that direction. Just as European explorers searched for allies in Islam's rear, so the Chinese needed to gather intelligence and identify potential sources of help in areas to the Timurids' south and west. The Indian Ocean, which was to provide easy pickings for Portuguese imperialism a hundred years later, was already highly vulnerable to a predator willing to back commercial initiatives with force. The trades of the region were highly lucrative and included spices, fragrant hardwoods, valuable medicinal drugs, and exotic animal products; the ships of the Chinese naval expeditions were called treasure ships. Moreover, the years of most intense long-range naval activity, from 1402 to 1424, coincided with the reign of one of the most expansionist, aggressive, and maritime-minded emperors in Chinese history. The Yung-lo emperor revived much of the tone and some of the projects of Kublai Khan's day. He restored the capital of Peking, invaded—and for a time appeared to have conquered—Vietnam, and intervened in the politics of the Malacca region and beyond. For a time even Japan was drawn out of isolation by the eagerly proffered opportunities for trade. Chinese coin hoards from medieval Japan, accumulations of both commerce and piracy, hint at the importance of relations with China for the islands' economies; but official trade was sanctioned only in short bursts, interspersed with periods, on Japan's part, of defiant autarchy.

The chosen instrument of his maritime ambitions was a Muslim eunuch of Mongol descent known as Cheng Ho. Every element in this admiral's prosopographical description marked him as an outsider of the Confucian scholar élite that contended for power with the eunuch establishment at court. His appointment in 1403 to lead an ocean-going task force was a triumph for linked lobbies whose interests offended Confucian values: the commercial lobby, which wanted to mobilize naval support for Chinese Indian-Ocean traders; the imperialist lobby, which wanted to renew Mongol visions of conquest; the religious lobbies, which wanted to keep state funds out of sceptical or anti-clerical Confucian hands by diverting them to

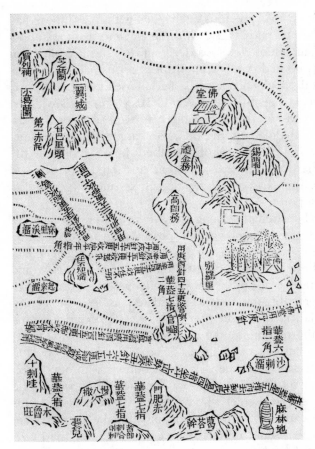

Though official records of Cheng Ho's voyages were destroyed by the anti-imperial lobby at court, charts which illustrate his overall survey of the ocean's shores reappeared in a printed work on warfare in 1621. Like early western portolans, these are diagrams of sailing directions rather than scale maps. In the section shown here, tracks annotated with compass-bearings are shown linking ports on either side of the Arabian Sea: Cheng Ho's surviving sailing directions are all in the form, "Follow such-and-such a bearing for such-and-such a number of watches." Each port is marked with its latitude according to the elevation of the Pole Star above the horizon, which Cheng Ho verified by means of "guiding star-boards"—ebony strips of various breadths held at a fixed distance from the observer's face to fill the space exactly between the star and the horizon.

other enterprises. Cheng Ho led seven expeditions from 1405 to 1433, six of them under Yung-lo's patronage.

Their scale and range were massive. The first was said to comprise sixty-two junks of the largest ever built, 225 support vessels, and 27,870 men. The vessels—to judge from a recently discovered rudder post—justified the awed terms of contemporary assessments, displacing perhaps 3,100 tons. According to the best available estimate, the seventh voyage—probably the farthest-penetrating—sailed 12,618 miles. The voyages lasted on average two years each. They visited in all at least thirty countries around the rim of the ocean, as far south as Zanzibar, as far north as Hormuz, and as far west as Jiddah.

Mutual astonishment was the result of contacts on a previously unimagined scale with peoples whose previous exchanges with the Chinese had been limited or mediated by middlemen. In the preface to his book about the voyages, Ma Huan, an interpreter aboard Cheng Ho's fleet, recalled that as a young man when he had contemplated the seasons, climates, landscapes, and peoples of distant lands, he had asked himself in great surprise, "How can such dissimilarities exist in the world?" His own travels with the eunuch admiral convinced him that the reality was even stranger. The arrival of Chinese junks at middle eastern ports with cargoes of precious exotica caused a sensation. Ibn Tighri Birdi described the excitement at the Egyptian court when news arrived that junks had anchored off Aden and that the captains of the ships had asked the Mameluke sultan's permission to approach the nearest port to Mecca.

Despite their formidable strength, Cheng Ho's voyages were designed to show the flag, not erect it permanently as European voyages of exploration did, in token of affected sovereignty. They distributed fabulous gifts to foreign potentates and shrines and garnered tribute in return, which would boost the emperor's prestige at home. These exchanges were themselves a form of commerce, probably intended to stimulate trade of a more conventional sort. They did, however, demonstrate China's potential as the launching bay of a seaborne empire: the capacity and productivity of her shipyards; her ability to mount expeditions of crushing dimensions and despatch them over vast distances. Cheng Ho's encounters with opposition unequivocally emphasized Chinese superiority. On the first expedition he was waylaid by a Chinese pirate chief who had set up a bandit state of his own in the sometime capital of Srivijaya in Sumatra; the pirates were slaughtered and their leader sent to China for execution. On the third voyage the Sinhalese king of Ceylon tried to lure Cheng Ho into a trap and seize the fleet; the Chinese dispersed his forces, captured his capital, deported him to China, and installed a pretender in his place. On the fourth expedition a Sumatran chief who refused to cooperate in the exchange of gifts for tribute was overwhelmed, abducted, and ultimately put to death.

Cheng Ho's own perception of his role seems to have combined an imperialist impulse with the peaceful inspiration of commerce and scholarship. A stela he erected in 1432 began in jingoistic vein: "In the unifying of the seas and continents the Ming Dynasty even goes beyond the Han and Tang. . . . The countries beyond the horizon and from the ends of the earth have become subjects." But he added, in deference to traders and geographers, "However far they may be, their distances and the routes may be calculated." The voyage on which Cheng Ho was engaged when the stela was erected was to be his last, and the last of China's official maritime programme. A promising imperial effort was abruptly aborted and never resumed. China's manifest destiny never happened, and the world predominance, which for a time seemed hers for the taking, was abandoned to other contenders from the west. To understand why, it is necessary to go back to the origins of the dynasty Cheng Ho served.

THE BRIGHT DYNASTY

Peasants make poor revolutionaries, except under a messianic leader in a millenarian cause. Normally, they can only be incited on empty stomachs, for peasant revolts born in prosperity tend to propose conservative objectives. In the middle of the fourteenth century, swarms of conscript peasant-labourers, assembled to repair the Grand Canal that carried essential food supplies to Peking, were convulsed by classic peasant discontents and classic peasant expectations.

They were victims of the grinding structures of economic misery, which had reduced the population of China, by some calculations, to half what it had been at its height; they were survivors of conjunctures of disaster—the Yellow River flood of 1344, the persistent droughts of subsequent years, the local famines exacerbated by decayed communications. The rhythms of peasant life are so slow and so changeless that hope is commonly deferred and promises of improvement tend to get discounted. The usual response is to wait and pray for the millennium, the occasional response to try and trigger it. The most explosive popular movement among the canal workers of 1350 had started as a quietist sect of Buddhism nearly nine hundred years before, watching patiently for the longed-for reincarnation of the Lord Maitreya. Now belief in the imminence of that consummation was honed with a political edge: the reincarnate Lord would give his followers power over their oppressors. This closely paralleled the contemporary millenarianism of the Fraticelli in the Christian west, who expected a cosmic hero to wrest new treasures from the depths of the earth, enrich the poor, put down the mighty from their seat, and exalt the humble and meek. But the cult of the White Lotus had become more than a popular religious movement; it was now a subversive secret society with a mass membership, comparable to political freemasonry in parts of eighteenth-century Europe or the Italian *carbonari* or the Chinese Communist Party in the 1930s.

Two similar movements coincided and to some extent combined with it. A dualist tradition identified the Lord Maitreya as Ming Wang, the Prince of Light, whose promised coming would put a triumphant end to the cosmic struggle of good against evil. At the same time a folk memory hankered for the Sung Dynasty, extruded by the Mongols nearly a hundred years before. Again, this is characteristic of peasants' revolts all over the world. They are often revolutionary in the most literal sense of the word, trying to turn the world back full circle to an imagined or misremembered golden age. A conspiracy launched by the White Lotus apologist Han Shan-t'ung exploited in

Despite the commonly asserted insularity of Chinese taste, Buddhism was a foreign religion which not only attracted Chinese adherents but also induced pilgrims to leave the country and influenced politics and the arts. This gilt-bronze Buddha of 1396 is of Chinese workmanship, but is heavily dependent on an Indian model. Yet, despite the huge contribution Buddhist ideology made to the rise of the Ming—galvanizing support and even contributing the dynasty's chosen name—the conservative Confucianism of the scholar-class reasserted itself once the new dynasty was securely enthroned. See p. 148.

combination all three of the myths current among the peasants: messianic, millenarian, and revivalist. Proclaiming himself the rightful heir of the Sung, his blood-brother Liu Fu-t'ung, he "sacrificed a white horse and a black ox and swore an oath to heaven and earth and planned to raise armies with a red turban as their sign." Han's execution in 1351 provoked an insurrection among the wearers of the red turban, who were suddenly able to call into the field armies scores of thousands strong.

These peasants were selected by their circumstances to be the fodder of war: displaced from their homes by natural disasters and forced-labour projects. They were joined to a surprising degree by townsmen. Civic patricians had generally felt neglected or impeded by the dynasty of Kublai Khan, which had an atavistic attraction to pastoralism and a preference for foreign counsellors. In the chaos of social upheaval, however, lords of misrule rise. The Chinese equivalent of Jack Straw or Huey Long was Kuo Tzu-hsing, a fortune-teller's son and butcher's apprentice who drank in low dives with his ragged bodyguards. He was typical of the charismatic up-starts who wrest power in riots by talk and toughness and run cities by mob violence. In 1352 he took over the town of Haochou in north-central Anhwei province. Most rabble-roused city-states falter or fizzle out; this one was to grow into an empire.

The founder of the Ming Dynasty was a bodyguard and fellow-drinker of Kuo's called Chu Yüan-chang. He was another of the peasant-emperors who occasionally streak across Chinese history, of whom Mao Tse-tung was, in a sense, the last. Promised to a Buddhist monastery as a boy, he led the disreputable life of an itinerant monk—a stock character of ruffianly villainy in Chinese fiction. This was a suitable background for a member of Kuo's entourage. His master took a fancy to him and gave him his adopted daughter in marriage. Fascinatingly tall and ugly, intimidatingly daring and strong, Chu was able to build up a personal following, thanks in part to his responsibility for recruitment to Kuo's band. No one could stop him from seizing the authority Kuo left at his death.

Haochou was only one of a string of bandit-states thriving in central China in the 1350s and 1360s, protected by the Red Turban rising which raged to the north. Twice the rebels were saved from destruction by the emulous politics of the imperial court, where strongmen who might have secured victory were disgraced or murdered, or both. The dynasty of Kublai Khan was flung back on its Mongol heartlands. Meanwhile, the states built up by Chu and his fellow-upstarts grew, merged, and toughened. By 1360 effective power was disputed among the three strongest warlords of the Yangtze region. Chu's forces were numerically the weakest of the three; he was poorly provided with ships—which might be expected to be decisive in river warfare; and the central position of his realm exposed him to attack on two fronts, though, perhaps, offered him a compensating advantage

conferred by interior lines of supply and communication. Coming from behind, he had less to lose than his enemies in campaigns of almost reckless
daring. Seizing initiatives against the odds, embracing a strategy of *toujours
de l'audace,* he pulled off a series of brilliant successes: in 1360 he beat the
neighbouring warlord at Nanking and captured over a hundred ships
grounded in mud. He could carry his own counter-campaign upriver in
1361–62 and in the following year established an unconquerable advantage
over his competitors in a running battle at P'oyang which lasted almost
without respite for nearly four weeks.

He was still careful to represent himself merely as a servant of the empire
of the Red Turban; but the untimely death of the imperial figurehead in
1366 created an opening Chu could not forbear to fill. In 1368 he proclaimed the inauguration of a new dynasty and the era of his own rule, under the imperial name Hung Wu, or Plenteous Victory.

Like all the best parvenu dictators, he was a clever manager of the coalition that had brought him to power. One thinks of Napoleon, juggling with
monarchists and Jacobins, or of Franco, playing off fascists and traditionalists. Chu respected all the ideologies that had been wound into the Red
Turban. He compared himself to the founder of China; he restored the
court ceremonial of the Tang era; he kept up the military command structure of the previous dynasty and even affected some habits of Mongol
dress; he balanced these features of his style with concessions to the Confucians, restoring the public examinations for the civil service. The cult of
Maitreya was explicitly abjured, but only after Chu had made it clear that he
had already fulfilled its expectations. In adopting the name of Ming for his
dynasty, he was arrogating the "Bright" attribute of the reincarnate Buddha
for himself.

Tentatively, slowly, the era of the Hung Wu emperor marked the beginnings of China's return to the Confucian values which came to dominate
the modern history of the empire. As a peasant and an ex-Buddhist monk,
Chu can hardly have been expected to embrace the Confucian heritage with
unqualified enthusiasm. He had the typical contempt of the self-educated
man for the academic establishment. His animadversions on the uselessness
of the "scholar-gentry" would sound plausible in the mouth of Newt Gingrich (ironically, a former professor of history). "Chewing on phrases and
biting on words," they did no good, he asserted, even to their own students.
"All they know is writing on paper. They have never had any practical experience of affairs. . . . When you examine what they do, it is nothing."

In practice, Chu, like Mr. Gingrich, realized that the academics did have
some forms of exploitable expertise and that a vast, literate empire needed
a bureaucracy disciplined by a traditional ethical code. But he kept the various power-centres in and around his court in balance: the Confucian bu-

reaucrats, the military top brass, the eunuch establishment, the foreign advisers, the Buddhist and Taoist clergies, the merchant lobby. His successor was a Confucian tool—one is tempted to say "enthusiast," but enthusiasm would be an un-Confucian emotion. The reign, however, was brief, and the great outward-going era of naval display, burgeoning commerce, and long-range exploration in the early fifteenth century was the achievement of the equipoise bequeathed by Chu Yüan-chang.

It could not last. In the 1420s and 1430s the balance of power shifted. When the Hung-hsi emperor ascended the throne on 9 September 1424, one of his first acts was to cancel preparations for Cheng Ho's next projected voyage. In his one year on the throne he restored Confucian office-holders whom his predecessor had dismissed and curtailed the power of other factions. In the next reign, the military establishment lost face through defeat in Vietnam: Montgomery's law of war—"Never invade Russia"— should be extended to reflect the experience the Chinese have shared with French and American successors (see Chapter 21). In 1429 the shipbuilding budget was pared almost to extinction. Revulsion from Buddhism and Taoism, except as pabulum for the masses, increasingly marked the emperors of the dynasty.

By the mid-1430s the Confucians had not definitively won the factional struggles, but their values were well on the way to a near-exclusive triumph. The abrogation of overseas expansion, the demotion of commercial values, and the renunciation of shipbuilding became such important badges of identity for the scholar-élite that bureaucrats destroyed all Cheng Ho's records in an attempt to obliterate his memory. The examination system and the gradual attenuation of other forms of recruitment for public service meant that China would increasingly be governed by a code of scholars, with their contempt for barbarism, and of gentlemen, with their indifference to trade.

In a far-off future, the galactic historians may come to see China's maritime self-restraint as a clever long-term strategy. While other powerful states of what we call the modern period concentrated on the creation of far-flung empires, briefly profitable but impossible to sustain, China turned back to her traditional arena, expanding at the margins, Sinifying the minorities, and creating, in very recent times, controllable empires, first at the expense of contiguous Muslim communities and then in Tibet. Among the effects, it may come to be said, have been a homeland more defensible, a heartland more unified, a culture more durable, and a power more concentrated than those of rivals from the Christian west whose dominance seemed, for a while, so spectacular. Certainly, China has been remarkably exempt from the empire-shattering convulsions of the late twentieth century and seems, as I write, immune from the processes of fragmentation which are afflicting many other modern super-states. On the evidence of the events of the early fifteenth century, in the world east of the Bay of Bengal—the world "behind the wind," as Arab navigators called it—China could have had a seaborne empire for the taking; she might then have established a commanding lead in the early modern space race for a world-wide role. Her forbearance remains one of the most remarkable instances of collective reticence in history.

Chapter 5

A SMALL PROMONTORY OF ASIA: LATIN CHRISTENDOM IN THE LATE MIDDLE AGES

The Stranger in the Glass—The Enlarged Horizon—
Enemies of Promise—The Divisions of Latin Christendom—
The Age of Fool's Gold—The Errant Spirit

THE STRANGER IN THE GLASS

A mule was as good as a woman for the Basques' perverted purposes, and—according to the same twelfth-century pilgrims' guide—the Navarrese poisoned their rivers in order to increase the sale of their wines. These jottings from an early ethnographer's copybook may sound conventional or quaint—snippets from a tradition in which national characteristics were crushed into gnomic stereotypes to boost the observer's sense of superiority. Taken in context, however, they belong typically to Latin Christendom's era of self-discovery in the late eleventh and twelfth centuries, when, impelled by the process of identity formation described in Chapter One, writers turned inward to find and describe Europe's inner barbarians: the remote peoples of forest, bog, and mountains, the imperfectly assimilated marchland dwellers whose evangelization was sketchy at best and whose habitats were often blanks on the map.

The expansion of Europe of the late middle ages and early modern period was preceded by—in a sense, began with—this exploration of the interior and threshold, the secret recesses, the unfrequented edges of

Christendom. In the twelfth century the riverbankers of Latin Christendom conquered the wild wood. In 1122, Abbot Suger's search through the forests for trees mighty enough to frame the roof of Saint Denis symbolized a vast project for the domestication of little-explored and under-exploited environments. Gothic architecture, erected by means which economized on wood, was a style adapted to shrinking forests. The growth of the Cistercians, the most dynamic religious order of the century, made rough places plain, driving flocks and ox teams into wildernesses where now, all too often, the vast abbeys lie ruined in their turn.

The peoples brought by this process into the candle-glow of scholarship had, for the writers who contemplated them, a variety of uses. Adam, bishop of Bremen, wielded his image of the pagan Prussians as a weapon with which to belabour the moral shortcomings of his fellow-Christians; without the advantage of access to the gospel, they shared their goods and despised gold and silver "as dung." For Barbarossa's encomiast, the poet Gunther of Pairis in Alsace, the Poles were just the opposite; savages despite their Christianity, with their wolves' voices and unkempt coiffures. Perhaps the Polish élite, who despite their impeccable Slav credentials fostered a myth of their descent from "Sarmatian" nomad-warriors, brought such misjudgements on their own heads. For the pilgrim-guide writer known as Aiméry Picaud, the mountains and forests that had to be crossed by pilgrims to Compostela housed misplaced exotics, whose unnatural lusts—sodomy and bestiality—licensed pornography.

Yet among the distractions of these partial purposes, medieval ethnography was able to achieve some real fieldwork and to construct some realistic images of marginal peoples and their societies. Before looking outward, through the windows opened by colonial and commercial expansion towards Asia and Africa, scholars turned to contemplate alien faces in a mirror of their own, among dwellers in the frontiers and fastnesses of their own world. The most representative enquirer, perhaps, was Gerald of Wales, whose journeys through Wales and Ireland really were projects of self-encounter, as this Normanized, Anglicized scholar searched out his Celtic roots. From his career in the royal administrative jobs in which he specialized, he often returned to his native country on missions of espionage or diplomacy. When he went back for good in 1199 as a canon of Saint David's, he was vulnerable to political slander, denounced by his enemies "as a Frenchman to the Welsh and to the French as a Welshman." His preferred habitat was comfortable, scholarly, and urbane. His self-satisfied account of the reception of a lecture he gave before the masters and doctors of Oxford in 1184 is one of the earliest pieces of evidence of the existence of the university. His account of a meal of barnacle-goose, shared at Canterbury on a fast day with cathedral clergy who convinced themselves that they were eating a kind of fish, is a masterpiece of satirical irony.

Transferred from the fleshpots to the frontier, Gerald beheld the wilderness of his birth with the nostalgia of a returnee and the discomfort of a misfit.

Gerald inherited a dilemma from classical tradition. He could never rid his mind of the conviction that sedentarism was civility and transhumance was savagery. Yet he was also susceptible to the myth of Arcady and inclined to see his fellow-Celts as revelling in a bucolic idyll. Thus he suppressed or overlooked the substantial sedentary and arable sectors of the Welsh economy and depicted the whole country as pastoral, with sidelines in brigandage and rapine. He condemned the Welsh as incestuous and promiscuous, the Irish—conveniently for their would-be conquerors in England—as wild infidels. Irish barbarity was typified by two hairy, naked savages fished up in a coracle by an English ship off the Connaught coast and astonished by the sight of bread. On the other hand, the Welsh had the conventional virtues of a shepherd race, among whom "no one is a beggar, for everyone's household is common to all. They prize liberality, especially generosity, above all virtues. Here the courtesy of hospitality is enjoyed by all, so much that it has neither to be offered nor requested by travellers." Genuinely torn between conflicting perceptions of his subject-matter, Gerald evolved a model of social development of great sophistication. "The Irish," he wrote,

> are a wild race of the woods . . . getting their living from animals alone and living like animals; a people who have not abandoned the first mode of living—the pastoral life. For when the order of mankind progressed from the woods to the fields and from the fields to the towns and gatherings of citizens, this people spurned the labours of farming. They viewed the treasures of the city with no ambition and refused the rights and responsibilities of civil life. Hence they did not abandon the life of woods and pastures which they had led up to then.

The Irish proved peculiarly intractable, but in general, in the course of the first half of the millennium, Latin Christendom's internal and frontier barbarians became integrated with their neighbours. Hungary, which Otto of Freising in the mid-twelfth century thought too good for the Hungarians, became in the fifteenth a cradle-land of the Renaissance. Basque lineages, so despised by Aiméry Picaud, supplied a new aristocracy to the rest of Spain in the fourteenth century. Dwellers in remote or inhospitable areas never escaped urbane contempt, and rarely matched the doctrinal standards of zealous evangelists, but the quest for the barbarian was increasingly turned out of doors to the world outside the boundaries of the Latin west. In the course of the twelfth century, moreover, two movements widened the mental horizons of Christendom. The crusades alerted westerners to the vastness of the world and to the smallness of the corner they

The measurable cosmos. The architect of the universe uses dividers to check the exactness of its proportions. The sun, moon, and stars have just taken their places and an earth "without form and void" is congealing. The illuminated caption at the top explains that the heavens and the elements are also being made. In the pre-Copernican universe, man is often said to have exaggerated his importance, but this illumination from a French bible of the thirteenth century shows how puny creation seemed in the hands of God.

occupied in their "small promontory of Asia." The progress of scholarly humanism in recovering classical learning animated the science of geography and painted in some of the details of the expanding image of the world.

The Enlarged Horizon

The end products were the marvellously comprehensive schemes of knowledge and faith elaborated by the encyclopaedists of Paris in the thirteenth century. The results can be seen today depicted in the decorative scheme of the Spanish Chapel in the Dominican church of Florence, where the contents of the mind of Thomas Aquinas are painted onto the walls—a panoptic vision, in precise categories, which reaches out to include everything known by experience or report. On a smaller scale, the Hereford Mappamundi maps the growth of the sort of mind which made it—the mind, probably, of a secular priest from Lincolnshire. Like its predecessors in the Christian world-map tradition, the Hereford specimen presents an ordered world to the devout beholder, in an image designed for the decoration of an altarpiece. Yet liberties are taken with the traditional scheme to reflect real knowledge, with Jerusalem slightly displaced from the central position demanded by purely devotional purposes, and the explored world fringed with speculative lands and beings, sometimes fantastic but always documented.

On the frontiers of Christendom, an astral observer might have been pardoned, in the thirteenth century, for supposing that this world was poised for further expansion. The population of western Europe may have doubled between the early eleventh and mid-thirteenth centuries. Restrictive inheritance customs had released or driven excluded sons from their patrimonial lands into frontiers of conquest and settlement. Behind the expanding frontier, modest technical revolutions were increasing productivity: large ploughs with curved blades bit deeper into the land; more efficient mills, more exact metallurgy, and new products, especially in arms and glassware, extended the range of business and the flow of wealth. The impetus of the crusades was halted and reversed in the eastern Mediterranean, but at the other end of that sea spectacular gains were made at Muslim expense in the Balearic islands and the Iberian peninsula. On the northern frontier, planned towns such as Elbing in Prussia and New Brandenburg were laid out with the measuring-rod and peopled by wagon trains, bringing the human flotsam of recruitment campaigns in the Rhineland and northern France. They bear the gridplan-brand of the colonial city throughout history—the same rectilinear image is stamped on the face of Melbourne or Lima.

Beyond these pickets of a new political order, merchants spread their more adventurous colonies. Those of Genoa had the most impressive range—serving Mongol khans on the northern shores of the Black Sea or Moorish sultans in Seville and Malaga, without sacrifice of Genoese identity; indeed, in Kaffa the streets were named after those back home. They sold— for oriental spices, Danubian forest products, or African gold—the output of Europe's first industrial revolution: fine cloths made by scientific breeding and fulling, by long-range trade and specialization. In the thirteenth century the long-severed economies of Mediterranean and Atlantic Europe were reunited when Mediterranean shippers unstoppered the Straits of Gibraltar, forcing their way through against the racing current. Now English wools could be transferred to sophisticated centres of production in northern Italy; dyestuffs from Phocaea could be carried to the cloth-makers of Flanders. This proto-capitalism, in turn, inspired proto-imperialism, as merchant families sent out cadets to establish new markets on and beyond the edges of Christendom.

The tone of life in a Genoese colony of the day, beyond the frontier of Christendom, is captured, for instance, in a precious series of notarial records from Tunis, covering roughly the first six months of 1289. The value of the 133 surviving documents of the notary Pietro Batifoglio lies in their chronicle, day by day and, on some days, hour by hour, of the life of the Genoese merchant community in one of the major Muslim ports of the west. They evoke the huge scale of the Genoese operation in Tunis. The numbers of notaries mentioned implies a colony of several hundred persons. Not only was it a large community, but also a settled one. The sons of resident or formerly resident fathers were often in business there. Some merchants had established households with womenfolk of their own. Waldo di Budi's was a temporary arrangement: his form of marriage to a former slave girl was annulled on grounds of her previous marriage in her homeland. Others were more permanent: a Genoese woman living in the Marseillais quarter of the city—presumably as a result of a marriage—claimed burial in the Genoese cemetery; Jacobina de Savignano stayed on after her husband's death and married again.

It was a society with established rituals and a well-defined élite. Most business was conducted in the "old warehouse of the Genoese," where the first merchant quarter had been founded in the twelfth century and which it had now far outgrown. But particularly solemn acts might be recorded in the Genoese church or major disputes with the local authorities in the amir's palace. Occasionally an urgent matter connected with an arriving or departing ship might be transacted in the open on the quayside. A more popular venue was the wine warehouse, the natural rendezvous of Latin expatriates in a Muslim state. Everything worthy of report—whether a purchase on credit, the acknowledgement or liquidation of a debt, the formation of a company, the registration of a shipping contract, the acquisition or

"He shall pass into the country of strange peoples. He shall try good and evil in all things." In the only surviving illumination that illustrates his report, Friar William of Rubruck looks alarmed at King Louis's instructions for a mission to the Mongols, but sets out purposefully enough. His journey of 1253–55 took him as far as Karakorum and generated an account full of vivid and faithful detail. No text better illustrates the broadening horizons and widening eyes of people in Latin Christendom in his day. See p. 158–59.

sale of a house, the making of a will, a divorce or a deposition of paternity, a dispute or demand addressed to the Muslim authorities, the conferment of a power of attorney, the attainment of majority—all passed before the notary to be inscribed and witnessed with prolix formulae.

The triad of notables—the consul, the priest, and the leading merchant—were often at the notary's elbow. Tealdo, the priest, was an universal helpmeet, witness, or proxy in nearly 20 per cent of recorded transactions, frequent donee of powers of attorney or commissions as agent in particular matters. A single family—that of Cibo da Cibo—were the most important of Batifoglio's clients, but the acknowledged leader of the community was the consul, Balianno Embronio. The fact that he was sought after as a witness even more than the priest reflects his presiding godfatherly role. His practical importance lay in his duty of representing the common interests of the community to the amir.

This was no easy job. In the brief spell covered by these records, Embronio had twice complained about breaches of Genoese treaties with Tunis. He resisted attempts to interfere with the established procedures for purchasing and selling wine by putting up the tax or rent on the warehouse; he locked the premises and gave the key to Tealdo until the status quo was restored. He upbraided customs officials for exceeding their powers and was obliged to denounce the amir's refusal to give him audience twice a month in accordance with agreed practice. Strained relations overspilled into violence on 3 May 1289. Two days previously, the consul had gone to the amir's palace to claim the revenue owed to Genoa on the sale of oil by some Genoese merchants; part of the tax had to be remitted to the Genoese state, and it seems that the merchants concerned withheld it for that purpose. The Tunisian authorities refused to yield their right to the amount in question, except to the Genoese head of government in person, and sent a force armed with stones and clubs to impound the oil against full payment of the tax. According to the notary's account, the Tunisians threatened to act "by force and even contrary to the law"; presumably, he was putting these words in their mouths, but the tone of shock is genuine enough. By the hour of vespers the siege was over. The prudent consul had capitulated, and the merchants agreed to foot most of the bill, referring the consul "to the court of Tunis or the purchasers of the oil" for the recovery of the disputed share of the tax.

Lives like these—perilous, strenuous, companionable—were led by merchants who got even farther afield, along the "road safe by day or night" that led, according to a fourteenth-century merchant's manual, to Peking. This was the road that took Marco Polo to the court of Kublai Khan where he seems to have served as a sort of male Scheherazade, gathering entertaining tales for the delectation of the Khan as he travelled about the empire on official business. He was a banal observer but an enchanting raconteur. He offered practised evocations of the embraces of whores in Hangchow, or of Tibetan sexual hospitality; he presented candid assurances of the existence of islands of tailed men or of Amazons who admitted males only to breed. Such sensationalist snippets justified the reputation he acquired back home as a mere travelling fable-monger. While he was in the Orient, a galley fleet set out from Genoa for the same destination by sea— "to the regions of India by way of the ocean," anticipating Columbus's similar venture by just over two centuries. Success might have pre-launched Europe's great age of maritime exploration, but the voyagers were never heard of again. Still, overland communications with China remained active

Ambrogio Lorenzetti could represent as an event of universal significance the massacre of some of the earliest Franciscan missionaries at Ceuta. A whole human gallery surveys the scene, including Blacks, Jews, a helmed Mongol, a Turk, a Chinaman, and what is probably meant for a Persian. This represents not only the vast range of the Franciscans' evangelical ambitions but also the diversity of the artist's interest and information about the panorama of mankind.

for over a hundred years more, and, until well into the fourteenth century, the dynamism of Latin Christendom generally seemed unarrested. In the 1320s, when Ambrogio Lorenzetti decorated a church in Siena with a great vision of the martyrdom of Franciscans at Ceuta, he was able to allude to a vast, familiar panorama of mankind, with a Chinese observer, among those of other races, studying the scene as if from a gallery within the painting.

ENEMIES OF PROMISE

The finest of all surviving medieval maps, the Catalan Atlas made in Majorca in the late 1370s or early 1380s, is as rich and intricate as a spilled

Plausibly attributed to Cresques Abraham of Majorca, the Catalan Atlas of the late 1370s or early 1380s is one of the glories of the medieval mapmaker's art, as intricate as a spilled jewel-casket. The depiction of a caravan bound for Cathay, with companionable merchants following well-laden camels, reflects the confidence in long-range trade expressed by Francesco Balducci Pegolotti, servant of the house of Bardi of Florence, in his handbook for merchants of about 1340. On the silk road "safe by day and night," he advised, "you must let your beard grow long" and take: a woman "if the merchant likes," a dragoman, and two servants with flour and salt fish. "Other things you will find in sufficiency, and especially meat."

jewel casket, resplendent with images of exotic beings and untold wealth. In the representation of the Atlantic Ocean, just off the bulge of Africa, a well-equipped galley is depicted, embellished with the legend of the disappearance of Jaume Ferrer, an explorer from Majorca, who perished on that coast in 1342. His voyage is unknown from any other source, yet it belongs in a context which makes it believable, of a sudden and rapid Majorcan gold rush towards the middle of the fourteenth century, when sailing licenses for exploratory voyages into the African Atlantic were granted in profusion.

It was a moment of promise in a land of medieval *Wirtschaftswunder*. Ramon Muntaner was, of all Catalan chroniclers, the most indiscriminate in his praise and the most ready with superlatives. But the breathless encomium of Majorca he penned about 1325 rings true. It was "a goodly isle and an honoured one." The king had made "great grants to all his men and great graces. And he peopled the said city and isle by means of more exemptions and privileges than any other city in the world; wherefore it has become one of the good cities of the world, nobler and of greater wealth than any, and all peopled with Catalans, all of honoured provenance and good worth, whence have descended heirs who have become the most

In Pere Nisart's altarpiece dedicated to St. George, the "City of Majorca," now called Palma, looks like a feudal fairyland, dominated by the towering Almudaina Palace, the warlike walls and the oratory in the middle ground. The countryside seems tended more for pleasure than profit and on shore only the windmill hints at its economic productiveness. The profusion of small vessels, however, is a clue to the basis of Majorca's medieval *Wirtschaftswunder* and to the limits of its competitiveness in the emulous Mediterranean world: a huge class of independent small shipowners had plenty of enterprising spirit but lacked the collective muscle of, say, the Venetian patriciate. See D. Abulafia, *A Mediterranean Emporium* (1994), pp. 127–28, 168.

businesslike and best endowed people of any city there may be in the world."

The concentration on the city of Majorca, despite the rest of the island, is revealing. When outsiders thought of Majorca, they thought only of its entrepôt, just as today they think only of the tourist complex, on the same coast, centred on the same city. Muntaner also accurately perceived the conditions that enabled Majorca's economy to thrive: the economic freedom and low taxation that accompanied a sustained effort to draw settlers to the island. The municipal accounts of 1349 capture the epicene contentment of the city fathers. Theirs was a world of status linked to consumption, measured in costly feasts and ostentatious displays of loyalty to the mainland rulers in Barcelona who had replaced the native line. At least seventy-six craftsmen and decorators—some Moors, some Greeks, a few specifically slaves—were hired to adorn the city chambers for the banquets.

Two "painters of altarpieces and battle flags" decorated hangings to celebrate the obsequies of the mainland queen. And the large sums spent on defence against the pretensions of the extruded island dynasty included the pay of eleven surgeon-barbers to serve the fleet. A society so abundantly supplied with quacks and craftsmen must have wallowed in surplus wealth.

Such complacency must have been, in the long run, an enemy of Majorca's promise. But a deadlier and faster-working enemy already lay in wait. In the very year of those self-satisfied accounts, Majorca was just emerging from the grip of the Black Death, a visitation of plague of a severity unparalleled in the past but often to be echoed in the future. The plague was general throughout western Christendom and the middle east, but Majorca, which lost perhaps a third of its population, was scythed with particular thoroughness. Records of voyages of exploration vanish from the archives. In the second half of the fourteenth century, almost the only Majorcan voyagers in the African Atlantic were missionaries, with their message of hope in the next world, in place of the merchants and gold-hunters, whose optimism in the early 1340s had been more nearly and more narrowly focused.

The descent of the Black Death was only the most conspicuous of a series of setbacks which muffled European initiative in the fourteenth century. In 1303 a pope's health was wrecked by the terminal shock of irreverent French knights who invaded his bedchamber. The unity of Latin Christendom never looked quite so impressive again, as western churches became increasingly "national" in character and personnel. Between 1304 and 1307 a Franciscan *enragé* improbably called Fra Dolcino proclaimed a millenarian republic of the foes of Antichrist in an Alpine valley; it was one of a convulsive series of social rebellions and radical religious spasms. In 1315–17 the dead of an exceptionally lethal sequence of winters of famine and floods were mourned from the Elbe to the Loire. It was a centrepiece of a climatic change now called the "little ice age," which marginalized some areas of settlement and emptied others; the frontiers of Christendom gradually withdrew, in the fifteenth century, from their outposts in Greenland and the Baltic, while in the heartlands hill farms became untenable. The Icelandic annals recorded the islanders' last venture to Markland in 1347.

The impersonal enemies—plague, famine, and cold—were supplemented by human foes. In 1354 a violent earthquake demolished the walls of Gallipolli. Turks were waiting to take over the ruins, inaugurating a history of European anxiety about the defensibility of the eastern Mediterranean frontier which would last, with fluctuations, for over two hundred years. Meanwhile, in the north-east, pagan Lithuanians eroded the conquests of the Teutonic Order along the Baltic. When the Greenland colony was finally extinguished in the fifteenth century, it was by mysterious raiders of savage ferocity known as Skraelingar. By comparison with this general repulse, the check suffered by Latin Christendom in the Holy Land in the twelfth century was minimal. Indeed, like so many other imperial checks—to Rome in the last Punic War, to the Ottomans by Timur, to Britain in the American revolution—it seems, in retrospect, more like a respite than a repulse, a starting-point of further greatness, a pause for the rewinding of springs. The fourteenth-century experience—in which Latin Christendom's expansion slowed and sloughed—had no such redeeming features. Its incapacitating legacy made western Europe in the fifteenth century the least promising of the world's civilizations and, to objective scrutiny, among the worst equipped to profit from the world's "age of expansion," which began with initiatives weighted in favour of China and Islam and—as we shall see in the next chapter—with states of greater dynamism in Africa and the Americas than any visible in the Latin west.

THE DIVISIONS OF LATIN CHRISTENDOM

In June 1417 a powerless papal legate took refuge in the Castel Sant'Angelo—the fortified Roman mausoleum which was the invariable refuge of popes in times of danger. From outside its walls, in the camp of an ambitious mercenary captain called Braccio da Montone, siege catapults pelted him with excrement. Braccio, whose career in warfare had begun when he was an impoverished exile from Perugia, had carved out a fief for himself in Umbria amid the distractions and opportunities of war between powerful rivals. He seemed to be close to usurping the traditional temporal power of the papacy and turning the old patrimony of Saint Peter into a principality of his own.

That a contemptible adversary could pose such a threat—and fling such an insult from his siege engines—showed how nearly the papacy had been broken on fortune's wheel since 1378, when a schismatic election had split the allegiance of the curia and of Christendom and undermined papal prestige. Since 1409 there had been three popes simultaneously, all with creditable claims and sizeable followings. In the summer of 1417 it looked as if there would be little left to contend for if the dispute were not soon resolved.

In November of that year, with the rivals deposed or held to have abdicated, an ecumenical council, which had met at Constance to refashion the government of the church, allowed the cardinals to elect Martin V, an unspiritual bureaucrat from one of central Italy's oldest aristocratic dynasties. At first, Martin had to endure the barracking of the street-urchins of Florence, with their chanted taunts that he was not "worth a farthing . . . our friend Braccio takes all." Braccio could not be defeated; he could, however, be reconciled with bribes. By concentrating on administration, Martin rebuilt the patrimony and, to a great extent, the power of the office he occupied, with surprising speed and completeness.

Yet even as it resolved one schism, the same council opened another by condemning the doctrines of the reluctant Czech heresiarch Jan Hus. Like the founder of English Lollardy, by whom he was deeply influenced, Hus was a donnish figure with a talent for *haute vulgarisation;* he began by challenging academic orthodoxies and ended by subverting the dogmas of the church. Early fifteenth-century Prague possessed, in the Bethlehem Chapel, a lively setting for popular sermonizing, where Hus was one of a series of star preachers whose appeal might stand comparison with that of today's tele-evangelists. There was a big demand for devotion in the vernacular among an urban class of half-baked sophistication—artisans, modest merchants, women—who could read their own language and nothing more. In this atmosphere, and even beyond this clientele, Hus's doctrines ignited an incandescent response. Some of his teachings—in favour of the use of the chalice by the laity at communion and of the Czech tongue in church—touched disciplinary rather than doctrinal raw nerves. He went on, however, to challenge the nature of the church as traditionally understood by conceiving it as the community of an unknown, predestined few, with little need of its traditional institutions and wealth. In a further development of his ideas, he threatened the whole basis of social and political organization by questioning—albeit less contumaciously than his accusers claimed—the right of the sinful to property and power. Hus was lured to Constance by a safe-conduct and lulled by lodging with a friendly widow; but he was burned under a dunce's cap, and his ashes were strewn in the Rhine to deny his followers relics.

In Bohemia his appeal was not so easily extinguished. The aristocracy favoured the secularization of church property. The intelligentsia favoured access to the chalice. The urban well-to-do wanted to worship in their own language; and radical heretics and peasant rebels could exploit Hus's message in their own causes. Though divided in itself and exposed to crusades by neighbours, Bohemia became the first state within Latin Christendom to secede from the Roman communion: the Bulgaria of the Bogomils in the ninth century was scarcely within the allegiance of Rome; neither the Provence nor the Aragon of the Cathar era had quite proclaimed independence from the Holy See. The Bosnian autocephalous church of the fourteenth century was probably not heretical and perhaps not intentionally schismatic. Until the Reformation, about a century later, no other state would follow Bohemia's example.

It would be a mistake, however, to see Hussitism as an isolated phenomenon which left the unity of western Christendom unimpaired. Lollards, whose doctrines overlapped with Hussitism, almost captured the English state in the early fifteenth century. Lollard knights were numerous in the

Reynard the Fox celebrating mass is a commonplace of anti-clerical art in the late middle ages. The fact that, like scenes of sexual impropriety involving priests and nuns, it could appear in church—in stained glass or, in this case, in a misericord in Worcester Cathedral, shows that it was a kind of humour which its own victims could enjoy. It illustrates a fairly common Reynard tale in which, surprised in the act of stealing, he masquerades as a priest to dupe the parishioners and make off with his prey. As well as traducing clerical rapacity and cunning, this image is outrightly blasphemous: the sheep's head Reynard is consecrating is unmistakable as a coarse allusion to the figure of the Lamb of God.

royal entourage. Henry IV himself wrote a will steeped in their characteristic language of self-deprecating piety. In 1409 the crown was saved from an attempted Lollard putsch. A Lollard joke—a fox celebrating Mass—even found its way into the carving of a misericord in Worcester cathedral: the fox was a stock image of deceitfulness in folk-art and sermons of the time.

Though heresy made no political conquests, it wrinkled the face of Christendom. It became rife at every social and educational level, especially in urban settings, detectable wherever the authorities were disposed to persecute it. Where it could not be contained, it was comprehended by the elasticity of the church establishment, which could domesticate dangerous movements by granting them status and encumbering them with jobs. In the thirteenth century the potentially revolutionary Franciscan movement was absorbed and became a powerful instrument of orthodox evangelization. In the fifteenth century the New Devotion, which anticipated much of the tone and teaching of Protestantism, electrifying personal piety through mental prayer and opening up direct channels of communication between the believer and God, was organized as an arm of the church

Meanwhile, an economic fissure opened between the eastern and western lands of Latin Christendom. The line of the Elbe and Upper Danube became a cultural fault. In the west, the effects of demographic decline were to diversify forms of tenure, liberate peasants, and convert arable land to pasture. In the east, which gradually replaced the Mediterranean as Europe's great granary, serfdom was enforced and extended, although in parts of the Middle Mark of Brandenburg depopulation was so acute that noble proprietors took to the plough themselves. Even free towns, in what are now Poland, eastern Germany, Czechoslovakia, and Hungary, lost their rights of jurisdiction on a massive scale to aristocratic or princely litigants and usurpers. Duke Casimr of Pomerania, for instance, encountered "ferocity like the Hussites" when he sought to enforce the taxes of Stettin in 1428: the ringleaders' bones were crushed and a castle raised to tower above the town. When the Margrave Frederick of Brandenburg came to power in 1440, he withheld the traditional vow to the saints when confirming the privileges of Berlin. In following years he appeared in arms at the gates, seized the keys, appropriated the town hall, and began to build a formidable, overawing castle. The citizens responded by undermining the foundations, breaking the doors, and burning the archives. The threat of arms was enough to reduce them to submission: Frederick subjected the city to total control, appointing its aldermen, creaming its revenues, and disposing at will of individual citizens' property.

The economic and social divergence of east from west may have been accompanied by a divergence of ethos. Hard times in the late medieval west were times of economic opportunity for those with the skill or luck to exploit them. High mortality created gaps in the élites. Government was revolutionized in the fourteenth century by the use of paper, which made the commands of princes cheaply and speedily transmissible to the farthest corners of every state. The consequent bureaucratization added another avenue of social advancement to the traditional routes via the church, war, and commerce. The magnate ranks of most western countries were almost entirely replaced with new men in the course of the fourteenth and fifteenth centuries. To suit their self-perceptions, western moralists embarked on the redefinition of nobility. "Only virtue is true nobility," proclaimed a Venetian patrician's coat of arms. A Parisian academic in 1306 declared that "intellectual vigour" equipped a man best for power over others. A German mystic a few years later dismissed carnal nobility, among qualifications for office, as inferior to the "nobility of soul." "Letters," according to a Spanish humanist of the fifteenth century, ennobled a man more thoroughly than "arms." Gian Galeazzo Visconti, the strong-arm man who seized Milan in 1395, could be flattered by an inapposite comparison with the exemplary self-made hero of humanists, Cicero. Antonio de Ferrariis (1444–1517), a humanist of Otranto who defended the authenticity of the Donation of Constantine and whose very obscurity is a guarantee that he was typical, declared that neither the wealth of Croesus nor the antiquity of Priam's

"Only virtue is true nobility": the Venetian family motto distills the meritocratic ethos that western moralists developed in the late middle ages, overthrowing Aristotle's definition of nobility as "ancient riches" and the modern secular heresies that made it unattainable except by prowess or blood. Latin Christendom never got an "open élite," but there were more avenues of access to its highest ranks—through the Church, war, law, financial management, trade, exploration, and even, by the end of the period, art—than in most other cultures.

blood could substitute reason as the prime ingredient of nobility. In eastern Europe these re-evaluations were hardly heard. For Ctibor of Cimburk, nobility was divinely apportioned and signified exclusively by right of blood. This was what his audience wanted to hear in Bohemia, where the traditional aristocracy had subordinated the throne, pillaged the church, burdened the peasants, and emasculated the towns. East of the Bohemian forest, nobility was ancient blood, and that was that.

Scored by heresies, cracked by economic fissures, trenched by conflicting social values, the unity of Latin Christendom was compromised by nothing so much—in comparison with some other major civilizations—as the strength of its component states. I mean strength in relation not to their own subjects—for pre-industrial states all over the world were weak in practice in that respect—but to each other and to institutions which claimed a higher allegiance. By the late middle ages no part of the world except south-east Asia had a state system as richly variegated as that of western Europe. The sometime unity of Islam had crumbled by the start of the millennium, but the Ottoman Turks were at work restoring a large measure of it. China seemed to seek, as if by some mysterious natural process, through all its divisions, a unity which the Ming were reconstructing. Eastern Christendom, after the disappearance of the Byzantine commonwealth, could never be tightly reunited, but the empire of Muscovy was growing to control most of what remained outside Ottoman hands and to dominate much of the rest. Even the volatile Indian subcontinent enclosed a dominant state, the Sultanate of Delhi. Fifteenth-century Mesoamerica became overawed by an Aztec hegemony, and the Andean culture-area, almost simultaneously, was unified by the rapid rise of the Inca Empire. In contrast to these imperial worlds, western Europe was an exceptional arena of discrete territorial states.

This ought to be a matter of surprise. Everyone at the time who thought about it, and who recorded his opinion, recalled admiringly the unity imposed by Rome and felt a reluctance to shelve the pretence that the Roman Empire still existed. In a sense it did still exist. The styles of "King of the Romans" and "Holy Roman Emperor" belonged to the elective head of the loosely agglomerated states of Germany and of some neighbouring territories. Whenever the holder of such titles had enough clout of his own—enough *Hausmacht*, inherited along with his particular dynastic territories—optimists surfaced to acclaim the potential restoration of the empire of Augustus or Constantine or, at least, of Charlemagne.

For a brief spell early in the fourteenth century, for instance, when Emperor Henry of Luxemburg was marching on Italy, Dante envisaged an era of universal peace, justice, and happiness under imperial rule. In the early sixteenth century, when Emperor Charles V united in his person more power, dynastic and elective, than any of his predecessors since Charle-

The apocalypse was fervently expected in late medieval Latin Christendom but never imagined, perhaps, with as much frenzied vigour as by Dürer in the series of woodcuts of staggering virtuosity with which he illustrated *The Apocalypse* in the 1490s. In this scene the sixth trumpet sounds and the angels of the Euphrates settle to their work of slaughtering a third of mankind. Dürer packs in a good deal of conventional moralizing: among the victims are a pope, a bishop, a knight, a merchant, and Jews. On the left, an angel aims a blow at a codpiece, a swooning victim exhibits a busty cleavage, and one angel seems to be shearing a magdalen's hair.

magne, an Extremaduran conquistador, an Italian cardinal, and Spanish and Belgian courtiers echoed this sort of language without embarrassment. In the intervening period, imperial resources could hardly justify such pretensions. The grandiloquence was unbacked by grist. Territorial princes, however, remained wary of imperial potential. When Emperor Sigismund V visited Henry V of England, his ship was met by a knight who waded out with the tide to demand his prior renunciation of any superior rights over the kingdom. A long tradition of eschatological prophecy fed hopes of the reunification of Christendom by a Last World Emperor whose cosmic battle with Antichrist would usher in the millennium. Holy Roman emperors—even feeble ones—tended to attract the expression, at least, of such expectations, but they were commonly aroused in the entourages of French and Aragonese kings, too.

Under the spectral shadow of Rome, and the remote goad of the apocalypse, the chief executives of western states got on with their own business and concentrated sovereign power within their frontiers. Fourteenth-century Castilian kings and a sixteenth-century English one called their kingdoms "empires." Evolved in the fourteenth century, applied in the fifteenth, the doctrine that the kings of France were emperors in their own realm spread and enhanced the self-perception of most western monarchs. Ideological strategies devised by propagandists to enhance the image of kings included the notion that the French king's office was miraculous, endowed by God with "such a virtue and power that you perform miracles in your own lifetime," and the formula, tediously repeated in the fifteenth century, that the authority of the king of Castile was "sovereign and absolute."

Territorial sovereignty became entrenched as the functions of the state changed. Traditionally, the business of government was jurisdiction, and law was a body of wisdom handed down from the past, not a continuous area of innovation. As states grew in size and complexity, and as their technical resources expanded, the range of their stewardship extended—over the vast vistas of common life and public welfare displayed in Ambrogio Lorenzetti's panorama of good government on the walls of the Signorie of Siena. Husbandship of the commonwealth in all its aspects became the goal of kings who had the example of Joinville's Saint Louis before their eyes; his *Life* was the ultimate mirror for princes, more influential on late medieval European government than any work explicitly of political theory. Accompanying the enlarged vision of the scope of the state, and perhaps in partial consequence, laws and administrative regulations multiplied.

Statute-making began, in the fourteenth century by my reckoning, to displace jurisdiction as the principal job—indeed, the defining characteristic—of sovereign authorities. Law-making bodies—kings and representative assemblies—came gradually to monopolize sovereignty which had formerly been shared: with rival sources of jurisdiction within the realm, with feudal suzerains outside it whose jurisdiction overlapped, and, above all, with popes who performed a supranational role as a court of final appeal in cases belonging to their sphere. In 1476 the monarchs of Spain began to use the printing-press to circulate their huge legislative and administrative output. At the height of legislative activity in the England of Henry VIII, eight sessions of parliament in eight years produced the unprecedented total of 333 new statutes.

Was the state system of Latin Christendom a source of weakness or strength? Investigators of the European miracle—the process by which western European civilization overtook more promising rivals for world hegemony in modern times—have often stressed the benefits of competition between rival states for control of world resources and for establishment of worldwide empires. Yet the disadvantages—of divided command, of limited resources, of effort and manpower wasted on internecine wars, of vulnerability to outside predators—seem to weigh more heavily on the other side of the balance. Certainly, the expansion of parts of the Latin world, when it resumed on the grand scale in the sixteenth century, was the work of individual states, not the sort of collective enterprise the crusades had been. The empires it threw up were Spanish and Portuguese, followed in the next century by Dutch, English, and French, each jealously guarded from its European rivals and, at times, bloodily coveted. There was, in that sense, no European expansion, as we might speak of the expansion of Islam or of China. There was only the imperialism of particular peoples.

Yet connections with the state system are hard to find. All the European overseas empires were to be established by the almost unaided initiatives of private enterprise, with little or no state patronage. No royal jewels were pawned for Columbus; the Portuguese crown spent more money on junketings for royal festivities in the sixteenth century than on Africa, India, and Brazil combined; the most successful of early English emigrants were fugitives from, not agents of, the home government.

The poverty and remoteness of the states from which the early imperial initiatives came are the best clues to their nature. Portugal and Castile were small countries, sparsely populated and scantily endowed with sources of natural wealth. Their precocious interest in long-range imperialism was like the desperate remedy-seeking of emergent nations today, drilling for offshore resources with foreign capital and foreign savoir faire. Much of the investment and personnel which launched both empires came from traditional medieval centres of capitalism and enterprise in northern Italy and the southern Low Countries—home territories, respectively, of Columbus and Ferdinand van Olmen, who tried to anticipate Columbus's voyage in Portuguese service. The Iberian "cradle of empire" stood, in relation to the rest of Christendom, much as did the Latin west in relation to the rest of the civilized world: an ill-favoured salient occupied by poor, marginal communities, coming from behind.

The great age of European expansion was no outpouring of pent-up dynamism. It was launched from the insecure edges of a contracting civilization. It was a slow and sometimes tortured recovery from the crisis of the late middle ages. Fifteenth-century Europe—still to our eyes a place of prospects and promise—will appear, to the galactic museum-keepers of the future, if they notice it at all, stagnant and introspective. Its population was barely recovering to the levels prevalent before the Black Death. Some new mineral resources were being exploited in central Europe, some new soils turning under the plough in the Atlantic and the east; but the economy as a whole still suffered a permanently adverse trading balance with Islam and could not guarantee the feeding of the population. None of the states among which the civilization was divided appeared really robust. Of the three great medieval trading empires of the Mediterranean, the Catalan was in collapse—enfeebled by its colonial "ulcer" in Sardinia; the Genoese was in retreat from the eastern Mediterranean; and the Venetians were turning to their own hinterland with an air of *il faut cultiver notre jardin*. The great land empires of the previous century—the English in France, the Teutonic Knights' in the Baltic—collapsed or faltered in the first half of the century. None of the states of the Iberian peninsula resumed their earlier histories of growth, and all were rent by civil wars. The union of Poland and Hungary, which had once looked formidable, broke up. France made spectacular gains, but not until late in the century did these begin to exceed the limits of the high-medieval kingdom; nor were they to be sustained into the next century or projected overseas.

The picture would look almost unrelievedly bleak—except, it might be objected, for the phenomenon we now call the Renaissance.

THE AGE OF FOOL'S GOLD

Only a few elegant remains can be seen above ground today at the site of the old palace of the kings of Hungary at Visegrád. In the forecourt, however, a very young Hercules wrestled with the Hydra in a version of one of the labours which formerly decorated the great bronze doors. Hercules—a mortal whose virtue raised him to the rank of the gods, a warrior whose prowess was unconquerable, a toiler who resisted the temptations of Pleasure with the fortitude of an honorary stoic or even, perhaps, of a prefigured Christian—was a favourite hero of fifteenth- and sixteenth-century Europeans. He was explicitly the role model recommended to King Matthias Corvinus of Hungary by the court humanist Bonfini. We shall never know whether the Visegrád palace really matched the description recorded by

The ruins of the palace of Matthias Corvinus at Visegrád require an effort of imagination to call up a sense of what this centre of Renaissance patronage was like in its great days, when the Hungarian king, who ruled a state of dynamic—if short-lived—vitality, recreated Pliny's country villa for his amusement. The podium of the Hercules fountain described in the text is in the foreground.

Bonfini. In conception, at least—or, rather, in the humanist's perception—it was modelled on a prototype ideal for the country dwelling of a Renaissance prince: the most famous private house of antiquity, the Laurentine villa of Pliny.

Room by room, Bonfini takes us through Matthias Corvinus's place of retreat—high-vaulted rooms, some set aside for summer or for winter use, the bathroom equipped with hypocaust, the loggias, and a library full of Greek and Latin books where "the sky could be seen," prudently painted on the ceiling rather than exposed to a risky skylight. The bedrooms were said to be golden chambers with beds and chairs of silver. In deeply hidden alcoves, undisturbed by "the noise of the servants, nor the murmur of the sea, nor the roar of storms, nor the flash of lightning," morning slumberers could "see the sun only through unshuttered windows." In patronizing architecture like this, the King was staking a claim to fame as enduring as that of the Romans. As Bonfini echoed his aspirations, "When you read that Romans created gigantic works which proved their magnificence, you do not endure, oh invincible Prince, that their buildings should surpass yours in their majesty, but you revive once again the architecture of the ancients." Matthias Corvinus called on all the resources of the Renaissance to project and perpetuate his self-image. "His triumphs over the enemy will not perish owing to virtue, bronze, marble, and writing."

Promoted in most of western Europe as part of the theatre of despotic display, the Renaissance was also a product, in some places, of strenuous civic pride and private investment. The towers of the little town of San Gimignano near Florence—fifteen survive of a sometime seventy-two—are reminders of the world which bred it: emulous, crowded, dangerous, where rivals lived under each other's gaze and outfaced their enemies across squares and streets. In Florence, the Medici, the Rucellai, the Albizzi, and the Pazzi complemented their sometimes violent political rivalries by contending in the endowment of ostentatious religious foundations. Similar rivalries were enacted on a civic scale: Siena's tower of Il Mangia was designed to dwarf that of Florence's Signorie; Brunelleschi was employed by Florence to give the cathedral a more conspicuous dome than Siena's.

The art sustained by these traditional, medieval rivalries was character-

The skyline of San Gimignano with its emulous towers has come to symbolize the stimulating rivalry of the aristocracies of late medieval Italian towns, many of which still bristle with these relics of mutual defiance. Civic rivalry of a similar sort thrust ever-bigger spires and domes into the skyline all over Europe—at least, wherever the wealth of local communities permitted them to engage in this expensive game—and helped to build up the pace of patronage of the arts.

ized, for the most part, by traditional, medieval taste. Though the Medici palace displayed to visitors an ostentatiously classical atrium, filled with Roman bric-à-brac and lined with looted inscriptions, the family's private space, the little oratory, was decorated by a conservative painter in the style and colours of a rich gothic tapestry, with Medici portraits in the guise of the gospel magi. The Medici, as good businessmen, wanted value for money. And money was suggested best by expensive use of gilding and lapis lazuli. They spent more on jewels than on the contemporary art of their day, and the family interest in antiquity seems to have sprung at least in part from the investment value of antique gems. The realistic style of painting which we call Renaissance probably developed under mendicant patronage, to provide the poor, urban congregations to which the orders

The Medici have a reputation as patrons of Renaissance style. In fact, they spent more on jewels than on painting and if there was such a thing as Medici family taste in the late fifteenth century it inclined to favour old-fashioned painters, whose style sparkled with the gem-like details of the tradition of Gothic illumination, like Pinturicchio, Baldovinetti or—as here—Gozzoli. Still, in this detail of the decoration of the small private chapel of the Medici palace, where the family self-perception is revealed with peculiar intimacy, the portrait of Lorenzo the Magnificent in the guise of one of the three Magi does reflect the subject's admiration for antiquity: the horse is modelled on a classical example—that of Marcus Aurelius on the Capitol or the horses of San Marco in Venice (See p. 76).

ministered with vividly intelligible images of the Christian story. That Renaissance art was in some special sense secular is a myth, fed by the minority taste for recherché erotica and pagan symbolism such as Botticelli supplied in the Medici country villa. Even Botticelli turned away from such subjects in the 1490s when Florence was ruled by a dictatorship of the godly; this was not a Renaissance but a period of born-again revivalism.

The recovery of the learning, values, and tastes of classical antiquity was a very long process. The fifteenth century perhaps marked a quickening of pace but not a new departure or change of direction. In about 1200 an English visitor to Rome called the Spinarius "that ridiculous Priapus, looking down at his large genitals." Driven "by some magic or I-don't-know-what" he went to see the naked Venus on the Quirinal three times, like a tripper in modern Copenhagen, lured into a peep-show. His account of his visit was called "An Account of the Marvels of the City of Rome: Whether Produced by Magic Art or Human Workmanship." By 1500 few educated pilgrims would have been so naïve, but "Master Gregory's" bafflement and titillation were possible only because of the continuous history of reverence for antiquity—which had inspired popes to collect ancient art and successive revivals in Rome to imitate it. All over western Christendom, throughout the middle ages, artists had copied Roman models whenever they could lay their hands on them. A lost Laocoön inspired an eleventh-century capital in Frómista in north-east Spain, nearly five hundred years before the same subject became a favourite source of Renaissance artists. A Roman aqueduct suggested the arcading of Autun cathedral, a classical sarcophagus the frieze of Saint Gilles. Brunelleschi mistook the Church of San Miniato in Florence, which was only about four hundred years old, for a classical building.

The impact of the Renaissance has been exaggerated in intellectual history, as in the visual arts. Humanists reformed the curriculum—at least in the limited range of institutions they influenced—but, like modern curriculum reformers, had little influence on standards or values. Some orthodoxies about the importance of the Renaissance hold true. The range of classical and patristic texts available to scholars increased enormously in the fourteenth and fifteenth centuries, thanks to the lucubrations of scholars in little-quarried libraries. The linguistic tools for reading them accurately and interpreting them sensitively were sharpened. Towards the end of the century, the printing-press assisted scholarship by providing standard texts. Yet almost all the ancient authors and most of the specific works to have moulded modern intellectual traditions were either never lost or long recovered before the Renaissance is conventionally held to have begun.

Aristotle, for instance, exceeds all other classical writers in his effects on us. When W. H. K. Guthrie was a schoolboy, he was entranced by the extraordinary way in which Aristotle seemed to anticipate modern thought;

The Resurrection of the Dead, made in c. 1320, on the façade of Orvieto Cathedral, by Giovanni Pisano, who, with his father, Nicola, established one of the most determinedly classicizing schools of sculptors of the middle ages. The bodies are modelled with a realism and fluidity that show the sculptor's familiarity with classical types and the sarcophagi seem to be copied directly from genuine relics of pagan antiquity. Though other fashions came and went, medieval sculpture never lost touch with the inspiration of the classics.

only in maturity did he realize that this was because so much modern thought derives from Aristotle. Yet most texts of Aristotle were known by the twelfth century and thoroughly assimilated in the western tradition by the end of the thirteenth. The *Politics* informed the political thought of Aquinas. The ethical and scientific works gave Albertus Magnus his categories. The logic was already the basis of the popularity of the Parisian lectures of Abelard before 1121. Indeed, reception of the essential techniques of Aristotelian logic had been ensured since the turn of the millennium, when Gerbert of Aurillac taught an influential generation of pupils from synopses of Aristotle and Plato collected in Rome five hundred years before. By the middle of the thirteenth century, a glorious library of Roman literature was available to Richard of Furnival, chancellor of Amiens cathedral, who arranged his catalogue of three hundred books in the form of a garden, plot by plot. Renaissance scholars thought they were doing something new; but scholars always think that, and every generation likes to spotlight its own modernity against the darkness of the past. We should not be taken in by the self-perception of the original Renaissance men. The excitement with which western European writers around 1500 anticipated the dawn of a new golden age is intoxicating to readers today, who scan the past for signs of Europe's awakening to a destiny of world dominance. But the gold was fool's gold. By the end of the sixteenth century, the pendulum of fashion had swung right back. Disillusioned artists made a cult of melancholia, and writers rattled the shackles of their "age of iron."

THE ERRANT SPIRIT

If there was some special spirit abroad in late fourteenth- and fifteenth-century Latin Christendom, which helped to make up for the divisions and the debilities of the civilization, it should not be sought in the worlds of scholars and artists, who contributed little to the hard work of launching European expansion, but in the mentalities of navigators, explorers, and settlers. These were the modest heroes who conquered the only new frontier to be added in the period to this otherwise inert or contracting culture area: a zone of navigation and new exploitation in previously uncharted waters, bound by the Azores in the north, the Canaries in the south, and the Iberian and African coasts in the east. Most were unknown pilots. Many known by name are recorded only or chiefly on maps. Of the Portuguese Diogo Silves, who may have established the true lie of the Azores in 1427, the sole memorial, on a Majorcan map, was accidentally blotted with ink by a clumsy gesture of George Sand's during one of her winters of dalliance on Majorca with Chopin. However, just as their efforts can be reconstructed from the maps, so their profiles can be built up from a few surviving documents.

They came, to begin with, mainly from Majorca and Genoa, homes of the art of the "conners of the sea," and—later and increasingly—from Portugal and Andalusia. They often had crusading experience, like the Poitevin adventurer Gadifer de la Salle, who went to conquer a kingdom in the Canaries in 1402, or Joan de la Mora, who was the king of Aragon's captain in Canarian waters in 1366. They sought "rivers of gold," like La Salle, or sources of slaves, like the Peraza family of Seville, who promoted a series of raids and conquests from 1393. They sought to win fiefs or create kingdoms, like La Salle's partner, Jean de Béthencourt, who had himself pro-

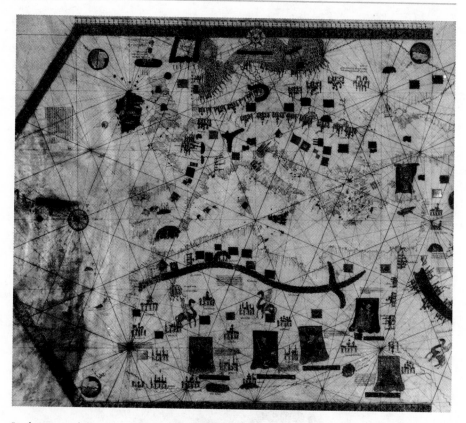

In the map of the Atlantic made by Gabriel Vallseca in Majorca in 1439, the treatment of the Azores seems based directly on the report of the otherwise-unknown navigator named in the cartographer's annotation: Diogo Silves, pilot of the King of Portugal. The islands had been mapped before but always with bewildering inaccuracy: here they appear, strung out in clusters from south-east to north-west, just as they would to a conscious explorer unequipped with means of verifying his position on the open sea but determined to rough out bearings that would help find them again. The two westernmost islands, Flores and Corvo, remained unrecorded until the 1450s.

claimed King of the Canaries in the streets of Seville, or the "knights and squires" of the Infante Dom Henrique of Portugal (1394–1460), who felt called by his horoscope to the accomplishment of great deeds. Or else they were missionaries, like the Franciscans of the Canarian bishopric of Telde, who sailed to and from remote and savage islands for nearly forty years until they were all massacred in 1393. They came from a world steeped in the idealization of adventure: the Perazas' squalid wars against stone age aboriginals on the island of Gomera were celebrated in chivalric verse; the coat of arms of the Béthencourt family was charged with wodehouses in tribute to Jean's wild adversaries. They bore or appropriated storybook names such as Gadifer and Lancelot and, in the case of an unsavoury thug who served Henrique, Tristram of the Isle. They aspired to fame, and most have been forgotten.

They shared, and strove to embody, the great, unifying aristocratic ethos of the later middle ages in the west: the "code" of chivalry. Their role models were footloose princes who won themselves kingdoms by seaborne deeds of derring-do in popular chivalric romances; figures such as the me-

The wild man or wodehouse was *par excellence* the knight's adversary, challenging with passion and savagery his civilized restraint, contending for possession of lands and ladies in hundreds of surviving works of art. On the frontiers of Christendom, his imagined participation in territorial wars could turn squalid adventures into chivalric escapades. This example, armed with club and shield, surmounts a silver-gilt ewer, probably commissioned in 1500 by the Master of the Teutonic Knights—the order that had been responsible for the frontier against the "barbarism" of the pagan Lithuanians. The wild man's appearance in this context carries the same implications as on the scutcheon of Jean de Béthencourt mentioned in the text.

dieval Brutus who, when Troy was lost, found a realm in Albion, or Prince Amadis of Gaul, who battled with giants and won an enchanted island. Their spokesman was the Castilian knight Count Pero Niño, whose chronicle, written by his standard-bearer in the second quarter of the fifteenth century, mixes history, romance, and chivalric discourse. *El vitorial* celebrates a knight never vanquished in joust or war or love, whose greatest battles were fought at sea, and "to win a battle is the greatest good and the greatest glory of life." When the author talks of the mutability of life, his interlocutors are Fortune and Wind, whose "mother" is the sea "and therein is my chief office."

Columbus, whose life's trajectory startlingly resembled the plot of a chivalric romance of the sea, probably had similar role models in his mind. He arrogated to himself the prize for sighting land on his first Atlantic

Far from keeping parvenus in their place, the code of chivalry has encouraged and equipped enterprising men who have risen in western society for centuries. Columbus, in a workaday sixteenth-century engraving, and Cornelius Vanderbilt, in a Tiffany window in the most socially respectable church in Newport, Rhode Island, both appear helmed and armed and attended by Christian symbols. It would be appropriate enough for Vanderbilt to imitate the other all-American hero; in fact, however, both images are independently inspired by the chivalric ideal: the New England *nouveau riche* and the visionary weaver's boy both appropriate the outer crust of chivalry. Columbus called himself "captain of cavaliers and of conquests." Vanderbilt puts on the "whole armour of God."

crossing, less perhaps out of naked greed than because his journey, though without precedent in fact, was precedented in literature. In a Spanish version of the medieval Alexander romance, Alexander makes his own discovery of Asia by sea and, the poet emphasizes, was first, before all his seamen, to see it. Chivalry has been a powerful and enduring spur in the west. In the nineteenth century it could still cram Victorian gentlemen creaking into their reproduction armour. In the twentieth it could still compensate the "knights of the air" of the Battle of Britain for their generally modest social origins. In a stained-glass window in one of America's most socially accepted churches, it clads the image of Cornelius Vanderbilt in unconscious self-mockery. In the late middle ages it was still strong enough to inspire the vanguard of Europe's overseas expansion, as characters in search of the denouement of their own romance reached out from their "small promontory of Asia" to touch the opposite shores.

PART TWO

THE SPRINGS UNCOILED

Nequiquam Deus abscidit
Prudens Oceano dissociabili
Terras, si tamen impiae
non tangenda rates transiliunt vada.

HORACE, *ODES,* I, 3

In vain God in his wisdom planned
The ocean separate from the land
If ships, defying his intent,
Cross the forbidden element.

translation by JAMES MICHIE

When the waters saw you, they writhed in anguish.

PSALM 77

Chapter 6

SHY AND RETIRING EMPIRES: EXPANDING STATES IN LATE MEDIEVAL AFRICA AND AMERICA

The Maya Renaissance—The Screen of Hindsight—
The Black Empires—An Empire Built on Sand—
The Aztec Memory—The Frustrated Empires

THE MAYA RENAISSANCE

Near the north-east corner of Quintana Róo, where the Gulf of Mexico joins the Caribbean, not far from the sleekly manicured tripperland of Cancún, the ruined, late Maya city of Tulúm stares out to sea from a lofty promontory. The twin city of Edzná, on the opposite side of the peninsula, so impressed passing Spanish explorers in 1517 that they called it "the Great Cairo"—a name synonymous with infidel opulence. When first glimpsed by Christian visitors, these cities would have struck just that sort of rich, exotic, menacing note. Gaudily painted, decorated with traditional Maya aesthetic values—which often seem more terrible than beautiful to western eyes—towering over the sea, walled and apparently fortified, Tulúm was the most impressive artifice of man that European invaders had yet seen in the New World.

Now its staring eyes are blind, black cavities in the sagging, buckled façades; and the brilliant colours have faded from all but the most sheltered patches of plaster. Those who behold Tulúm today, in its ruined state, perhaps at the end of a tour of Maya sites which began far inland among the

The tallest temple of Tulúm occupies a conspicuous position on the summit of the crag—a beacon to commerce that knew its way around the reefs to the beach in the foreground, where the trade of the Bay of Honduras met that of the Gulf of Mexico.

much grander and splendidly restored monuments of earlier periods, see it as evidence of Maya decline. But to those who saw the cities fresh, with the eyes of 1517, they were emblems of promise, civilized and redoubtable. To its inhabitants in its day, Tulúm displayed symbols of what may have been a conscious resurgence, based on memories of a great past and hopes of a great future. It was already undertaking a modest colonial expansion of its own, reoccupying the inland city of Cobá and re-dedicating its ruins to the cults, and with the icons, of Tulúm. Through Tulúm's low, dark doorways we can began an approach to some little-known but vigorous cases of state-building and, in some instances, empire-building in the recesses of late medieval Africa and America.

The people of Tulúm were different from the Maya of earlier ages of greatness: shorter and less well fed, to judge from their remains. They in-habited different spaces—lower-built and lower-ceilinged—and ascended by shorter steps stacked in more modest flights. They occupied a quite dif-ferent type of city from the ceremonial centres of earlier phases of Maya history. Tulúm had streets like those of towns in many cultures, rather than plazas and clusters linked by processional walkways and causeways. The excavated site was enclosed by a wall of immense thickness but apparently modest height, pierced by five narrow gateways. This may have been for defence or perhaps to differentiate a sacred or socially elevated centre from profane suburbs. A particularly select quarter in the very middle comprised two substantial and lavishly decorated palaces, a temple, and a small but dignified house built over a rich grave. From an imposing position near the cliff edge, another, more substantial temple dominated the town. All interior chambers were modest and poorly lit: the élite of Tulúm did not enjoy the spacious way of life of, say, the rulers of seventh-century Palenque with their halls and baths; but it was in the Maya tradition to combine mean, functional, and austere interiors with splendid outdoor spaces in which life was lived in public.

Although Tulúm has none of the vast piazzas of ancient Tikal or Quiriguá, for example, the better of the palaces is set back from the road behind a pillared arcade, and the lesser palace has a small grove of columns to one side of it. A broad boulevard links the residential centre to the cliff-side temple, but Tulúm was not designed primarily for ritual. Whereas in older Maya cities comfort and convenience are subordinated to the demands of display, mass sacrifice, or perhaps, in some cases, geomancy, Tulúm is arrayed for commerce and security. The approach from the open sea is guarded by deadly reefs. The access for the canoe-borne cabotage that supplied the city's wealth is easily controlled. The beach and cove immediately under the town were as good for trading then as they are for bucket-and-shovelling today, and the thick walls that surround the town centre would help to protect off-loaded goods from land attack. Tulúm in the fifteenth century was well placed to be an entrepôt along the trade route that linked the Gulf of Honduras, via Cozumel, around the Yucatán peninsula, with Xicalango and the Aztec world.

Although they lived differently from their forebears, the Maya of Tulúm were not insensible of the past. They cherished in their central temple a stela of 564 CE; they respected the ancient buildings of Cobá; and, both as a badge of their own identity and a remembrance of things past, they adopted the figure known to archaeologists as the Diving God. Recessed in niches and sculpted in stucco over some of Tulúm's most eminent doorways, he descends, with bulging eyes and arms akimbo, legs doubled and drawn in like wings. He is hurtling rather than swimming; his bee's wings, jutting from below his arms, make his motion unmistakably one of flight. The image of "diving" suits Tulúm's cliff-side position, but to his devotees he might as well have signified a falling star or a descending intercessor. His cult was not unique to Tulúm—other similar cults could be found elsewhere in Mesoamerica. In the ball court of Tajín in Vera Cruz, a site before 600 CE, a creature like the diver of Tulúm descends to devour sacrificial victims. The last occurrence of a comparable cult before his re-emergence at Tulúm was not later than the twelfth century, at Sayil, the red-earthed city in the dry limestone Puuc hills of Yucatán, where, without his wings, he adorns the façade of the largest building.

It was characteristic of Maya history that political revolutions and cultural revivals were accompanied by changes in the celestial imagery promoted

The Diver of Tulúm is so prominent in the decorative scheme of the main buildings in the town that it is hard not to think of him as its patron deity and as the symbol of a strong civic identity. His cult was revived here, it seems, after centuries of obscurity: despite the discontinuities of Maya history, long memories are characteristic of Maya culture, in which time is reckoned in aeons, astronomical records and predictions encompass hundreds of thousands of years, and historical and prophetic events are fused in a characteristic literary genre—the *Books of Chilam Balam* —which has a long tradition behind it.

by the state. During what we think of as the high middle ages, the creation of the great cities of Yucatán was marked by the progressive rise of the cult of Kukulcan, the feathered-serpent god from central Mexico, to equilibrium with, and then supremacy over, the indigenous gods of earlier traditions.

Kukulcan can be found at Tulúm, but only in a modest role. Chaac, the square-eyed deity with the long, curling proboscis, whose masks smothered the most intricate of Maya façades at Kabáh in about the eleventh century, and who had once been dominant, and always present, in traditional Maya iconographic programmes, disappeared from Tulúm. The Diver, who plunged other gods into obscurity, was a strong symbol of identity to his adherents; yet he was revived, not contrived, after an interval of three or four centuries, a link between the squat tradesmen of Tulúm and their heroic predecessors in the great age of the Puuc.

The Maya are most familiar to us as the makers of a classic period of monumental building and high art between the third and tenth centuries of our era, when their gleaming cities rose above the rain forests of the Usumacinta and Motagua valleys and in the Petén, or as the builders of the "post-classic" centres which defy the arid climate and dense bush in Yucatán. Nothing created by the descendants of the Maya after the thirteenth century equals or remotely rivals the triumphs of human will over hostile environments represented by the scale and majesty of these early groups of cities. Nevertheless, the sort of revival achieved in Yucatán in the high middle ages could have been repeated later in a new location. The ruins of Tulúm suggest that a genuine Maya renaissance was under way, to be cut short, for unknown reasons, at about the time of the arrival of the Spanish invaders in Mexico.

The fate of this Maya renaissance was typical of African and American experience: vigorous and promising initiatives, in state-building or cultural achievement in the period corresponding to the late middle ages, were frustrated or defeated. Some of them, however, generated cultures of expansion as impressive and dynamic as anything produced in the Old Worlds of Europe or Asia at the time. In simply quantifiable terms, like range of reach and military effectiveness, some African and American empires outclassed anything attained in western Christendom. A number of aggressive states arose suddenly and expanded rapidly in the fourteenth and fifteenth centuries. Properly considered, their stories should modify our conventional picture of an "age of expansion" disputed among old powers, with inevitable victims rather than active contestants in the new worlds opened up by old-world explorers.

THE SCREEN OF HINDSIGHT

An astral observer, privileged to behold the fifteenth-century world with cosmic vision from a commanding height, would first have noticed, perhaps, the rapid, dramatic, and far-reaching expansion of the Ottoman and Muscovite states. The next most conspicuous examples would have drawn his gaze to Mesoamerica, where the Aztec world expanded from the valley of Mexico to fill the land between the oceans; to Peru, where the Inca empire spread over thirty degrees of latitude and enfolded almost all the sedentary peoples of the Andean valleys south of modern Colombia; to west Africa, where Songhay was transformed from a subject-state of the remarkable Mali empire into its rival and potential successor; to Ethiopia, which overspilled its traditional highland fastnesses to hold sway from the Red Sea to deep in the Rift valley; and to Mwene Mutapa, a new empire of the Zimbabwean plateau which established control from the Zambezi to the Limpopo.

By comparison, no western European effort would have appeared very remarkable. Latin expansion had been reversed in the Levant and was checked in the Baltic. The Mediterranean empires of Genoa and Barcelona were stagnant or declining, that of Venice turning to its Italian hinterland for growth. English domination of France was laboriously established and extremely short-lived. Portuguese penetration of the Atlantic—though our cosmic observer, if also endowed with foresight, would have appreciated its significance—was still feeble, shallow, and slow, and its main colonies had been erected on previously uninhabited islands, where there was nobody to resist them. The Spanish empire of the future was barely foreshadowed until the closing years of the century, except in the Canary Islands, where the stone-age occupants were remarkably successful in withstanding Spanish arms, from the establishment of the first permanent European settlement in 1402 until the submission of the last island-conquest in Tenerife in 1496.

As well as the then conspicuous but now forgotten empires of the fifteenth-century Third World, there were remarkable cases of promise in parts of Africa and America where, in any event, no great empire emerged. In the southern Niger region and on the lower Congo, states were developing which, in different circumstances, could have come to play major roles in their regions and beyond. In its little world of city-states Benin might have become the Genoa of west Africa; or, in a region of fiercely disputed territory, Kongo another Mwene Mutapa. In Mesoamerica the Maya renaissance faltered. On the banks of the middle Amazon, a remarkable sedentary rain-forest culture, populous and militarily strong, was observed by the first Spanish visitors in 1542, but it had disappeared—perhaps wiped out by European diseases—a generation later. In north Africa, Mameluke Egypt evinced promise but declined an imperial destiny until Ottoman expansion overwhelmed it. Morocco's age of expansion was deferred until the late sixteenth century and launched with only limited success.

None of these cases—neither those of promise nor those of achievement—has ever received much attention from writers of world history. Except for the Inca and Aztecs and, in an earlier period, the Maya, they are usually unknown or unrecalled. The history we learn, or to which we ascribe importance, is screened through a film of hindsight, which filters out the stories of undeveloped potential. Because of the long-term success of European imperial initiatives, we study the origins of European expansion to the exclusion of parallel phenomena in other societies. A vital part of the reality of the past drops out of our picture.

By looking at some of the shy and retiring empires, which generally forgo their proper place, we shall be better able to see the late middle ages and the early modern period for what they really were: eras in which a number of expanding civilizations in different parts of the world clashed as their dynamics drove them into collision. The traditional picture, of a largely passive extra-European world, which awaited, in retreat or decline, in stagnancy or arrested development, the imprint of an uniquely vital force from Europe, will have to be discarded in favour of a more fluid image of the past.

THE BLACK EMPIRES

The king most noted for his riches, in the opinion of a Majorcan mapmaker of the late fourteenth century, was to be found neither in Europe nor Asia. None of the long-established civilizations which had dominated the first third of the millennium could compete for reputed wealth with the recently arisen empire of Mali, where, deep in the African interior, across the glare of the Sahara and against the darkness of the jungle, between the grassland of the savannah and the scrub of the Sahel, the glint of gold began in the 1320s to attract the admiration and cupidity of the Mediterranean world.

In 1352 the most travelled individual in the Muslim world set off from Tangier on his last great journey across the Sahara desert to see this empire for himself. Though Ibn Battutah was said to have only "a modest share of the sciences," he was a conventionally well educated scion of the Maghribi aristocracy of service who had developed, on a pilgrimage to Mecca, a passion "to travel through the earth." His stories, received with stupefaction at his patron's court in Fez, were embellished with repetition. The account which survives from his own hand, however, is almost entirely convincing. By the time he crossed the Sahara he had already been to east Africa, India, Arabia, Persia, the lands of the Golden Horde, and, allegedly, China, and his powers of observation were at their height.

His route south was through Sijilmassa to Taghaza, "an unattractive little town with the curious feature that its houses and mosques are built of blocks of salt." From here he planned to travel south with the gold caravans of Mali, reputedly so rich in gold that the salt tripled or quadrupled in value as it crossed its territory. Ibn Battutah still had an arduous journey ahead of him. The desert had to be crossed by marches of ten nights, a stretch without water, eating "desert truffles swarming with lice" in a land "haunted by demons. . . . There is no visible road or track in these parts—nothing but sand blown hither and thither by the wind."

The heartlands of Mali were in a landlocked but river-bound realm between the Niger and the Upper Senegal, roughly in the extreme south-west of the present state of the same name. Its Mande-speaking élite governed a savannah homeland and an empire that covered the Sahel, stretching into the desert in the north and the rain forest in the south. Across the land of Mali, through the hands of canny monopolists, gold passed on its way north to the Saharan merchants whose caravans bore it to Mediterranean ports. Its location was a closely guarded secret. Procured—according to all accounts written perhaps from convention rather than conviction—by "dumb" trade in which goods were exchanged by being left exposed for collection, the gold generated bizarre theories about its origins: it grew like carrots; it was brought up by ants in the form of nuggets; it was mined by naked men who lived in holes. Its probable real provenance was mainly in the region of Bure, around the upper reaches of the Niger and the headwaters of the Gambia and Senegal rivers. Additionally, some may have come from the Volta valley. The middlemen of Mali never succeeded in controlling the production of the gold; whenever their rulers attempted to exert direct political authority in the mining lands, the inhabitants adopted a form of passive resistance or industrial action, suspending mining operations. But Mali controlled access from the south to the emporia of Walata and Timbuktu, on the fringes of the Sahara. Marketing was therefore in the power of rulers who took the nuggets for tribute, leaving the gold dust to the traders.

As the remotest place on gold-road to which the gold could reliably be traced, Mali became famous in the Mediterranean world in the fourteenth century. Its ruler, known as the Mansa, attained legendary proportions as a result of diffusion of knowledge of the Mansa Musa, who reigned from about 1312 to 1337 and undertook, in 1324, a spectacular pilgrimage to Mecca, which spread his renown far and wide. He was one of three Mansas to make the hajj. This alone indicates the substance and stability of the Mali state, as the pilgrimage took over a year. Musa's trip was undertaken in particularly lavish style and with conspicuous effect. It was remembered for centuries in Egypt, where the Mansa stayed for three months and distributed gold with so generous a hand that he caused inflation: by various accounts, the value of gold in Egypt fell by between 10 and 25 per cent. He gave fifty thousand dinars to the sultan and thousands of ingots of raw gold to the shrines which received him and the officials who entertained him. Though he travelled with eighty or a hundred camels, each weighed down with three hundred pounds of gold, he was obliged to supplement his finances by borrowing on his homeward journey. It was said that on his return to Mali he repaid his loans at the rate of seven hundred dinars for every three hundred he had borrowed.

Ibn Battutah encountered the first outpost of Mali officialdom at Walata. "It was then," he complained, "that I repented of having come to their country, because of their lack of manners and their contempt for white men." Culture shock struck quickly. The visitor was disgusted by the food, not realizing at what cost precious millet was brought from far away. Outraged by a spectator when he relieved himself in the Niger, he subsequently discovered that the man was on guard to protect him from a crocodile. The brazen womenfolk and the sexual freedom alarmed him, but he was impressed to find children chained until they learned their Koran, and he praised the Blacks' "abhorrence of injustice."

When he reached the Mansa's court, he was annoyed by the contrast between the ruler's personal meanness and the copious displays of gold. A gold bird bestrode the Mansa's parasol; his skull cap, quivers, and scabbards were of gold; but the Mansa had to be shamed into generosity: "What am I to say of you before other rulers?" Some of the opulent rituals seemed silly, especially the antics of the poets dressed in thrushes' feathers "with wooden head and red beak." Cannibal envoys, whom the Mansa presented with a slave girl, appeared at court to thank him, daubed with the blood of the gift they had just consumed. Fortunately, "they say the white man is indigestible, because he is unripe."

Yet in spite of himself, Ibn Battutah could not help being impressed by the ceremonial magnificence of the court of Mali. The Mansa, he found, commanded more devotion from his subjects than any other prince in the world. Black states did not normally attract respect from Arab writers; this makes the goggle-eyed awe of Ibn Battutah or his fellow-observer, Ibn-amir Hajib, all the more impressive in this case. Everything about the Mansa exuded majesty: his stately gait; his hundreds of attendants, bearing gilded staves; his indirect method of address through an intermediary; the acts of humiliation—prostration and dusting of the head—to which his interlocutors submitted; the reverberant hum of strummed bowstrings and murmured approval with which his words were greeted at audience; the capricious taboos which enjoined death for those who entered his presence in sandals or sneezed in his hearing. This exotic theatre of power had a suitably dignified stage setting. The Mansa's audience chamber was a domed pavilion in which an Andalusian poet sang. His bushland capital had a brick mosque.

The empire had reached this apogee of power and opulence after less than a century and a half of existence. Its founder in the early thirteenth century was known by tradition as Sundiata, a culture-hero of ideal type, a boy-cripple whose mother was mocked by the king's other wives and who

A terra cotta horseman from a grave in the Dienne/Mopti area between the Niger and Bani Rivers, probably late thirteenth or early fourteenth century. Aristocratic cavalry was the effective arm of the military expansion of Mali in the Sahel. Ibn Khaldun ascribed the era of conquest to the reign of Mansa Uli, who made a pilgrimage to Mecca "during Baybars' reign in Egypt"—that is, 1260–77. "During his powerful reign their dominions expanded and they overcame the neighbouring peoples . . . and all the nations of the lands of the Blacks stood in awe of them." The elaborately carved harness, the bracelets, the helmet and body armour all contribute to an image of combined might and wealth.

returned from exile in Ghana to reconquer his homeland and overthrow its oppressors. The strength of his army and of those of his successors was cavalry. Images of Mali's mounted soldiery survive in terracotta. Heavy-lidded aristocrats with protuberant lips and haughtily uptilted heads, crowned with crested helmets, ride rigidly on elaborately bridled horses. Some have cuirasses or shields on their backs or strips of leather armour worn apron-fashion. Their mounts wear halters of garlands and have decoration incised in their flanks. The riders control them with short reins and outstretched arms.

By the middle of the fourteenth century, the power of these warriors had established the Mansas' rule from the Gambia and lower Senegal in the west to the Niger valley below Gao in the east and from the upper Niger in the south to the Sahara in the north. Trade followed and overtook their standards. Mali was an empire not only of war but also of commerce. The merchant caste, called Wangara or Dyula, thrust colonies beyond the reach of the ruler's direct authority, founding, for instance, a settlement at Begho, on the north-west border of Akan country, where they bought gold from chiefs of the forest regions. When the Portuguese established a gold-trading factory at Elmina, a hundred kilometres west of the mouth of the Volta, in 1482, they found themselves negotiating with a ruler called the Karamansa, whose title faintly echoed the greatness of the old rulers of Mali. The fourteenth-century Mande were like their closest contemporary European counterparts, the Catalans, a commercial and imperial people in equal proportion, strong in war and in wares.

Like many empires of promise in out-of-the-way worlds in the late middle ages, Mali became a victim of its own relative isolation. Mansa Musa recognized this weakness of his empire, whose inhabitants were "a vast multitude. . . . Yet if you compare it with the Black populations which surround it and stretch to the south, it is like a little white spot on a black cow." Eroded by rebellions and incursions at its edges, it was weakened by rivalries at its heart. From about 1360 a power struggle pitted the descendants of Mansa Musa against those of his brother, Mansa Sulayman. At about the end of the century, Songhay, the people lowest down the Niger, broke away, and Gao was lost to Mali. This was a serious blow, for Gao was one of the great entrepôts between the forest and the desert, and it was now possible for Mali's monopoly to be outflanked. In the 1430s, Tuaregs from the desert seized Walata and Timbuktu. Two decades later, when Portuguese expeditions pushing up the River Gambia made the first recorded direct contacts between outposts of Mali and European explorers, the Mansa's power was virtually confined to the old Mande heartlands.

The stroke of fortune which deprived the European interlopers of the opportunity of seeing a great Black empire at the height of its glory seems, in retrospect, one of the most tragic ironies of history. While known only by report, Mali had projected a splendid image. In Majorcan maps from the 1320s and most lavishly in the Catalan Atlas of about 1375–85, the ruler of Mali was portrayed like a Latin monarch, save only for his Black face. Bearded, crowned, and throned, with panoply of orb and sceptre, he was perceived and presented as a sophisticate, not a savage: a sovereign equal in standing to any Christian prince. Against this background of expectation, the discovery of Mali in decline was a source of bitter disillusionment. Familiarity bred contempt, and the heirs of the Mansa came to be seen as stage niggers—crude racial stereotypes, dangling simian sexual organs. Mali survived until the end of the sixteenth century, barely enduring its mutually

"This Black lord is called Massa Melly," reads the legend accompanying Mansa Musa's portrait on the Catalan Atlas (see p. 160), "lord of the Blacks of Guinea. This lord is the richest and most noble lord of all this region owing to the abundance of gold which is gathered in his land." Reputation inflated his wealth to exceed that of all other kings. The European-style regalia and ample beard are compliments bestowed by an artist who had not yet learnt to despise Black kingship. Cresques Abraham's depiction of the Sahara is dominated by a cameleer in a litham—the veil-like headgear that was the privilege of the élite and conferred an almost divine character. The figure depictured here, who also wields a knotted whip, a mythical weapon of enchantment "like cattle's tails," is probably intended for the great Sanhaja hero, Abu Bakr bin ʾUmar al-Lamtuni, who founded Marrakesh in 1070, fought the jihad on all fronts and was supposedly killed in 1087 by a poisoned arrow in the "Mountains of Gold" near the sources of the Nile.

exhausting conflicts with Songhay, but it never recovered its former power or prestige.

In Black political worlds that were disappointing or declining, European visitors decided that Blacks naturally lacked political capacity. The Portuguese crown in the late fifteenth and early sixteenth centuries strove hard to impose on fellow-Europeans a keen appreciation of the level of civilization of the Black cultures to which it introduced them. For instance, in an extraordinary political pantomime in 1488, King João II entertained an exiled Wolof potentate to a full regal reception, for which the Black guest was decked out with specially borrowed European clothes and silver plate. Kings of Portugal long kept up the convention of addressing the Manicongo of Congo as "cousin," building him a palace modelled on that of Lisbon, shipping his heirs to Portugal for education, and reprimanding Portuguese on the spot for contempt of the Blacks. None of these devices worked. With the exception of some of the missionaries, all the Portuguese who went out to the Congo to serve or trade conceived a pejorative image of their hosts and spread it back home. Expectations shattered by the first encounters with Black societies could never be restored. Had the first encounter with an important Black polity happened a century earlier, when the grandeur of Mali was at its height, the whole subsequent history of Black–White relations might have been different.

The African state best equipped in the late middle ages to impress Europe with an image of Black dignity was perhaps Ethiopia. "Although the Nubians are Blacks," said an Aragonese geographical compilation of the late fourteenth century, "yet they are endowed with the faculty of reason, like us." Negroid physical features, such as low brows, flat noses, and thick lips—which, in a tradition of psycho-physiology popular in late medieval Europe, were associated with beastly qualities of sensuality, prurience, indiscipline, and stupidity—were happily rare among Ethiopians. Moreover, they were zealous custodians of an ancient Christian tradition, which gave them a claim on the fraternal sensibilities of the Latin west and made them members not only of that vague juridical category, admitting so many invidious distinctions, known as the *communitas mortalium,* or community of mankind, but also of the *communitas fidelium,* or community of the faithful, whose rights were well defined.

Thanks to sporadic diplomatic contact from the time of the Council of Florence in 1439 and frequent cases of study and pilgrimage via the Ethiopian religious community established by Pope Sixtus V in the Church of San Stefano dei Mori in Rome, learned and enterprising examples of Ethiopian churchmanship became well known in the west by the late fifteenth century. The image Europe got of Ethiopia was of the kind expressed in an Ethiopian miniature in the Bibliothèque Nationale of Paris, in which the patron, sumptuously clad, prostrates himself before Christ-in-blessing, shown bearded and Father-like, in a lozenge supported by the symbols of the evangelists, while a small Black acolyte, bare from the waist up, stands by with a long linen stole. Despite the doctrinal heterodoxies known to characterize a church which had been Monophysite for centuries and got its patriarchs from Alexandria, Ethiopia appeared as a rich land of strong devotion and liturgical propriety. The information was supplemented by Christian merchants who were sporadically willing to brave the hazards of a voyage through Muslim territory along the Nile, across country by caravan to the Red Sea to take a ship for Massawah, and thence by perilous defile to the highland empire.

The glimpses of Ethiopia which such sources disclosed seemed highly

The early sixteenth-century Coptic psalter of the Ethiopian priest Nicholas who performs a proskynesis—perhaps commemorative of his ordination—while an acolyte waits to garb him with his stole.

promising. The Negus—*Negushta Nagast,* or king of kings—was presumptively identified with the legendary Prester John of the Indies whose help in the world conflict against Islam had been frequently hoped for and sometimes sought since the mid-twelfth century. For most of the late middle ages the rapid and irresistible rise of Ethiopia seemed to justify expectations that the Negus would prove a powerful ally. Since the accession of the Solomid Dynasty in 1270, the empire had been organized for war, its court turned into an army and its capital into a camp. The monasteries of Debra Hayq and Debra Libanos, the little world of religious communities on the islands of Lake Tana, became schools of missionaries whose task was to consolidate Ethiopian power in the conquered pagan lands of Shoa and Gojam. Under the Negus Amda Siyon in the 1320s and 1330s, the frontier was extended to the south and east. A new route to the sea through Zeila, to supplement the long road north to Massawah, became a major goal of Ethiopian policy. Access, at first enforced by raids, was secured by conquest under Negus Davit in 1403. By then, Ethiopian rule stretched into the Rift valley south of the upper Awash. Trade north along the valley in slaves, ivory, gold, and civet was largely in Ethiopian hands, funding defence of the empire and fuelling expansionist ambitions. The same sources of wealth arrayed the court in trappings of exotic splendour. With perhaps calculated exaggeration, the Portuguese embassy of 1520 reported the "countless tents" borne by fifty thousand mules, the crowd of two thousand at an audience, the plumed horses, caparisoned in fine brocade. The letters the Negus despatched to Portugal, which treated their recipient with magnificent condescension, played shamelessly on the Prester John legend, vaunting "men and gold and provisions like the sands of the sea and the stars in the sky."

Defence, however, had become progressively more difficult as the frontiers grew. The motive of Ethiopian appeals to Portugal was to secure help in the task. Expansion was hard to sustain with an emulous élite, a disputatious clergy, and a divided imperial family. Ethiopia was cursed with a system of dynastic instability tempered by exposure of royal infants. Succession conflicts plagued it. Conquered pagans were readily assimilated by conversion and colonization, wherever wholesale enslavement and deportation of the existing population proved insufficient; Muslims, however, were more intractable, and the failure of Ethiopia's overstretched evangelists to make any impression on the deep-rooted Islam of the Adel in the early fifteenth century, when they had the chance, was to prove almost fatal in the long run.

In the early sixteenth century, when Ethiopian energies faltered and the initiative passed to pagan and Muslim tribes on the southern and eastern frontiers, it was among the Adel that a strong, wily, and charismatic leader emerged, bent on vengeance. Ahmad Ibn Ibrahim, known as Gragna (often rendered "Grange"), the left-handed imam of Zeila, was able to secure Turkish money and arms for his campaigns and to coordinate his attacks with other regional adversaries of Ethiopia. In the 1520s the defences of the empire crumbled with terrifying suddenness, and Imam Ahmad's raids reached to the monasteries of the north. An Arab chronicler who claimed to have accompanied the expedition vividly captured the moment of the fall of the monastic complex of Lalibela on 9 April 1533:

The rain was falling. The Imam marched all night, forcing his pace. The extreme cold caused many men to perish. They arrived at the church. The monks had gathered there resolved to die for the place. The Imam beheld such a church as he had never seen before. It was hewn out of the moun-

Though Great Zimbabwe is the most impressive of the stone-built sites of the region it is typical in a general way of building technology in the late middle ages south of the Zambezi, before the political centre of Mwene Mutapa got displaced northwards by the expansion of the fifteenth century. This funnel-shaped turret overlooks the walls of a large oval enclosure standing under an abrupt granite hill, 350 feet high, that holds a formidable citadel.

tainside; its pillars were carved from the rock. There was nothing of wood save their images and their reliquaries.

Normally the imam's habit was to set a torch to churches, and the monks would "hurl themselves into the flames like moths at a lamp." Here, there was nothing to burn. After an exchange of challenges to an ordeal by fire between Christians and Muslims, Ahmad "put their relics to the sword and broke the idols of stone and took all he found of vessels of gold and stuffs of silk." During the next ten years of fighting, the empire was rescued from its own embers by the energy of the Negus Claudius and the intervention of a Portuguese volunteer force; but it never again attained its past glories and its devolved system of government, often likened to feudalism by western historians, kept its élite divided and its power weak.

The examples of Mali and Ethiopia seemed to convey a general rule about the instability of Black empires and the unsustainability of African achievements. The mid-sixteenth-century Portuguese historian João de Barros reported the ruins of Zimbabwe with awe—they were "of marvellous grandeur, without any mortar or tar at the joins," beyond comparison with the humble castle-building efforts of the Portuguese themselves at Sofala, and "perfect, whether in the symmetry of the walls, or the size of the stones or the dimensions of the colonnades." Yet he was scornful of the suggestion that they might have been of indigenous construction:

To say now how and by whom these buildings could have been made is an impossible thing, for the people of this land have no tradition of that sort of thing and no knowledge of letters: therefore they take it for a work of the devil, for when they compare it with other buildings they cannot believe that men could have made it.

In fact, stone Zimbabwes were common and widespread settings for political and administrative centres south of the Zambezi between the twelfth and sixteenth centuries. As well as Great Zimbabwe, an impressive site has been excavated at Mankweni, south of the River Sabi, and relics of others are scattered over the land. The displacement of the centre of power of the Zimbabwean plateau region northwards in the mid-fifteenth century, to an area of less durable building materials, was caused not by a decline in the power of the state or in the level of material civilization, but by the military expansion of the empire of Mwene Mutapa into new and highly attractive territory. The colonists of the north were drawn, not driven, although a decline in the navigability of the River Save may have helped to stimulate the move. Indeed, the great age of both Great Zimbabwe and Mankweni was in the fifteenth century, when building was done in dressed stone with regular coursing and the beef-fed élite were buried with gifts of gold jew-

This image of the might of the empire of Mwene Mutapa appeared in André Thevet's *Cosmographie universelle* in 1575, the year the attempted Portuguese conquest was beaten off. Thevet's text is rambling and barely coherent, but the engraver had a clear, if inaccurate, perception of the state and its ruler. The elephant and palm trees are exotic conventions. The thatched huts are realistic enough but the Monomotapa advances on them as a foreign conqueror, bringing a higher level of civilization with him. The engraver mistakes him for a Muslim and gives him and his men an oriental air and arms. The attendant pack of hounds is a sign of nobility any European would recognize. The suppliant subjects suggest the ruler's role as dispenser of justice. The naked savages fighting each other in the background convey the impression that the Monomotapa is approaching in strength as peacemaker as well as conqueror.

ellery, jewelled ironwork, large copper ingots, and Chinese porcelain, no doubt brought across the Indian Ocean through Kilwa and Sofala. The abandonment of the sites regretted by Barros and by subsequent European commentators marked not the extinction or eclipse of Mwene Mutapa, but a shift in its centre of gravity.

The shift is associated by tradition with the campaigns of the second quarter of the fifteenth century by the Rozwi chief Nyatsimka Mutota, who conquered the middle Zambezi valley, a frontier land at the northern edge

Amazons have always tended to be popular with illustrators. Columbus had reported Amazons in the Caribbean and Francisco de Orellana had collected rumours of their rich and powerful realm in the valley of the river he named after them in 1542. The Monomotapa probably really did have a female bodyguard. In the nineteenth century the "Amazons" of the court of the Kabakas of Buganda exerted a similar fascination. Representations of all these subjects became muddled with each other and confused with the Amazons of classical myth. Despite the exotic environment depicted in this Dutch engraving of 1707, the artist is chiefly interested in the torsos of the Amazons, who remove their right breasts to facilitate archery. The operation is taking place on the left and its effects are modeled by the consciously classical, mannequin pose of the warrior in the right foreground.

of the Zimbabwean plateau, rich in cloth, salt, and elephants. The ruler acquired the title of Mwene Mutapa, or "lord of the plundered peoples," which became extended to the state. From the mid-fifteenth century the pattern of trade routes altered as the conquests spread east towards the coast along the Pungwe and Save rivers. Travellers to Mwene Mutapa in the sixteenth century normally went up the Zambezi River to the confluence with the Mazoe, from where it was five days' trek through the Mazoe valley to the trade fairs where the gold of Mwene Mutapa could be acquired. By then the empire occupied all the territory its rulers wanted. Their frontiers to the north and south were protected by tsetse-infested rivers. The Kalahari Desert lay to the west, and on the east they had the natural defences of the Inyanga mountains to fall back on, well behind the limits of their advance. A direct outlet to the sea was probably of no interest to a native mercantile community which did very well out of the middlemen of the coast and had no experience of oceanic trade.

There were extraordinary structural similarities between Mwene Mutapa in the late fifteenth century and the Mali of a hundred years before. Both were the products of sudden and rapid expansion. Both were landlocked empires whose economies depended on control of routes of gold and salt. Both were big enough to be vulnerable to secession and putsch from within. Both were surrounded by cupidinous enemies. Both were isolated and hard of access. It may have been Mwene Mutapa's formidable natural defences that saved it from Mali's fate. The most determined onslaught, by the Portuguese from 1571 to 1575, was beaten off and ended in a commercial accommodation. The admiration that Portuguese writers withheld from other Black states was conceded selectively to Mwene Mutapa, which was identified with the realm of Sheba and with Ophir and was even proposed, after the near-collapse of Ethiopia, as the true prototype for the kingdom of Prester John. The Monomotapa's female bodyguard of a hundred strong—purportedly converted to Christianity by a Jesuit in 1560—aroused the curiosity of humanists keen to aetiologize the Amazon myth. The empire never utterly succumbed but rather faded away as its component communities grew more and more self-assertive—increasingly falling prey in the seventeenth century to "men who would be king": Portuguese desperadoes "going native" and carving out bushland fiefs for themselves. Still, its precarious existence continued until the 1830s when it was swamped by the surge northwards of the Ngoni of Natal (see Chapter 14).

An Empire Built on Sand

The vitality of some sub-Saharan states in the late middle ages makes the quiescence of North Africa in the same period seem surprising. Egypt and Morocco, at least, were equipped for a greatness never quite fulfilled. Between their repulse of the Mongols in 1260 and their submission to the Turks in 1517, the Mameluke rulers of Egypt had a secure, rich, and populous state at their disposal; its imperial potential was sensed by its founder, Baybars the Great, who boasted that he could play polo in Cairo and Damascus in the same week. Although Cairo's skyline is dominated by the antique grandeur of the pyramids and the modern pretensions of Mehmet Ali's acropolis, its best buildings, after the mosque of Ibn Tulun, are late-medieval glories of Mameluke mosques and madrasas. The most lavish expenditure—and therefore perhaps the richest era—was in the reign of Qaʾit

The mausoleum of the Mameluke sultan Qaʾit Bey, the prodigious builder, seventeen of whose buildings survive in Cairo today. The elegance of the minaret and dome, the luxury of the striped masonry and spangled roof of the burial chamber are typical. This is the finest of the twenty tomb complexes of Mameluke rulers that form the "City of the Dead." They were also built to house the living, with apartments for the reception of family members who came to pray, and often had a pious foundation attached, such as a school, collegiate mosque, public fountain and resting place, or Sufi community. Qaʾit Bey's has all these dependencies.

Bey, which ended in 1496, less than a generation before the collapse of the state.

Egypt's inability to convert this wealth into power may have been partly due to a structural defect in the state which also afflicted Morocco. Both states were dominated by armies of distinct social composition: Morocco was ruled by tribal vanguards, Egypt by a military caste; both provided excellent light cavalry but depended on feeble levies, unreliable Christian renegades, and treacherous Turkish mercenaries for infantry and artillery. The consequences could be fatal. In 1557 one of the most effective sultans of Morocco was assassinated by his Turkish gunners, who sent his pickled head to Istanbul. The history of sixteenth-century Morocco could be characterized as a search for means to adapt the new technologies of warfare with which Spain, Portugal, and the Ottoman Empire threatened the Maghrib. Despite her enviable position, with Mediterranean and Atlantic seaboards that gave her, like France and Spain, an unusual advantage in the late-medieval and early-modern scramble for oceanic resources, Morocco was also inhibited by the lack of a maritime tradition and the contempt for the sea that made Moroccans dismiss the Ottoman Empire as a fishermen's enterprise.

Still, Morocco had to the south a sea of sand with an inviting shore. Like Spain's Atlantic, Morocco's Sahara was an obstacle course, which could be crossed only with danger, difficulty, and expense, to a land of gold. In the late middle ages, Morocco's chances of founding a trans-Saharan empire were slight. The way to the gold was guarded by the daunting strength of Mali. The imperial ambitions of the Marinid dynasty, which reigned from 1269 to 1465, were absorbed in dreams of reconstructing a Maghribi and Andalusian state, like those of earlier desert conquerors; but they were enervated by sedentarism and in the fourteenth century, increasingly, because of retiring habits and royal minorities, tended to withdraw into the life of the palace and the seraglio, abandoning government to their hereditary vizirs, the Banu Watta.

The rule of the palace by mayors nearly always ends in a coup. When the Wattasids seized sovereignty, they had to struggle to assert their legitimacy against pretenders sprung from desert sects and, allegedly, from the stock of the Prophet of Islam. These religious movements were dangerous when disunited, indefeasible when fused. In the first years of Wattasid rule, the followers of a murdered Sufi charismatic called al-Jazuli spread rebellion by touring the realm with his embalmed corpse. They were narrowly defeated but had demonstrated how the renown of a holy man could animate a political movement. In the second decade of the sixteenth century, the mantle of al-Jazuli passed to a family from Tidsi which claimed the Prophet as an ancestor and organized a tribal confederacy into a rival of the Wattasid state. They drew support by proclaiming the holy war against Christian adversaries, but their real enemies were the ruling dynasty of Morocco. Spain and Portugal, their nominal foes, in fact supplied them with firearms. In 1541 they turned these weapons on the Portuguese garrison of Agadir. Enriched with booty and ransom, enhanced in prestige by a victory over the infidel, they went on to conquer the rump of Wattasid Morocco and unite the country under their rule in 1549. Their leader, Muhammad al-Shaikh, still reeked of the desert but, following precedents set by previous Maghribi conquerors of the coast, succumbed to the allure of Mediterranean civilization, taking lessons in deportment from servants of the ousted sultan of Fez.

As soon as the war with the Wattasids was over and the united might of Morocco became available for a new enterprise, Muhammad al-Shaikh began to plan the conquest of the Sahara. In 1557 an expeditionary force from Morocco briefly seized Taghaza, the salt-mining town deep in the desert. The logistical problems of desert campaigns, and distractions on other fronts, deferred further progress until the 1580s, when the vision of an empire of gold captured the imagination of the sultan Ahmad al-Mansur.

He urged a campaign in the south against the doubts of his followers and the advice of his counsellors. He took the need for expansion for granted. The way north was blocked by the Habsburgs; the east was guarded by the might of the Ottoman Empire. The land of the Blacks was richer than that of the Maghrib; its conquest would yield a profit which lands of easier access could never provide. The desert was not impassable. What the merchant-caravans accomplished a well-organized army could achieve. Ahmad al-Mansur slavered at the prospect of the havoc his army would wreak on the Blacks, for his firepower was now fully arrayed, with 2,500 Christian renegade or Morisco marksmen under a Spanish captain and a train of camel-mounted artillery. In 1588 he demanded from Songhay a new and exorbitant rate in gold for consignments of Saharan salt. It was a deliberate provocation. The defiant reply from Songhay was a present of javelins and a sword. Nine thousand camels accompanied the Moroccan task force on a march of 135 days across 1,500 miles, mostly of desert. Half the force is thought to have perished on the way, but the survivors dispersed the hosts of Songhay as efficiently as previous conquistador vanguards had shattered the Aztecs and Incas.

The parallels with Spanish experience continued. Over the next twenty years Morocco turned the Sahel into a colony settled with twenty thousand men. After the death of al-Mansur, the settler communities, often marrying locally, created creole and mestizo states of their own which gradually slipped out of Moroccan control. The gold that passed through their hands trickled to other destinations. The biggest shipment back to Morocco arrived on thirty camels in 1599, valued at £604,800 by an English merchant in Marrakesh; but that scale of return was never repeated, and by the late 1630s Morocco's reserves of gold were running out.

At about the same time, the Spanish Empire was experiencing a similar crisis as the level of bullion shipments from America slid to its lowest level ever and as the "creole patriots" of America, especially in Mexico and Peru, developed identities and political myths that prefigured, if they did not immediately precipitate, severance from Spain (see Chapter 11). Yet Spain's empire proved more resilient than Morocco's, despite serious relative weaknesses in its structure and origins. The distances over which its communications stretched were much greater; it had been established with relatively less manpower, more thinly spread; and it had confronted indigenous adversaries of formidable power and unrestrained aggression, to whom we must now turn.

THE AZTEC MEMORY

Why did Cortés in Mexico or Pizarro in Peru not suffer the fate of Magellan, who died, overestimating his prowess, at the hands of native warriors in Cebu? Or of Captain Cook, who was cut down and bludgeoned on a beach in Hawaii? Or of the Portuguese of Cristovão da Gama in Ethiopia in 1542, where three hundred of a force of four hundred were slaughtered by the tribesmen of Adel? Or—to take some examples where the technical disparities between the contenders were even greater—why were they not destroyed like Chelmsford's men at Isandhlwana or Gordon at Khartoum or Custer at the Little Bighorn or any one of many "thousand pounds of education" felled by "a ten-rupee jezail"?

But for the experience of the Spanish in the New World, and a very few other similar examples, our perception of the ease with which expanding European societies of the modern period asserted their supremacy over technically inferior indigenous civilizations might be far less clear. Weight of numbers or ferocity of commitment would be seen frequently to triumph over the generally modest technical advantage which armies from Christendom could bring to bear, before the era of steam power, rifled guns, and gatlings. European successes in the third quarter of our millennium, "western" world hegemony in the last, would no longer seem the foregone conclusion for which they have been taken.

Yet the true history of the creation of the Spanish Empire in America does not support the inferences usually drawn from it. Outside the cases of Mexico and Peru—conspicuous because of the glitter of the gold and the dramatic possibilities of the stories—conquest was normally painful and slow. The Maya of Yucatán defeated repeated Spanish incursions and, after the conquest of most of their land, maintained a rump state of their own in the depths of the Petén until the 1690s, when a Spanish friar convinced them that submission would be in accordance with their own oracles. The Seminoles of Florida went on fighting until the Spanish Empire crumbled away. The Araucanos of Chile kept up their resistance throughout the history of the Spanish monarchy and then, with characteristic perversity, continued it in that monarchy's name against the successor-republic. Many forest tribes of central South America were irreducible except by the peaceful methods of missionaries. On the northern frontier of New Spain, Indians who had never responded to the force of Spanish arms were induced to follow Spanish policy in the eighteenth century only by means of laborious parleys on equal terms, called *parlamentos*.

The final triumph of this collaborative approach was spectacular. Its results can be admired, for instance, in the decorative plan of the settlement of San Juan Bautista in Texas in 1754, in the Archives of Simancas, where

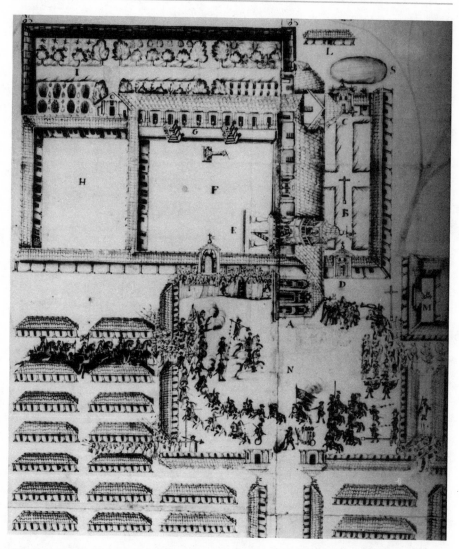

The main square of San Juan Bautista, Texas, 1754: the collaborative approach by which the Spanish monarchy eventually won over native communities who could not be reduced by force. By a policy of "attraction," Indians were drawn into rationally planned settlements. The drawing was made as an official record but seems obviously idealized. It shows the consecration of the main square by the erection of crosses at its corners. The mission is at the top, with its garden and magnificent church, and the town hall is to its right. A community of religious sisters, with the children of their school, emerge from the mission buildings to attend the ceremony. Parties of Indians are arriving at all the main entrances to the square, while Spanish troops and native auxiliaries parade and fire salutes.

José Gabriel Condorcanki, "Tupac Amaru II," self-proclaimed restorer of the Inca empire, a wealthy landowner of the Cuzco region who mobilized a "general rebellion" in
Peru in 1780 by awakening memories of sixteenth-century resistance to the conquistadors. Although this Jesuit-educated revolutionary dressed in European clothes, Inca
fancy-dress was the favourite style for the portraits of descendants of the native élite in
eighteenth-century Cuzo. José Gabriel fought a long lawsuit to assert his descent from
the last ruling Inca and was inspired by reading the utopian accounts of Inca history that
were popular with creole readers. The goatskin painting was done more than a generation after his brutal execution—by bodged dismemberment—in 1781. See p. 222.

through the neat files of the colonnaded streets, processions of Indians and Spaniards thread, with their traditional arms and dress and music, to meet the mission-folk in the main square and erect celebratory crosses in each of its corners. Yet the process had been neither quick nor easy, nor, ultimately, had it been procured by any Spanish superiority, technical or moral.

Nor have the conquests of the great Amerindian civilizations of Mexico and Peru generally been fairly represented. That of Peru was not quick and that of Mexico was not easy. An Inca state held out in the forests of Vilcabamba until 1572. Like the Roman Empire in the middle ages, that of the Inca continued a sort of phantasmagorical existence until the revolt in 1780 of José Gabriel Condorcanki Tupac Amarú, who, combining the appearance of a Spanish gentleman with the blood of an Inca emperor, proclaimed himself "José I, by the grace of God, Inca-King of Peru." In one of Hergé's Tintin stories, the hero discovers an active Inca court in the depths of the South American forest; the fantasy has just enough plausibility to make it powerful. The Aztec Empire was more quickly overthrown and more thoroughly expunged; but, as we shall see, it was no less vigorous an enemy and in its way just as tough a conquest.

"In war," said Napoleon, "the morale is to the materiél as ten to one." The conquistadores of Mexico had neither sort of advantage. The events of the conquest unfolded rapidly, but as strenuously and terrifyingly for the Spaniard as for their opponents. Cortés landed with what was supposed to be a reconnaissance force at Veracruz in August 1519. Abjuring the authority of his superior in Cuba, he constituted his men as a civic community and had himself elected mayor: it was a reflex action. When Spaniards met on a wild frontier, they founded a city, just as Englishmen in similar circumstances would found a club.

Beaching his ships, he proceeded "with no fear that once my back was turned the people left in the town would betray me." Rumours of Aztec wealth steeled a resolve which, with the ships grounded, was literally to conquer or die. "Trusting in God's greatness and in the might of their Highnesses' royal name," 315 Spaniards struck inland to seek Montezuma "wherever he might be." The route was consciously chosen to penetrate the most inaccessible patches in the Aztec world, where the Aztecs' most reluctant tributaries and most defiant enemies would be found. They climbed from Jalapa by "a pass so rough and steep that there is none in Spain so difficult," emerging with the conviction that they were now in the Aztec realm. "God knows," wrote Cortés, "how my people suffered from hunger and thirst and . . . hailstorms and rainstorms." They fought their way through the land of Tlaxcala, where their courage was rewarded by the alliance of the fiercest pocket of resistance to the Aztecs between Mexico and the coast.

The thread by which their morale hung frayed quickly. They were farther from home than any man had been before by way of the west. They were cut off from hope of help, and they knew that if a force followed them from Cuba, it would be to punish them, not to assist. They were surrounded by a hostile and awe-inspiring Nature and hundreds of thousands of menacing "savages" whom they could not understand. They had to breathe an unaccustomed, rarefied atmosphere; to endure extremes of heat and cold; to eat a debilitating diet without the red meat and wine that Spaniards considered essential for good health and high status. They were at the mercy of native guides and interpreters who might choose to betray them at any moment. At Cholula, where the feathered-serpent god had his principal shrine, Cortés resorted to methods of terror. To pre-empt, he said, an Indian conspiracy but, more convincingly, to alleviate the Spaniards' stress, he massacred, by his own admission, more than three thousand citizens.

Even when they got to the lakebound fastness of Tenochtitlán, where they were ceremoniously received and comfortably accommodated, the conquistadores remained jittery and psychologically insecure. It is important to remember that before the conquests of Mexico and Peru, Spaniards had not yet fully formulated the god-like self-perceptions that came to them so easily in the wake of victory. The stories of superhuman prowess were not yet on record, such as that of Hernán Sánchez of Badajoz at the siege of Cuzco in 1536, when he climbed a scaling ladder, deflecting a hail of stones with his shield, in order to squeeze into a tower through a window, beyond which, after routing the Indian defenders at that level, he seized a dangling rope and hoisted himself to the top, braving more stones on the way, to encourage his comrades to follow him. Tales like this, reminiscent of modern comic-strip heroes with "special powers," whether true or false, can only be told in an atmosphere of sublime self-confidence. The conquerors of Mexico were digging the foundations of the myth of Spanish invincibility and could get no comfort from it themselves.

It is true that they spoke a language in which the word for "arrogance" denotes a virtue. They came from a people accustomed to self-assertion, whose most distinguished historian of the time had argued that Spaniards were superior to Italians because the Goths had vanquished the Romans, and whose representative at the Council of Basle had settled a dispute over precedence with the English delegation by overturning the bench on which their rivals were sitting. Spanish arms had, moreover, a creditable record in the half-century before the conquest of Mexico. Their prizes were the western Canary Islands (1476–78), the Kingdom of Granada (1482–92), Naples (1497–1503), Melilla (1497), Oran (1509), Algiers and Bejaia (1510), southern Navarre (1511–14), and in the New World, Hispaniola (1495–96), Puerto Rico (1508), Jamaica (1509), Cuba (1511), and Castilla del Oro (1512–17).

None of these, however, had constituted a precedent for the predicament faced by Cortés and his men. The Old World conquests were effected with relatively short lines of communication and relatively concentrated and well-equipped forces. Those in the New World so far had faced relatively feeble foes and had been backed by at least some logistical support. Cortés had not only to overcome a populous and powerful enemy without any such advantages; he had also to defeat his own potential allies before they would join him and vanquish the forces sent after him from Cuba before he could impress their aid.

The conquistadores in Tenochtitlán developed some curious psychological strategies to cope with their isolation and exposure. Bernal Díaz del Castillo—who, as an old soldier, left astonishingly vivid memoirs—took refuge in a chivalric fantasy. His first sight of Tenochtitlán was like a glimpse of an enchanted city; Montezuma, in his eyes, was an exotic prince whose accolade he prized as proof of his own nobility. Pedro de Alvarado, whose long career in the New World would bring him one of the cruellest reputations, tried to repeat the terror tactics of Cholula, provoking a sanguinary reaction from the Aztecs by massacring a group of nobles of Tenochtitlán. Some of the force resorted to the consolations of religion: the appearance of Saint James alongside them in battle lent their struggle the flavour of a crusade; Cortés himself grew progressively more religious in the course of the conquest, ending with a vision of the future of Mexico as the homeland of a new "apostolic" church. Some deified their leader, singing campfire songs of his prowess in his presence. Fear underlay all their reactions: fear legible between the line of Bernal Díaz's dry-throated accounts of the anguish of witnessing human sacrifice or of the nice balance of battles from which every Spaniard emerged wounded.

Nor were the Spaniards invincible in practice. Their first major encounter with hostile Aztecs resulted in abject defeat on the *Noche Triste,* or "grim night," of 30 June 1520, when, expelled from Tenochtitlán with heavy losses, they picked their way across the causeways of the lake under heavy fire. "God alone," said Cortés, "knew how difficult and dangerous it was." Even when Cortés had raised the tributary subject-peoples of the empire and returned with thousands of native allies to get his revenge for him, the Aztec capital could not be subdued by force. The technical advantages commonly imputed to the Spaniards counted for little: horses were unsuited to street-fighting in the middle of a lake; steel blades, however superior to the obsidian-studded clubs of the enemy, were held in too few hands to make much difference, as were crossbows and guns, which depended on limited supplies of munitions. Not even the nine sailing brigs which Cortés built to patrol the lake were decisive. Instead of being overwhelmed by superior morale or superior technology, Tenochtitlán was starved and plagued into surrender. An empire nourished by tribute could not survive the severance of supply. A densely populated community crowded onto a small island could not endure without the huge inputs of food the empire supplied.

The power of the Aztec state to levy tribute was both the source of its weakness and a daunting measure of its strength. Only the scale of consumption among the hegemonic communities in and around Lake Texcoco can show the degree of their dependence on the resources of the hinterland. According to the surviving tribute-lists, which may not be complete, Tenochtitlán received annually, in units probably of about a bushel and a half, 140,000 of maize, 105,000 of beans, 105,000 of sage, 90,000 of purslane, 4,000 loaves of salt, 980 loads of cacao, and 320 baskets of maize flour and other powdered foods. Bernal Díaz witnessed 1,000 daily meals served to Montezuma's retinue and 300 dishes for the ruler at each meal. These included stewed fowl, stewed turkeys ("double-chinned chickens," Bernal said), pheasants, "partridges of the country," peccary, quails, wild and domestic duck, venison, fried songbirds, pigeons, what looked like hares and rabbits, "and many sorts of fowl and things that grow in this land. . . . I heard tell that they used to cook boys of tender age for him and, since he had so many different types of stews and other things, we were not able to see if it was human flesh or something else." When the chieftain had finished, his household was given "jugs of foaming chocolate, more than 2,000, with infinite fruit." The palace of the allied city of Texcoco was said to have absorbed daily, in the mid-fifteenth century, tribute amounting to up to 1,200 kilograms of maize, 143 of beans, 32,000 cocoa beans, 100 turkeys, 20 loaves of salt, 40 baskets of chillies, 10 baskets of tomatoes, and 10 squashes with, reputedly, 400,000 tortillas. When this empire of greed had to withdraw its tentacles, when it could no longer reach out, across and beyond the valley of Mexico, for the tribute on which it gorged, it was doomed. Cortés did not have to kill it; by raising its subject and tributary peoples he cut it off from its sources of life. What his Indian allies failed to accomplish, unseen allies finished off: the debilitated and undernourished city was ravaged by disease before it finally gave in.

Early colonial society in Mexico was divided about how to explain the conquest. For the conquistadores, embittered by the paucity of their rewards, in the submissions they wrote for the Spanish courts in pursuit of their claims on the crown, it was the sum of their individual acts of valour. For missionary friars, like the redoubtable Toribio de Benavente—who took in Nahuatl the surname of Motolinia, or "he who is poor"—it was ordained by God for the conversion of the Indians. For the Indians of Tlaxcala, who supplied the vital native levies that enabled Cortés to overawe other potential allies, it was a Tlaxcalan victory over Tenochtitlán, in which some others, including the Spaniards, played an ancillary role. In a legal brief prepared to plead for the reward of tax-exemption, they showed pictures of their chiefs negotiating with Cortés through his Indian interpreter-mistress,

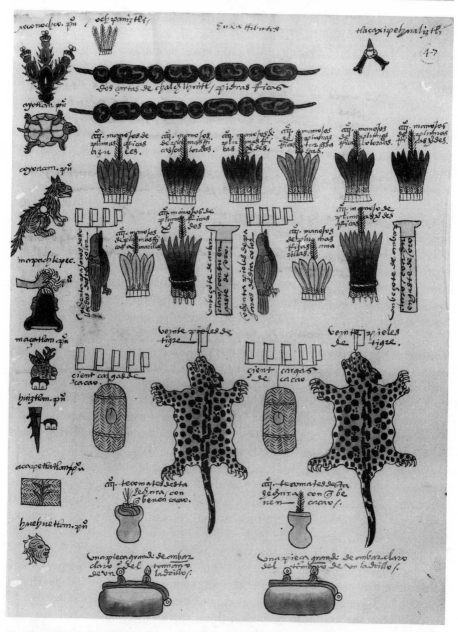

The tribute-roll section of Codex Mendoza conveys a sense of the great reach of Aztec power and the complexity of the network of tributary relationships which held the hegemony together. The glyphs at the top and along the left-hand margin show the names of remote places which owed tribute to Tenochtitlán. The prickly pear–glyph at top left, for instance, stands for Xonconochco, the most southerly of the Aztecs' tributary states, on the Pacific coast. The tribute due annually is vividly depicted, with amounts specified (each flag-like glyph stands for twenty units): jade beads, rich feather war bonnets, exotic birdskins, phials and chunks of amber, jaguar pelts, baskets of cacao beans, and chocolate-drinking vessels.

who always occupied the centre of the composition; they displayed scenes of the triumph of their warriors, with Spanish horsemen bringing up the rear, like the Duke of Plaza Toro. Most explanations, however, divided the responsibility between the inherent virtues of the Spaniards and the supposed crisis of morale which was thought to have racked Aztec society in its final years of self-rule.

The image of Aztec decision-makers hamstrung by a sense of impending doom and of an Aztec world resigned to its own failure derive from two partial sources: Cortés's own reports and an early-colonial myth. Cortés first put into Montezuma's mouth, in his account of their first meeting, an admission that power would have to be surrendered to strangers from the sea, representatives of a departed culture-hero of a remote past, "and according to the things this captain has said of the Lord and King who sent him here, and according to the direction whence he says he comes, I am certain . . . that this is the same lord for whom we have been waiting." This seems no more than a device by which Cortés justified his naked usurpation, on the King of Spain's behalf, of the Aztecs' apparently legitimate sovereignty in their own land. Yet it appears to be confirmed by the description of Aztec religion and mentality found in early colonial ethnographic sources, and especially in the greatest of all such compilations, the *General History of the Things of New Spain* of the Franciscan missionary Bernardino de Sahagún. In this tradition, the Aztecs are depicted as a doom-fraught people; some chiliastic consummation seemed always to be just around the corner, and their powers of resistance to the conquistadores were sapped not only by the story of a returning god, for whom Cortés was mistaken, but also by a series of portents and auguries which convinced them—in the language of the sandwich-board—that the end was nigh.

Sahagún's prestige as an ethnographer has made these disclosures appear credible. Yet, from a lesser source, it is hard to believe they would carry much conviction. The myth of a "god from the sea" is found all over the world but, in other cases, only among coastal peoples. The portents recorded by Sahagún as harbingers of the conquest read more like a mishmash of classical and late antique prophecies of the fall of Rome and Jerusalem than a genuine Aztec tradition. They include strange lights and fires in the sky, cases of spontaneous combustion, isolated lightning strikes, comets, earth tremors, ghostly wailing, and monstrous deformations.

To identify the tradition to which these devices genuinely belong, it is sufficient to turn to Shakespeare's *Julius Caesar*, where the prodigies feared by Casca and Calpurnia exactly parallel every one of the signs recorded by Sahagún. The friar's informants and interpreters were his pupils in the College of Santa Cruz in Tlatelolco—the lakebound community that adjoined Tenochtitlán: grammar-school boys, as it were, educated, like the actor from Stratford, in "small Latin" but in strong reverence for classical literary

The *Lienzo de Tlaxcala*—the main source of the Tlaxcalan view of the conquest of Mexico—has been destroyed but a copy survives, in which Tlaxcalan warriors dominate most of the scenes of fighting while Spaniards bring up the rear. The picture-history was drawn up for submission in the Spanish courts as part of the Tlaxcalan's case for exemption from tribute in recognition of their vital role as the Spaniards' allies. Even in scenes of negotiation, like this one, in which no Tlaxcalans appear, Cortés (mounted on the right with a romantically helmed Spanish cavalier behind him) plays a role subsidiary to that of his mistress and interpreter, Doña Marina, a Nahua princess who had learned Chontal Maya as a captive in Tabasco. Here she negotiates the alliance of the Otomi community of Atleuçian. There is no evidence that she spoke Otomi but Nahatl was a *lingua franca* in the area.

models. At the same time they were young nobles, conscious of their Aztec ancestry and anxious to vindicate Aztec civilization by the standards of Renaissance humanism. For them, Tenochtitlán was both the Rome and the Jerusalem of their forefathers. The tails of those comets must be liberally

The mythical foundation of Tenochtitlán—the opening leaf of Codex Mendoza. Year-glyphs representing the count from 1325 to 1376 CE form the border. At the top, the signature of André Thevet can be seen (see p. 219), marking his ownership of the manuscript after French pirates had captured it on its way from Mexico to Spain. The central scene—in which the native artist has been influenced by European heraldic conventions—shows the eagle nesting on a prickly pear in an island on Lake Texcoco, at the confluence of two streams: this was the omen which directed the culture-hero Tenuch (distinguished by the sacred blacking on his face) to the right spot. The skull-rack to the eagle's right represents both the charnel of the eagle's eyrie and its perpetuation by the Aztecs, who built piles of the skulls of sacrificed captives.

sprinkled with grains of salt. Our picture of corroded Aztec morale at the time of the conquest derives from the efforts of mixed-up kids of early colonial New Spain to understand the conquest in terms of an alien heritage.

There is, however, a source of which we can turn for an uncorrupted Aztec memory of the last years before the conquest. Sometime in the early 1540s—he could not remember the exact date—a Spanish settler in Mexico, Gerónimo López, entered the studio of an Aztec "master of painters" called Francisco Gualpuyogualcal. He was evidently on terms of intimacy with the artist and apparently in the habit of dropping in for a chat. The painter confided that he was engaged on a secret commission from the viceroy himself in which, López reported, he had—in the form of a picture-story, not unlike a comic strip—"to put all the land . . . and all the lords who had ruled it until the coming of the Spaniards . . . and the division made of these peoples and provinces by Montezuma among the leading men of this city of Mexico." The object of the exercise was to show that the system by which the land and people were exploited was not a Spanish device, unlawfully contrived by the conquerors, but a tradition inherited from the Aztec past.

Instead of this intended work of colonial propaganda, Gualpuyogualcal produced a triumphant vindication of his own people, in paintings firmly executed in an indigenous style, hardly corrupted by the Renaissance aesthetics which the Spaniards had introduced to native painters. His work displayed the glory and suggested the legitimacy of the Aztec state. The first decorated leaf of the surviving version sums up the character of the image of the Aztecs which the artist wanted to transmit to posterity. It depicts the foundation of the Aztec capital, Tenochtitlán. In the centre, the city's name-glyph in the Aztecs' proto-writing-system—a prickly pear growing from a stone—is surmounted by a huge eagle, whose animated realism, with wings outspread, beak parted, head poised to strike, and talons rampant in a fashion which might betray heraldic influence, is the only echo of European conventions of painting on the page. The image alludes to the foundation myth of the city, in which the Mexican culture-hero Tenuch was guided to the spot chosen by the gods. It is closely guarded by symbols of war: a shield adorned with clumps of eagle's feathers and a stack of barbed and feathered throwing-spears; a skull-rack for the display of the heads of sacrificed captives. The surrounding lake and intersecting canals of the city are schematically depicted, and Tenuch and his nine companions squat around on status-conferring rush mats, facing the central foundation scene. Below begins the Aztec career of conquest, which forms the subject of the next twenty leaves, as huge Mexican warriors, standing erect with obsidian-blades swinging, vanquish puny enemies who crouch, doubled up in humiliation, almost in a foetal position of fear.

The surviving manuscript—which, if it is not Gualpuyogualcal's secret commission, is something very like it—passed through the hands of French pirates, who captured it at sea, to those of André Thevet, the French cosmographer-royal, who sold it to Richard Hakluyt. The publicist no doubt hoped it would yield intelligence useful to England in war against Spain, whereas John Selden—through whose collection it passed to its present home in the Bodleian Library, Oxford—scoured it in the course of his comparative study of writing systems. Thus, all its owners, from the patron who commissioned it onwards, had their own expectations of it; and it defied them all, serving its author's purpose and his people's cause. It makes an ideal source for the study of the Aztec past as seen by an educated Aztec of the early colonial era.

Few single texts have as much power to undermine our received picture of world history in the sixteenth century. The Aztecs depicted in Gualpuyogualcal's studio were not cowed by oracles, waiting resignedly for their fate. The reality of their attitude was the very opposite of what has commonly been supposed. The main lesson the work conveys about the Spanish experience in Mexico is that the conquerors were not drawn into a vacuum as if by an abhorrent nature but clashed with a competing culture that was also expanding rapidly and aggressively.

Throughout the codex the triumphalist mood of the first page is sustained. Though occasional Aztec defeats are recorded, the story is saturated in the "honour code," the victory-ethic which drove the Aztec élite. In page after page of pictures of broken, burning enemy temples, it recounts the Aztecs' inexorable rise. Ultimately unsuperable, their warriors parade in lavish suits of war-feathers or tower over timid adversaries, sometimes satirically portrayed. A rebellious chief of Tlatelolco flings himself in defeated shame down temple steps, foaming at the mouth with the pulque-glyph, which is the sign of drunkenness. Of the Aztec chiefs, the reigns are numbered in two ways only: by regnal years and by conquered towns. On the whole, the number of conquests mounts, reign by reign. And the last reign—that of Montezuma, the leader who was supposedly resigned to an adverse fate, whose reign was overshadowed by portents of doom—appears as the most dynamic, the most aggressive, the most triumphantly self-confident of all. His total number of conquests—forty-four towns—was slightly behind that of a predecessor, Ahuitotzin; two earlier rulers were slightly ahead in terms of average numbers of conquests per year. The relative efficacy of such operations may be judged by the fact that Montezuma and Ahuitotzin both had to return to reimpose their authority on already conquered communities only four times in the course of their reigns.

Where Montezuma incomparably outstripped all his rivals, however, was in the range of his campaigns, which took him with amazing rapidity from the River Pánuco in the north, on the Atlantic coast, where those cunning craftsmen, the Huastec, dwelt, to Xoconusco on the Pacific in the south—back and forth between frontiers enclosing over 200,000 square kilometres of territory. It could be objected that the very rapidity and scale of this expansion must have over-extended and weakened Aztec power. This evidence cannot, however, be reconciled with the view that the Aztecs were morally enfeebled or that their dynamic and dominating urge was exhausted.

The contemporary Spanish commentator who annotated the manuscript summed up well the stature of Montezuma's reputation among the Aztec survivors of his day: "in comparison with his predecessors, there was none who attained to the fourth part of his great estate and majesty." Compared with the timid and fatalistic Aztecs familiar from most accounts of the conquest, the burgeoning, vital Aztec world depicted in the pages of Codex Mendoza was at least as vividly perceived and may have been more accurately remembered. The final irony of the conquest of Mexico is that when the Spaniards took over from the Aztecs as the imperial master-class of the

Codex Mendoza displays Aztec self-perceptions with candour. Heroic warrior-priests, heavily armed and in divine disguises, tower over the puny enemies whom they capture for sacrifice. One of the priests carries a shield adorned with the eagle-down clumps of Huitzilopochtli, the deity particularly identified with Tenochtitlán. His colleague at bottom right wears the jaguar costume and carries the sun-ornament shield of Tonatiuh, a god identified with the sun. Notice the feather-burst standards and the clubs studded with black blades of obsidian.

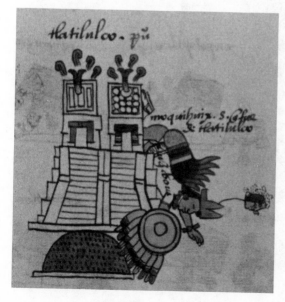

The suicide of Micuihuixtl, chief of Tlatelolco, the community which neighboured Tenochtitlán. The earth-mound is the place's name-glyph: the distinctive twin temples for which Tlatelolco was famous are shown burning as a sign of the conquest by Tenochtitlán. From the conquest-roll section of Codex Mendoza, in which Aztec history is represented as an almost uninterrupted parade of triumphs.

Nahua world, the dynamism and expansion did not cease. In a sense the last Aztec conquests were those launched from the Valley of Mexico, under Spanish command, by overwhelmingly Nahuatl-speaking armies, to conquer Guatemala and Honduras in the 1520s and Yucatán in the 1540s. The last Aztec emperor, formally so-constituted, Cuauhtémoc, was murdered by Cortés on their march, as companions-in-arms, to Honduras.

The Frustrated Empires

The Aztecs ruled only one of a number of rapidly expanding civilizations of the late middle ages in Africa and America. The closest parallel is with the Incas of Peru, whose state and society were very different and whose eclipse by the rising Spanish Empire was neither so sudden nor so total, but whose imperial age was of similar duration and whose growth—judged by the standards of every other contemporary empire except Spain's—was similarly spectacular. The expansion of the power of the Aztecs in central Mexico is traditionally dated from the subjection of her previously hegemonic neighbour-city, Azcapotzalco, in 1428; the rise of the Incas is con-

The typical eighteenth-century portrait of Tupac Yupanqui's father, the Inca Pachacuti, is arrayed in the fancy dress affected by the mestizo élite for special occasions, with his renown as a conqueror unconvincingly alluded to in the diminutive axe and shield.

Balsa-wood rafts of the Peruvian Indians, like these engraved for Girolamo Benzoni's mid-sixteenth-century polemic against Spanish imperialism, encouraged Thor Heyerdahl to believe that stories, recorded early in the colonial era, of Tupac Inca Yupanqui's seagoing missions of exploration could be true. He was not the first: in the late sixteenth and early seventeenth centuries Spanish expeditions combed the Pacific for the Incas' "Isles of Gold." See pp. 262 and 661.

ventionally dated from 1438, when Inca Pachacuti was said to have conquered Chava and to have begun to spread Inca rule beyond the valley of Cuzco. The rapidity of the growth of the Aztec Empire is echoed in the Incas' case by the period of the conquests of Pachacuti and his heir, Tupac Inca Yupanqui, who, in a meteoric career in the last third of the fifteenth century, campaigned deep into Chile, reputedly reaching the River Bíobío, and was said to have discovered rich islands in the Pacific. Although the Incas were rent by civil war by the time Pizarro invaded, and they were no longer sustaining the sort of advance continued by the Aztecs up to the moment of their collapse, their military effectiveness was undiminished. A few years before the coming of the Spaniards, Inca Huayna Capac slaughtered 20,000 Caranqui Indians in what was probably the bloodiest encounter in the history of the pre-Hispanic New World and had the bodies flung into Lake Yahuar-Cocha. This destructive power was accompanied by terrible administrative efficiency. The Incas maintained a road network over 30,000 kilometres long with teams of runners capable, on favoured routes, of covering 240 kilometres a day. They organized exchange across the climatic tiers and varied environmental zones of which their long, high empire was composed. They were capable of uprooting and relocating labour on a vast scale. In the first quarter of the sixteenth century, Huayna Capac colonized the Cochabamba valley for maize production with fourteen thousand settlers from all over the empire. On the Moho, when Pizarro announced, "The time of the Inca is over," almost the entire population rose, gathered their belongings, and left for the distant homes from which they had been resettled. Of course, no empire could be so large and diverse without serious structural problems and internal strains; but the conquistadores were lucky to be, in Peru as in Mexico, the beneficiaries—almost the bystanders— of an Indian civil war, which enabled them to seize control, like a coal from the flames.

None of the frustrated empires of late medieval Africa and America may seem to have come to very much. Some, like Mali or the Maya, tottered or faltered before facing the blows of rivals from Europe. Others were extinguished or outstripped by European imperialism. Ethiopia, exceptionally, was rescued with European help from what threatened to be terminal difficulties, but never recovered. Morocco and Mwene Mutapa survived European expansion—both, indeed, fended off Portuguese attempts at conquest in the 1570s—but were unable to make much progress in competition with it. It would be a mistake, however, to underestimate either the dynamism of these societies in their day or the effects on the subsequent character of world history.

Morocco's late and barely glorious empire in Black Africa, for instance, was part of a bigger and more influential phenomenon: the meteoric expansion of late medieval and early modern Islam (see Chapter 9), which has helped shape the modern world just as much as the contemporary and parallel movement from Christendom. Though their renaissance faltered, memories of a great past remained alive among the Maya throughout centuries of survival as a people of distinct identity in the Hispanic world, and helped to inspire a long series of political movements: rebellions against Spain in the seventeenth and eighteenth centuries; the "caste war" against the state of Mexico in 1847; the Cruzob movement, which created an independent state, surviving in the jungles of Quintana Róo until 1905, under leaders inspired by a "Speaking Cross." Aztec myth and imagery have been appropriated in the making of a Mexican national identity (see Chapter 11), and the Inca phantom empire which reappeared in the 1780s, despite a mixed appeal in Peru, remained an influential idea ever after. In a recent important Peruvian textbook, the entire colonial period of the country's history is conceived as an era of reconquest from a foreign foe. After a long period of immolation in academic study and folk-memory, some of the great Black states of medieval Africa have been recalled to provide names, with varying degrees of aptness, for their modern successors. Though the name of Mwene Mutapa has not been revived, that of Zimbabwe has the right archaizing flavour. Songhay is absent still, but Mali, Ghana, and Benin are all on the modern map, somewhat displaced from their original locations (see Chapter 18). The name of Kongo, ironically, which acquired for African nationalists unacceptable resonances through its retention under a colonial regime, has been discarded by the state which now occupies its former territory.

Yet however feeble these echoes of past greatness seem, however easily the remote empires of the late middle ages were absorbed or outstripped by those of the sixteenth century and after, however flawed they were by isolation, over-extension, internal division, and external threat, it is important to restore the imperial careers of these African and American states to their place in the commonly received record of the past. Without the examples of the rapidity of their growth or the reality of their promise, the relatively static nature of fifteenth-century Latin Christendom and of much of Asia can hardly be appreciated; without a broad picture of the expanding and convergent movements which met in the "age of expansion," the nature of the world moulded by European initiatives in the second half of our millennium cannot be fully grasped, nor the scale of the achievement realistically envisaged.

Chapter 7

THE REACH OF CONQUEST: IMPERIALISMS OF THE EARLY MODERN PERIOD

The Turtle Armada—The Corners of the Carpet—
The Colour of the Bear—The Impossible Empires—
The Highway of the World

THE TURTLE ARMADA

"The deepest caves of the mountains and the reach of oars at sea" represented the ambitious limits of a survey of Japan proposed by the military dictator Hideyoshi in the 1580s. It was to include the dimensions and soil quality of every rice-field and the location of every irrigation-channel. Villagers who withheld information would be crucified; landowners who failed to cooperate would be put to the sword. Begun in 1583, driven by demonic energy, and hurried by unpitying force, the job was finished by 1598. The very idea of a comprehensive survey of the empire would have been barely conceivable a generation before, when Japan was divided among scores of mutually hostile warlords, whose truculent independence in diminutive territories was the result of two hundred years of civil wars. Japan had been ground into ever smaller fragments.

The trend of two centuries was reversed in the twenty-odd years from 1560, to the point where Hideyoshi could survey the country and project the conquest of the world. To a remarkable extent this concentrated achievement was the work of one man: Oda Nobunaga, a warlord in whose service

Shinsen Dainihon Zukan (Revised Map of Japan) of 1687. The maps generated by Hideyoshi's survey have not survived, but this is one of a series derived from them. Each province is marked with the name of its *daimyo* and the amount of his salary. At the top right it is evident that the cartographer is in some doubt about the nature of the Oshima peninsula and its relationship to the rest of Hokkaido. The placard at the top lists topographical information, including place-names, temples, and shrines, by provinces. The blank land to the left of it, labelled Chosenkoku, is Korea.

Hideyoshi had outstripped his modest origins and learned his military craft. Warlords had often dreamed of restoring imperial unity to their own advantage—much as some Renaissance princes dreamed of unifying Italy. Nobunaga was able to realize the dream partly by exploiting the overconfidence of his competitors—for he started from a small and ill-favoured power base in Owari, halfway up the Pacific coast of Honshu. His battle tactics were characterized by unmitigated nerve: in his first major battle he is said to have routed an army of more than eight times his own strength before they had time to sort out their weapons. His political strategy combined ruthless methods and objectives unrestrained: his campaign in Echizen choked the streets with corpses, and the fugitives were hunted "hill by hill, valley by valley." His seal was inscribed, "Rule the empire by force." An inventive streak, a technical flair, gave him an advantage over rival warriors: he helped to revolutionize Japanese warfare by organizing the manufacture of firearms copied from Portuguese prototypes. In 1568 he captured

the sacred but retiring person of the emperor, which enabled him to legitimate his desires and outlaw his enemies. By the time of his death in 1582
he had brought about half the provinces of Japan under his control.
Hideyoshi, securing the uneasy compliance of Nobunaga's other great lieutenant, Tokugawa Ieyasu, was able quickly to halt the disintegration that
immediately began, and rebuild and enlarge his master's legacy with relative rapidity.

Hideyoshi's letters to women—to his wife, to his mother, to his thirteen-
year-old future concubine—capture the calculations of a mind poised between amoral pragmatism and visionary madness. Waiving the formalities
which make most Japanese correspondence of the time inscrutable, he declared policies and passions in simple language with alarming indiscretion.
The immolation of hostages and the self-disembowelment of a rival were
described with frank glee. Unease at the onset of grey hairs and fear of his
wife's displeasure were confessed with equal candour. In a letter of 1583 he
declared his ambition to rule Japan. By 1587, writing to his wife, he extended the same ambition to grasp Korea and China. The momentum of his
success must have made all things seem possible.

The passion for conquest became an obsession reminiscent of the worldwide vocation of a thirteenth-century Mongol khan. Hideyoshi sent demands for submission to the kings of Indo-China and the Spanish governor
of the Philippines. He proclaimed himself the gods' choice for the mastery
of the world. In some ways foreign adventure was a rational policy in the
circumstances. The long civil wars had militarized Japanese society; professional warriors needed employment; the armaments industries required a
market; the energies of warlords had to be redeployed. Unlike China,
which could supply her own wants, Japan relied on commerce; warfare
was one way of securing supply. The piracy which had siphoned surplus
wealth from China and south-east Asia on an increasing scale in the fifteenth and sixteenth centuries could have become the prelude to empire,
like so much piracy around the world—that of the Vikings and Genoese
earlier in the middle ages, for example, or of the Portuguese in the fifteenth
century and the English and Dutch in the sixteenth. Korea produced
surplus grain. Chinese cities—sometimes far inland—could be held to
ransom. China was raided almost every year from 1545 to 1563. On one occasion raiders seized Nanking. Hideyoshi's ambitions, however, seem to
have exceeded rational bounds, and to have spilled over into a form of
rabid folly.

He imagined the future of his potential conquests vividly. They would
form not just a personal trophy but a thoroughbred empire. The Koreans
and Chinese would be "taught Japanese customs." A policy of indoctrina-
tion was actually begun in the early, successful stages of the invasion of
Korea, and native children were selected to learn Japanese. The land of

China would be partitioned among Japan's notables and the Japanese emperor invested with the mandate of Heaven.

While Japan had been steeled by long civil wars, Korea had enjoyed two centuries of unprecedented peace. The rulers dismissed Hideyoshi's threats as incredible; the generals submitted to them as irresistible. By comparison with the Japanese task force, reputedly 300,000 strong and equipped with firearms, the Korean forces were feeble and antiquated. The invaders reached Seoul in twenty days. Within eight weeks the Korean court had been forced to a refuge on the banks of the Yalu River, barely clinging to the kingdom. The only serious landborne opposition came from bandits temporarily transformed into guerrillas.

At sea, however, Korea was better prepared. Her navy had continuous experience of action against pirates and a lively tradition of technical innovation. The notion that the object of a sea battle was to sink the enemy's ships was only in its infancy in the western world but had been fully grasped in Korea. The use of heavy guns as ship-killing weapons, as well as of smaller firearms as man-killers, was being developed; ships specially adapted as gun-carriers, known as turtle ships, were under construction at the very moment when the Japanese invasion struck. The turtles had reinforced hulls, dragon's-head prows formed to conceal cannon, and decks covered with iron spikes to deter boarders. Six guns were arrayed on each broadside, protected by an upper deck in the shape of a turtle's back and directed through portholes. Overall dimensions were small by comparison with European standards—very small by those of Chinese warships. But it suited a potential ship-killer to sling its guns low, near the enemy's waterline. A Korean eyewitness of the war recalled how the turtles "could get among the enemy at will and make easy prey of them all." In reality there can have been too few of them in service to make much material difference to the outcome, but they form a representative instance of Korean naval élan.

The success of the Korean navy, however, seems to have depended on the personal genius of its commander, Yi Sun-shin, who has left war memoirs of Attic pithiness, which hardly ever stoop to self-aggrandizement. When jealousy of his victories compelled his retirement, to write poetry in the ranks at Chokye, fortunes were reversed and the navy reduced, reputedly, from more than two hundred ships to twelve. King Sonjo wrote to him, "It was due to my lack of wisdom that I replaced you. . . . I can find no words to repent for my wrong-doing towards you. . . . Again I beseech you to save the country." After Yi's rehabilitation, a mood of misery, an intensified fatalism, pervades the diaries; yet he remained a man of action. He was uninhibited by his faith in divination through dice and book, his anxious interpretations of his dreams, his bouts of heavy drinking, and his emotional dependence on a much-loved mother who died at a critical moment of the war. He was enough of a realist to appreciate that with a depleted fleet and much territory in enemy hands, Korea could survive only with Chinese intervention. Collaboration between Yi and his Chinese counterpart, Chen Lin, made Japanese communications unsustainable. With nicely judged theatre, Yi fell in the last battle of the war, in November 1598, confident of victory.

Hideyoshi had died the previous September, leaving—by his standards—a defeatist testament anticipating withdrawal. By one of the curious coincidences history sometimes throws up, another practitioner of *Weltpolitik,* Philip II of Spain, died within a week of the same date, surrounded by the stench of his own putrefying body and the disillusionment of aborted conquests. His council had also considered the prospects of conquering China earlier in the decade, and a party of would-be conquistadores had actually reconnoitred Cambodia and made the first known report of Angkor by Europeans; but like Hideyoshi's, Spanish invasions had got stymied nearer home, in the Netherlands, France, and the English Channel. Like Japan, Spain would begin the new century with sights adjusted to more modest targets. World imperialism was going out of fashion. That did not mean, however, that the age of worldwide imperial expansion was over.

In the context of Japanese history, Hideyoshi's abortive imperialism can be seen as an uncharacteristic twitch. No programme of Japanese conquest outside the home islands resurfaced for three hundred years, and in the interim the Japanese diverted chiefly to enrichment and amusement the energies they had formerly employed in fighting each other. The military caste rusted and sold their possessions. Impoverished samurai were lampooned in literature, just like the poor hidalgos made redundant by "the decline of Spain" on the other side of the contemporary world. With less justice, Chinese imperialism is commonly said also to have been paralysed in the same period by isolationism and inertia. Although the Chinese congratulated themselves heartily on turning their enemies away in Korea, they are said to have been enfeebled and ultimately disheartened by the cost of the war. Even when a new dynasty seized power in 1644—the Manchu Dynasty of interlopers from the northern steppes, heirs, it might be supposed, to the boundless imperial ambitions of previous nomadic conquerors—no change of ethos ensued, and the "timelessness" of China ticked over to the rhythms of the prosody favoured by scholar-mandarins.

In fact, the frontiers of China continued, quietly and intermittently, to expand in the seventeenth and eighteenth centuries. The Korean adventure was typical of the pattern of Chinese aggression: it was a war waged for security. But many empires have been founded in the pursuit of security. For security, the Romans took their boundaries over the Danube, and France in modern times sought natural frontiers along the crests of mountains and the lines of rivers. For the security of possessions in Mexico, Spain in the eighteenth century reached as far into North America as Nootka Sound. In the name of security, the Turks reluctantly took over Hungary in the sixteenth century. Conquests have been justified on grounds of security from the ancient Egyptian subjugation of Syria and Palestine under the New Kingdom to the establishment of the beleaguered little Zionist Empire in the same region in our own day. Within a generation of their conquests of outlying or recalcitrant parts of traditional China, the Manchus were pre-empting or pursuing Russian rivals in new territories to the north. In the late seventeenth century, the road which led to the war zone against Russia on the Amur River frontier was kept smoother—according to Ferdinand Verbiest, who travelled along it with imperial hunting parties—"than our Catholics in Europe keep the road on which the Sacrament is to be conveyed." The Treaty of Nerchinsk of 1689 formalized Chinese claims to vast unexplored lands of doubtful extent in the north-east of Asia, where some cartographers imagined a huge proboscis pointing to or even joining America. Before the end of the century, outer Mongolia had been crudely incorporated into the empire. In the south-east, where the Manchus had barely maintained their authority during rebellions of the 1670s and 1680s, consolidation rather than expansion was enjoined by circumstances, but China met fears of a Tibetan resurgence by seizing Tsinghai in the 1720s.

Paradoxically, the era of greatest Chinese complacency was also that of fiercest aggression. Perhaps the episode of eighteenth-century Chinese history best known in the west was the celebrated rebuff of the Ch'ien Lung emperor to Lord Macartney's trade mission in 1793 on the grounds that China already had everything she wanted. The remark came at the end of a period of dynamic expansion which, since the middle of the century, had extended Chinese rule or protectorates as far as the Tien Shan and the Himalaya and had launched invasions of Nepal, Burma, and Vietnam. The conquering habit was as deeply engrained in early modern China as in any part of the west. Indeed, no potentially imperial power in any part of the world was untouched by it. Of all the influences—including the colonization, evangelization, and trade that are the subjects of the next three chapters—which brought the world's major civilizations into mutual touch between the sixteenth and eighteenth centuries of our era, none was more dynamic than the impulsion to conquest, none more pervasive than war.

THE CORNERS OF THE CARPET

Its central plaza was seven times the size of the Piazza di San Marco. The goalposts installed there for games of polo were of marble. At one end the great mosque, the Masjid-i Shah, was offset at an angle to guarantee a good view of the dome and minarets, displayed behind a gate twenty-seven metres high. The patron who commanded its erection had no time to heed

A mounted archery context on the polo court of the main piazza of Isfahan, engraved in the 1680s, illustrating Jean de Thévenot's travels in Persia. The Masjid-i Shah is the building at the end of the square.

his architect's warnings of the dangers of subsidence; to save time, substance was sacrificed to superficial splendour, and painted polychrome tiles replaced mosaics. In the city as a whole, according to a usually sober European visitor, there were 273 public baths and 1,802 caravanserais. The Isfahan of Shah Abbas (1588–1629) was unmistakable evidence of the power, wealth, confidence, and dynamism of Safavid Persia.

Like so many Islamic dynasties—like Islam itself—the Safavid house had been founded by warrior holy men who galvanized under-evangelized tribesmen from deserts or mountains into formidable armies. The first shah was a precocious visionary, crowned in 1501 at the age of fourteen, who held private conversations with an apparition of Ali and who appears, from his powerful egocentric poetry, to have considered himself an incarnation of God. To a Venetian traveller it seemed that "the name of God is forgotten throughout Persia and only that of Ismail remembered." He inaugurated the policy, which distinguished his dynasty and gave Iran its peculiar character among Islamic countries, of imposing Shiism by force. When counselled in moderation, he threatened to put the entire population to death unless it shared his faith. Naturally, he thought himself invincible, and it is true that under his rule and that of his successors, until well into the seventeenth century, Safavid armies displayed remarkable versatility. Baghdad was twice seized, though never retained. Scores of thousands of Georgian, Armenian, and Circassian prisoners were incorporated into the élite slave-families of the shahs. But Iran's potential was always limited by its position, squeezed between two imperial giants of the Islamic world: the Ottoman Empire in the west and Mughal India in the east, which unrolled from their centres like huge prayer-rugs to reach into the corners of the Islamic world. When Ismail's wild horsemen were stopped by Ottoman guns at Chaldiran in 1514, he went into mourning and flew black banners inscribed with the word "Revenge." Though Shah Abbas was able to make gains on the Ottoman front, the retribution Ismail envisaged was never easy or lasting. At an early stage of the formation of the Mughal Empire, Persia played host to an exiled emperor but was unable, partly from scruples of religious purity, to exploit the potential advantage. The shahs were compelled to scrutinize each neighbour in turn; with less apprehension, we must do the same.

The India of the Mughal Empire is best evoked by two ruins in contrasting environments. The shattered fragments of the city of Vijayanagar are scattered through an almost abandoned landscape of hump-backed hills on the banks of the Tungabhadra; the remains of Shahjahanabad are crammed among the teeming streets of Delhi. Vijayanagar is a departed seat of Hindu power, in a part of the country where it is almost impossible to avoid a vegetarian meal. Shahjahanabad was a Muslim capital, pervaded today by the aroma of meats from Kumar's Grill. By the time Shahjahanabad was built in the 1640s, Vijayanagar had been destroyed for nearly two generations, emptied and wasted by Muslim raiders from the north. Today sugar cane grows wild between the elaborately wrought temples. Meanwhile, what was once the central boulevard of Shahjahanabad, the Chandni Chowk, is choked with cars and bicycles. After the fall of Vijayanagar, no Hindu state of imperial potential arose again until the twentieth century. The Mughal unification of the peninsula proceeded from north to south, and the successor-states of the Mughals—the British Raj and independent India—ruled from the same northern site. Yet for a time in the fifteenth century, Vijayanagar seemed to demonstrate the vitality of the south and centre. Its aggressive ethos was proclaimed in its name, which means City of Victories. Its defensive capabilities were declared by its sixty-mile length of sevenfold walls. It impressed a Muslim visitor in 1443 as finer than Herat—indeed, "such that the eye has seen nothing like it." When power had shifted definitively northwards, Shahjahanabad attracted even more emphatic praise. It was "an inhabited Eden," the "foundation of the eighth heaven," the "centre of the earth" or—as a Hindu declared in celebration of the inauguration of the

The ruins of a Jain temple in Vijayangar, in desolate surroundings, contrast with the continuing life in the Chandni Chowk—formerly the central boulevard of imperial Shahjahanabad, dominated by the domes, minarets, and walls of the Jumma mosque.

palace in 1649—"the abode of the sun, so full of pleasure that its avenues are like paradise."

If its founder's engaging memoirs can be trusted, this empire, which ultimately acquired such splendid solidity, was established in a mood of distraction. Babur (1483–1530) was an adventurer from central Asia, in the mould of his ancestor Timur. In the volatile world west of the Hindu Kush, he raised war-bands and exchanged kingdoms with a rapidity of turnover unattainable elsewhere. Yet he was constant in his dream of reconstituting a Timurid empire based on Samarkand. It was, he claimed, only when he had won and lost Samarkand for the second time that he heard of India, from a crone in Dekhar, 111 years old. She told him stories garnered from relatives who had accompanied Timur's Indian campaign of 1398. The seed thus implanted in his mind grew into an ambition of conquest, which he pursued single-mindedly from 1519. Once in India, like so many modern visitors, he was seduced by the country. He was almost poisoned owing to his partiality for Indian dishes. He rebuked Afghan followers who preferred Kabul where he had been "the sport of harsh poverty." After 1526 he never left India, though he could never banish from memory "the flavour of melons and grapes."

Though he conquered more of India than any one man had ruled for more than a hundred years, his empire at first looked typically fragile and probably ephemeral. A story told of the birth in exile of his grandson, Akbar, illustrates the fragility and foreshadows the recovery. Driven into penury in Persia, Babur's heir distributed a crushed pod of musk among his few remaining followers, saying, "This is all the present I can afford to make to you on the birth of my son, whose fame will, I trust, be one day extended all over the world, as the perfume of the musk now fills this apartment." The prophecy was duly fulfilled. Akbar's father met the death of a well-established emperor, falling from his library steps, which he had ascended to observe the rising of Venus, six months after the recapture of Delhi. Akbar himself was too busy fighting to acquire his father's and grandfather's literary flair. A monarch, he thought, "should be ever intent on conquests." Too unskilful or too impatient to handle books himself, he had them read to him, like Charlemagne, at meals. By concentrating on the practical and bloody arts of leadership, he established his dynasty so securely that it lasted for three hundred years and dominated India for two hundred.

It was always an imperfect form of domination, exercized from a place as far as possible from the sea, with a landsman's perspective. The Mughals never ruled the coasts, leaving the edges of their world to the charge of tributaries of suitably maritime inclinations. In consequence, just as Iran was contained by political constraints, the Mughal Empire kept within its natural frontiers: the geographical obstacles that define India, the mountains of the north, the desert of the north-west, the jungle of the north-east,

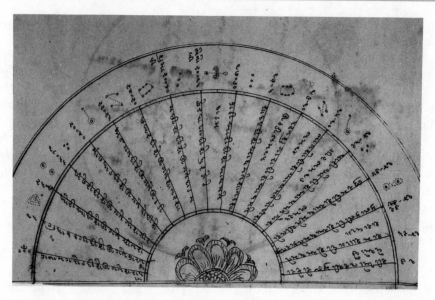

A diagram annotated in Kutchi with sailing courses from Socotra to ports around the
Arabian Sea. Stellar bearings, latitudes, and surface distances are given. Indian mariners
are not known to have made sea-charts before the introduction of European influence,
though charts were common in east Asia, and Indian methods of navigation yielded to
none in sophistication: diagrams like this may have made conventional maps otiose.

and, around the rest, the circumvalatory ocean. On the fringes of the
Mughal world, some fine marine charts were produced. A Gujarati chart of
1664, annotated in the Kutchi language, shows the southern cone of India,
with Ceylon rather oddly displaced; sailing courses were recorded in diagrammatic form with abundant practical information: star bearings, latitudes, and surface distances. But the Mughals had no access to a realistic
image of the world. A brass "earth-ball" in the Museum of the History of
Science in Oxford, made in 1571, with names inscribed in Sanskrit for
places in India, shows the limits of timeless Indian cosmography: it depicts
the traditional Buddhist world of four island continents radiating from a
mountainous core.

To be a world-conqueror, as Ottoman sultans aspired to be, it is not essential to be up-to-date with world mapping. But it helps. From Constantinople, a city founded to be a universal capital, generosity of perspective
was easier to achieve. The interest of the Ottoman court in monitoring
worldwide discoveries is displayed on the walls of the Topkapi Saray, in
the greatest cartographical treasure of the sultans' palace: the western portion—all that survives—of the world map made in Istanbul in 1513 by Piri
Re'is. The map exhibits the influence of the captured Spanish charts on
which it was based. It presents a detailed report of the findings of Colum-

An Indian bughola or earth-ball of 1571, engraved with Indian place-names in Sanskrit but reflecting a conventional world picture: the post-Vedic "Four Continents," reflecting perhaps a schematic version of a world centred on the Himalayas. A mountainous core is surrounded by concentric circles of rock, from which the four zones radiated.

bus and delineates those of Vespucci. If its purpose was connected with Turkish anxieties that Christian navigators would divert the spice trade from Ottoman territories, the sultans need not have worried. Demand for spices worldwide in the sixteenth and seventeenth centuries was supply-led, and the total volume of trade increased so much that the traditional caravan routes expanded their capacity in spite of the competition from the new oceanic highways. If, however, the map was produced by a general concern at the long reach of the infidels from their Atlantic-shore bases, it attests to a remarkable degree of far-sightedness in Istanbul. By any standards, the Ottoman Empire remained highly dynamic until well into the seventeenth century. In terms of territory added to their sovereigns' sway, the achievements of Columbus and Cortés were eclipsed by their Turkish contemporaries.

By turning from the contemplation of the Piri Re'is map to a perambulation of the palace which contains it, a vivid impression of the political nature of the Ottoman Empire can be conjured. The throne room is a pavilion, and many apartments are kiosks scattered through the grounds, like the tents of a nomad camp. The imperial stool is capacious enough for a sultan of the most morbid corpulence. For this was an empire which sustained memories of its nomadic origins through long centuries of sedentary solidity. In the warren of the harem, with its lavish alleys and secretive culs-de-sac, the ar-

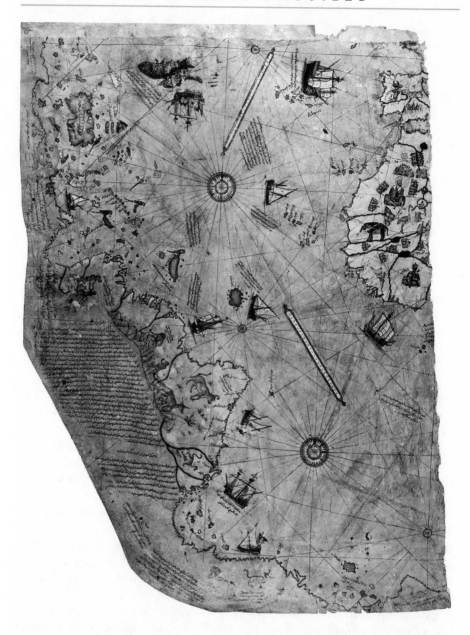

Despite their land-borne traditions, the Ottoman Turks adapted with speed and skill to the demands of sea warfare when their conquests reached the Mediterranean. If they were never able to make up for their limited access to the world's oceans and their late start in oceanic exploration, it was not for want of interest, as the global range of the geographical work of Piri Re²is in the early sixteenth century shows. The surviving portion of his world map of 1513 records Columbus's discoveries, with the aid of Spanish documents captured at sea and translations of the printed versions of Columbus's reports and probably those of Vespucci.

cane methods by which the empire was regulated can be sensed: here pillow talk was of politics, and women and eunuchs conspired to secure the succession for a potential patron from among the sultans' brood. In the gilded "cages" where, when parricide was out of fashion, unelevated princes were confined, a knocking at the door might be a summons to the throne or the rap of the executioner: Ibrahim I heard both and mistook each for the other. Access to a sultan's favoured womenfolk was an avenue of political influence, though this more often meant his mother than his wife or concubines. For much of the seventeenth century the effective chief executives of the state were queen-mothers who knew nothing firsthand of the world beyond the harem walls.

The harem could accommodate two thousand women, the stables four thousand horses. The scale of everything in the Topkapi Saray attests to the size of the empire and the effectiveness of Ottoman authority. The grounds of 700,000 square metres enclosed ten mosques, fourteen baths, and two hospitals. The kitchens were equipped to serve five thousand diners daily and ten thousand on holidays; the head cook had a corps of fifty sous-chefs, the chief confectioner thirty assistants and the chief taster a hundred subordinates. Wood for the kitchen fires was carried by one hundred carts. Daily deliveries were taken of dates, plums, and prunes from Egypt, honey from Romania or—for the sultan's own table—from Candia, oil from Coron and Medon, and butter from the Black Sea, packed in oxhides. In the early seventeenth century the daily intake of meat comprised 200 head of young mutton and 100 of lambs or kids in season, 330 brace of fowl, and 4 calves for the eunuchs' anemic veal. Like the products for the kitchens, the personnel of the palace came from all over the empire. The harem was an ethnic melting-pot, and the janissaries were drawn from infidel minorities, mainly in the European dominions, for re-education under arms. As well as a fortress-palace, the Topkapi Saray was a sanctum and a shrine. The bustle of the outer courts, where the kitchen noise competed with the clatter of the janissaries, contrasted with the inner silence of the sacral spaces where the sultan was cocooned, close to his prodigious collection of relics of the Prophet. Here, according to the traveller Tournefort in 1700, "even the horses seem to know where they are."

Though western visitors all went away heady with the exotic scents of palace life, the Ottoman state from the fifteenth to the seventeenth centuries could outstrip in efficiency and match for adaptability its western competitors, many of whose traditions it shared. When Mehmet II conquered Byzantium and occupied Constantinople, he saw his empire at one level as a continuation of that of Rome; in his portrait by Bellini, he displays the profile of a Renaissance prince who employed Italian humanists at his court. Other empires of nomadic origins failed when faced with the need to adapt to new military and naval technologies, whereas the Ottomans instantly became a naval power when they reached the Mediterranean shore. "Horses," they might have said, "is my occupation, but the ocean's my hobby." They could batter the walls of Byzantium or blow away the Safavid cavalry, thanks largely to their engineers' quick grasp of gunnery. The direction and balance of their conquests, which in the fifteenth century were heavily tilted towards the heart of Europe, gave them access to huge numbers of Christian subjects, reared in distant successor-states of Rome. In the sixteenth century, Turkish political thought kept pace with developments in western Christendom. The jurist Ebu us-Sud produced a justification of absolutism that revealed a thorough command of Roman law. Even allowing for the inevitable inefficiencies that arise when commands are transmitted by pre-industrial technologies over vast distances, the dominions of Murad IV, because they were conceived as a whole, were more tightly reined to the centre than those of his Habsburg counterpart Philip IV, who ruled multiple kingdoms with the aid of an up-to-date bureaucracy but without an overarching source of authority. And unlike Christian rulers anxious to extend their patronage, sultans had no need of a Reformation; though they had to be wary of the moral vigilance of their clerical establishment, they controlled its power structure themselves.

Beset as the Ottomans were by enemies on every side, only a state of extraordinary resilience could survive, only a state of extraordinary efficiency could expand. The armies of Suleiman the Magnificent (reigned 1520–66) had to shuttle back and forth across the empire in successive seasons to keep the Habsburgs intimidated and the Safavids at bay. In 1529, Suleiman was called from the siege of Vienna to the eastern front, while a Turkish flotilla raided Valencia. In 1538, in a single season, Ottoman forces conquered Moldavia, besieged Diu, and wrecked a Christian fleet in the Ionian Sea. Until Suleiman's death, the pace of conquest was prodigious: from Egypt, conquered in 1517 and cleverly exploited for huge annual fiscal surpluses which sustained campaigns elsewhere, he extended his protectorate and, in some sense, his authority over almost the entire southern shore of the Mediterranean, where the Barbarossa brothers—corsairs from Turkish Rumelia—organized a seaborne empire of war-galleys and pirate-havens. He conquered Iraq and most of the shores of the Red Sea, while exerting more informal lordship over much of the rest of Arabia. What began as a punitive expedition against Hungary ended as a conquest. The degree of imperial authority could hardly be uniform in the outlying parts of so extensive an empire, but it was felt everywhere. The younger Barbarossa, known as Khair el-Din, who ruled the remotest outposts on the Maghribi coast, was loosely called a "king," even in Turkish annals; he recruited ships and men with his own resources, won his victories by his own prowess, and sold Christian captives "at an onion a head." He was more a collaborator than a client of the Sultan's. In the Maghrib, legitimacy was established by the sword. Yet when Suleiman summoned him to Istanbul, he did not hesitate to obey.

If the pace of expansion was slower in subsequent reigns, it was because of diminishing returns on remoter conquests. But every generation brought a net gain of territory until the last years of the seventeenth century, and only the treacherous cleverness of hindsight has made historians anxious to antedate the "decline." When Austrian diplomats wrote off the "sick man of Europe" in 1721, the patient continued to defy the slavering surgeons for two hundred years more. In the interim, only dispensable extremities were amputated. What is remarkable about the Ottoman phenomenon is not the long sickness but the long survival, not the wasting disease but its robust resistance in an enduring frame.

The Colour of the Bear

In a popular English joke, a yokel troubled for the best route to a passing motorist's destination replies, "I don't rightly know, but if I was you I wouldn't start from here." For all the Turks' success in the lands and seas within their reach, to build a worldwide empire, Ottoman Turkey was the wrong place to start from. Access to the world's oceans was controlled by enemies through easily defensible straits. Piri Re'is could map the world from Istanbul in evident chagrin at the rich and easy pickings available to more favoured states. Much the same limitations afflicted the world's fastest-growing land empire of the period. When Sigmund von Herberstein visited the court of Muscovy as ambassador of the Reich in 1517, Russia was already an eye-catching giant of an empire, which during the previous century had outpaced every other state in the world in growth. As Herberstein tried to assess its true extent, its edges seemed to fade into fable; he doubted the reliability of his Russian itinerary, with its exotic description of the attributes of the River Ob—"such as men being dumb, dying and coming to life again, the Golden Old Woman, men of monstrous shape, and fishes having the appearance of men." Yet this icy version of Eldorado was far beyond the limits of the Russians' real control, and a grossly fat Tatar, taunted by his Russian captors, could still score debating points by affecting to assume that they had insufficient land to nourish them. By the time Herberstein returned in 1526 as envoy of Archduke Ferdinand of Austria, the Russians had embarked on a series of campaigns which would bring the territory of the most impressive Tatar state, the Khanate of Kazan, under their rule and reverse the terms of the joke.

By early in the second half of the century, the Volga had become a Russian river, and the entire route for the products of the north to the Caspian was under a single political authority. It was therefore remarkably fortuitous that in 1553, at the opposite end of the great Russian river system, on the shores of the White Sea, by the mouth of the Northern Dvina, a "discovery of the kingdom of Muscovy" should have been made by merchant venturers who were able to put the Volga valley in direct touch with their own native kingdom of England. Richard Chancellor was the navigator appointed to take an expedition from London to Cathay around the north of Russia by a putative route. His companion ships were lost in a storm, but according to his own account, "Master Chancellor held on his course towards that unknown part of the world, and sailed so far that he came at last to the place where he found no night at all, but a continual light and brightness of the sun shining clearly upon the huge and mighty sea. At length it pleased God to bring them into a certain great bay, whereinto they entered." The inhabitants received him almost as the natives of the Bahamas treated Columbus, caught between awe and fear, prostrating themselves and kissing his feet. This was every bit as much a new discovery as that of Columbus, for it was an exploitable route, previously unknown, between mutually useful economies. The growth of the Muscovite state progressively enhanced its importance and increased the scope of the English commerce that now began to approach Russia and Asia through the White Sea. Tsars entertained English merchants with personal embraces and dinners off gold plates, for they had opened the only outlet to the world's seas that Russia would have until the eighteenth century.

The existence of the new routes increased demand for northern products, especially the "very rare and precious skins" coveted by Master Chancellor. The hopeless project for the navigation of the Arctic drew eyes towards Siberia. An empire which spanned the land from the White Sea to the Caspian had every incentive to increase and extend its control towards the north and east. In 1555, Ivan IV began to call himself Lord of Siberia. From early in the 1570s he encouraged colonists beyond the Urals. In 1580 or 1581 the first campaign of conquest began, like so many of the great maritime conquests of the imperial powers of western Christendom at the time, as a private enterprise. It was funded and equipped by fur and salt merchants and manned by cossacks. The drawings—of more than a hundred years later—which illustrate one of the chronicles of the conquest show how it was done: by river barge and firearms, as the waterborne conquerors exchanged bullets for bow shots with the natives on the banks. The defenders in their turnip-shaped helms suggest the nature of the enemy. The first object of the conquest was not to vanquish the primitive Ostyaks and Samoyeds who ranged the tundra but to eliminate the only state that could rival Russia in the region, the Tatar khanate of Sibir which dominated the eastern tributaries of the Irtysh. Thus the conquest was sold as a crusade. On the chronicle's title-page, gospel texts are spread through the flatteringly overdrawn settlements of Siberia by rays from the eye of

In the Remezov Chronicle of 1700 the conquest of Siberia is seen as an evangelizing and civilising mission. The words over the title-page read, "From the beginning of time, the All-Seer . . . decreed for the gospels to be preached throughout Siberia to the ends of the universe and the limit of the mountains to the famous city of Tobolsk," which is flatteringly depicted at the bottom while rays from the gospel spread to twenty-one other towns. Among the legends inscribed around the eye of God is, "He will dwell in righteousness and towns will arise to the Lord." The hen is an evangelistic topos, "gathering chicks under her wing."

Christ. Tatar resistance was soon reduced to the level of guerrilla activity, but it was not finally crushed until 1598. Even then the sheer hostility of the environment impeded the Russian advance. The Pacific was reached at Okhotsk only in 1639, Cape Dezhnev—the furthest extremity of Siberia—by sea in 1648. The image of Siberia as a rich and strange new world was spread by scientific expeditions and commercial ventures. Peter the Great presented a pair of brown Siberian bears to the menagerie of the Dutch head of state. The accomplished marine painter Sieuwart van der Meulen mistook them in his search for models and over one of his arctic whaling scenes lowers a polar bear of the wrong colour. Bering's expedition of 1733 incorporated a scientific detachment which provided the world with more or less definitive images, in maps and sketches, engraved and printed.

Russia's reward for this long and painfully sustained enterprise was the only enduring empire of the early modern period. Russian Siberia has remained Russian, outlasting all the maritime empires of western powers and the land empires of the Ottomans and the Ching. It survived the breakup of tsardom and of the Soviet system. Its full potential has still not been realized, nor, in all probability, the extent of its hidden wealth uncovered. Yet

Sieuwart van der Meulen, *Dutch Arctic Whaling Scene*, 1699, with the Siberian brown bear, drawn from the pair given by Peter the Great and mistaken by the artist for a polar bear. The brown bears currently exhibited in Amsterdam Zoo are said to be descendants of the Tsar's gifts.

the conquest did not mark the climax of Russian expansion at the time; it was only a springboard to eighteenth-century imperialism in Alaska and along the Pacific shore of North America. On the western frontier of the empire in the eighteenth century, Russia made what seemed at the time more important gains, which gave access to the Baltic, at Swedish expense, early in the century, and to the Black Sea, at the Ottomans' cost, towards its end. In the same period, the Russian frontier leapfrogged the Pripet marshes, when Poland was partitioned between her powerful neighbours. When Russian expansion finally skidded to a halt in the early nineteenth century, it took the concerted diplomacy of all the other major powers to keep her out of the Mediterranean.

One measure of the breadth of Russian imperialism in the early modern age is the number of other expanding empires its frontiers had touched by the eighteenth century. It met China's in central Asia and at the Amur. In the 1680s the fort of Albazin was destroyed and rebuilt almost yearly as Russians and Chinese succeeded each other along a wavering frontier. West of the Tola, however, according to a Scots traveller early in the new century, "neither party thought it worth while to dispute about a few hundred miles of property." Russia's expansion met Turkey's in Bessarabia and the Black Sea, Persia's along the Caspian, Sweden's in the Baltic, Prussia's in Poland, Holland's in the northern whaling grounds, Spain's and Britain's in North America. Ironically, in 1812, when the Grande Armée was starving in Russia, Spaniards pityingly fed the Russians' own starving garrison in their furthest imperial outpost, a hundred kilometres north of San Francisco. With Britain, Russia disputed influence in central Asia and Afghanistan (where its sphere also approached that of the Mughals) and, briefly, rights in the Ionian Islands. At the very end of the period, the French revolutionary and Napoleonic wars, which took French troops to Moscow and Russian troops to Paris, even brought expanding Russia up against French imperialism. The only great empire of the period whose extremities remained remote from Russian outposts was Portugal's.

THE IMPOSSIBLE EMPIRES

In 1594 the commander of a little Portuguese fort on the mainland of Persia wrote an ill-destined report to his king. He began by complaining that his fort was of mud and had to be rebuilt annually after the rains. He went on to explain that his garrison consisted of seven Portuguese and twenty-five native mercenaries and that with these he had not only to defend his position but escort caravans bound for Hormuz, punish raiders and bandits, and keep the local satrap intimidated. Moreover, he was troubled by a shortage of munitions—not because of problems of supply of powder and shot, for he hardly aspired to such luxuries, but because of the irregular consignment of arrows for his men's bows. The catalogue of troubles ends with the worst of all: he could not guarantee his men's supplies of opium. An irresistible picture emerges of life in the farthest border-station of an impossible empire, where the reality of the defenders' predicament was too hopeless to face and where the morale of doomed heroes could only be sustained by doses of dope. A clinching irony makes the document tragic: the report never reached home. Victim of the fragile communications which held the Portuguese empire together, it was captured at sea by English interlopers and ended up docketed with other enemy intelligence in an archive in London.

No document brings home so clearly the tenuous nature of Portugal's world-enterprise. For most of its history it was an empire of outposts—of frontiers without hinterlands. Its memorials are the ruins or rebuildings of the forts and trading posts that clung to the extremities of the winds and sea lanes or to the points where these met continental trade-routes controlled by other hands. Where the Atlantic meets the Sahara, Arguim was the first, inaugurated in 1448 in the hope of drawing some of the Saharan gold trade west from Wadan. Elmina, the next great emporium to be opened, on the underside of the west African bulge, in 1482, was for its

"A sort of Camelot with Blacks": the fort of São Jorge da Mina, later called Elmina, founded in 1482 and grandly depicted nineteen years later on a map purchased in Lisbon by the Duke of Ferrara's agent, Alberto Cantino.

time and place an impressive affair, erected by a hundred workmen and depicted by early cartographers as a sort of Camelot with Blacks; the present edifice, however, is of largely Dutch construction, like Bertie Wooster's cow-creamer. It bears scars of eighteenth- and nineteenth-century wars between the Dutch, the British, and the Ashanti, in which the extruded Portuguese played no part. On the other side of the continent, the castellations of Mombasa or, at the furthest eastward reach of the empire, the backless façade of the Church of Saint Paul in Macao show how in the sixteenth century the Portuguese system of seaborne, seaboard imperialism was stretched to just short of breaking point. The seaboard remains are interspersed with seaborne wrecks. The blackest spot on the *Carreira da India,* the route back and forth that joined Lisbon to the Indian Ocean, was the deadly lee shore of the Transkei, where the frequency of shipwreck inspired a new genre of "tragico-maritime" Portuguese literature in the sixteenth and seventeenth centuries—tales, cautionary or inspiring, of ships that went down with their pepper-clogged pumps, and of survivors' treks

Jan van Linschoten's travels in the Portuguese trading places of the east were an intelligence-gathering mission which helped to launch Dutch overseas expansion. The engravings which illustrated the published versions were based on drawings he claimed to have made from life. Despite the obvious idealizations, the depiction here of the street life of Goa at the end of the sixteenth century is convincing in detail. Notice the business being recorded at the table of the public scribe and the merchants gathering around it, the unsuccessful pedlar of stuffs in European dress, the madam selling a concubine on the left, and that characteristic institution of Portuguese colonial life, the alms house, on the right.

overland to await rescue in Delagoa Bay. Reflected in hopeful eyes at home, this empire of tatters and patches was seamlessly perfect: on a globe which illuminates the title-page of a chronicle for a royal patron, flanked by armillary spheres and angel musicians, the empire covers part of North America and the Antilles as well as Brazil, and enfolds the Atlantic, stretching over an Africa and an Asia which are emblazoned with the royal arms.

The showpiece of the empire was Goa, the seat of the Viceroy's court of Portugal's *Estado da India*. When Saint Francis Xavier sailed into its harbour on 6 May 1542, it had been a Portuguese city for a little over thirty years and was still being reclothed in western fashion. In the foreground of the approach were gratifyingly exotic landscapes—palm-thatched native huts, rice fields, mango trees, and coconut groves—but as one came in on the western road, evidence appeared of an environment warped to Portuguese purposes: the arsenal and workshops, the shipyard by the beach of red sand, the long jetties supported on arches, the prolific shipping where carracks jostled with dhows. Then the city walls appeared, low enough to reveal the white houses and unplanned streets behind, which showed that this was an old settlement reclad, not a colonial foundation newly built on a rational plan. At the far end of the harbour were a fortified jetty and the customs house. Dominating everything, lining the skyline, were the churches: the chapel of Nossa Senhora da Piedade, announcing the town from far off; the white, spireless shrines of Nossa Senhora do Rosario and

Nossa Senhora do Monte on twin hills, framing the town; the spires of the Franciscan church and the bulk of the cathedral rising above the streets in the centre. This was substantially the view sketched by João de Castro in 1539, though some new building had been completed even since then. A close-up of the seething life of the streets two generations later is provided by the engravings which illustrated Jan van Linschoten's account of his service in the city, where tall stone houses form the backdrop to richly appointed vendors' stalls, approached by clients equipped for the tropics with parasols and palanquins.

Goa stayed Portuguese until the 1960s; the colonies that eventually took shape around outposts in Angola and Mozambique remained until the 1970s, adorning imperial posters in provincial sub–post offices that proclaimed Portugal "Not a Small Country." Macao, as I write, has still not reverted to China. These startling cases of longevity or arrested development make the Portuguese empire of the *Carreira* seem deceptively strong and stable. The frail reality, however, was exposed in the seventeenth century, when much of its trade and most of its forts fell to the first determined and sustained onslaught, mounted by Dutch interlopers and predators. In the interim it was expanded and sustained by the tolerance of host-communities in the hinterlands of Portuguese outposts and by the verve and nerve of a series of visionary viceroys, impractical men, unhampered by common sense, who made up in conviction and ruthlessness what they lacked in resources. Afonso de Albuquerque, who in campaigns at either end of the Indian Ocean connected up the ends of the network of the Estado da India between 1510 and 1515, trapping enough trade to make it viable, inherited Columbus's dream of conquering Jerusalem via the Orient. António Galvao initiated the evangelization of the Pacific at a time when only the sketchiest notion of the ocean's limits was available. It is often supposed that the Portuguese succeeded by terrorizing their hosts and destroying their opponents. It is true that the calculated display of force was often a useful gambit in initiating trade or seizing a toehold and that, at least in the Indian Ocean, the Portuguese showed repeatedly a reassuring naval advantage over regional opponents. The truth, however, is that the Portuguese were too thinly spread and too exposed to counter-attack to succeed by force; the self-romanticization of swashbuckling writers and the condemnations of moralists have given us an exaggerated impression of the role of violence in what was essentially a peaceful enterprise. The Portuguese slotted into existing patterns of trade, or augmented native societies' prospects of self-enrichment, by creating new routes (see Chapter 10). It was worthwhile for most of their hosts, most of the time, to allow them to retain their coastal conquests.

Like so many early-modern empires, the Portuguese got a second wind after seventeenth-century troubles. The seaboard empire of the Indian

The austere temple of Mammon and the sumptuous church of the apostle of poverty: the chaste exterior of the Stock Exchange of Oporto contrasted with the lavishly gilt decor of the church of São Francisco round the corner.

Though Aleijadinho's most admired work in Minas Gerais is at Nossa Senhora do Carmo, at Ouro Preto, his embittered, contorted style is at its most extreme in his last sculptures, a series of twelve prophets on the terrace of the church of Nosso Senhor do Bom Jesus de Matosinho, in Congonnas do Campo. The animation, emotion, and decorative detail displayed, for instance, in this portrayal of Ezekiel would have been impossible for the sculptor's crippled hands but for the soapstone of Minas Gerais, which is soft when freshly quarried and hardens on exposure to air.

Ocean was shattered, but in the next century Portugal developed a vast, rich domain to landward in its previously neglected outpost of Brazil. A claim in Brazil was staked as early as 1500, when an India-bound fleet found land in the course of a wide sweep into the South Atlantic for a westerly wind. Tentative exploitation—at first for logwood, casually harvested, and later, from the 1580s, for sugar, laboriously planted—created a coast-bound colony little more substantial than those of the Indian Ocean. The interior was largely abandoned to slavers and plunderers of Spanish bullion routes, until the gold and diamonds of the Matto Grosso alerted the metropolitan élite to its unexploited asset.

The effects can be measured in the depth of gilding which coats countless Portuguese baroque church walls. Oporto exhibits the full range of the metropolitan response, with beguiling irony. In the gloomy, cavernous interior of the Church of Sao Francisco, the layers of dust are penetrated, the layers of dark dispelled, by the gleam of an almost totally gilded interior, as if Midas had become a troglodyte and chosen it for his abode. Around the corner, the sparsely ornamented Stock Exchange was built by John Carr of York, with all the pedimented severity of northern classicism, under the patronage of a merchant class conscious of its imperial responsibilities. Thus the temple of Mammon displays Roman austerity, while the church of the apostle of poverty is smothered in the gleanings of wealth. The most startling counterpart to these monuments in Brazil is the lively, original rococo of the mulatto cripple, Aleijadinho, who carved his masterpieces outside the Church of Nossa Senhora do Carmo at the end of the century, with chisel tied to half-paralysed fingers.

One might almost say it became fashionable in the eighteenth century to found land empires far from home. The British did it in India; the French and the Dutch attempted it, with disastrous consequences, in North America and Java, respectively. Up to that time it was a trick only Castile had successfully performed. If Portugal's was an empire of the impossible—spread so far, from a home base so small and underpopulated—Castile's seems an empire of the inexplicable: unprecedented in its own time and, strictly speaking, unparalleled thereafter, for it was the only global empire of land and sea created with pre-industrial resources. The great French and British empires of the nineteenth century, for instance, which excelled it, were procured with the magic of modern technology: latitude-finding devices, anti-scorbutics, malarial suppressants, rifled breechloaders, gatlings, steam power, electric telegraphs, and the sort of tropical kit formerly sold to the newly graduated members of an imperial master-class in army and navy stores or Walters of Oxford. By the time even the earliest of those aids became available, the Spanish Empire had already unfolded to its fullest extent. By the 1770s it reached from Manila to Naples and from the Upper Missouri to Tierra del Fuego, without interruption except where the sea separated Spanish territories.

Visitors today, uninstructed in its glorious past, would never suppose that the Botanical Garden of Madrid was once, in a literal sense, the nursery of this unique empire. It resembles, rather, a well-kept municipal playground, the resort of courting couples, raucous children, and friendly neighbourhood cats. Its stocks of flowers are neat and copious, but unremarkable. In the half-century after its foundation in 1756, and in the generation after its establishment at its present site in 1781, it was one of the grand ornaments of the European Enlightenment. By the end of the century it formed the last link in a chain of gardens of acclimatization, in Manila, Lima, Mexico, and Orotava in the Canary Islands, which made it possible, at least in theory, to cull samples of the plant life of every climate the monarchy occupied and centralize them in a single place of research.

The Spanish crown was stung into starting the project by the criticisms of Linnaeus, who, in his great botanical compendium of 1736, had deplored the lack of scientific publications on the florilegia of Spain. The monarchy hired one of his disciples, Pehr Loefling, to ensure the collection was organized on Linnaean principles. He was sent to Venezuela to continue the work Spanish savants had begun of cataloguing and propagating the plants of the empire. Loefling died on the job, but his samples reached Spain and formed the kernel of the Botanical Garden's Americana. Thereafter, official commitment to the project was unwavering. In a work of 1811, the great naturalist Alexander von Humboldt praised Spain for spending more on botanical science than any other government in the world. Some idea of the scope and fruits of the labour of successive expeditions, of increasing cost and scope, can be obtained from dialogue with their ghosts and from inspection of their specimens in what survives of their gardens. But the publications which record their work provide a more vivid guide, together with the huge piles of meticulous drawings, still in manuscript, which were collected in the Botanical Garden's archive.

From Peru, for instance, a thousand coloured drawings and fifteen hundred written descriptions of plants arrived in 1783. The collection—eleven hundred more plates—of the leader of one expedition, who also helped to establish the Botanical Garden of Mexico, was almost lost when he fled with it to Switzerland during the Napoleonic War; when the Spanish government demanded their return in 1817, 120 ladies of Geneva made copies of the lot for the local Botanical Society to keep. Perhaps the most important collections were those of Hipólito Pavón, whose expedition to Chile and Peru of 1777–88 gave him the chance to indulge his personal passion— the study of the therapeutic properties of plants—and to produce the most comprehensive study of quinine yet attempted. Perhaps the most beautiful were those of Humboldt's vital collaborator in botany, José Celestino Mutis, who presided over scientific life in one of the heroic outposts of the civilized world at Bogotá from 1760 until his death in 1808. This is what imperialism at its best could mean in the early-modern world: to be able to cull the flowers of empire from an astonishing diversity of climes and make them bloom together in scientific proximity.

Subject-peoples proved less amenable than plants to the processes of centralization, transplantation, classification, and experimentation practised upon them by overambitious imperial governments. In the late eighteenth and nineteenth centuries all the big empires created in the early-modern period were to be destroyed or transformed. They were succeeded by new forms of imperialism, enforceable by industrial technology. The Spanish Empire almost disappeared in a series of convulsions which arrested the

The "snooty elegance" of the main square of Mexico City, painted by Cristóbal de Villal-pando, in 1695. The metropolitan air with which colonial cities were depicted and de-scribed is a clue to the ambitions and limitations of colonial mentalities, determined to ape Europe in a hostile environment. In 1526, the historian of Santo Domingo, Gonzalo Fernández de Oviedo, described it as "far ahead of all the towns I have seen." As early as 1554, Cervantes de Sálazar had extolled *Life in the Imperial and Loyal City of Mexico*, in a Latin dialogue, for its paved stone streets, grand portals, uniform houses, classical proportions, the "artistically made architraves" of the viceroy's palace, and the excel-lence of a university allegedly equal to any in the empire of Charles V.

growth of the Dutch Empire, obliterated the Mughals', shattered those of France and Britain in America, sheared those of the Ottomans, Russia, and Portugal, and reversed the expansion of China. When Columbus launched the Spanish overseas enterprise, he called his achievement "the conquest of what appears impossible." While it lasted, the empire seemed just that, typ-ified by the monumental cities, which defied hostile environments. Mexico City reproduced, at 7,350 feet, every amenity, every urbanity of an old-world metropolis. It had a university, a printing-press, and a cathedral long before Madrid. It complimented itself on the snooty elegance of its social rituals, meticulously painted, for instance, by Cristóbal de Villalpando in 1695. The still inhabited ruins of Antigua in Guatemala evince the breath-taking self-confidence of a society willing to build and rebuild under the volcano, with reckless expenditure on daring colonnades. There, in the eighteenth century, the nuns of Las Capuchinas could meditate with equal serenity in their earthquake-proof cloister or their lavatory-equipped cells.

THE HIGHWAY OF THE WORLD

The spread of imperial contagion had left pock-marks in some odd places. I do not mean the effects of smallpox—they belong in the next chapter—but, for instance, the unfilled breaches in the walls of Vijayanagar, the emptied treasure-chambers of the Temple of the Sun at Cuzco, the permanently depopulated villages of Khorchin, and the gaps in the picture galleries of Munich and Prague left by the passage of Swedish troops in the Thirty Years' War. Sweden may seem an unlikely place to be the metropolis of an empire. The examples of the Portuguese, the Castilians, and the Dutch show that a small, poor, peripheral, and unpopulous home base is no necessary disqualification, but to a twentieth-century reader it is the Swedish "image" that is likely to be unconvincing. Nowadays the nation's associations are with benevolent neutrality, anodyne social democracy, and complaisant sociologists of impeccable reputation. In the seventeenth century, however, it had its lost moment of imperial possibilities, when three rulers—Gustavus Adolphus, Queen Christina, and Charles XII—were able to profit from a recrudescence of energy unexampled since the Vikings or, as Swedes preferred to think, since their even remoter legendary ancestors, the Geats. Looking down on the world from their northern vantage point, they could now behold their potential oyster. Sweden's imperial achievement was the more remarkable because it happened during another century of "little ice age," which sent areas of glaciation creeping along the mountain valleys of northern Europe, smothered some fertile lands, penned seaports behind pickets of ice, and even occasionally provided ice-passages for Swedish troops across the Danish Baelts.

In common with other imperial peoples of the early-modern age, the Swedes had some medieval colonizing experience behind them. Their enterprise in Finland from the thirteenth—perhaps the twelfth—century was advertised as a crusade. It subjugated the agrarian Suomi and brought lands of the hunting Tavastians under the plough, reached Karelia, and disputed a frontier on the Neva with Russians before running out of steam. This tradition, such as it was, helped determine the direction of Swedish ambitions. When imperial expansion resumed under Gustavus Adolphus, it was backed by firearm technology and efficient battlefield organization to maximize its effects. The king's technical flair helped give the Swedes an advantage which their limited manpower could not confer. The range of the provenance of the artistic loot they accumulated in the Thirty Years' War—

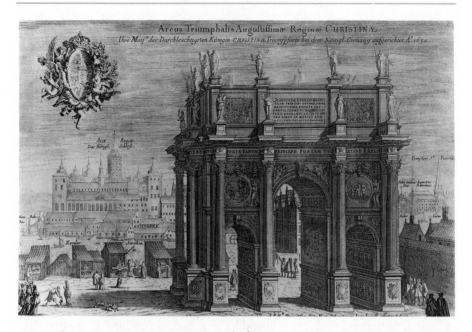

Queen Christina's coronation procession of 1650 approached the royal palace of Stockholm under a trompe l'oeil arch of wood and canvas, held together with gum and resin designed in imitation of the Arch of Constantine by a Parisian *arbiter elegantiae*. It was surmounted by twenty-four statues, of wood painted to look like stone, representing virtues. Like Constantine, Christina was to make the journey from the north to Rome and be seduced by Mediterranean culture and religion.

from Russia and Lithuania, Franconia and Alsace—suggests that their power to expand could have been pursued in any direction. The glorious art collections of the Bavarian elector and the emperor of the Reich disappeared comprehensively on northbound barges to enrich a palace where there had formerly been only one picture. With their share of the plunder, the Swedish nobility moved out of their rustic hovels—single-storeyed and thatch-roofed—into baroque palaces where they vied to learn French dances and cultivate suitable artistic tastes. For her coronation in 1650, Christina entered her palace through a wood-and-glue mock-up of the Arch of Constantine suitable to a twentieth-century motion picture production.

In practice, however, though they might go anywhere as the allies or mercenaries of others, Sweden's soldiers were used primarily to build up a Baltic empire. Charles XII frittered away his manpower fighting an interminable war against Russia. It was the wrong direction in which to head. Sweden, had her armies turned west to conquer the Atlantic seaboard of Scandinavia, might have employed her energies better participating in the seaborne imperialism of Europe's oceanside powers. Her merchants reached

Guinea and North America, and traded in South Africa and Canton in the seventeenth and eighteenth centuries; the Swedish West India Company even acquired a sugar-island of its own in Saint Barthélemy in the 1780s; but it was left to Denmark to sweep up the pickings let fall by others in Greenland, Saint Thomas, the Faroes, and Norway.

Sweden's brief imperial spasm is often cited, together with the mercantile and colonial precocity of the French, English, and Dutch, as evidence that the commonly perceived shift of initiative in favour of western Europe at the expense of other world civilizations was accompanied within Europe by a transference from the old, southern, Mediterranean powers towards the north. It is even used as evidence that Protestantism was superior to Catholicism as an imperialist faith and as proof that Protestants inherited the talents for capitalism that in the middle ages had been particularly attributed to Jews. Every part of this thesis seems to me misguided. If Europe's centre of gravity moved, it was not from the south to the north but from the Mediterranean to the Atlantic. The English, French, Dutch, and Danes participated in the benefits, but at a lower level and to a lesser extent than Castilians and Portuguese. The southerners' Atlantic empires started earlier, reached farther, lasted longer, and yielded better returns than those of the north. The preponderance of northern powers in nineteenth-century world struggles did not begin or even show signs of beginning nearly as early as is commonly supposed. It is a common failing of historians to overlook the speed with which change happens and to trace "origins" over meaninglessly long aeons. Nor, by the way, did northern capitalism—to judge from the religion of leading northern capitalists of the

A Scottish pistole of Darien Company gold, minted in 1701, and worth twelve pounds Scottish. The company's badge—a sun rising from the sea, an emblem of the western empire that was never won—can be seen under the portrait bust of William III.

time, generally ecumenical, latitudinarian, moderate, and unreceptive to predestinarianism—have much to do with any particular Christian tradition, certainly not a radical one. In making conquests, in the early-modern period, to be Catholic was no impediment, any more than to be Muslim or Russian Orthodox or Chinese.

What mattered was the geographical position of the potentially imperial societies. What the seaborne empires all had in common was their starting-place on the shores of the Atlantic. For the Atlantic, in the age of sail, was a highway that led not only to the immense, under-exploited, defenceless resource-base of the Americas but also to wind-systems that linked up with the rest of the world. The monsoonal regions of the Indian Ocean are cut off to the south by a belt of storms; to those approaching round the Cape of Good Hope it was worthwhile to weather those latitudes, whereas the native navigators who trafficked with the monsoons had no need or incentive to brave them. From China or Japan the vast and unprofitable expanses of the Pacific were not worth crossing on a regular basis. Via the Atlantic, however, the world became accessible to explorers who cracked the codes of the wind-system. The westerlies of the south Atlantic, discovered at the end of the fifteenth century, led to the Indian Ocean by a route opened by the Portuguese, and to the roaring forties, pioneered by the Dutch. The central Atlantic trade-wind route, discovered by Columbus, took Spaniards to Mexico, from where the shortest—indeed, under sail, for long the only viable—trans-Pacific routes in both directions could be operated.

Even Scotland, the smallest and poorest of the Atlantic-side European kingdoms of the period, tried to exploit these possibilities. In 1695, William Paterson, who invented the Bank of England, proposed a Scottish company that would establish a colony in central America to trade with the East Indies. Unable to share the burden with hostile English investors, Scotland subscribed half her available capital to the enterprise. It was a ludicrously optimistic scheme. There were some prospects for trade with Africa, which yielded the company's only profits and produced, in 1701, the wherewithal for the last gold coins struck by the Scottish mint. But the site at Darién for the intended "Emporium and Staple of Both Indies" was unhealthy and exposed to Spanish attack. Nearly all the 3,800 colonists perished of wounds, disease, or shipwreck during flight home. The company was bought out and killed off by an embarrassed English government. All that remains of the venture is the moat around the ill-fated fort, still used by Indian canoes, and the name Puerto Escocés on the map.

Chapter 8

THE TOUCH OF EMPIRE: COLONIZATION ON EARLY MODERN FRONTIERS

Lands So Wonderful—The Pioneer Mind—The Involuntary Colonists—
The Indigenous Victims—Touchpoints at the Rim of Empire

LANDS SO WONDERFUL

There is an adage that in Sinkiang even a beggar must ride on a donkey. "Otherwise," explained a truck driver in a story, "having eaten his fill in one village, he will starve to death in the next. . . . If you don't come west to Sinkiang, you will never realize how big your country is." The driver had started his own life on the frontier in 1960 as a migrant without papers. "Sinkiang had been living in my imagination through a song we sang in school: 'Sinkiang, O Land So Wonderful.' So to Sinkiang I decided to go." Labour was so short that the recruiters would overlook lack of documents "as long as you have all your limbs intact." A middle school diploma was enough to secure a teaching job.

It was the last phase of China's conquest of her wild west. The driver was a participant in a process of colonial expansion across the Gobi desert that began in the seventeenth century and took off in 1759, when the conquest of the area was completed. The beginnings of the transformation of Sinkiang occurred during an era of colonization worldwide, or at least world-wide-spread, that peopled the penumbras of the expanding empires of the early-modern period and lined with settlers the political frontiers, whose growth was followed in the previous chapter. Painstakingly procured and thinly spread, colonists barely began to extend the limits of the inhabited world; in some areas they were a destructive presence whose wars and diseases actually eroded the frontier. But at the edges of the empires to which they belonged, where they reached out to touch the outposts of other expanding peoples, they helped to mesh the world together.

When the scholar Ji Yun made his journey of exile into Sinkiang in 1769, he felt the awe of entering "another world" that Chinese commonly sensed beyond the Pass of Jiayuguan. From a distance, at first sight, he mistook the Turkestani Uighur merchants for women because of their long sheepskin coats of dark green and rosy purple. Yet he soon settled down on a frontier that was being civilized with remarkable rapidity. The hick-town capital of Urumchi had housed bookshops, selling classical texts, for two years when he arrived. He was able to send home to his wife seeds from the huge chrysanthemums and marigolds he grew in his own garden. The peaches planted by a sub-prefect and the peonies of a fellow-exile gave Urumchi scents and sights of home, though some of its flavours were elusive, particularly as pork—the Chinese celebratory meat—offended the local Muslims. Particoloured little Nang cakes became a shared local taste. Meanwhile, about as far to the west as the empire ever reached, the poppies at Ili were famed for their size, and in the same town an emancipated convict was able to make a fortune by opening a shop selling Kiangsu-style delicacies in 1788.

By the end of the century at least 200,000 Chinese immigrants had been drawn into Sinkiang by a mixture of selective deportation and inducements to voluntary settlers. Plenty of criminals and political undesirables were sent there by force, but for merchants the opportunities were so profitable that they were punished for wrongdoing by being sent back home. Bona fide migrants had their path sweetened by a government which reimbursed travel costs and offered loans for seeds, livestock, and housing, with a grant of four and a half acres of land per family and temporary exemption from tax. In some respects the economy was a continuation of that of the earlier, southerly frontier of Kweichow—a get-rich-quick economy based on logs floated out on the rivers and the products of mines: lead, copper, iron, silver, mercury, and gold. But in Sinkiang settlement concentrated on arable lands north of the Tien Shan, where market towns mushroomed into being. The lead and iron mines of Urumchi, in contrast to those of Kweichow, produced nothing for export; all the materials were absorbed by the frontier's own boom. Convicts worked the ores for base metals, but wage labour teased out the veins of copper and gold. Production depended on colonization. The natives, who could not "smell" the copper, left its exploitation to the Chinese.

The swelling population of the empire, which more than doubled during

The Tien Shan—the "Celestial Mountains" which screen the Takla Makan desert to the north—are one of the world's most formidable mountain barriers, ringing Sinkiang to the north and west: 1,800 miles long and up to 300 miles wide, they occupy nearly a quarter of the province. The highest peak is over 24,000 feet. The extraordinary environment the mountains enclose is made odder still by the deep depressions which punctuate the mountains: that of Turfan drops to more than 500 feet below sea level.

the eighteenth century, helped keep up similar colonial pressure on all fronts. The Manchu conquest of Szechuan had been exceptionally savage, eliminating—so it was said—three-quarters of the people and undoing the laborious medieval colonization described in Chapter One. Yet between 1667 and 1707 more than 1.5 million settlers had been lured by the promise of fiscal immunities. Here and on the south-east frontier the pressure of intensive new settlement provoked a cycle of conflicts and solutions ominously familiar to students of New World colonialism: rebellious aboriginal tribespeople were penned in reservations. Militarized agricultural colonies grew wheat, barley, peas, and corn while keeping the natives suborned. Schools were erected to bring Chinese language and values to the tribes. On the southern edges of the empire the only exception to the pattern was in Taiwan, where at first the Manchu government used the native deer-stalkers to repress the suspect immigrant population in an offshore province whose resistance to Manchu conquest had been strong. By the mid-eighteenth century, however, deer stocks were dwindling, and Chinese farmers were allowed to move in as tenants of the natives.

To the north of traditional China, in the borderlands of Mongolia and Manchuria, colonization proceeded on a different footing. The Manchus came to power in China convinced that their own heartlands had to be preserved as a reservoir of Manchu identity, where warriors, unsullied by Chinese ways, uncorrupted by Chinese contact, could continue to breed for the service of the dynasty. In the only schools in eighteenth-century Manchuria, the curriculum was limited to horsemanship, archery, and the Manchu language. Chinese immigration was, at different times, actively discouraged or peremptorily banned. Yet the Manchu were Sinicized and the frontier domesticated despite imperial policies. The dark, generous soils of a land reasonably close to the competitive, thickly settled world of northern China were an irresistible incentive.

From the point of view of local officials, the exploitability of illegal immigrants made them welcome. The earliest colonization had inevitably the flavour of contemporary Canada or far Siberia—a camp-life quality of roving communities of ginseng-diggers and *coureurs des bois*. Farmer pioneers, however, came not far behind. Under the Ming Dynasty, the stockade of the Manchurian Pale—the frontier loop around the Liao valley—was designed to keep Manchu out; under the Ch'ing, its purpose was to keep Chinese in. The distinctive character of unofficial colonial society was apparent in the unkempt look of the frontier town at Ninguta (northeast of Kirin, on the River Hurka), compared with the sedulous coiffure of neat Urumchi. In the generation after its foundation in 1660, only four hundred households dwelt inside Ninguta's collapsed wall of mud. There was "no person of leisure" and the exiles' womenfolk, "descendants of the rich and honourable families of China," slid barefoot down the icy hillside under the burden of water from the only well.

Yet even in this environment some metropolitan values triumphed, while others were overturned or blown away by the winds of change. Anyone with scholarly pretensions—let alone attainments—was prized in Ninguta. An exile's visitor in 1690 was impressed by the deference the natives accorded to the Chinese and the prosperity accumulated by settlers, compared with Manchu officers. The older merchants even "greeted the military governor as a younger brother." The hierarchies of home, in other words, persisted alongside new rankings evolved by the emerging society of the frontier.

From the point of view of the ruling dynasty, colonization of the frontier was too important to be left to the Chinese. In a reshuffling of tribal peoples, reminiscent of the frontier defence strategies of the late Roman Empire, the Ch'ing moved Mongol bands about like knights on a chessboard, shifting some between weak points along the borderlands, inducing others into the empire from outside. In an affecting ceremony in Peking in 1771, the Ch'ien-lung emperor welcomed back into the imperial fold the Khan Upasha of the Torghut Tatars, who had abandoned Russian suzerainty in the Volga valley to return to Dzungaria, the homeland they had left more than a century before. They had been wheedled back by long wooing, begun by a diplomatic mission of 1712 which had sensed the Torghuts' nostalgia. Meanwhile, the remaining natives of Dzungaria had been virtually wiped out in the course of the Chinese conquest, and the imperial government had tried to repeople the land from every quarter of the empire—from other nomads' grazing grounds as far as Manchuria itself, as well as with ethnic Chinese convicts, exiles, and peasant migrants. Cultivable steppe could accommodate large numbers when converted from nomadic to sedentary use, especially with the efficient new crops that were introduced. Maize, potatoes, and peanuts were made available through the transoceanic network of ecological exchange that was a by-product of early-modern imperialism.

THE PIONEER MIND

In 1595, in Callao, Peru, Don Álvaro de Mendaña and his formidable wife were recruiting in the streets while their ships made ready in the harbour. They were planning the colonization of the Solomon Islands, which had been discovered twenty-seven years before and unvisited since, ninety days' sail away on the far side of the Pacific Ocean. Peru was already, as far as its inhabitants knew, on the furthest rim of their world; its settlers were mostly first-generation pioneers; its own hinterland was undeveloped and beckoning; and yet the Mendañas were able to raise a following of three hundred prepared to venture across another ocean, to a land so far away that even the promoters of the enterprise had only a vague idea of how to find it. For the tragedy of their voyage was that its destination eluded the venturers, and most of them perished in search of it.

This mind-boggling wanderlust was the essential ingredient of the settler-societies of the early-modern world. Each new frontier was settled by the flotsam of the last. Many of the Spanish settlers of the Caribbean came from Extremadura and Andalusia, the last frontiers of Spain's own medieval history of "gigantic and uninterrupted" colonization; colonial societies in Mexico and central America were founded from the Caribbean. From those early mainland colonies came the vanguard of the conquerors of the Inca world, who in their turn launched colonial enterprises in Chile and Tucumán. Ferdinand Verbiest was shocked by the Chinese policy of destroying villages in Manchuria so that the people exported to the next frontier along the Amur would be unable to return home. The first band of Russian conquerors in Siberia was composed of cossack frontiersmen with recruits from an armed fur-trapping company including "men of Lithuania, foreigners, Tatars, and Russians." When John Winthrop's colonists arrived in Boston in 1630, they found the site already occupied by a pioneer who sold up and moved on. Later in the century, English North America was boosted by the arrival of emigrants from the West Indies. Deserters and runaways from Portugal's forts and factories left to "go native" in the interior of Africa, where in the seventeenth century some of them ended up ruling chiefdoms in and around the former lands of the enfeebled empire of Mwene Mutapa. Or else, in Asia, they formed the personnel of a "shadow empire" of traders operating beyond the political frontier and the reach of official treaties.

Neither economic determinism nor dialectical materialism can explain the range or nature of early-modern colonialism, because so much of it was produced by the unpredictable impulses of spirit. Something more than quantifiable exigencies or rational calculations must have driven or drawn participants in enterprises which led sometimes to fortune but more often, in this period, to disappointment or death. The importance of quirks of individual psychology, in what were world-remoulding but rarely numerous settler-groups, make generalization hazardous; restless implacability, however, does seem to have been a vital part of the pioneer profile. Ultimately, the only answer to Horace's question

> . . . *quid terras alio calentis*
> *sole mutamus?*

—which might be paraphrased, "Why do some of us bother with alien climes?"—is, "Because some of us are like that." A large proportion—in the New World, by far the larger part—of early-modern colonization was enforced under the sanctions of slavery; a great deal more was state-sponsored. But it all depended on the availability of pioneering manpower in home societies that were not always overpopulated or inhospitable. The move to the frontier was, as an English promoter of American colonization said in the 1640s, "the resolution of free spirits."

Yet it is still helpful to set the pioneers' aspirations against the background of their home societies. Those who started from the Iberian peninsula seem often to have been animated by a form of *folie de grandeur* transferred from the traditions of an urban, aristocratic, chivalric, and crusading world of values. When in 1606 Pedro Fernandes de Queiros, the self-styled new Columbus, thought he had discovered the Great Unknown Southern Continent, which had eluded earlier explorers for the simple reason that it was not there, his first acts were to found a city which he called New Jerusalem and to knight every member of his crew, down to his Black cooks. In 1499 the captain of the little island of São Tomé in the Gulf of Guinea, at a time when his complement of colonists amounted to fifty criminal exiles, announced his intention of building a city "which after it is finished will be one of the most magnificent works one could find" with a church bigger than Saint Peter's. Spanish archives are full of requests from disappointed conquistadores of undistinguished ancestry, petitioning the crown for the right to erect coats of arms over their doors or to wear a

The domination of Trujillo's main square by the statue of Pizarro is no more than just. The wealth reflected in the surrounding palaces and civic buildings came from Peru; a web of networks between returnees and emigrants ensured that Trujillo went on benefiting for generations and the conquest of the Incas was the biggest source of benefaction for a town whose local hinterland was poor.

sword in the street. This was an empire of Sancho Panza as well as of Don Quixote. A spell in America was a standard means of escape or attempted enrichment for the low-life heroes of Spanish picaresque novels. Sancho's pleas to the Don to make him "governor of some island" or "of some tiny bit of the sky" were realistic enough to be funny.

Trujillo in Extremadura is little bigger today than it was in the sixteenth century, when it supplied Peru with many of its conquerors and settlers. Here, in the mirror of a returnee society, colonists' hopes are reflected. The irregular square is dominated by the statue of Pizarro, who by conquering the Inca Empire made the whole town's fortune. Returnees' palaces are dotted around: the Pizarros' own, with submissive Incas at the cornerstones. Modestly tucked away, through an archway that leads under the town hall, is a sumptuous little Renaissance palazzo—perhaps the finest of the lot— built by a conquistador who came straight back with his loot from Atahualpa's ransom and bought himself the meaningless lordship of a deserted village. Of the 1,021 sixteenth-century immigrants to Peru, only sixty-two returned permanently, but they took over the town, buying up titles and offices, founding churches and a hospital, flinging rich dowries to the hungry marriage market. Those who stayed in Peru exerted influence from afar, shipping out their kinsmen or calling on the wealth of the New World to correct the balance of the old. In 1574, Inés de Cabañas from Lima sent for her brother "because it pains me to hear that you should be in anyone's service."

In some settings, French and English colonists could be influenced by the same sort of self-perceptions. Eighteenth-century Canada had its *bourgeois gentilshommes,* and James I thought colonization could be stimulated by the grant of titles such as Baronet of Nova Scotia. When the ill-fated Thomas Wentworth arrived to govern Ireland in 1633, he was disgusted by the pretensions of the New English settlers who, with parvenu relish for the opportunities of the frontier, had transformed themselves from penniless adventurers by the purchase of titles and the affectations of display. It was thought to be a good destination for "such younger brothers as were wont to be thrust into abbeys," and, indeed, the English upper classes do seem to have been exceptionally philoprogenitive in the late sixteenth and early seventeenth centuries. In Ireland, honours came cheap and offices abounded. The wife of one recipient of James I's patronage could not re-member the names of her husband's three bishoprics, "they are so strange, except one, which is Derry: I pray God it may make us all merry."

For would-be colonists who were economically motivated and nothing more, Ulster was close enough and remunerative enough to monopolize migrants from Great Britain. English colonial endeavour further afield needed the impetus of some greater cause, and it was fortunate for England that the era of her efforts coincided with Europe's age of religious wars. English America was peopled with the jetsam of confessional struggles. This did not necessarily mean that they were all religiously motivated. The 130 Englishmen who were massacred by Indians on an arm of the Amazon in 1618 were the disbanded garrisons of Dutch hostage towns. Many of the Germans, Dutch, and Scandinavians who boosted the meagre populations of Dutch and English colonies were prisoners taken or refugees expelled during the Thirty Years' War. Although English Catholic gentry founded Maryland as a refuge for their persecuted co-religionists, they were com-pelled to recruit mainly Protestant labour to serve them.

Yet there were many colonies that got all their energy from faith. In the Virginia Company's original charter, the investors' businesslike aims were uncorrupted by reference to religion, but their manpower was recruited en-tirely by preachers, who represented Virginia as Canaan and the company's mission as akin to that of Joshua in the land of the Perizzites. Winthrop's founders of Boston arrived there, they believed, "under the eyes of God." Increase Mather's horrifyingly satisfied account of the extermination of the Algonquin Indians is presented as proof of divine favour to "the English Is-rael." In the innumerable engravings of his treaty-making with the Indians, William Penn appears hatted, not out of disrespect for his treaty partners but as a symbol of Quaker identity. Sir Connor O'Brien surrendered the independent Irish colony on the Amazon to Portugal in 1629, in defiance of English demands, to spare the Indians from becoming heretics.

Many pioneers were obviously practising evasion; some were avoiding work—for that, as Hollanders in North America admitted in 1628, "they might as well have stayed at home." Others were avoiding their wives or complex matrimonial imbroglios, for bigamy was one of the commonest of colonial crimes. Others were avoiding the burdens of lords or masters at home, though many, especially in English colonies, were willing to buy their freedom by long spells under indenture in the plantations. Yet even these needed some source of commitment to emigration as a preferred means of escape. A sense of mission and an exalted self-perception were, from one point of view, rational strategies for coping with the demands of a hostile and barbarous environment. Winthrop's colony, for instance—though it was in one of the more salubrious locations—was tried through its first winter by dysentery, scurvy, bitter weather, storms, raging fires, and the depredations of wolves; by the end only about six hundred of the original thousand colonists were left. Yet Winthrop felt he had "never fared better in my life."

Similar fortitude was shown by the Austrian Lutheran colonists of Ebenezer, Georgia, in 1737, who, "carrying home the little corn that the worms have left them," declared "their contentment and satisfaction with what God has given." The profane equivalent of these impressive consolations can be tracked down in a corner of the present Mexican republic. When the Montejo family completed their laborious, costly conquest in Yucatán in the 1540s, they were well aware that they were the also-rans of the race for riches in Mexico, relegated to a peripheral province with no mineral wealth and no established cities, only dry limestone tablelands and artesian wells. Yet they could console themselves by building a palace in Mérida which still proclaims the success of their quest for self-ennoblement through great deeds. Athwart a façade smothered in Renaissance strapwork, helmed and armoured conquistadores tower over vanquished savages, while the inscription, without conscious irony, proclaims the conquering power of Love.

Clearly, to be a colonial pioneer in the early-modern world required not only good health and a robust frame but also a vivid imagination; an imagination like Alonso de Lugo's, which plotted out the main plaza of La Laguna but left it rough-hewn, with one side planted with vines; an imagination like that of Columbus, who expected to see his colony open trade with the oriental merchants, in their Aladdin hats, who appear in the engravings illustrating his first report; an imagination like Jan Coen's, who dreamed, with his monsoon-soaked, grog-sodden garrison in Indonesia in the 1620s, of capturing the whole trade of China by force; an imagination

A bank now occupies the Montejo palace in Mérida, built by the family of the founding conquistadors and endowed in self-praise with this lush mannerist facade. It was a typically dismal conquest, hard fought and destructive, which claimed perhaps 60,000 lives to war, dislocation, and imported disease before the population began to recover; but the legend over the door of the Palace reads, "Love Conquers All." Notice how the portrayal of the conquistadors and their victims continues to be influenced by the medieval iconography of knights and wild men: see p. 180.

like that of Bryan Edwards, who believed in the 1790s that breadfruit could turn Jamaica into a hive of industry.

One of the most useful resorts of the colonizing imagination was the ability to idealize an unpleasant, unpropitious or exacting environment. At the mouth of the Orinoco, Columbus supposed he was close to the site of the Garden of Eden, and Thomas More's *Utopia* was inspired by Vespucci's description of an adjoining coast. "Acadie" was adopted as the inappropriate name of a French colony frozen out of Canada in 1610 as an obvious orthographical slip. Religious and secular utopianism joined to direct ex-

"The city of Melilot in the Province of Remarin of the Kingdom of Apalache," Charles Rochefort's fantasy-capital in 1681, imagined to bolster his campaign for a Huguenot settlement in what is now Georgia. The prim settlement can be seen in the valley, marked C, founded by refugees in amity with the natives whose forbiddingly fortified temple looms on the mountain-top, looking suspiciously like a medieval European city. The wigged and robed figures in the foreground are examining a plant with marvellous prophylactic properties. This scene should be compared with later cases of utopianism in America, see p. 503.

pulsees from Boston, in strenuous pursuit of the millennium, towards New York or Rhode Island. Or it could make Mexico the imagined setting of a new apostolic age of the church. When disappointed by experience, colonial projectors transferred their hoped-for utopias to beyond the next horizon. Sixteenth-century explorers sought the fountain of eternal youth in Florida, the realm of the "White King" in the Chaco, the fabulous City of los Césares in Patagonia, the Seven Cities of Cíbola in the Arizona desert, and the kingdom of El Dorado in the jungles of Guyana. Charles Rochefort, a Huguenot promoter of colonization of the late seventeenth century, described and even illustrated the city of Melilot, capital of the imaginary kingdom of Apalache. In a fantastic landscape worthy of a Flemish primitive, lush with miraculously therapeutic plants, Huguenot pioneers hobnob with natives, crowned with oriental hats and wrapped in robes out of the court of Louis XIV, under a citadel dominated by a Temple of the Sun. The supposed location of this paradise was the present state of Georgia.

In 1747 the enlightened French naturalist Georges-Louis Buffon lost patience with the utopian tradition of depictions of the New World, which, it must be admitted, owed a great deal to the promotional purposes of the imperialist patrons of such literature. He sketched out an alternative America, a dystopia of adverse climates, dwarfish beasts, stunted plants, and degenerate men. Successors developed the attack, and the most virulent of them, Corneille De Pauw, who believed that the western hemisphere was irremediably brutalizing to anyone foolish enough to venture there, wrote the article on America in the supplement to the bible of the Enlightenment, the *Encyclopédie*. These views attracted disciples, stimulated controversy, and provoked scientific enquiry into the concept of noble savagery, to which we shall have to return in its place (see Chapter 15). But it left the pioneer spirit undaunted. Among those who replied to Buffon was Thomas Jefferson. He pointed out at a dinner in Paris that all the Americans present were taller than their French hosts, and compiled lists of American species to show that they were at least as big as those of Europe. Might the current European stereotype of American taste—warped by quantitative values— have its origin in that philosophical dinner party?

THE INVOLUNTARY COLONISTS

The first man to farm wheat in Mexico was Juan Garrido. This conquistador-companion of Cortés had seen Tenochtitlán submit, made an expedition to California, and was custodian for his fellow-citizens of the aqueduct of Chapultepec which supplied Mexico City with water. He was also Black.

He was not unique among people of his colour in establishing a position of responsibility in colonial society in Spanish America; he was, however, to say the least, highly exceptional in making his life there of his own accord. However strong the pioneer spirit in the metropolitan bases of early-modern empires, the home countries—except perhaps for China—were insufficiently well populated to supply the labour needs of their colonies themselves. In some areas because of the emptiness of the colonial lands; in others because of the intensive labour demands of successful cultigens; in others, because of demographic catastrophe, slaves became essential to the sustaining of colonial enterprise in the sixteenth and seventeenth centuries.

The only source which could supply them in adequate quantities was Africa. As a consequence—though Black slave labour remained important in parts of India and, in some contexts, in Europe and China, while a sig-

Dalzel's *History of Dahomey* of 1793 was a slaver's apologia and the engravings reflect the author's prejudices. The royal court of Dahomey is presented as a contemptible blend of despotism, daftness, and debauch. By contrast, the King of Dahomey who graces Duclos's *Histoire du costume* of 1780 is a dignified figure, a "society huntsman," in a mixture of European and Turkish dress above the lower legs which were bared by a royal taboo.

nificant new market was created in the seventeenth century by Dutch spice-planting enterprises in the East Indies—the biggest single transference of population in the course of early-modern colonization was from Africa to the Americas.

The slaves came—in varying degrees at different times—from Atlantic-side Africa, especially the west African bulge, the Congo, and Angola. Overwhelmingly, they were obtained by their Black vendors by war and raiding, which reached many hundreds of miles into the interior. Despite the breadth of the catchment area, it is hard to believe that the export of manpower on the scale demanded cannot seriously have affected the victim-societies. Most slave communities in America did not reproduce naturally, for reasons which are still little understood. Constant new imports were therefore required just to maintain labour levels. To augment economic activity substantial inputs were needed. Over 1.5 million Black slaves reached the New World by the end of the seventeenth century, and nearly 6 million more in the eighteenth. The numbers shipped out of Africa were somewhat larger, for the passage across the Atlantic was fatal to many. From the best available figures, something approaching 400,000 of those exported from Africa during the eighteenth century never reached America. The demographic and economic impact is hard to assess. For a time the Angola region seems to have developed a marked excess of females over males; on the fringe of Black slave-trading societies, some areas may have been depopulated. The political effects are glaring in some instances, however, and can be followed, for example, in the history of the rise of the kingdom of Dahomey.

Two images of Dahomey were projected to eighteenth-century Europe. In one engraving which illustrated a contemporary history, King Agaja (reigned 1708–40) affects the posture of a society huntsman's portrait, as he leans on one of the long muskets that constituted the basis of Dahomey's military might. He wears a white tricorne, a richly embroidered Turkish silk shirt, and a long robe with gathered sleeves like a western university doctor's gown. With his fine-bridged nose, butterfly lips, and Mediterranean complexion, he is as far removed as may be from a White stereotype of the Black; the naked savage peeps out of his attire only below the knee, where bare legs are shod in the sandals which were a privilege of royalty. This is the Agaja who was said by a French visitor to resemble Molière and who asked European traders to bring him a suit of armour. In a rival depiction of "the King of Dahomey's Levée," published by a slave-trader in 1793, a Stepin Fetchit in a feathered straw hat lolls drunkenly among his simpering, bare-breasted women, sucking at a long pipe while he receives the comic salutations of grovelling subjects. To an extraordinary degree, for White visitors, this realm combined extremes of civility and savagery. Guests dined with silver-handled forks on the dishes of their homelands, prepared by cooks "instructed in Europe or, at least, in the different forts," but had to approach the king's chamber over a path of skulls and were obliged to witness the human sacrifices with which the Dahomeyans celebrated royal funerals and annual commemorations of former kings.

Dahomey lived by war, and all other values were subordinated to a ferocious warrior-cult—"the insatiable thirst after blood, the barbarous vanity of being considered the scourge of mankind, the savage pomp of dwelling in a house garnished with skulls and stained with human gore." The kingdom arose in the interior of the present state of Benin in the early seventeenth century, founded, according to tradition, by exiles from the dynastic conflicts of the rich city-state of Allada. By the 1640s, Allada was already a magnet for European slave-traders; its port, with its nearby rival at Whydah, gave the area the name of Slave Coast. Around the middle of the century, Dahomey began to accumulate European muskets for slaves, obtained by raiding further north. The eighteen tributary communities subject to King Wegbeja (c. 1650–80) had grown to 209 in Agaja's time. His greatest prize was the coastland between the rivers Ouémé and Mono, conquered—he told European traders—to give him access to the outlets for slaves.

With a productive home territory in an area with a long tradition of middle-range commerce, Dahomey cannot be said to have depended on slaving, which may have accounted for no more than a fortieth of the economy. Slaving apologists frequently pointed out that Dahomeyan aggression was inspired by a less discriminating lust for conquest and that war captives were prized more as potential sacrifices than as slaves. It was claimed that slave-traders performed a work of mercy by redeeming their victims from certain death. Yet the facts are clear: Dahomey rose and fell with the rhythms of the slave trade, and the cult of ferocity coincided with the market for captives of war. The economics of the trade obliged its suppliers to be warriors or bandits. The prices Europeans paid made it worth raiding but not worth raising slaves. They were a form of livestock profitable only when rustled.

From Agaja's time, Dahomey was overshadowed by an even greater kidnapper-kingdom, the Oyo state, which had its heartland around the headwaters of the Ogun, south of the now-dessicated Moshi River. Just as Dahomey relied on the slave trade for its supply of muskets, so, indirectly, Oyo sold slaves to finance its own technology of warfare, which was based on the horse. Europeans brought a few horses as gifts, but the cavalry of Oyo was mounted on purchases from the savannah lands further north, paid with the profits of slaving. Their trade was so copious—especially after they captured Porto Novo, about 100 kilometres west of Lagos, and opened a direct route to the sea—that as well as raiding slaves they imported them from Hausa country. When Oyo attacked Dahomey to safeguard its own access to European posts, the mounted lancers proved superior to Dahomeyan musketeers. This seems a curious inversion of the trend in the rest of the world but is probably accounted for by the Dahomeyans' lack of bayonets—they preferred to close with axe or cutlass—and inexperience in shooting to kill. The object of their warfare, after all, was to take prisoners for slaves or sacrifice. They could never cope with horses: on ceremonial occasions their king had to be propped up in the saddle by flanking attendants on foot.

Further west, the history of Ashanti shows that state-building on an even greater scale was possible with resources other than slaves. Gold was the basis of Ashanti's spectacular rise from the 1680s to the dimensions of a great kingdom by the mid-eighteenth century, occupying 10,000 square miles of present-day Ghana and commanding a population of 750,000. The royal chest was said to be able to hold 400,000 ounces of gold. The throne was a golden stool said to have been called down from the sky. The court sheltered under parasols as big as trees. For the annual yam ceremony, the capital at Kumasi housed 100,000 people when the king's tributaries gathered with their retinues. More adaptable than Dahomey, Ashanti was able to use firepower to defeat mounted armies from the savannah, while coping with a variety of environments and fronts. Part of the armies' success was owed to outstanding intelligence and logistics, with fast runners operating along cleared roads. Even Ashanti, however, became increasingly reliant on slaving to supplement its riches in tributary gold. To the east of the gold coast, Akwamu was another substantial slave-stealing state, of a distinct character: its ruler enslaved large numbers of subjects by arranging trumped-up denunciations for adultery—a crime punishable by servitude in many African states—and by mobilizing gangs of "smart boys" to carry out abductions.

Our traditional images of the horrors of the middle passage and the degradation of life in slave communities derive from slaves' memoirs and abolitionist tracts. Sceptics have wondered whether shippers can have been so careless of their cargo as to tolerate—and even invite—heavy losses of life en route; yet evidence such as the often-reproduced deck-plan of the slaveship *Brookes* in 1783, where the slaves were stacked "like books on a shelf," or the tell-tale case of the Liverpool captain in 1781 who had 130 slaves thrown overboard for the insurance confirm the horror stories of the slaves who survived. Some shippers had more rational policies for the protection of their investments, but the extent of both inhumanity and inefficiency in the trade are enough to shock moralists and pragmatists alike.

At their destinations the slaves were usually the great majority of the colonial population: 45,000 to 8,000, for instance, in Jamaica in 1700. In 1553—when Blacks in Mexico were doing little more than domestic labour—the Viceroy was afraid that White settlers would be swamped. In much of the hemisphere, Blacks came to outnumber the indigenous popu-

Don Francisco Arove and his sons, leaders of the Cimarrón community of Esmeraldas in what is now Ecuador, who submitted to the Spanish crown by treaty in 1599. The painting was commissioned by a government official and judge in Quito, Juan del Barrio de Sepúlveda, for presentation to Philip III. The mixed culture of the republic of runaway slaves they headed is reflected in their exotic appearance: the black faces, the rich attire of Spanish noblemen, the costly ear and nose ornaments borrowed from native American tradition.

lation, too: in North America from Virginia southwards, in most of the West Indies, in some coastal areas of Central America and Venezuela, where plantation economies gradually grew up, and in the sugar lands of Guyana and Brazil. These disparities gave Blacks a potential power which was seldom realized; drawn from too many places and nations they were rarely able to adopt solidarity. When they did, the results could be such as were captured in a painting by Adrián Sánchez Galque of Quito in 1599. The three Black leaders of a Cimarrón community—a republic of runaway slaves in the interior of Peru—are shown richly robed and bejewelled, with extravagant ruffs at their collars and gold nose- and ear-ornaments of Indian workmanship, each dignified with the style of Don, the prefix of nobility. The canvas commemorates the treaty by which they rejoined the Spanish monarchy, retaining local power in their area for themselves. These—and there were many like them—were the spiritual forebears of Toussaint l'Ouverture and Nat Turner.

Even in tightly controlled plantations, slave communities were able to create autonomous institutions: in Jamaica, the British were never able to eliminate the secret power of the "Obeah-men" and "Myal men" whom they denounced as sorcerers, or curb the benches of elders which were the self-regulating judiciaries of the slaves. Though the issue is much debated by the specialists, the social orders of plantation life—the family structures, the regulation of relationships, the behavioural norms—seem, where the evidence has been studied in British North America, to have been evolved by the slaves themselves. Moreover, outside the reach of Spanish religious orders, most slaves were, at best, lightly evangelized until the nineteenth century. The result wherever slaves were congregated was that in the early-modern New World colonial society was more African than European.

North and west of the plantation world, Blacks were already an ethnic minority, composed of domestic servants, concubines, freedmen in unpopular occupations (especially at sea), or—if they came from the right part of Africa—technicians in the mining industry. Paradoxically, the fewer they were in relation to other colonists and natives, the easier for them to integrate or introduce offspring into the White and mixed-race élites. Under the Spanish and Portuguese crowns, at least, the descendants of free Blacks enjoyed equality with Whites before the law: spectacular cases of the exploitation of these rights include Dom Henrique Dias and Dom João Fernandes Vieira, ennobled for their services in Brazil's War of Divine Liberty against Dutch invaders from 1644 to 1654. Generally, however, administrative discrimination and knee-jerk racism kept them repressed.

Depictions of the life of Black societies in their American heyday range from the idyllic through the picturesque and the satirical to the horrific. But the crack of the cat can be heard between the lines even of William Beckford's idealized account of the Jamaica in which he was a slave-owner in 1788. In South America no area had a rosier reputation than eighteenth-century Minas Gerais for the degree of "liberty" attainable within a slave's condition; yet even here, slaves were free chiefly to obtain their gold quotas by extortion or prostitution. Whites preserved order by techniques of selective terror, exploitation of enmity between rival Black nations, and copious ministrations of rum and tobacco.

THE INDIGENOUS VICTIMS

His father took no notice; his mother professed her ease; yet this six-year-old was covered in pustules, with swollen arms, dry mouth, and an urgent fever. It was the spring of 1718 in Istanbul, where his parents had come on a mission from London. The boy's mother was Lady Mary Wortley Montague, and she had volunteered him as a guinea-pig in an experimental inoculation against smallpox.

The embassy physician described the technique of the "old Greek woman, who had practised in this way for many years," selected by Lady Mary to perform the operation, "so awkwardly by the shaking of her hand." She "put the child to so much torture with her blunt and rusty needle that I pitied his cries." Yet the experiment was a merciful success, and when London was threatened with an epidemic in 1721, Lady Mary repeated it on her daughter, converting society to the practice in consequence. Previous efforts by savants to introduce vaccination had been "regarded as virtuoso amusements"; now, however, Lady Mary fulfilled an ambition she had conceived as a patriotic duty, on seeing an inoculation performed at Adrianople, "to bring this useful invention into England."

It may seem ironic that one of the great benefits spread by modern and western science should have originated as a Turkish folk-remedy. A grimmer irony still is that smallpox had already played its part in the worst single demographic disaster ever to have befallen mankind: instead of increasing the population of the New World, in accordance with the known precedents, colonization had nearly destroyed it, and the great reserves of indigenous labour on which early colonial promoters had relied were, in many areas, enfeebled or annihilated. Epidemiology is a notoriously difficult subject to set in historical perspective because the tiny organisms which cause disease are often in a volatile state of evolution. It does seem, however, that smallpox, in a virulent form, fatal to the immune systems of unaccustomed populations, was among the earliest and most effective killers.

Demographers have been unable to produce convincing figures for the extent or duration of the collapse, but even at the most optimistic estimates the population of Hispaniola, where New World colonization began, was virtually wiped out, and those of the densely settled and exposed areas of Mesoamerica and the Andean area were reduced by more than 80 per cent before recovery began—very patchily and intermittently—in the 1570s; generalized, uniform recovery cannot be said to have started before the very late seventeenth century. Even the more spacious environments of North America bred diseases as devastating. The influenza introduced by Cartier on the Saint Lawrence in 1535 and the nameless plague spread by de Soto's exploration of the deep south in 1538 began a lamentable history in which almost every attempted European settlement infected the natives. The first English attempt to settle Virginia spread a quick-killing disease "so strange that they did not know anything about it or how to cure it." By the time a successful colony was initiated on the Chesapeake a generation later, the Indians were complaining of the destruction wrought in the meantime; depleted by periodic wars of mutual destruction between natives and settlers, the Chesapeake Indians had disappeared by the end of the seventeenth century. Meanwhile, in the tropics, "the breath of a Spaniard" was said to be enough to make an Indian die. The first Spanish navigators of the Amazon, in 1542, beheld stilt-raised cities on the banks, fed by the intensive cultivation of bitter manioc and by turtle-farming. The Spaniards did no more than pass through; by the time of the next visitors, a generation later, that populous world had disappeared. When a plague struck Bahia in 1563, José de Anchieta, the Jesuit "apostle of Brazil," could make no sense of symptoms which rotted the liver and produced a noxious pox, but he treated Indians by bleeding and peeling "part of their legs and almost all their feet, cutting off the corrupt skin with scissors." Even if we assume that native American societies were like the rest of the world and had suffered undocumented pestilence before, it seems incontestable that the diseases brought by colonization were new and the effects unprecedented.

For the natives, the colonial experience was unmitigated even by the most benevolent attitudes on the part of the colonial authorities. The Ch'ing favoured the natives of Taiwan, but that did not prevent the depletion of the deer herds. No empire has ever legislated so persistently or so ineffectually for the benefit of its victims as Spain's in the New World. In these cases the effects were no better than if the regimes had been hostile or indifferent, as in English and Portuguese America. It is impossible to imagine a system more benevolent—in paternalist fashion—than that of the Society of Jesus in the vast area of Brazil and Paraguay hived off by the Spanish crown from Spain's secular dominions for the sake of an experiment in the building of a Christian republic. A picture in a work of propaganda in praise of this enterprise, dated 1700, displays its millenarian inspiration: a jaguar lies down with a tapir and a little child leads them. Somehow this utopia had got mislaid. The baptismal records showed that by 1650, of the 150,000 people the Jesuits had baptized in their missions in the four most forward frontier provinces, only 40,000 survived the depredations of Portuguese slavers and the visitations of plague.

It was a long-lasting matter of debate in Spanish policy-making circles whether Indians should be spared contact with Spaniards or exposed to the improbably improving effects of Spanish "conversation." In practice, the Spanish habit of leaving a good deal of judicial, policy, and administrative functions to local communities produced a self-regulating Indian hinterland in most colonies, not unlike the effectively sovereign tribes who, as allies or expulsees, fringed the French and British colonies in North America. In very selective cases the Indians were left in no-go areas for lay Spaniards, under the protection of missions or in territories delegated to religious orders. The interpenetration which more usually prevailed, however, worked in the long run despite the friction and contagion which ensued. The improvement—economic and demographic—of the lot of Indian communities under the Spanish crown in the eighteenth century was checked in some areas by new fiscal demands in the last years of the century, but they lasted on the whole until independence, when power passed, in most of the former empire, to the mixed-race élite that was an enduring consequence of the intermingling of immigrants and Indians.

In the archives of Simancas, among the documents which chart the re-

On the title page of his life, the Jesuit missionary João de Almeida seems to contemplate England and Brazil as mission-fields on an equal footing. He was particularly praised for his asceticism, fasting, and the practice of mortification. A hair shirt is over his arm and a scourge for his own back in his hand, along with the crucifix.

vival and renewal of Spanish America in the eighteenth century, lies a curious artefact: an eight-pointed star, with a red cross at the centre, picked out in gold and silver braid, and surrounded by a garter bearing the words, *"Honi Soit Qui Mal y Pense."* The insignia of the garter had been presented to Esteban, chief of the Moscos Indians on the Mosquito coast of Guatemala, by British interlopers anxious to ingratiate themselves with the natives. The British withdrew in 1783, in accordance with the terms of the Peace of Versailles, and Esteban had handed his medal in as a sign of his continued fidelity to the British crown. Immigrants were procured from Asturias to replace the departing British. Similarly, at about the same time on every frontier, by attracting Indians to parleys and to purpose-built settlements, on principles similar to those applied by the Chinese in Dzungaria, or by repopulating deserted areas with Catholics recruited in the old world, or by profiting from the natural increase of population which was now at last general and substantial, the Spanish monarchy was making a new colonizing effort and consolidating its grasp at the edges of its empire. At last, imperialism was beginning to justify itself as a going concern even in areas remote from the superficial attractions—the gold, silver, and furs—of the

The insignia of the star and garter presented by British invaders to Esteban, Chief of the Moscos Indians on the Mosquito Coast of Guatemala and surrendered by him on the British withdrawal in 1783 as a pledge of loyalty to Spain.

early days, or the laborious enterprises—sugar, dyestuffs, tobacco—that had made costly extensions of the frontier seem worthwhile in the seventeenth century.

Historians' favourite question about early-modern colonization is whether it created "frontier" societies—removed from their metropolitan models by generation gaps and pioneer radicalism—or printing-block impressions of home, transplanted old-worlds equipped, to adapt a phrase of Braudel's, with cultural heavy baggage (see Chapter 22). The answer, of course, is that they were both. Moulded and changed by new challenges and opportunities, settler communities usually continued to tug at nostalgic images of a home they resolutely aped or unconsciously mirrored. An early Spanish imperial apologist conceived it as the colonists' obligation to rebuild New Spain in the image of the old. Hence Spaniards built arches in earthquake zones. Even Puritans, who really did consciously want to make something New of New England, set about it by planting and fencing.

Yet the results nearly always did mark fresh departures. There were more innovations than continuities. Colonies had to adapt to new environments and, in many cases, to the presence of new neighbours. Sectarian communities, democratic commonwealths, and plantation economies were all new to the English experience. A bureaucratic state, with little devolution to nobles and towns, was unprecedented in Spain. Slavery on the American scale had antecedents but no nearly exact prefiguration in the middle ages. The huge mixed-race populations of Spanish and Portuguese America, meticulously classified by administrators fascinated with the gradations of colour, had never had a chance to emerge before. To return to one image, the new lands were a distorting mirror, which reflected the old worlds without reproducing them. To hazard another, they were products of an alchemy wrought by their environments, which transmuted the people in them.

TOUCHPOINTS AT THE RIM OF EMPIRE

The New Worlds of the early-modern era had taken a long time to build and had exacted a terrible price. Just when the enterprise could be seen to have succeeded and might be expected to have earned praise, its critics were at their fiercest. Rousseau and Dr. Johnson, who agreed about little else, united in condemning the discovery of America as a disaster for mankind, which had degraded the noble savage and despoiled the environment. Since then, the pursuit of happiness with intent to destroy has become a theme tediously familiar in the historiography of America, reformulated in eco-speak in our own day. Yet when the galactic museum-keepers look back on it, they will reckon that until the nineteenth century the exploitation of most of the colonial frontiers had hardly begun. No

QUEBEC, *The Capital of* NEW-FRANCE, *a Bishoprick and Seat of the Soverain* COURT.

1. The Citadel. 2. the Castle.
3. Magazine. 4. y Recolets.
5. Ursulines. 6. Jesuits. 7.

7. Cathedral of Our Lady.
8. The Palace 9. y Seminary
10. The Hôtel Dieu.

11. S.' Charles River.
12. The Common Hospital.
13. The Hermitage of the Recolets.

14. The Bishop's H. se. 15. The Parish Church of the Lower Town.
16. The Upper Town v. y Lower Town.
18. The Platform & Battery of Cannon.
19. The Isle of Orleans. 20. Point Lieve.

Quebec engraved by Thomas Johnston of Boston as a propaganda piece in celebration of the British conquest in 1759. Advertised as based on "the latest and most authentic French original," it was in fact copied from an inset on a French map published forty years earlier. As usual, the image projected by colonialism on a wild frontier seems distorted by *folie de grandeur*. The grandiloquent terms of the title—"Capital, Bishopric and Sovereign Court"—match the splendour of the skyline with its many-storeyed buildings and huge spires and the river full of big ships.

recorded crossing of North America was made until 1793. Knowledge of the interior of the hemisphere was so ill recorded that patriots in Washington were unsure of the location of the Rockies and savants in Europe had to wait until Humboldt's voyage of 1800 to learn that the Amazon and the Orinoco were connected. Only a beginning had been made. Yet what had been achieved did matter.

Early-modern imperialism had crossed the chasms of the world, though it had not filled in its gaps. There were touchpoints of empire, at which the colonialisms of rival powers met in some of the most impenetrable places of the globe. In the late eighteenth century, Chinese and Japanese agents vied to collect tribute from chiefs in Sakhalin, where Russia was also beginning to cast covetous looks. In the depths of Brazil, Portuguese soldiers wiped out the last Jesuit missions in 1755, with Spanish connivance, in a murderous rationalization of a previously vague frontier. In 1759 tiny French and British armies settled the fate of Canada under the remote but respectable spires of Quebec. In 1762–63, the British occupied Spanish Manila, on the edge of the South China Sea, where the purely commercial maritime expansion of China had met the rival, armed imperialisms of Portugal, Holland, England, and Spain. In 1788 a French expedition anchored off Botany Bay to find that a British colonizing venture—using convict-exiles, in time-honoured fashion—had just beaten them to it. In 1790, Britain and Spain almost went to war over the confiscation of British ships, despatched from Sydney, at Nootka Sound. In 1796 the Spanish crown's glib Welsh agent, John Evans, persuaded the Mandan Indians of the Upper Missouri to hoist the Spanish flag, defining a new frontier with the British Empire, represented by the formerly French fort of La Souris, two weeks' march away. The hand of early-modern colonialism may have lain feebly on some of its lands, but it stretched long fingertips over the world.

Chapter 9

THE EMBRACE OF EVANGELIZATION: REFORM AND EXPANSION OF EARLY MODERN RELIGIONS

The Road to Bali—The Infidel Within—The Spiritual Conquests of Christendom—The Scales of Faith

THE ROAD TO BALI

Malacca is a mess. On the receding waterfront, which has left the fort high and dry, out of cannon-shot of the shore, ramshackle huts with tin roofs greet dirty coking-junks. Most of the modern town beyond is low-built in nothing better than concrete. The most monumental space, the Stadthuis square, seat of government during Dutch rule from 1641 to 1800, looks tawdry in its clashing shades of pink.

Before the Dutch, the Portuguese were here. A dignified trace of their presence is a fragment of their redoubtable fort of A Famosa; but this solid, sombre, heraldically emblazoned gateway is all that survived the dynamite of the last imperial masters, the British, who blew it up in 1801. The Chinese were here before them all, but, despite the continued presence of a large community of Chinese descent and the Chinese habit of ancestor-veneration, the cemetery founded by a Ming princess on China Hill is neglected and unkempt, its inscriptions, four or five hundred years old, fading into illegibility. Brighter reminders of Malacca's Chinese past can be seen in the Cheng Hoon temple downtown, which keeps—among brittle idols and pastel joss-sticks—a stela, left by Cheng Ho, marking Malacca's sudden ele-

The Stadthuis Square of Malacca, the town's "most monumental space," engraved a few years after the British took over from the Dutch. First erected in the mid–seventeenth century, the Stadthuis served the British as "treasury, post office, and government offices generally." In 1883 Isabella Bird described its "faded stateliness": its Dutch courtyard-garden, its forty-odd rooms, the great arched corridors, "and all manner of queer stair-cases and corners. Dutch tiling and angularities and conceits of all kinds abound." See K. Singh Sandha and P. Wheatley, eds., *Melaka*, ii(1983), 536-7.

vation in the early years of the fifteenth century from a fishing village to a kingdom and great emporium.

A fifteenth-century sultan is said to have claimed he could build gold and silver bridges, but they never materialized. Today, it is hard to imagine the glorious period in which such a boast might have sounded plausible. Yet at its height, according to one observer, four thousand foreign merchants were lodged in the city's billets and eighty-four languages could be heard on its streets. For "commerce between the different nations for a thousand leagues on every hand must come to Malacca." Here the state provided underground storage for merchants' wares from the Indian, China, and Java seas, while they waited for a wind, poised between the monsoonal systems that meet in the straits.

Though geography helped, the greatness of Malacca was made by Chinese. Their political clout gave the city power. Their commercial know-how gave it prosperity. According to the Malay Annals, the ruling dynasty descended from Alexander the Great, transformed into Rajah Iskandar; but the founder, Paramesvara, was down on his luck, driven from his own king-dom into lightly disguised banditry. In his search for a new stronghold, the swampy site of Malacca was made to seem auspicious by the toughness of a mousedeer which resisted his hounds. His fortune was really made when Cheng Ho brought him the seal and robes of kingship in 1409. He went to Peking to pay tribute in person and established a client-relationship with China that guaranteed his own enrichment. Chinese trade over the Indian Ocean demanded the creation of a secure emporium in the straits. Selection for this role enabled Malacca to throw off the overlordship of Siam and to begin a career of commercial empire-building of its own.

As China turned away from long-range imperialism, her tutelage slack-ened. More important in the long term were the links Malacca forged with a source of influence that was expanding from the west. A battered tomb-stone from Terengganu on the Gulf of Thailand suggests that Islam may have had royal adherents on the Malay peninsula in the early fourteenth century—at about the time of the earliest Islamic epigraphy of Sumatra. When Paramesvara wedded a Muslim Sumatran princess in 1414 and adopted her faith, the spread of Islam became linked to the growth of Malaccan power. Both took off together. The first Muslim ruler of Pahang, a substantial state in the interior of the peninsula, was a son of a sultan of Malacca. When he died in 1475, his grave was marked by a tombstone of a type imported in bulk from Cambay, with inscriptions almost completed, save for blanks left for inserting the name of the deceased. So many of these stones were stockpiled that when the Portuguese seized Malacca in 1511, they used them in building improved fortifications.

Islam was not spread by dynastic tentacles alone. That would have made it a religion of courts and élites, as it was in much of India, unlikely to strike popular roots or to endure future political change. In what were to become Malaysia and Indonesia, as in the other great arena of Islamic ex-pansion at the time, in Africa, the means of propagation were threefold: commerce, conscious missionary effort, and Holy War. Trade shunted living examples of Muslim devotion between cities and installed Muslims as port supervisors, customs officials, and agents to despotic monopolists. Mission-aries followed: scholars in search of patronage discharging the Muslim's obligation to proselytize on the way; spiritual athletes in search of exercise, anxious to challenge native shamans in contests of ascetic ostentation and supernatural power. In some areas, crucial contributions were made by the appeal of Sufis—Islamic mystics who could empathize with the sort of pop-ular animism and pantheism that "finds Him closer than the veins of one's neck." Sufis cannot be shown to have played a part in the conversion of Malacca, but they congregated there and, after the city fell to the Por-tuguese, fanned out through Java and Sumatra. In the late sixteenth and seventeenth centuries, Aceh in north-west Sumatra was pre-eminent in the incubation of Sufi missionaries; when they emerged or when their writings circulated, they disseminated fervent mysticism of sometimes dubious orthodoxy, like that of the millenarian Shams al-Din, who saw himself as a prophet of the Last Age and whose books were burned after his death in 1630.

Although trade and proselytization were far-reaching and insidious, the progress of Islam was steady rather than spectacular, patchy rather than systematic. The ruler of Macassar, in distant Celebes, was converted in 1603, but eastern Java enclosed a Hindu state until 1614. Even peaceful missionaries tended to see themselves as warriors of a sort, waging the "jihad of words." In the course of the seventeenth century, perhaps under the goad of competition from Christianity, the "jihad of the sword" grew in importance, and the extension of the frontier of Islam became increasingly de-

Photographed in 1958, Aya Raka Purnami, aged twelve, Princess of Bangli. Hinduism informs and fashions Balinese dances, which are usually enactments of sacred myths. The dance shown here, however, the *Legong Kraton* or Dance of Heavenly Nymphs of the Palace, tells a secular story of the twelfth or thirteenth century CE: the King of Lasen in East Java found a maiden lost in the forest and locked her in a house of stone. In order to possess her he went to war against her brother and fulfilled the oracles by dying in battle.

pendent on the aggression of sultans, especially from central Java. One spot in the island world, however, remained unconquerable. Bali, just east of Java, had an odd history and was uniquely equipped to resist.

Watching the traditional dancers, their sinuous allure, their forbidding formality, one can almost sense the suppleness and strength of the island's indigenous culture. The source of Bali's special power to remain peculiarly itself can be approached, in a landscape of green and grey, near Gunung Kawi, above the Pakrisan River, where rock shrines hewn from dark, damp stone are mildewed and beslimed with the muggy dankness that clots the atmosphere. In a royal burial chamber, austere outlines of a huge stone helmet frame a faceless black aperture; priestly cells are carved with gyrating ancestors of today's dancers. These graves were dug in the eleventh century, at the end of India's great era of cultural expansion, when Bali was one of the last overseas territories to be incorporated into the Hindu world. Most areas of south-east Asia, evangelized earlier, housed only small Hindu élites; in Bali, however, it is said the missionaries deliberately laid the basis of a profoundly popular religion, enjoining the erection of three temples in

As Buddhism and Islam spread in south-east Asia and the archipelagoes in what we think of as the late middle ages, an island of Hinduism remained unengulfed in Bali, where the rock tombs and priestly cells of Gunung Kawi—the "Mountain of the Poets"—were dug in the eleventh century: this was the last and most enduring frontier of India's great era of overseas cultural expansion.

every settlement. All over the island to this day, the triple nest of temples can be seen in every village; a profusion of shrines embellishes every home and public building. The persistence of Hinduism in Bali is reminiscent of parts of India where Muslim rule made little difference to traditional devotion. Wherever Hinduism was popularly rooted, Islam was unable to replace it.

As in south-east Asia, on Islam's farther front, in Africa, the retreat of paganism was undisturbed by the arrival of European interlopers in the early-modern period. Except in the coastal toeholds of Christendom, the dominance of Islam was ensured by the same combination of merchants, missionaries, and warmongers who spread the faith on the eastern fringes of the Indian Ocean. A fateful coup ensured that the major power of west Africa in the sixteenth century would be a militant Islamic state: Sonni Ali, the founder of the nascent empire of Songhay and architect of its role as the successor of Mali, was an imperfectly converted "magician king," denounced by imams for the pagan impurities of his personal religion, but the general who seized power on his death in 1493 was heartily committed to Islam. Muhammad Ture, upstart and usurper, needed legitimation by some venerable and numinous source of authority. A pilgrimage to Mecca made him hallowed; diplomacy en route gave him international recognition. Maghribi intellectuals were easily procured to qualify as holy his wars against the heirs of Sonni Ali and against neighbouring states.

In practice, however, religious pretexts rarely transformed warfare into a genuinely useful tool for spreading the faith. At least until the late eighteenth century, merchants and missionaries seem to have been far more effective. In about 1500, Timbuktu became the centre of custodians of Almoravid tradition (see Chapter 3); from this relatively southerly spot they were able to influence the frontier. Merchant clans or classes, like the Saharan Arabs known as Kunta, who made a habit of marrying the daughters of holy men, were the advanced guard of Islam. The Black wandering scholars known as the Toronkawa incited revivalism and jihad in Hausaland from the 1690s. Schools with an extraordinarily wide—almost humanistic—curriculum played a vital part in diffusing Islam among the Hausa, scattering pupils with a multiplying effect. A sheikh who died in 1655 was able, at school in Katsina, near the present border of Niger and Nigeria, to "taste to the full the Law, Koranic exegesis and prophetic tradition, grammar, syntax, philology, logic, study of grammatical particles and of the Name of God, Koranic recitation and the science of metre and rhyme." Paid by donations according to the pupils' wealth, the master of such a school sat on a pile of rugs and sheepskins before his niche of books, equipped with his tray of sand for tracing letters with his finger. He might have his brazier in winter and perhaps his spittoon for the husks of cola nut. Students' manuscripts survive, smothered in annotations from the teacher's commentary, which

Katsina: the Yandaka Gate in the city walls. As well as for the long tradition of learning alluded to in the text and still vigorous in modern times, Katsina was famous for its redoubtable defenses. By the end of the seventeenth century, when it was the hegemonic state of Hausaland, controlling the caravan routes to the north, Katsina had eight miles of walls which proved impregnable until the Fulani jihad overwhelmed them in 1807. Even then, the defenders held out until a lizard inside the town fetched fifty cowries and a vulture five hundred. See F. D. F. Daniel, *History of Katsina* (n.d. 1937?), p. 16.

was often in a native language. At the end of the course the student acquired a certificate attesting that he had received the teaching of a long pedigree of named scholars going back to Malik ibn Anas, the eighth-century codifier of Islamic law.

THE INFIDEL WITHIN

In 1559, Saint Teresa of Ávila, the exemplary mystic, had her first direct experience of Christ after listening to the preaching of a Franciscan lately returned from the New World to raise money for missions. "There is an Indies here in Castile," was the burden of the apparition's message, "also waiting to hear the gospel." For Saint Teresa, as for many godly reformers of the early-modern period—not just in Christendom but in the domains of other major faiths including Islam and Buddhism—the call of the infidel within was at least as urgent as the summons to evangelize more widely. Clerical élites everywhere encountered similar sources of dissatisfaction as they scanned the profane worlds with which they were surrounded. There were areas to which the doctrines of their respective faiths had barely penetrated, because of inhospitable terrain or shortage of trained manpower; there were rural communities where "popular" religion persisted, more actively concerned with survival in this world than salvation in another. There were growing towns, breeding rootless masses wrenched from the traditional rhythms, rites, and moral discipline of their former villages; there were educated laities craving a more active and fulfilling religion, a more personal relationship with God than established churches had provided for the relatively undemanding followers of earlier periods. Wherever the critical eye sought to detect them, there were practices—recreational, therapeutic, celebratory, commemorative, social, and sexual—which were condemned as survivals from a pagan past.

At one level, this was a conflict of two types of culture: élite culture seeking to remodel popular customs in its own image, not unlike the attempts of the BBC in Britain or Public Broadcasting in America to "improve" twentieth-century taste; at another, it was a meeting of two sources of accelerating demand: laymen's demand for more access to the mysteries of religion, and clerical demand for a more responsive congregation and a more committed flock. The parallel nature of élite attacks on vulgar traditions in contrasting environments is illustrated by stories juxtaposed in Peter Burke's brilliant book, *Popular Culture in Early Modern Europe*. Both date from the mid-seventeenth century. Here is a Catholic curé in a village outside Paris:

> I remember that being warned one feast day that wandering actors were playing a farce on a stage they had erected, I went there with some officers of the law. I climbed onto the stage, tore the mask from the face of the leading actor, took the fiddle away from the man who was playing and broke it, and made them come down from the stage, which I had the officers overturn.

He had a contemporary counterpart in the Russian Archpriest Avvakum, who was a conspicuous figure in the history of his country as a leader of moral reformers and liturgical conservatives:

> There came to my village dancing bears with drums and lutes, and I, though a miserable sinner, was zealous in Christ's service and I drove them out and I broke the buffoon's mask and the drums, and two great bears I took away—one I clubbed senseless but he revived and the other I let go in open country.

With scarcely greater urgency, with no livelier sense of duty, did any Puritan ever chop down a maypole or deface a Madonna or harry witches out of town. No New World missionary put more zeal into smashing an idol or burning a "sorcerer's" almanac.

Everywhere in the early modern world, reform of religion was inseparable from reform of manners. Ming intellectuals were as revolted by the irrational rituals of popular Buddhism and Taoism as they were by the
superstitious beliefs which were thought to underlie them. The Wahhabi
zealots of eighteenth-century Islam denounced impurities of belief but directed their violence against those who exhibited impure lives. The struggle
of the church against the "Old Believers" of seventeenth-century Russia was
inspired by a search for truth in texts purged of error by rigorous scholarship, but it got bogged down in conflicts about outward ceremonial forms.
The Spanish Inquisition was supposed to be a tribunal for the scrutiny of
faith but spent more of its time excoriating lax morals.

For most adherents of most systems, religion is not primarily a matter of
belief; if it were, it would probably not be such a potent force in human affairs, with the energy to create misery and happiness, war and peace. Few
people know the doctrines or dogmas of their faith, and fewer really care
about them, sharing the indifference of the headmaster in a play by Alan
Bennett who, when a catechumen asked about the Trinity, replied, "Trinity?
Three in One, One in Three. Any doubts about that—see your maths master." Religion shapes society not because it is about belief but because it is
about behaviour. Your religion is part of what you do, how you do it, and
whom you do it with.

For instance, within a few paces' walk of each other among the immacu-
late shops of a fashionable London boulevard are two huge old churches,
known respectively as the Brompton Oratory and Holy Trinity, Brompton.
In outward appearance they are similar—of respectively classic and gothic
monumentality, solid elegance, domed and pinnacled grandeur. Inside,
their layout, furnishings and appointments are closely comparable, though
the first, which is Catholic, has more Italianate splendour and more prolific
imagery than its Church of England sister. Their likeness is the result of
conscious emulation. In terms of class or education, of wealth or occupation, there is nothing to choose between their respective congregations:
both are well heeled, well spoken, well educated, drawn from business and
the professions, although Holy Trinity's is conspicuously the younger.
Though they belong to different Christian traditions, those few worshippers
who can give you a coherent account of the doctrinal issues between them
will play these down, stressing the common core of commitment to the divine and human Christ.

Yet the way they behave among themselves makes it impossible to imagine them ever combining. The atmospheres they contrive in worship are
echoed in their language of lips and body. Mass inside the Oratory is
hushed, reverent, adoring; numinous music makes it exquisite, and lachry-
mose art makes it pensive. By the decent obscurity of a learned language
its mystery is enhanced. When it is over, the congregation consort with re-

"It must be admitted," says the official guide to the London Oratory, "that there is some element of pastiche in recreating an Italian church interior in London." The ensemble is conceived as an unashamed assertion of universal Catholicism, without concessions to national taste. Pozzi's painting of 1925 shows the Oratorians' founder, St. Philip Neri, in one of the ecstasies which came on him while saying mass and which sometimes lasted so long that the altar-server would leave the sanctuary for two hours at a time and still be sure of returning in time to resume his duties. His vocation was typical of sixteenth-century evangelization. Like St. Teresa, he felt a call to be a missionary in "the Indies at home"—in his case, in Rome itself.

The Oratorians' tradition of splendid music in worship gave the world the art form known at the Oratorio; their London neighbours at the Church of Holy Trinity, Brompton, prefer the workaday spirituality of an ensemble of instruments and voices borrowed from jazz and pop and rigged to electric amplifiers. In contrast with the Oratory, the flags of St. George and the Union strike a self-consciously Anglocentric note. Though the interior is designed as a galleried hall—on a model which became normal in post-Reformation England and America—it is in its own way almost as grand as the Oratory, with an uncompromisingly glorious altarpiece of Christ in Majesty. The performers, though ostentatiously open-necked, all adopted an inhibitedly formal pose.

strained good humour and with mutual solicitude tempered by reserve. At Holy Trinity, however, the services are brisk and breezy, with a lot of cheerful noise and lusty congregational participation. Sermon and prayers are contrived in *actualisé* language, which makes the experience of church seem immediate and "relevant." The rite of coffee afterwards is celebrated with the same earnest cheeriness, the same hearty bonhomie. No member of either congregation could feel wholly comfortable with the other. The difference between them is not the difference between the churches of Rome and of England. The atmosphere of the Oratory is replicated nearby, for example, at the Anglican Saint Mary's, Bourne Street; that of Holy Trinity is imitated in many Catholic parishes. Worshippers align themselves—usually, given freedom of choice—with kindred spirits, not with schools of dogma.

In highly fissile religions, sectarian and doctrinal differences do overlap, and it is possible—indeed, it is traditional—to define the differences between Protestantism and Catholicism in confessional terms. Yet this sort of litmus often displays puzzlingly muted hues. The doctrine of salvation by faith alone is often said to be essential to Protestantism, but it was espoused in the sixteenth century by Catholics of unimpeachable stature, including Reginald Cardinal Pole, who presided over the burning of many English Protestants. Catholics are often thought to be distinguished by their literal-minded interpretation of the presence of Christ in the sacrifice of the Mass; yet it was Martin Luther, the initiator of the Reformation and founder of Protestantism, who carved or chalked, "This Is My Body" on the table at a conference with a fellow-reformer. Few adherents of either tradition understand the difference between Luther's eucharistic doctrine of "consubstantiation" and the reference to "transubstantiation" with which Catholics explain how the bread and wine they share are transformed into the real flesh and blood of Christ.

Other common ways of characterizing what sets Catholics and Protestants apart are almost equally unhelpful. Protestants—Quakers apart—defer to the authority of scripture, Catholics to the collective wisdom of the church; but this distinction, which looks fine in theory, crumbles in practice because the Bible is a palpably human document, full of obscurities and contradictions which cry out for interpretation. Protestant churches have developed institutions for authorizing interpretations and excluding heretics who do not accept them. Protestants pare down the sacramental life of their churches—the ritual channels by which grace is mediated to believers—and short-circuit the mediators and intercessors, in the form of priests and saints, who get between the individual and God. Yet the most devotionally effective way round the church to a direct experience of God is mysticism, in which the Catholic tradition is immensely richer than that of Protestantism, though American fundamentalism, with its glossolalia, snake handling, and personal testimony, is making every effort to catch up. All religions seem to need saints in some sense; Protestants have not extruded them from Christianity any more effectively than the Wahhabis, who attempted something similar, in Islam. Luther's peasant followers venerated cheap engravings of their master. Luther was driven from the church less for heresy than for arrogance; advocates of equally subversive doctrines have succeeded in squeezing them inside the elastic girdle of Catholicism by deferring to popes, councils, and inquisitors. Yet Catholics have no monopoly on humility.

We search for ways of explaining differences which still seem important to us and which mattered enough to our forebears to make them kill for them. The galactic museum-keepers of the future, however, will surely abandon the search in ennui, on the grounds that the distinctions of sect from sect, tradition from tradition, beheld from a distance, are insignificant. The movements we call the Reformation and the Counter-Reformation will be seen as two aspects of a single, powerful urge to evangelism which dominated the history of the planet in the early-modern period. Luther began with himself: a conviction of his own sinfulness and of his own redemption by unprompted grace. He looked out to the church, to his fellow-priests, religious, and teachers in need of reform. His great effect, however, was on the broad, lay public that he discovered late in the course of the history of his vocation, as he spread the gospel to parts of Christendom other publicists had been unable to reach—not just in under-evangelized places and classes but within individuals whose Christian awareness he enhanced. When Dürer thought the reformer had been kidnapped, "Oh, God," he exclaimed, "if Luther be dead, who will expound to us the Holy Gospel with such clearness?" His fellow-citizen of Nuremberg, Hans Sachs, the doyen of the Meistersinger, celebrated in doggerel the transforming impact of a teacher who had communicated directly a revelation of his own: "Luther spoke, and all was light."

Luther's revolution in Christian communication was shared with his fellow-reformers and with Catholic publicists who were equally evangelical in inspiration. One of Luther's most cutting weapons was the yellow-press language he crafted himself, vivid beyond crudity in images, for example, of the whore of Rome copulating with Antichrist or of the pope shitting lies. Apologists on the other side gave as good as they got. Movable type is always acknowledged to have been vital in spreading Luther's message, but the simpler technology of the woodcut was more important still in penetrating layers of society that were still barely literate. Protestants banned graven images from worship but knew their worth as propaganda. Considered from one point of view, the conflict of Reformation and Counter-Reformation was a woodcut war. In some areas the Protestant attempt to make Christianity accessible had been anticipated by the Roman church. Cardinal Cisneros, for instance, who was Grand Inquisitor of Spain from 1507, had cheap editions of vernacular devotion published to wean readers from the pulp fiction of the day.

Christian experience, directly communicated in simple language, is the subject of all the vast output of sixteenth-century evangelical publishing, from Protestant and Catholic presses alike. Often, the content is ideologically indifferent. Work by the late-sixteenth-century Franciscan Diego de Estella, who has never been surpassed as a popular homilist for the beauty of his language or the accuracy of his common touch, had—among many others—a Protestant English translator who explained in his preface that "though he be a papist," the friar's writings were full of wholesome devotion. In the second half of the sixteenth century, catechisms were the most prolific genre of printed books in western Christendom—a sure sign of a civilization gripped by mission fever.

The farther a message reaches, the more it gets modified on the way. In the course of the sixteenth and seventeenth centuries, Christianity was re-expressed, to and by different audiences around the world, in strange new ways. Jesuits in China accommodated it to Confucian rites of ancestor-veneration. Translated into the Quechua tongue, the "congregation of the saints" came out as the saints' "merriment." To the Tupinamba of Brazil, God was revealed under a name which in their language meant Thunder. An Indian artist in seventeenth-century Guatemala framed a picture of the Blessed Virgin with a rain-god mask. Just as Saint Paul gave Christianity a new flexibility when he first stretched its message to embrace gentiles, so the early-modern evangelists—often in the face of reluctance from church leaders—felt its clay quicken in their hands.

The demotic language in which Luther recast Christian verities had its parallel in European painting. When Matthias Grünewald died in Halle in 1528, his drawing of the Trinity was so subversive that he left it undisclosed to other eyes, in a nailed drawer: it took to extremes the artist's pious right of making God seem human. The Father was wizened and ugly, the Paraclete warty and chinless, the Son low-browed and unkempt. Yet by the last decade of the century, Caravaggio could bring the inhabitants of heaven down from the clouds with impunity and clothe them in the flesh and garb of ordinary men. His Supper at Emmaus is a meeting of peasants, his Last Supper a scene of tavern low-life. This was the last frontier of the evangelical impulse, where sacred images were redrawn to make them identifiable with the lowliest onlooker. It is a frontier being re-explored today in American tele-evangelism and the crudely demotic language of *The Living Bible*. In 1531 in the Valley of Mexico, an Indian boy called Juan Diego effected a similar transformation of a remote mystery into the imagery of his own world when, on the site of a pre-Christian deity's shrine, he gathered petals which impressed a miraculous portrait of the Virgin onto his cloak.

No artist has ever depicted so uncompromisingly human a God as that of Matthias Grünewald: his dying Christ is peculiarly twisted and agonized; his dead Christ decayingly dead—and no condition is less divine and more human than death. His drawing of the Trinity—a work so shocking that it had to be locked away in his lifetime—takes the habit to an extreme unprecedented then and unparalleled since: "the Father wizened and ugly, the Paraclete warty and chinless, the Son low-browed and unkempt." This is a God who shares our nature unreservedly.

Just as Europe's overseas expansion was preceded and accompanied by internal exploration, so the Christian age of worldwide missions was preceded and accompanied by evangelization at home. The mission to the infidel within—to the patches and imperfections inside Europe, and to the pagan in every man—was paralleled in other religions. In China, Chu-hung (1535–1615) and Te Ch'ing (1546–1623) re-presented Buddhism as a religion for practice "at home," filletting out the hieratic character that had formerly made it seem inaccessible and unintelligible to lay followers. Profanity was no bar, priestliness no magic; lay devotees could perform the same rituals at home as monks in a monastery. Laymen could worship Buddha, fast, adopt vegetarianism, and even don the saffron robe that signified a religious vocation. In the eighteenth century, P'eng Shao-sheng took the same line of reform further by explaining techniques of mental prayer, unprompted by images. In eighteenth-century Islam, two evangelical movements collided much as Protestantism and Catholicism had in western Europe: the Wahhabi reformists rekindled Islamic consciousness by fierce anti-clericalism, ferocious iconoclasm, immolations of heretics, and purgations of saints; a Sufi revival responded as the Catholic church had in Christendom by recommending the disciplined use of traditional mediants between God and man, including sacred places and people, mystical contemplation and meditation.

In seventeenth-century Russia and Japan, comparable movements began with the re-examination of ancient texts, much in the spirit of what in a western context would be called "humanism." In Japan, the Buddhist monk Keichu (1640–1701) was a pioneer in the recovery of authentic texts of the *Manyoshu,* poetic Shinto scriptures of the eighth century CE, which with the myths collectively known as the *Kojiki,* of comparable antiquity, constituted the basis of a born-again Shintoism, stripped of the accretions of intervening centuries and of influences from outside Japan. Among his successors in the following century, Matoori Norinaga (1730–1801) used the *Manyoshu* as Protestants used the gospels—to reconstruct a model of pristine purity and to denounce the degeneracy of the latter days. In eastern Christendom, reform and schism went together as they did in the west. In 1648 the clerical brotherhood known as the Zealots of Piety captured the Tsar's attention, and the vulgarities of popular culture were banished from court. Minstrelsy was banned as a presumed survival of paganism. Within twenty years the clergy who had triumphed together in championing these changes fell out among themselves over a further proposed stage of the elimination of impurities: the standardization of texts and the harmonization of rituals. The leader of one party was exiled in 1666, that of the other burned at the stake in 1681.

THE SPIRITUAL CONQUESTS OF CHRISTENDOM

In Chucuito, on the western shore of Lake Titicaca, in a commanding position high above the lake, an unpaved square used as a playground marks the site of an Inca ceremonial centre. On the east side, fragments of Inca masonry support an austere little bell tower, of two tall storeys, topped by a shallow dome. The adjoining structure, with a roof of corrugated iron, which would once have been thatched, looks from the side like an enormous barn. The entrance arch, however, betrays its true nature, with its frame of entablature and pilasters under the remains of a pediment cocked like a quizzical eyebrow. This is the church of Santo Domingo, the oldest church in the province, built for the Dominican mission in the early 1550s. On either side long arcades, now crumbling, are thrust out to define a vast atrium and to display with multiple arches the superior building technology of conquerors. All the churches the Dominicans built in this part of the world are essentially similar: bafflingly big, austerely classical, triumphs of defiance of the environment in what in its day was Christendom's farthest frontier.

Not only the size but also the number of these churches is baffling. In the second half of the sixteenth century there were never more than forty Dominicans in the province, yet they built a total of twenty-two churches in seven towns strung out along the lake, mobilizing by exhortation, without explicit threat of force, a workforce of up to two thousand Indians at a time.

From other frontiers in the early-modern period similarly spectacular evidence can still be seen of the reach and depth of the work of other orders of spiritual conquistadores. The Franciscan mission headquarters at Izamal

The church of Santo Domingo, Chucuito, crushing under the weight of its enormous stones the pagan deities who made its high lakeside site holy before the coming of Christianity. The churches of Chucuito are puzzlingly vast and numerous, perhaps because their Dominican builders needed a pretext to keep Indian labour from being forcibly exploited on secular projects.

Santa Barbara Mission, California: the garden still tended by the Franciscan community established by Junípero Serra in 1782. It was one of a string of ten missions stretching from San Francisco to San Diego founded to keep the wilderness, paganism, and rival empires—British and Russian—at bay. The garden was a vital source of sustenance; with only intermittent openings to the outside world, the missions were maintained by an autarchic economy with introduced crops.

in Yucatán was opened soon after the Dominicans reached Chucuito. Yellow stucco smothers the Maya masonry of which it is built, though fragments of carving still show in some of the paving-stones, under spires and arcades raised above the town on the towering base of a demolished pyramid. From start to finish of the history of mainland Spanish America the Franciscans continued to build in the same tradition. From 1769 to his death in 1784, Fray Junípero Serra extended the Spanish empire beyond its remotest garrisons, founding a string of missions along the coast of Upper California, where hot desert and cold ocean meet and an annual ship was the only contact with the rest of the civilized world. Here he converted the environment as well as its inhabitants, wrenching the Indians out of nomadism, wresting unaccustomed food crops from the soil. At Santa Barbara, where he settled Chumash gatherers in what has become one of the world's richest towns per capita, friars still dig the cloister-garden he planted and dust off the battered statues of Saint Michael and Saint Barbara that survive from the original pedimented façade. At the other end of the empire, where the Jesuits tended the frontier until their expulsion in 1768, dozens of ruins of mission churches have been restored in recent years. All are astonishing—none more so than in the impoverished railway town of San José de Chiquitos, in the remotest interior of Bolivia, where the forests the Jesuits knew have been slashed and burned to dry scrub. Four broad stone façades fill the east side of the square. Their false fronts contain the only dressed stone for many miles. Behind, the structures are wood and mud under tin roofs, still housing the madonnas and archangels the Jesuits left behind.

These were militant missionaries; though they came unarmed they were genuine conquerors. Eight or twelve Franciscans were for long stretches the only Spaniards holding some 200,000 Maya in submission in Yucatán; they went alone or in pairs to places where no White man had ever been, dethroned idols and challenged shamans to contests of holiness. Izamal in the third quarter of the sixteenth century housed one of the most violent of the lot. Fray Diego de Landa was an admirable missionary of unquestionable dedication who formed relationships of confidence with his flock, loved their land, and respected features of their culture; but in 1562, when he suspected that they had deceived him and continued to worship idols in secret, he unleashed a terrible inquisition in which 4,500 Indians were tortured—158 to death—in three months. A witness at the ensuing inquiry claimed that "the friars ordered great stones attached to their feet, and so they were left to hang for a space, and if they still did not admit to a greater quantity of idols, they were flogged as they hung there and had burning wax splashed on their bodies." The missionary had cracked under the strain of impossible responsibilities but was eventually exonerated and returned to Yucatán as bishop, after writing its praises in prison.

The Jesuits of Canada admired the Huron but could also be driven to uncharacteristically brutal excesses of correction. In Brazil, Paraguay, and Uruguay, where their duties encompassed secular government as well as the normal sphere of missionaries, they became the staff officers of Indian wars and ministers of defence against lay incursions. In 1637, the Jesuits in the Uruguay valley lost patience with the depredations of slavers in their mission lands and armed the Indians. The habit spread, and by the end of the decade mission Indians were beginning to win battles against invaders. Guaraní Indians armed with bamboo guns wrapped in oxhide were trained by Jesuit ex-soldiers and led by a talented native captain, Ignacio Abiaru. In a series of canoe-borne battles along the Acaragua River, Saint Francis Xavier "guided the balls." As well as spiritual conquests, the work of the religious orders created colonial ventures of a sort, "attracting" desert and forest Indians to agrarian settlements and sedentary lives.

The effectiveness of the "spiritual conquest" of the New World is a matter of debate. Sometimes external forces impeded it. The Puritan preacher John Eliot began an extraordinary campaign among the Algonquin Indians of New England in the second half of the sixteenth century. Inspired by the conviction that they were a lost tribe of Israel, he initiated the only Protestant enterprise in America comparable for energy and sincerity with the efforts of Catholic religious. His translations into Algonquian began with the catechism and ended with the complete Bible. His Christian communities led by native pastors in "praying towns" were exemplary essays in reorganizing Indian societies in the image of those of European colonists. They met twice on Sundays to "praise God in singing, in which many of them are excelling" and to hear a reading and sermon "after the manner of the English." Lay enemies doomed the experiment in wars of extermination as unremitting as those of the slavers against the Jesuits. Conflict ingrained the Indians' image as unassimilable heathen in most settlers' minds.

Not even the absence of external enemies could guarantee the missions' success. Diego de Landa's experience—alienated from his congregation by the discovery of "idols"—was common enough. The first Franciscan missions were inspired by an urgency which made them careless—a millenarian conviction that God's purpose in exposing so many million new souls to the light of the Gospel must be quickly accomplished in preparation for the imminent end of the world. Peter of Ghent, who launched the Franciscan mission in Mexico, performing fourteen thousand baptisms a day, had no time for sophisticated catechism classes. He aimed to get four points across: a single creator God of wisdom and goodness; the Blessed Virgin; the immortality of the soul; the devils and their temptations. Here, even Christ was included only by implication. If the Franciscans had really baptized, as they claimed, more than a million souls by 1541, most instruction can hardly have been much more detailed. The order's specialist colleges—

The steps of the church of Santo Tomás at Chichicastenango in the highlands of Guatemala, where Fray Francisco Jiménez, the editor of the *Popol Vuh*, the "sacred book" of the Quiché Maya, was parish priest. He suspected his flock of covert idolatry and the region has had a reputation for syncretic distortions of Christianity—and for survivals of outright paganism—ever since. The exotic rituals outside the church, where shamans perform censing ceremonies while members of orthodox fraternities in colourful indigenous uniforms perform counter-ceremonies with indistinguishable incense, create an atmosphere of sacred obnubilation. Other worshippers scatter flower-petals, rum, and candlewax.

like that of Santa Cruz de Tlatelolco (see Chapter 6) where young Aztec nobles became consummate Latinists and performed the Last Judgement as an
end-of-term play—had a disappointing impact and were gradually wound
up.

The church in frontier zones was always short-handed, and the quality of
the manpower was patchy. Frontiers attract the best and the worst. In
Manila in 1617 an Augustinian friar administered the sacrament of reconciliation to his inconveniently reformist superior while murdering him by
strangulation. In Lima in 1580 the mad Franciscan Fray Francisco de la Cruz
was interrupted in a plot to proclaim himself pope and emperor in a revolutionary creole theocracy. The case of Diego de Landa shows that Jekyll
and Hyde characters could coexist in a single friar. Even allowing for the
missionaries' saintly self-sacrifices and miraculous energy, they were too
few and too thinly spread to do more than make a start. The traditions they
established in the early days, in the Caribbean, New Spain, Central America,
and the Andean region, came from an unreformed old-world Catholicism,
before the Protestant threat and example had shaken up the standards of
evangelization and before the Council of Trent had set new benchmarks of
doctrinal purity and dogmatic awareness.

As the missionaries' own standards of expectation rose, they seemed
never to get much further with their flocks. It was like aiming at a receding
target. An early eighteenth-century parish priest such as Father Francisco
Jiménez in what is now Chichicastenango in the Guatemalan highlands
made the same complaints of the imperfections of his flock's grasp of their
faith as his predecessors uttered nearly two hundred years before. In a series of cases in early eighteenth-century Peru, "superstition" and demonic
delusion became the obsessive allegations of hag-ridden prosecutors, or
formulaic denunciations in neighbourly quarrels. In 1701 a good Christian
of twenty years' standing was gaoled on evidence solely of unorthodox
medical prognoses; in 1723 an Indian's private chapel containing six Christian images was condemned as a shell for idolatry; in 1710 a cause célèbre
arraigned Juan Básquez, a button-maker with a miraculous reputation in
the streets of Lima, who relied on Christian creeds, confessions, and acts of
contrition in a healing ministry which, he claimed, had been inspired by
Saint John: he made no charge for his services, but dissatisfied patients still
accused him of collusion with demons and worship of pagan gods.

Periodic official investigations into the church's penetration of the native
world throughout the colonial period have left plenty of evidence for anthropologists and sceptics who regard the post-conversion religion of the
Indians as pagan or "syncretic," in which the old ways were influenced but
unsupplanted. Yet the missionaries' labour was like that of a dog walking
on its hind legs. As Dr. Johnson said, one should not expect it to be well
done; it was remarkable enough to see it done at all. If Indian peoples'

Christianity remained idiosyncratic, that made it no worse than the religion of rural communities in Europe in the same period, where simple people still lived in worlds full of spirits and demons, and where natural forces were personified and placated. In Spain, where most of the missionaries came from, trials of rats and exorcisms of locusts were practised in the seventeenth century. Fray Benito Feijóo (1674–1764), the mouthpiece of the European enlightenment in Spain, found the countryside full of rivals to the clergy: diviners, phoney prophets, quack magicians, wise women, and folk-healers. In adding new layers to people's understanding of the transcendent, evangelization was more effective than in eradicating popular traditions, in the Old and New Worlds alike.

The Philippines, where Christianity was in direct competition with Islam, make a good place in which to test the effectiveness of the spiritual conquistadores. The islands lay at the farthest reach of both religions, at the ends of the uncoiled springs of Christian and Muslim expansion. The church started late and could apply some lessons learned in America: to instruct only in native languages, to take the task slowly, and to bring existing power-structures and social networks into the framework of parishes and confraternities. In the first five years of their mission the Augustinians baptized only about a hundred individuals. After twenty-five years, the number of missionaries had increased from 13 to 267, and the number of converts to 288,000. Some techniques were little changed. A Dominican flung the sacred treasures of his flock into a ditch through which the sewer flowed, to impress children with contempt for the old gods. "No-go areas" for laymen were set up where mission culture could thrive without adulteration from profane examples or friction with exploitative colonists; in general, the relatively low numbers of Spanish colonists put the Philippine church at an advantage compared with those of the New World. In the Philippines, the settler-population introduced under the colonial regime was overwhelmingly Chinese, who tended to keep to ghettos of their own.

Missionary work was backed by ethnographical enquiry: Fray Miguel de Talavera, a denizen of the islands from childhood, was the author of a still-fundamental source for students of the customs and language of the Tagalog, who have become the modern Philippines' most important ethnic group. As in China, compromise was accepted with ineradicable native rites, substituting for the sacrament of extreme unction a ceremony of invocation of Jesus, tolerating traditional sexual irregularities, and moderating some penances. Over the era of Spanish domination as a whole, the legacy was laid of the islands' vibrant and idiosyncratic Catholic culture today, which can be experienced by any visitor who samples the luridly dyed delicacies—bright blue bananas and red rice cakes—which round off the most characteristic of Filipino devotional exercises: daily dawn Mass throughout advent, which crams churches as first light seeps through the dense, rich atmosphere of the tropical night. The Philippines, in consequence, is the only Christian country in Asia. Only in Japan was the Christian message received with comparable popular enthusiasm in the same period; and there it was a victim of its own success, expunged by an alarmed official reaction of unsurpassed thoroughness.

Even in the Philippines, Christian success in direct competition with Islam was limited. In the Sulu Islands, where Muslim missionaries were active within reach of protection from a strong Islamic state in Brunei, the threat could be met by force of arms but not eradicated by preaching. In Mindanao, Muslim interlopers were not reported until the 1580s, when they came from the small but immeasurably rich spice-island sultanate of Ternate. Here the Christian mission had barely begun and could not be sustained. In the late sixteenth and early seventeenth centuries, it was all the Spanish garrisons of the main islands could do to keep at bay hotheads

Generally, in direct competition with Islam for the allegiance of souls, Christianity has a poor record of success except in the Philippines, where the distinctive Christmas customs include the dawn-mass breakfast described in the text and the habit, shown in this photograph taken in 1960, of hanging lanterns and palm-wreaths in star-shapes outside homes.

who ventured jihads against Luzon. It was enough to ensure that the eastern frontier between Islam and Christendom was drawn across the outer fringes of the Philippines and that the two great offshore archipelagoes of Asia—Indonesia and the Philippines, both fabulously rich, teemingly populous, and still of unfulfilled potential—would be divided accordingly. When it was suggested to Philip II of Spain that the islands were not worth the effort and that the Philippines should be abandoned on economic grounds, he replied that he would rather spend all the gold in his treasury than sacrifice one oratory where the name of Christ was praised.

THE SCALES OF FAITH

Until the latest incarnation, the only non-Tibetan Dalai lama was the fourth, Sümer Dayicing Qung Tayiji (1588–1616), the son of a Mongol prince. His training for his role took place in Mongolia, amid scholars engaged in the systematic translation of the vast corpus of Buddhist scriptures into Mongolian. The context which makes these extraordinary events intelligible is that of one of the most effective instances of missionary enterprise in the early modern world: the Lamaist mission to the Mongols, which began in 1576 and continued into the nineteenth century.

Tibetan monks had shown sporadic interest in converting the Mongols at least since the time of Kublai Khan. The decisive initiative of the 1570s, however, seems to have come from within Mongolia, from the court of Altan Khan (1530–1583), at Koke Khota, the Blue City he had founded as a fixed capital, to which the Chinese gave the name of Kui Hua, or Return to Civilization, near the present border between Inner and Outer Mongolia. The cultivation of Buddhism gave his khanate, which occupied a swath of territory along the northern loop of the Yellow River to the border of Tibet, an identity distinct from that of China's marchland client-states. Altan Khan had the form and habits of an inveterate pagan, who treated his gout by paddling his feet inside the cleft body of a human victim, but he founded monasteries, sent for scriptures to Peking, and commissioned translations on tablets of polished apple-wood. On the mountain slopes around his capital, shrines and hermitages pullulated.

Under his guidance and the stimulus of visits from the third Dalai lama in 1576 and 1586, at least the letter of Mongol laws and customs was reformed. Human sacrifices were forbidden and blood-sacrifices of all sorts curtailed. The Ongons—the idols of felt in which spirits reposed except when liberated by shamanistic rites—were ordered to be burned and replaced by the intimidating statue of Mahakala, the seven-armed protective lord of Lamaism. This was a reformation too radical to happen quickly. The new religion was at first an aristocratic indulgence, but over the next cen-

The Ongons or Ongghot, small figures of felt or wood kept in a box or—like these, dangling from a tent-pole in a felt pouch—are the most conspicuous distinctive feature of Mongolian shamanism, noticed by almost every recorded observer since the thirteenth century. The souls of the dead "become ongghot" with the power both to help and harm living people. Using the little images rather as mediums, the shaman, in his ecstasy, can tease—as it were—the presence and power of these spirits into himself. William of Rubruck thought they were analogous to the "household gods" of classical antiquity; Marco Polo mistook them for effigies of deities.

tury Buddhism spread down through society and out, north and east, across almost all the pagan Mongols' vast lands.

Young noblemen were inscribed into the priesthood to be ministers of the new faith and agents of its propagation. Altan Khan had a hundred ordained to celebrate the third Dalai lama's first visit. From the 1630s a mission organized by a West Mongol prince, Neyici Toyin (1557–1653), took Lamaism to the remotest east "among the ten banners of the Khorchin," building the great Yellow Temple in Mukden to house a Mahakala statue centuries old. He worked by "miracles" of healing, which may have been grounded in the superiority of Tibetan and Chinese medicine over the unscientific therapies of the shamans. Manchu political power reinforced the mission: the emperors perceived the Buddhist clergy as pacifiers and potential imperial agents. This had, in the eighteenth century, a warping effect on the nature of the mission, for imperial favour selected lamas from Tibet who were unlikely to evince atavistic Mongolian separatist sentiment. Like the Catholic missions in the New World, those of the Lamaists among the Buddhists were shadowed by political conquistadores and spearheaded by spiritual torchbearers vigorous in the selective use of violence. Neyici Toyin burned before his tent a pyre of Ongons four tent-frames high. The advice to missionaries on the farther front, among the Ili of the extreme west of Mongolia in the mid-seventeenth century, was, "Whoever among the people whom you see has worshipped Ongons, burn their Ongons and take their horses and sheep. For those who let the shamans and shamanesses perform fumigations, take horses. Fumigate the shamans and shamanesses however with dog dung." In practice, of course, the old gods did not altogether disappear, re-emerging as Buddhist deities, just as in Christian America they survived as saints and advocations of the Virgin. They continued to mediate between man and nature while the lamas did the same job between man and God. In parallel with official Islam, Christianity, and Buddhism, "popular" religions continued to confront the transcendent, or apparently transcendent, forces of this world.

Despite the shortcomings of the missionaries or of their congregations, the enormous extension of the frontiers of these three religions remains one of the most conspicuous features of the early-modern history of the world. Buddhism and Islam expanded into territories contiguous with their existing heartlands; by overleaping the Atlantic and Pacific oceans, Christianity registered a spectacular difference. Islam, however, had the advantage of expanding in the demographically vigorous worlds of Africa, Malaysia, and Indonesia; the millions won for Christianity in America were delusively promising shoots, quickly withered; the territories won for Buddhism were vast but sparsely populated.

In the long run, the sheer size of the New World counted for most. By Catholic domination of the American missions, the losses of followers and revenues inflicted on Rome by the Reformation in Europe were reduced to the proportions of a little local difficulty. The exclusion of Islam from the western hemisphere helped to ensure that when the Americas made up and exceeded their demographic lost ground in the eighteenth and nineteenth centuries, Muslim preponderance among world civilizations slipped. In the scales of faith, there is perhaps little to choose between religions, except to a partial eye. In the balance of resources, Christendom acquired, in the era of evangelization, vital extra weight.

Chapter 10

THE TANGLE OF TRADE: EARLY MODERN LONG-RANGE COMMERCE

Chinese Fortunes—Outcasts of the Islands—The Venice of the North—The Feast of the Dead—The Age of Irish Madeira

CHINESE FORTUNES

Except on Jewish holidays, a fat man could be found almost every working day in front of a particular Doric column in the south-east corner of the London Stock Exchange. From the close of the Napoleonic Wars until his death in 1836, Nathan Rothschild maintained his perch with what became proverbial regularity, except on the day in 1833 when a practical joker, by rising early, beat him to the spot and forced him to withdraw, flustered and blustering, to the benches at the back. Mr. Rothschild and his twin "pillar of the Exchange" became inseparable subjects of caricaturists' double portraits. When he died, Thomas Jones drew the column attended by his shadow.

Even more perhaps than his unprecedentedly rapid rise to fortune, what surprises about Rothschild is his success in English institutional life. To become a "pillar" of the economy and the government was an unpredictable achievement for this unmodified outsider, with his indecent corpulence, his blubbery lips, his reputedly coarse table manners, his German accent, his alien faith, and, from 1822, an Austrian title which he never dared use in English society. He succeeded by being necessary. As the London representative of the firm of M. A. Rothschild and Sons of Frankfurt, he was at the nerve-centre of a system of intelligence-gathering and information-

"The death of Mr. Nathan Rothschild," reported *The Times*, "is one of the most important events for the City, and perhaps for Europe, which has occurred for a very long time. His financial transactions pervaded the whole of the Continent. . . . No operations on an equally large scale existed in Europe previous to his time." His shade—clutching the four keys that symbolized his brothers—still seemed to the caricaturist Thomas Jones to haunt his usual pillar in the Stock Exchange.

exchange which enabled him to make unerring judgements in the money markets, to transfer gold and cash around Europe on an unrivalled scale, and, during the critical period in which the Rothschilds became "the richest folk in Europe," to preside over the financial business of the allied war effort against Napoleon. He handled money on the London market for the Prince of Hesse-Kassel and the King of Prussia—exploiting war conditions to cream huge earnings from delays in the transmission of funds. He raised the loans which kept Wellington's armies paid in the Iberian peninsula. He devised the routes by which British subsidies reached continental allies and the means by which British goods beat Napoleon's attempted blockade. When the war ended, he was the fixer who provided capital for projects of reconstruction. In 1825–26, his intervention was said to have halted the London banking crash single-handedly. Though his secretive methods make an assessment difficult, his capital has been plausibly estimated at over £28 million sterling in 1828.

No circumstances could be more propitious, no eye more discerning, for making a fortune in Europe in the early nineteenth century. The Americas could produce no rival, though the Astors demonstrated the wisdom of investments in Manhattan real estate. Yet the single richest private citizen in the world at the time was probably neither Rothschild nor any other business magnate of the west. The name of Wu Ping-Chien has been virtually forgotten. Even under his trading soubriquet of Howqua, he is today an obscure and neglected figure. His portrait pops up in some surprising places. Above the fireplace of the family room in one of the oldest mansions of Newport, Rhode Island, the King family—physicians, traders, and mariners—accorded pride of place in their house to an icon of this meagre, grave old man, with wispy beard and capacious robe. A version of the same portrait hangs in the East India Hall of Fame in Salem, among much larger pictures of local merchants who rose to prosperity in trade with the far east in the early nineteenth century. The private houses and public spaces of many New England merchant communities of his day are adorned with his image. They had much to thank him for: his power and generosity eased their entrée into the richest trade in the world at the time.

Howqua was born in 1769; Napoleon and Wellington were among his almost exact contemporaries. Like Rothschild, he benefited from a background of family business: the Wu formed the most extensive merchant clan of Canton and the Fukien coast. Until 1789 his father was one of the handful of merchants privileged to trade with the foreign factories of Canton, where the world clamoured for admittance at China's barely opened door. All the trade of Europeans and Americans in search of Chinese tea, silk, rhubarb, and porcelain was funnelled through this narrow aperture. The barbarians paid in silver, for they had no goods China would officially accept in bulk. Over this unique opportunity of enrichment, Howqua in effect presided from early in the new century until his death in 1843. Wealth attracts predators, and like other privileged Chinese traders, he had to endure persecution from the mandarin élite. His father was forced to surrender his trading privileges because of punitive taxation, which fell so heavily on the top traders of Canton that Howqua alone, of all of them, was able to maintain his solvency throughout his career. In 1831 his youngest son was imprisoned on charges of opium smuggling. His unease at the snobbery that merchants suffered beneath the mandarins' haughty nostrils is betrayed in his nickname, which means Great Official. In China such a title had a mocking resonance when applied to a mere merchant, however rich in informal power. His dearest wish was that his eldest son should join the ranks of the scholar-bureaucrats, but the boy disappointed him by failing the examinations.

The scale of his fortune and the nature of the reputation on which it was founded are apparent in the many stories of his honesty and generosity.

Howqua's portrait in the East India Hall of Fame, Salem, Massachusetts: his features are a common sight in New England, where merchants engaged in the China trade had good reason to be grateful for his favour. His career as a leading merchant of Canton in the late eighteenth and early nineteenth centuries, which brought him, by repute, the world's biggest fortune, coincided with a revolution in the terms of trade between China and the west. By the 1870s, China's favourable trade balance had disappeared.

"You and me Number One olo flen. You belong honest man," he said in his characteristic pidgin to an American trader whose promissary notes he tore up. When the price of quicksilver rose unexpectedly, he paid an American vendor at the new price. The loans he advanced to fellow-merchants were of up to a million silver dollars at a time, and his share of shipments was regularly three or four times higher than that of his colleagues. His public benefactions were enormous. In 1831 he repaired the Pearl River dikes at his own expense. He laid out millions for improved fortifications when war threatened, and after the Opium War of 1839–42 he subscribed 1,100,000 silver dollars towards the reparations.

During his career he saw the favourable balance of China's trade eroded by opium, smuggled into or forced onto the Chinese market from its place of production in India by British purveyors. Opium was the only foreign product, controlled by western suppliers, which Chinese consumers wanted or came to want in large quantities. As with the milder drug exported in exchange—the tea which was said to have been discovered by Buddha to banish sleep—its demand seems to have been led by supply. When China first banned the trade, in 1729, imports were reckoned at two hundred chests a year; one thousand chests were recorded in 1767; by the time the trade assumed war-threatening proportions at the end of the 1830s, over ten thousand chests a year were entering China. Its exclusion for the Chinese government was a matter both of economic interest and moral rectitude; for Britain the accessibility of the Chinese market was not only a material imperative but also a symbol of freedom of trade. When China tried actively to halt the imports, Britain invaded.

China's defeat was one of the great decisive events in the economic history of the world. Howqua's heirs were able to carry on lucrative business in traditional products, but they would never again be able to patronize the western barbarians: the dependency relation was permanently reversed. Howqua died in a shattered world, and his corpse was consigned to turned worms. The terms of trade, blighted by increased volumes of opium, were made worse still by relaxations of tariff barriers generally, which, as industrialization spread in the west, favoured western products of enhanced competitiveness. At the worst moment for China, new tax-farming policies made the Thai kingdom lose interest in trades which had favoured the merchants of the celestial empire. Within a generation, China's favourable trade balance narrowed almost to nothing and, in the 1870s, disappeared.

Since the remotest antiquity—persistently and urgently since the time of Marco Polo—the extreme orient had evoked images of enviable wealth for mankind's poor relations in the west. Western trade was the "barbarian" client of the Chinese Empire. Western silver drained eastwards, and when Europe grabbed the silver of America, the effect was to enrich China further. A seventeenth-century Jesuit observed that China had more riches in a street than Flanders or Italy had in a city. When Matteo Ricci redrew his Great Map of a Thousand Countries for the Chinese court, placing China in the middle, he was not only pandering to Chinese self-esteem but reflecting the facts of where the world's economic centre of gravity was located. Ac-

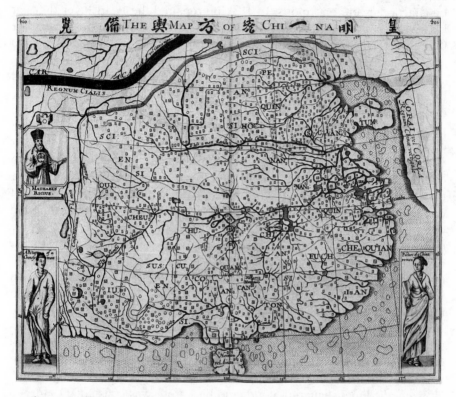

In 1601, the Chinese court annals reported, "the eunuch Ma Tang of Tien Ta'in brought to the court Li Ma-tou, a man from the western ocean, who had some rare gifts for the emperor. The emperor sent the eunuch's memorial to the Board of Rites, who replied, '. . . The images and paintings of the Lord of Heaven and of a virgin which Li Ma-tou offers as tribute are not of great value. He offers a purse in which he says there are the bones of immortals, as if the immortals, when they ascend to heaven, did not take their bones with them . . . He should be sent back to his own country.'" Nevertheless, it was the start of a fruitful relationship between Matteo Ricci and the Chinese court. He became esteemed in particular for his skill in western cartography. His map of China was the first drawn on a global projection. It was, however, based on a prototype by Chu Ssu-pen (see p. 137). The Gobi Desert appears as a black band, the Great Wall as a curling palisade. Ricci's portrait in a cartouche implies that he was the acknowledged author after whose work this engraving was made for Samuel Purchas's great compendium of travel literature. By his own account Ricci's world map caused a scandal: "When they saw the world so large and China appearing in so small a corner, the more ignorant made fun of the map."

cording to one of Louis XV's ministers, what eighteenth-century France needed was "an injection of Chinese spirit." From the same period a memorandum which survives in the Central State Archives in Moscow records a similar recommendation: the Russians should be like the Indians and Chinese who sell to the west for cash and "by the method adopted by these nations ever since they have been known to history" purchase almost nothing in return. Napoleon's conviction that he had to transfer his base of operations to the Orient because "it is in the east that great reputations are made" was founded not only on memories of Alexander and Genghis Khan but also, perhaps, on a rational calculation of where the potential initiative in his era lay.

The invasion of the Pacific and Indian oceans by European interlopers in the sixteenth and seventeenth centuries has left a false impression of the balance of economic power in the period. The presence of these parasites was a compliment, not a threat, to the wealth of the host-cultures. Most trade originated outside European empires; most was carried by native shippers and handled by native merchants. The trade of Canton could inflate the wealth of Howqua beyond the reach of western avarice because it was restricted to a few privileged individuals, but it was exceeded in total value by the commerce of the Fukien coast, where, on average in the seventeenth and eighteenth centuries, 200,000 tons of cargo annually included millions of silver rials and tropical imports from south-east Asia. In many colonial outposts, though the nominal authority, the garrisons and the guns were European—or at least under European officers—the real colonists, who settled the towns in large numbers and exploited the economy on a grand scale, were Chinese. Without a metropolitan government of their own committed to overseas imperialism, they used western empire-builders as surrogates to protect and promote their own activities.

No example is better than Batavia. Old Batavia—the predecessor of modern Djakarta, which encloses the site on the north coast of Java—bore the Roman name for Holland because it was the overseas capital of the commercial empire of the northern Netherlands in the seventeenth century. Dutch merchants were able to break into the spice trade suddenly and with devastating effect because by 1616 they had opened a new fast route across the Indian Ocean, sweeping far to the east from the Cape of Good Hope with the roaring forties, emerging in the Sunda Strait and outflanking Malacca. The site of Batavia was unpromising—low-lying and marshy—but its geographical position was ideal. Its conceiver and commander was Jan Pieterszoon Coen, a warrior by vocation for whom the town was at least as much a serviceable corsair-nest as an emporium of trade. The entrepreneurs of the colonial settlement, the creators of local and regional economies which sustained Batavia in its great days, were Coen's two principal Chinese collaborators, his dinner-host Su Ming-kang, vulgarly known as Bencon—the godfather-figure of the Chinese community—and the energetic labour broker called Jan Con.

The entrance to Bencon's country house was flanked with lanterns inscribed The Original Founder of the Region. In Chinese eyes, the Dutch role was ancillary. While Bencon was the town's fixer, Jan Con was its mover and doer. He was a Muslim artisan who came to Batavia in 1619 or 1620 in response to Coen's policy of attracting Chinese settlers. Nostalgia never left him, and when he became rich, he made regular remittances home in compensation for his unfilial departure. Most of the money went straight into the corrupt system of Chinese fiscal extortion. The initial source of his capital is unknown. He was first recorded, borrowing a grove of coconut trees, in August 1620 and within months was a leading local capitalist, farmer of the gambling tax. In 1624 he added the cattle tax farm to his stable. He seems to have owed his rise to Bencon's favour: in 1622 he kidnapped the man who had cuckolded the godfather and extorted compensation from him on Bencon's behalf. By the complaisance of the Dutch governor, who knew he depended on the goodwill of the local Chinese, neither career was impeded by this high-handed zeal for justice.

Jan Con's main business was importing labour, hiring coolies year by year in Fukien for the canals and defence-works that made Batavia first viable, then impregnable. He was also a comprador who advised the Dutch merchants on markets and, in his own right, a developer of the hinterland of the colony where he started sugar plantations and harvested lumber. His empire expanded to include saltpanning and the minting of lead coins, which gave Batavia a brief and rickety boom in the 1630s. But he was already over-extended, kept going only by the perpetually renewable commission to build and extend the defences. By the time of his death in 1639 he was broke—defeated by a combination of poor sugar yields, unrecoverably high costs in salt production, and the devastating policy by Batavia's English competitors of dumping lead coins. The authorities had not even suspected his plight. His Dutch creditors lost fortunes.

The Dutch never fully trusted Chinese entrepreneurs again. But the Chinese character of the colony was already indelibly printed. It was part of what in the twentieth century would be called an "informal empire" in which a local source of authority—in this case Dutch—shouldered political responsibility while China creamed off the profits in the form of remittances home, trading surpluses and returns on investment. The Chinese community grew, especially when the mainland government eased restrictions on overseas migration in 1684; in the eighteenth century, when the general population fell, Chinese numbers went on rising. The Chinese shipping in the harbour normally outnumbered that of any other country by at least two and a half to one.

Meanwhile, Batavia was being destroyed by ecological change. Over-exploitation of the hinterland for sugar consumed the forest, poisoned the water, and transformed the city—in contemporary perceptions, between the late seventeenth and late eighteenth centuries—from "the best town in the world" to a graveyard, protected from attack only by its reputation for unhealthiness. While Batavia remained great, the Dutch depended on Chinese trade and labour; only in decline could they afford to lose patience with their collaborators. The brutality of the massacre of 1740 in which perhaps ten thousand Chinese died was recalled with shame by participants such as the apprentice carpenter Georg Schwarz, who took advantage of the chaos to steal his Chinese neighbour's fat pig. "When my boss, the master-carpenter, saw this, he slapped me and told me to kill the Chinese first and then to plunder. I therefore took a rice-pounder and with it beat to death my neighbour with whom I had so often drunk and dined."

In the nominally Spanish Philippines, a series of similar massacres—occasionally commuted, in the Spanish style, to mere expulsions—was the result of comparable Chinese preponderance in the commerce and, to some extent, the production of those islands. Some Filipino cities have a Spanish air, just as Old Batavia had the neat streets, steep roofs, and bulbous pediments of old Holland. In Manila the swags and curlicues that decorate the

This part of the fort of Santiago, Manila, now houses a popular theatre. St. James the Moor-Slayer appears over the gate: this turned out to be an appropriate image when the Philippines became a frontier of conflict between Islam and Christendom (see p. 305). The site, by the muddy mouth of the Pasig River, was the location of the pre-Hispanic stockade; but the fort's reputation in colonial times was rather as a prison, where the dungeons flooded at low tide and José Rizal, awaiting execution, wrote his valedictory poem, *"Mi último adios."* Notice the squat conquistador carved in indigenous style on the pilaster furthest to the right.

sanctuary of the Church of San Agustín have survived nearly four centuries of earth tremors; the heavily fortified angles of the polygonal fort of Santiago enclose memorials of Spanish rule, from armorially stamped gun barrels to the yellowing collars of José Rizal, preserved like saintly relics of the hero of Filipino nationalism.

The élite in colonial days vaunted the Spanish character of their islands and perhaps really saw no other. In an elaborate allegory illustrating commercial theses defended in 1759 in one of the archipelago's two universities, the Philippines are shown as the pedestal on which the worldwide Spanish monarchy is supported. Yet, in reality, the islands nearly always represented a net loss to the imperial treasury. Though at intervals in the eighteenth century a tenuous link was attempted directly with Spain, around Cape Horn, the only effective and regular trade of the Philippines

"Striking is the correspondence of the feet of this symbolic figure of the Hispanic World, which are these Philippine Islands . . . with the feet of the chaste Judith. For as that which most ravished the soul of Holophernes . . . were Judith's sandals, so Lucifer is most terrified by these islands, as the sandals of the Hispanic World." The implicit message of Vicente de Memije's explanation of his allegorical figure of the Spanish monarchy is a plea for more resources for the defense of the Philippines.

with the rest of the monarchy was borne by the annual galleon that plied between Manila and Acapulco, exchanging Mexican silver for Chinese silk.

By comparison, the Philippines' links with China were immeasurably more important, and the Spanish colony was numerically insignificant compared with the vast numbers of Chinese settlers who came, under Spanish protection and at Spanish mercy. Indeed, while Japan remained a participant in trade, even Japanese shipping and settlement also eclipsed those of western arrivals. The islands' reliance on Asiatic and half-breed traders is nicely illustrated by the failure of the policy of a mid-eighteenth-century governor who expelled them all—except, fortunately, for a thousand-odd whom the Dominicans contrived to keep, on the grounds that they were undergoing catechism—and founded a joint-stock company of Spaniards and acculturated half-breeds to replace them. When the capital was exhausted, the religious orders were plundered to keep the venture going; even then, it had to be wound up after a further year of losses.

Other indigenous trading communities were less robust than the Chinese, but if they succumbed to outside rivalry in the course of the seventeenth

Vestigial ruins of the English trading factory on the shore at Hirado, where foreigners were welcomed in the early seventeenth century by Matsura Hoin, the daimyo, who hoped the foreigners would restore the fortunes of his port after the damage inflicted by competition from Nagasaki. The English stayed only ten years, withdrawing in 1623 after contributing, by their failure in attempts to market woollens, to the general demise of Japanese overseas trade.

From 1592, Hideyoshi issued foreign trading ventures by Japanese ships under the "Red Seal." At first they relied on Portuguese pilots, later supplanted by the Dutch; but native pilots soon became proficient. Licensees included daimyos and high officials as well as merchants. Until the abolition of the trade in the 1630s, about ten voyages a year took craft goods, copper, silver and foodstuffs mainly to Macao, Vietnam, Siam, and the Philippines, in exchange for silk. On this silk scroll of about 1630, the red seal ship of the Chaya family of Kyoto is towed into the river-mouth by Vietnamese galleys. The umbrellas indicate the market in front of the Japanese quarter. The three long houses across the river represent the Chinese quarter.

century, it was as much to Chinese as to European competition, or else, in the case of the Japanese, it was a self-elected withdrawal from an abhorred arena. In the era after Hideyoshi's death, Japan did not at once lose all taste for empire or all sense of the value of trade. The Ryukyu Islands, which stretch like the tips of a fan between Japan and Taiwan, were conquered in 1609 in the last twitch of the corpse of Hideyoshi's imperialism. They became a useful and enduring entrepôt for trade with China: in 1719 a sedan-bearer on a Chinese mission to Okinawa had in his baggage 45,000 pieces of benzoin—used in the manufacture of scent and incense—and 80 pairs of spectacles. This fitted into the pattern of Japan's foreign relations as it evolved and dissolved in the seventeenth century.

Tokugawa Ieyasu—effectively, Hideyoshi's successor as the strong-man of all Japan—began his rule as shogun with abounding faith in trade. Dutch and English factors were welcomed to Japan. A few courses of dressed stone on the shore at Hirado recall how well built were their trading posts. Japanese ships frequented Macao, Taiwan, the Philippines, and Siam. The reversal, when it came in the 1630s, was a product of cultural rather than commercial revulsion: the decrees which forbade the Japanese to trade abroad were accompanied by others rewarding denunciation of Christians and expelling half-breed children. From 1639, contact with the west was confined to a tiny Dutch trading post on a comfortless island—"or, rather, prison," according to an early inmate—off Nagasaki. For Chinese trade the Ryukyus were used as a similar airlock against impurities from outside, while commerce with Korea—had there been any with that equally fanatical isolationist state—was limited to Tsushima. Marginal luxuries, such as clocks and narwhal tusks marketed as unicorn horn, were exchanged for the copious silver and copper which Japan produced.

OUTCASTS OF THE ISLANDS

Normally, in eastern and southern Asia, the European barbarians were good for local and regional trade. They increased demand by their own presence and by linking existing trades into long-range oceanic networks. In the early seventeenth century, Portuguese hands controlled 10 per cent of the pepper of Malabar in a good year. This was probably enough to supply western European needs but left largely unimpaired most of the age-old trade of the traditional handlers to the middle east. The major impact of the business of the Portuguese derived not from the Cape route they had created but from their new initiatives in long-range trade within the traditional arenas of the Indian Ocean and China Seas. Sometimes Portuguese who "went native" outside their own colonies pioneered new routes or traffic between regional destinations. Half-breeds found in commerce a route of escape from restricted social opportunities, to the common enrichment of the regional economy.

Chances multiplied for those long-standing guests, the Gujeratis, Armenians, and near-easterners whom the sources call "Persians." The Armenians' versatility equipped them for the role of intermediaries wherever there were new trading partners, separated by religion or politics, to be brought together. They were, declared an East India Company representative in 1697, "the world's oldest traders," who had presided over the textile trade since the first cloth was woven. They linked Protestant trading posts in the Malay islands to the impenetrably Catholic Philippines and worked their way inside the barriers of isolationism and protectionism. In 1724 an English supercargo in Canton complained that all the tea in the port had been pledged to Armenians.

There were a few cases, however, where indigenous or established merchant-communities suffered from the competition or hostility of the European newcomers. In the long run—perhaps also from the perspective of historians looking back at our millennium from far in the future—these exceptions would come to establish a new rule. The fate of the great maritime tradition of Java and Sumatra is the most conspicuous example. The raffish Venetian adventurer Lodovico Varthema, who claimed to have been here in the early sixteenth century, found the seas dominated by the masters of these islands, with their "wonderful knowledge" and accurate maps, which the first Portuguese interlopers copied. Until well into the seventeenth century, their role was little changed. The vast junks of Japara—as big as the Dutch and Portuguese carracks that were built to cross two oceans—kept Makassar and the Spice Islands supplied with basic foods. Jambi, a pepper land on the Batanghari river, benefited from the ruthlessness of Dutch business methods: when the Dutch forced the Chinese from the river, men of Jambi took their pepper to Batavia in their own junks. Aceh, for the first three decades of the century, succeeded by Bantam for most of the rest, was an emporium which handled more traffic—in terms of tonnage, if not of value—than Malacca or Batavia. But even in a world of expanding markets, competition brings losers as well as gainers. By 1657, Japara had to get Dutch or Eurasian pilots in to guide its fleets "because the sea is large and the Javanese cannot sail it." Jambi rarely had the freedom to trade to competitors of the Dutch.

Bantam, like other states in what would become Indonesia, boomed with the increased demand for pepper in China and Europe in the sixteenth century. Land was converted and the country became a net importer of food. When the Dutch arrived in 1598, they found well-established merchants operating on a vast scale, such as Sancho Moluco, who dressed in velvet and could supply 200 tons of pepper at a time. Eighteen thousand bags of pepper of unspecified size were being sold annually to China and 3,000 to Gujerati merchants for trading on elsewhere. The Dutch could handle only nine thousand a year but could not be indifferent to the scale of Bantamese production, which gave the natives and their oriental customers too much control in pricing. After a series of disputes, Jan Pieterszoon Coen decided to use the shipping strength and firepower of Batavia to destroy Bantam's trade. The war waged intermittently but ruthlessly from 1618 reduced the sultanate's pepper production to less than 8,000 bags in all by 1629. Ironically, Lim Lakko, the ruler's Chinese adviser who had organized the pricing cartel that broke Dutch patience, was obliged to move to Batavia, "utterly down-and-out," to found a new fortune trading with Taiwan. Bantam switched to making sugar for the Chinese market. When pepper production revived for English customers in the 1670s, the Dutch moved in again and forced the sultan into a humiliating treaty at gunpoint in 1684.

Makassar—a small sultanate on Celebes, out of the way of the destructive mutual rivalries of the Javanese states—was one of the most tenacious survivors of the early-modern era in eastern seas. Refugees from Dutch aggression elsewhere gave her a dynamic "frontier" culture in the seventeenth century. Malays swelled her ships' crews, Moluccans brought savoir faire in spices, and Portuguese from Malacca introduced their long-range trading contacts. It became their "second and better Malacca" and, by the reckoning of a Dominican who visited in 1658, "one of the great and pleasant places . . . one of the greatest emporia of Asia" with a ruler who wore a European coat over his bare midriff, collected a library of Spanish books, and kept a globe and a striking clock. The career of the Portuguese adventurer Francisco Vieira de Figueiredo was representative of the range of opportunities, if exceptional in the scale of its achievements.

Like many impecunious Portuguese soldiers in the east, he resorted to trade to make a living. He was a chameleon who moved with ease through the particoloured islands between the Indian Ocean and the South China Sea. He served in 1642 as the envoy to Cambodia of the Spanish governor of Manila, and even when the Spanish and Portuguese crowns—united from 1580 to 1640—had been irretrievably sundered, he continued to partner Spanish dignitaries in trading ventures. While a truce prevailed between the Portuguese and the Dutch, he worked happily with the Dutch East India Company, and when a diplomatic revolution made them enemies, he continued to sell them sandalwood even while they were hunting and burning his ships. He became the intimate adviser of the King of Makassar, the envoy of the Nawab of Golconda, and the commercial collaborator of both of them. In 1652 he showed he could glide out of prison as easily as he could shimmer into a court: his baulked gaoler, the ruler of Mataram, blamed the English agent, whom he tortured, and Javanese servants, thirty-six of whom he put to death.

Vieira's object, according to English reporters, was "the gain of wealth"; yet he was so useful a political agent of Portuguese interests that the Viceroy forbade him to go home; and he proved the validity of his reputation for Catholic piety by telling his royal and Muslim patron that Muhammad was burning in hell. Like Howqua, he delivered. "I always made a maxim of scrupulously observing my promises," he said. Though he often talked of returning to Portugal, he was so much in his element in the east—where he could affect the rank of a gentleman and presume on the friendship of a prince—that it is hard to imagine him in any other setting. He was a model of happy deracination, his life adapted for mobility: in Makassar, like the other foreigners, who were forbidden to build solidly or evince permanence, he lived in a bamboo shack, but his real palace was his magnificently appointed yacht.

As a trader his first interest was in the textiles of Coromandel, where his fortune inflated like an early pumpkin. He specialized in the sandalwood of the Lesser Sunda Islands but also handled gold and silver from Sumatra and the Philippines, sappanwood from Indo-China, and Moluccan cloves, which were the centrepiece of Makassar's emporium trade in his day. Jealousy over spices was at the root of the Dutch–Makassar war which broke out in 1652, but the immediate provocation was the confiscation of Vieira's ships—in which the King of Makassar had a big interest—by Dutch authorities seeking to exploit the end of their truce with Portugal. Vieira armed a galley fleet to harass the foe and stoked the war with well-meant but ultimately vain promises of Portuguese intervention on Makassar's behalf. When the new young king, Hasanuddin, sued for peace in 1656, with "no powder left, no munitions, nor anyone who could supply them," the natives were inclined to blame Vieira as the sole cause of the conflict. Dutch arrogance led to renewed fighting in 1659. "Do you believe," Hasanuddin demanded, "that God has reserved for your trade alone islands which lie so distant from your homeland?" The size of the naval task force the Dutch had waiting in Batavia seemed to justify that arrogance. The peace they imposed involved the expulsion of all the Portuguese. Vieira went, dragging his heels, to Timor in 1664, while his compatriots, with English and Malay expulsees, dispersed to Siam, India, and Macao. When he died in 1667—struggling to pacify the warring Timorese tribesmen in the interests of sandalwood production—Makassar was being reduced to a Dutch colony.

It was the most important of a string of conquests which turned the Dutch from interlopers in commerce into controllers of production. Makassar, when it fell, was already full of refugees from earlier wars. In 1628, Sultan Agung had abandoned his vision of reunifying Java when he failed to take Batavia. In 1646, when his successor made peace with the Dutch, the newcomers could still be regarded as "powerful vassals ruling lucrative but uncivilized coastal districts." Like the Spaniards in Mexico or Peru, the Dutch were few enough and insidious enough to worm their way into local wars which they could direct and exploit. Once Makassar was reduced to subservience—its forts fired, its walls undermined—in 1669, only Bantam, of the major spice producers, still enjoyed effective independence. By 1683 its resistance had been worn down and its pepper output was in pawn. An "age of trade" came to an end as indigenous cultivators "retreated from the world economy," abandoning valuable cash crops which had once enriched their cultivators but which seemed now only to attract foreign predators. In 1686 the Dutch found the nutmeg and clove trees of Magindanao uprooted by the disillusioned inhabitants in an attempt to make their land unattractive.

In the end this sort of imperialism did the Dutch little good. Their strength was in their shipping, and a seaborne and piratical empire suited their talents and technology. Their weakness was in manpower. Territorial acquisitions, for which appetite grew with eating, gradually overstretched and exhausted them. They had—it could be objected—no choice: unlike the Spaniards and Portuguese, they had little or no access to marketable assets, such as mineral wealth and slaves, which could be exchanged for the

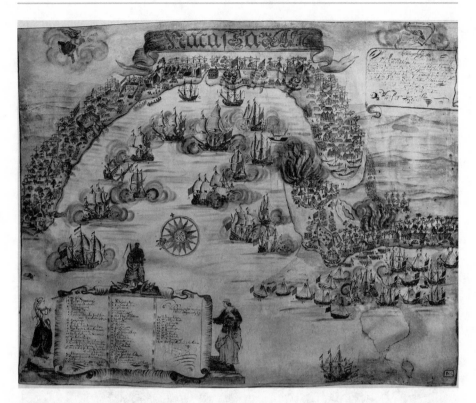

The fall of Makassar, 12 June 1660, painted on vellum by Fred Woldemar. Vieira's ship is on the left; Portuguese colours are also trailed by a prize the Dutch had already taken. Samboupo Castle, the palace of Hasanuddin, is exchanging fire with the Dutch ships. The English factory, neutral by treaty, flies the flag of St. George. The decisive moment of the encounter is recorded: the garrison of the fortress of Pankoke march out to the sultan's aid, allowing the Dutch to land a storming party and seize the stronghold.

riches of the east. They had to take the spices, or the land on which to grow them, by force. They ended with an empire whose costs exceeded its profits: the gap was only closed in the eighteenth century by the conversion of much of Java to the cultivation of coffee—the counter-opiate of the rococo west, the potential home-breaker satirized in Bach's *Coffee Cantata*.

Meanwhile, the Dutch in the East Indies whirled in a vicious spiral, obliged to operate on a war footing, at huge costs, which could only be paid for by enforcing high prices. As they devastated rivals' lands, uprooted surplus crops, and destroyed competitors' ships, they ran the conscious risk of ruining the entire region and being left profitless "in depopulated lands and empty seas." The practical limits of their victories saved them from the adverse consequence of too much success. Even at its height their would-be monopoly of the rarer spices—cloves, nutmeg, and mace—was a leaky vessel, and their shipping never accounted for more than a seventh of Asia's total. Makassar's reduction to subject-status, for instance, did little damage to resident native shipping business.

Yet the fall of Makassar, however modest its effects on some local lives, did change the world. It completed the Dutch ring of force around the spice islands: now the Dutch could control supply at the source of production and the first level of distribution. Their response was ruthlessly destructive, and plantings of clove, nutmeg, and mace rapidly fell to a quarter of their former levels. Hitherto, the new routes tacked to world trade by European interlopers in the east had been like the epicycles added by pre-Copernican astronomers to the theoretical movements of the planets; they had supplemented and confirmed the existing system, and expanded its to-

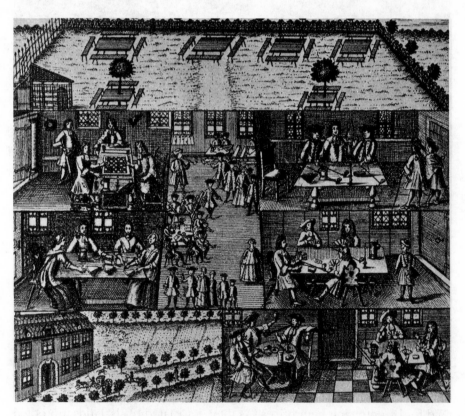

Bach's *Coffee Cantata*, "a satire on the counter-opiate of the rococo west," defended the new beverage against allegations that it undermined family life, distracted women from their wifely obligations, and consumed time in fastidious rituals. The dedicatee owned the coffee house at number 14, Catherstrasse, Leipzig, and another, shown here, the Kuchen Garden in the suburb of Gaststäte.

tal volume, without modifying its essential character or shifting its centre. Now a valuable slice of the gorgeous east really was held in fee, and the economy of part of the Orient was impoverished for the benefit of the stockholders of the Dutch East India Company. This was a reversal of the aeons-old balance of trade, which had enriched the east at western expense.

So far, the effects were limited to where Dutch imperialism could be made to work: the Dutch had only a toehold in Japan; they were nearly banned from China and Indo-China; they were gradually forced out of most of their positions in India and Ceylon. The products they largely controlled were of high value but represented only a fairly small portion by volume of the total world trade in spices—for pepper, of which they never had a thorough grasp, normally amounted to 70 per cent of the whole and continued to grow almost uninterruptedly, steadily increasing the sum of global commerce and keeping traditional routes and handlers supplied. The Dutch had set a fateful example, however, of how to chop and bludgeon a suppliers' economy to suit a customer's needs: in India in the second half of the eighteenth century, and in much of the rest of the world in the nineteenth, other European powers would find the means and opportunity to effect similar refashionings. That is why the galactic museum-keepers are more likely to attend to what happened in the Banda Islands and the Celebes in the early-modern period than to the fate of European rebellions or the posturings of European kings. Neither the English civil war nor the wars of Louis XIV will seem to be worth so much space in the vitrine. Meanwhile, Dutch imperialism was also changing Europe, for the fat of the spice trade, which had enriched Lisbon and Antwerp or ended up by adding to the girth of subjects of Venetian portraiture, was now getting under the belts of the burghers of Amsterdam. God has taken their riches from other cities, declared a popular guidebook of 1662, "and spilled them into our bosom."

THE VENICE OF THE NORTH

"'Tis commonly said that this city is very like Venice. For my part I believe Amsterdam to be very much superior in riches." At the upper levels of society this observation of a seventeenth-century English traveller could not be verified: patricians of Amsterdam, at the end of the century, had, on average, little more than half the assets of their Venetian counterparts. The Englishman, however, was more impressed by the diffused prosperity which put peasants allegedly worth £10,000 in his way. Certainly, in relative terms, the riches of Amsterdam had grown so prodigiously in the course of the century—"through the hand of God," said the guide of 1662, from 30,000

The habit of withdrawal to the countryside on the profits of business conducted in towns even affected Europe's most business-conscious élite: the bourgeoisie of early-modern Amsterdam. Some of the most sumptuous villas were on the Vecht, like Gunterstein Manor, built by the city councillor Ferdinand van Collen (1651-1735) as a summer resort.

inhabitants in 1585 to equality with Venice at about 130,000 in 1650—that the favourable comparison with the static wealth of Venice was understandable.

The two cities had more peculiarities in common than just canals and spices. Their élites shared a republican and civic ethos and a culture of consumption. To be sent to The Hague was exile for an Amsterdam patrician, who needed to be near the Bourse and the harbour, but at least a third of the city's office-holders in the late seventeenth century had pleasure-houses along the Amstel; by the mid-eighteenth century owners of country houses comprised more than 80 per cent of the patriciate, and the town council met rarely in June and August. On the smaller scale which befitted Amsterdam's narrower hinterland, this shift to a seasonal Arcady matched the flight of Venice's aristocracy to Palladian villas in the *terraferma*. Accompanying both movements was a trend in the economic status of patricians from entrepreneurs to rentiers.

Taste is the best clue to values, and in all Europe, according to one of the most perceptive economic theorists of the late seventeenth century, "you will find no private buildings so sumptuously magnificent as a great many of the merchants' and other gentlemen's houses are in Amsterdam." The burghers managed to retain their traditional image of parsimony because a great deal of the display was withheld for the inside of their dwellings. Planning regulations kept façades narrow, though the determinedly ostentatious could create double-width garden fronts or double their frontage by collaboration with a neighbour. Exteriors could be enlivened by armorial gables, richly moulded entablatures, or decorative urns and busts, of the sort favoured by the early seventeenth-century arbiter of elegance, Hendrick de Keyser. There are examples still standing today on the Keizersgracht and the Herengracht. Generally, however, the buildings of Amsterdam dressed modestly, with clean lines, chaste mouldings, and plenty of neatly glazed windows. Only the baroque taste of an Andries de Graeff could rival the denizens of Venetian palaces of the same period.

By comparison the seventeenth century has the reputation of a lean time in the history of Venetian palace-building, but the seven palaces of that era attest to enduring wealth, often underrated by historians anxious to write off "declining" Mediterranean powers. The most daringly baroque in spirit, however, reflect the variable fortunes of the families that commissioned them. The Palazzo Pesaro with its strangely textured façade, unconventionally placed rustications, and intense contrasts of light and shade celebrated in 1652 the abiding status of one of the city's self-styled oldest families, which traced itself back to "Jove, King of Tuscany and Emperor of the World": but their finances were rickety and the palace remained unfinished until 1710. The other great palace commissioned from the inventive architect Baldassare Longhena was the Cà Bon: similarly delayed by the debts of the patron, it was still without furniture when its heirs sold it to the upstart Rezzonico family in the eighteenth century.

Whereas the grandeur of Amsterdam was solidly based, the splendour of Venice has been ascribed to spendthrift abuse of credit masking real decline—a thin layer of gilding over wormwood. There were undeniable economic advantages to being in business in northern rather than southern Europe in the sixteenth and seventeenth centuries. Inflation, built into the economy as a regular feature unprecedented in history, flowed from south to north, stimulated by new sources of bullion, by new forms and expanded levels of credit, and by the demand created by an increase of population. The northerners used their price advantage to break into the Mediterranean in the late sixteenth century, where they were helped by demand for their shipping: to bring in grain to meet food shortages, to counter losses to Muslim corsairs. The Dutch became familiar newcomers, much like the Portuguese in the late middle ages, and with similar consequences: the expanding orbit of the shipping of these previously poor and marginal peoples carried them on to a role as worldwide empire-builders.

The Dutch had a long apprenticeship as dominant carriers and fishers in the Baltic in the sixteenth century; they were the *orang laton*, the sea-gypsies of the west, with the relevant experience and equipment to benefit when longer sea-lanes opened to them. Their penetration of the Mediterranean, the Atlantic, and the Indian Ocean looks at first sight all the more remarkable for having occurred during their long struggle, from 1572 to 1648, to separate themselves from the Habsburg monarchy, but the effect of the war was positive in crucial ways: it steeled enterprise, stimulated piracy, justified interloping in Spanish and Portuguese waters, and above all was accompanied by a shake-out of population which sent some of the great capitalist families of the southern Netherlands scurrying northwards to the safety of Amsterdam. The grave of one of the greatest of these migrants, Isaac Le Maire, proudly records the wounds of entrepreneurship—the loss of one and a half million guilders. The infusions of cash the migrants brought made it possible for Amsterdam to grasp the historic opportunity of the early seventeenth century. It was a triumph of business values allied to cheap money. At 2½–5 per cent, interest rates in seventeenth-century Amsterdam were the lowest in the world.

Even at the time it was suspected that the Dutch had an ideological or psychological advantage as well. "What has made that contemptible spot of earth so considerable among the powers of Europe," suggested the author of *The Fable of the Bees,* "has been their political wisdom in postponing everything to merchandise and navigation and the unlimited liberty of conscience that is enjoyed among them." Though proof is lacking, it seems that some rich immigrants to the northern Netherlands were attracted by religious toleration or at least repelled by the arbitrary penalties of Inquisitions elsewhere, which almost attained the status of extra commercial risks. Venice, too, was notoriously unzealous in persecuting heresy. In Amsterdam, the Protestant Venice, the prevailing ethos, the tone of the homilies which everyone had to hear, is sometimes thought to have favoured capital accumulation in two ways: by promoting a Puritan aesthetic, hostile to the cost of luxury, and by devaluing personal charity on the grounds that salvation cannot be bought by works. Burgher spending habits, however, seem to show that sermons in early-modern Amsterdam were as ill heeded as sermons generally are.

THE FEAST OF THE DEAD

The biggest, costliest apartment in the Hospital de Caridad in Seville is the chapel. In the late seventeenth century the power of prayer was probably as effective as any other therapy; the inmates for whom this chapel was designed were derelict with age, terminally sick, or otherwise beyond human help. The foundation existed to cure the souls of the caretakers as much as the bodies of the patients. The decoration of the chapel was carefully contrived to make the worshippers feel better, guiding them as they approached the altar and returned to their places on a sacramental journey to a glimpsed heaven and back. The same journey can be made by an unhurried visitor today.

As you enter at the west end, you are caught between two of the most disturbing paintings in the world: the reminders of death painted by Juan Valdés Leal in his typically impatient, stabbing brushstrokes. One is dominated by a skeletal reaper, with limbs outstretched, surrounded by the respectable vanities of this world—the books of the wise, the arms of the valiant, the memorials of art, the arch of triumph. Opposite, a knight putrefies on his deathbed. The worshipper's pilgrimage up the aisle therefore begins with a summons to repentance. A little nearer the altar, the works of mercy are spread out for view, depicted by Murillo, whose creamy, comforting paint is as reassuring of the hope of salvation as Valdés Leal's fierce style is threatening of hell. The uncompromisingly catholic message is of faith fortified by effort. Not all the original paintings have survived, but the emphasis is obvious on vocations proper to the work of a hospital, as, over the south aisle, Saint Elizabeth of Hungary beatifically picks over the headsores of the poor. It was an obligation of the rich and noble members of the hospital confraternity that they should tend the sick with their own hands. Nearer still to the sanctuary, sacred allegories of the Eucharist are mounted high on the walls: Murillo's scenes of the children of Israel refreshed in the desert and of the miracle of the loaves and fishes. For a dying worshipper prepared to receive the sacraments by contemplation of the images of retribution and salvation which line his approach, no scene could be more sympathetic than that which adorns the high altar, where one of the most dramatic compositions of the skilful baroque carver Pedro Roldán displays Christ at his most human: the dead Christ, just descended from the cross, surrounded by the inhabitants of heaven in extremes of worldly agony. Identified with his savior, the communicant turns from the altar to contemplate overhead a triumphant vision of the exaltation of the cross. He can return to his seat, shriven, exhorted, edified, comforted, fed, and reassured.

In this decorative scheme can be read not only the predicament of the sick and the theology of the church but also the economic fortunes of seventeenth-century Seville; evidence that though the new transatlantic trade of the early-modern period was small in volume—like the rest of the world's intercontinental trades in their early stages—it could, where its impact was concentrated, be formidable in its effects. The hospital was created with money accumulated in boomtime by "nabobs" of the Atlantic trade, to help assuage the social consequences of the mid-century collapse and the late-century crisis. Seville was a western canton with a monopoly of the trade of the Spanish New World. In the second half of the sixteenth century, when the veins of the world's richest silver mines in Mexico and Peru poured unstaunchably into the Atlantic, Seville became a bonanza-

Burial of the dead—plague-stricken or impoverished—was one of the obligations of the brethren of the confraternity which ran the Hospital de Caridad in Seville. Pedro Roldán's sculptures on the high altar therefore depict the entombment of Christ. Roldán was one of the last great sculptors of the Sevillan baroque: in the ethereal setting designed by Bernardo Simón de Pineda this altarpiece represents a characteristically emotional baroque conceit: the paradox of inhabitants of a glorious heaven sharing the miseries and suffering of an earthbound life.

town, the "thieves' Babylon" of Cervantes, settled in suburbs and shanties by 100,000 rootless poor from a deprived hinterland. Seventy religious communities, by 1610, had moved in to evangelize them. The "golden age" painters of the generation of Velázquez's friends and contemporaries worked frenziedly to manufacture appropriate devotional aids.

By the 1640s the mood was changing. Bullion imports fell as production problems multiplied at the mines while the New World economies grew and absorbed more specie. Devastating mid-century plagues destroyed confidence. The age of religious foundations gave way to a new devotional era, dominated by the chillingly penitent confraternities whose sacrificial holy week calvaries are still an inescapable part of everyone's image of the city. Francisco Zurbarán and Francisco Herrera the elder—the most sought-after painters of the previous generation—first turned to the export market, then died in poverty. The gilded youths of the boom years became the sombre confrères of the Hospital of Charity, burying the plague-dead and tending the buboes of the poor with their own hands. Their prosperity had turned, like Don Juan's revelries, into a feast of the dead.

Within Europe and in the east, between Europe and Asia, early-modern developments changed old patterns. The Atlantic trade was altogether new and might therefore be expected to have more potential to reshape the economies it affected. Throughout the period, silver was America's main product, and nothing is more powerful than specie in disturbing prices or unlocking, in turn, more new sources of wealth. Colonization in America— a project which was almost a Spanish monopoly until well into the seventeenth century—created a captive market for the supplies and manufactures which could not, at least at first, be locally supplied. Yet the silver slipped through Spain like jollop through a defective digestion, and no industrial revolution or agrarian boom happened, except in a few limited areas, in response to the needs and opportunities of empire. In the world's most privileged economy, capitalism did not succeed imperialism. It was the imperial laggards, England and Holland, who developed East India companies and Banks of England and of Amsterdam—institutions which had no genuine or enduring parallels in the more precocious empires of Spain and Portugal.

Historians have scattered blame with the accuracy of carpet-bombers. Contemporaries, influenced by stoicism and Christianity, enviously eying saddlebags too fat for the eye of a needle, inculpated the corrupting effects of Spain's inordinate wealth, which became a sort of Midas curse. Later analysts have blamed bureaucracy, hidalgo values, the Inquisition, excesses of deficit finance, and the "colonization" of Spain's home economy by foreign bankers—German, Italian, and French—who creamed off the profits of a surrogate empire. In reality, however, American products and markets developed too slowly to have spectacular effects, except concerning bullion. Apart from Newfoundland cod and the sugar of Brazil and Hispaniola, America was relatively undeveloped for other large-scale export products until well into the seventeenth century. The diversified New World which took shape in the seventeenth and eighteenth centuries, with its widely separated centres of production and its huge output of natural products and cash crops of low unit value, could not be controlled by one power or exploited for the benefit of one country. Spain kept control of the bullion shipments with remarkable tenacity; throughout the period of her supposed decline, her convoys were almost invincible. But she cheerfully farmed out the trade in slaves and abandoned to competitors, with insouciance, sugar and tobacco lands along the Atlantic coasts.

THE AGE OF IRISH MADEIRA

The development of the Atlantic economy has been suggested by various measures: of the growth in numbers of New World slaves and the depletion—perhaps the retardation—of the economies from which they were exported; of the stimulated output of metalwares and cotton textiles in proto-industrial Britain, where the export of these manufactures to North America and the West Indies accounted for most of the mean annual rate of growth of trade of 1½ per cent over the eighteenth century; or of the pace of emergence of a political consensus in Britain where "only Jacobite cranks fumed in the wilderness against Britain's 'blue water' policy." The "Americanization of British trade," according to its most judicious scrutineers, turned Britain from "simply part of a traditional European trading network with growing interests in American and Asian markets" into "the centre of an Atlantic economy."

The complexities, however, of Atlantic trade in the eighteenth century can best be appreciated from inside the tightest part of the tangle—from the perspective of a dynasty of Irish merchants established in the port of Orotava, on the island of Tenerife, at the heart of the Atlantic wind-system. Until recently their activities were almost unknown to scholarship, yet their place in the commerce of the day was primordial in importance as well as central in position, and their enterprises touched almost every inhabited Atlantic shore from New England to Brazil and from Waterford to Guinea.

The founder of the dynasty was a refugee from the Protestant ascendancy called Bernard Walsh Carew (1663–1727). From 1692 he combined the lives of exile and trader, fixing his residence first in Nantes, then moving south to Lisbon in 1707 and Tenerife in 1714. He was a sickly, gouty melancholic with a taste for spacious dwellings, thickly planted gardens, and good books. The houses he built in La Laguna and Tenerife were famous locally for their gardens and their libraries. He collected only religious pictures and continued in exile to pile endowments on the family foundation, the Hospital of the Holy Spirit, back home in Waterford. His son, who inherited his aristocratic tastes, successfully applied for a patent of nobility under the Spanish crown.

The real continuator of the family fortunes, however, was John Colgan White, who married Walsh's granddaughter in 1742. From his native Dublin he had joined an émigré branch of the family in Cadiz—which by then had taken over Seville's monopoly of the New World trade—and got his commercial apprenticeship trading between Spain and Mexico. His business practices reflected the advantages of being Irish. Clannish solidarity and exiles' fellow-feelings gave him an entrée into Irish circles in every useful port. He could buck the laws of mercantilism by exploiting the privileges of a Castilian subject in the Spanish monarchy and the rights of a Briton in colonies of the British crown, though his private loyalties were Irish and Catholic. Where his grandfather-in-law had been an aristocrat manqué, a trader by compulsion, he was one of nature's entrepreneurs, who made his capital grow at between about 10 and 25 per cent a year by taking risks: he often had over 60 per cent of his capital tied up in stock-in-trade until he diversified into banking. His European business went mainly to the Channel and North Sea; his letters of credit circulated among London, Amsterdam, and Hamburg. His American marketplaces included New England and New Spain, and his correspondents could be found in a string of ports from Boston to Caracas, with an inland outpost in the silver-mining centre of Zacatecas in Mexico.

The basis of his business was Canary wine, which could be loaded in Tenerife for a relatively short passage to America or India or for the gratification of specialized tastes in Europe. The Malvasia grape had been carried from the Ægean to the islands by Genoese planters in the fifteenth century; its cultivation expanded as New World demand grew and as northerners came to appreciate its sweet, liquorous, well-travelling products. The "cup of Canary" appreciated by Falstaff and Sir Toby Belch was the islands' main export in Shakespeare's day. To Bostonians of the late seventeenth century, the archipelago was known as the Isles of Wine. Charles II's historiographer-royal, James Howell, praised this "richest, most firm, best-bodied and lastingest wine, and the most desecated from all earthly grossness." But in John Colgan's time the long-prosperous trade was threatened by the competition of Madeira, which displaced Canary in northern esteem and, with its unique adaptability to tropical temperatures, monopolized the East India market. Tenerife had always manufactured a wine from second-class grapes, known as Vidueño, cheaply produced with indifferent results and reserved for the domestic and South American trades. Whether or not it was Colgan who first had the idea of turning these wines into a sort of phoney Madeira to undercut the Portuguese suppliers, it was he more than any other individual who dedicated himself in the 1750s and 1760s to the perfection and promotion of Tenerife's new wine.

Colgan saw to it that his product had the requisite body and colour; he offered it at competitive prices in pipes an eighth larger than those of Madeira. From 1766 he exported it to British East India, at £10 a pipe to Madeira's £24. This "monstrous" difference, he hoped, would induce the East India Company "to send all their ships to this island, at least when the Gentlemen Directors are acquainted with its quality." As a promotional ploy he held a tasting on a merchantman bound for Madras, "the quality whereof, the Captain and Gentlemen assured, pleased them as much and even better than any Madeira they have ever drank."

White's cartel of wine buyers outraged the indigenous aristocrats who grew the grapes. The Marquess of San Andrés accused him of "squeezing the land like a sponge, and draining its life-blood like a leech." For the Marquess of Villaneuva del Prado he was a "mercantile despot." But his fake Madeira helped to salvage Tenerife's economy. Its market penetration was never very strong within Europe, but in the English American colonies it enjoyed enormous popularity, which the American War of Independence could only boost. Colgan's efforts in East India had some success. His "Madeira" established itself as a sundowner's tipple—a cheap flavour of metropolitan life in distant colonies.

Seville never recovered her old place in this new Atlantic world of eroded mercantilism. The bullion flow recovered in the second half of the seventeenth century, but it was diverted to Cadiz from the silted Guadalquivir, and at intervals during the eighteenth century the outward trade of Spain to America was opened up to other ports. Seville's elegantly pedimented mint, where once the bullion was turned into coin, is today a suitably dilapidated symbol, a warren of ramshackle housing and sweaty taverns, due for refurbishment and embourgeoisement, as I write, into a tourist attraction and pricey flats.

PART THREE

THE ATLANTIC CRISIS

Western Civilisation? I think it would be a good idea.

attributed to GANDHI

Chapter 11

THE ATLANTIC CHASM: FISSURES AND FRACTURES IN THE ATLANTIC WORLD

The New Canaan—Self-Evident Truths—
The Fine-Feathered Serpent—The Creoles of Yankee Country—
Riding the Crocodile—The Spittle of Democracy

THE NEW CANAAN

One substantial knot in the tangle of Atlantic trade in the late eighteenth century was tied by John Brown of Providence, Rhode Island. In 1771, knowing "what property was and consequently what a despicable figure in life I would cut without a share thereof," he left the security of the family business, which made candles from whale blubber, and launched himself into a series of speculative commercial ventures with almost uniform success. He dealt in slaves and rum, pig iron and whale products, then pioneered the China trade of Providence; among the luxury goods his ships brought home was his porcelain punch bowl, painted with the blue façades and tiled terrace of the American factory in Canton, which he helped to found. The enduring symbol of his wealth is the palatial house he built on Benefit Street in his home town. This is the street which bills itself as the oldest in the United States because of its unrivalled sequence of unspoilt eighteenth-century buildings. Even in such company the John Brown House is uniquely conspicuous.

He called it a homestead, a noun which evokes affected simplicity and a

339

John Brown's porcelain punch-bowl, acquired late in the 1780s or early in the 1790s: a luxury item of the sort he imported from China to New England. The decoration shows the American *hong* in Canton, overlooking the Pearl River. The imperial and Swedish factories are on the left: the French and Spanish factories were among those occupying buildings on the right. See p. 311.

world of all-American values. More just, however, were the assessments of visitors who called the house, for instance, "one of the grandest in the country," marked by "magnificence and taste" which "would appear considerable, even in Europe." A visitor from Philadelphia—then universally regarded as the biggest and best-built city in the states—exactly identified its inspiration when she observed that it was "built after the plan of some of the noblemen's seats in England and far surpasses any I have seen." On the outside, the house looks like a transplanted bit of old England, with its Georgian symmetry, its reticent mouldings, its classical details. Inside, it was extravagantly papered and dazzlingly carpeted; the tables were set with English silver and Chinese porcelain. Nothing was provincial, let alone colonial in flavour; though the cabinet-makers were from Newport, with a distinctive style of their own, the firm of Thompson and Goddard was unsurpassed for craftsmanship or artistry anywhere in the old world.

Yet in this temple of Atlantic civilization, the severance of the political links that bound the colony to England was plotted and celebrated. John Brown was among the fiercest of American patriots, who had anticipated the War of Independence by raiding a revenue ship in Narragansett Bay in 1772. He was a signatory of the Declaration of Independence, an intimate of George Washington, whose image he hung in the house, and the host of Washington and Jefferson at a grand dinner in his home to celebrate Rhode Island's rather tardy adherence to the Constitution of the United States in 1790.

This was a typical Atlantic story. Colonies laboriously created, meticulously embellished in the image of metropolitan society, gradually grew away from home and eventually broke free. Creole sentiments and values began to emerge almost as soon as colonies were established. Atlantic civilization was under notice to quit for the first three hundred years of its existence. It began to take shape around the shipping lanes opened by

The study of John Brown's "homestead" in Providence—a classic case of the imitation of a metropolitan aristocracy by a colonial thalassocracy. His other building projects in Providence included the wharfs that served his ships, a bridge that cut the distance to Newport by a mile, and a passage through a hill to the waterfront.

Columbus in central latitudes, by Cabot in the north and by Cabral to the south, in a concentrated spasm of exploration between 1492 and 1500. Between them, these three explorers found and recorded the routes that were to link the shores of the ocean for the rest of the age of sail. Traffic in goods, ideas, and people made it possible to think of a single civilization spanning the ocean. But the links were tenuous, the future insecure; some settlers came to escape their mother countries; others, determined to remould the frontier in the image of home, were none the less seduced by the novelties of the New World, turning their backs on the ocean, striking inland, and seeking a new identity. In some ways the New World tended to drift away from the old almost as soon as the shores were linked; newly tied moorings began to slip. Internal economic systems developed, followed by new loyalties and finally political independence.

The America that broke away from Britain in the war of 1776–84, for instance, was in many ways a brand-new society, though its origins had been laid more than 150 years before. Until the middle of the eighteenth century settlements were sparse and dispersed, clinging to the rim of the continent. As a destination for migrants, mainland North America was outweighed by the attractions of the British West Indies. After a hundred years of colonization, the total white population was less than a quarter of a million. Most of the successful colonies had been conscious experiments by utopian projectors and pilgrim communities; economic self-betterment had been the explicit aim only of those desperate enough to sign away their liberty and labour for the term of an indenture in order to buy a passage from home and a few tools and clothes with which to start an independent life when their bond was paid. In the eighteenth century, as the colonial horizon broadened and the prospects of a good life in America became better defined, the mood of migrants changed and their numbers exploded. By the eve of the Revolution, the total population was probably near two and a half million.

This astonishing increase—by a factor of ten within three generations—had no precedent or parallel elsewhere in the New World. It was an accelerating process, most of which was crammed into the last third of the entire short period. Between the middle of the century and the outbreak of the Revolution, the number of annual foundations of towns in New England trebled, as did roughly the populations of Georgia and South Carolina. In the 1760s the population of New York rose by nearly 40 per cent and that of Virginia more than doubled.

The migrants who stimulated and swelled this growth came from societies which were not particularly populous, though they were beginning to experience the demographic buoyancy which inspired Malthus and fuelled the Industrial Revolution. Scotland was disproportionately represented and, within Scotland, the western Highlands and Isles. Here depopulation was both a cause and an effect of ruin. Around the trauma of the uprising of 1745, when a Highlander army almost conquered the rest of Great Britain, the anxious victors inflicted destruction on clans, derogation or exile on chiefs, massacre or expropriation on landsmen—vivisection of a whole people by an English and Lowland establishment understandably fearful of a culture of rebelliousness in a society organized for war. Emigrants from England were almost all young men, of the sort society had always willfully wasted in war. From western Scotland, whole families went to America, eroding the demographic base at home and contributing to the creation of a stable and settled tenor of life in the colonies.

In America, the results included the burgeoning world and dilating frontier described with astonishment by writers in the generation before the Revolution. From about 1760 a rush of settlers scaled the previously unpassable west wall of the Appalachians to found "a new land of Canaan" between the Susquehanna and the Ohio. Michel-Guillaume-Jean de Crèvecoeur, who was to become one of the architects of American identity, imagined himself joining a mass of migrants heading out from Connecticut to the wilds of Pennsylvania, where he found "a prodigious number of houses rearing up, fields cultivating, that great extent of industry opened up to a bold and indefatigable people." On the day the land office opened at Fort Pitt in 1769, 2,790 claims were staked; 10,000 families were living on this frontier by 1771. The most adventurous imaginations were over-stimulated by what they saw. George Washington dreamed in the 1760s of laying "with very little money the foundation of a noble estate" on the Ohio. He was disappointed and had to make do, after an interval, with the presidency of a fledgling democracy instead.

Self-Evident Truths

The aristocratic pretensions of George Washington and the nobleman's plan of the John Brown House are reminders of the depth to which the North American élite was still steeped in old-world values. Even at a time when the struggle for independence was stimulating the search for a distinctive American identity, the new Canaan was full of Pharisees. The aspirations of American revolutionaries were unoriginal. Demands for fiscal exemption would not have shocked a noble *frondeur* of the mid-seventeenth century. That institutions representative of the people should at least share sovereignty with the crown was a shibboleth of English Whigs. The Minutemen who stood shoulder to shoulder on Lexington Green were in the tradition of the citizen armies idealized by Renaissance humanism. In their world, the language of rights and republicanism—a secular language, traceable through a succession of writings by "commonwealthmen" back to the English revolutions of the seventeenth century—reverberated in an atmosphere of religious sectarianism, which was strong enough and fanatical enough to supply manpower for revolutionary armies. At one level, the American War of Independence was one more English revolution, at another—the level of many of its rank-and-file—it was a "war of religion" in an old European tradition. The new demands of the pre-revolutionary years came from an England anxious to exact efficiency from her empire, and it was the threat to the colonies' comfortable habit of effective self-rule and cheap government which provoked confrontation. Washington and Jefferson were provincial English gentlemen only somewhat further removed from court than the leaders of country parties traditional in English politics. The official rhetoric of the revolution was borrowed from Europe, and its leaders were pursuing an old-world image of themselves.

The point could best be proved by textual analysis but is best illustrated by a look at Thomas Jefferson's strange country house, which has recently re-emerged in its sometime glory under the restorers' hands. Jefferson was his own architect, and Monticello says as much about his peculiarities of character as about the ideological context of the revolutionary élite as a whole. On a giant scale, it is the eccentric folly of an enlightened amateur. It was its owner's obsession, which took fifty-four years to build and re-build, embellish and perfect. By siting it on a mountain top, 867 feet up, Jefferson proclaimed its oddity and determined its strenuous, quirky character. He built in lots of challenging innovations of his own design: the almost unnavigably steep, narrow stairwells which are the only access to upper floors; the alcove beds; the two-storey windows; the semi-octagonal rooms, added as an afterthought; the expensive domed room, which had to be de-moted to playroom or storeroom because it was so hard to get at; the gadgets which minimized labour by Rube Goldberg means—from hoisting wine from the cellar to duplicating documents.

It is a perfectionist's house: the pillars of the colonnade had to be dis-mantled and re-erected half a dozen times to get them quite straight; but, even more, it is an idealist's house, modelled on pattern-book Palladianism in conscious revulsion from the practicality and charm, of English inspira-tion, which characterized Virginian gentlemen's dwellings and public build-ings at the time. In describing the lofty setting, Jefferson used the languages of enlightened science—"to look down into the workhouse of nature"—and of the late eighteenth-century cult of "Enthusiasm"—to cultivate "emo-tions arising from the sublime." But he was also straightforwardly applying Palladio's advice to "build on an eminence."

Inspired by Italian writings and engravings, Monticello was thoroughly revised after Jefferson had served as U.S. minister in Paris; he returned with copybooks full of French recipes, a French chef at $300 a year, 250 bottles of Château d'Yquem, and a determination to remodel Virginia in the tradi-tions of Parisian comfort and in the image of Roman Nîmes. Simultaneously, perhaps paradoxically, Jefferson was groping for an American identity and displaying his patriot pride. His domestic museum was rich in American specimens and native artefacts. His hall was hung with painted buffalo hides and inhabited by "savage" carvings excavated in Tennessee, rather as the atrium of a Renaissance palazzo might be filled with Roman inscriptions and statues. He ordered his booksellers in Paris and Madrid to send him everything on America, and he decorated Monticello with portraits and busts of supposed makers of the New World—Columbus and Vespucci, Raleigh and Franklin, Washington and Lafayette. Yet his was always a heav-ily European America, inhibited by a sense of inferiority. He imposed on Virginia a state capitol in the style of a Roman temple to show "honour to our country, taste in our infancy."

In some ways the thirteen colonies, strung out along the Atlantic sea-board, were fertile in revolutionary notions precisely because of their expo-sure to old-world influences; similarly, in South America, revolution was to

The hall of Jefferson's Monticello was decorated to celebrate a specifically American enlightenment, hung with indigenous trophies and native art "rather as the atrium of a Renaissance palazzo might be filled with Roman inscriptions and statues."

spread outwards in the second decade of the nineteenth century, from Caracas and Buenos Aires, promoted by readers of Rousseau, Machiavelli, and Tom Paine, and borne in part by soldiers of fortune recruited in Britain, Ireland, and Germany. The patriot fathers who employed these volunteers were, in some cases, so saturated in European precedents that they devised constitutions like the first Colombian republic's, described by the acclaimed founder of the nation as "a Greek temple on a Gothic pedestal." The economic policy which united revolutionaries throughout the Americas was free trade—which in practice might be expected to multiply transatlantic contacts, even if independence meant the severance of some traditional ties.

In Canada, the King of England's newest subjects—the French Canadians acquired by war and treaty in 1763—preferred, as a lesser evil, the rule of London to that of Boston or Philadelphia and stayed aloof from the revolutionary war. Elsewhere in the Atlantic world, however, ocean-spanning unity depended on the fellow-feeling that joined colonies and parent-states.

A sense of distinct identity, a "creole consciousness," was a prerequisite or at least an essential ingredient of successful revolution throughout the hemisphere; to document its emergence, it is best to start in the south.

THE FINE-FEATHERED SERPENT

"Let's go and see" was the practical response of the Jesuit Manuel da Nóbrega when he was told of a rock near Bahía in Brazil which bore the impress of the feet of Saint Thomas the Apostle. The crisply defined prints, with well-dug-in toes, immediately convinced him. The conviction was re-inforced by the discovery that the local word for shaman was *zume:* to his ear this was too similar to "Thomas" for the etymology to be in doubt. The miraculous rock became a place of pilgrimage, where Jesuits and their In-dian neophytes gathered to sing hymns and erect crosses.

Traces of the apostle in Brazil were surprising but not altogether incredi-ble. The tradition that Saint Thomas was the original evangelist of India was well established and had been confirmed by the discovery of his supposed followers and presumed shrine in Mylapore. The relation between India and the hemisphere which Europeans called the Indies had not yet been clarified by exploration, and it was possible for Nóbrega honourably to overestimate the accessibility of Bahía from Asia.

Still, it would have required firmer proof or more obvious self-interest for the cult to grow. The proof was never forthcoming; indeed, as knowledge grew of the size of the world and as pious frauds were subverted by schol-arship, the scope for Saint Thomas's presumed mission in America shrank. Yet the self-interest of the cult's adherents did accumulate with time, and slowly but surely the doctrine that the saint had preceded Columbus grew to assume, for its believers, the quality of a dogma.

First to sense the potential usefulness of the notion were missionaries confronted by evidence of what seemed to be a partial revelation of the truths of Christianity to the pagans of the New World. In the sixteenth cen-tury, awareness of a supreme being, for instance, was attributed to the Arawaks, the practice of confession to the Aztecs, baptism to the Maya, and tonsure to the Tupinamba. For missionary purposes these prefigurations of Christianity among the Indians became protective talismans, with power to ward off the depredations of slavers; according to legal traditions estab-lished by the thirteenth century, pagans could not be enslaved "by reason of their paganism alone" but had to be guilty of crimes against natural law to justify their victimization. Evidence of the natives' sense of justice or truth—naturally derived or imparted by God—elevated them above the herd of beast-men inherently suited to slavery. One apologist of the six-teenth century even argued that human sacrifice, which seemed to be a blatant offence against natural law, was proof only of immoderate piety. This was the start of a line of thinking which would eventually seek to exonerate human sacrifice as a distorted memory of the Eucharist.

One reasonable conclusion from such evidence was that there was a common core of "natural" religion accessible, like natural law, to all reasonable men and all fully human societies. Gullible or adventurous intellects were prepared to go further, however, and postulate Saint Thomas as the source of foreshadowed Christianity in pagan America. One of the fullest expositions of the theory was that of the Augustinian father Antonio de la Calancha in 1639. His response to sceptics who had dismissed it was animated by a spirit of charity reminiscent of Erasmus's reply to Luther. He took scripture as his starting-point, arguing that the evangelical prophecy that Christ's word would be heard throughout the earth was meant to be fulfilled in apostolic times; America could not therefore have been exempt from such a blessing. Like Erasmus, he went beyond hermeneutics to appeal to Christians' sense of the loving nature of God. Just as Erasmus refused to accept that a loving Father could damn his children capriciously, so Calancha found it incredible that an equitable God should deprive one part of mankind for so long of the light of His word. Calancha evinced no vulgar enthusiasm; he took it that Thomas's mission was only "probable," but he followed the saint's footsteps through shady sightings and across rock-top impressions from Brazil through Paraguay to his own province of Peru.

Already by Calancha's time the controversy over Saint Thomas was acquiring political overtones. Spain's dignity and prestige among the nations of the old world derived in part from her privileged past as the chosen object of an apostle's ministry. Saint Thomas could do for America what Saint James did for Spain. To the missionaries' interest in propagating the cult of Thomas was therefore added an even more powerful interest: that of creoles who demanded greater autonomy for the colonies and equivalence in the allocation of offices with peninsular appointees. In creole hands the image of Saint Thomas was curiously remoulded. He became identified with a god or culture-hero from the depths of the Mesoamerican past: with Quetzalcoatl or Kukulcan, the best-known figure in the pre-Columbian pantheon, who is usually depicted as a feathered serpent.

This transformation can be followed in the sources in minute detail. For a Dominican missionary of the late sixteenth century, the Toltec culture-hero Topiltzin seemed to resemble Saint Thomas. He lived in chastity and penitence in a cell, prayed on his knees, and taught his followers to pray and preach. He also foretold the Spanish conquest, as Quetzalcoatl was said to have done in other traditions. In texts based on the Dominican's, this Topiltzin, with his Thomas-like characteristics, is identified as Quetzalcoatl by another name. The leap to assuming that Quetzalcoatl and Thomas were one and the same had then to span only a narrow logical chasm. By the 1740s it was taken as a matter of course that the apostle was "to the Indians, the Feathered Serpent."

But the myth of Saint Thomas–Quetzalcoatl was never as popular with Indians as with creoles. Its explosive political power became apparent in 1794, when a Dominican firebrand called Servando de Mier made it the theme of the official celebratory sermon, preached annually by custom to all the notables of Mexico City, on the feast of Our Lady of Guadalupe. He argued that the cult of Guadalupe was a legacy left by Saint Thomas, then concealed for hundreds of years during the time of Indian apostasy. Mier was already known as an admirer—with reservations—of the American and French revolutions, who was said to be "opposed to the rights of the king and to Spanish dominion." From the furore unleashed by his sermon he escaped to France and then to the radical, "constitutional" Spain of the period of the struggle against Napoleon, where he served as a colonial representative in the constitutional assembly. He returned to Mexico to join the rebellion against Spain which broke out in 1810; as a member of the constituent congress he helped to shape independent Mexico's republican destiny. He never ceased to advocate the cause of Saint Thomas–Quetzalcoatl, who, as well as a culture-hero, became a sort of honorary founding father of Mexican nationhood. Meanwhile, the peasant armies who fought for Mexican independence were inspired by a similar syncretic deity with whom Mexicans could identify as their peculiar patroness: they entered battle with the cry, "Long live Our Lady of Guadalupe!" At the end of the struggle, captured Spanish flags were laid in her shrine.

Mier, a member and spokesman of the creole élite, professed belief in his own descent from an Aztec emperor. His resentment of intruded peninsular officials began in his Dominican order, where he and his fellow-creoles felt excluded from power. It spilled over into the broader political arena. "America is ours," he wrote, "because we are born in it" by "the natural right of all peoples in their respective regions. God has separated us from Europe by an immense sea and our interests are distinct." The Atlantic, which had joined the shores it lapped for the three hundred years since Columbus, was now being seen once again as separating them.

The growth of creole awareness was not uniform throughout Spanish America. Peru and Costa Rica had independence thrust upon them by their neighbours; Cuba and Puerto Rico perceived the advantages of staying in the Spanish monarchy as almost unique purveyors of colonial produce under protected terms of trade. All the mainland colonies, however, were effectively independent by 1828.

In developing political self-consciousness, the most surprising laggard was Portuguese Brazil, where independence was bloodlessly conceded in 1822. This was a huge world, riven into isolated and self-regarding commu-

"Civilized savages"—a Paulista Bandeira in battle with Botocudo Indians, drawn by J. Debret from his own observations in Brazil in the 1830s. The cumbersome muskets seem old-fashioned but produce an impression of deadly superiority. The quilted body armour is proof against arrows.

nities by its intractable geography. São Paulo, already in the seventeenth century, was the capital city of a culture of truculence: the Paulistas, in their remote fastness, with their autarchic economy, were unencumbered by sentiment, ruthless in the pursuit of self-interest, unrestrained by laws, and barely touched by the institutions of government. Engravings of travellers' encounters with them, until well into the nineteenth century, show how they looked and how they lived: big men, well nourished, and bulgingly muscular, their girth enhanced by folds of quilted armour, bristling with arms and shaded by hats of roughly woven reeds, confidently terrorizing natives. They prospered by enslaving Indians in technical defiance of the law. Theirs was an anarchical society—a state of nature which worked because of a general equilibrium of terror among the bosses. If they never proclaimed their independence, it was because it was not worth asserting in theory what they enjoyed in fact. When they did rebel in 1710, it was in defence of their traditional, informal polity in the face of hectic immigration drawn to the region by recently discovered mineral wealth.

In other parts of Brazil, detachment from metropolitan culture was slow to emerge. The two colonial provinces of Maranhão and Bahía were closer, in terms of days of sail, to Portugal than to each other. Most Spanish mainland settlements were much farther from home in terms of travelling time. Portuguese community of feeling could more easily embrace the whole of a relatively compact Atlantic empire. In the Spanish colonies creole sentiment was nourished among colonials, who had never seen the mother country, by large, rich universities capable of generating as much self-pride in their alumni as almost any in the old world; the Brazilian élite, however, had to complete its education in Portugal, cultivating a sense of belonging which could be sustained an ocean's breadth away.

Not until the very late eighteenth century did a form of Brazilian identity emerge that could seriously threaten imperial unity. As in the British and Spanish empires, provincial feeling was aroused by intrusive reforms. Local academies and literary societies sprang up to supply the want of an intellectual focus for creole patriotism. In 1788 a rebellion inspired by the American Revolution broke out in Minas Gerais under a banner bearing an Indian breaking his chains. The governor of the area thought that it would be ungovernable even with a gallows at every crossroads. In 1790 a report from Rio de Janeiro accused Brazilians generally of disloyalty to the crown. Americans, it was said, had an inflated idea of the greatness of their homeland and believed Portugal would be nothing without the wealth of Brazil.

The development of an openly rebellious spirit was checked by the flight of the Portuguese court to Brazil during the Napoleonic wars. Yet not all the effects of this enforced proximity were positive. Portuguese, who had always cultivated a comic stereotype of colonial bumpkins, projected an offensive air of superiority. The lampoons in the 1820s of the English consul's wife, Maria Graham, in which Brazilian courtiers are depicted as dwarfish grotesques, cringing, stunted, and simian, are in the tradition of affected metropolitan superiority and nicely capture its sneering, racist tone. A broadsheet of 1830 calling for a Brazilian-born emperor of Brazil shows how Brazilian feeling had caught up with the creole precocity of the Spanish colonies; but it also shows its lateness and its limits. By then, Brazilian independence had been won under a cadet dynasty of the Portuguese royal house, and the prince hailed in the broadsheet as a "darkie [cabra] like us" was the blue-eyed, golden-haired boy-prince Pedro.

THE CREOLES OF YANKEE COUNTRY

Michel-Guillaume-Jean de Crèvecoeur had frequent identity crises. He changed his name back and forth between English—Hector St. John—and French versions. During and after the American Revolution, he wavered between loyalist and patriot sympathies. He assumed so successfully the character of the narrator of his most famous book, *Letters from an American Farmer*, that readers were misled in his day and ever since. He reclaimed

French nationality after adopting British and made a fundamental contribu-
tuion to the invention of American identity along the way.

He was hardly suited to this role. In some ways his idea of America was
as European as Jefferson's. He got his arcadianism and his belief in noble
savagery from the French Enlightenment; he thought American freedom
was a transplantation of English "national genius." He was at best an equivocal American. In 1782 he escaped with evident relish from the rural America he praised to the Parisian salons he preferred. The experience of the
revolutionary war corrupted his idyll, and his later "sketches" of American
life are bloodstained by horror stories. After the 1793 edition, the work
which contributed so much to the self-definition of U.S. citizens, and which
attracted the admiration of a range of luminaries encompassing the Comte
de Buffon and Benjamin Franklin, was not reprinted again until 1904.

Yet he was a precocious and inspiring spokesman for the American
dream. He invented the image of the "melting pot," the ethnic cauldron into
which the "poor of the world are gathered together" and stirred, like a
magic brew, into transmuted nationhood. The American, he declared, is
"neither an European nor the descendant of an European. . . . Here individuals of all nations are melted into a new race of men, whose labours and
posterity will one day cause great changes in the world." He captured the
tones in which Americans have identified themselves with liberty:

> Here are no aristocratical families, no courts, no kings, no bishops, no ec-
> clesiastical dominion, no invisible power giving to a few a visible one . . .
> no princes for whom we toil, starve, and bleed; we are the most perfect
> society now existing in the world. Here man is free as he ought to be.

He was prophetic, too, in his emphasis on religious tolerance, born of the
mingling and intermarriage of sects.

Crèvecoeur was a misfit in his own utopia—a French Anglophile of
Catholic origin and Quaker sympathy. Joel Barlow was better qualified by
birth and background to be a Yankee creole spokesman, though his analysis of what it meant to be an American was less shrewd and less clear-
sighted than Crèvecoeur's. He was a Connecticut puritan of modest background, a Yalie educated above his talents and below his ambitions. His
belief in meritocracy arose from his self-pity, deprived, as he claimed, of
friends and fortune; but he took comfort from the conviction that "if ever
virtue is to be rewarded, it is in America." He had the vocation of a poet
without the gifts. The quantity of his output, however, served in the place
of quality, and after publication of his proto-epic *The Vision of Columbus* in
1797, he enjoyed, in a restricted circle, the reputation of Poet Laureate of all
America.

The choice of Columbus as hero is puzzling. The mystical Genoese

Catholic who founded a Spanish American empire and never came near the future United States had no genuine quality to commend him to a Yankee revolutionary. Yet at the time of the revolution there was a strong sentiment in patriot ranks that identified Columbus as a fellow-founder of the new America. Jefferson, as we saw, had his portrait on the wall. In Baltimore, Maryland, where Columbus had many co-religionists, his statue was erected by public subscription in 1792. In Barlow's poem his Catholicism was suppressed, along with whatever else the author thought a human vice; the Reformation was among the events he was made to foresee with approval. This poetical Columbus sought "a happier shore, from lust of empire free" and hailed the United States "with a father's smile." Barlow's America had some of the same defining characteristics as Crèvecoeur's:

> As the glad coast, by Heaven's supreme command,
> Won from the wave, presents a new found land,
> Yields richer fruits and spreads a kinder soil,
> And pays with greater stores the hand of toil,
> So, call'd from slavish chains, a bolder race,
> With statelier step, these fair abodes shall trace;
> Their freeborn souls, with genius unconfined,
> Nor sloth can poison, nor a tyrant bind.

In speaking of "race" Barlow was proposing a distinctive doctrine: the improving environment of America would combine with the civilizing effects of settlement to work at once on the natives and colonists, producing a new breed without the squalid necessity of miscegenation. With help from sedentary culture, "milder arts," social joys, and "new beauties in the growing mind," tribes "who display the wild complexion of the place/Shall flush their features and exalt the race." Meanwhile, on arrival in the New World, "fair Europe's noblest pride" will acquire "a ruddier hue and deeper shade" and "stalk in statelier figures o'er the plain." The thesis is supported by a footnote claiming that Americans are darker-skinned than their European relations. The insistence on Americans' "stateliness" is intelligible in the context of the eighteenth-century debate about which hemisphere bred the bigger and better specimens of the species (see Chapter 8). Here is a form of creole identity, elicited *à parti pris* by mis-observation.

RIDING THE CROCODILE

Colonies that did not want or win independence might be disowned by mother-countries turning from the Atlantic in revulsion. After a French expeditionary force had succumbed to yellow fever in Haiti, Napoleon decided that most of what was left of France's American empire was best abandoned. Except to the king, the loss of thirteen colonies in North America seemed to the English a matter of indifference. While the probable main reason for the rebels' surprising success was England's inability—for once, in all her eighteenth-century wars—to distract her Bourbon adversaries with a continental coalition, it remains true that on the British side the war was fought half-heartedly and aborted with relief. Renewed war against the states in 1812–14 was fought with the savagery of revenge, not the hope of reconquest. Although the Spanish crown was reluctant to write off the American empire, most subjects on the eastern side of the ocean shared the sentiments of a Barcelonese merchant in 1813 who "could not care less if we separated from that rabble."

The Americas could be said to have been separating from a Europe that was in the grip of a period of self-absorption of exceptional intensity—a sort of breathing space between two ages of expansion. In the middle ages "Europe" had been a geographical expression, encompassing the heartlands of what, in parts one and two of this book, could be treated as the two separate civilizations of western and eastern Christendom. This usage was now challenged or supplemented by a new one in which the term acquired meaning as the name of a culture perceived as distinct and coherent. In the late seventeenth and early eighteenth centuries, Queen Christina of Sweden and Peter the Great of Russia wrenched at the frontiers of "western" and "Mediterranean" taste and ideas to include their formerly marginal realms. Stockholm and Saint Petersburg acquired a look of Paris or Rome, with baroque buildings and shaven boyars. In the same period, religious toleration began to glue back the shards of schisms. The international status of the French language, the shared cults of reason and experimental science, and the uniformity of enlightened, classicizing taste made it possible to glide between widely separated frontiers with little more cultural dislocation than a modern traveller feels in a succession of airport lounges. Midway through his *Decline and Fall* Gibbon was able to formulate a "European ideal": "It is the duty of a patriot to prefer and promote the exclusive interest of his native country: but a philosopher may be permitted to enlarge his views, and to consider Europe as one great republic, whose various inhabitants have attained almost the same level of politeness and cultivation." Belief in this common European culture was long inseparable from a conviction of European superiority, "distinguished above the rest of mankind."

In the early years of the nineteenth century, Napoleon Bonaparte almost gave political form to this European ideal by creating a Europe-wide empire. He was a Corsican adventurer, propelled to power in the chaos of post-revolutionary France by unrivalled military gifts. His own talent and the invincible might of the mass armies the revolution threw up gave him a chance to conquer Europe piecemeal; only at its extremities, in Spain and

Ingres' *Dream of Ossian.* Ossian's works—which contributed so much to the formation of the romantic spirit—were forgeries by James Macpherson. Napoleon was one of many readers deluded by them and in 1803 he commissioned Girodet to paint the bard welcoming a Napoleonic army into Valhalla, surrounded by Valkyrie. This absurd mixture of Celtic and Tutonic myth formed the romantic counterpoint to the classical and Roman iconography typical of Napoleonic propaganda. Ingres' painting, produced in 1813 for Napoleon's palace in Rome, echoed the theme.

Russia, did his reach become overextended. He was an opportunist whose ambitions were unrestrained by finite goals; but he had ideals, too, which overlapped with those of the revolution he claimed to fulfil. He was a child of the Englightenment, who read Rousseau in his youth and picked cherries, like a Rousseauan hero, with his first girlfriend. And he was a technocrat who rose to command in the artillery and won campaigns by meticulous attention to logistics. In some ways his was an avowedly barbaric empire, descended as much from Charlemagne's as from Rome's. It was beheld from heaven—in propaganda images painted by the promising young Ingres—by Ossian and the Valkyrie. Its appeal was at least as much to the rising romanticism of the nineteenth century as to the fading rationalism of the eighteenth. But Napoleon's vision was of a Europe engineered with a gunner's precision, levelled by uniform laws. From 1802, when he decided to sell Louisiana to the United States, until 1814, when he briefly contemplated retirement in America, he had no time for the New World.

If Europe could affect indifference towards America, it was hardly possible for America to respond in kind. In eighteenth- and early nineteenth-century allegories, America was commonly depicted as a gorgeous, strapping native

"America the Rich" engraved by G. B. Goëtz in about 1750. The parrot and crocodile represent savagery domesticated. Her cornucopia promises wealth. Her feather-wear echoes the exoticism of her surroundings. The arrival of Columbus, imitated from a famous sixteenth-century engraving by De Bry, is shown on the left. African, Asian and American natives combine to guard the globe in the foreground.

in a feathered head-dress, usually accompanied by similar figures symbolic of other continents, emphasizing the interdependence which worldwide trade had brought. The allegory could be made to look alluring. In a mid-eighteenth-century version by Gottfrid Goëtz, America extends her arms in a welcoming embrace, offering, along with her own dusky good looks and bejewelled and feathered nakedness, armfuls of riches and a sinuous cornucopia of rare fruits. Only the growling maw of the crocodile she rides reminds the beholder of the risks of conquest. But this was an outsider's image. Most of the élites who ran post-colonial states in the New World could not usefully or convincingly adopt an indigenous self-image.

They were too White, too close to their European roots, and in most cases too implicated in hostility to the Indians. Even in Bolivia and Paraguay there was little enthusiasm for a sense of nationhood purged of European impurities. Simón Bolívar, the "Liberator" after whom Bolivia was named, imposed on the country a rhetorical tradition steeped in Caesar and Solon but innocent of Pachacuti and Tupac Yupanqui. Even the Andean republics, with their glorious pre-conquest civilizations, were slow to exploit the indigenous past for creating national myths. In post-liberation Argentina the dilemma to be resolved was not whether the new state should avow an

Just after the natural inferiority of the New World had been proclaimed by Buffon and De Pauw (see p. 269), spectacular archaeological finds in Xochicalco and under the paving-stones of the main square in Mexico City seemed to vindicate pre-Columbian America's claim to house great civilizations. The Aztecs' apologist, Antonio León y Gama, professed peculiar satisfaction with this sun-stone or "Aztec Calendar," unearthed in 1790, because it seemed to demonstrate mathematical proficiency, elevating its makers from "superstition" to "science." The calendrical glyphs surround an image of the deity Tonatiuh (see p. 221), who is crowned with a sunbeam and arrayed with images of a jaguar's head and claws, a sky serpent, a feathered shield with an emblem of the sun, and a basketful of the detritus of a human sacrifice.

Atlantic or transatlantic identity but whether it should be dominated by the European civilization of the cities or the Asiatic barbarism of the pampas, where the wild gauchos, powerful enough to impose dictators of their choice on the country, were likened by sickened city-slickers to Tatars of the steppes.

The ruins of Palenque were among the most exciting of a series of dramatic archaeological finds in late eighteenth-century Mexico: a splendid city, largely of the seventh and eighth centuries CE, on the edge of the rain forest, near the Usumacinta River in Chiapas. The tomb of King Pacal (r. 615-83), whose dynasty was responsible for all the monumental building, is on the right, facing the curious tower of the palace complex. In 1787 Charles III of Spain—who, as King of Naples, had become used to the custodianship of antiquities even before his accession to the Spanish throne—ordered Antonio del Río to survey the remains.

Only Mexico felt confident about returning to its pre-conquest roots in search of a serviceable national myth. The legend of Saint Thomas–Quetzalcoatl helped. So did the fact that the Virgin of Guadalupe had chosen to reveal herself to an Indian. So did the willingness of the creole ruling caste to acknowledge its own Indian blood. Decisive was the copious evidence of the superior material culture of ancient Mesoamerican civilizations with which Mexicans were surrounded. Archaeology was not neglected among the sciences patronized by the late eighteenth-century Spanish monarchy; but this disinterested scholarship had a partisan effect: the scholars' trowels turned up objects of patriot self-pride.

Three discoveries, of many, were perhaps of outstanding importance. In 1784 a splendid palace emerged from the ruins of Xochicalco, which, in the opinion of local scholars, definitively exonerated the Aztecs of the charge of barbarism. An exiled Mexican Jesuit took the opportunity to point out that the highest achievements of civilization were attainable to all races in all climates, but for the strict purposes of creole patriotism it was not necessary to go that far. In 1790, during paving work in the main square of Mexico City, a great cache of buried Aztec masterpieces came to light, including the calendar stone and other calendrical materials. Now Mexicans could look up to their Aztec predecessors for their science as well as their arts. Meanwhile, in the far south of the country, royal curiosity had been aroused by the rediscovery of the lost ruins of Palenque, a sumptuous Maya city, mainly of the eighth century AD, on the edge of the rain forest. An expedition made detailed drawings, which, though unpublished until 1838, convinced savants that the glorious antiquities of Mesoamerica were not confined to the environs of the valley of Mexico but spread over a vast range of contrasting environments.

In partial consequence, Mexicans were able to interpret their experience in terms accessible only to themselves. Their independence was a Reconquista and their state a successor to ancient glories; the first effectively independent modern Mexican state called itself an empire, and its seal—with eagle surmounting a prickly pear—reproduced elements of an Aztec glyph (see above, p. 218). By comparison, in other "liberated" parts of the New World, the regimes seemed prolongations of the colonial past.

THE SPITTLE OF DEMOCRACY

The fledgling United States had no Aztec-style past to look up to. The carvings in Jefferson's hall aroused in his visitors curiosity or disgust but never awe or admiration. Instead, the new republic gave itself identity, common purpose, and a special place in the world by creating a new political culture.

It was not a democracy at first. Though the principle of elective office was firmly rooted and widely spread, the franchise was restricted. Even before the revolution, its limits were more generous than in Europe, embracing, state by state, perhaps 60 to 80 per cent of the adult white male population. Nor was democracy a dirty word as it was in Europe. Democratic reform was implicit in some of the guiding assumptions of the late-colonial society: the notion of universal—that is, of course, White male—citizenship; the conviction, inherited from Renaissance humanism, that citizenship conferred a share in civic duties; the belief, made explicit in the Declaration of Independence, in common "rights of man," equally distributed; the Puritan doctrine of "calling," which summoned men to social duty as well as to membership in the church. When Rhode Island, the last state to conform to democracy, introduced White manhood suffrage in 1842, until then limited by the 1663 state charter to freeholders and their sons, it was represented in the preamble to the legislation as a reversion to the ideals of Roger Williams, the Baptist founder of the Providence plantations.

The 1830s were the decade in which democracy took off, because levels of participation expanded to match the gradual extensions of the electorate. Two and a half million voters took part in the elections of 1840—more than twice as many as in 1832, whereas the population in the interim had increased by 30 per cent. Democracy was a style of politics as well as a doctrine. The barnstorming populism—even the vulgarity—of Andrew Jackson, who was elected president in 1828, set a new tone. This Cincinnatus of Tennessee, this old soldier recalled from his farm to civic duty, with his plain words and uncouth manners, ignited the hip-hooray and ballyhoo of mass enthusiasm; his methods defined the world's image of presidential campaigning until the late twentieth century, when rallies and conventions were sanitized to make safe television.

Alexis de Tocqueville was able to record American democracy in its cradle when he came, resolved to make a scientific study of American society, in 1831. Like other visitors he was critical of American manners; the want of an aristocracy to elevate common standards was sadly felt. The results included dull cities, pompous oratory, forward women, and barbarous table manners—meat served before fish and oysters for dessert. All travellers of the period found American habits crude; even in the best society, wads of tobacco were chewed and the yellow juices revoltingly expectorated. Dickens, who visited in 1842, found the White House rugs beslimed with spittle. There seems hardly to have been an observation of the United States recorded in the period in the old world without an animadversion on the hypocrisy of a people who talked equality and practised slavery. On the whole, however, Tocqueville returned home feeling that he had seen the future and found it to work. Dickens was more sceptical: "a lover of Freedom, disappointed" by what he saw; but even he found the effects of spitting and slavery mitigated by model prisons, decent schools, enlightened madhouses, and moral factories.

Tocqueville was aware of the dangers of democracy: in ignorance and equality, a people might elect a tyrant. But in his prescience he felt America was proof against the risk and that other societies where aristocratic privilege was entrenched would sooner or later follow its example. The sense of being an example to the world formed Americans' image of themselves and sustained the union through all the trials of the century down to and including the civil war. From an objective standpoint it may seem that only brazen hypocrisy could enable Lincoln to justify fratricidal war and defiance of states' rights on the grounds that "government . . . by the people shall not perish from the earth." Yet against the background of Americans' self-perceived vocation as torchbearers of republicanism and democracy—at a time when democracy was still unique to their own country and the world still seemed far from safe for republicanism—the apparent paradox made perfect sense.

In the long run, the spread of democracy would help to re-establish the

Manifest Destiny, The Spirit of "American Progress," depicted by John Gast in 1872, hovers over the westward march of White settlers, trailing a telegraph wire, as the land behind her is turned to tillage. Symbols of technological advance race across the plains. Rather than leading the march, the Native Americans on the left are fleeing, casting apprehensive glances at their pursuers. No irony was intended: centennial fervour was building up.

moral unity of Atlantic civilization, which the revolutions of 1775 to 1828 had strained or shattered. Indeed, no sooner was the crisis of Atlantic civilization over than its fragments began to reassemble. Noah Webster, the lexicographer, who set out to reform the language of America in order to make it less like England's English, repented of his decision; Anglo–U.S. political collaboration helped to ensure rebel victory in Latin America's wars of independence. After Britain had "called the New World into existence to redress the balance of the old," she busily set about a strategy of economic recolonization on her own behalf of the former Spanish empire. As we shall see, economic links, intellectual exchange, and the human contacts that multiplied with the hugely increased volume of transatlantic migration in the nineteenth century were all greater after independence than under colonial rule.

Meanwhile, without forgetting the ocean, America turned west. Although the U.S.A. kept her moral distance by affecting a lofty attitude towards European imperialism, she practised an imperialism of her own in pursuit of her "manifest destiny" in her own hemisphere. In the popular propaganda images, Manifest Destiny appears as an angelic figure, spreading beneficence as she guides settlers forward; but she appeared as an angel of another sort to the expulsees from Eden who were crowded onto the edge of the engraving, as the United States engorged Native American, Canadian, and Mexican lands.

Ironically, American imperialism was sanctified by democratic instincts. When a hundred and fifty years ago William Hickling Prescott published his *History of the Conquest of Mexico,* there was another conquest of Mexico in the offing. Prescott, as befitted a sober and scholarly Bostonian, had no journalistic sensationalism. He neither loved nor needed topics of current interest; but when in the late 1830s, towards the end of a decade's labours on *The History of the Reign of Ferdinand and Isabella,* he was looking for a new historical theme, it seemed increasingly certain that war between the U.S.A. and Mexico could not be long delayed. On 2 March 1836, Texans of U.S. origin had proclaimed their independence from Mexico; after the humiliating defeat of the punitive expedition which ensued and the capture of the Mexican leader, General Antonio de Santa Anna, who commanded it, the United States had recognized Texan sovereignty. In 1838, when Prescott decided to devote his next project to an earlier conquest of Mexico, the Texan war flickered on, never officially renounced by either side. Less than two years after the appearance of Prescott's book, the United States announced the annexation of Texas, and on 13 September 1847 a new army of gringo conquistadores marched into Mexico City.

Like other New England intellectuals, Prescott was equivocal about the morality of his country's policy. He did not go as far as Thoreau, who withheld his taxes and urged others to do the same, but when invited to write the history of this "second conquest" of Mexico, he replied, "I had rather not meddle with heroes who have not been under the ground for two centuries, at least." The success of his account of the first conquest benefitted, none the less, from its adventitious topicality, and despite Prescott's avowed aim of judging the past by its own standards, his view of the subject was occluded by gunsmoke from the south. The Aztec Empire was condemned by Prescott's democratic lights:

> Its fate may serve as a striking proof that a government which does not rest on the sympathies of its subjects cannot long abide; that human institutions, when not connected with human prosperity and progress, must fall—if not before the increasing light of civilization, by the hand of violence, by violence from within, if not from without. And who shall lament their fall?

Thus, subtly and without obvious violence to Prescott's vocation as an historian, the story of the conquest of Mexico became a tract for the times, the example of Cortés an encouragement to the Texan rebels, and the fate of Montezuma an admonition to General Santa Anna.

There was of course no necessary connection between imperialism and democracy; universal manhood suffrage was briefly introduced into European constitutions by the widespread—and uniformly unsuccessful—"intellectuals' revolutions" of 1848. Indifferently, it spread relatively early to a declining seat of empire such as Spain in 1868 or to mother-countries of burgeoning empires such as France and Britain in 1871 and 1884, respectively, or to anti-imperialist polities such as Switzerland in 1874. This painful headway was made against deep prejudice. Although democracy was hallowed by origins in the universally admired world of classical antiquity, well-educated gentlefolk could hardly forget Aristotle's warning that "extreme democracy is tyranny" or Plato's that "democracy is the worst of good constitutions, though the best of bad ones" or Homer's that "it is not good to have the rule of many." A democratic franchise in a monarchical state was, according to ancient wisdom, the worst of mixtures: this was a big deterrent in nineteenth-century Europe, where Switzerland was the only state to remain a republic throughout the period. Disraeli, who as prime minister of the United Kingdom enormously widened the British franchise, identified the "fruits of democracy" with the typical rational reluctance of the European élites: impatience at taxation and increases in expenditure; impassioned wars ending in ignominious peace; devalued property; and diminished freedom. From our late twentieth-century vantage point, when democracy has been laundered of all the blemishes of a once-dirty word, we forget how long it took for democracy to get to the top of the "greasy pole" of competing political systems.

The slow extension of the democractic principle continued in Europe until after the First World War, when it was boosted by the enormous political influence wielded by American armies (see Chapter 13): democracy in Europe did not perhaps need American patronage to triumph, but it certainly helped. Even then, the east side of the Atlantic was not safe for democracy until a virulent anti-democratic reaction was spent. Most of the major powers of continental Europe abjured democracy at some time between 1918 and 1940; in western Europe it was not generally restored until after the Second World War, and even then it remained precarious in France and was kept out of the Iberian peninsula. Most of the countries of the southern shore remained undemocratic or imperfectly democratic until the 1970s; some did not return to the fold until the 1980s or 1990s. East of the Elbe, democracy was only restored after the revolutions of 1989–91 (see Chapter 16). Nevertheless, democracy did become a defining feature of "the western world"—imbedded in the political culture of some peoples, such as the British and Swiss, emblazoned as an ideal on that of others, such as the Hungarians and Czechs. Early in the twentieth century—and with renewed commitment after the Second World War—democracy became the cement of an Atlantic alliance which linked like-minded states on both sides of the ocean in a programme of defence and a sense of shared values (see Chapter 13).

From the perspective of that period, when Atlantic powers huddled round the ocean, while the links that bound Atlantic peoples in amity were fully restored by the world wars and the cold war, Atlantic civilization, from its inception halfway through the millennium, seemed to have grown inevitably to dominate modern history. *The Rise of the West* and *The Triumph of the West* were the titles of two of the most brilliant and successful accounts of world history to be written during that period. Yet the fragility of the bonds of the "west" in its first three hundred years, the depth of the chasm opened by the revolutionary era, and the slow process by which moral unity and political interdependence were restored will perhaps make the galactic museum-keepers see things differently. To them, the ocean-straddling colossus will be a late arrival among the wonders of the world, with a very short-lived supremacy. The next few chapters—this part of the book and the next—will pick a way, over the bridges and fissures of Atlantic civilization, through its long period of climacteric.

Chapter 12

VOYAGES OF BOUNTY:
THE REDISTRIBUTION OF
WORLD RESOURCES

Empires of the Dandelion—The Precious Commodities—
The Industrious East—The Growl of the Tiger—The Industrial West

EMPIRES OF THE DANDELION

Suppose Columbus had been right. Suppose the enterprise on which he sailed in 1492 had been practical and his geographical assumptions correct: a world 25 per cent smaller than it really is; a world without a New World; a direct passage from Spain to China or Japan with no intervening hemisphere; an easily accessible Orient, prematurely reported and vividly depicted in his early reports from America, where Asiatic merchants in funny hats appear, engraved in a woodcut, hobnobbing with naked natives.

Had there been no New World to redress the economic balance of the old, western Christendom might have remained in the position of inferiority traditional in her relationship with Islam and China—and perhaps stooped to one of subordination. Columbus, had he been able to reach Japan, would have been greeted as an exotic freak and derided for eating with his fingers; and in China he would have been received as a primitive tributary, bearing risible gifts. As it was, shortly after gaining control of much of the vast, under-exploited resource-base of the Americas, western European peoples went on to establish the farthest-flung empires the world had ever seen and, collectively, the most thoroughgoing hegemony any civilization

Although no galley could have made a crossing of the Atlantic, the artist of this woodcut from an early Basle edition of the first printed report of Columbus's discoveries chose this image to suggest the lucrative commerce which, the report claimed, could be found in the New World: "both with the mainland on this side of the ocean and that on the far side belonging to the Great Khan great trade and profit will be had." The figures in oriental headgear are presumably meant to represent merchants from a supposedly nearby Asiatic civilization.

had ever attained. Since the late eighteenth century, successive observers of the "rise of the west" have asked whether there is some link between the acquisition of America and the revolution in resources which made age-old supremacies vanish.

A privileged observer at a critical stage of the trend was the Scots economist Adam Smith, whose *Wealth of Nations* appeared in the year of the American Declaration of Independence and whose name has been synonymous ever since with the cause of worldwide free trade. As a foe of mercantilism, he could hardly be a friend to imperialism. He claimed that Britain would be better off with an independent America than with an expensive and resentful empire. He complained that "it was not the wisdom and policy, but the disorder and injustice of the European governments, which populated and cultivated America." Yet he could not join so many other moralists of the European enlightenment in condemning Europe's

American enterprise utterly. He regarded the discovery of a way across the Atlantic, together with that of a sea route from Europe to Asia, to be the most important event in history and was convinced of its general benefits. In particular he saw American bullion as the starting-point of reversed fortunes, helping to make up Christendom's adverse trade balance with Islam and China, while copious natural resources and burgeoning new markets were put in the exclusive reach of western and central European industries.

It is hard to fit the detailed facts to this hypothesis, despite its common-sense appeal. The New World markets, as we have seen, were small and as they grew became increasingly detached from their parent-economies. The bullion barely enriched its handlers, and much of it ended up benefiting exporters in the far east. It is true that lands unsurpassed anywhere in the world as food-producers are concentrated in unrivalled amounts in the North American midwest and athwart the River Plate, but these regions were not exploited until well into the nineteenth century. Colonial America was established on relatively inferior soils.

The real treasure of the New World is sometimes said today to have been the indigenous food crops—above all, maize and potatoes—the sustaining stodge which revolutionized old-world diets. As we shall see in a moment, that is a persuasive view, but the civilization of western Europe was not the only beneficiary of such treasures. If America made a difference, it was a difference longer deferred and compromised by more complexity than is commonly acknowledged. It has to be understood in the context of a very slow shift—uneven in pace and sometimes forced by fitful accelerations—in the balance and distribution of the world's resources.

Even in our own times, markets bombarded by statistics make impressionistic judgements and stocks or currencies rise or fall as much on their rumoured prospects as their recorded performance. For most of our millennium, reputation has been worth more than objectively measured wealth, and therefore, for the historian, qualitative evidence is better than quantitative. Even where economic historians have scraped up the statistics, the crunched numbers tell us less—as they tire us more—than the guesswork of contemporaries which really influenced events. The revolution in economic reputations between, say, China and the west during the second half of our millennium is reflected in the awestruck stares of what we might call the window-shoppers of history, amazed at other people's plenty.

An early window-shopper in China, for instance, was Fernão Mendes Pinto, the Portuguese Sinbad, who from 1521 to 1558 claimed to have sailed the east as a soldier of fortune, penetrating every cranny of the accessible Orient, surviving en route more shipwrecks, enslavements, slaughters, storms, and changes of fortune than any reader could reasonably believe. His account of his adventures is a masterpiece of picaresque literature with many delicious asides, both sententious and satirical. Though his description of China is no more verifiable than the rest of his book, it fairly reflects the country's image with his contemporaries. In the tingle of senses excited by the excess of everything, it rings true as the relation of an eye-witness, walking round the markets of Peking, for example, "as if in a daze" at the quantities of "silk, lace, canvas, clothes of cotton and linen, marten and musk and ermines, delicate porcelain, gold- and silver-plate, seed-pearls and pearls, gold-dust and gold-bullion"; and as for the base metals, gems, ivory, spices, condiments, and foods—"well, all these things were to be had in such abundance that I feel as if there are not enough words in the dictionary to name them all."

Fernão Mendes, who could never forgo irony for long, felt obliged to ex-cuse himself from cataloguing the riches of China "so that everyone will see with what generosity the Lord our God has shared out with these benighted people the fruits of the earth he created. For which generosity, let his name be praised for ever." Yet this land of plenty gradually became a land of penury in western eyes, where nowadays an average citizen survives on two-thirds of the daily calorific intake of an American and where visiting western students find themselves feeling faint after a few days' eating in a university canteen. A few years ago, when the wife of the American jour-nalist Fox Butterfield dined with a friend in a provincial restaurant, "eight other customers, all men dressed in patched and faded blue clothes, pulled up their stools in a semicircle around the foreigners' table to watch. Some of them were picking their teeth. 'We got the feeling we were the nightly entertainment.'" The jealous, hungry eyes Fernão Mendes once turned on Chinese markets are now reflected back at visitors from the west. Over the same period of four centuries or so, the same contrast could be illustrated in the relative economic esteem evinced in western sources for India and some parts of the Middle East, which once excited western greed and now evoke western pity.

By narrowing the focus to the late eighteenth and early nineteenth cen-turies of the Christian era, the historian can actually discern the transition in progress—can actually capture some of the relevant changes happening in a period which seems to have been crucial in the realignment of the tradi-tional balance of production and terms of trade. Here statistics can be ten-tatively called in to help confirm what impressionistic evidence suggests—an increase in the numbers of mankind over a very broad front. In almost every place and period, except where statistics to the contrary are incontro-vertible, sources can be found to lament depopulation and shortage of manpower; when contemporary observers unite, or at least join freely, to claim the opposite, they therefore command respect. The eighteenth cen-tury had plenty of prophets of depopulation, especially in particular rural areas from which migrants flew or in the urban areas where thousands were immolated by plague. Overwhelmingly, however, the general trend

Thomas Malthus, portrayed by J. Linnell as the ageing sage of international renown in 1833, the year before his death. His eminence was based only on the *Essay on Population*, which remained his sole substantial work. The son of a Rousseauan perfectibilian, he formulated his doom-fraught version of mankind's future in reaction against the philosophy on which he was weaned. His statistical projections were borrowed from the arch-optimist of the Enlightenment, the Marquis de Condorcet. In fact, Condorcet's interpretation of rapid population increase as symptomatic of a stage of "progress," reversible as prosperity increases, has proved to be more consistent with the observed trends since then than Malthus's conviction that only disaster could prevent overpopulation (see p. 723).

was acknowledged to be upwards. In many places it was going up far enough and fast enough to inspire Malthusian nightmares.

In the second half of the century, wherever demographic change can be documented in detail over a large area, population boomed. In 1837 a British investigator reported that the population of the lower Ganges delta had doubled during the British domination, since 1765, while that of Madras was increasing at about the same rate as Wales. According to official census figures, which were of course subject to under-reporting, the population of the Chinese Empire rose from 275 million in 1779 to 430 million in 1850; an even sharper rise in about the previous half-century is probable but, owing to the deficiency of the data, hazardous to compute. Economic theorists in China vied to congratulate themselves on the increasing numbers of producers or to predict Malthusian effects. In eastern and western Christendom combined, numbers have been reckoned to increase in the century after 1750 from something over 140 million to a figure approaching a quarter of a billion. The doom-fraught theories of Thomas Malthus were therefore of their time—a voice crying for the want of a wilderness, an earnest, rational clergyman peering with anxious charity into a grave new world of overpopulation tempered by disaster. In the Americas, where the much smaller numbers were disproportionately influenced by immigration, the total doubled in the second half of the eighteenth century, then more than doubled again to an estimated 59 million in 1850. For Islam west of India the evidence is inconsistent—collapse in parts of Iran, Syria, and Palestine, slaughter in plague-rife cities which "devoured" people, buoyancy in rural Egypt and European Turkey; but generalizations in the past about overall decline have been too glibly made.

Neither the spread nor the pace of the demographic leap forward has been convincingly explained. General phenomena demand general explanations, but this growth of population happened in too many different environments and too many diverse economic contexts for such explanations to be credible. Some consequences are clearer than the causes: over the eighteenth and nineteenth centuries as a whole, despite the big rises in population in some parts of Asia, Europe's relative share in the world's human resources rose dramatically, from around a fifth to over a quarter. If the United States and the other Atlantic destinations of European emigrants are included, the component-states of the "Atlantic civilization" probably contained over a third of mankind by 1900. Much of this relative growth was at the expense of parts of Islam: the slow reordering of the relative demographic ranking of Islam and Christendom, which as we saw above (Chapter 3) seems to have begun in the late middle ages, picked up speed. It helps, for instance, to understand the fading of the Ottoman Empire among the great powers of the world, to know that the ratio of its population relative to that of Europe as a whole dropped from perhaps about 1:6 in 1600 to about 1:10 in 1800.

Space makes people philoprogenitive. The increase of population in the Americas was boosted by exceptionally high birth rates as well as by immigration. The New World can therefore be said to have added to the human resources of western civilization by adding to its resources of space. Moreover, in the temperate parts of the Americas (and in the lush lands farther afield in New Zealand and south-east Australia), space could be colonized by European food crops and livestock which eventually made these regions purveyors of food to the world.

In this transplantation of old-world ecosystems, wheat was of paramount importance; worldwide it remains, by preference, easily the dominant staple food of mankind. Almost equally important were weeds, especially purslane and Englishman's Foot, which created what Alfred Crosby brilliantly christened "empires of the dandelion." Weeds "healed raw wounds invaders tore in the earth," bound soil together, saved it from erosion and desiccation, refilled "vacated eco-niches," and fed imported livestock. Not far from the empires of the dandelion were the supply-lands of the Kingdom of Sweets. The fantasy land of Hoffmann and Tchaikovsky was supplied from the New World with transplanted coffee and sugar and indigenous chocolate. Of the products which performed the kingdom's courtly dances, only tea was without New World associations, and even this

"The supply-lands of the Kingdom of Sweets." Where they could not control production or transfer to territories they ruled, Europeans remained suppliants for exotic produce throughout the early-modern period: whether negotiating concessions to buy nutmeg and mace, as in the seventeenth-century Dutch engraving of a merchant bargaining with the Sultan of Ternate (see pp. 321–27), or in the early nineteenth-century scene of European merchants in top hats haggling over samples in a Chinese tea warehouse.

had a comparable history—transplanted from China to India and converted by plantation production into an article of mass consumption.

Two caveats, however, should be borne in mind: first, the incorporation of American space only contributed to a "western" advantage in power over other civilizations very gradually, in the course of the nineteenth century, as the most productive spaces were colonized and as the value-chasm, which divided the Atlantic world, was re-spanned. Second, an important part of the extra productive capacity of the New World consisted not in the extent of the soil, nor even its quality or adaptability to an imported ecology, but rather in the indigenous crops which sprouted from it and which could be grown elsewhere. In other words, this was an exportable form of productive capacity. In China, where space was by no means abundant, even in the colonized fringes and uplands of the early-modern era, population growth was materially assisted by the new food resources adapted from America. In the eighteenth century, maize and sweet potatoes became the poor men's foodstuffs of widely separated provinces.

THE PRECIOUS COMMODITIES

The impact of these crops was registered in a Chinese countryside convulsed by a disturbing and sometimes violent tenurial revolution. An incident from 1645 shows what was going on: a powerful clan's rural poor relation called Huang T'ung planned an attack on his urban kinsmen in revenge for the desecration of his father's grave. Joined by tenants "for the pleasure of working off their petty grievances," he broke into the county capital and, after looting and blood-letting, tore down part of the walls. Serfdom, undermined by peasant revolts in the 1640s, was abolished by stages. In 1681 peasants could no longer be sold along with the land they farmed but must be free to "do as they please." The last vestiges were swept away in the early eighteenth century. The landlord life became less attractive in consequence. Land was still valued as a source of prestige or security, but agriculture was despised as "the labour of fools" while peasant truculence made rent collection a "path to be feared." Estates broken up by partible inheritance were no longer restored by individuals determined to accumulate traditional patrimonies. Eighteenth-century China became increasingly a "world of smallholders." Rural investment took the form of pawnbroking by city-dwelling loansharks, lending for seed-grain. A history of enmity between town and country began which continues to this day.

These conditions favoured the spread of crops of American origin, perhaps because their cultivators could exploit otherwise marginal lands, out of the reach of trouble, or because growing peasant independence facilitated experiments in planting. Occasionally production was promoted by officials anxious to feed expanding populations while boosting their own fiscal returns. In 1594 it was said to be a governor of Fukien who recommended sweet potatoes when more conventional crops failed. In the 1770s officials in Hunan, urgently promoting double-cropping on rice paddies, advised that the lack of available wasteland for increased output could be compensated by growing maize and sweet potatoes on the hills.

These crops had reached China amazingly quickly after their discovery in America—so quickly, indeed, that some scholars insist on an undocumented earlier transmission. They were treated at first as exotica of only marginal practical utility. Maize, known as "precious grain," had arrived perhaps by two independent routes: overland from the west, as a tribute-plant brought by western frontiersmen and first recorded in 1555; and by sea to Fukien, where a visiting Augustinian saw it cultivated in 1577. It rated no more than a footnote in a standard agricultural compendium of the early seventeenth century. The sweet potato, first reported in Yunnan near the Burmese border in the 1560s, may have come overland from the south. Its flavour had a bad reputation with Han Chinese, but it was favoured, especially in the hill country of Fukien, by immigrants and, later, in Hunan by natives and foreign settlers. In the eighteenth century, in alliance with maize, it transformed vast areas of China. The uplands of the Yangtze basin, formerly covered with forest, were developed for cash crops—indigo and jute—by "shack people" who lived off maize planted on the sunny side of their slopes and sweet potatoes on the shady side. Similar results flowed from the complementarity of these crops in Fukien, Szechuan, and Hunan. By the end of the century sweet potatoes had conquered palates sufficiently widely to be sold boiled and roasted by the street vendors of Peking.

Even in China, maize and sweet potatoes were only a supplement—not a substitute—for the native staple, rice; they had the effect of extending, not replanting, the cultivated soil. In the rest of the world their effects were even more limited. India spurned them both, and nowhere did sweet potatoes get taken up as in China. In the Middle East by the end of the eighteenth century, maize became the staple of Egyptian peasants, who grew other grain only to pay their taxes, but it remained a marginal crop in the rest of the region. In Europe, which had privileged access to New World agronomy, maize was unsuitable for the climate of much of the best land, and unpalatable to the people of much of the rest. It had a restricted but vital importance in the Balkans, where it made life possible at relatively high altitudes in the eighteenth century, nourishing effectively autonomous communities beyond the grasp of Ottoman tax-gatherers and the reach of Ottoman administrators, weaning the future political independence of Greece, Serbia, and Romania from their mountain cradles. Thus in this corner of Europe an American resource really can be shown to have made a direct contribution to the adjustment of the frontier with Islam in Christendom's favour.

In nutritional value, maize is exceeded by the potato. Both crops have a significantly higher yield of calories than all other staples except rice—which is roughly equivalent—but the potato, unlike maize, supplies unaided all the nutrients man needs. Thanks to the adaptation of this Andean tuber, the influence of New World crops on regional agronomies of the old world was probably highest in northern Europe, where the potato attained a mastery maize could never achieve in China, supplanting rye as the food base of a vast swath of mankind from Ireland across the northern European plain to Russia. It was spread by war, for peasants, eluding requisition with the aid of a crop that could be left concealed in the ground, survived on potatoes when other food was in short supply.

Essayed with success in the Basque country and Ireland, the potato began its war-linked career of conquest in Belgium in the 1680s under the impact of Louis XIV's drive for a rational French frontier. The troubles of the next century sowed it in Germany and Poland, and the Napoleonic wars took it to Russia, where it conquered a territory Napoleon was unable to subjugate with the entire Grande Armée. The acreage planted with potatoes increased with every European war down to and including the Second World War. On its way, it was helped by the patronage of savants and monarchs. Catherine the Great advocated it in 1765. Marie Antoinette—unfairly cast as a promoter of cake for the masses—advertised its merits by wearing potato flowers in her dress. It fed some of the industrializing, urbanizing, surplus populations of the nineteenth and twentieth centuries in Germany and Russia. In Ireland its failure in 1845–46 released emigrant labour for the British and North American industrial revolutions. It can therefore be said to have helped make possible the new means of production which gave the nineteenth-century west an advantage in competition with the rest of the world.

Other New World products, without attaining the status of staples, achieved mass markets and helped to modify cultures. Peanuts fascinated the Chinese because they were "born from flowers fallen to the ground" and had seeds like silkworm cocoons. They were ideal for the sandy loams south of the Yangtze and might have been exploited as a basic food, but perhaps because of their mysterious generation they remained a luxury, invested by reputation with magical properties—"longevity nuts," considered essential at Peking banquets in the late eighteenth century. Tomatoes tinted the palette of Mediterranean cuisine, and chilies accentuated the preferences of Indian and Thai cooks in a part of the world where other American crops found surprisingly little favour.

Two other New World products made important contributions in the long run to the redistribution of the world's resources. The first was tobacco. A weed destined to vanish in smoke was a suitable symbol of vanity in early-modern Europe. A Dutch emblem-book of 1627, for instance, showed Cu-

Tobacco-emblem from Jacobo Cats's illustrations of popular moral philosophy, *Proteus ofte Minee-Beilden Verandert in Sinne-beelden* (1627). Tobacco's properties were thought to be digestive rather than erotic; Cupid carries the smoker's pipe and pouch because tobacco, like love, is an evanescent pleasure which quickly goes up in smoke.

pid as a natural tobacconist. But as the means by which the opium habit spread—for the smoker's pipe in which opium was mixed proved an ideal inhaler for the drug—tobacco had a major part in reversing the traditionally favourable terms of China's trade in the nineteenth century (see Chapter 10). Quinine, too, played a vital role in the "rise of the west" by helping to equip the white man for mastery of the tropics. A native American remedy for malaria, borrowed by a seventeenth-century viceroy of Peru desperate to save his wife's life, it was transplanted to India in the nineteenth century and grown in plantation conditions for industrial processing.

QVESTION MORAL.
Si el Chocolate quebranta el
ayuno Eclesiastico.
Tratase de otras bebidas j confecciones
que se vsan en varias Provincias
A D. Garcia de Avellaneda y Haro Conde
de Castrillo de la Camara de su Mag.
Comendador de la Obreria de los
Consejos de Estado y Guerra
Castilla y Camara y Governador
del Real de las Indias.
Por el Lic. Antonio de Leon Pinela
Relator del mismo Consejo.

En Madrid. Por la Viuda de Iuan Gonçalez. Año. 1636.

The "moral problem" posed by chocolate and addressed by Antonio León Pinelo in this work of 1636 was whether a cup of chocolate could be taken before mass without fast-breaking. But he took a wide view, suggesting that chocolate was morally threatening not only because it was sustaining but also because it was luxurious. The controversy was serious: it provoked the disorders in Mexico described in the text.

Meanwhile, in a story curiously parallel to that of quinine, chocolate, discovered by conquistadores at the court of Montezuma, was turned from a luxurious beverage to a concentrated source of energy for mass consumption in the west by industrial processes. Early doubts among westerners who tried it about whether it was really a source of food are illustrated by a curious seventeenth-century controversy over its permissibility during fasts. In a work of 1648, which is usually credited with introducing England to the merits of chocolate, Thomas Gage reported the repercussions of this controversy in a remote diocese of New Spain, where the bishop had tried to prevent ladies from refreshing themselves with cupfuls during mass. When excommunication failed, he provoked a riot in the cathedral by ordering the priests to prevent chocolate from being served, and when he died mysteriously, rumour insisted that a poisoned cup of chocolate was responsible. "And it became afterwards a proverb in that country, 'Beware the chocolate of Chiapa!'"

The new beverages generated by imperialism and global trade created new social rituals as well as reinforcing old ones. Tea, coffee, and chocolate demanded to be elaborately prepared and decorously served. In these eighteenth-century Catalan tiles the beau who has no cup of chocolate has more difficulty attracting a lady's attention than his better-equipped counterparts.

Though to Gage, who knew chocolate in its natural habitat, it seemed a good, cheap stimulant, he also conveyed its adaptability to a luxury market. He described concoctions mixed with cinnamon, cloves, and almonds, which would appeal in Europe, as well as the stews of bitter chocolate and hot chilies which were traditional indigenous recipes. The elevated status of the beverage in eighteenth-century Europe surrounded the consumption of chocolate with rituals of social differentiation and images of wealth. In Barcelona's Ceramics Museum, painted tilework of the time in honour of the chocolate cult shows cups of the stuff being offered by bewigged gentlemen on bended knee to sumptuously attired ladies, beside the fountains of a pavilioned *hortus conclusus*.

To exploit its potential as cheap food it was necessary to create mechanized factories for pressing the cocoa bean; such factories existed by the last decade of the eighteenth century in Barcelona and Bologna, but they were still producing an expensive product for an exclusive clientele. It was also vital to contrive the right cultural climate. The technology came from continental Europe—from Spain and Italy, where cocoa presses were first mechanized; from Holland, where Conrad van Houten created cocoa powder; from Switzerland, where the Caillier and Nestlé families, united by marriage, combined in business to make milk chocolate. But it was English Quaker manufacturers of cocoa who did the most to revolutionize social attitudes.

In eighteenth- and early nineteenth-century England, civil disabilities forced Quakers into business. The chocolate business attracted them particularly because of cocoa's potential as a temperance beverage. To drive the price and accessibility of the product down to the level of the mass market was an ambition which, for families like the Frys of York or the Cadburys of Bournville, united God with gain. The chocolate bar, first marketed by Frys in 1847, was the natural outcome. The entire history of chocolate, from colonial crop to industrial product, is encapsulated in Roald Dahl's fictional chocolate factory, inspired by the work of the American inventor and caramel millionaire Milton Snavely Hershey. Here magically supra-modern technology combines with the labour of a tiny race of slaves. The full effects were not felt for nearly a century after the first bars: in the Second World War, quinine pills and Hershey bars helped Americans wage successful campaigns in tropical environments.

THE INDUSTRIOUS EAST

Quinine and chocolate—plants from the colonial florilegium, transformed by technology, in long stages, into powerful extensions of the resources of

Roald Dahl's hero Willie Wonka steps onto the banks of the chocolate river "where everything was eatable" to recruit "hundreds and hundreds of tiny oompa-loompas" for his chocolate factory. The oompa-loompas are a rather equivocal image of the effects of the exploitation of colonial environments for consumer products: in Mr. Wonka's chocolate factory they are effectively imprisoned and enslaved, yet they effuse happiness and loyalty. The illustration is Michael Foreman's to *Charlie and the Great Glass Elevator*.

Atlantic civilization—are reminders of how much the Industrial Revolution contributed to the material advantages of the western world in the recent past. Yet as recently as the eighteenth century the great industrial centres of the world were in China and India, where traditional technology could support enormous concentrations of production and remarkable degrees of specialization. There was as yet no "workshop of the world," but the world's biggest workshops were to be found in the east. According to memories recollected in the early nineteenth century, for instance, the Beneficial and Beautiful wholesaling firm, founded two hundred years previously by Mr. Wang of Hangchow, built up its cloth sales to a million lengths a year by making audacious rebates to tailors. Mr. Wang employed 4,000 weavers and several times that number of spinners. His dyeing and finishing were organized in a great centre of the trade, outside the Ch'ang Gate, where 10,900 workers were gathered in 1730 under 340 contractors, "and for two hundred years now there has been no place, either north or south, that has failed to consider Beneficial and Beautiful cloth to be lovely."

Other trades were organized on a similar scale. A porcelain centre in eighteenth-century Kiangsu province "made the ground shake with the noise of tens of thousands of pestles. The heavens are alight with the glare from the furnaces, so that one cannot sleep at night." There were ironworks in Szechuan that employed two or three thousand men. In Kwangtung water-driven hammers pounded incense "without any expenditure of muscular effort." In Kiangsi similar machines for husking rice were lined up by the hundred. In Fukien water-driven paper-makers hummed "like the whirr of wings."

Chinese industry may have been in a class of its own at the time for technical proficiency, but in terms of volume of production and degree of specialization, some Indian industries in the eighteenth century were scarcely less impressive than those of China. In Bengal, where it seemed to a British scrutineer that "every man, woman, or child in every village was employed in making cloth," each major variety was produced by a particular subcaste. In Kurnool on the Krishna River 30,000 to 60,000 miners were said to be gathered in a town of only 100,000 people in all. At their peak of production, in the mid-seventeenth century, the shipyards of the Maratha states were said to have produced 200 warships for King Shivaji. A Dutch silk factory at Kasimbazar in Bengal, with 700 or 800 workers, was modelled less on European precedents than on the official textile factories sponsored by the Mughals to supply the imperial wardrobe with fine stuffs.

Although by the conventional economic standards of Europe, the fiscal demands of the Mughal state, exacting perhaps 50 per cent of the gross product of the empire, might seem depressing to any nascent industrial spirit, it may actually have favoured the concentration of production by concentrating demand and creating a huge administrative class with surplus spending power. Although most Indians were, by European standards, scantily clad, sparingly shod, and sketchily housed in a land where, according to a sixteenth-century envoy, "the swine lie better than any man," the sheer size of the market ensured high levels of demand. The habit of hoarding no doubt inhibited trade, but one aspect of the prevailing value-system favoured the output of artisans in a society where women went "fettered with gold and silver, the meaner with brass and glass" and where it was *de rigueur* to wear ornaments of gilt, or at least of copper, ivory, seashell, bell-metal, or tin "though the whole family should die of hunger."

In consequence, eighteenth-century India was an enormous exporter of manufactures—the Mughal Empire was almost certainly the world's most productive state in terms of manufactures for export—despite the modest technical equipment with which her industries were generally supplied. Indian workers cut screws without a lathe and made muslin without a spinning wheel. Water-powered mills were rare, cast iron unknown. Even the Maratha shipyards were scratch affairs with an *ad hoc* workforce. In 1675 the English physician John Fryer watched fascinated as a Hindu coral-worker in Surat bent over his task with "hands and feet being all the vice and the other tools unshapen bits of iron." Nearby a Muslim cut every kind of gem except diamonds with a wheel whetted with melted lac and powdered stone.

Some of the same inducements and inhibitions overhung the industrial development of the nearer east. Here raw materials were also abundant; the vitality of the luxury market impressed every European visitor. The selectivity of Turkish talent for industry and the retardation of technical inventiveness in important trades were well described by an acutely critical observer of 1807, at a time when the empire seemed to be tottering from the effects of Wahhabi revolt:

> I know not whether Europe can equal, but certainly it cannot surpass them, in several of their manufactures. The satins and silk stuffs and the velvets of Bursa and Aleppo, the serges and camelots of Angora, the crapes and gauzes of Salonica, the printed muslins of Constantinople, the carpets of Smyrna, and the silk, the linen and the cotton stuffs of Cairo, Chios, Magnesia, Tocat, and Castanbol, establish a favourable but not an unfair criterion of their general skill and industry.

"In many of the inferior trades" Turkish workmen were equal to those of France, but as in India, their methods were hidebound. "They still practise all they found practised, but from an indolence with respect to innovation have not introduced or encouraged several useful arts of later invention."

Such industrial promise as the region still possessed was destroyed by European competition. According to a voyager in mid-eighteenth-century

"Britannia Receiving the Riches of the East" by Spiridione Roma, 1778. Commissioned by the East India Company for the ceiling of the Revenue Committee Room at the company's headquarters in Leadenhall Street, London, the painting is an odd mixture of the classical and the exotic. The river god in the foreground is modelled on Father Tiber. Hermes directs the queue of tributaries, headed by India, bearing pearls, with other bearers presenting Chinese porcelain, a case of tea, bales of indeterminate contents, spice pods, an elephant and a camel.

Bairam, the expansive spending habits of local notables mainly benefited French importers. In the second half of the century the carrying trade of the Ottoman Empire passed entirely into foreign hands—mainly French, English, and Venetian; in 1775 Tunisian shippers abandoned a heroic effort to overcome Marseillais protectionism and commercial dirty tricks. Persian silk and Egyptian linen dwindled or disappeared from export lists.

Although India was hardly better equipped than the Middle East to experience an industrial revolution, the extent of her own industrial collapse in the same period is astonishing. The ancient drain of westerners' silver into India was reversed in Bengal by the 1770s. In 1807, John Crawfurd reported that useful trades in Bengal had been supplanted by "kite makers, falconers, astrologers, and snake charmers. Such is the state of the arts in British India." A French missionary's analysis was candid and cogent:

Europe no longer depends on India for anything, having learnt to beat the Hindus on their own ground, even in their most characteristic manufactures and industries, for which from time immemorial we were dependent on them. In fact, the roles have been reversed and this revolution threatens to ruin India completely.

With an exactness rare in history, India's industrial debacle coincided with the establishment of British rule or hegemony over most of the subcontinent and, in particular, over its former industrial heartlands. The rapidity of the transformation took contemporaries by surprise. For Edmund Burke this was one of the "stupendous revolutions that have happened in our age of wonders." Its dual nature, political and commercial, decorates the ceiling of East India House in London's Leadenhall Street, where Britannia, enthroned, receives the riches of the east from an abject procession led by India, negligently inspecting the proffered platter of jewels and pearls. The question naturally arises: how, if at all, were India's political and economic fortunes connected?

Economic explanations of India's industrial frustration are best approached by way of a comparison with China, where industry was similarly productive and specialized and, in a technical sense, even more proficient. Indian technology may have been caught, like China's, in what Mark Elvin has called a "high-level equilibrium trap." Industries which were meeting huge demands with traditional technologies had no scope for increasing output by mechanization. Britain, starting from a low threshold, could triple cotton production between the 1740s and the 1770s. A similar rise in Chinese output would have glutted the world. The entire world supply of raw cotton would have been insufficient to meet a comparable increase in Chinese demand. In about the 1770s or 1780s a single Chinese province imported yearly, on average, six times as much cotton as the whole of industrializing Britain. Cheap labour is good for an industrial revolution, but cheap capital is better. In the "teeming" worlds of India and China, the cost of labour relative to that of capital may have been too low for industry's good. There was no point in expending the latter to economize on the former. Identified by Elvin, "a rational strategy for peasant and merchant alike tended in the direction not so much of labour-saving machinery as of economizing on resources and fixed capital." This trap was typified by the experience of a Chinese official in 1742 who proposed to save peasants in his charge four-fifths of their labour by installing copper pumps at a well-head; aghast at the immobilization of so much hard wealth, the peasants preferred to continue to draw water by hand. The frustration some of us feel today at our continued dependence on the internal combustion engine and fossil fuels shows how progress can be arrested by the inertia of inferior technologies which, like evil, are sufficient unto their day.

Explanations like this, which focus on the immobility of certain Asian economies or the traditionalism of some Asian technologies, can satisfy curiosity about the limits of the spread of the industrial revolution. They seem inadequate to explain the extinction of Indian industry, the "de-industrialization" of India under British rule. Some contemporaries tried to exonerate the new masters by explaining that the economic problems had started before they arrived. The decline of the Mughal Empire—skewered at its heart by Persian and Afghan invaders, shredded at its edges by usurping officials and tribal wars—had deprived native industries of courtly markets. After Nadir Shah looted £30 million from Delhi, the nobles could no longer buy the products of Bengal.

Even in Britain, industrialization was in its infancy and was probably not advanced enough to smother Indian textiles by dumping before the 1820s. Still, British policy was to favour home produce by tariff regulation, and in the internal Indian wars which dispelled producers and choked demand, a British official confessed that "we have had too large a share." It is therefore possible that political change lay at the root of India's economic problems and that the redistribution of the resources of the world was politically weighted. In any case, the extension of British mastery in the subcontinent is a vital part of the story because India was Britain's base for the cultivation of tea and opium, which together reversed the terms of trade with China, and for the quinine planting which helped fortify English sahibs for wider empire in tropical climes.

THE GROWL OF THE TIGER

Hector Hugh Munro, who died fighting in the First World War, signed as "Saki" the best and most delicately subversive English short stories of the Edwardian era. In "Sredni Vashtar," perhaps the most frequently anthologized of them all, a boy's vicious, slinky pet polecat kills an ungenerous aunt, recalling in warped form an incident in 1792 when Munro's namesake and collateral ancestor was savaged to death by a tiger in Mysore.

Saki's story was not the only work of art inspired by the event. It has been commemorated in a great range of media from Staffordshire pottery to modern collage. One of the grisliest memorials was a gigantic mechanical toy which reproduced the scene life-size to the accompaniment of screams from the victim and growls from the tiger emitted through organ-pipes inside. The sense of humour titillated by this device belonged to Tipu Sultan (1749–1799), ruler of Mysore, whose emblem was the tiger and whose enemy was the British. The tiger's victim was the son of a British general to whom Tipu had reputedly lost ten thousand men. Tipu intended to imitate its action in springing to his own voracious revenge.

Munro's death in a tiger's jaws in 1792 became a symbol at Tipu's court of the coming defeat of the British at the hands of the sultan, whose name meant "tiger" and who adopted the beast as his badge. Another version of this grisly mechanical toy at Edinburgh Castle shows the victim as a soldier.

His gorgeous and defiant world comes to life in the booty of his realm, collected today in the Victoria and Albert Museum, London. He was obsessed by tigers. Of his throne, "the proud monument of his arrogance," broken up at its capture before even the British governor could see it whole, only a gold tiger's head and paws survive. He was guarded by tiger-striped guards behind fretwork shutters that imitated the scratch of a tiger's claw. Even the hammer of his blunderbuss had the form of a tiger in blue steel with gold and silver damascening.

He dreamed dreams and embodied an ideology. His dream-book in the India Office Library includes scenes—amid emeralds, tiger-shoots, and white elephants—of French troops and the expulsion of the British from India. In his portrait, his epicene body is swathed in green and his pale, wispily moustached face is turbaned in the same sacred colour of Islam. His banner was a calligraphically stylized tiger's head forming the words "The lion of God is conqueror." Yet his anti-British policy, idealized as a holy war, was underlain by political realism: by the last decade of the eighteenth century it had become obvious that the British could no longer be accommodated in the traditional Indian commercial and political frames. They had to be expelled or obeyed.

They had not come as conquerors. Although, as we saw above, land empires became fashionable diversions for European states to pursue overseas in the eighteenth century, the British Empire in India does seem to have been acquired, or at least initiated, accidentally, almost in a fit of absence of mind. As late as 1750 the East India Company insisted that its officials think of themselves as "the factors and agents of merchants" rather than as a military colony. The circumstances of violent competition with French interlopers, however, were already forcing the men on the ground to reappraise their role. Young Robert Clive, for instance, shipped out by his family to be a clerk in Madras because he was considered too hopeless for any more ambitious occupation, spent his leisure reading military history and, when fighting broke out, found soldiering was his true métier. His happy attributes of luck and pluck drew his superiors' attention and got him a peacetime job as a commissary. This was his chance to make the rapid fortune that was every Indian official's ambition and to return to an independent life in England. But the onset of the Seven Years' War in 1756 and the chance of an independent command sent him back to India.

It was Clive's audacity and opportunism that turned what was intended as a punitive expedition against the Nawab of Bengal into a campaign of conquest—an almost uniquely clear case of the influence of an individual personality on history. But the impact of the "great man"—great, in this case, at least in greed and grasp and grip—depends on interplay with forces both personal and impersonal. The Nawab had incurred an exceptional degree of English resentment by allying with the French, seizing Calcutta, and allegedly conniving in the maltreatment of prisoners. In dealing with him, the usual prudence of English policy was replaced by passion, and Clive enjoyed greater licence in the pursuit of vengeance than frontier colonels were commonly allowed. Despite their better form, the French were the wrong horses for Indian princes to back: during European wars, the English could rely on continental alliances to keep them distracted. Furthermore, Bengal was riven by internal dissent: Hindu resentment of Muslim rule, warlord rivalry with the Nawab, popular resentment of exploitative taxation, and military unrest at arrears of pay.

Clive blundered into this tense arena like a typical conquistador. His barely professional army of a little over one thousand Europeans and two thousand native trainees was outnumbered in the field by over twelve to one and had hardly any technical advantages; the disparity in equipment was probably less significant than that with which Cortés had faced the Aztecs. The Nawab had French guns and gunners when most of Clive's artillery was mired. But as with so many conquistadores, his role was not necessarily to defeat the enemy but to divide them. He succeeded as the catalyst of a coalition against the Nawab, who was ousted at Plassey in 1757 by what was effectively a battlefield putsch.

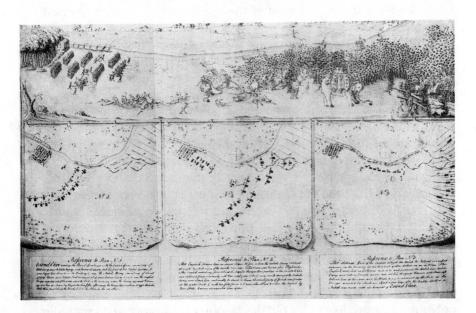

"A successful propaganda-image": a contemporary plan of the Battle of Plassey, representing it as a triumph of a rationally disposed British-led force over the chaos of a native army. In fact the weakness of Clive's position is obvious, with his back to a wood and the River Hugli straddling his line of retreat: a fleet of boats tactically positioned is visible. The building on the edge of the wood is the Nawab's hunting lodge, which Clive used as his ammunition dump.

Like the Spaniards in Mexico or Peru, the British in Bengal were the beneficiaries of internecine conflicts. Traditionally, the battle of Plassey has been represented as symbolic of the superiority of the white man's technique, whereas in reality it only proved the superiority of some Bengali factions over others. A delightfully illustrated plan made at the time to celebrate Clive's heroism displays the successful propaganda-image. Clive's army is drawn up in neatly ordered lines of fire, with arms borne in disciplined uniformity. The Nawab's force is a straggly tangle, presenting itself for slaughter, naked cannon fodder first. Its war elephants are dying or disordered. The supplies of humpbacked cattle on the hoof emphasize the picture of rusticity. The impression conveyed is not entirely bogus: at the Ardya River in 1746, a French force had shown that, with the advantage of terrain, controlled volleys of musketry could thwart a traditional Indian army of greatly superior numbers. This was not, however, what happened at Plassey. Clive had no advantage of terrain. With a wood and a river to his rear, and one flank totally exposed, he started the battle in a tactically hopeless position. Nor was his confidence well judged in the conspiracy of which he formed part, for most of the conspirators were out to cheat the others, and even as the battle unfolded, the allegiance of key players was doubtful. In any event, the conspirators' nerve held while the Nawab's broke; he fled in ignominy after little more than exchanges of cannon fire and skirmishing. That is not, of course, how it appears on Clive's drawing, where the enemy appear to flee before an inexorable British advance.

Bengal was easily the richest of the fragments into which the Mughal Empire had dissolved. Clive's attitude to loot was lofty; faced with all but the highest bribes, that is, he was "astonished at my own moderation." Booty never cloys the appetite it feeds. Clive's men almost mutinied at dissatisfaction with a share that made them all rich; the East India Company almost collapsed in 1772 from the overstimulated expectations of the market. Yet, well managed, Bengal was the biggest prize of any pirate since Pizarro. The East India Company, which had previously had minimal landward revenues, raised £2 million in 1761–64 and almost £7.5 million in 1766–76. The riches of Bengal paid for the conquest of other Indian principalities. By 1782 the East India Company, whose maxim had once been "trade, not war," was keeping an army of 115,000 men. Indeed, the British Raj was only the latest product of an old theme of Indian history: the establishment of hegemony over the subcontinent from within one part of it, usually to the benefit of foreign military élites.

The reminder of the conquistadores is again irresistible: the British first installed a puppet ruler, then used the profits of confiscatory policies to conquer the Ganges valley and the shore of the Bay of Bengal, as the Spaniards used the wealth and manpower of the Nahnatl-speaking highlanders of Mexico to conquer the Maya. As with the model-cases of Mexico and Peru, the speed of the intruders' triumph gave it the illusion of inevitability. Once the accumulation of a land empire had begun, it had to continue: security always demanded control of the next frontier. The Indian *ancien régime*, in which native princes arbitrated among western buyers and shippers, became intolerable to the British in the aroma of a scented monopoly. Under cover of the Napoleonic Wars, which again neutralized the French threat, Britain's coalition of native clients and payees defeated piecemeal the only regional powers capable of reversing the trend. Tipu Sultan, besieged in Seringapatam in 1799, killed himself; the Maratha states in the Deccan accepted client status after a defeat in 1806.

THE INDUSTRIAL WEST

Britain's India was the first big European empire on the mainland of Asia. Much of its land could now be appropriated or cleared to grow the products which suited the new masters. The potential competition of its indige-

The industrialization of the nineteenth-century west would have been impossible without the exploitation of the labour of women and children, but it brought them long-term dividends in the form of prosperity and emancipation. Even at the relatively low social and economic level at which this soap advertisement was directed, the emergence of a new ideal of womanhood—decorative and unproductive—can be detected in a period of oppression of the sex. A similar change affected children, who became, during the period of industrialization, at once an exploited underclass, a lumpenproletariat, and a source of images of angelic innocence. See S. P. Carteras, *Images of Victorian Womanhood in English Art* (1987).

nous industries could be stifled. No single episode was more decisive in shifting the balance of the world's resources than this shift in the sources of their control.

It was at once the last of the old conquistador conquests, achieved without conspicuous technical advantages, and the first of the new industrial conquests made crushing, in the nineteenth century, by revolutionary technology. There were no machine guns or ironclads or quinine pills in industrial quantities; steam power and rifles were in their infancy; but the conquest of India was the work of an industrializing power whose factories produced standard ordnance so superior to the native product that the finely embellished cannon of Tipu Sultan were good to the conquerors only for scrap.

Mechanization multiplies muscle. Vivid indices, very fashionable with scholars today, are the histories of slaves, women, and children in industrializing societies, which—with much moral self-congratulation—were able to abolish slavery and invent or impose new ideals of womanhood and childhood, decorative and unproductive. Illustrations abound in European and American art and literature of the nineteenth century, but none is more expressive than an advertisement for Sunlight soap which hangs in my lavatory at home. This product was the subject of one of the great success stories of the nineteenth century, manufactured in the model industrial community of Port Sunlight, contributing a fortune to the Lever family and to the industrious masses an economical means of keeping clean and healthy. Its profits erected Thornton Manor in the Gloucestershire country-side, where Lord Leverhulme could revert to the rural type of the English entrepreneur and emphasize his personal asceticism by taking baths on the balcony; the surplus was lavished on philanthropic projects typical of their era, from Congregationalist chapels and temperance hotels to salubrious dwellings and scientific research. The advertisement shows a housewife magicked into a fairy princess by the power of industry.

The industrial revolution confirmed and extended a shift that was already in progress and gave the civilization which sponsored it a decisive advantage over others. Europe's head start, though closely followed by North America and East Asia, helped shape what remains on the map one of the most conspicuous features of the modern world: a zone of fairly densely clustered industrial cities from Belfast and Bilbao to Rostov and Saint Petersburg. Even today, in the last decade of our millennium, when the world has had time to catch up and the technology of the industrial revolution is itself out of date, the legacy of early industrialization gives the European economy a distinctive profile, with an industrial zone more concentrated than in North America, more extensive than in Japan.

Flattering reasons are sometimes adduced for the priority of Europe's, and in particular Britain's, industrialization on the assumption that industrialized societies are better, more "progressive" than those which leave industry in the hands of traditional artisanates. In the nineteenth century in Europe even socialists, who deplored the supposed effects of industrialization on workers' lives, revelled in the march of history towards a teleological climax. Nowadays, when we are still clearing up the detritus of the industrial revolution, the progressivist fallacy is more easily eluded. The people responsible for it are no longer likely to be credited with superiority of intellect, morals, or imagination over the rest of mankind. Nor is there any demonstrable correlation between industrialization and an identifiable set of social values.

Britain was in some respects well suited to be a "steam intellect" society, where invention could be mothered by taste rather than necessity, but the values of the élite in most of the country remained profoundly rural throughout the industrial revolution; for captains of industry, industrial wealth was typically a means to the creation of a rural idyll; their managers, who could not afford country estates, simulated the longed-for way of life in garden suburbs. The industrial revolution was not strictly a British phenomenon but a regional one; the southern part of the country actually experienced a de-industrialization, like India's in miniature, as its traditional industries were replaced by the new mechanized versions taking shape in the midlands and the north. Britain was briefly "the workshop of the world" but remained the world's insurer and rentier for much longer.

Industrialization in nineteenth-century France, formerly condemned as backward by native historians in the grip of an inferiority simplex as they looked across the Channel, has now been elevated to its due rank among the olympians. Here, too, the industrialists often reflected the values of the society around them in evincing scorn for the enterprise that made them rich. In 1836 a member of a great textiles dynasty of the north went on a pilgrimage "to obtain illumination from the Holy Ghost so that we should never undertake anything in business above our strength, lest we should be troubled by hazardous speculations." When François Wendel died in 1825, he left a fortune of four million francs from his ironworks but claimed to regret this avocation from his envisioned destiny as a soldier or sailor; he ended up, "against my will, iron master and owner of several firms which have prospered despite and against all." An "enterprise culture" did come to exist in nineteenth-century Europe, but it seems from the chronology to have been the child, rather than the begetter, of industrialization—another mass product, factory-produced and widely circulated.

The philosophies which seem best to characterize the industrial phase of western history—utilitarianism, pragmatism, Marxism—were among its results, not its causes, and their opposition is profound to the disembodied rationalism, disinterested science, and disinterred classicism which ruled western intellects on industrialization's eve. Mr. Gadgrind's curriculum of facts was as far from the humanist tradition as you could get. Individualism is admittedly a good ethos for an industrializing society and may have helped to impel mechanization by raising labour costs in Britain, say, or North America. In Japan, conversely, individualism has never been a prominent part of prevailing values, but the country was as avid as any in embracing industrialization. If propitious social values and intellectual trends were sufficient conditions of industrial advance, Egypt, where Islamic apologists had written capitalism into the prevailing scheme by the late eighteenth century, might almost have been expected to rival Britain as the first industrial nation.

It may be helpful to see the western "barbarians" from an oriental perspective and acknowledge that the industrial revolution, like the "expansion of Europe," was an initiative launched from a civilization coming from behind—evidence in some respects of the inferiority, rather than the superiority, of the early industrializers. Where rates of production were so low

The beauty of Bliss Valley Tweed Mill, an outstanding example of a "cathedral of indus-try" in 1872, has not been enhanced by its recent conversion to "luxury flats." The de-velopers' concept, however, of the mill as a setting for a privileged rural way of life, was consistent with the ethos of nineteenth-century factory building, which imitated palatial traditions in architecture. The publicity emphasizes the sporting facilities and healthy amenities. The showhouse is decorated in a pastiche of the English "country-house" style.

there could be no "high-level equilibrium trap" to snare developing tech-nologies. Where rising population teetered on a delicate fulcrum, stimulat-ing demand without glutting the labour market, mechanization was an obvious option. The passion in the west in the eighteenth century for the ingenious gadgets despised in China arose not from the bolder spirit or cleverer brains of the inventors but from the marketability of their con-trivances. All economies tend to get the technology they need and to shelve the surplus; otherwise, the Incas would have had the wheel and axle, and the ancient Greeks steam power.

Rather than speculating about the causes of industrialization, it may be more fruitful to try briefly to evoke it through its effects. Those on the world outside Europe belong in future chapters (see Chapters 14, 20, and 21). In its heartlands, the spread of the revolution has been measured in various ways: by planting pinheads in the map to show the proliferation of

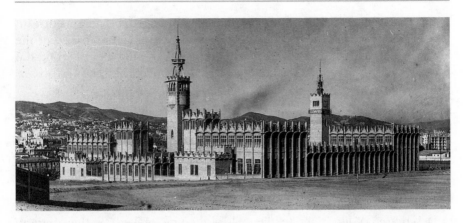

Barcelona's factories made perhaps the most extravagant ensemble anywhere of "palaces of progress." The Casarramona factory of 1910, on the carrer de Mèxic, was designed by Josep Puit i Cadafalch, a figure of heroic stature in antiquarian scholarship, art patronage, and Catalanist politics, as well as an architect of high repute and enormous influence. He experimented with a variety of medieval sources of inspiration and made this textile factory—utilitarian within and supported by steel girders—into a Moorish fantasy castle, with trefoil castellations, elegant pilasters, and minaret-like towers.

steam-powered factories or railway termini; by counting profits and collating statistics of output; by chronicling the disease and disorders that incubated in the fearsome early-industrial wens of Europe, overcrowded and under-sanitized; by enumerating the heroes of "self-help" who created wealth through enterprise or invention and spread it through philanthropy or enlightened self-interest; or by echoing the volume of the cries of the urban slum-dwellers, deracinated and relocated in ruthless environments, like the Manchester of Engels or Mrs. Gaskell or like Zola's mines or like the Chicago of Upton Sinclair or the New York of Theodore Dreiser.

Another method is to read the implicit messages of the industrial revolution's most solid monuments, the great factories, where they survive. The best examples still visible today are often in uncharacteristically rural settings. Just outside a country town in Oxfordshire, north of where I live, one of the "cathedrals of industry"—Bliss Valley Tweed Mill of 1872—has just been converted into luxury flats. It was made to resemble a grand château in a parkland setting, with a balustraded parapet and corner towers crowned by urns. In the central dome and elegant tapering chimney-stack, a church or abbey is vaguely suggested. In a rural setting on the Marne, the Menier factory still looks much as in engravings of the 1860s: the main building is an iron-framed palace incongruously perched on the weir which gave it power, decorated with the fussy geometry of the mansions and civic monuments of the northern European tradition.

Sometimes the factories' messages to onlookers are made explicit in contemporary accounts of these unprecedented buildings. The notions that informed them were captured, for instance, in a newspaper's praise of the factories of Sabadell, outside Barcelona, in 1855: the nobility of work, the power-hunger of a meritocratic bourgeoisie, the puritanical morals of bosses' paternalism:

> And these factories, grand and elegant . . . are sumptuous palaces which ought to inspire their owners and all the people with pride. . . . These palaces house no pharaohs, no orgies, but are a means of life for hundreds of families. These palaces are not there to inspire vanity or arrogance, but love of work and respect for effort and for merit.

Description of life in the textile mills of the time reeked, on the contrary, of the "sweat of the common man." But the praise offered here was not disingenuous. Factory builders sensed a genuine contrast between the common good served by their edifices and the vainglory all past ages had produced on a similar scale. Theirs were the first palaces of production in a history of palaces of consumption. Barcelona's Casaramona factory of 1911, now a police barracks, expresses this ethos perfectly: two fairy-tale campaniles preside over a battlemented skyline, below which huge windows in ranks of slim bays flood the large interior spaces with light. Churches, castles, palaces, and artists' studios are all archly quoted or brazenly trumped. Templeton's carpet factory of 1889 still stands on Glasgow Green, a Venetian palazzo built in brick to be "the finest thing outside Italy" and enriched with turquoise mosaics and twirling pilasters, guelfic battlements and spiralling towers.

Finally, one can try to interrogate the ghosts of the pre-industrial past, to conjure the "world we have lost": the ways of life and social structures eroded or destroyed by the new organizational imperatives of factory-based production. The nearest thing to a factory in pre-industrial Britain was the perhaps fictional—certainly romanticized—"great household and family" of Jack of Newbury, who was supposed to have employed six hundred people on two hundred looms in a single building in the reign of Henry VIII. But the terms applied by the poet who recorded it in 1619 reflect the model on which industry was commonly organized—the "household and family" in which master and apprentices worked together, with a shared life in a homely setting. In the opinion of the historian who has made a famous study of it, the scale and intimacy of the pre-industrial era are so lost to us in the "developed" world today that we know them only from prompts to "folk memory," such as Grimm's fairy tales and the cartoon films of Walt Disney.

One way of quantifying the change is by measuring the decline of guilds. In Barcelona, for example, the bridle-makers had 108 members in 1729, 27 in 1814. The cloth-dressers, about 700 strong when the eighteenth century began, had only 3 members left, all too old to work, by 1825. The carders ranged from 28 to 65 years old in 1719 and from 51 to 78 years old in 1793. Their vanishing world was buried in the seismic upheaval which raised factories over the old city like smoking volcanoes and flattened the "vertical" structures of traditional society. Instead of identifying with communities that encompassed people at all levels of rank and prosperity—neighbourhoods, cities, provinces, sects, orders, lineages, clans, capacious "households"—people uprooted and regrouped in industrial centres came to place themselves in society in horizontally ordered tiers, defined by wealth or class. Now that the industrial revolution is over, people seem uncomfortable with this legacy. "Class" is disappearing from our active vocabulary, and historians are being asked to write a new kind of social history in which people are placed in the intricate, overlapping contexts of the company they keep.

Meanwhile the benefits of economic change had been concentrated disproportionately in western Europe and North America. The consequences form the subjects of the next two chapters. In the nineteenth and twentieth centuries, thanks to a new series of ocean-spanning trends, the Atlantic world recovered the unity that had seemed to be threatened with severance. Enriched by the profits of the voyages of bounty, empowered by the muscle of industrialization, people in parts of the world favoured by these changes went on to build world empires. From the perspective of the galactic museum-keepers, their supremacy will look feeble and short-lived; but, while they lasted, their empires lamed their victims and endowed their master races with a false sense of superiority. For a while, the "Rise of the West" seemed to be the end towards which all "the course" of history had flowed.

Chapter 13

THE CHASM SPANNED: THE SURVIVAL AND REVIVAL OF ATLANTIC LINKS

The Era of Elvis—The Habitat of the Blue Bloom—
Coming to America—Business Imperialism—Coming from America

THE ERA OF ELVIS

I was an anti-American boy. Even before the Vietnam War made anti-Americanism an almost ineluctable fashion in European schools and universities, I shared, from viewpoints on the Atlantic edge of Europe in England and Spain, growing resentment of the power of the United States; the hegemony of the world as far as the frontiers of communism; the size of an economy which dwarfed those of Europe and of the dwindling British Empire; the political interference which helped to emasculate European empires while legitimizing illiberal regimes in eastern Europe and Spain; the magnetism of the trashy culture of hamburgers and rock 'n' roll; the presence—irksome reminder of western Europe's military impotence—of GIs who were, according to a popular joke, "overpaid, overfed, oversexed, overconfident, and over here."

The menace and allure of America in Europe were both represented in the late fifties by the image of the rock king Elvis Presley. He combined an effortlessly sensual voice with provocative on-stage athletics and starred in a series of intellectually feeble films, including one suggestively called *G.I. Blues*. His appeal in America was said to be based on the "American

"All American Boy." Elvis Presley kissing a fan on his discharge from military service in February 1960. Fans resented his being drafted in 1958—"Would you draft Beethoven?" one is supposed to have said, but Presley's compliance was one of his shrewd career moves, which gave him respectability with adult audiences back home. The Communist *Neues Deutschland*, however, typified European suspicions: it published a picture of him on a date with a sixteen-year-old German girl and called him "a cold war weapon . . . puffed up like a peacock, hooting like a ship-warning buoy." See S. and B. Zmijewsky, *The Career of Elvis Presley,* pp. 50-58.

dream" of a poor boy elevated to riches by the buoyancy of talent in a free society. In Europe the same dream-figure looked nightmarish. His style, which made fans swoon and scream, summed up the American threat. The offhand manner seemed morally polluting, the pelvic gyrations sexually alarming, the catch in the voice insinuating, the glamour delusive, the art meretricious, the arrogance typical. He was drafted for the American army and served in the ranks of the Atlantic alliance in Germany. His discharge was greeted by mass hysteria. Beached by the new wave of the sixties, stranded in middle age, he eventually indulged himself to death in 1977 after a drug-aided decline, inspiring an extraordinary posthumous cult among fans, now transformed into followers, who still hold vigils at his graveside, record apparitions, and rewrite the story of this unholy child of licence as a genius sanctified by suffering. His death was, as some wit remarked, "a great career move."

To me, in what might fairly be called the Elvis era, the anti-American French leader Charles de Gaulle was a Samson in Dagon's temple, struggling to push apart the "twin pillars of the Atlantic alliance" and expel the Philistine. In a sense he was himself a product of the Atlantic unity he detested. In the darkest hour of the Second World War, when his country was overrun with shattering ease, he was transformed by British patronage from a general of small importance to the unchallengeable leader of "Free France." American power restored him to his homeland as a liberator. Free French units led the allies into reconquered Paris in 1944. American support fell short, however, of keeping a Chauvin in the Elysée Palace. When de Gaulle was summoned by acclaim to almost dictatorial powers in France in 1958, it was as a phoenix, rekindled from rejection—like his old comrade and rival, Churchill, in Britain in 1940—by a crisis so terrible that it had daunted or discredited every other contender: Algeria, the colony in which France had invested most effort and emotion, was about to fall to independence-fighters. In the meantime, the United States had incurred de Gaulle's hatred by expropriating the French Empire in Indo-China, undermining it at Suez and eroding its credibility and diplomatic support. The purity of the French language was being polluted by Americanisms, the influence of French culture drowned by the loud voice of *le monde anglo-saxon*. In place of the Atlantic alliance, an arch of two pillars, de Gaulle proposed a house of many mansions: "Europe from the Atlantic to the Urals." At the time it seemed like an evasion; now, in the 1990s, it looks increasingly like a prophecy.

The Atlantic dependence I resented as a child was the outcome of Europe's period of "civil war" from 1917 to 1945. The coherence of Christendom was denied or disputed, as never before in the internecine conflicts of the eighteenth, nineteenth, and early twentieth centuries, by advocates of ideologies which claimed to generate distinct cultures of their own. Nazism's racial basis and communism's class basis were incompatible with old ideas of a civilization inclusive enough to embrace everybody. In the late 1940s Europe was left divided—apparently for a long time—between armed camps. Clinging to the western edge of the continent or the northern shore of the Mediterranean, on one side of the "iron curtain," were a few countries unoccupied by Soviet forces or communist militias. Blitzkrieg had shown how easily a military debacle could happen and how quickly tank armies could roll up the remaining continental territory outside Moscow's control. Only alliance with a power big enough to strike a "balance of terror" could provide security.

The Atlantic, across which goods and ideas had been exchanged between peoples who consciously belonged to the civilization of the west, now became the lake—or, as they affectionately said, the "pond"—around which they huddled for defence. This new Atlantic Order was paid for by the Marshall Plan—a vast programme of American economic aid for war-shattered economies. It was good-naturedly resented by American taxpayers and satirized by Irving Berlin in *Call Me Madam*—a deceptively charming musical comedy of 1951 about the romantic spin-off of an American aid mission to a petty European monarchy. "Do you need any money today?" sings the ambassadress. "Take all you want. When it's gone you can come back again." America paid jovially because aid was part of the grand strategy of self-defence, buying a front line far from home in an age of increasingly long-range bombing. Nor was it only the missiles that had to be kept at arm's length; Americans feared Russia as a source of moral subversion, cultural pollution, propaganda, and espionage. In any case, there was more to Marshall aid than this. Economic recovery and political stability in Europe were equally in America's interest. But once Stalin had refused American money for his zone of influence and control, the accountants' rulers began to underscore the line of a frontier against communism which the Eisenhower Doctrine declared immutable.

The strategy only half-worked. Western Europeans resented the insecurity of life in what seemed like a buffer zone between superpowers or a bridgehead ready for the next world war. Yet the need for western solidarity became ever more apparent during the 1950s and 1960s, for all the dislike in Europe of American seniority, as the brutality of Soviet rule was exposed by the blighted "springs" of Berlin, East Germany, Hungary, and Czechoslovakia, successively blockaded, bludgeoned, or reoccupied by armies commanded from Moscow. Meanwhile, belief waned that Britain and France could ever muster deterrents independent of America's. The crushing superiority of what was called the Soviet bloc grew and grew in numbers of men and weight of weapons. In 1964 a new British prime minister proposed a "technological revolution" of "white heat" in an effort to catch up with the pacemakers in eastern Europe. From the perspective of the 1990s, when the countries who formerly terrified the west are begging for technical aid from erstwhile enemies, it seems like a joke, but it was in deadly earnest at the time.

The political unity of the Atlantic world had never been so perfect since the American Revolution, nor its cultural unity so sedulously recommended. Winston Churchill, Britain's wartime prime minister, with his Anglo-American parentage and aristocratic fear of the tumbrils of Bolshevism, toyed with the idea of reunifying the United Kingdom with the United States. A more scholarly Spanish equivalent of his *History of the English-Speaking Peoples* was the collaborative *Historia de España y de América* planned in the fifties by the Catalan historian Jaume Vicèns Vives. He was no friend of Franco's, but his project suited the Spanish dictator's policy of cultivating a pan-Atlantic Hispanic community of nations, and showed how desire for Atlantic security and belief in Atlantic unity transcended political divisions on

From the White Cottage
to the White House

THE CAPITOL, WASHINGTON

BELFAST

GALWAY

DUBLIN

Céad Míle Fáilte
a Seán

DUNGANSTOWN

CORK

THE KENNEDY HOMESTEAD
CO. WEXFORD

Seekers after "roots" criss-crossed the Atlantic with ties of sentiment and lines of pilgrimage after the Second World War. A famous and influential case is illustrated by this souvenir postcard of President Kennedy's visit to what was presumed to be his ancestral home in Ireland in June 1963. The words of Irish say, "A hundred thousand welcomes, John."

the ocean's western rim. Other historians discovered "Atlantic civilization" as a subject whose origins deserved research. Mass tourism brought Americans from almost every level of society to the homelands of their ancestors, many of them in conscious exploration of their "roots," like the presidential Kennedy family in 1963, making a pilgrimage to the Irish homestead which was the supposed birthplace of their dynasty, carrying the glamour of local boys made good.

It would be unfair, however, to dismiss the unity of the Atlantic world as the invention of a desperate generation, a short-term expedient extemporized as a means of escape from the postwar crisis. The unity compromised or cracked by the revolutions of 1774 to 1828 had been slowly re-established in the interim in a variety of ways. The Second World War and its aftermath confirmed a trend discernible for at least a hundred years before, as cultural movements were shared, large numbers of people exchanged, communications improved, investment multiplied, and, at last, common interests identified between kindred peoples on both sides of the ocean. The redistribution of world resources recounted in the last chapter was accompanied and succeeded by a redistribution of culture and of values, which is the subject of this chapter and the next, and of which the reforging of Atlantic civilization—the restoration of the moral and cultural unity of great stretches of the ocean's shores—was one of the most conspicuous aspects.

THE HABITAT OF THE BLUE BLOOM

As historical periods go, in the European experience the "long nineteenth century" from, say, 1792 to 1914 was an extraordinarily well-defined period, separated from its neighbours by the troughs and trenches of war. It was made in the crucible of the Napoleonic Wars, unmade in the cataclysm of 1914–18. The prevailing mood of the nineteenth century was romantic, sentimental, enthusiastic, numinous, nostalgic, chaotic, and self-critical, whereas that of the eighteenth, at its most characteristic, had been rational, passionless, detached, precise, complacent, ordered, and self-assertive. The change that overtook Beethoven's music or Goya's paintings during the Napoleonic Wars was symptomatic of the transformation of an entire culture.

Some of the new tones and tints were made, or at least mixed, in America. The landscapes of the New World began in a small way to mould the romantic imagination almost from the moment of their first discovery by European eyes. Most early explorers ignored them. Columbus, writing what was effectively promotional literature, indulged in vague superlatives. Vespucci, who had a genuine observer's eye, included some rhapsodical descriptions. Sensitivity to the beauties of nature was, however, a rare quality among sixteenth-century laymen. Gradually, the Franciscan idea of the beauty of creation, supplemented by realistic Renaissance aesthetics, began to influence perceptions of the New World. The first attempt to depict the American landscape feelingly, with an accent on the appeal of the grandeur of the wilderness, was made by Jan Mostaert, Margaret of Austria's court painter. Beginning in the 1520s, on the basis of reports from Mexico, and continuing into the 1540s, when he may have worked on eyewitness reports of a Spanish march from New Spain to Kansas, he filtered his hearsay sources through the typical colour-screen of Flemish landscape-painting of the day and added much that was fantastic and incongruous.

It was only when transmuted by the eighteenth-century cult of sensibility that the landscapes of the New World came to occupy a permanent place in the romantic imagination. The tradition began with the beautiful and exciting drawings made during their scientific expedition to Quito by Jorge Juan and Antonio de Ulloa, first published in 1752. Their mission was a copybook case of eighteenth-century empiricism: the Spanish marine officers were barely out of their teens when they were appointed to accompany

Jan Mostaert's scene of an encounter between natives and conquistadors, painted in the early 1540s, in tribute to the achievements of the House of Habsburg, inaugurated a long tradition: romantic and fantastic treatment of New World landscapes. Curiously, the Spaniards are on foot, though Mostaert had been reading about Coronado's cavalcade to Kansas.

representatives of the Académie Royale des Sciences of Paris to resolve discrepancies (accumulated over half a century's work towards the surveying of France and the construction of an accurate world map) in the measurement of a degree of latitude along the surface of the earth. If successful, their readings taken near the equator, in combination with others made simultaneously in the Arctic, would determine the true shape of the world, the form in which it deviates from the perfection of the sphere.

Their representations of their observations often took the ostensible form of scientific diagrams but were always calculated to arouse the senses with awestruck reverence for untamed Nature. Their drawing, for instance, of Cotopaxi erupting, with the phenomenon, depicted in the background, of arcs of light seen in the sky on the mountain slopes at Panambarca, combines diagrammatic precision with rugged romance. The Andean settings they recorded remained the source of the most powerful romantic images of America. Cotopaxi became the favourite subject of American landscape-painters. The high point of the tradition was marked by the illustrations from journeys in mountain regions, especially of the Andes, by Alexander von Humboldt in *Vues de Cordillères,* published between 1806 and 1814.

Born in the same year as Napoleon, Humboldt was a Napoleonic figure, with the same world-conquering ambitions in science as Napoleon had in war. He worked to classify natural phenomena at the highest possible level,

Jorge Juan and Antonio de Ulloa accompanied La Condamine's expedition to verify the shape of the world in 1735. The idea was to compare measurements of a degree along the circumference of the earth at the equator with others taken at the same time by an expedition near the Arctic circle, in order to determine whether the world was a perfect sphere or, if not, in what way it was distended. Juan's and Ulloa's extraordinary drawings, like this one which combines an eruption of Cotopaxi with the appearance of arc-lights in the sky and on mountain slopes at Panambarca, combined scientific rigour with romantic flair and helped to fix images of the New World in the romantic imagination. With Chimborazo, Cotopaxi became a symbol of the unconquerable yearning that characterized romantic sensibilities.

where the whole cosmos could be arrayed in a single coherent scheme. Yet this detached scientist, whom Darwin called "the greatest scientific traveller of all time," was first inspired to travel by desire to see "Nature in all her variety of grandeur and splendour." His journeys in America were undertaken by accident, in substitution for frustrated plans to go to Egypt. At his own expense and with the goodwill of the Spanish crown, he made a hero's progress and a triumphant return. Literally the high point of his endeavours was the ascent of Cotopaxi's twin peak, Mount Chimborazo, in the summer of 1802. It was then thought to be the highest mountain in the world, the untouched summit of creation. Humboldt's account of his climb, cleverly restrained, is a poignant litany of the cult of the unattainable so characteristic of romanticism, so essential to its spirit. Sickened by the altitude, racked by the cold, bleeding copiously from nose and lips, he was forced to turn back just short of the top by an impassable crevasse. In his visual record of the mountain, he appears stooping in the foreground to pluck a botanical specimen. In 1800 the introspective but influential German poet Novalis

Humboldt stoops to pluck a botanical specimen near the foot of Chimborazo. A detail from the most spectacular of the engravings in Humboldt's and Bonpland's *Vues des Cordillères,* Humboldt had the original hung in his study.

created one of romanticism's most potent symbols, the *blaue Blume,* the elusive flower that has symbolized romantic yearning ever since. Surely the Blue Bloom of Novalis grew among the florilegia of the New World.

Views such as Humboldt's of the Andes defined a romantic image of America for subsequent painters. Thomas Cole (1801–1848), the founder of the Hudson River school, started a vogue for South American settings as scenes of cosmic high drama. His vision of Eden with the expulsion of Adam and Eve was painted in 1828 after a long sketching tour in the West Indies. Because "preserved untouched since the creation," America's mountains were "hallowed to [his] soul" in a continent where "all nature is new to art." For these heart's reasons, no old-world landscapes had a comparable influence on romanticism, not Ossian's Highlands nor the forests of the

Thomas Cole's *Expulsion from the Garden of Eden,* 1828. No artist was better able to wring romantic potential from New World scenery, perhaps because in his life, the inspiration of the landscape came first and the painter's vocation second. From the 1830s his interests gradually shifted to historical, allegorical, and religious subjects; but he had founded a school and tradition of North American scenery-painting which remained passionately attached to the "wild and rugged grandeur" of nature.

Brothers Grimm, nor even the Alps of Wordsworth. When those wicked angels of romanticism, Mesdames de Staël and Récamier, made an excursion to Mont Blanc in 1807, they turned back, discomforted by sunburn on their daring décolletage, without even reaching the Mer de Glace. The guide urged on them their obligation to Nature in the poetry of the phrase book. "You could repeat yourself in all the languages of Europe," de Staël replied, "I should still go no further."

In the Andes such indifference, such superior ennui, would have been unthinkable. Sensibilities staled by custom in the old world were rekindled in the New. Although romanticism was not American in origin, it had become American in inspiration. With economic liberalism at the start of the century, with industrialization and democracy by the end, it took its place as a lively part of the distinctive culture which bound Atlantic civilization together and differentiated it from the rest of the world.

COMING TO AMERICA

On the morning of 3 January 1842, a small knot of travellers stared apprehensively into

> a long, narrow apartment, not unlike a giant hearse with windows in the sides, having at one end a melancholy stove, at which three or four chill stewards were warming their hands; while on either side, extending down its whole dreary length, was a long, long table, over which a rack, fixed to the low roof and stuck full of drinking glasses and cruet stands, hinted dismally at rolling seas and heavy weather.

Charles Dickens and his fellow-voyagers were contemplating in disillusionment the saloon of the *Britannia*, first of Cunard's new breed of packet-steamers, fast and reputedly luxurious, that were to revolutionize transatlantic communications. The bleak berths, cramped quarters, and pig's-face-and-potato dinners that dismayed Dickens were forerunners of the grand-hotel luxury, palatial space, and haute cuisine to which transatlantic passengers would be treated in the 1930s, when newsreel footage of voyages by the

In the Hollywood age, svelte voyagers like Fred Astaire and Ginger Rogers shared passage with our parents and made the feel and flavours of ocean-liner life familiar to us. The still is from *Shall We Dance?* (1937, directed by Mark Sandrich. Music and lyrics by George and Ira Gershwin.) This was the most unashamedly opulent of all Fred's and Ginger's films: the plot takes them from riches to riches, eschewing the "rags to riches" storylines of so many of Hollywood's feel-good contributions to the Depression era (see p. 497). The luxurious liner, in which glass doors slide open from the state rooms onto the deck, carries them from Le Havre to New York.

Duke of Windsor was blended with the movies of Fred Astaire (or perhaps it was the other way around) to make the feel and flavours of ocean-liner life familiar to a generation.

The early steamers sailed in all weathers, for regularity was as important as speed to the commercial appeal of the service. The discomforts experienced by Dickens are brought home by a series of paintings—portraits in action—of Atlantic steamers through the centuries, collected in the Peabody Museum, Salem, Massachusetts. The *Britannia* is among her sister-vessels as they plunge and buck through stormy seas. Sometimes, in the propaganda-spirit of the artists' commissions, they outperform sailing rigs; sometimes the painters include symbolic hints of better times—a shaft of sunlight, a glimpse of blue sky; sometimes they stick to the bland ease of summer. The best and most dramatic pictures, however, share the "staggering, heaving, wrestling, leaping, diving, jumping, pitching, throbbing, rolling, and rocking" of Dickens's crossing. His vision of the ship braving the headwinds "with every pulse and artery of her huge body swollen and bursting" is recognizable from some of the canvases. The rhythm of the *Britannia*'s progress is captured in his evocations of seasickness. The ups and downs are relived in the description of his comic attempts to catch up, brandy in hand, with fellow-sufferers borne away to a sofa by the pitching of the vessel.

Britannia, the Cunard Line's flagship packet-steamer, painted by Fitz Hugh Lane in 1842, the year Dickens made his crossing in her. The stormy scene recalls Dickens's woebegone description of a crossing wracked by *mal de mer*. Yet this is still a propaganda image, designed to suggest the superior performance of the steamship over the sailing-vessel foundering in the background.

The coming of the steam packet was part of a long and, at first, uncertain history of improvement in Atlantic travel. Regular packet lines operated under sail with speed and economy. The first opened in January 1818 between New York and Liverpool; there were two more from 1822, and thereafter their numbers seemed to multiply freely. Steamships were at first such poor performers by comparison that many early examples suffered the fate of the *Savannah*, the first steamer to cross the Atlantic, from Georgia to Liverpool, in twenty-seven days, in 1819; she had her engine gutted and was sold as a sailing ship after spending only eighty hours of her crossing under steam.

Gradually, however, technical improvements to the propulsion and fuel-consumption of the steamers confirmed where the future lay. The first more or less regular transatlantic steam packet service began in 1838. Cunard started operating out of Boston in 1840 and out of New York in 1848. The ten- or twelve-day crossing became the norm. The prestige and progressiveness of steam was confirmed by the intense competition of the 1850s between Cunard and the Collins Line, heavily subsidized by the U.S. Congress as a standard-bearer for all-American values of speed and comfort until time-saving maintenance procedures drove two Collins ships to the bottom in spectacular tragedies which put customers off.

It was aboard a sailing packet between Le Havre and New York in 1832 that Samuel F. B. Morse got the idea for another revolutionary contribution to communications, his electric telegraph. He was turning away at the time from the frustrations of his vocation as a painter, admired but unsold. As an after-dinner diversion from the longueurs of the passage, a fellow-passenger showed him an electromagnetic apparatus purchased in Europe. Morse devoted the rest of the voyage to frenzied sketchings of ideas for harnessing its power to intelligent communication over vast distances. At first he could transmit no farther than a few yards, but collaboration with other workers in the field created a system that was operational on the first long-range telegraph line between Washington and Baltimore in 1844. In combination with submarine cables, first laid across the bed of the Atlantic in the early 1870s, this invention shrank the ocean to the dimensions of a pond that could be crossed by messages at the speed of light. Marconi, who bridged the Atlantic by radio in 1901, perfected the process by bringing every point of either shore into potential mutual touch.

People and goods are more effective culture-carriers than telegraphy, even in the radio age. Ship-borne communications made the most difference to the Atlantic world in the nineteenth century because they carried immigrants and trade. Migration, until the last third of the century, was essentially a phenomenon linking a few western European countries to the United States. There were patchy exceptions: in 1823–30, when only 6,230

German immigrants were recorded in the United States, some 10,000 of their fellow-countrymen migrated to Brazil; especially from British ports, many of those destined for the States went first to Canada and stayed there. But Canada was often a way station, and the South American republics, despite determined efforts, only gradually attracted masses. In the main destinations, Argentina and Brazil, numbers of immigrants per decade remained below six figures until the 1860s. Meanwhile, in the United States, net gains exceeded 128,000 people in the 1820s, leapt to over half a million in the 1830s, nearly trebled in the next decade, and, though arrested by the civil war and the depression of the seventies, remained at between two and three million until a further big leap to over five and a quarter million in the 1880s.

Most of them were English, Irish, Scots, and, in greatest numbers, German. Other nationalities, until near the end of this period, were statistically marginal. A good place to see them settling and becoming American was Milwaukee, an essentially immigrant community where foreigners always outnumbered natives—including the immigrants' own children—from 1835, when land plots were first offered for sale, until well into the last third of the century. Its healthy site at a confluence of important waterways, handy for the Canada traffic and the Chicago road, helped make it a boomtown of 20,000 people by 1850, over 45,000 by 1860; and it had the curses of all frontier boomtowns—shortage of women and surfeit of drink. In 1846 a butcher drowned, drunk because his wife and children refused to join him from Germany. In 1860 it was reported that "young girls go like lager beer." The taverns which welcomed and exploited fresh arrivals off the jetties specialized in clients from Ireland, Germany, England, and, in one case, Lincolnshire in particular. But by early in the second half of the century Milwaukee was predominantly a German-American town with a German press, stomping bands, and a *gemütlich* atmosphere.

Germans had been there since 1835, but in local lore the archetype of German settlers was Matthias Stein, an instrument-maker from Washington, who claimed to have taken early-morning exercise with Andrew Jackson and who reputedly got stuck in Milwaukee by accident when boiler trouble crippled his boat in 1837. The "deluge" of his successors in the first half of the 1850s was typical of the sharp increase in German emigration at the time, which is generally linked by historians, without much direct evidence, to the failure of the 1848 revolutions and the exodus of disillusioned liberals. The reputation of Milwaukee in the old country was spread by individual recommendations and the systematic advertising of two enterprising migrants who set up as estate agents. The Catholic bishop's efforts to raise subscriptions for his diocese in south German parishes helped to spread its fame. It could not be recommended, as some reporters observed, to seekers after high culture, but a distinctive tone was achieved in Karl Julius Stern's Latin Grocery, where "an aristocrat, whose schemes for a fortune from land speculation ran afoul of his lust for gambling, offered tavern service in German, English, French, Latin, and Greek."

Though political and religious exile were important motives for migrants, most were "sons of hope," seeking "rewards of thrift." Their motives were typified by the Scots emigrant of 1848 who, taking his first morning walk in America, passed twenty-six houses and was encouraged to hear the breakfast-pan sizzling in seventeen. But, as all printed advice to emigrants stressed, real experience was varied, and the immigrants' lot commonly included odium and exploitation. The sufferings of Irish migrants, as a class, may have been exaggerated by a myth which has helped to forge Irish-American identity; but it is true that in the mid-century, for areas in which studies have been done, the Irish seem to have been concentrated at the lower levels of achievement and prosperity, where, as in their home country, they commanded relatively low wages and specialized in jobs others would not do in a still privileged labour market. George Fitzhugh, the Carolina philosopher who first used the word "sociology" in America, became an advocate of slavery after seeing the conditions of Irish workers on a visit to the North in the 1850s, which left him revolted by capitalism and unpersuaded by socialism.

Irish Americans' problems of status were inseparable from the anti-Catholic prejudice rife in the élite of the time. Guardians of American values commonly supposed that Protestantism was fundamental to them, that civil liberties grew out of freedom of faith, and that despotism and popery were natural allies. Contempt for the Irish was one of the values inherited from the old country by some Americans of English descent—and with it went suspicion that allegiance to the pope was incompatible with loyalty to the state. The German-American minority was divided along similar lines by confessional hatred, which surfaced in the old homeland in the *Kulturkampf,* a government-sponsored campaign against the freedom and social influence of the church in the 1870s. Anti-Catholicism united with ex-immigrants' natural antipathy to the rivalry of more recent newcomers in a political movement, which came officially to be called the American Party but which revelled in the ironic soubriquet of the Know-Nothing Party. Samuel Morse was one of its candidates, and his propaganda brings out the programme and tone. "Can one throw mud into pure water and not disturb its cleanliness?" he asked before arguing that America was the target of a Jesuit plot. A wave of anti-Catholic feeling flowed from President Franklin Pierce's decision to appoint a Catholic cabinet member in 1852. The coalition of anti-immigrant and anti-Catholic forces was apparent, for instance, in the *North Carolina Weekly Standard*'s "Know-Nothing Menu," which in-

Her creation was a stupendous feat of engineering, but assembling the Statue of Liberty once it had arrived was also a major undertaking. It involved erecting acres of platforms supported on elaborate scaffolding. The crook of Liberty's arm and the massive hand can be seen poking through the scaffolding among the large numbers of workmen and the staggering amount of rubbish. The cost of the pedestal was the sticking-point which delayed the operation until enough subscriptions were shamed out of the public by Joseph Pulitzer's publicity campaign.

cluded as puddings, after "Fried Nuns, very nice and tender," "Rich Irish Brogue" and "Sweet German Accent."

The United States depended heavily on immigrants to fuel expansion and industrialization. While immigrants continued to flow in and to account for a considerable proportion of the nation's citizenry and manpower, Know-Nothingism had to fail. The counter-triumph of awareness of America's nature as a land of immigrants seemed to be symbolized in 1886 by the erection of the Statue of Liberty, with its incised welcome to the "wretched refuse" of the poor and oppressed. Yet from the first, the giant structure cast a dark shadow. It had been proposed in France in 1865 for the purposes of French rather than American politics by Frenchmen who wished to liberalize the regime of Napoleon III, to express solidarity with republican traditions and to curtail imperialistic adventures. Four hundred thousand dollars had been raised; the artistic flair and engineering genius of F. A. Bartholdi and Gustave Eiffel had been commissioned, and the problems of design and construction had occupied nearly twenty years when the finished work was presented to an American envoy on 4 July 1884, to be shipped across the ocean in 214 crates. Enthusiasm was much less at its destination than in its country of origin. The delicately articulated structure—the central iron pylon, the complex, flexible trusswork innards, the teguminous cladding of hammered copper—seemed destined to remain crated for lack of funds with which to supply a pedestal, until Joseph Pulitzer's newspaper campaign shamed the public into raising the $100,000 needed to put the statue in place.

From her perch on Bedloe's Island, Liberty presided over a new era in American immigration. At her feet was Ellis Island, where, from 1892, immigrants were processed as to suitability, and undesirables—mostly the carriers of suspected disease, but also including political suspects, such as anarchists, or moral rejects, such as prostitutes and polygamists—were filtered out and where ever-narrower quotas were enforced. The Statue of Liberty had arrived just in time to witness the erosion of liberality in America's immigration laws, under the impact of a migrant movement hugely bigger in numbers, vastly more extensive in range of provenance, than had been experienced before. Between 1890 and 1920, migration brought the United States a net gain of 18.2 million people—more than in the entire previous history of the country. The newcomers came from ethnicities new to American experience or previously little represented, from areas deep in Europe beyond the western-seaboard states which had formerly predominated. From 1899, when Jews were first separately enumerated, until 1924, 17 per cent of arrivals were Italians, 14 per cent Jews, and 17 per cent Slavs, of whom nearly half were Poles.

By the start of this period, though the United States remained a uniquely powerful magnet for migrants, a substantial portion of the overflow of Europeans was spilling into other parts of the Americas, especially to Canada and the fabulously fertile River Plate region of Uruguay, Brazil, and, above all, Argentina. Between 1857 and 1930, Argentina's net gain totalled 3.5 million migrants; immigration supplied 60 per cent of the total population increase, and by 1914, when 13 per cent of the population of the United States was foreign-born, the corresponding proportion in Argentina was 30 per cent.

In overall statistics, Argentina's newcomers were more homogeneous than those of the north: 46 per cent Italian, 32 per cent Spanish, communicating in *lunfardo,* the Italo-Spanish argot still spoken in Buenos Aires' docklands. The same length of reach and the same cosmopolitan flavour, however, could be found in Buenos Aires' brothels, famous or notorious according to taste, which made the Argentine capital the "sin city" of its day. Of registered prostitutes in Buenos Aires between 1889 and 1901, 19 per cent were born subjects of the Russian empire; 36 per cent came from Europe east of the Rhine; 13 per cent from Italy. In the lurid *demi-monde,* where tales of white slavery abounded, the pimps, procurers, and madams were at first predominantly French and Italians, later, increasingly, Hungarians and Poles, especially Jews, who, as ever, tended to get marginalized in respectable trades and professions.

BUSINESS IMPERIALISM

In the prostitutes' case the distinction was perhaps blurred, but traffic in migrants was matched by traffic in goods. Growing trade was a world phenomenon. Just as transatlantic migration was part—the biggest part—of a worldwide picture, which included export of labour on a large scale from India and China, so the growth of the Atlantic economy in the nineteenth and twentieth centuries took place against a global expansion of trade which gave the term "world economy" a resonance it never had in the early-modern infancy of worldwide exchange.

The figures look different according to whether they are reckoned up by volume or value, but acceleration was most conspicuous in the 1850s and 1860s, when the increase by value was of the order of 80 and nearly 100 per cent, respectively. In the trough of the last quarter or so of the nineteenth century, just when migration was at its most intense, world trade roughly doubled in volume and increased by a third in value. Even at this checked rate of growth the range and intensity of economic activity were powerful agents of change. Between 1870 and 1900, while 21 million Europeans emigrated to other continents and world industrial production may roughly have quadrupled, world shipping nearly doubled to about 30 million tons net. The division of the world into primary producers and manufacturers made inter-regional trade vital in a new way.

Within the emerging global economy it was Atlantic-side economies that became most closely tied to one another, especially those of western Europe with North America and with some other parts of the American hemisphere. Argentina's was again the most spectacular case. From being a net importer of cereals in the 1860s, she developed an export trade of 100 million bushels of wheat and maize annually by 1899. Refrigeration, introduced in 1883, made possible a similar sudden rise in beef and mutton exports. Argentina's foreign trade almost trebled in the last three decades of the century. Like comparable booms in other Latin American economies, this was led by foreign capital. A new form of clientage to international big business arose to elude the Monroe Doctrine, the ban unilaterally decreed by the United States against European colonialism in the New World.

Participants in the Atlantic economy inherited habits of inter-dependence from the colonial past. In Latin America the wars of independence inaugurated a new era of economic colonialism. The new republics, after spending heavily on the fight against Spain, were obliged to go on maintaining

big armies in wariness of one another. They started life under a burden of
debt still familiar today. Having fought Spanish monopolists under the banner of free trade, they were unable to protect native industries against European imports.

Capital projects always had to be financed from outside—overwhelmingly, over the nineteenth century as a whole, from Britain, with significant
inputs from the United States, Germany, and France. For most tastes this
chapter must already be overburdened with statistics, but a few more will
make the point concisely. Between 1870 and 1913, British investments in
Latin America rose from £85 million to £757 million; this amounted to about
two-thirds of the total foreign investment in the continent. British companies controlled over half the tonnage of Argentine and Brazilian ports. Railways, which made export booms possible by linking areas of potential
production to the ports, were, over much of the continent, a British preserve. They absorbed nearly half of Britain's total overseas investments. The
railways of Argentina and Brazil were almost wholly British-owned. Even in
North America, British capital tied up in railways amounted to £400 million
in 1900; indeed, the United States was itself an arena for business imperialists, differing chiefly from Latin America in finding more productive and industrial outlets for massive foreign loans.

"Business imperialism" was in no sense naked exploitation. Like other
forms of more overt imperialism practised elsewhere in the same period,
which are the subject of the next chapter, it was a collaborative project of
locals and outsiders—in this case local élites and foreign capitalists. A typical story is that of the Rosario Water and Drainage Company between 1870
and the eve of the Second World War; it was a British firm founded to provide Argentina's proud second city with amenities to match its pretensions.
The local authorities demanded a high level of investment from their guests
and a high share of the yield for themselves; only gradually was the company allowed even to make a profit. In Brazil, exploitation by British coffee-
shippers was a common source of complaint in the late nineteenth century.
American buyers and consuls fomented it, fearful of the rate at which export cartels were buying out impoverished producers. There were some
grounds for anxiety. English absentees did exercise over their plantations
the kind of paternalism-in-paradise encountered by Billy Bunter in Frank
Richards's best book: his funny evocation of a schoolboy holiday on an
English-owned *fazenda*. As in the novel, the locals responded with fawn-
ing deference or covert resistance. But by 1911 only 8,000 coffee plantations out of some 57,000 were in foreign hands. In Mexico, Weetman
Pearson, Lord Cowdray, was one of the most notorious "exploiters," especially when he moved from engineering and construction projects to oil ex-
traction in 1909. As a liberal MP in Britain he was lampooned as "the
member for Mexico" and emblazoned his coat of arms, on elevation to the

Billy Bunter, "the fat owl of the Remove," the most prolific schoolboy anti-hero of the century, visits a school chum's fazenda in the company of a range of stereotypes. The ranch manager, standing, on the right, is the epitome of the oily Latin; the Indian paddlers are timid and spineless; the English schoolboys, animated by a spirit of adventure, brave an exotic environment full of bandits and beasts. From *Billy Bunter in Brazil* (1949) by Frank Richards, illustrated by R. J. Macdonald. See also p. 460).

peerage in 1910, with the image of a Mexican peon. He was said to have looted more from Mexico than any man since Cortés, yet he was a philanthropic employer and copious reinvestor, whose success was owed to a mutually advantageous relationship with the dictator Porfirio Díaz.

Latin America became littered with the failures as well as the fortunes of business imperialism. The young English adventurer Hugh Pollard met some of them during "a busy time in Mexico" in 1910, when he stayed on to get mixed up in the revolution. Dismissed from a clerkship with an agricultural machinery firm in the wilds of Tapachula, a gun-slinging outpost of the Pan-American railway near the Guatemalan border, he found a country where "everybody has something in the way of a concession and only needs a little capital to become a millionaire." The flotsam included the German hotel-keeper of the town, "who should have been a millionaire, but for a mania for worthless mining claims"; "broken gentlemen" with

"El Foxchase," photographed to illustrate Hugh Pollard's account of his adventures in Mexico. "There were no foxes and no hounds: a drag had been tried, but the altitude with its sharp night frosts and morning sun was fatal to the scent. The idea of a gallop remained, and the 'sport' was obtained by fastening a silver-mounted fox brush on to the left arm of an ambitious horseman, who was chased by the remainder of the club. . . . To English eyes the whole proceeding was a brilliant burlesque. The weird horse and still weirder costumes . . . belonged to either the circus or Margate sands—no hunt on earth had ever been so brilliant in costume."

public-school reminiscences; rubber-concession con men and "experts . . . who will report on a plantation for a five-dollar bill"; and an ex-Guardsman, who claimed to be an aviator, attracted by cheap drink and playing poker for peanut shells.

Yet Pollard could also mix with a quasi-colonial beau monde, riding to "el foxchase" in Chapultepec Park in an eccentric shade of pink, or sallying forth with an animal-loving friend to start café brawls with bullfighters. He was impressed with the superiority of the English-owned railroad, which seemed "quite home-like" after the "appalling food and worse company" of the Pan-American system, where the first-class accommodation was so filthy that "no English workman would tolerate [it] for half an hour's ride." And he concluded that the best destiny for Mexico would be incorporation into the British Empire.

As Pollard regretfully realized, Britain had been pre-empted by the United States. Mexico had been victimized by her northern neighbour through European-style business imperialism, for Yankee investments exceeded Britain's by half as much again and *gringos* were scythed along with

other exploiters by Death the Bicyclist in one of José Posada's macabre caricatures. But there was more to it than that. Between the Mexican War and the Mexican Revolution, the United States had appropriated half of Mexico's national territory, occasionally encouraged secession, and intervened repeatedly by armed force in the republic's troubles. From the 1890s, Yankee imperialism in Latin America would get more strident and far-reaching, with arbitration of Venezuela's border (1895), annexation of Puerto Rico and a protectorate over Cuba (1898), dismemberment of Colombia and administration of the Panama Canal Zone (1903), armed interventions in the Dominican Republic, Haiti, Mexico, and Nicaragua between 1905 and 1916, and incorporation of the Virgin Islands (1917).

Nothing so overt by way of new imperial initiatives had been attempted from the other side of the Atlantic since Napoleon III's intervention in Mexico in 1861. In a sense the French adventure had a direct link with "business imperialism," for its pretext was to secure Mexican government debts held in France, Britain, and Spain. Installed by the French as emperor of Mexico, Maximilian of Austria, a Habsburg gilded youth, was driven from his palace bed by fleas and from his throne by inveterate nationalism; when Yankee demands obliged French troops to withdraw in 1867, he was executed by firing squad. The alien nature of his intrusion seemed symbolized by the local embalmer's difficulty in finding a blue eye to replace one that had been shot out.

If the limits of European neo-imperialism in the Americas were set by the United States, this discipline had an obverse. The restraint was mutual. By self-denying ordinance, the United States was committed to refrain from in-

José Posada, *Las bicicletas* (1913). A version of the horsemen of the apocalypse for an industrializing society. In ascending order of guilt, their victims are declared to be dishonest businessmen, prostitutes and their clients, bar-room bravos, corrupt politicians, Yankee imperialists, and "bad Mexicans who help the foreigners." Medicine, legal cunning and piety are dismissed as defenses useless against the skeleton bicyclists.

tervention in Europe. The declaration of President Monroe in 1823, in which the United States first claimed a free hand in the western hemisphere, had been explicit on that point, and every subsequent American government upheld it. "Isolationism" was an ingrained part of American political culture, and Atlantic civilization perhaps could not be considered fully restored until it was renounced. In the words of the song sung by the troops who broke the taboo in 1917, "We won't be back 'til it's over over there."

Ten years later a conspicuous transatlantic event commemorated their achievement when Charles Lindbergh made the first solo airborne crossing of the ocean. His was really a modest achievement, for numerous aviators had made the journey in pairs, but in a mythopoeic press campaign he was hailed as a "new Christ" who had "conquered death"; at Le Bourget the unprecedented crowds venerated a boy who glimpsed the hero from his father's shoulders; at Croydon spectators were trampled in the rush. The fuss was partly contrived, but Lindbergh's arrival in Europe did symbolize a genuinely popular ideal of a narrowed Atlantic—an alliance kept taut by a flight "guided," according to the American ambassador in Paris, "by the same sublime destiny" as had directed the allied armies in the First World War.

COMING FROM AMERICA

On hearing that my wife had a degree in war studies, an interlocutor at a cocktail party asked her ingenuously, "What really did cause the First World War?", adding, "I've always wanted to know." His small talk was deplorable but his bafflement excusable. Few questions have generated so much futile debate. Much of it has been moral debate about who was to blame. Much has been philosophical—about the nature of historical causation and how long it takes "origins" to mature into wars. The war has been ascribed to small causes, such as the inflexibility of railway timetables which governed the mobilization of armies or the unpredictability of holiday-season decision-making in the summer of 1914. It has been ascribed to great, structural causes, such as the supposed warlike proclivities of capitalism or the violent deficiencies of the collective culture of an unregulated international society. It has been blamed on German lust for conquest, French thirst for vengeance, Austrian irresponsibility, and Russian insecurity. The moral position of the British government, which contrived a pretext for joining the war after it had started, has been shown to be little better.

The diplomatic context of the outbreak has been sought on the Austro-Italian border or in the zone of Russo-German rivalry in the Balkans or among areas of overseas competition among the British, French, and German empires. Responsibility has been pinned on the logic and momentum of the arms race and on the unreason and inertia of incompetent statesmen. It has been understood as the "muddle" of "men who foundered" and as the long-term design of planners who conspired. Underlying the search for an explanation of impressive weight is the conviction that a cataclysmic event must have a conspicuous cause. "There has been a tendency to argue," a clear-sighted analyst points out, "that because the war caused such great and lasting damage, because it destroyed three great empires and nearly beggared a fourth, it must have arisen from causes of peculiar complexity and profundity, from the neuroses of nations, from the widening class struggle, from a crisis in industrial society."

One useful way of reformulating the question is to ask, first, what caused each of the distinct wars of which the First World War—which is really an umbrella name—was composed. With Britain, for instance, Germany was impelled to war by different circumstances, and contending for different prizes, from those at stake in her war with Russia or Serbia (though the reader will be relieved to be assured that, for present purposes, each pair of adversaries does not have to be particularly scrutinized). Second, it is helpful to ask, "What made this a world war—or, rather, what makes us characterize it as such?—instead of just another European war like so many others?" Since truth is relative and the answer to every question depends on the perspective from which it is asked, we have to look at these questions from an American point of view in order to understand issues so compelling that they made the United States government of 1917 abandon isolationism and renounce long-standing ties of culture and kinship which bound many of its citizens to Germany, to launch a war of its own against the German Reich.

This involves laying aside the railway timetables and looking at the world map. In an age of burgeoning world trade, of which German industry was claiming an increasing share, and of worldwide imperialism in which Germans felt disadvantaged compared with Britain and France, Germany had no access to the ocean highways of the wider world except through narrow seas easily policed by British rivals. Whatever the particular quarrels which set Germany and her continental enemies at loggerheads, this alone made a global showdown between Britain and Germany predictable.

In terms of strict Staatspolitik, Germany might have counted on American backing. Britain was ahead in the races for space and trade, and an enemy who checked her would benefit all her rivals, including the United States. There were flashpoints of German–American rivalry in the Pacific, but generally, where imperial interests clashed, there were far more rasps of friction between America and Britain than between America and Germany. In the western hemisphere, where America exercised conscious political guardianship, Britain was a colonial power whereas Germany was not. In ideological terms, America's choice was more evenly balanced, for whereas France and Britain shared democratic credentials with the United States, Uncle Sam had a historic anti-imperialist commitment to maintain; America's own imperialism—by then overspilling the hemisphere to include, since 1898, the Philippines, Hawaii, Guam, American Samoa, and other Pacific Islands—made this seem more or less humbug to an objective scrutineer, but it remained a moulding influence on American policy, which targeted the biggest empires, those of Britain and France, as the most urgent cases for dismemberment. Moreover, at the critical time, American decision-making was in the hands of an academic élite, led and typified by the professorial President Woodrow Wilson, who, while detesting Germany's perceived militarism and despotism, revered the liberal German professorate.

Yet as well as the advance of democracy and the retreat of empires, American interests were perceived in the States as demanding world peace and freedom of the seas. In these connections, Germany was easily branded as aggressor and transgressor. Coming from behind in the arms race, she forced the pace in the pre-war years. Faced with enemies on two fronts, she had to cultivate a militaristic ethos to survive. Squeezed between Russia and France, she felt compelled to act pre-emptively on at least one front once war became inevitable. Since the maritime status quo was to Britain's advantage, it was Germany that appeared as the disturber of the peace of the seas. Once the war was under way, Britain continued to enjoy access to Atlantic trade—which became a lifeline of supply—while Germany was compelled to resort to submarine warfare to break the blockade of her home seas. U-boat attacks, because of their unseen and unfamiliar power of sudden destruction, aroused barely rational moral resentment; when American shipping figured among the victims in 1917, the United States was already looking for a pretext for war.

In the first two years of the Anglo-German conflict, under the shell of neutrality, America's war-willingness incubated. The United States was tied ever more tightly to Britain. By 1914, American industrial production had already overtaken Britain's in crucial areas—fuel products, iron, and steel; but the American economy continued to carry a huge burden of indebtedness to British financial institutions. It was therefore unthinkable that America should press neutrality to the point of withholding supply from her creditor; on the contrary, the war could be and was exploited to reverse the relationship of debt.

America needed a long war and an eventual Franco–British victory. Once revolution had knocked Russia out, the German preponderance in numbers—324,000 more bayonets in the field on the western front by March 1917—had to be redressed if the western allies were to escape defeat. As German policy-makers realized the growing likelihood, the ultimate inevitability of American intervention, they plotted to defer it by manipulating German–American lobbyists and negotiating with enemies of America in Mexico and Japan. Like the submarine campaign, these excesses only helped to provoke an American reaction in Britain's favour. Meanwhile, a further peculiarity of American society contributed to force the pace of intervention. As the empires of eastern Europe crumbled at the edges, the migrants and descendants of migrants who were so numerous in America glimpsed the chance of future freedom for their homelands. An American war of liberation in Europe therefore became—counter to the isolationist tradition—an increasingly popular cause.

When American intervention came, it was not on behalf of France and Britain but for America's own objectives: crushing German militarism, freeing the seas, weakening European empires, lifting America's debts, and "making the world safe for democracy." When Germany was out of the picture, Wilson intended to turn to deal with Britain and France. As he confided to his envoy in Europe, "England and France have not the same views with regard to peace that we have by any means. When the war is over we can force them to our way of thinking." Technically, the United States did not become an ally of the entente governments but an "associated power." In the 1920s the American staff was turning out contingency plans for wars against Britain and France.

April 1917: American help for the western democracies issues, in a German cartoonist's depiction from Simplicissimus, from the maw of hell, depicted as a Leviathan with a stovepipe topper, against a backdrop of a futuristic American cityscape.

These realities were smothered by the rhetoric of amity that accompanied allied euphoria at American intervention: a decisive accession of strength at a critical juncture of the war inspired Britain to take up the happy cry, "The Yanks are coming!" For another songster, the biggest problem would be

> How ya gonna keep 'em down on the farm
> Now that they've seen Pa-ree?

Those Americans who saw one bit of Europe or another amounted to three million men. A whole generation was refreshed with images of their parents' or ancestors' home. The convoys that bore them re-stretched an umbilical cord.

Like most wars, this war only confirmed the way things were already going. Staring at each other across the ocean, the faces of two hemispheres grew increasingly alike and saw reflected images of each other. By the end of the nineteenth century most western seaboard states of Europe—Britain, France, Spain, and Norway—were all as democratic, in terms of their franchise, as the United States. In terms of social legislation they were in some respects more advanced, and the unionization of their labour had, in most contemporary opinions, progressed much further. Meanwhile, the U.S.A. and, more selectively, Canada, while remaining major primary producers and exporters, had copied the manufacturing and industrial culture of western Europe. The States lost the distinctive look of a young country, a pioneer republic, a lone democracy. Developments on both sides of the Atlantic made the American "nations"—as, in imitation of Europe, they were now styled—more like the old countries from which they had for-

Manaus Opera House. Enriched with so much spendthrift zeal that it mocks, rather than imitates, old-world taste, with English engineering, Italian fixtures, and French fittings. The pneumatic tyre was invented in 1888; the rubber boom began in earnest two years later and the Teatro Amazonas was opened in 1896, by which time the area was producing 90 per cent of the world's rubber.

merly broken free. "Uncle Sam" became "Brother Jonathan," "a power among the powers."

Most of Latin America, with big Indian populations and structural economic underdevelopment, was not so easily recast in this standard "western" image but became increasingly adorned with its maquillage. In the short-lived rubber boom of the late century, Manaús on the middle Amazon acquired a splendid imitation of the Paris Opéra, now crumbling with neglect, wrinkled and warped with age. Madame Gautron took *haute couture* to Bogotá in 1840, and Elisa Lynch—reputedly—the first grand piano to Asunción in 1861. Guatemala City was dubbed "the Paris of Latin America." With the profits of guano and the advantage of fast travel, the bullring of Lima hired the best matadors from Spain. Even the Pacific shore of the American hemisphere was closely bound, more deeply drawn, into Atlantic civilization, and in 1914 the opening of the Panama Canal made the Atlantic, in travelling time, closer still.

Despite the conflicting interests which still divided the United States and the western European powers, partnership in a single civilization, shared by so many of the world's most resourceful and predatory states, confronted the rest of mankind with a source of cultural influence of peculiar force. Until the component states of Atlantic civilization started tearing each other's empires apart, they also posed, individually, a political threat—or an economic promise, from the point of view of those many who embraced western rule or influence with enthusiasm: a promise of a share in the fabulous material benefits this civilization seemed to confer on its home populations. In consequence, the world hegemony of "the west" was brief but real. Our next task is to try to evoke what it was like.

Chapter 14

THE MIRRORS OF IMPERIALISM: WESTERN REFLECTIONS ELSEWHERE IN THE WORLD

Refracted Images—The Industrial Advantage—
The Tomb of Radamès—The Hidden Hippopotamus—
The Meal of the Man-eaters—The Distorting Mirror

REFRACTED IMAGES

This is about as far as you can go. Here man's world stops. Beyond Dunedin, on New Zealand's South Island, as you look from the cape to the south-east, there are only ocean and ice. Yet the edge of the earth, in spots like this, is not just habitable but comfortable. Dunedin's skies, bright with an almost painful clarity unknown in the northern hemisphere, are lined with spires and trimmed with towers, as heavy with human embellishments as an alderman's robes. The solidity of the bluestone buildings—dark, beetling-browed, academic, civic, ecclesiastic—is as eminently respectable as anything in a late nineteenth-century English or Scottish city centre. Dunedin is a miraculous mirror, reflecting Victorian and Edwardian Britain from as far away as it is possible to get, through almost the whole length and density of the core and carapace of the earth.

The name of the city is an echo of Edinburgh's. The university, of 1869, is modelled on that of Glasgow. In the palatial railway station of 1904, which houses the last buffers before the Southern Ocean, "Gingerbread" George Troup gilded his architecture with loyal lions and lubricious nymphs, who

Larnach Castle, Dunedin, was begun in 1871, less than a quarter century after the founding of the colonial city, the remotest in the world, and ten years after the discovery of Otago gold. Two hundred workmen spent fifteen years building it at a cost of £125,000. This extraordinary gesture of confidence in Dunedin's future was paid for by the manager of the first Bank of Otago, who had married a French heiress with a dowry of £85,000.

roar and laugh at the monogram of New Zealand Railways, endlessly repeated in mosaic tessellations. Cathedrals and town hall proclaim with the same defiance the citizens' confidence in civilization's last stop. A photograph of Lower High Street in 1907 shows the Grecian telephone exchange facing the Italianate Fire and Marine Insurance Company, while the Flemish-baroque towers of the Chamber of Commerce rise in the background. The obligation to build was solemnly felt, though hard to express without the bathos of an adoptive local poet's cry:

> Go, trav'ler, unto others boast of Venice and of Rome,
> Of saintly Mark's majestic pile, and Peter's lofty dome;
> Of Naples and her trellised towers, of Rhineland far away.
> These may be grand but give to me Dunedin from the bay.

Perhaps the most expressive building is a private dwelling a little out of the centre: Olveston, built in 1904–6 to be the home of D. E. Thomin, a businessman who patronized painters and bequeathed his house to the nation, represents the perfection of Jacobethan nostalgia, inside and out. For Dunedin was built by men who thought edifices should edify. They laid out extravagant streets and squares in a wilderness of hills so inhospitable that in the opinion of an early surveyor "nothing save an earthquake coming to level them could ever make it suitable for the site of a town."

Like so many of the remotest European colonies, Dunedin blended nostalgia with escapism. In origin it was a refuge for marginalized radical Protestants, every bit as self-conscious and exclusive as the plantations of seventeenth-century New England. Its founders were purposefully re-enacting a seventeenth-century experiment. Its founding manpower was spilled out of Scotland by the presbyterian schism of 1843, and admission to the colony was originally confined to members of the Free Kirk. When the first 344 settlers sailed in 1847, purity had already been compromised by necessity. Of the 2,000 properties marked out on the map, only seventy-two had been sold, mostly to absentee speculators. The project had two guarantees of success: an inspired leader, the Free Kirk minister Thomas Burns, nephew of the great poet whose statue dominates Dunedin's octagonal piazza; and abundant pasture to turn into wool. "Sheep," a local paper improbably declared, "are the pioneers of civilization." Seven hundred new settlers arrived in 1848 and 1849. Modest prosperity had already been achieved, and the Free Kirk was outnumbered by gentiles of other communions, when the gold rush of 1861 crammed the town and caused a typhoid epidemic.

By then a similar story of sheep and gold on the rim of the world had turned Melbourne from a small town of 23,000 people in 1850 to a "metropolis" of 126,000 in 1861. Its growth could be calibrated in statistics, but its success was also an immeasurable *succès d'estime*. A returnee of 1858 recalled it in the typical language it inspired: "utterly surpassing all human experience" in growth "unparalleled in the annals of the world." Where "twenty-two years ago the Yarra rolled its clear waters to the sea through the unbroken solitude of a primeval forest," he remembered the crowded wharves, handling £13 million a year in exports, the "waterworks constructed at fabulous expense," the steamships, the theatres, the "scream of the engines, the hubbub of the streets," and the "black swarming masses" on the corner of Bourke Street. "All the town lay at my feet, and the sun was going down behind the distant mountains; I had just crossed from the front of the new Houses of Legislature, and had nearly been run over by a great omnibus."

Founded as a rudimentary settler village in the year of Queen Victoria's accession, Melbourne fulfilled the best and the worst of Victorian values, surviving all the risks of rampant speculation, acquiring all the beatitudes of the Gospel of Work, all the beauty and ugliness of the unrestrained pursuit of progress. The auctioneer at the first land sales in 1837 bought two lots for himself at £54; when he died in 1881 they were worth a quarter of a million. The last decade of the century would be disfigured by a slump, but by 1891 Melbourne had over 800,000 inhabitants and the third highest property tax revenue in the British Empire after London and Glasgow.

To travel from England to Melbourne today seems at first like falling into a mirror. After a journey long enough—for most tastes—to land you on another planet, you emerge in a city with fish-and-chip shops, where lawyers wear wigs. The buildings of Collins Street "would not disgrace Saint James's"—a boast first uttered in 1858—and the tables in the Athenaeum Club are laden with cruets, sauceboats, and épernes statelier and more elaborate than in the homonymous establishment in London. It looks, as it did in 1885 to J. A. Froude, whose relish for professional enmity made him a misfit at home, like "English life over again." Yet even in Froude's day— even before the elastic immigration policies of the twentieth century spangled or spattered the streets with a bewildering ethnic diversity and enriched or encumbered Australian radio waves with broadcasts in a babel of tongues—the differentness of Melbourne was apparent to an accustomed eye. The grid plan stamps the city with a colonial branding iron. The low-built sprawl of old suburbs like Fitzroy and Saint Kilda's has a Latin American tang. To Sir Charles Dilke, Australian rules football was more like a bullfight than anything back home.

Most mime ends as burlesque. Even the most faithful colonial imitations of metropolitan societies produced warped or refracted images. The very

Collins Street, Melbourne, in 1857, looking east from the Wesleyan Chapel on "buildings that would not disgrace St. James's," with street lighting, a phaeton, and a rider and dog modelled on one of Orme's English sporting prints.

intensity of colonial nostalgia for the mother country is a measure of the disparities imposed by the effects of distance and of new environments. Charles Kingsley's brother Henry came home from unsuccessful foraging in the Australian goldfields in 1858 voicing perhaps the sentiments of the hero of his novel of colonial life: "Don't let me hear all that balderdash about the founding of new empires. Empires take too long in growing for me."

His novel tingles and pricks with the newness of Australia. European fashions are unshaped and begrimed by heat. Hostile animals menace life; uncatalogued plants provoke academic debate; the bush, tamed by farmers or turned into sheep stations, fights back with omnivorous fires. People are changed: old convicts into ornaments of society, exiles into aristocrats, promising youths into demoralized wrecks. And on the margins of the White world he depicts, the "blackfellows" roam. A few resist, waiting in the ranges with poised spears; others exploit the enemy, using their spears only on stray and wild cattle; one or two are active collaborators, drawn into the settlers' service by drink or religion. The transformation can be seen in explorers' paintings, from the tense, naked, bristling assailants who confronted Thomas Baines in 1855 to "Dick, the brave and gallant native guide" sketched by his master, relaxing, tankard in hand, a few years later. In all the environments transformed by nineteenth-century colonialism, the existing populations had formerly been the most powerful ingredient. In

Thomas Baines's painting of his own encounter with Aboriginal warriors in 1855. He was a sympathetic antagonist and these are noble savages, whose poses seem based on those of classical javelin-throwers.

Dick, the brave and gallant native guide whose talents were left idle in the base camp, while Burke and Wills hurried ahead to their deaths on their disastrous trans-Australia expedition of 1860. A sympathetic portrait by Dr. Becker, the expedition's official artist and scientist.

Australia, New Zealand, Patagonia, some Boer lands, and the North American west, they were condemned to be victims by their paucity, too easily exterminated, expropriated, or penned up in uncongenial wastes. Here Atlantic civilization was most faithfully mirrored and the indigenous people could only respond, feebly or fiercely, to White initiatives.

According to the conventional wisdom, other colonial frontiers of the time, in Africa and south and south-east Asia, were almost as thoroughly remodelled in a "western" image, despite the presence of dense indigenous populations and robust native polities. No one, indeed, can fail to be impressed by the strength of the colonial legacy today in surprising places. In the middle of Singapore, cricket is played on an ersatz village green, under the spire of an Anglican cathedral. Bagpipes drone at the inauguration of Pakistani presidents. Indian army mess-menus still feature the dish that E. M. Forster saw as encapsulating the expatriate imperialist tragedy: roast chicken and green peas. Filipinos, who suffered two colonial regimes, eat Spanish *cocido* and play American baseball. African legislatures still gather around the Speaker's mace or tinker with the code Napoléon. In the Central African Republic, when Jean Bokassa wanted to be an emperor, he ordered Napoleonic uniforms from a Parisian couturier. In Malawi, at the Kamuzu Academy, Latin is taught at the behest of a dictator who believes that "every educated man should know about Julius Caesar." European tongues are official languages in many African and Asian states. Even Bangkok, which never experienced a colonial regime or a sustained invasion, is held up in our day for its shops and fashions, as an example of the pervasive nature of the cultural influence of Atlantic civilization borne abroad in the great age of imperialism. Yet if we shift focus and look closely at the colonial empires from the point of view of those who experienced their effects, or step back and try to imagine them from the perspective of a remote future, when only very long-term trends will be worth noticing, these surface reflections of the western world may seem shallow by comparison with the slower changes and longer continuities that went on underneath.

THE INDUSTRIAL ADVANTAGE

As Atlantic civilization scattered excess people and capital over the world, the victims of imperialism seem to have absorbed them with reluctance forced—it is now commonly said—by the White man's unchallengeable technology. Even where they were numerous, victim-peoples could not resist conquerors borne on steamboats, fortified by quinine pills, and armed with steel guns. Certainly the White man's industrial prowess was feared and imitated. Even without coercion by superior force, it therefore helped to spread western influence.

The royal barge of the Lozi, in a photograph published in 1907. A steersman seems to be trying out his place in the stern. The canopied deck-pavilion is ready for the launching, which will take place when the flood comes up, and a rich rug is being unrolled in preparation for the king's arrival.

A story from Zambia illustrates this charmingly. In 1889, François Coillard, an evangelical missionary, was invited to see the new royal barge of the king of the Lozi. "Everyone wanted to make me share their admiration and enthusiasm," he reported. "'Well, *moruti* [teacher], what do you say of *Nalikwanda*? You see what the Lozi can do. The Lozi!' and a clicking of the tongue told the rest." The missionary introduced the king to the European science of boat-building, and thereafter there were always two barges, bigger than formerly, one built in traditional fashion and the other with nails. Displays of technical prowess, without violence, could procure temporary and localized ascendancy, especially in Africa: David Livingstone's reputation as a great chief derived from his skill with fireworks and magic lantern; Joseph Thomson survived as an explorer among the formidable Masai and Kikuyu of Kenya in 1882–83 thanks to conjuring tricks with a false tooth and Eno's Salts. In 1878, Andrew Mackay, the Calvinist missionary, became the "great spirit" of Buganda, one of the most impressive kingdoms of central Africa, by installing a pump that worked "like an elephant's trunk."

Empowered by industrial technology, White imperialism was certainly hard to resist, whether by weight of numbers, extreme fanaticism, or sophisticated statecraft. The helplessness of the Chinese Empire in the opium war; the havoc wrought by a single gunboat on the road to Mandalay; the hecatomb of dervishes at Omdurman all demonstrated that bloodily enough. White supremacy was patchy at first, for technological differentials were slow to mature. In the 1840s, for instance, gunboats and screw-elevated cannon made up huge disparities in numbers when the British fought the Chinese, while in the Sikh wars, the invaders' firepower could almost be matched by the defenders. In some places, however, the simplest technological advantages were already decisive in the early stages of the industrial revolution. In the 1830s, for instance, the relatively modest iron-barrelled guns of Boer farmers were sufficient to check the expansion of Black Africa's most promising native empire. The history of the rise and fall of the Zulus illustrates the growth of the technical gap.

At the time, the might of the Zulus was itself based in part on a technical revolution in the design of their traditional weapons, attributed to one of the most conspicuous heroes of African tradition. Shaka was named after a kind of beetle that was said to cause menstrual irregularities; such was the dismissive language in which he was repudiated in the womb by his Zulu father. He invented his heavy-bladed thrusting spear in the service of another chief, developed the intensive drills, and revived the traditional tactics it demands. When he reclaimed his Zulu inheritance in 1816, the clan had perhaps about 350 warriors. The best measure of the growth of his power is the extravagance with which he mourned his mother's death in 1827: the corpse of the woman the tribe had spurned was guarded by 12,000 men, supplied by 15,000 head of cattle. For a year no crops were to be sown or milk drunk, and all pregnant women were to be put to death with their husbands.

The following year Shaka was murdered by a family conspiracy of a sort common in the history of Ngoni peoples; by then he was ruler of about a quarter of a million subjects and dominated the emulous, militarized world of south-east Africa from a territorial state that stretched between the Pongola River, central Natal, and the Drakensberg. The Zulus could massacre the Boers of Natal with initial impunity. Boer revenge took ten years to equip and organize, but when it came, in 1838, it was irresistible; the Zulu spearmen barely got within thrusting distance of the gun-barrels. In 1840 the Boer puppet Mpande was installed as Zulu chief and ruled a truncated state in peace, growing so fat that he had to be carted round his kraal.

The Zulus' neighbours were not yet convinced, however, that the superiority of White weapons had been adequately emphasized. In the Boer republics and crown colonies that grew up to the south and west of Zululand, or among the Swazis to the north and the Kaffirs who were already under colonial rule, the Zulus were still objects of fear and suspicion, with their 50,000-strong army of "celibate, man-destroying gladiators." In 1879 they were shamelessly provoked into war by an unreasonable British ultimatum after a trifling border incident. By then a vast technical chasm between the foes had been opened by the power of rapid-firing rifles, combining American mechanisms and steel barrels, which could not be copied or mended by African artisans. Lord Chelmsford expected his command to be easy, and the outcome was indeed a foregone conclusion. The mettle of Zulu resistance was demonstrated on the way at Isandhlwana on 22 January. The temerity of a Zulu attack on an exposed British forward camp struck a staff officer as "most amusing," but of 1,800 men caught between the horns of the Zulu impi, only about 350 escaped.

It was a pyrrhic victory. Reinforced, a second invasion destroyed the Zulu army a few months later. Thereafter, for the rest of the century, most resistance in the field was crushed by imperialist forces in the same way. In 1880, for instance, General Julio Argentino Roca machine-gunned his way through the Indians of the pampas. In 1884, Admiral Amédée-Anatole-Prosper Courbet's guns silenced opposition to a French protectorate in Indo-China. Sir Harry Prendergast bombarded the kingdom of Burma out of existence in 1885. Between the Rhodesian settlers' cynical shoot-out with the Ndeble in 1893 and the subjection of the impressive confederacy of Fulani states in what is now northern Nigeria in 1903, most of the remaining field armies of Black Africa were scattered by the Maxim gun. In a typical gesture of despair, Ngoni diviners in Mozambique threw away their bones after defeat by invincibly well-armed Portuguese in 1895.

On the other hand, technical superiority could be eluded by guerrilla tactics, as against the British among the Afghans or against the French in Algeria; or it could be successfully imitated, as in Japan; or brought in from Europe, as in the Ethiopia of Emperor Menelik, or fended off by diplomacy. Occasionally traditional armies triumphed through tactical superiority or the favours of the terrain. Usually such victories were isolated. Zulu independence was not won, though the day was won at Isandhlwana, when traditional weapons cut against the grain; nor did Crazy Horse's victory at Little Bighorn in 1876 save the Sioux. Even the success of a sustained campaign, such as the Maoris' at Te Ngutu in 1868, could not keep White invaders at bay for long. Yet the example of the Battle of Adowa in 1896, which ended Italy's attempt to conquer Ethiopia, shows that the imperialists' prey could turn against the predators with decisive effect. Outside imperialists could maintain their technological advantage only where arms supplies to potential enemies could be controlled.

Instead of assuming the conquerors' superiority, historians of imperialism today are therefore looking inside the victim-societies to expose reasons for collaboration, submission, or the limitation of resistance. As more work is done, the victims look less and less powerless. Not even the overwhelming technical might of the intruders stripped indigenous societies—at least in the early stages of the colonial experience—of their power of initiative. The arena which most abounds in helpful evidence is Africa. This was *par excellence* the new frontier of nineteenth- and twentieth-century colonialism, where earlier empire-builders from outside had stopped short at the coasts but where, in a notorious scramble, in little more than a single generation's span from 1880, ten million square miles of territory were reallocated on the map among eight powers. Yet far from being passive recipients of an alien impress, indigenous states can now be seen as participants in the process and native peoples as its exploiters and manipulators, as well as its victims. Even under imperialism, African history was made in Africa.

The balance of alien input and local initiative is well represented by the adventures of Edgar Wallace's fictional hero in "Sanders of the River." To his readers in the 1930s he was the epitome of a gunboat colonialist; yet he ruled his patch of colonial West Africa by a typical mixture of technological superiority and responsiveness to local needs. In one guise he was made insuperable in palavers by the chatter of the gatling, manned by Hausa gunners and mounted on his steam launch; in another he was the objective arbitrator, welcomed as a wise man, almost as a holy man, able to mediate between rival potentates and irreconcilable systems of law. Sanders's world was still recognizable between the lines of Lord Hailey's report on "native administration" in British west Africa in 1951.

There were ways round naked force: among the Gogo of Ugogo in east Africa, for instance, in 1895, the German practice of exacting tribute by beating the chief was met by the expedient of putting up a false chief to take the beatings. Where brutal methods of control were tried—by the Germans in east Africa, by the British in Rhodesia—the consequences usually included a bloody and costly revolt, followed by a political accommodation. Wherever the White man was useful, however—and he was usually, at least, useful—his power could be enhanced by connection to the structures and tuning to the requirements of indigenous societies. If imperialism was a crime, there were some guilty native states, acting as principals as well as accessories—instigators and fautors as well as quislings and dupes. Those Africans who emulated or anticipated the imperialists, those who colluded and those who resisted, were all retaining and exercising forms of initiative.

The Tomb of Radamès

In 1871 when *Aïda* opened in Cairo, Giuseppe Verdi already had a reputation as one of the most radical, as well as one of the most talented, composers of the day. His operas were sought by impresarios, applauded by the public, and suspected by despotic authorities. Since his first great triumph, *Nabucco,* in 1842, he had cloaked a series of pleas for revolutionary causes in historical costume: attacking slavery, absolutism, feudalism, racism, and clericalism, advocating republicanism, nationalism, humanitarianism, tyrannicide, and freedom of conscience. He had set to music the work of liberal romantics such as Schiller, or radical exiles such as the Duque de Rivas, or social critics such as Victor Hugo. Yet this innkeeper's son, who consorted with grocers, got commissions from European kings and emperors. When the Khedive Ismail of Egypt wanted a new work to be premiered at the Cairo Opera House, he selected Verdi without a qualm; it was the composer who evinced some reluctance. First Verdi temporized, then he demanded the unrealistic fee of $20,000. The khedive, an ascetic aesthete who combined personal austerity with prodigal profligacy, agreed murmuringly.

The opera Verdi wrote has often been hailed as a musical and dramatic masterpiece. It was certainly a masterpiece of political deftness in which every production can stress the message its audience wants. In Mussolini's Italy, it was performed as a Blackshirt extravaganza in praise of racist supremacy; recently, in Frankfurt, I saw a pacifist, gay-rights version. It has plenty of Verdi's political and sentimental stock-in-trade: sympathy for the underdog; pity for the victims and captives of war; hope for suppressed nationhood; anti-clerical odium. In human terms it is a story of the conflict of love and duty—parting in life, reuniting in death a captive princess and a susceptible general—while at a further level of tragedy armies tramp to victory unaffected by the individual sacrifices of the main characters. The explicit focus is just where the patron wanted it: on a history of successful Egyptian colonial warfare in the south; a celebration of a war of conquest in which the Ethiopian enemy is crushed. Ismail relished it, unaware of the

Radamès and Aïda surprised in unpatriotic proximity. This wonderfully rich set was used for a production at Her Majesty's Theatre, London, in about 1879. Even for patrons neutral in the Khedive's quarrels with the Negus, the opera was fascinating in an age of exotic and specifically Egyptian taste: see pp. 689–94.

subversive subtext. Yet the tomb of Radamès, in which the hero is immured at the end of the opera, could have been an augury of the immolation of his own ambitions.

For the ruler of Egypt was one of the indigenous imperialists in whom nineteenth-century Africa abounded. Some native monarchs were already doing their best to carve up the continent before Europeans joined in with sharper slicers. Not that Ismail would willingly be classified with them. He called himself a European and proclaimed his country "part of Europe." Egypt, as one of the frogs in the Mediterranean "pond" of Socrates, was indeed closer to Europe than to the Black world which happened to share its continent. It was largely Islamic and Arabic-speaking and nominally belonged to the Ottoman sultan, whose hereditary viceroy Ismail was. Yet the passage of Napoleon's armies had inflicted on it the influence of one of the great common experiences to befall European peoples in the late eighteenth and early nineteenth centuries. By the 1860s, when Ismail came to power, cotton revenues, boosted by the effects of the American Civil War, seemed to create an opportunity to "modernize" in the European image.

Borrowing at ruinous rates of interest he erected docks, sugar mills, the Opera, and a school for girls. The Suez Canal was completed. No country outside Europe except Japan responded with greater enthusiasm to European ideas.

In one respect Ismail anticipated his European friends. He realized that steam power made the interior of Africa accessible to political control as well as commercial penetration. He believed, too, that he could create an empire for Egypt among the remotest reaches of the Blue and White Niles by exploiting western sentiment: the revered explorer and missionary Dr. David Livingstone had excited a mood of crusade against the slave trade. Egypt, posing as the policeman of the slave routes, would get the finance for her empire-building from philanthropists in Britain and France.

Ismail used a series of imported White "pashas" to organize what he called the "province of Equatoria," beyond the cataracts, in a world of great lakes and waterfalls that were only just beginning to find their way onto maps. Here he was defeated by the environment. Along the Blue Nile and the Red Sea, where his potential victims were the relatively populous and prosperous Coptic principalities of the Abyssinian Highlands, he was checked by determined resistance. For here he trespassed on the home territory of Africa's most explosive indigenous empire. Three times in the nineteenth century highland chiefs knocked their neighbours into unity and recreated the semblance of the old Ethiopian Empire (see Chapter 6). The first, Tewodros (1855–68), who likened to the creation of Adam his sudden rise to power "from the dust," killed himself, despairing of the survival of his vulnerable state. The second, Yohannes IV (reigned 1871–89), beat off the Egyptian threat and fell in battle against fanatical Muslim raiders. Both relied on Ethiopia's ancient ideology of Holy War to mobilize antiquated armies. The last, Menelik (1889–1913), was an Ethiopian Meiji who beat the European imperialists at their own game and emerged from the scramble for Africa with a bloated Black empire, an invincible reputation, and an army of 600,000 men armed with rapid rifles, machine guns, and cannon.

Menelik was a compulsive, if cosmetic, "modernizer" with a weakness for gadgets, the sort of man, opined a European courtier, who "would build an escalator to the moon." Buoyed by expanding foreign trade, his reform of the fiscal system provided the means to buy in European technology; by the time he had to confront Italian invaders he had perhaps 100,000 modern rifles. A painting in Addis Ababa university shows the victors of the Battle of Adowa led by traditional heroes with swords and bucklers, under the protective nimbus of a mounted Saint George. This is not an entirely misleading image: Menelik's campaign against the Italians was the triumph of collective defence by tribal warriors, guarding their homes against an unprincipled and opportunistic interloper. But it was also a genuine conflict of Caesars, between two calculating imperialist powers. The outcome was

In contrast to the Ethiopian version of the Battle of Adowa described in the text, the European press managed to invest the Italian defeat with the heroic quality of a last stand against overwhelming odds. In this typical example from *The Graphic*, the light is falling on the Italians' gleaming uniforms, which convey an impression of civility and almost of sanctity, in contrast with the demonic savagery of their assailants. They are surrounded by spent cartridge cases. The figure on his knees on the right, with a transfixed look and prayerful posture, is trying to reload despite a mortal wound. General Baratieri, outlined against gunsmoke, on a rearing charger, raises his helmet in a gesture of encouragement and of salute.

procured by Menelik's modernizing—both of the army's weapons and of its commissariat. He demonstrated that a Black state could participate on equal terms in the carving-up of the continent.

Respecting the established European colonial territories to the east, he was rewarded with huge gains as far as Lake Rudolf to the south and the swamplands of the upper Nile to the west. European observers recorded his methods of conquest and control. Campaigns began with obsessive chants of self-praise from the troops and ended in "terrible butchery by soldiers drunk with blood." The acculturation of the vanquished began. In pagan communities Christianity was introduced, "not always by persuasion"; the manners, dress, and language of Menelik's native principality of Shoa were spread; fortified garrisons dotted the mountaintops. In consequence of this thorough job, Ethiopia's empire lasted longer than that of any other participant in the scramble for Africa.

No other African ruler succeeded in a similar enterprise. Khedive Ismail's effort from Egypt snapped, enfeebled by financial mismanagement and broken by Islamic revolt in the Sudan from 1881. Of his two greatest White pashas, one was killed off in Khartoum, the other cut off in Equatoria: Charles Gordon, who had been sustained in the desert by brandy and Bible, passed into legend as an "eminent Victorian," martyred by a sense of duty; meanwhile, Eduard Schnitzer, known as Emin Pasha, fed European fantasies about the governability of darkest Africa by keeping up a dwindling, isolated shadow-state just north of the equator, between Lake Albert and Rejaf, until 1889. Egypt itself, by then, had fallen under British occupation and tutelage, as European paymasters lost confidence in Ismail's will—not only his ability—to repay his loans. The khedive was dethroned in 1882 by a "stock-jobbers' war."

Similar fates eventually befell the other states that might have matched Ethiopia's achievement. In the sultanate of Morocco, memories of the imperial past (see Chapter 6) infused the ambitions of Mulay Hassan (reigned 1873–94), who tried to pre-empt European empire-builders in the Maghrib by claiming an ill-defined mandate over the Sahara. He was, in his own estimation, the rightful ruler of "all the tribes not subject to another sovereign" and of "the country of all the tribes who mentioned the Sultan in their prayers." In practice, however, the desert Arabs acknowledged "no other chief than Allah and Muhammad." The real nature of authority in the desert is suggested by a French traveller's account of a visit to the great holy man, Ma el Ainin, in 1887. His capital was "a multitude of tents on a vast plain, surrounding a larger, splendid one of European construction." Conspicuous in his bright blue turban, with the pious look that perhaps gave him his nickname of "Water of the Eyes," he received pilgrims who kissed his hands and begged grains of sand made miraculous by his breath. A few years later he organized resistance to French and Spanish incursions and built the fortress-city of Smara, still a grim reminder of the desert dwellers' defiance of outsiders. As Mulay Hassan's crescent waned, his pretensions seemed mere moonshine. After his death, usurpation by rebellious sheikhs and erosion by jealous European powers weakened Morocco to the point where, in 1904, the country was effectively partitioned by France and Spain.

What Mulay Hassan dreamed in the desert was imagined in the jungle at about the same time in central east Africa by Said Barghash, Sultan of Zanzibar. He was, according to his flatterers, "chosen by Providence to found a great African kingdom which will extend from the coast to the great lakes and beyond to the west." His project was in some ways comparable to Khedive Ismail's, aimed towards the same mysterious region, rich in ivory and rumours of great mines, on the shores of Lake Victoria and the arc of lakes around it. Like Ismail, Barghash realized that he was most likely to succeed with the approval of European powers; he therefore posed unconvincingly

Tippu Tip, "the biggest slaver of them all," whose activities on behalf of Barghash of Zanzibar almost succeeded in pre-empting European imperialism, before he became a collaborator in the empire-building efforts of King Leopold. In the opinion of Jerome Becker—one of Leopold's agents in the Congo in the 1880s—"From his immense plantations, cultivated by thousands of slaves, all blindly devoted to their master, and from his ivory trade, of which he has the monopoly, he has in his duplex character of conqueror and trader, succeeded in creating for himself in the heart of Africa a veritable empire."

as a foe to the slave trade. This encumbered his plans with a fatal contradiction, for it was the slavers' routes that linked the lands he coveted, while the slave-economy gave them potential unity. He did not want Ismail's kind of empire—European in tone, centralized, uniform. He was as interested in fiscal yield and commercial profit as in territorial control; instead of White pashas, he used Black and Arab agents who were left to run their fiefs to suit themselves. His most useful agent in the interior was the biggest slaver of them all, Tippu Tip, the small, Black Arab, ever-smiling fixer with "eyes full of fire," who claimed his name derived from the sound of his rifles.

Barghash's imperialism clung to the region like an Arab garment—loose-fitting, free-flowing, responsive to the wind. It looked well on the map and sounded impressive to small native polities deep in the interior, where, in the early 1880s, Zanzibar was the cynosure of commerce and a reputed fount of power. It was vulnerable, however, to despoliation from within and depletion by conquest. Barghash's vassal in Ugogo, for instance, Mwinyi Mtwana, imposed a fairly effective hegemony over local chiefs but, unrestrained by the sultan's orders, provoked European traders by extortionate caravan tolls. It was a perfect pretext for German invaders, who put him to death and took over the territory. From the mid-1880s, when the German government came to see Zanzibar's empire as ripe for takeover, Barghash's system was doomed. By the time of his death in 1888, his possessions had been dismembered by agreement between Britain and Germany.

THE HIDDEN HIPPOPOTAMUS

A debate among the early nineteenth-century Xhosa, near the southernmost extremity of Africa, polarized around the figures of two prophets. Makana was the "prophet of resistance" to the incursions of White men; Ntsikana was the prophet of "controlled accommodation" who was attracted by Christianity and who perceived that White neighbours could be useful as well as dangerous. From the 1840s in west Africa, the rich and populous city-state of Abeokuta admitted missionaries and grew cotton for Lancashire in exchange for ordnance from Lagos; but these policies rapidly became controversial and were eventually reversed. In 1847, El Haj Omar, the creator of a theocratic state on the Upper Niger and Senegal, proposed collaboration with France: the French would supply the arms to help him conquer Futa Jalon, while he would guarantee order and licence trade. When imperialist appetites in Europe were only faintly beginning to stir, Africans were inciting intervention by an understandably equivocal attitude to what was still an undetectable or barely detectable threat.

In the last quarter of the century, when European imperialism was extended in earnest throughout the continent, it still depended almost everywhere on local abettors. Sometimes Black collaborators were shipped in from far away. When Frederick Lugard marched into Uganda in 1890, he had a Somali chief porter, a Sudanese sergeant, and Zanzibari riflemen; on arrival he trekked to the far shore of Lake Albert to recruit a Sudanese army. When Henry Morton Stanley blasted his way through to claim the lower Congo for the king of the Belgians in 1880, a party was already in possession on behalf of France, commanded by Sergeant Malamine, a Senegalese who normally dressed in "dirty African rags" and who declared "in all seriousness that, being the only White man there, he was glad to see others arrive to keep him company." Among the promoters of British colonialism in west Africa was the Black settler community of Sierra Leone, introduced by the British from the jetsam of abolished slavery. This "creole" élite included some radical thinkers but embraced thoroughly collaborationist cultural values. The first arrivals were often cast ashore naked from their ships, but they strove to acquire Sunday costumes from England and raised a generation of dandies in stiff collars, bow ties, and "primrose kids," lampooned in a local paper in 1868. Their capital at Freetown became al-

The Freemason's Lodge of Freetown presents an address to the Duke of Connaught, 15 December 1910. The White ladies, in their tea-dresses under the marquee, and the top brass with ceremonial swords and pith helmets, look positively informal by the standards of the Black dignitaries, who wear what appears to be full evening dress in the heat of the tropical day. It would be hard to find a more telling image of determination to defy the environment.

most as faithful a travesty as Dunedin, with garden parties, lecture circuits, "mind-uplifting concerts," and a temperance union. At Sawyerr's Bookshop in the 1880s you could buy *The Ballroom Guide* and *Etiquette and the Perfect Lady*.

In other places, empires were sustained by the kind of collaboration which comes when imperialists divide to rule. Kaffirs were armed with Martini-Henrys to shoot at Zulus; Hausa gunners—confirmed in their affectations of superiority by British patronage—were the "sepoys" of British dominion over other west African peoples. The French conquerors of Tukolor on the Niger in 1889 incorporated thousands of wild Bambara tribesmen into their force; when the Bambara mutinied, the Tukoloros were enlisted to put them down.

Overwhelmingly, however, it was minutely local acquiescence and help that sustained European empires in Africa. The real arbitrator of the boundary between the French and Belgian spheres on the lower Congo was no European power but a local chief called Ngaliema, whom Stanley depicted as a simpleton but who extorted fabulously rich gifts of trinkets, silks, and rifles from both sides. The imperialists succeeded best when they applied the advice formulated by an English parliamentary committee in 1898: "adopt the native government already existing; be content with controlling their excesses and maintaining peace between them." Without acquiescence, imperialism was too expensive; it was probably only marginally cost-effective in most places at best. In the seven million square miles of French territory in Black Africa in 1914 there were 2,708 White officials supported by 230 Black interpreters, 5,989 Black police, and 14,142 Black troops; there was only one White battalion, garrisoned at Dakar. Captain Richard Meinertzhagen, the future Zionist who had 100 men to police 300,000 people in early twentieth-century Kenya, thought expectations of "control" were "absurd" and "laughable."

"Acquiescence" is a passive term. African collaborators often chose forms of cooperation which enabled them—according to their own perceptions—to retain at least some initiative. The mental strategies by which they made sense and use of what befell them are hard to reconstruct today, but anthropologists, who are cunning in the recovery of discarded cosmologies, can help us retrieve frameworks of reinterpretation. A representative case to have emerged from recent work is that of King Lewanika of the Lozi, who dealt with the rise of Rhodesia in the early 1890s by imitating the action of the hippopotamus in the proverb: "He jumps, the hippopotamus of

Mr. Elliott Lochner, the agent of the British South Africa Company, in June 1890, at the interview with King Lewanika of the Lozi, described in the text. The crowd in the background are not waving at the camera, but uttering the royal acclamation, the *Shoalela*.

Libonda, when he swims; he sees a canoe on the riverbank, he swirls the deepest waters."

Early in the second half of the 1880s, Lewanika decided to use British power to protect his lands from his surrounding enemies: the Portuguese, the Ndebele, and the Boers. A photograph survives of his first serious negotiations towards a satisfactory relationship with the British crown, conducted with a representative of the British South Africa Company in 1890. Dressed in a bowler hat and linen jacket, the king faces his interlocutor, who wears a pith helmet, at the edge of a sandy piazza occupied by musicians. A large crowd supervises the negotiations—people on one side, chiefs on the other. On that occasion the company cheated the chief into conceding wholesale his country's resources, but Lewanika's subsequent repudiation of the agreement was upheld by the crown. By 1897 he had acquired the services of a British resident and a portrait of Queen Victoria. Meanwhile, his Ndebele enemies had been broken and his power among his own people enhanced. In a part of Africa where the intensity of imperial rivalry had condemned neighbouring peoples to exploitation and massacre, he was one of the most satisfied clients of imperialism. When he visited England in 1902, he was deservedly dubbed a "dusky Disraeli."

THE MEAL OF THE MAN-EATERS

The diary was often a rather misleading confection, but, for what it was worth, under the date 13 June 1880, Pierre Savorgnan de Brazza, the explorer who was racing Stanley to the lower Congo, recorded a typical foundation-ceremony. To a salute of rifle-rounds, "In the name of France," he declared, "I here plant the flag. Long live France! Long live the Republic!" His men went down on one knee as he added, "May God protect the first French station founded in the west of Africa!' The chiefs of the surrounding area, he claimed, were present and received gifts. Like a French wedding, the civil procedure was followed by religious lip-service. The cult of the flag and the canting gestures of legality towards the expropriated locals were obligatory embellishments. He gave the place the name "Francheville" in imitation of places such as "Freetown" and "Libreville," but it soon got corrupted into the nationalistic "Franceville." There was not much to it: a stockade, in what may be a flattering early engraving, with a big, open loggia and a few huts.

Flag-raising was sometimes treated by local people as if it really made a difference to the status of the place or to the nature of authority. The Baganda up to the time of Lugard had a superstitious fear of foreign flags, which they would not allow to be imported, let alone raised. Gradually, even the colonialists came to view such ceremonies with derision. In the

Niger region in 1898, Lieutenant James Willcocks devoted a campaigning season to lampooning French *pavillons* by putting up Union flags in alternate villages. Confronted at Kanikoko in his worn khaki by a resplendent French officer who turned up to repudiate the insult from a station only two miles away, he avoided disaster by getting his antagonist to share the joke and a drink.

The fun of flag-waving could be indulged because European imperialism made little political difference, on the whole, in most of Africa. Planting flags was a sterile form of farming; like other temperate products, they did not do well in tropical soils. Clan loyalties survived, as had similar structures under a more brutal assault in eighteenth-century Scotland. Traditional identities throve—sometimes incubating under the shell of repression—to re-emerge like those of eastern Europe in the twentieth century when the Soviet Empire receded; and traditional centres of power shifted or submerged, like the hippopotamus, in a flurry of white sand, without quitting or dying. Chieftaincies and sultanates were changed but rarely expunged. They survived as the scaffolding by which White magistrates clambered up to their judgement-seats.

The resilience of political structures is astonishing when one reflects how Christianity destroyed so much of the surrounding and supporting fabric, social and ritual, where it existed: human sacrifice, twin murder, infanticide, trial by ordeal, and the practise of witchcraft. New élites were raised up under colonialism—especially by education in mission schools—but only very slowly. In most of Africa it was decolonization, early in the second half of the twentieth century, that broke with the past, crunching traditional polities into improbable "nations" and federations, overlaying tribes with "parties," and intruding new languages of identity from Marxism, pan-Africanism, and secularism. The colonial era was no benign golden age and should not be romanticized in retrospect, but neither should the succeeding period.

The effects of imperialism, modest in the political sphere, were none the less enormous in spreading revolutions in economics and technology. Few parts of Africa that could produce or might demand what the rest of the world wanted or supplied were left unintegrated into the global economy. The traditional traders were condemned with astonishing speed to extermination or extinction. The face of the continent was scarred and pitted with roads, railways, and mines, or rouged and rubbed with new plantations and crops. In all these effects the mixed motives of the imperialists were revealed. A "civilizing mission," sincerely espoused, might mean despoliation in practise; some traders suffered because they were slavers, others because they got in the way of armed greed. Though it would be naïve to see imperialism as the mere overflow or appetite of capitalism, the scramble for Africa was, in part, a scramble for resources.

The face of Africa, scarred and pitted by colonial exploitation: open-cast diamond mining in the "blue earth" at Kimberley, 1872. At that early stage—not much more than a
year after the first diamond was discovered on the De Beers farm—the diggings were
checkered with the square plots of individual prospectors. The difficulty of exploiting
small plots to a considerable depth led to consolidation and the formation of De Beers
Mining Company in 1874; by 1914, the hole had grown to the largest man-made crater
ever dug.

Not even war against the slave trade was morally unequivocal. In 1879,
Charles Gordon delegated the drive against the slavers of southern Sudan
to a ruthless subordinate, Romolo Gessi. The leading trader was hunted
down and shot without trial; the slavers' womenfolk were slaughtered to
stop them from breeding. Thousands of slaves were abandoned to starvation by caravans disrupted or destroyed. Gordon, riding out on a tour of inspection of his men's work, was sickened by the skulls and skeletons. The
war waged on the slavers of the Congo in the early 1890s was little more
than a pretext for ivory-grabbing. Most traditional inland commerce was in-
extricably linked with slaving, and the human traffic could not be curtailed
without filching legitimate lines of trade from its practitioners. Nor were indigenous traders spared, even when largely innocent of slaving. Palm oil
from the upper Niger was traditionally handled by coastal middlemen, like
those of the city-state of Brass, "the Venice of the Niger Delta," whom the
Niger Company beggared into a bloody rebellion in 1895. Sobered by fear

of retribution, King Koko apologized for the attack on the company, "particularly in the killing and eating of parts of its employees. . . . We now throw ourselves entirely at the mercy of the good old Queen, knowing her to be a most kind, tender-hearted, and sympathetic old mother."

If the prostration of the Brassmen symbolizes the economic ordeal of the native traders, it is tempting to choose a metaphor from the landscape to symbolize the impact of imperialism on the African environment. "The Flame Trees of Thika," for instance, look highly suitable: an ordered avenue in the wilderness of Kenya, leading to a White-settler household, where Elspeth Huxley was a girl, and a plantation growing alien coffee. Or the blue earth of the Kimberley mine, scoured by industrial diggers, might make a more ruggedly realistic image. Or, for a townscape, "the rubbish-dumps of modern colonial towns" might serve—though urban development on any significant scale was, on the whole, a late phenomenon under colonialism. Or the image of a particular pioneer—such as Stanley, dynamiting roadways along the Congo to earn the natives' nickname, "Breaker of Rocks"—could suggest the transforming, destructive thrust of White technology.

Stuffed and mounted in the Field Museum of Chicago, the lions of Tsavo look comic. As a 1925 museum guide said with exaggeration, "When the visitor . . . pauses before the life-like forms of the Tsavo man-eaters, it will be hard for him to realize that these two ferocious brutes killed and devoured, under the most appalling circumstances, one hundred and thirty-five Indian and African artisans and labourers . . . in a regular 'reign of terror' when they finally succeeded in bringing the railway works for a time to a complete standstill."

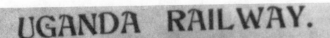

UGANDA RAILWAY.

THE HIGHLANDS OF
BRITISH EAST AFRICA
AS A
WINTER HOME FOR ARISTOCRATS
HAS BECOME A FASHION.

SPORTSMEN in search of **BIG GAME** make it a hobby.
STUDENTS of **NATURAL HISTORY** revel in this **FIELD** of **NATURE'S** own **MAKING.**

UGANDA RAILWAY, BRITISH EAST AFRICA.

UGANDA RAILWAY Observation Cars
pass through the Greatest Natural
GAME PRESERVE in the **WORLD.**

For reliable information, etc., address;
PUBLICITY DEPT. UGANDA RAILWAY,
DEWAR HOUSE HAYMARKET, S.W.

The story of the Tsavo lions became so famous that the Uganda Railway's publicity found it easier to cash in on the curiosity and blood-lust of big game-watchers and hunters than on the commercial benefits that were supposed, at the railway's inception, to justify its cost.

The most surprisingly evocative symbol perhaps is not found in Africa at all but stuffed inside two mangy pelts in the Field Museum in Chicago. These huge monsters of the taxidermist's art are all that remain of the notorious man-eating lions of Tsavo, who terrorized the camps of coolie labourers during the construction of the East Africa Railway in 1898 and 1899. They ate twenty-eight labourers and a White superintendent of railway police, disrupted and, for a time, halted construction, and made most of the workforce defect in terror. They became a worldwide attraction for big-game hunters, who made their killing-grounds a macabre holiday resort and stalked them without success. The lions defeated every defensive precaution the railwaymen could devise. They outflanked every picket posted against them and sprang every trap. They eluded trackers and seemed to dodge the bullets. The chief engineer who eventually hunted them down after an obsessive nine-month odyssey was almost disposed to share his men's belief that they were not flesh-and-blood lions, except in their appetites, but demon visitants: the "angry spirits of two departed native chiefs" protesting at a railway in their country. Thus they were made to symbolize African resistance as well as the mutual opposition of nature and technology, raw tooth and polished steel.

The lions were only the most spectacular of the barriers erected by nature and eventually—at heroic effort and murderous cost—overcome by the builders of what anti-imperialists called "the lunatic line." Workers were immobilized in the hundreds by malaria as they began the coastal section out of Mombasa; in the first year of construction, only twenty-three miles of line were laid. Then the deadly environment of the Taru desert had to be crossed. Tsetse flies killed off most of the animal transport. Raiders and rhinoceroi supplemented the work of the lions. Throughout 1898 the railhead advanced through a disaster zone of drought, famine, and smallpox. Almost as soon as its laborious climb had reached 6,000 feet in the spring of 1899, devastating rains alternated with crippling droughts to undermine the rails and destroy embankments; not until the spring of 1900 were broadly favourable conditions encountered. The railway only reached its projected terminus at Port Florence on the shore of Lake Victoria on 20 December 1901, and was not fully operational for another two years. This monument to technical mastery of the wilderness is still there: a gash on the cheek of Africa, like the parody of a tribal scar.

THE DISTORTING MIRROR

When Lord Delamere, the first great settler of the "White man's country" of the Kenya highlands, arrived to set up home in 1903, he excused himself from dining with the governor on the grounds that the correct clothes were

Gauguin's *Nevermore* (1897), one of his Tahitian *majas*, which have come to seem representative of the "sexually delusive" images of paradise which helped to make colonial postings seem both alluring and threatening.

not yet unpacked. The colonial passion for keeping up standards was a mechanism of defence against the two most feared effects of the frontier: deracination and demoralization. Going native in the sexually delusive paradise of Tahiti, Gauguin transmitted images of the inseparable menace and allure of a brown *maja*. Algeria created the "stranger" type of Camus's play—a man "put to death for not crying at his mother's funeral" because settler morale was too fragile to withstand indifference, let alone dissent. Adjusting to the environment was like being suckled by wolves: survival could be uncivilizing. In an extreme case, like that of Conrad's chilling hero, Falk, a Christian could turn into a cannibal.

Sometimes—in a curious inversion of the imperial ideal—outcasts purged by colonial exile could bounce back home and help transform the metropolis. Richard Hannay, the hero of *The Thirty-nine Steps,* can stand for this type. Returning "home" with a colonial fortune, he is shunned in the old country until he saves the empire from foreign spies. It is an incredible plot but a typical life-trajectory. Sir F. D. Lugard arrived in Africa after failing in an attempt at suicide and ended up in honoured estate in the House of Lords, moulding imperial policy; yet his years in Africa, issuing orders and shedding blood, never endeared him to *salon* society. Cecil Rhodes, who never learned to pass for a gentleman, became the most commemorated alumnus of his old university—but only because he was the richest—and had two countries named after him. He was at least an Oxford man. Many of the proconsuls and merchant princes of British Africa had no background in the spawning-beds of the establishment: Jews and Scotsmen were disproportionately numbered among them. Stanley, the workhouse boy, could break the rocks of Africa but never shifted the chip from his own shoulder, and found all his achievements barely enough to win the consent of the woman he loved. Everywhere empires opened careers to the talents and conferred power and fame on the escapees of worlds of restricted opportunity at home.

The literature of colonialism is full of Tarzan myths: the natural aristocrat unsullied by the jungle. The success of some penal colonies even suggested that the experience of a savage frontier could have redemptive qualities. If there was ever a potential Eden-in-reverse, a "paradise regained," where the bite might be put back into the apple, it was surely the last frontier to be colonized by White settler-farmers, the "Happy Valley" of upland Kenya in the early twentieth century. It promised to be a land of beauty honed by toughness; for a while Theodor Herzl even envisaged it as the new Zion for international Jewry, though his scheme came to nothing. It was the retirement choice of the founder of the Boy Scout movement and became a fashionable place for spoiled public-schoolboys to be sent to grow up.

In a sense the founder of the colony was living proof of its improving properties. Lord Delamere had left Eton at sixteen years old, an uncontrollable vandal, an incorrigible truant, and an irrational gambler. His decision to tame the Kenya wilderness was capricious: one of his gambler's hunches that cost him his inherited fortune. The setbacks and sufferings he endured did not cure him of all crankiness. He had to start each day at Equator Ranch by playing *All Aboard for Margate* on the gramophone; he liked racing trains on horseback; in respectable middle age he used to continue to lead drunken brawls in the streets of Nairobi, shooting out the bottles in the bars. Yet he proved he had guts. He started work at four every morning and joined in the physical labour of the ranch. When disease killed his cattle, he tried wheat; when fungus killed the wheat, he tried ostrich farming; he borrowed to develop a strain of the cereal that would survive and diversified into maize, barley, potatoes, timber, wattle, oranges, and pigs.

Once Delamere had broken the back of the land and shown the way to make it productive, his successors had life too easy. The monstrous fertility of some soils bore forty-pound sweet potatoes and, reputedly, brussels sprouts 6 feet tall. The generation who came out in response to Delamere's propaganda were "hardly colonists," as one of them admitted, but "wanderers, perhaps, indefatigable amusement seekers . . . misfits, neurasthenics, of great breeding and charm, who lacked the courage to grow old, the stamina to pull up and build anew in this land."

In the opinion of the Delameres and the stiff-lipped governor's set, the rot really set in with the arrival in Happy Valley in 1923 of Josslyn and Idina Hay, soon to be Earl and Countess of Erroll. Children of earls, they were fugitives from society's disapproval of the adulterous elopement with which

Idina Erroll was a singularly unphotogenic beauty, whose surviving photographs, like this one of 1933, project, instead of the sensual vamp who caused so much erotic havoc in Happy Valley, an unseductive image: hard-faced, heavy-breasted, carefully coiffured.

their romance began, evaders of the restraints of rectitude. Idina, who was on her third marriage, was morbidly devoted to sexual indulgence, cultivating her desirability in the heady air and quivering heat of the highlands. A house guest described her sultry performance, lounging in red and gold kekoi: "The flames flicker; her half-closed eyes waken to our mute appeal. As ever, desire and the long-drawn tobacco smoke weave around her ankles . . . around her neck it curls; a shudder, eyes close. Contentment! Power!" The Errolls' house spread the cult of sexual licence through long weekends of partner-swapping games. The Muthaiga Country Club in Nairobi, conceived as a colonial Hurlingham, was abandoned in the mid-twenties by day to the infantile horseplay of roisterous Lost Boys and to games of clanging bedroom doors by night. The Kenya highlands became synonymous with the depravities of demoralized expatriates. It got worse as like attracted like. The corrupting effects of so much self-indulgence seemed to rot the settlers' depths: fascism was cheered, settler self-rule plotted.

War in 1939 with an Italian army just across the Ethiopian border had a sobering effect. But it took a scandalous society murder to make responsibility fashionable again in Happy Valley. The victim was Josslyn Erroll. He had divorced Idina in 1930; his second wife had died, riddled with heroin abscesses, in a stench of vomit and champagne. He lived on her dwindling money and amused himself by seducing the wives of friends and acquaintances. Life turned serious for him towards the end of 1940 when the fast young wife of a newly arrived baronet embroiled him in a definite commitment. Sir Jock Delves Broughton professed acceptance of the couple's decision, but on the night of a tasteless, hard-drinking celebration of his wife's new source of happiness, a bullet from his revolver was found in Erroll's dead body.

The fabric of imperialism rotted away even without the corrosive effects of settler demoralization. The petit-bourgeois values that animated some would-be French colonists were no more conducive to success in the long run than those of Kenya's raffish aristocrats: applicants for concessions in Guinea included a commercial traveller from Bordeaux whose wife was a housekeeper in Paris and a young man "who wanted to set up a cotton industry but knew nothing about the business." Except in Algeria, the French Empire had to settle for "Black Frenchmen"—a type of solution to which the British would not stoop. But by 1946, when French citizenship was extended to the empire's Black subjects, it looked like a desperate expedient, reluctantly espoused. Resistance movements were catching up with the ageing "technological advantage." The moral bankruptcy of imperialism was the negative side of a long-accumulated account, not just the result of the excesses or inadequacies of settler communities and colonial regimes. It can only be understood against the next background to be examined: a grinding realignment of prevailing values, which started in science early in the second half of our millennium, spread slowly to affect morality, and like most intellectual and moral movements, took longest to permeate politics.

PART FOUR

THE TWIST
OF INITIATIVE

*Nous autres civilisations, nous savons désormais
que nous sommes mortelles.*

PAUL VALÉRY, *La Crise de l'esprit*

*Écoutez le monde blanc
horriblement las de son effort immense . . .
écoute ses victoires proditoires trompeter ses défaites
écoute aux alibis grandioses son piètre trébuchement.
Pitié pour nos vainqueurs omniscients et naïfs!*

AIMÉ CÉSAIRE, *Cahier d'un retour au
pays natal*

*As to our civilizations, we know from now on
that we, too, are mortal.*

*Listen to the white world,
Horribly enfeebled after an enormous effort . . .
Hear their treacherous victories trumpet their defeats.
Listen to them stumbling blindly over elaborate alibis:
Have pity on our conquerors who are so knowing and so naïve!*

Chapter 15

GRAVEYARDS OF CERTAINTY: THE DECLINE OF CONFIDENCE AND THE EROSION OF EMPIRES

Empires of Certainty—The Ordered Universe—The Obedience of the Corpse—The Included Ape—States of Nature—Eating People

EMPIRES OF CERTAINTY

Like Cleopatra's, his nose was wrong. Cleopatra's was fascinatingly wrong and changed the fate of Rome. Darwin's, which "foretold a lack of energy and determination," deterred students of physiognomy and almost wrecked his future as a scientist by putting off an early patron. In 1831, when Darwin was twenty-two years old, Captain Robert Fitzroy was in a position to give him his first great chance in life by taking him as resident naturalist aboard the *Beagle* on a projected circumnavigation of the world. Luckily, despite misgivings induced by the sight of his face, Fitzroy was unable to find a replacement and had to put up with the unpromising proboscis looming across the captain's table at every mess.

The two fellow-travellers never established mutual confidence. Their politics were irreconcilable. The captain was moody and self-important, obsessed by an ultimately self-fulfilling fear that he was congenitally suicidal. Nearly thirty years later, Fitzroy, then an admiral, would intervene in a public debate on evolution, brandishing a Bible and adjuring the audience to believe God rather than Darwin. The voyage of the *Beagle,* however, gave Darwin his start in science. He was able to collect the specimens which were distributed with his calling-cards among learned societies. He accumulated some of the insights and data which helped, after a long interval imposed by caution and reflection, to revolutionize man's sense of his place in nature.

Almost nothing commonly believed about Darwin is strictly true. The theory of evolution—that all species descend from, at most, a few common, rudimentary ancestors—was already well established before he contributed to its refinement. His great addendum, the doctrine of natural selection or "the survival of the fittest," was never meant to be an all-encompassing explanation of how evolution works. It was disregarded by some of his closest supporters. Thomas Huxley, for instance, who was justly acknowledged as a mouthpiece of Darwinism and who preferred an ape to a bishop as a remote progenitor, never believed in natural selection. Darwin himself was barely faithful to it, at times preferring "sexual selection"—the elimination of unfavoured types in the joust for mates—as the "main agent" of evolutionary change. Theories of evolution were in the air of his day—such as Mr. Casaubon's "key to all mythologies" and Mr. Lydgate's search for "the common basis of all living tissues." Other researchers were on the track of natural selection or had adumbrated the idea when Darwin published. He was less important as an original thinker than as a cogent publicist.

The image projected by his friends and family of Darwin as the embodiment of Victorian philanthropy and natural charity was a propaganda device, a campaign promise of a candidate for hero-worship honoured in the breach. Despite his great wealth, he was prudent with it to the point of miserliness. His treatment of Alfred Russel Wallace, the poor scholar who shared with Darwin initial credit for unveiling the principle of natural selection, was shabby and evasive. While making a calculated display of generously conceded co-equality with a fellow-discover, Darwin withheld scientific information and withdrew an offer of employment. His attitude to St. George Mivart, the Catholic evolutionist who deserted the Darwinians' anticlerical crusade, was small-minded and vindictive: he incited hostile reviewers and blackballed Mivart for his club.

Nor was Darwin's science more politically dispassionate, more socially disinterested, than any other. It was a product of its time and circumstances and served the interests of a particular race and class. There was no clear dividing line between "scientific" and "social" Darwinism. The founder of both doctrines was a child of an inbred family and compounded the tradition by marrying a cousin. He was tortured by ill health, often in pain, given to bouts of vomiting which lasted for weeks at a time, and troubled by anxiety over the weakness and vulnerability of his own children. His interest in scientific breeding and the survival of the fittest had an obvious resonance in his own predicament. His conviction of the unity of creation

A Fuegian on the frontispiece of Fitzroy's *Narrative of the Surveying Voyages of* Adventure *and* Beagle (1839). "Nothing," wrote Darwin in his *Beagle* journal, "is more likely to create astonishment than the first sight in his native state of a barbarian—of man in his lowest and most savage state. One's mind hurries back over past centuries, and asks, could our progenitors have been men like these, men who do not appear to boast of human reason. I do not believe it is possible to describe or paint the difference between savage and civilized man . . . It is greater than between a wild and domesticated animal." The remarkable environmental adaptation that made the Fuegians impervious to cold was one of the observations that prompted Darwin's thinking in the direction of a theory of evolution.

was, in part, the result of social observation: contempt for the savages of Tierra del Fuego, encountered on the *Beagle,* persuaded him that unaccommodated man was just a bare, forked animal. The official artist of the *Beagle* drew the natives with depressing realism: shaggy and simian-featured, knock-kneed and woebegone, the epitome of ignoble savagery.

As his work proceeded, Darwin grew increasingly committed to the search for a theory which would explain the evolution of social structures, manners, morals, and the properties of the soul—including conscience and shame, the human fruits of the apple trees of Eden. "Oh, you materialist!" he reproached himself—partly because, having lost his faith in an accession of bitterness when a loved daughter died, he wanted to eliminate Providence from history as from creation; partly, too, because of the influence of a model before his eyes, of a competitive world and an emulous society, selecting ranks and races just as the brutal, beautiful justice of Nature selected species.

Reflecting on his notes from aboard the *Beagle* in 1839, Darwin made the parallel explicit. "When two races of men meet, they act precisely like two species of animals. They fight, eat each other . . . But then comes the more deadly struggle, namely which have the best fitted organization or instincts (i.e., intellect in man) to gain the day." Blacks, he speculated, would have evolved into a distinct species had imperialism not ended their isolation. As it was, they were doomed to extinction.

He repeated almost exactly the same views at intervals until 1881, the year before his death. Though Darwin took no lead in applying the theory of natural selection to the justification of racism and imperialism, he concurred in the efforts of the many contemporaries who did. The British, who succeeded in an amazing variety of environments, seemed chosen by Nature and tried in the struggle, as the Jews had once seemed chosen by God and tested in faith. It was therefore fitting that despite his apostasy Darwin should be buried in Westminster Abbey, the pantheon of specimens of British superiority.

In the same year as Darwin, the Comte de Gobineau died; relying more on what was then beginning to be called anthropology than on biology, he had worked out a ranking of human races in which Aryans came out on top and Blacks at the bottom. Two years later Gregor Mendel died, the Austrian monk whose experiments with peas established the foundation of the science of genetics. The implications of his work were not followed up until the end of the century, but when drawn, they helped to complete a trend to which Darwin and Gobineau had contributed. Among the results, the most socially influential was the scientific basis on which, in combination with the effects of Darwinism, racism could seem to rest.

Genetics provided an explanation of how one man could be inherently and necessarily inferior to another by virtue of race alone. The anthropology of scholars in the tradition of Gobineau supplied what passed for evidence. Darwin helped provide a justification for the subjection of naturally inferior races to those better adapted. In partial consequence, the first half of the twentieth century was an age of empires at ease with themselves, where critics of imperialism could be made to seem sentimental or unscientific, in a world sliced by the sword and stacked in order of race.

No previous age had been able to formulate racist doctrines so completely or so convincingly. Early modern empires had been erected with much less comprehensive theories—of the rights of tutelage of developed cultures, or the limits of the protection of natural law; the appropriation of untenanted territory, or the fiction of purchase from unsophisticated occupants; the imperfection of the sovereignty of pagans, or Aristotle's doctrine of the "natural slavery" of conquered men. Now, just when White power was at its most penetrative and most pervasive, scientific theory helped to ram it home. Imperialists from the White west could confront the rest of the world in confidence.

It might be objected that racism, in one form or another, is ancient and ubiquitous. It is said that most human languages have no term for "human being" except that which particularly denotes the members of the tribe or group; identity has always been nourished by hatred for outsiders; contempt is a common mechanism of defence against the stranger; what the nineteenth century called "race" had been covered in earlier periods by the discourse of "lineage" or "purity of blood." Still, the assumptions of modern imperialism were uniquely arrogant. They can be glimpsed in stark relief in the pages of children's literature, in the treatment of the image of the White child in Black worlds. Paternalism was an old device of empire, and sixteenth-century Spanish theorists, adapting a metaphor of Aristotle's, had likened the development of human societies to the ages of man: "primitive" societies were immature and could be guided to adulthood under the guardianship of responsible elders, who might be missionaries, settlers, or colonial administrators appointed by the Spanish crown. In nineteenth- and twentieth-century works, the paternalism could be exercised by White child-heroes, so hopeless seemed the arrested development of the societies to which authors transferred them. The schoolboy protagonist of G. A. Henty's novel of the Ashanti War learned that Blacks can never be fit for self-rule. Hergé's boy hero, Tintin, in a representative image, took on the role of teacher in a school in the Congo.

Yet history never moves in only one direction at a time, and even while theoretical justifications of imperialism were being extemporized, longer-term trends in science were undermining it at a deeper level. Darwinism itself was ambiguous. It was ambiguous about Providence, for whereas Darwin and Huxley conceived evolution as a mechanism for eliminating the need of God, the likes of Mivart and Charles Kingsley hailed it as God's way of mediating His purpose. Darwin, the exponent of a deadly ecology, red in tooth and claw, was buried to the strains of an anthem to Nature whose "ways are ways of pleasantness, and whose paths are of peace." Even the politics of Darwinism were ambiguous, for a common origin joined men of different races in real, if remote kinship, and evolution placed civilization in an uncomfortable continuum with savagery. The ultra-racist Anthropological Society of London, which shared Gobineau's sort of outlook, was dissatisfied with Darwin's message because its members wanted Blacks to be relegated to the safe reaches of separate and inferior creation.

Considered from one point of view, imperialism was a confidence trick perpetrated on the rest of the world by a small, swaggering, self-assertive

From *The Adventures of Tintin in the Congo*, after Hergé's artwork for the serial *Tintin au Congo*, which appeared in the Belgian children's paper, *Le petit vingtième*, in 1930. The lesson Tintin gives in a mission school in the Congo is remarkable not only for the inversion of roles—among young Blacks, a young White becomes sage and teacher— but also for the key assumption of Belgian colonialism: the colony is an overseas extension of the metropolis.

part of it. The resources which went into the empires of the Atlantic powers were barely adequate to make and sustain them for long. Psychologically, the whole enterprise rested on the self-faith of the confident few. It was nurtured on certainty: certainty about progress, embodied in the history of western civilization; certainty about the verifiability of assumed truths, informing traditional western values, laws, social structures, and moral precepts; certainty about the superiority of some ways of life, some uses and perceptions of the world over others. Occasionally a Darwin or a Mendel or a Gobineau might boost this vital confidence; ultimately, however, it was doomed. Gradually, fitfully, but with increasing pace and force during the second half of our millennium, evidence accumulated to shatter it.

We are now uncertain about everything: about science, religion, morality, philosophy, politics, and economics. We doubt whether we can tell truth from falsehood in any field, or even whether such a distinction might mean anything, if we found it, or could be meaningfully expressed. Faith in science, logic, and mathematics as means of telling the truth has in some ways been more thoroughly undermined than faith in religious texts or churches. Imperialism, I want to suggest in this chapter, bereft of its sustaining certainty, has been one of the conspicuous casualties in recent times of epistemological upheaval. It would be naïve to look for the start of the process; today, however, in the second half of the twentieth century, when certainty is dead and buried, we can exhume it and pick out some of the oldest worms in the corpse.

Bartolomaeus Spranger, *The Triumph of Wisdom*, perhaps intended as part of the decoration of the projected memory-theatre of Rudolf II in the Hradschin Palace, Prague. Bellona, similarly armed, is in the left foreground. Some of the Muses gaze up at Wisdom, though Clio is absorbed in her book and Urania, holding aloft a celestial globe, stares out of the canvas, perhaps in order to catch Rudolf's eye, as astronomy and astrology were favourite interests of his.

THE ORDERED UNIVERSE

At times, he painted the erotic scenes in which the emperor delighted; at others, his propaganda pieces depicted victories. Among his biggest canvases of the 1590s, however, Bartolomaeus Spranger, court painter of the emperor Rudolf II, has left *The Triumph of Wisdom*. It is an accomplished but unoriginal work, full of mannerist clichés: Minerva, in a contorted pose, with elongated toes and neck, tramples ass-eared Ignorance in the presence of the Muses. In the Faustian world of Rudolf's palace in Prague, wisdom was occult knowledge. Here magi gathered to elicit "secrets" from nature and to practise esoteric arts, including astrology, alchemy, cabbalism, magic, and pansophy—the attempt to classify and master knowledge and so unlock the key to control of the universe. Spranger's painting was probably intended as part of a decorative scheme which would turn the palace into a large-scale version of the "memory theatres"—the magicians'

By the time Andrea Cellari published this dramatic engraving of the heliocentric universe in 1660, Copernicus's model, with adjustments made since his time, was generally accepted. But for a century after its first appearance, the Copernican theory figured on the syllabus of no university except Salamanca, where no students are known to have studied it. See D. Goodman, *Power and Penury: Government, Technology and Science in Philip II's Spain* (1988), pp. 52–53.

data-banks in which knowledge was comprehensively arrayed and through which the ambitions of Faust could be realized. Science and magic were indistinguishable pursuits, aspects of a single project to bridle nature's power.

The magical universe could be controlled because it was orderly, articulated by the couplings of divine artifice. The drive to find the secrets of control was rendered more urgent in Rudolf II's day by the challenges to old certainties mounted by reformers in religion and politics and by Copernicans in cosmology. The shift of focus from the earth to the sun was a strain on eyes adjusted to a self-centred galactic outlook. Terrestrial exploration was already making the planet seem to grow. Though geographers persisted in underestimating its size and Saint Francis Borgia's nephew,

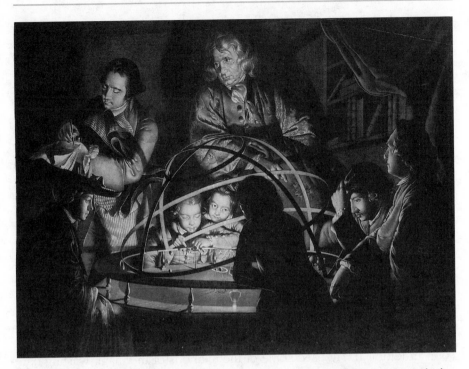

Joseph Wright of Derby, "A Philosopher Giving that Lecture on the Orrery in which a Lamp is put in Place of the Sun" (1766). The brass ball which normally represented the sun was replaced by a wick floating in a glass (just visible behind the female figure) in order to demonstrate an eclipse. The earth and moon can be seen to the left, Saturn and its rings behind them. Wright had an opportunity to see this sort of clockwork contrivance in 1762, when James Ferguson lectured in Derby "to explain the Laws by which the Deity Regulates and Governs all the Motions of the Planets and the Comets by Machinery." The figure taking notes is modelled on the surveyor and mapmaker, Peter Perez Burdett, whose friend, Earl Ferrers, made an orrery of his own and bought this picture for £200. Rather than a realistic depiction of a public lecture, this work represents a symbolic enlightenment: a practical demonstration can make the wonders of the universe accessible to all—including women and children. See D. Fraser, "Joseph Wright of Derby and the Lunar Society" in J. Egerton, *Wright of Derby* (1990), pp. 15–19.

thanking his uncle for a gift of a globe, was surprised to find it so manipulable, travellers chased receding horizons. Copernicus's theories were formulated tentatively, propagated discreetly, and spread slowly. He received the first printing of his great book on the revolutions of the heavens on his deathbed in 1543; it took nearly a hundred years thoroughly to remould men's vision of the universe. In combination with the work on the mapping of orbits around the sun published early in the seventeenth century by Johannes Kepler, the Copernican revolution expanded the limits of the observable heavens, substituted a dynamic for a static system, and wrenched the perceived universe into a new shape around the elliptical paths of the planets. Within a hundred years more, the shape of the earth had been re-defined, squashed out of the spherical by the rival forces of gravity and centrifugal distension. These reformulations did not make the cosmos any less orderly than it had seemed in the past; they did, however, make the order more complex, more elusive, harder to comprehend.

The search for order, the disclosure of ever greater complexity, continued to characterize the history of western science almost until the end of the millennium. The conviction that order lurked in or presided over creation retained for scientists the force of a faith, and, at first, reason and experiment both seemed to confirm it. The underlying, permeating "secret" which had eluded the Renaissance magi seemed to have been discovered in a bout of furious thinking and experimenting, beginning in the mid-1660s, by Isaac Newton, who imagined the cosmos as a mechanical contrivance—like the wind-up models of the solar system, in brass and gleaming wood, that became popular toys for gentlemen's libraries in the next two centuries. It was tuned by a celestial engineer and turned and stabilized by an ubiquitous force, observable in the swing of a pendulum or the fall of an apple, as well as in the motions of moons and planets.

Newton's project was not essentially different from that espoused at the court of Rudolf II. He used some of the methods of the magi, wasting time in alchemical lucubrations and heretical tinkering with sacred chronology. He had, however, the advantage of another hundred years of work to build on, and his discourse, because it was so influential for such a long time, has always sounded more modern to the ears of later historians than the hermetic language of some of his predecessors.

As well as belonging to a tradition, his work was both genuinely pioneering and embedded in a broader context of English and Scottish thought of the time: empiricism—the doctrine that reality is observable and verifiable by sense-perception. The universe consisted of events "cemented" by causation, of which Newton found a scientific description and exposed the laws. In the praise of a great poet sparing with praise, "God said, 'Let Newton be!' And all was light." It turned out to be an act of divine self-effacement. Deism throve in the eighteenth century in Europe, partly because the mechanical universe could dispense with the clockmaker after He had given it its initial winding. By the end of the century, Pierre-Simon Laplace, who had formulated ways of interpreting almost every known phenomenon of the physical world—broken down into the attraction and repulsion of particles—could boast that he had reduced God to an unnecessary hypothesis.

That was the high noon of certainty. When the shadows began to fall, Laplace's world-view was the first to be darkened by disrepute. His critics complained that he had oversimplified the nature of light, imagined "imponderable fluids," overlooked the atomic basis of matter. All nature was not yet manageable enough to fit into a single clock-case. Newton's mechanism, however, continued to work: it answered every query, predicted every result. Even without help from the theory of evolution it was impressive enough, inviolable enough to make the entire nineteenth century part of the age of certainty. When, almost at the very end of the century, scientists strayed into experimental terrain where its predictions began to break down, the catastrophic effects were all the more deeply felt.

The Obedience of the Corpse

The University Museum in Oxford is a sort of cultural fossil, a well-preserved relic of the age of faith in science. Shaped like a cathedral, it is held up by angels' wings which were forged in the cast-iron technology of the industrial revolution, rather than the flying buttresses of the first gothic age. Inside there are shrines to great saints and patrons of science and piles of bones to venerate. The displays are static, didactic, as if established by changeless decree.

The Boston Museum of Science breaks all the conventions of the nineteenth-century world in which its Oxford cousin is stuck. The building is messageless; it could equally well be an airport or a shopping mall or a multi-storey car park. The displays are interactive, vital, mobile, ephemeral, theatrical. The stuffed animals smell. The Van der Graaf generator crackles and booms with thunder flashes. There are, of course, good commercial and pedagogic reasons for both museums to be the way they are, but those reasons only make perfect sense in their cultural contexts. Between the eras of the Oxford and Boston museums, the culture of science had changed, along with scientific understanding of the cosmos, as certainty exploded out of sight and reach.

With a narrower focus, the revolution can be seen, in decisive concentration, in events of the first decade and a half of the twentieth century, after which "not one of the fields of mechanics, atomistic chemistry, thermodynamics, or electromagnetic theory rested on the same bases." In 1905, Einstein emerged suddenly, like a burrower from a mine, to detonate a terrible charge. At the time he was a Class II technical officer in the Swiss Patent Office—penned in a corral for the containment of genius. He had been expelled from school as disruptive; suspected at university as arrogant; excluded from the academic world by jealous professors. His ambitions remained irrationally unrestrained and undaunted by these disappointments. He wanted "to know how God created this world. . . . His thoughts. The rest are details."

His three papers of 1905—especially the one in which he formulated the

University Museum, Oxford: "a cathedral held up by cast-iron angels' wings" with "shrines to great saints of science and piles of bones to venerate." Designed to house "all the materials explanatory of the organic beings placed upon the globe," the building was as competition-piece, the work of Benjamin Wood, in 1853. The steep arches in red and buff stone suggest the influence of Ruskin's *Stones of Venice*, which had just appeared, but the revelling in industrial technology reflects rather the values of Ruskin's friend, Dr. Henry Acland, the Reader in Anatomy, whose brainchild the idea for a museum was. It proved, he thought, that "Gothic art could deal with these railway materials—iron and glass."

outline of what would come to be known as the Special Theory of Relativity—opened a new perspective on the universe. The scientific world was troubled by rogue results as technology improved and the range of experiments widened. In particular, the speed of light could now be measured against moving objects; contrary to traditional assumptions, it never seemed to vary, however fast or slow the motion of the source from which it was emitted. Einstein himself was enough of a traditionalist to assert that what had been proved by experiment must be true; he was revolutionary enough to draw the consequences.

If the speed of light is constant, time and distance must be relative to it. At speeds approaching that of light, time must slow down and distance shorten. Our working assumption, that time and space are given—"absolute," in Newton's terms—is practical only because, compared with light, we never go very fast, never fast enough to detect the effects. Einstein, who had been a railway buff from childhood, liked to explain the theory with fantastic analogies with trains, but his most graphic illustration, extemporized at a meeting in answer to a hostile question from the floor, was the paradox of the twins: the sister, say, who departed for space on an ultra-fast journey would return home younger than the immobile brother. If Copernicus's universe had seemed dynamic compared with its predecessors, how much more so was Einstein's, where every appearance deceived, where energy and mass were mutually convertible, and where common-sense perceptions skidded away, as if down a rabbit hole to Wonderland.

Though Einstein upset Newton's world, he was engaged on the same project: the quest for what is now called a theory of everything, the baring of cosmic order, the retuning of celestial harmony. Like Jackson Pollock, who tried to paint the concept, he thought chance was only "so-called" and that "God does not play dice." The comprehensive theory proved elusive, perhaps chimerical. Scientists still had some hopes of it, even in the second half of the century when the genius of the Cambridge professor of theoretical physics, Stephen Hawking, briefly excited expectation. Gradually, however, suspicion dawned that order could not be wrested from the universe because none was there. Erratic wisps of data kept sticking out of the package. One of the most intractable emerged from work on the structure of atoms between 1911 and 1913, when it became apparent that electrons slipped capriciously between orbits around the nucleus. The phenomenon resisted all attempts to find a formula which would predict or explain it.

The grounds of certainty were quaking with seismic upheaval even before the First World War. It is tempting to see the terrible catastrophe of 1914–18—cataclysmic, unpredicted, destructive of four empires and of a whole generation of Europe's élite—as a volcano which buried any lingering feelings of security under layers of lava. By the mid-1920s, Einstein was feeling alienated from a tradition he had started, as Niels Bohr and Werner

Heisenberg (see Chapter 23) worked towards a principle actually called Uncertainty. Shorn of technical language; rescued from in between the differences of formulation passionately debated between Bohr and Heisenberg; abstracted from the particular context in which it unravelled—the experimental problems of measuring position and momentum in quantum mechanics—this debate produced a far-reaching epistemological revolution. Scientists who thought about it came to realize that the observer is part of every experiment and that there is no empyrean level of seclusion at which his findings become objective.

If this were not shattering enough, in 1931, Kurt Gödel proposed a theorem which stultified the ideals of maths and logic. Neither system—indeed, no formal axiomatic system, according to Gödel—can operate without tripping over internal contradictions. The computer scientist Douglas Hofstadter has likened Gödel's perception of math to Escher's drawing of a staircase: tied in a "strange loop," trapped in the circularity of a self-referential paradox. When the mathematician makes a statement of number theory or of mathematical logic, he is like Epimenides the Cretan, branding all Cretans as liars.

Meanwhile, the limitations of language in handling truth were being exposed by linguistic philosophers, developing an insight that Ludwig Wittgenstein received in the trenches during the First World War. Its essence was akin to the teaching of medieval nominalists: on this very day in March 1993, as I write these lines, the greatest of nominalists, the "subtle doctor" John Duns Scotus, is to be beatified in Rome. The doctrine in which he anticipated Wittgenstein was that words signified only themselves, not any independent reality, and statements referred only to their own terms. Amid the decaying confidence of the 1920s, this old doctrine had a new impact. Some students in Wittgenstein's tradition in England tried to salvage the certainties of English empiricism from the shipwreck, under the aggressively cocksure name of "logical positivism"; but the pretence that truth could be elicited by linguistic rigour and empirical tests collapsed under the subtle critique of French and American scholars. What became known as the structuralist school recovered the lessons of Wittgenstein and left intellectuals of the late twentieth century peering into the dark glass of self-referential language.

The *Gymnasium* which had been unable to contain Einstein taught the traditional discipline of the military academy: the *Kadwergehorsamkeit,* the "obedience of the corpse," unquestioning acceptance of received wisdom, the schooling of a conquering master-class of unscratched confidence. Here knowledge was arrayed, straight and stiff, in an undrooping line, like the waxed moustaches of a row of Potsdam grenadiers. After the work of Einstein's successors and the parallel movements in mathematics and philosophy, education could never again be convincingly presented in the same

M. C. Escher's *Concave and Convex* (1955): as Douglas Hofstadter's Tortoise said, "Two internally consistent worlds when juxtaposed make a completely inconsistent composite world." *Gödel, Escher, Bach* (1977), p. 107.

way. If by the end of the first half of the century substantial ruins of old certainties in science were still visible, they were pounded into rubble from the 1960s onwards by bombardment from the "new science" of chaos which discovered random events in supposedly determined dynamic systems, including Newton's working models: the oscillations of a plumb-line and the motions of the solar system.

As the epistemological empires of certainty buckled and crumbled, the human and territorial empires of the Atlantic powers teetered and tumbled. I think these were not just similar or parallel but actually linked phenomena. Imitating and influenced by other disciplines, economic, political, and moral certainties dissolved during the same period; therefore, the self-confidence of imperial élites, on which empires depended, disappeared. The links between science and empire are best pursued in the context of the history of anthropology, the discipline which, in a sense, formed the

most conspicuous link and taught imperial masters to fancy their own superiority.

There could, indeed, be no western supremacy without such a sense of
superiority; anthropology, which at times served to reinforce it, ended by
undermining it—discovering the sufficiency of other cultures, understanding them in their own terms, acknowledging their equivalent wisdom, and
presenting the western world with their lessons. White supremacy is impossible now, when Parisian women squat to give birth in imitation of Australian aboriginals or Californian college professors consult a Yaqui shaman.
This is the end of a longer history than is commonly supposed; to make
sense of the alternations of certainty and uncertainty in the White world's
view of the rest, one must look back to the ethnographic prehistory of anthropology in the western middle ages and at distant forerunners of Darwin, who puzzled over man's relationship to apes.

The Included Ape

By comparison with the hierarchy of evolution, which ranked species in ascending order and threatened inferior races with relegation to a separate division, ancient and medieval ways of classifying creation look seamless.
There were fewer discontinuities along the ladder of nature; the great chain
of being was held together by stronger links—at least in the stretch shared
by apes, angels, and the beings in between.

Man has always looked over his shoulder at the other apes. The kinship
is too obvious to be ignored. Darwin liked to visit Jenny, the London Zoo's
little orangutan, and to see her behave uncannily like a human child, responding with apparent understanding to her keeper's threats and promises,
cajoling and collaborating in the hope of reward, showing off her human
dress at her presentation to the Duchess of Cambridge. His sympathy with
the creature had been anticipated by medieval artists, such as the illustrator
of Breydenbach's pilgrim guide of the late fifteenth century, who showed a
baboon taming a camel with lead and stick. Whereas Darwin looked at
man and saw an evolved ape, medieval naturalists looked at apes and saw
degenerate men. In what has been called a theory of devolution, they described a ladder of creation in which the nether rungs were filled with descending sub-men, including wodehouses, homunculi, hybrid beast-men,
sciapods, "the anthropophagi and men whose heads do grow beneath their
shoulders," monstrous races and apes.

This made it impossible to draw a definitive line between men and non-
men. Whenever new breeds of men or new types of ape were discovered,
a rational debate ensued on whether to classify them as human or not. The
American Indians were officially included in mankind by papal fiat in 1533;

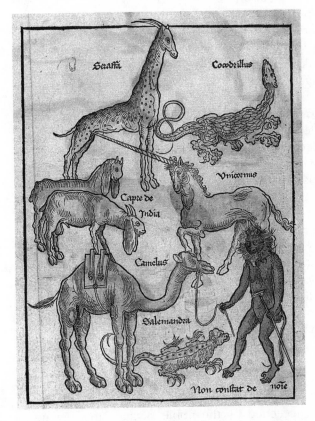

"These animals are faithfully depicted as we saw them in the Holy Land," reads the caption to this illustration in Breydenbach's pilgrim guidebook of 1486. The illustrator admits that the baboon is unknown by name, but confusion between the various species of ape was perfectly understandable at the time. The baboon, the orangutan, and the gorilla have all been considered at different times to be part of mankind: this specimen's human faculties are suggested by his use of a stick as a tool and his ability to domesticate a camel.

about the Hottentots opinions were divided, but Sebastian Cabot's world map of 1544 idealized them as participants in a Renaissance *conversazione,* wearing decent breeches and wielding tools. In the late middle ages, indeed, jurists and theologians seem to have been working towards a world in which no "barbarians" were excluded from the *communitas mortalium,* the category which included all mankind—in which, according to a famous sixteenth-century tautology, "all the peoples of mankind are human."

Darwin preferred little Jenny, with her pretty clothes and tentative self-control, to the intractable Fuegians, but earlier observers had been less fastidious, representing classical postures and physiques around the Straits of Magellan, where Darwin saw only a difference between savage and civilized man "greater than that between a wild and domesticated animal." Early observers had beheld the practice of social nakedness with awe, as a survival from a golden age of sylvan innocence, of which classical poets sang, or as evidence of almost pre-lapsarian sinlessness. To Darwin, the same phenomenon was another instance of animal adaptation, which enabled the Fuegians to endure, unclad, the bitter cold of their habitat.

As natural man wavered in scholars' esteem, the apes rose to meet him. About a generation before Darwin's meeting with Jenny, Thomas Love Peacock had written a novel in which an orang-utan was hero. Peacock was a comic genius and a maker of history, a satirist of "steam intellect" and a promoter of steam navigation. His simian character Sir Oran Haut-Ton exposed the dilemma of making a firm distinction between the savage and the beast. Because Sir Oran seemed to have every rational faculty except the use of speech, he developed a reputation as "a profound but cautious thinker"; then he was elected to parliament and elevated to the baronetage. The punning name played on the idea that orang-utans can be taught to play the flute, a view sustained by the great advocate of the ape's humanity, Lord Monboddo (d. 1799), whose theory of social development, gradually elevating man from a beastly condition, was similar and perhaps contributory to aspects of Darwinism. It was appropriate that this species of ape should have been so tenacious in thrusting himself into man's company, for the Malay root of the name *orang-utan* means "man of the woods." Potentially, if orangs could be welcomed into the fold of humankind, pygmies or Hottentots or any unfavoured group could be excluded; in practice, however, albeit with many exceptions, pre-evolutionary methods of classification tended to err on the inclusive side.

STATES OF NATURE

Later, natural man was succeeded by the noble savage—the exemplary primitive whose social and moral world could teach his civilized cousins how to behave. But his rise was not smooth or swift or unopposed. The outsider, whether good Samaritan or good barbarian, had always been used by moralists to point up the deficiencies of audiences and readerships; however, the idea that primitives could supply useful social models does seem genuinely to have arisen in western Christendom in the late medieval and early-modern periods as a result of the unprecedented range of contacts between travellers or settlers and cultures they perceived as savage. In a famous phrase, Jules Michelet characterized the Renaissance as the period of "the discovery of the world and of man." He meant the individuality of man and the newly perceived nature of man's superiority to the rest of creation, the concept of "the measure of all things" and the vague, collective narcissism of "What a thing is man!" He was coupling geographical discoveries with what were really no more than the speculations (or maunderings) of moral philosophy. But there was a "discovery of man" in another sense, too. The geographical discoveries brought anthropological revelations in their wake. By widening the terms of reference of discussion of the

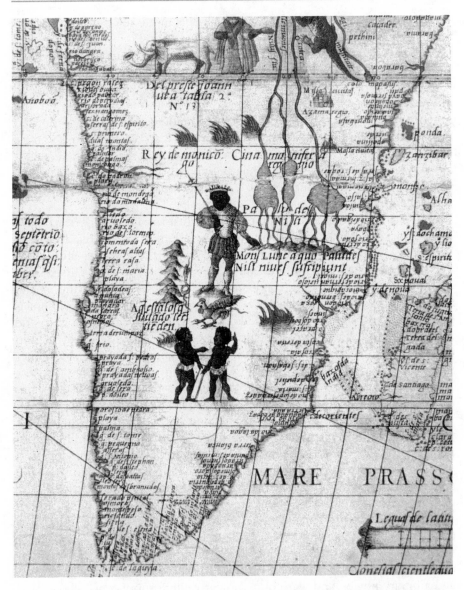

If there was doubt about the relationship between men and apes, it is not surprising that some newly encountered races of the late middle ages took some time to establish their place in the panorama of mankind according to European schemes of classification. Sebastian Cabot, in making his world map of 1544, seems, however, to have been in no doubt of the status of the Hottentots, whom he equips with sticks and shows engaged in civilized conversation.

nature of man, these contributed to adjustments in the self-awareness of the philosophically inclined.

The origins both of scientific ethnography and of the myth of the noble savage—to take two contrasting examples, rich in implications for the development of traditions on the relationship of man to the created and metaphysical worlds—are commonly traced back to the discovery of the American Indians and the debates they engendered. Like most supposed features of the Renaissance, the "discovery of man" in this sense can be found deeper in the middle ages. A decisive start was made in the encounters with Blacks and, more particularly, with aboriginal Canary Islanders, which occurred in the course of early Atlantic exploration in the fourteenth and fifteenth centuries.

When their heartlands and home societies first became exposed to European explorers, Blacks, as individuals, were a familiar sight, readily classified, in a category not far removed from that of the apes, as men made degenerate by sin. The tradition that the sons of Ham were cursed with blackness—as well as being condemned to slavery—reinforced the mental associations evoked by a "diabolical" colour, generally preferred for depicting demons and signifying sin. The Portuguese chronicler Gomes Eanes de Zurara found the first slaves directly shipped from Africa "so deformed in their faces and bodies as almost to resemble shadows from the nether world."

Despite, or perhaps because of, direct contact with Black societies, images like these were hard to dispel (see Chapter 6). The Venetian traveller Alvise Da Mosto, writing early in the second half of the fifteenth century, was almost uniquely sensitive to the merits of Black civilization, as observed among the Wolof of the Senegambia region. Though their cities and villages were only of grass huts, they were recognizably urban. And the chiefs were genuine "lords," for "such men are lords not by virtue of any treasure or money but on account of ceremonies and the following of people they may truly be called lords." Da Mosto emphasized the impressive court ritual of the chief he called Budomel, of whose friendship he spoke with pride. Budomel rode on horseback, went everywhere with two hundred men in attendance, struck fear into his subjects by his haughty mien and arbitrary power, and was courted by grovelling supplicants who dusted their heads continually while addressing him. On the other hand, Da Mosto seems to have harboured no doubts about the Blacks' general inferiority. He derided their scanty attire, despised their bestial table manners—"they eat on the ground, like animals"—dismissed them as cheats and liars, and apostrophized them as incorrigibly lascivious. Budomel, impressed at the White man's arcane knowledge, begged Da Mosto to tell him how to satisfy more women.

Even to minds accustomed to the pliant and useful categories of men and sub-men devised or inherited by medieval encyclopaedists, the discovery of the Canary Islanders was a sudden and startling phenomenon. The native races have died out and the evidence of their origins conflicts, but they were probably a pre-Berber north African people, similar perhaps to the Znaga of the western Saharan coast today. When European visitors began to make ethnographical observations in the fourteenth and fifteenth centuries, they generated far more interest than the Black societies; the Canary Islanders provided much better copy for humanists and missionaries susceptible to the glamour of natural man. The author of the earliest known account, like Columbus confronting the Tainos of the Antilles 150 years later, noticed their nakedness first. Giovanni Boccaccio, who copied the text in 1341, took this to signify innocence rather than savagery: gold and silver coins were shown to them, but they took no notice. They were equally innocent of the knowledge of weapons. They respected natural law. They seemed to know nothing of individual property but divided everything equally. They spoke a "polite" tongue like the Italians, sang sweetly and danced "almost like the French." Their houses—really caves or huts—were said to be "of wonderful contrivance." Their "temple or oratory" was adorned with a suspiciously classical-sounding statue, the image of a man sculpted in stone with a javelin in his hand.

Finally, as if these assurances were insufficient, no room was left to doubt the human status and rationality of the natives. They were physically "normal"; this was important as the encyclopaedist Albertus Magnus had denied that reason could subsist in a monstrous frame. And they were "of great understanding." The humanist Utopia envisaged by Boccaccio, who turned this first account of previously unknown primitives into a setting of the golden age and an admonition for his times, was an influential image. In the early fifteenth century, when the first permanent European settlements were erected in the archipelago, the illuminator of the Vienna codex of the *Roman de la Rose* apparently chose the Canaries as the setting for his version of that blissful time, with hide-clad aboriginals dwelling in peace amid trees and mountains.

Not all perceptions were equally generous, however. During the fifteenth century, missionary and humanist writers had to defend the native Canarians against the rival observations of slavers, conquerors, and colonists, who likened them to dogs and monkeys and accused them of barking or howling speech, disgusting table manners, and eating uncooked food, similar to Sir John Mandeville's hairy race of islanders who "eat both flesh and fish all raw." The traditional heraldic wild men (see Chapter 5) became near-naked islanders, supporting the scutcheon of one conquistador family. In practice, negative assessments of the Canarians prevailed. By the time the interest of missionaries and humanists had been deflected by the discovery of more numerous and promising primitives in America, the Canary Islanders were

The setting of the Golden Age of this fifteenth-century manuscript of the *Roman de la Rose* represents a rosier version of the wild-man image than was usual at the time. See p. 180. Here, the natural activities in which these happy savages are engaged include hunting, gathering, and love. The landscape and the combination of cave-dwellings and rudimentary huts, combined with the peaceful innocence of the people portrayed, suggest the influence of Franciscan and humanist accounts of the world of the recently rediscovered Canary Islands.

nearing extermination. While debate about the American Indians raged, the Canarians' relevance was almost forgotten.

Towards the end of the sixteenth century, when the islanders were already nearly extinct, antiquarian *amateurs* compiled some ethnographic information, perhaps in imitation of the great compilations of missionaries in the New World. In a work of the 1590s, a Dominican apologist, Alonso de Espinosa, tried to demonstrate the natural piety of the natives before the conquest. In other literature spawned by reports or memories of the Canarians, their image became altogether abstracted from reality and assimilated to commonplaces of another popular genre of the time: pastoral literature. In a play of Lope de Vega, and in the poems of pastoral elegists of the early seventeenth century, the Canarians led not real lives but those of a bucolic idyll, in idealized simplicity, enlivened by coy love affairs. "Natural man" had yielded to another, even less apposite literary stereotype.

In the meantime, however, America had renewed demand for appreciative images of the primitive and refreshed the sources of supply. Almost immediately on first meeting people of the New World, Columbus, wrestling mentally to fit them into his received panorama of mankind, developed three mutually incompatible ways of looking at them. At one level, their nakedness suggested beastliness, fit only to be exploited or enslaved; at others, it reminded him of the nakedness of Saint Francis of Assisi, who stripped off in the public square to signify his total dependence on God, or of the unclad simplicity of the golden age, guileless and almost guiltless. From that initial conflict of perceptions arose all the subsequent inconsistencies of Columbus's native policy, which was genuinely torn between reverence and contempt.

The same uncertain range was echoed by the voices in the ensuing debate about how to treat native American peoples. Their sheer diversity was bewildering. Even in the course of his first short Caribbean cruise Columbus had been aware of big differences between the simple and impoverished material culture of the Bahamas and the relative opulence of Hispaniola, with its stone courts, carved thrones, and formal political ranks. The mainland enclosed examples of every kind of polity known to man, including some—city-dwelling, stone-building with specialized economies, and large professional and learned classes—which seemed to demonstrate arts and virtue recognizable to European onlookers as of the highest sorts. Albrecht Dürer thought the plunder of the Aztecs equalled any workmanship he had ever seen; his ideal city seems to have been modelled on reports of Tenochtitlan. For the capitals of his palace, begun in 1527, a bishop of Liège was inspired by Aztec masks.

Amid this diversity, the search was still on for genuinely "natural" man, hunted, like the Amazons, in the abiding blanks on the map. Even as Miranda imagined man's potential, Caliban's snuffles could be heard in the background. The idealized portrait of natural man with which observers from Christendom approached the New World in the sixteenth century was of an instinctual being, regulated by passions rather than laws, who could, according to the prejudices of the beholder, demonstrate the universally fallen condition of man or, more often, his God-given goodness in a state uncorrupted by society. Such expectations were dispelled by the disappointments of experience and the priorities of imperialism. In the 1530s the first detailed attempt at a total history of the New World, encompassing the description of the environment and of the inhabitants, represented them rather as unnatural than natural men, given to sexual and dietary perversions which put them outside the pale of natural law. Missionary-ethnographers who worked among native peoples or interpreted the findings of such field workers garbed even the most savage communities of hunter-gatherers in rudimentary civil institutions and equipped them with a past.

Though almost every social projector of the seventeenth century called

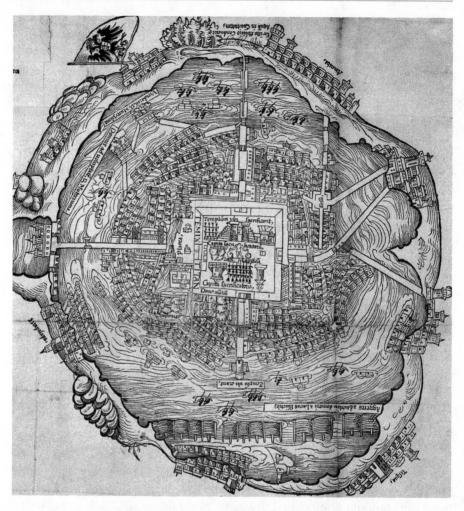

Cannibal capital or ideal city? Cortés claimed that Tenochtitlan, before he razed it to the ground, was the equal of any city in Spain. The plan of it published to illustrate the 1524 edition of his reports from Mexico has affinities with late-medieval models of town planning: Eiximenis, for instance, recommended that four main streets should radiate from a central square to gates at the cardinal points. The magnificent towers and spires of the cityscape presented here demonstrate a conviction of beauty and opulence attuned to European taste. On the other hand, the temple of human sacrifices, the skull racks, and the elegant headless corpse in the centre are all given prominence.

on Amerindian examples—to supply rhetorical vocabulary, locate common-places, and support nostrums—confidence ebbed in the utility of the New World as a laboratory of the state of nature. When Thomas Hobbes wanted to vindicate strong government in the aftermath of the English Civil War, he presented sovereign power as men's collectively chosen refuge from primeval insecurity, when every man's hand was raised against his neighbour. He got little assent, however, to his claim that peoples without government—"except the government of small families, the concord whereof dependeth on lust"—could be found to prove his case in the New World.

EATING PEOPLE

Meanwhile, another tradition in New World ethnography was elaborating a concept which was incompatible with imperialism in the long run: cultural relativism. The first glimmerings came in the work of missionary-ethnographers of the sixteenth century, who realized that in order to be converted, a culture had first to be thoroughly understood in its own terms. *"Tout comprendre, c'est tout pardonner,"* and most of the early ethnographic compilations evince a generous spirit, especially since the missionaries applied the technique Anthony Pagden calls "attachment" to understand alien societies: "recognizing" echoes of their own culture in their new environment and consequently acknowledging the natives' possession of equivalent elements of civilization. When we look at some of the barbarities depicted in the illustrations to their work, we have to try to see them with the missionaries' eyes. Codex Mendoza (see Chapter 6), for instance, includes an ethnographic compendium in which scenes of the upbringing of boys and training of male oblates evoke spine-chilling horror, as the victims are beaten with sticks, savaged with maguey spikes, singed with brands, and made to inhale smoke by having their heads thrust above choking fires. The purpose of these inclusions was not to excoriate Aztec savagery but to praise Aztec discipline: the missionaries belonged to ascetic orders with rigorous standards of penance and came from a society in sixteenth-century Spain where enthusiastic flagellation was a popular devotional practice.

Even the most sensitive missionaries, however, could not quite bring themselves to endorse the notion of the moral equivalence of pagan and Christian societies. Cultural relativism, *tout court,* was a conclusion they left to their readers back home. While missionary writers spread the laudable principle that alien societies had to be judged on their own terms, it was secular readers who inferred that, from a neutral standpoint, every human society was as good as any other. Montaigne's defence of cannibals was a conspicuous early example. His source on the anthropophagous habits of the natives of Brazil was the Protestant pastor Jean de Léry, who mildly deprecated cannibalism as the product of superstition and fear. Montaigne went further: European practices of torture and massacre were, at one level,

A leaf from Codex Mendoza (see pp. 218–22) shows the training of an Aztec oblate, probably depicted under missionary influence. The young man is shown carrying supplies and weapons for the battlefield and being disciplined by beating with sticks, having blood drawn with maguey-spikes and hair singed with brands before, his initiation having been completed, he can set off for the temple by canoe. This should not be seen as an attempt to denounce the barbarities of the Aztec priesthood but to commend its prudent severities, reminiscent of the mortification esteemed by some Christian religious orders at the time.

no better than cannibalism and, at another, more deeply vitiated by hypocrisy. "There is more barbarism in eating men alive than to feed upon them being dead."

For a long time cultural relativism was embedded in other traditions: the myths of the good Samaritan and of the noble savage. Montaigne combined them, chastizing his contemporaries for falling short of savage standards and declaring, "If my fortune had been to live among those nations, which yet are said to live under the sweet liberty of Nature's first and uncorrupted laws, I assure thee, I would most willingly have portrayed myself fully and naked." More than a hundred years later, Dryden enmeshed the same three traditions in a pair of couplets (placed, perhaps surprisingly, in the mouth of Cortés):

> Wild and untaught are terms which we alone
> Invent for fashions differing from our own.
> For all their customs are by Nature wrought,
> But we by art unteach what Nature taught.

Relativism emerged more strongly in the early eighteenth century in the work of Louis Armand de Lom d'Arce, who called himself by his family's alienated title, Sieur de Lahontan. He not only read Jesuit accounts of North American Indians but gathered ethnographic observations of his own before his expulsion from Canada in 1693. He walked in the woods with Hurons. He was an anticlerical freethinker who was not above using his native interlocutors as mouthpieces for his own irreverent messages. "How should I believe in the truth of these Bibles," asks his "savage of good sense," if they were "written so many centuries ago, translated from so many different languages by ignoramuses who had no understanding of their original meaning or the liars who have changed, increased, or diminished the words which we find today?"

Like many enthusiasts for noble savagery Lahontan had a prurient interest in sex and esteemed societies in proportion to the freedom with which they practised love. Engravings of the courtship rituals he described came deliciously embellished for an eighteenth-century readership, with delicate eroticism and decorative classicism. A Huron who looks like a revivified Greek statue enters his lady's chamber carrying a torch; the lady signifies assent by blowing out the light.

Lahontan transmitted attractive images of freethinking and free loving to scrutineers of savages among the philosophers of the Enlightenment. His native companion, Adario, was the source of Voltaire's "ingenuous Huron." Uncomplicated connubiality was part of the allure for Rousseau, the greatest exponent of the ideal of the noble savage, who wanted western contracts of concubinage to have the same directness as Lahontan had ascribed to those of native Americans. Rousseau foresaw, if he did not found, the scientific anthropology which was to evolve from the ethnographic and ethnological traditions inherited from the middle ages and the Renaissance. He called for philosophical voyagers, freed from "the yoke of national prej-

"Enthusiasts for noble savagery . . . esteemed societies in proportion to the freedom with which they practiced love." Bernard's engravings are supposed to illustrate Lahontan's descriptions of Huron courtship rituals. From *Cérémonies et coutumes religieuses de tous les peuples idolâtres* (1723–43).

udices," to study *in situ* the diversity of human societies and classify them "according to their likenesses and their differences."

The stock of images was topped up in the late eighteenth century by the extended exploration of the Pacific. The nobility of the savage was confirmed by the specimens that explorers brought home. Omai, a restless misfit in Polynesia, was lionized in England in 1774–76, praised by duchesses for his naturally gracious manners and painted by Sir Joshua Reynolds to represent the equipoise of uncorrupted dignity. Lee Boo, from Palau in Micronesia, was even more adept in the assimilation of gentlemanly accomplishments; when he succumbed to smallpox in 1783, he was buried in Rotherhithe churchyard under the inscription,

> Stop, Reader stop! Let Nature claim a Tear—
> A Prince of *Mine,* Lee Boo, lies bury'd here.

Visitors to the Pacific found a voluptuary's paradise, painted by William Hodges, who sailed with Captain Cook in 1772. His image of Tahiti is of a ravishing habitat for the nymphs in the foreground: one invitingly presents

William Hodges' vision of Tahiti, remembered from the artist's experiences as resident artist with Captain Cook's expedition of 1772: "a voluptuaries' paradise . . . a habitat for nymphs." Cf. Gauguin's Tahitian icon, p. 448.

a tatooed behind; another swims supine, under a diaphanous film of water. The sexual hospitality of the island tried the discipline of Cook's men and broke that of Bligh's. The Pacific, in short, had just the combination of liberty and licence which ennobled the savage in the eyes of the suitably disposed.

The self-styled "scientific anthropologists" of the nineteenth century reacted against the subjective unrealism of the noble savage and related traditions. Like the missionary-ethnographers who were their remote intellectual ancestors, they constructed sequences of development in human culture: from—for instance, in the 1870s—promiscuity through polyandry to monogamy, from animism through polytheism to monotheism, from savagery through barbarism to civilization. Whereas earlier models of social development had emphasized common humanity by suggesting that European societies had been through the same stages as those encountered overseas, the implications of the new anthropology were racist. The fashion for cranial calibration convinced many practitioners that the more developed races had the biggest brains. Imperialism was implicitly endorsed and much of the world condemned to servitude or subjection.

The tendency of ethnology to press the message of cultural relativism was only recovered in the last decade of the century, thanks in large part to an under-sung hero of the western liberal tradition, Franz Boas. This German Jew, who became the doyen and presiding spirit of anthropology in America, not only exploded the fallacies of racist craniology but also out-

"I lived like a visiting young village princess. I could summon informants to teach me everything I wanted to know: as a return courtesy, I danced every night." The photograph shows Margaret Mead in native dress relating to her subject on Vaitogi, with her collaborator Fa'amotu. Fieldwork seems to have been a liberating experience for the anthropologist.

lawed from the biggest, fastest-growing and most influential national school of anthropologists in the world the notion that societies could be ranked in terms of a developmental model of thought. People, he concluded, think differently in different cultures, not because some have superior mental equipment but because all thought reflects the traditions to which it is heir, the society by which it is surrounded, and the environment to which it is exposed. Boas was a fieldworker in his youth and a museum-keeper in his maturity—always in touch with the people and artefacts he sought to understand; his pupils had native American peoples to study within little more than a railway's reach. The habit of fieldwork, shared by British anthropologists who made use of access to a vast empire in Africa and Australasia, tended to reinforce the relativistic tendency by piling up enormous quantities of diverse data intractable to the crudely hierarchical schemes of the nineteenth century.

After long exclusion, the noble savage reappeared among anthropologists drawn back to the Pacific like the lovestruck mariners of the eighteenth century. Perhaps the most influential of all anthropological books was Margaret Mead's *Coming of Age in Samoa,* published in 1928 and based on fieldwork with pubescent girls in a sexually unrepressive society. Whether the paradise depicted was real or imagined has been much debated by critics. The image, however, was seductive, of an uncompetitive world, creatively fertilized by freedom, protected from the agonizing restraints and inhibitions which psychoanalysts were busy uncovering in western cities and suburbs. The extent of the influence imputed, if not attained, can be inferred from the ferocity with which the work was attacked during a reaction, soon after Mead's death in 1976, against the social and educational nostrums which in the meantime had reshaped western adolescence: uncompetitive schooling, rod-sparing discipline, and cheap contraception.

Mead had certainly been an advocate of and lobbyist for these innovations, though the implication that her scholarly work helped to lubricate their flow, rather than reflecting a permissive *zeitgeist,* may have been exaggerated. She was accused of falsifying evidence, projecting a spinster's frustrated fantasies onto her interviewees, and importing into Samoa the hang-ups and hedonism of twenties America. The status of her reputation is still a matter of doubt. Her story shows how cultural relativism drags moral relativism in its wake. If what is wrong for one society can be right for another, then what is wrong for one generation can be right for the next. If western educationists could learn from the wisdom of Samoan adolescents, what right or hope had the white masters of dying nineteenth-century empires? In a world without barbarians and "savages," where the differences between "primitive cultures" and "advanced civilizations" were reformulated, in value-free language, as "elementary and complex structures," no such empire could survive. Where all peoples had their collateral share of earthly bliss, invidious distinctions withered.

Chapter 16

THE STUMBLERS' ALIBIS: DOMESTIC DIFFICULTIES IN THE MODERN WEST

The Skeleton of Pessimism—Nervous Disorders—Militant Tendencies—Today, the Struggle—Barbarism, Freedom, and Technology—The Enemy Bereft

THE SKELETON OF PESSIMISM

On the evening of 27 June 1787, Edward Gibbon, who epitomized the self-assurance of an enlightened gentleman, reported a stroll around a covered walk of acacia trees in his garden in Lausanne. "The air was temperate," he said, "the sky was serene; the silver orb of the moon was reflected from the waters, and all Nature was silent."

He was a scrupulous historian but an untrustworthy autobiographer, and it is impossible to take this tissue of commonplaces literally. The *locus amoenus,* the sympathy of man and his surroundings, the personification of Nature: all are splendid but conventional artifices of classical rhetoric which enhance enjoyment while corroding credulity. Even the acacias seem to have been exaggerated or misremembered. Gibbon had an acacia outside his window of which he was peculiarly fond, but according to his letters it was "too closely pruned" in March 1786 and did not recover "from the cruel shears of the gardener" until December 1792. In between, in Gibbon's mind, the single plant had blossomed to the dimensions of a walk.

The stroll was imagined to celebrate, with philosophical moderation, an important event: the completion of *The History of the Decline and Fall of the Roman Empire,* the world's most enduring history book, uniquely still read as such more than two centuries after it was written. The author can be pardoned or applauded for exhaling proper satisfaction in his personal achievement, but his was a pride that went deeper and wider. It embraced the civilization of which he formed part and penetrated to the marrow of the tradition in which he belonged. He was proud of his country and language, foretelling the benefits of the worldwide English-speaking community that was beginning to take shape in his day; he was especially proud of Europe and of the records of humane learning, public service, material progress, and *noblesse oblige* which had characterized a long period of the past of the continent, "elevating" its peoples, by their own reckoning, above the rest of mankind.

Gibbon was no imperialist. He knew too much about empires to like them; but he did relish the superiority of a civilization which reached across the world, manipulated the environments of distant places, and demonstrated a kind of mastery by mapping the whole. The world-view of his class and time is captured in miniature in an engraving which adorned the title-page of one of the atlases in his library: a cartographer's shop in which the world is docketed and arrayed for the instruction and amusement of bewigged ladies and gentlemen.

The decline of the Roman Empire was a subject of passionate concern to Gibbon's contemporaries because it seemed an exception to the course of history: a trough or loop in an otherwise linear progression, a check to the onward promenade of "improvement." Gibbon never uttered the glib gurglings of a Pangloss, smug in the enjoyment of "the best of all possible worlds"; he appreciated the fragility of progress and apprehended its arrest. He was happy to conclude, however, that

> the experience of four thousand years should enlarge our hopes and diminish our apprehensions: we cannot determine to what height the human species may aspire in their advances towards perfection; but it may safely be assumed that no people, unless the face of nature is changed, will relapse into their original barbarism.

The safety of that assumption was savaged repeatedly and left in shreds during the next hundred-odd years by the attacks of an inveterate barbarism, lurking under the skin of western civilization. Irregularly phased moons provoked the transformations of unpredictable werewolves: a famine or a mysteriously generated "great fear" could start a peasant rebellion; fast-growing towns could agglomerate dangerously rootless mobs; ruthless, rapid industrialization could throw up an uncontrollable proletariat; ideological passions could stir urbane élites into mutual malevolence

Atlas—once an image of a burdensome universe—becomes the handler of an accessible world in the engraving of the title-page of a Dutch edition of Guillaume De l'Isle's world atlas of 1730. The atlas was able to draw on the sharply enhanced image of the world compiled by the Académie Royale des Sciences in Paris, where readings of longitude and latitude made all over the world were collated. The scene depicted is a mapmaker's shop, with all the world docketed and arrayed—reduced to order by the scientific application of reason.

and make fanatics of sophisticates; wars could displace masses; ethnic hatred could hallow massacres. The monsters of earlier imaginations, prowling in the blanks on the map, were replaced by those of the nineteenth century, grown at home in the laboratories of Frankenstein or Dr. Jekyll.

At either end of the nineteenth century, peculiarly nasty wars nourished pessimism. In the beginning, the French Revolutionary and Napoleonic wars drove nails into the body of optimism, and at the end, the First World War hammered them home. Napoleon, who thought warfare was an art, "like everything that is beautiful and simple," wept at the scale of the slaughter on the field of Eylau in 1807. Goya, who decorated his dining-room with a scene of cannibalism, re-envisioned war, with the victims' starting eyes, as a giant wading in mud and blood. Unforgettable realism was also impressed on readers of Baron Larrey's chillingly surgical medical reports on the wounds of casualties from Napoleonic battlefields.

The optimism universal in Gibbon's generation became controversial after the conflicts of 1789–1815—conflicts more generalized and destructive

Goya's art began to desert the conventional subjects demanded by his early patrons in the 1790s, when, under the impact of the deflection of the Enlightened ideology into the dark and bloody channels of the French Revolution, he produced scenes of witchcraft and torture for the Duke and Duchess of Osuna. It was the Spanish War of Independence, however—the Peninsular War of 1808–14—that released from his imagination colossal monsters like this: an image of war wading through the land and overshadowing the wreckage of lives. This painting must have been done before 1812, when it appears in an inventory drawn up at the death of the artist's wife.

than any experienced in Europe since the fall of the Roman Empire. In 1816, Shelley's friend and contemporary Thomas Love Peacock gathered in his fictional Headlong Hall figures drawn from his circle of acquaintances and representative of the drift of debate. "Mr. Foster, the perfectibilian," continued to expect "gradual advancement towards the state of unlimited perfection," while "Mr. Escot, the deteriorationist" foresaw, with gloomy satisfaction "that the whole species must at length be exterminated by its own imbecility and vileness."

The facts piled up remorselessly on Mr. Escot's side of the argument. The dissolving confidence which was the subject of the last chapter was opposed by congealing pessimism. Paradoxically, in the nineteenth- and twentieth-century west, where more material progress was made than in the rest of the world and the rest of history put together, the very idea of progress was undermined. Even extreme optimism took on a strangely pessimistic form in the predictions of Karl Marx (1818–1883) and Herbert Spencer (1820–1903), who foretold the perfection of human society but expected things to get worse before they got better—and, in Marx's case, believed the happy consummation could only be brought on by a bloody cataclysm. A novelist from a neutral country who served in the First World War saw—in the flesh, it seemed—mankind herded towards Armageddon by apocalyptic horsemen. Sigmund Freud, who before the war had identified the sex urge as the motor of human conduct, revised his opinion to add the death-wish, Thanatos, alongside Eros, as co-ruler of the mind.

The greatest apostle of pessimism was perhaps Oswald Spengler (1880–1936); if Gibbon wrote the world's most enduring history book, the first volume of Spengler's *Decline of the West* was the most instantly successful. It sold sixty thousand copies in its first year—an astonishing tally for a demanding work which tortured the reader with grisly predictions, difficult allusions, and contortionist's prose. Gibbon's English was consistently stately and smooth, Spengler's German alternately sinuous and sinewy. Whereas Gibbon had his acacia walk, Spengler, who wrote on the eve of the First World War and published almost at its end, walked, as it were, through a *berceau* of barbed wire. In place of the linear, progressive history charted by Gibbon, he proposed tangled downward spirals of senescence and decay for civilizations which he conceived as analogous to living organisms.

Spengler denied that he was a pessimist at all—but that is a typical self-indulgence of a critic suspicious that even his own predictions are insufficiently bleak. He claimed to know remedies to reverse decline—but, as one of his many bitter adversaries said, "an element of blank despair is unmistakable in the activism that is left to those who foresee the future and feel instrumental in its arrival." His book was buried under shovelfuls of reviewers' abuse. He saw history with a hawk's eye view, in vivid detail, from a commanding height; he anticipated one of the most brilliant trends in modern historical scholarship by wresting alarming and unsuspected connections between different aspects of a culture: its science and its politics, its social structure and its art, its music and its religion. But these merits could not impress specialists (who noticed only the mistakes) or reconcile ideological enemies. Some of them, such as Hitler, got no further than the title before offering judgement. Reviled by liberals as a fascist and by fascists as a liberal, Spengler died, while the echoes of his éclat faded, in the misery which befits a pessimist.

His message, however, had got home. There were still optimists left, of course. Some thought the First World War would end all wars and that the west would climb back out of its trench. War-weary pessimism was largely confined to Europe and did not cross to the other shore of the Atlantic civilization until economic collapse followed a decade later. Even on the east bank of the ocean, the wreckage of the pre-war world looked well, at first, to those who had enjoyed little stake in its lost era of splendour: the poor, the previously suppressed nations, the hitherto unenfranchised, the political radicals and extremists. Spengler's great rival among popular world-historians, H. G. Wells, published the *Outline of History* in praise of progress in 1920; he was sexually predatory and tyrannically opinionated, but he was the seducer or spokesman of those emancipated by the effects of the conflict. In spite of him, in what John Maynard Keynes called "the

The look of a "Bright Young Thing" meets the lyrics of black despair. *Twentieth Century Blues*—first aired in 1931 and performed here in the film version of Coward's *Cavalcade* in 1933—was a song which seemed to sum up the Depression, from its opening line accusing civilization of making the world worse: there was, the song concluded, nothing left to live or love for, except the Blues.

dead season of our fortunes," pessimism prevailed. With recession and slump, it spread. By the end of the twenties the world was singing "Twentieth-century Blues" and the decline of the west was actively anticipated or believed to have begun. "Just wait for the next European war," threatened E. M. Forster's character, the amiable Doctor Aziz, in 1924, looking forward to dismantling western dominance and dismembering its empires.

When prophecies are believed, they become self-fulfilling; haunted imaginations get attuned to the rattle of the skeleton's bones. Behaviour responds, in anticipation, to feared but unfelt effects. In a series of "local difficulties," of which the First World War was the first, European powers bludgeoned the strength out of one another and Atlantic civilization unfitted itself for world supremacy. Almost before the gun smoke of the First World War had cleared, the overthrow of western hegemony was being prefigured: Gandhi returned to India in 1915; the Sarekat Islam movement in Indonesia mobilized a mass party for independence in 1916; the Pan-African Congress first met in 1919, and in that year the Egyptian Wafd was founded. Meanwhile, and over the next generation's span, western powers' retreat from imperial responsibilities was prepared by loss of nerve, dissipation of resources, and internecine strife. Atlantic civilization rehearsed and performed the drama of decline—rehearsal blending into performance—in civil wars and self-inflicted economic calamities. While the victims of imperialism braced themselves for freedom, the Black poet Aimé Césaire could hear "the white world stumbling in great alibis."

NERVOUS DISORDERS

To make the murder more shocking, Dorothy L. Sayers located the focal crime of her postwar detective novel, *The Unpleasantness at the Bellona Club,* during the two minutes' silence observed annually in England to honour the dead on the anniversary of the armistice. This added sacrilege to murder, tearing the mask of piety from pessimism. These dead, it seemed, had died in vain. To make her detective more interesting, she turned Lord Peter Wimsey—who was in every other respect the very model of aristocratic propriety, a scholar, athlete, and connoisseur, willowy and wan, without blemish or body hair—into a nerve-jangled victim of shell-shock, who had to be coaxed out of trench-bound nightmares by the soothings of his old batman.

Shell-shock was the *mal de siècle* of the postwar years, but it was only one of a startling range of neuroses induced by the strains or unearthed by the science of the period. Each disaster of the twentieth century in the west impacted on nerves disordered by the last. The strain was tightened and the effects heightened by the self-awareness which the growth of psychology and, especially, psychoanalysis encouraged. Freud was, in a sense, both the model and mentor of the age. In an experiment conducted on himself in Vienna in 1896, he exposed his own Oedipus complex. The therapeutic effect seemed to be confirmed in a series of patients who rose from his couch—or that of his mentor, Josef Breuer—and walked more freely than before. Women who only a few years previously would have been dismissed as hysterical malingerers became case studies from whose example everyone could learn. Freud generalized, from the evidence of a few burgesses of pre-war Vienna, to illuminate the human condition in general. Every child experienced before puberty the same phases of sexual development, and repressed similar fantasies or experiences. Hypnosis—or, as Freud preferred, the mnemonic effects in a stirred subconscious of the free association of images and memories—could retrieve repressed feelings and ease their nervous symptoms.

Freud was an unreliable scientist who had promoted the therapeutic use of cocaine without checking its consequences and who presumed to subject Leonardo da Vinci and Alexander the Great to his techniques of psychoanalysis; but he was a brilliant phrase-maker whose discourse became universal. Introspection became a rite in the modern west, defining this culture, as self-mutilation or dance or codes of gesture might define another. Repression became the modern demon and the analyst an exorcist. In urban America the rite of psychotherapy came to be practised by the second half of the century with the regularity of communion, by every generation of virtually an entire social class, in a world depicted from the inside by the film-maker Woody Allen, who appears in his movies, picking nervously at the threads of his own hang-ups.

This is not to say that the neuroses of twentieth-century westerners were unreal—only that psychology enhanced awareness of them and therefore, paradoxically, while contributing to their treatment, increased their effects. The material of the First World War is eye-catching because it can be computed in digits which take up a lot of the line: perhaps 10 million killed in action, 30 million casualties in all, 9 million tons of shipping sunk, for instance. The political consequences are conspicuous because they can translate into colours on a map: twelve new sovereign or virtually sovereign states in Europe or on its borders; frontiers reshuffled among a dozen more; three huge European super-states demolished, overseas colonies swivelled and swapped. Yet the psychological effects, which cannot be calibrated or mapped, make at least an equal impression on the reader of the sources. The dead left gaps which societies were convulsed to fit—replacing the dead with the young or the old, men with women, aristocracies with meritocracies. The survivors returned with mental scars which, if communi-

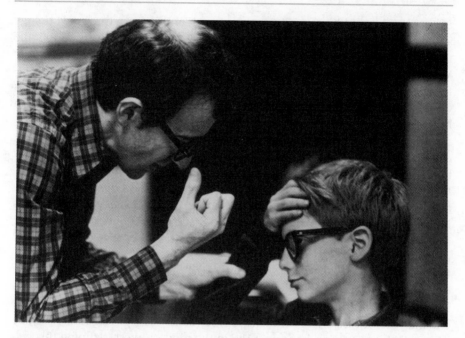

Neurosis is the subject most satirized in the films of Woody Allen. In this scene from *Annie Hall* (1977), one of his characteristic tales of love lost through self-absorption, the goal of psychoanalysis—the recovery of repressed memories—materializes as Woody encounters and interrogates his childhood self, played by Jonathan Munk.

cated, could change sensibilities and pass on, in chat or silence, art or verse, the effects of the war to future generations, even when harvests were back to normal and cities rebuilt.

It is conventional but wise to look for the evidence in the poetry written on the western front. After the Germans' planned knockout blow against France was deflected on the Marne by reinforcements ferried to the field in taxis, the armies of both sides got mired in unflankably long trenches dug from the Channel to the Alps. There poets lived a conducive life of leisure and peril, trapped, with no view any way but upwards, between earth and sky. For literature, which usually does well out of war, this scoured and blasted landscape was a productive environment. It is commonly said that realism—bloody and sordid—was the result, like the transformation of Goya's art by the experiences of 1808. Among the English poets, for instance, contrasts are drawn between three kinds of voice: the heroic rhetoric of those who never saw the war, such as Thomas Hardy in *Men Who March Away;* the poignant romanticism of Rupert Brooke, who died before joining combat; and the frank anguish of the poetry of real experience attributed to Isaac Rosenberg, say, or Wilfred Owen. We hear Hardy's trumpets, and "only the monstrous anger of the guns" in Owen or the "scrutting" of the rat at David Jones's feet; we scent the remembered flowers of England with Brooke, catch with the front-liners the urgent stink of gas or the pungent excretions of fear.

Yet our impression is an illusion induced by the power of the poetry. All the poets drew screens of romance and rhetoric across the horrors of the war, and Wilfred Owen himself was as evasive of the truth, as repressive of his own memories, as any child of a Viennese Konditorei. The very act of turning vicious memories into poetry clogged and padded them with softening wads of literary artifice. Associations with the sentiments, lovely or mawkish, evoked by most of earlier poetic tradition tugged writers and readers away.

Everyone who tried to write about the war with frank realism found that language filtered out reality. A typical hero, back among the comforts of Blighty, could not communicate about anything that mattered. The people he found there—only seventy miles, less than a day's journey, from his "stinking world of sticky, trickling earth"—had understandings grounded in an unoverlapping universe of experience; his was unfathomable and came to seem unmentionable in their company. Philip Gibbs and Robert Graves both found that they "didn't want to tell" what it was like at the front. In consequence, the societies of home were exposed to the nightmares and unvoiced horrors of repressive returnees. It was like having the hero of Kipling's prophetic *The Man Who Was* on every street corner. In a world grown accustomed to the wisdom of Freud, unspoken neuroses were the worst. The horrors of those who fought the war were answered by the guilt of those who missed it. Christopher Isherwood's generation, "suffering from a feeling of shame that we hadn't taken part," went on fighting "a subliminally persistent war." French memories of the war were nourished and transmitted by similar means. French psychiatrists turned *en masse* to blame the war for conditions familiar for years. French law developed the fiction of "tacit consent" to cuckoldry of those absent at the front. In 1920, France's postwar president retired to a mental home.

Nervous disorders naturally found their way onto canvas and collage as well as into print. Though governments had patronized conventional war artists, the characteristic art of the First World War was Dada: externalized disillusionment, contempt for order and tradition embodied in the deliberately meaningless name. After the war, in Germany, Kurt Schwitters scraped artworks together from the detritus of a broken world—bits of smashed machines, fragments of demolished constructions. The visionary painter Max Ernst exposed postwar nightmares in weird, sickening dreams of evil, sometimes pieced, like Schwitters's work, from scraps of ephemera, or itch-

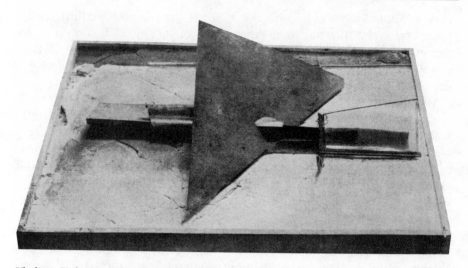

Vladimir Tatlin, *Painting Relief: Selection of Materials*, 1914. Russian art was enormously fertile in new ideas in the last years of Tsardom, and though Tatlin was an essentially practical man, incapable of *je m'en fichisme*—he was a merchant seaman and a fervent believer in the potential social usefulness of art—he anticipated the techniques of Dadaists and some of the sources of inspiration of Futurism and Vorticism, building up disturbing reliefs from bits of industrial detritus.

ingly textured by rubbing the paper over wires or sacking or unplaned planks. The jangle of nerves could be "heard" in music on the twelve-note system developed by Schoenberg in the early twenties.

The war-induced neurotic syndrome was feeble at first in America. The U.S. economy had been the great gainer from the war, bloated by reparations from the losers and repayments from the winners. Optimism here lasted as long as prosperity: the great era of American suicides did not begin until October 1929, and lasted until well into 1932.

The Stock Market Crash and the Great Depression were no less traumatic for being predictable. After the immediate postwar dislocation of a demobilized economy, the towns of the United States revelled in seven fat years from 1922—albeit without the lawful stimulus of drink, banned by constitutional amendment between 1920 and 1933. The farmers fed the fat years. High production and low prices were the war's legacy to agriculture. Other sectors were suckled by credit-led inflation. Between 1922 and 1927 annual output per industrial worker grew by an astonishing 3½ per cent, while wages rose by under 2½ per cent per annum. Automobiles became articles of mass consumption; construction flung "towers up to the sun." While share-ownership spread among the ranks of society and the levels of wealth, economic power became, paradoxically, increasingly concentrated.

Ford, Chrysler, and General Motors, for instance, edged all the middle-size competitors out of the automobile market; chain stores came to dominate the retail sector. "Pyramids" of millions of shareholders were bestrode by a few colossi, who controlled preferential stocks or manipulated their voters, just as in Europe dictators took over nominal democracies and ruled by charisma or demagogy.

As holding companies multiplied and stocks were revalued, a booming market seemed to offer the promise of literally universal riches. A millionaire genuinely believed that "every American could become rich" by investing small savings in the relentlessly upward mobility of shares. The market was overheated to the point of incandescence, while the nominally superrich fed the flames with paper profits: men such as Samuel Insull, the utilities king, who claimed at his trial, with some justice, that he had done only what "every banker and business magnate has done"; or the Van Swinbeuren brothers, who kept control of their railway empire by issuing stocks in effectively worthless holding companies; or Richard Whitney, reputedly the coolest hand on the Exchange, who was later exposed as a fraud who had raided clients' accounts. In 1924, 282 million shares changed hands on Wall Street; by 1929 the figure reached over 1.8 million. Prices doubled in the same period. The most revealing and the most frightening proof of the madcap momentum was the leap of loans to brokers to cover purchases of shares on the margin: from $3 billion in 1926 to $8.5 billion in 1929.

President Hoover, a cramped ascetic who always mistrusted the rich, received no thanks for impotently foreseeing the consequences. In 1926 he warned that "this fever of speculation can only land us on the shores of over-depression." Annually from 1927 the founder of the Babson Institute warned that "sooner or later a crash is coming . . . factories will shut down . . . men will be thrown out of work . . . and the result will be a serious depression." At the beginning of the year of the crash, one of Wall Street's most respected journals denounced the stock fever as "a menace to the entire community." Joe Kennedy sold out in the summer, his instincts alerted—he later claimed—when a shoeshine boy outside the Exchange offered him investment advice.

At first, the October crash seemed like an extreme instance of the habitual short-term fluctuations of the market. The comedienne Fanny Brice, who lost half a million on Black Thursday, invested her last $50,000 on Friday; she more than doubled it by two o'clock. In total, however, between 24 October and 13 November 1929, $30 billion was cut from the total value of American stocks—almost equivalent to the entire cost of America's war effort. When a further crash followed on 30 May 1930, recovery seemed impossible. The effects ricocheted off the rich to bounce the economy into recession, bounded across the Atlantic, and contributed to a series of European bank failures from 1931. Financial institutions slammed shut; govern-

ment spending programmes guttered. Suicide jokes became the humourists'
escape. An old colleague of Samuel Insull's, who had shared his fortunes
since their early days as, respectively, office boy and stenographer to
Thomas Edison, was one of the first to kill himself. Later, the contralto Au-
gusta Lenska threw herself under a streetcar in despair that Insull's opera
house would have to close. The president of a cigar company grappled
with a waiter to reach the ledge of a Manhattan hotel. In a typical instance
of the cycle of despair, when James J. Riordan, the president of the New
York County Trust Company, shot himself, the news brought on the nervous breakdown of his broker. America had joined the other half of Atlantic
civilization in a condition of nervous disorder.

Samuel Insull himself claimed to have attempted suicide three times on
his way back, extradited from Europe to stand trial. He was a tragic rogue:

Samuel Insull helped
through the gates of Cook
County gaol, Chicago, in
1934, shortly before his ac-
quittal on fraud charges involving $150 million.

the poor, bright boy whose mother had kept a temperance boarding-house and who grew rich by hard work before he got super-rich by phonus-bolonus. At the height of his success, bankers telephoned him with offers of loans, "the way," said his secretary, "the greengrocer phones my mother." His fall was due not to wickedness but to hubris. His methods were illegal but not flagrant enough to get a conviction, despite three separate prosecutions. Yet his obsessive desire to control all his own companies drove him to bankruptcy in an attempt to buy back his own stock at prices even he could not afford. He was always fastidious about his clothes. One of the most expressive images of the depression years, when cartoonists and photographers delighted in contrasts of rags and riches, shows him emerging from the gates of Cook County gaol for one of his trials: soft homburg, herringbone coat, white spats, and gleaming footwear; thin and trim-bearded with aristocratic stride. A chubby gaoler in a flat cap and woolly jersey holds the door, without deference but with a smile caught between kindness and satisfaction.

MILITANT TENDENCIES

Until he killed himself in 1907, Giuseppe Pelizza, the Milanese painter, searched restlessly for symbolic subjects to express huge moral and political messages. He tried religion and nature before turning, with greater enthusiasm but no more success, to socialism as a source of inspiration. In 1902 he exhibited an enormous painting, five and a half metres wide and

Pelizza's *Il Quarto Stato*. Reading Tolstoy gave the artist a conviction of the social role of his profession, which he expressed in an article written in 1889—the year before he began this painting—as educating, elevating, and inspiring other workers-by-hand; but it could only be done, he opined, by one born, bred, and living among the working class.

A design for Robert Owen's projected socialist utopia of New Harmony, Indiana. Owen's socialism had Christian origins, though the minaret-like towers and central pavilion give New Harmony a resemblance to Mecca. The symmetry reverts to classical models of an ordered life; the grandeur and fantasy are reminiscent of the "progress-palace" tradition typical of nineteenth-century factory architecture. Compare the even earlier American utopia (p. 268) and the factory (p. 391).

Babar's Célesteville: an ultra-rational utopia of benevolent despotism, dominated by the "Palace of Industry" and "Palace of Pleasure," coyly mistranslated in this illustration from the English-language edition. Babar's own residence is the one at top-right with the picture-windows so nastily typical of postwar taste. Despite its obvious similarities with other utopias, Jean de Brunhoff's ideal town, with its neat rows of round and oblong huts, seems clearly indebted to René Caillié's description and engraving of Timbuktu— the fabled "unattainable city," which came in the early nineteenth century to symbolize romantic yearning, but which Caillié reached, disguised as a Muslim pilgrim, in 1828.

Two masks of tyranny. Eisenstein's images of Lenin were appropriate for a phase of revolutionary violence. A dynamic force emerges from the darkness: a jerky, restless figure flickers on the screen. Stalin's image, in a design for an enormous poster, represents calm after the storm, reliability for an epoch of consolidation, a stout bastion for defence: placidly the leader contemplates a peaceful future in a landscape of purposeful activities and unruffled horizons.

nearly three metres tall, which aroused at the time only coldness and indifference in onlookers. The subject of *Il Quarto Stato* was a vast crowd of workers, advancing, the artist said, "like a torrent, overthrowing every obstacle in its path, thirsty for justice." Their march is certainly relentless, their solidarity intimidating, but except for a Madonna-like woman in the foreground who seems bent on a personal project, appealing to one of the rugged leaders at the head of the march, they are individually characterless, moving like the parts of a gigantic automaton, with a mechanical rhythm, slow and pounding.

No work of art could better express the extremes of grandeur and grind which are at the heart of socialism: noble humanity, mobilized by dreary determinism. In the history of socialism, the humanity and nobility came first. They were expressed in the ideals of equality and fraternity, proclaimed by utopians of the enlightenment and applied in the practices of sharing and cooperating attempted in early socialist communities in nineteenth-century America. You can still get a sense of what these were like from a few surviving fragments of doomed experiments—planners' drawings, propagandists' engravings, and even some decayed but undemolished structures. They slot into a long and continuing history of "backwoods utopias" strenuously constructed by religious fanatics, of a sort to be seen at Ephrata, Pennsylvania, where despite the early founders' exhortations to celibacy, an austere Eden lasted from 1728 to 1904; wooden buildings survive in the style of the prayer hall, built to the plan of Solomon's Temple, so that "neither hammer nor axe nor any tool of iron was heard in the house while it was building."

Socialism followed with secular utopias, which in the opinion of one of their great projectors, Étienne Cabet (1788–1856), would breed "true Christianity." The communities' other inspirers, Robert Owen (1771–1858) and Charles Fourier (1772–1837), proposed communal buildings for socialist families to share, whereas Cabet favoured individual but uniform dwellings. Owen's project for New Harmony, Indiana, looks like a mosque; an engraving of the site resembles an old English village in a Gainsborough landscape. A Fourierist plan for a "phalanx" in the wilderness is monumental enough for the Paris of Haussmann, with boulevards linking factories and people's palaces. Some of the neat, bleak houses of Cabet's disciples survive at New Icaria, near Corning, Iowa. The realm of Icarus must have resembled nothing so much as the benevolently planned capital of Babar's elephant kingdom. All the plans are geometrical and symmetrical, as unsuited to the realities of uneven sites as socialist utopianism to the limitations of real life.

Icarus was brought down to earth by Louis Blanc (1811–1882) and Karl Marx; the former convinced most socialists that their ideals could be entrusted to the state, to be imposed on society; the latter gave them a conviction of the historic inevitability of their triumph in a cycle of class conflicts, in which workers—degraded and inflamed by employers' ex-

La Pasionaria becomes an icon. Her nickname was itself an appropriation of religious imagery in the communist cause. Photographed in the streets of Madrid in October, 1936, her image replaces that of the Virgin in a version of one of the devotional parades traditional in a Catholic city. The red star, just visible in the background, occupies the place of the cross: the hammer and sickle usurps the role of the banners of religious sodalities.

ploitation—would establish a decisive advantage as labour wrested control of economic power from capital. Early socialist experiments had been peaceful, with no land to conquer except in the open spaces of the wilderness, no human adversaries except selfishness and greed. Transformed by language of conflict and coercion, socialism became an ideology of violence, to be resisted uncompromisingly by those who valued property above fraternity and liberty above equality.

The very conviction of ultimate victory helped socialist leaders in Europe restrain their hands. In most European countries they built up mass organizations for political and industrial action in the late nineteenth and early twentieth centuries, generally without risking premature revolutionary attempts. The first revolutions in which socialist inspiration played a major part broke out where the messages of socialism were muted by distance and its ranks thin through under-industrialization, in Mexico and China in 1910–11. The influence on the Mexican Revolution of the left-wing agitators who published, from havens in exile, the call to insurgency in the broadsheet *Regeneración* may have been exaggerated, but it was widely assumed at the time. When, for example, drunken brawlers threatened to "kill all the rich" in Lagos de Morena in August 1911, an informer reported that "someone has been filling their heads with socialist ideas." In Mexico, liberalism—if anything—was the avowed ideology of most of the urban revolutionary chiefs, while in the countryside the resemblances among socialism, Robin Hood banditry, and the values of an old-fashioned *jacquerie* may have been purely adventitious. In China, however, socialism was explicitly part of the inspiration of the revolutionary leader Sun Yat-sen (1866–1925). He rejected Marx's methods but shared his goals. He proposed handing out estates to peasants and nationalizing large industries: a programme of "levelling, not liquidating."

When socialist revolution did reach Europe, its force and rapidity were explosive. It defied Marx's own predictions. The misery which provoked it was brought on not by the excesses of capitalism but by the unmerciful demands of war—though theorists claimed these were the same thing. It was supposed to flow from vast, impersonal historic forces, yet it was acclaimed as the achievement of heroes: profane tsars, Lenin and Stalin, of contrasting charisma—the first the restless, active genie immortalized in Eisenstein's jerky cinematography, the second substantial and still, controlling by chill calm from broad billboards. The revolutions started in the unevenly industrialized environment of Russia, spread from east to west, and tended to get checked or domesticated wherever industrialization was most mature. In England and France, for instance, the progress of democratic socialism seemed to make revolution unnecessary; everywhere west of the Russias, in the first round of Europe's civil wars from 1917 to the early twenties, revolutionaries were defeated and socialist compromisers seduced by embourgeoisement. Militant socialism, however, retained or gained impetus for every subsequent stage of the conflict—the street fighting of the twenties and thirties, the Spanish Civil War, the Second World War—until its energies drained slowly away in the rechannelled hostilities of the cold war.

The fighting spirit of those who stayed or became loyal to Moscow could be illustrated from literally millions of individual stories. Perhaps none has more legendary status than that of "Dolores" Ibárrurri, a loud international voice of Moscow's for most of the century. She was cut out to be a figure-head. Her lumpy figure might have been carved from hardwood. In her early forties, her bulging breasts excited republican soldiers' passion. Her staring eyes held audiences spellbound. Even her characteristic posture—leaning forward to declaim, with out-thrust head—might have been designed to adorn a prow. She became the mascot of Spanish communism. She joined the party at its foundation and died at the age of ninety-three in 1989, when it was crumbling as fast as the Berlin wall. It brought her fame and failure, prominence but not power.

This daughter of a well-paid miner came to communism, tainted by the piety and prosperity of her pit-head childhood, when she married an impecunious revolutionary. She hated her husband but became wedded to his politics—perhaps in penance for her hatred. She was a frustrated priestess who served the party with the passion of a vocation transferred. Moscow became her Rome, Stalin her pope; inside the communist there was always a Catholic trying to get out. During the Spanish Civil War, the "priest-eater" of right-wing propaganda protected nuns and ransacked religious imagery for her famous speeches. Her real name was Isadora. "Dolores," like the highly exploitable pen-name of "La Pasionaria," was a nickname that evoked the sorrows of Holy Week.

She was the naughty Lola of the Left, practising what she claimed was politically correct sex with a lover twenty years her junior. Her choice, however, with his mudless boots and silk pyjamas, suggested some fatal tendency towards bourgeois deviation; she later came to see him as a traitor to the cause. She was a feminist who was good at knitting and who patched the holes in the commissar's jacket. Her revolutionary credentials were combined with old-fashioned values: she was flattered by a gift of perfume, and she hated women to smoke. She reminded some fellow-communists of a medieval queen, others of a sixteenth-century saint. She was Stalin's dupe but the authoress of her own personality cult. "You have such a famous mother," she told her children, "why must you behave so badly?" She stormed through the conflicts of militant socialism and snored through its senescence—noisily asleep, a returnee from exile in her eighties, on the back benches of Spain's Chamber of Deputies.

During its period of vigour, socialism, like any growing creed, was vulnerable to fracture by heretics and schismatics. The triumph of one of the

Nazi propaganda characteristically projected an image of Teutonic manhood, strenuous vision, irresistible strength, and national recovery from the "wounds" of Versailles; but it was also careful of the party's "socialist" image, presenting worker icons and promising "work and bread."

most militant fragments in the Russian revolution exacerbated enmities within the left, from where the sects would wage civil wars of their own while contending with external enemies. "Aren't we all socialists?" George Orwell naïvely asked during the gun battles of rival revolutionaries in Barcelona in 1937. This was like asking "Aren't we all Christians?" at the massacre of Saint Bartholomew. Whether fascism was a splinter of socialism or an independently evolved doctrine, or just a slick name for unprincipled opportunism, has been a matter of passionate debate. From the perspective of the future, the differences among all forms of violent political extremism will blur. The politics of twentieth-century Europe were horseshoe-shaped, and the extremists at both ends seemed close enough to touch. In practice, individuals moved between fascism and militant socialism as if by connecting channels. Mussolini was a socialist youth leader before he became a fascist *duce*. At least until Hitler's hijack and purge, many Nazis tried to make the party conform to its name: the German National Socialist Workers' Party. Britain's failed Man of Destiny, Oswald Mosley, was a socialist cabinet minister before he took to the streets. An aunt has told me that my father, who became one of Spain's most faithful voices for the cause of the western allies in the Second World War, carried a communist card and wore a Falangist uniform at different moments during the thirties.

Of course, it was equally possible to be attracted to fascism from other traditions, but the common ground among rival totalitarianisms was broad enough to be conspicuous to those who look back on it, perhaps even as far ahead as the era of the galactic museum-keepers. During and after its check in the 1940s, "fascism" became a term of abuse, signifying nothing about what it denoted except the speaker's disapproval; during its rise in the 1920s and 1930s it was presented by its spokesmen in calculatedly obscure rhetoric. Yet it can be usefully defined.

The doctrine of the omnipotence of the state it shares with the dominant tendency in socialism since Blanc. Its celebration of the sanctity of violence resembles the militancy of two strands in the ragged fabric of the far left: the anarchist tendency proscribed by Marx, and the zealots of perpetual revolution, who had Lenin's comrade and rival, Leon Trotsky, as their patriarch. The military model followed by fascists for the organization of society is, in one perspective, a model of fraternal community life. "Revolutionary discipline" was also demanded by Lenin. In the 1930s, the economic programme of fascism, summarized in Hitler's slogan, "*Arbeit und Brot*," included planned re-inflation and wealth distribution through public works—which was or became the orthodoxy of social democracy. I can imagine the galactic museum-keepers classifying fascism as a variant of socialism, adapted to the needs of a variegated electorate; for it is a verifiable fact that fascists mobilized small property owners from the petty bourgeoisie, as well as workers, by advocating policies which could be crudely reduced to "socialism without expropriation." Despite the relatively long eclipse of fascism, its potential is probably unexhausted in the 1990s; amid the ruins of militant socialism in parts of central and eastern Europe, textbook conditions exist for a fascist revanche, and the museum-keepers may come to see it as one of the more durable bequests of the conflicts of the twentieth century.

TODAY, THE STRUGGLE

The civil wars of Atlantic civilization were not just confrontations of left and right, nor simply struggles of the traditional mixed societies—with their irra-

This republican poster of 1936 seems to lack the killer instinct: the enemy is lampooned, not savaged. The ship of the "Nationalists" is full of foreigners: Jewish capitalist, fat Nazi, comic-opera Italian fascist, and—most suggestive of all in a Spanish context—African Moor. All but the first of these slurs stuck. Franco relied on German and Italian aid and on the crack reputation of his Maghribi recruits.

tionally evolved institutions, conservative habits, and liberal orthodoxies—fending off the attacks of radicals on either flank. The killing grounds were crossed with old enmities which the new lines of battle overlay. Among them were those of liberals for clericalists; local and regional majorities for their ethnic or racial victims; nationalists and imperialists for liberals and separatists; and neighbouring nations for each other. Age-old violence went on under the shell of pan-European conflict; secular hatred took on the language but rarely the forms of class war.

Between 1936 and 1939, for instance, young poets deferred their bicycle races through English suburbs to "explode like bombs" in a Spanish war, because they oversimplified it as a theatre of the fight between right and left. Most ended disillusioned, because the war was really fought between broad coalitions pursuing an introspectively Spanish agenda. The "national" coalition included virtual fascists but partnered them with an uncomfortable wagonful of fellow-travellers: traditional Catholics, fighting to save nuns from rape and churches from incineration; old-fashioned liberal centralists, who were equally numerous on the other side; romantic reactionaries, who in armed thousands yearned to restore a long-excluded line of the former royal dynasty; constitutional monarchists, who wanted to get back to the cosy, remunerative parliamentary system of the previous generation; worshippers of "the sacred unity of Spain," who thought they were fighting to hold the country together; *hispanizadores,* who wanted to purge supposedly Spanish virtues of foreign pollutants. On the other side, along with all the mutually warring sects of the left, were conservative republicans, who included Catholics as well as secularists; anticlericals of the liberal tradition; admirers of French and English standards of democracy; and right-wing regionalists, who, recognizing the nationalists as the greater threat, supported the republicans as the lesser evil.

Similarly in France the Second World War masked a civil war in which old enemies bared their knives. Here, however, the traditional divisions more closely matched those of left and right. Swathes of French society had never accepted ungrudgingly the republic that had been created after the last crushing defeat by Germany in 1871. Clericalists regarded the republic as an affair of freemasons; for royalists it was a thing of bad taste, symbolized by the frightful hat knocked from a president's head by a baron at the races in 1899. Bonapartists and other authoritarians deplored the successive governments' spineless record in foreign affairs. The symbolic "Marianne," nubile bearer of the tricolour at the barricades of the revolutions of the nineteenth century, was "the slut" in an aggressively nationalistic paper.

The acquiescence of a large part of this powerful lobby was secured through the glory and patronage accruing from an unwieldy empire in Africa and Indo-China; but disloyalty to the republic was too tightly entwined with some groups' hatred for others to be easily unravelled. The scale and tenacity of the hatred were brought home by the Dreyfus scandal of 1894–1906—a slow agony of national humiliation, mutually inflicted by rival interests in pursuit or defence of incompatible ideals of France. Alfred Dreyfus was a staff officer of creditable record but a double outsider: an Alsatian of German antecedents, when Germany was the national enemy, and a Jew at a time when anti-Semitism was inflamed against France's fastest-growing minority. Intelligence officers colluded with a real spy—who was also an aristocrat from a traditional army family—to indict the innocent Dreyfus for espionage. When a brother-officer, outraged by the injustice, leaked the decisive evidence, officialdom, denying its crime, refused even to admit its mistake. Lobbyists for justice were persecuted in their turn. The verdict was shored up with fabricated evidence and justice denied by delay. Dreyfus was returned for retrial, white and crushed, after three years' penal exile on Devil's Island. His sentence was lightened before he was pardoned; he was pardoned before he was officially exonerated. Meanwhile, the conspiracy against him had come to be seen by republicans as a reactionary plot against the constitution. The anti-*dreyfusards* saw the Dreyfus lobby as an unpatriotic gang. The issue was not, a propagandist said, "whether a wretched individual is guilty or innocent—it is whether the Jews and Protestants are or are not the masters of the country."

The civil war narrowly escaped in 1899 broke out in 1940, when the anti-*dreyfusards* emerged from the tumbledown woodwork of fallen France, some of them openly gloating. The name "Republic" was excised from that of the French "State." A government of old soldiers and Nazi sympathizers in Vichy "collaborated" with the Germans against their fellow-citizens; Jews and leftists were slaughtered and enslaved; Germany preyed on the economy, looted works of art, and exported hundreds of thousands of Frenchmen as labour. Feeble at first, the "Resistance" was transformed by the German invasion of Russia in June 1941. This released communists, previously quiescent on orders from Moscow, into the woods. The resisters were now a coalition reminiscent in its breadth and fragility of those of the Spanish Civil War, encompassing communists and Catholics. From 1943 the fascist *milice* fought a ruthless war in the wastes against the *maquis*. The Germans fled in 1944, leaving Frenchmen at each other's throats. Perhaps, more than by any other single influence, peace and democracy were restored by women's suffrage: the votes of widows and spinsters gave power to the Catholic centre and an opportunity to policies of reconciliation. Meanwhile, France was reduced to prostration, derided or pitied by the young Leon Brittan for "clapped-out Citroëns and filthy loos."

Though the United States got dragged into Europe's civil wars, which became civil wars of Atlantic civilization, militant socialism found it hard to cross the Atlantic. Marx set up the First International in New York, where in 1901 a publicist could "taste socialism in the price of beef." Socialists enjoyed some local electoral successes in the first two decades of the twentieth century. In 1920, Eugene V. Debs, an ex-railroad worker campaigning from prison, won a million votes as socialist candidate for the presidency. But the language of class war never caught on in a country where, even in the depths of the depression, nearly 80 per cent in an opinion survey considered themselves middle class. "Whatever happened to the socialist party?" asked one of James Thurber's cartoon women, shapeless but eagle-eyed.

Though European civil war could not be transferred to America, American power was potentially decisive in European conflicts. Americans had rationally unanswerable excuses for staying aloof. Fascism and communism were equally detestable, equally un-American creeds; from the moral perspective of Americans, collectively unable to admit their own imperialism to themselves (see Chapter 11), the imperialist democracies of Britain and France seemed hardly more worth fighting for. Migrants had "made America" to escape the class war, not to send their children back to fight it. In strict Staatspolitik, America's best interest lay in watching other contenders fight the Second World War, or, if that was impossible, concentrating on the defeat of Japan. America's rise would be proportionate to others' prostra-

"What ever became of the Socialist Party?"

In *Men, Women and Dogs* (1946), Thurber made fun of the demise of socialism in America: but it is a bigger historical problem than is commonly appreciated, in view of the intimate connection of American communal experiments with early socialism, and the high hopes still entertained by American socialist idealists at the start of the twentieth century.

tion. Emotionally, however, the Atlantic was a narrow sea (see Chapter 13). In broadcasts and articles, fund-raisings and speech-making, demonstrations and dances, "hearts and minds," Americans fought over the European wars before joining in earnest. Hitler is usually said to have made a mistake by declaring war first in 1942: indeed, he seems to have thought so himself, but he was only anticipating a predictable development.

Foreign involvement is a smooth-sided pit, and America found it hard to get out. It was not the demands of the war that kept America in Europe but the problems of maintaining peace when it was over. Even before American power began to tell, German resources already looked overextended. Germany was fighting simultaneously against Britain and Russia while taking up the slack of her half-hearted Italian allies' wars in North Africa and the Balkans. Once America was committed, only the degree and timing of German defeat were at issue. It was the inevitability of ultimate victory that made America give priority to the European theatre; the opening of continental fronts by Anglo-American invasion could be represented as a response to the gallant Russian ally's repeated pleas for help. At a deeper level, it was compelled by fears that Russian armies could conquer much of Europe alone or that Stalin would leave others to finish the job and make a separate peace with Hitler.

The peace was harder to win than the war. Protracted conflict threatened from three sources: continuing civil wars in "liberated" countries; Russian desire for security or power on her western borders; and the internationalist idealism of militant socialists—exploited but not really supported from Moscow—who wanted to take advantage of a "revolutionary situation" across the continent. Depending on his point of view, the onlooker could be disgusted by Stalin's greed or astonished at his moderation: the Soviet Union reabsorbed Ukraine, Estonia, Latvia, and Lithuania but did not try to annex Finland; of the nominally allied countries, Stalin occupied Poland but withdrew from Czechoslovakia and Yugoslavia; he garrisoned the territory of hostile belligerents in Romania, Bulgaria, Hungary, and eastern Germany, but cooperated with the other allied powers in the administration of Austria and Berlin. In practice, American decision-makers seem to have been willing to allow him more liberties than he took. In March 1946, Churchill announced the descent of an "iron curtain" across Europe, but it was still perforated by chinks and draughts.

The civil wars of Atlantic civilization did not end at that fleeting moment of possible compromise. The struggle became focused on Greece, where Stalin had promised Britain "90 per cent predominance" and where Britain was determined to exact her rights. There was no east–west confrontation, only a civil war settled by British intervention, in which the left was disarmed and destroyed. In the rest of Europe over the next few years, economic necessity imposed a fragile equilibrium. Economic aid was the best means of seducing former enemies into dependence. By the time the Marshall Plan was introduced in 1948 to fund European reconstruction from America and create "social and political conditions in which free institutions can exist," most of the central and eastern countries were already tied to the Soviet market by reparations debts or the want of alternatives. All of them, by choice or putsch, became "people's republics" and Soviet satellite-states—even Czechoslovakia, which was close to the west and had a long democratic tradition. Russian fear of prosperity bought with dollars showed in the attempt to force East German currency on West Berlin in 1948–49: the American response included the Berlin airlift to break the blockade and the formation of the North Atlantic alliance to oppose "the Kremlin's intimidation."

BARBARISM, FREEDOM, AND TECHNOLOGY

A Europe of armed camps and a heavily fenced Soviet Empire: like so many others, Europe's civil wars had resulted in partition. A prediction of Spengler's looked perilously close to fulfilment: after the decline of the west, the next dominant civilization would be Russian. Like Gibbon's Rome, the victims of these wars had seen—or been blinded by—a "triumph of barbarism." Believers in progress beheld in horror the evidence of inhumanities unearthed at Auschwitz and Katyn, the record of atrocities compiled in wars motivated more by hatred than self-interest. The barbarism that broke Rome had invaded from the outside, it was supposed; the new barbarism had welled up from within. Analysis of how it happened, whom to blame, and what to remedy was to pass through three phases before the end of the millennium, reflecting the tribulations of a culture struggling to recover its sense of being civilized.

In the early stages of the conflicts, blame tended to stick to those at or near the top of society. The caricatures of Georg Grosz, in which cannibal-capitalists are gorged with the food of the starving, are the best-known images, but more effective—because more subtle—is, for instance, T. C. Dugdale's *The Arrival of the Jarrow Marchers in London* of 1936, where the hungry are reduced to anonymous blobs, contemplated in boredom or disdain. Barbarism—these artists were saying—had not seeped up from the bottom of society; civilization had begun to slip from the top. The doctrine of "war crimes," by identifying individuals as guilty—most of them in positions of some responsibility—implicitly exonerated the masses. There was some irony in this, since at the Nuremberg trials "taking orders" was an inadmissible defence. The experience of war convinced some humanitarians that circumstances of deprivation or conflict could corrupt people not fundamentally flawed by turpitude, like the inhabitants of Cela's beehive or the

"The Arrival of the Jarrow Marchers in London" by Thomas Dugdale (1936). Dugdale was a dandy who proudly "flaunted a coloured handkerchief in his waistcoat" in reaction against the pale colours favoured by designers at the time. He knows the social world of the foreground—the cocktail shaker, the indifferent idler slumped in Oxford bags, the sinuous, languorously curious young woman—better than the contrasting world in the background, of the "hunger marchers" reduced to an anonymous blur and the line of mounted police, turned into diabolical shadows by the flare-light.

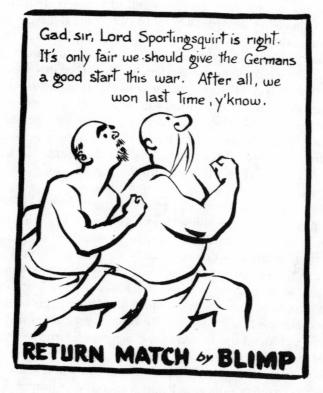

David Low's Blimp usually began his utterances by saying, "Gad, sir, Lord N is right," aligning his views with a brand of establishment convention; his milieu is the Turkish bath, for which he is always attired. His imagery comes from the playing-field—that vast swathe of old England which stretches from Clifton Close, via Plymouth Hoe to Eton— and his morality, though warped by all sorts of prejudice, is essentially the charming schoolboy "code" of fairness. But, Gad, sir, Low was right: the values of fair play did emasculate British policy and give Hitler an advantage. See also pp. 528–35.

victims of Camus's plague. In a more individual and accessible way, the moral corrosion of wartime ate its way into the fibre of David Low's splenetic cartoon character, Colonel Blimp, who became a symbol of the moral dilemma of the British officer class. In a film version of 1942 made popular by government disapproval, Blimp represented a pre-war honour code of military conduct and was unwilling to be dragged down to the moral level of the Nazis—but Dresden was razed by bombing anyway after a "realistic" decision.

After the war, in the perceptions of alarmed commentators, barbarism seemed an uncontainable genie, unwilling to get back in its bottle. Postwar prosperity did not make people better. Juvenile delinquency, soaring crime rates (especially among the young), brutalized manners, raucous excesses of popular culture, urban violence, racist outbursts, decayed values, and broken homes: these were the fodder of headlines all over the western world. Some of the alarmists may have misinterpreted matters of taste as matters of substance. I remember reading Richard Hoggart's *Uses of Literacy* and Denys Thompson's *Discrimination and Popular Culture* as a schoolboy and suspecting my schoolfellows who liked rock music of *trahison des clercs*. Others were misled by a natural phase of the demographic cycle: all wars produce baby booms, and all baby booms produce generation gaps. The youthful rebellions of the second half of the century in the western world differed from others chiefly in the huge spending power of young earners, which made them unusually ostentatious.

In the last years of the twentieth century, though perceptions of a generally demoralized society are still widespread, the evidence is inconclusive. High crime rates, for instance, reflect high standards in the reporting and classification of incidents—not necessarily an expansion of evil. More remarkable than the persistence of barbaric behaviour is the survival of traditional values. More impressive than the horrors of mob violence is the extent to which, in most western countries, they have been confined to minorities and contained on the streets. We can at least congratulate ourselves that we have improved the record of the biggest barbarian of the war era: the state. Many western states have willingly curbed their power to kill or maltreat the citizens they have at their mercy. Human rights movements have helped to transform policing habits, especially of former dictatorships in eastern and central Europe.

It can hardly be denied, however, that the moral effects of peace and prosperity, freedom and democracy, mass communications and mass education have been disappointing. The wartime analysis, which tended to blame barbarism on the demoralizing effects of conflict and misery, has been challenged by pessimists who regard human nature as incorrigible and by a powerful wave of conservative social philosophers who are aware of the limited power of politically engineered change. The most widely familiar form of the debate is trivial: sterile political cross-banter about whether unemployment is responsible for crime. At a deeper level, however, the drift of opinion has dangerous implications for the future. Those who begin by deprecating change may end by indicting it, and if we lose faith in freedom, we may get fascism back in its place.

One of the drawbacks of freedom is that free choices are regularly made for the worst, ever since the setting of an unfortunate precedent in Eden. To expect people to improve under its influence is to demand unrealistic standards from freedom and, ultimately, to undermine its appeal. Something similar could be said of the other victims of late twentieth-century disillusionment: prosperity, democracy, and education. Freedom, however, is uniquely intractable to political moulding, because in the recent past it has come to be influenced far more by technological progress than by political decisions.

The object of technology, in a sense, is freedom. By replacing or extending the power of brain and muscle it liberates people to do what they want instead of what they must. No statute or constitutional amendment has done more in the twentieth century for the freedom of ordinary people in the Atlantic world than inventions—to take a couple at random—such as the internal combustion engine and the mass-producible contraceptive. Yet neither has been unequivocally beneficent. The motor car rolled into the world, puffing and chuckling like a creepy fictional fat boy, just ahead of the present century. It began as a rich man's toy but gradually became accessible to people at almost every level of society in the Atlantic world. While conferring the unheard-of freedom to go where one liked when one felt like it, the car created aggressive drivers, demanded ugly roads, and polluted the world with its noxious fumes and stertorous noise. Contraceptives are often credited with liberating women for employment, but the enhanced freedom to choose sexual partners on an unprecedented scale fulfilled a more basic human craving. The effect has been equivocal on the spread and multiplication of sexually transmitted diseases. And rather than just facilitating family planning, it probably also contributed to the erosion of monogamy and the unforeseeable consequences, which await western countries in the next century, of families on new patterns, composed in a majority of cases of step-relations and single parents instead of the traditional "nucleus."

Technological change seems likely to take over from unaided human wickedness as the focus of fears of barbarism. The first indictments were uttered under the mushroom-cloud of the atom bomb, for weapons of mass destruction threaten civilization more radically than any brutality of manners. Technology too powerful for existing political controls can speed and spread familiar forms of brutalization: satellite-borne pornography outflanks the efforts of legislators. As the end of this millennium approaches, artificial intelligence researchers are poised to become the Frankensteins of the next; what Hitler could not achieve by exterminating under-races, eugenics engineers threaten by genetic manipulation; the complexities of defining life, the deftness with which it can be prolonged or terminated, has transferred a terrifying power over it into the hands of medical technicians. Embryos, for extermination and experiment, are the "persecuted minority" of a new form of inhumanity.

THE ENEMY BEREFT

In one respect, Atlantic civilization was strengthened by its squabbles. Though the world was full of other issues which divided the United States from the European allies and the Europeans from one another, they were all huddled together in fear of the Soviet Empire, crowded into the same corral by the danger of a communist stampede. The last of the "local difficulties" of the twentieth century—up to now, in 1993—was the collapse of that empire and the disappearance of the danger. It happened suddenly and was greeted uproariously, but by removing a common enemy it left the west with no principle of unity.

The huge postwar Russian penumbra in eastern and central Europe can be understood in two ways: first, as an unsurprising empire—typical of the entire recorded history of the region (see Chapter 2)—which reflected Russia's natural endowments for hegemony: huge population, untold resources, and an unassailable heartland. Such an empire had been foreseeable for centuries and might have taken shape more than a hundred years earlier, after the Napoleonic wars, when the opportunity of 1945 was startlingly prefigured. On the other hand, with equal conviction it could be claimed that Soviet power was a jerry-built edifice, ramshackle and extemporized, incapable of containing for long—much less, eliminating for ever—the inveterate national and religious identities of the subject peoples. Its collapse was predicted almost from the start, and it could be said that what was surprising about it was not its sudden demise but its long survival.

The bicentennial year of the French Revolution, 1989, was decisive in dismantling it. In June, in Poland, the Communist Party was swamped in the first free elections since before the war, while in Hungary the martyrs of resistance to Soviet domination were rehabilitated. In October the Communist Party in Moscow formally resigned its leading role. In November the Berlin wall—the concrete successor of the iron curtain—began to come down; by 22 December, when Romania's dictator was slaughtered after crowds rushed his palace, changes of leadership had occurred in almost all the Soviet Union's former satellites. At the time, the change was attributed to the economic deficiencies of state socialism and the cumulative toil of the democratic "dissidents."

Neither analysis was completely right. The Soviet Empire was, in a sense, the victim of its own economic success. Until the 1970s communism looked like "the future which works." Russia had escaped the slump of the early thirties and, despite the vulnerability of a command economy to policymakers' mistakes, had found means to score daunting technical successes after the war, symbolized by a terrible nuclear arsenal and the spectacle of the sputniks. In 1960 a Cuban cartoonist drew a Russian spaceship scattering stardust while an earthbound priest told a stupefied catechumen, "The Russians can't get to heaven." Throughout eastern Europe—as in the right-wing dictatorships which survived from the pre-war period at the other end of the continent, in the Iberian peninsula—prosperity created bourgeoisies which the regimes tried unsuccessfully to buy off. Russian surpluses, especially in energy, subsidized most of the satellites without impoverishing the home economy. The era of economic success seems, in retrospect, to have ended with the world economic crisis of 1973, when rising oil prices convulsed the energy market and contributed to unprecedented inflation.

Against form, capitalism now began to work better. The western world began a collective revulsion against the economics of intervention, which had prevailed since the slump. This was a phase of the predictable cycles of the history of economic policy. When the enemy is recession, the experts reach for the economic pump; when it is inflation, classical economics are revived. As a gap in economic performance opened—a pit before the iron curtain, separating the plush of the stalls from the backstage gimcrack—some of the company edged into the wings or switched to front-of-house. Satellites slipped out of economic dependence on Moscow and into heavy indebtedness to western bankers. The American administration of Ronald Reagan (president, 1981—88) boldly accelerated the arms race in an attempt to outstrip Russian paying power.

In 1985 the Soviet Union floated off the shoals, groaning with the grinding of its hull, out of port, and into the wake of the west, piloted by a leadership which, through a mixture of corruption and pragmatism, had ceased to believe the traditional socialist rhetoric. Some of the revolutions of 1989 were manipulated from Moscow, the last leverings of a doomed supremacy. The outgoing East German dictator blamed the Kremlin for his fall; in Prague the Soviet secret police engineered the outbreak of demonstrations fatal to the communists. The conspirators who took over Romania were recently back from Russia.

Moscow's was a rational but, in the circumstances, an overambitious ploy. The back fires lit from the Kremlin became part of a more general conflagration. Dissidents were on hand to take over the revolutions they had not started. Most of the new governments of the early nineties were clericalist or nationalist in different degrees. The satellite states zoomed out of orbit; Communist Party groups all over Europe—including the Soviet Union—were dissolved or rechristened. The two communist super-states—the Soviet Union and the Yugoslav Federation—collapsed like marble edifices, cracked along the veins.

In some ways post–Soviet Europe resembled that of the Treaty of Versailles, with images multiplying in a Hall of Mirrors. As in 1919, the super-states were broken up and the frustrated nations restored to indepen-

Empty conference chairs in the Hall of Mirrors of Versailles: a suitably illusionist environment for the Treaty of Versailles, which projected delusive images, proffered empty promises of peace, and multiplied the number of small, easily confused European states as if by recessive reflections.

dence—including some, such as Slovenia and Croatia, Slovakia and Ukraine, that had missed their turn in the sharing of sovereignty that followed the First World War. Eastern Europe seemed to have gone straight from the world of Marx to that of the Marx brothers, with bewildering new states bubbling like Duck Soup.

Coinciding more or less with the emergence, in the form of the European Community, of an agglutinative western Europe which excludes—and in the economic sphere is designed to compete with—the United States, the Soviet débâcle seems likely to pull Europe's centre of gravity eastward. The architects' plans are already being debated that will rebuild Berlin in a form fit to house Europe's potential capital—a nightmare vision of Hitler's transformed into a dream-city. The grappling-hooks of the Atlantic alliance, alternately tightened to straining point or dangerously slackened through the troubles of the century, may at last be due to be finally slipped.

Chapter 17

THE CASEBOOK OF FAILURE: FRAYING EDGES OF THE ATLANTIC

Tears for Argentina—John Bull's Second Childhood—The Mature Years of Marianne—The Maggot in the Apple

TEARS FOR ARGENTINA

The most aristocratic *faubourg* of the future—according to a cartoon which appeared in Buenos Aires in 1909—featured a shack made of flattened oil cans in a landscape of scrub strewn with rubbish, where smoke rose in parallel with the effluent from a distant factory chimney. In a similar satire on the patter of estate agents, a man with seven-league boots took "one step to the railway station" from a suburban development in the same city. Buenos Aires was booming, and the image of a miraculously lengthening stride seemed appropriate for Argentina. With rates of increase in population and production scarcely excelled elsewhere in the world (see Chapter 13), self-confidence swelled. The parvenu swagger for which Argentina became notorious was concentrated at the upper levels of wealth, symbolized in the woodcocks stuffed with foie gras served to twelve hundred guests at a senator's golden wedding in 1906. It reached down to the customers of the housing developers and the children in school. According to an oath to the flag introduced by an educational reform in 1909, the Argentine Republic was simply "the finest country on earth." With "blind faith in their glamorous destiny," Argentinians were encouraged to believe that they would "know no history without a triumph."

Disappointment is the usual reward of hope. The Spanish philosopher,

521

"The most aristocratic *faubourg* of the future" from *Caras y Caretas* (13 March 1909): the cocksure self-confidence of early twentieth-century Buenos Aires was its own undoing, setting an unsustainable pace and encouraging a corrupt market.

José Ortega y Gasset, who was fascinated by Argentina and who fancied himself a prophet, saw it coming in the late 1920s: "the promises of the pampa, so generous, so spontaneous, many times go unfulfilled.... Defeats in America must surely be worse than elsewhere. A man is suddenly mutilated, left high and dry, with no treatment for his wounds." When the American Hispanist Waldo Frank paid a return visit to Argentina in the early forties, he found that the "whitest," cocksure country he formerly knew had become self-critical and agonized. The most successful Argentine work of fiction of 1931, Raúl Scalabrini Ortiz's *El hombre que está sólo y espera*, depicted an unfamiliar Buenos Aires—noncommittal and withdrawn, practising a policy of Lock Up Your Daughters reminiscent of medieval Byzantium (see Chapter 2). The hero of Manuel Gálvez's *Hombres en soledad* concluded in 1935 that in creating Argentina "God made a mistake." Politicians and intellectuals—in Argentina, these formed cavernously overlapping sets—beheld in despair a country intractable to their dreams and efforts.

Intractable Argentina survived outside the metropolitan glitz of Buenos Aires; it was captured in a photograph taken on the upper Paraná in 1905—

shanties, caped Indians, a sailing brig off a beach, the unruffled river dwindling into the distance. Despair was expressed in tears or rage at the loneliness and isolation of a culture cut off from its roots, "shuddering" in a corner of the world map. "Europeans can hardly imagine how tragic is our loneliness," pleaded Carlos Gálvez in 1937. The tyranny of cartography, which showed Argentina tapering off the bottom of the world, became a symbol of the anguish of frustration. Nowadays you can get maps that show Argentina at the top, and the strutting manners of the soccer star Diego Maradona or the playboy Luis Basualdo are part of everyday images of Argentina.

The failure of Argentina in the twentieth century became an historical mystery, like the decline of Spain or the eclipse of German liberalism: a game of Clue which any historian could play and to which each brought a peculiar solution. Measured from the perspective of the second half of the century, the squalid picture of underdevelopment was depressing in a country which had once claimed the credentials of a potential Canada or

Diego Maradona greeting the winning goal in the Association Football World Cup final of 1986, when Argentina beat West Germany. His "strutting manners" seemed to symbolize the return of Argentinean national ambition, but he proved a tragically flawed hero, weakened by scandals alleging cheating and drug abuse.

Australia—even a U.S.A. In the 1960s, Argentina was a country of ageing automobiles, where only half the school-age population completed primary school and where the capital was enclosed by a mould-growth of 1.5 million shanties. I remember seeing it then, when I was in my early teens. Buenos Aires was a city of decayed gentility, struggling with hard times. At Harrods in the *calle* Florida, richly patinated steam-lifts, operated by flunkies in threadbare uniforms, swished shoppers between floors of shoddy goods. At street-café tables, antiquated fashions clustered round creaking soda-syphons. Even the graffiti all seemed sadly out of date, squeaking dull praise for Perón from under films of grime. People complained, with some justification, of recolonization by an informal empire of multinational companies: new enterprises, where they existed, tended to be foreign-owned. Half the top hundred manufacturing firms were in foreign hands by 1966.

Economic failure was certainly a symptom and perhaps a cause of Argentina's prolonged mood of disillusion. It used often to be said that the Great Crash and Depression of 1929–32 were the decisive turning-point. The voices of the outraged poor can be heard in *tango* lyrics of the 1930s— the ironic paeans to filth and money uttered by Discepolín, for whom "Jesus was worth the same as the thief"; "the anger," in a song of Celedonio Flores, "of men who are strong but have to sit helpless in the face of hunger." The statistics show, however, that Argentina was more resilient in the depression years than almost any other capitalist country, containing unemployment and raising exports. The structural weakness of an economy geared to dependence, producing cheap food for other countries' industries, was redressed at startling speed. There were 383,000 industrial workers in the whole country in 1914; by 1931, Buenos Aires wore the 'grey crown' of greasy smog typical of an industrial metropolis. On the eve of the world war, Argentine workers were almost as productive per capita as their French counterparts and well ahead of Austrians, Italians, and Japanese. Numbers employed in industry rose to over half a million by the mid-thirties and 830,000 by 1941, thanks especially to the development of native textiles. In 1943 the industrial sector overtook agriculture in terms of value of output.

Though the thirties were blamed as an "infamous decade" by writers who resented the power of domestic capitalists and foreign imperialists, the real "lost moment" of Argentina's economic history seems to have come later, during the Second World War and its aftermath. Until then, Argentina relied disproportionately on Britain as a market and source of investment capital. On the eve of the war, Britain provided a fifth of the republic's imports and bought over a third of her exports. The war crippled this main trading partner and produced no successor; Argentina was obliged to feed impoverished postwar Europe on credit in order to offload a surplus for which there was clamour without demand, need without means. The wheat producers of North America and Australia were chasing the same market. In 1948 the United States government decreed that Marshall aid (see Chapter 13) could not be used to buy Argentine produce.

Meanwhile the growth of industries—nurtured by governments, conservative and radical alike, in the thirties and forties—literally ate into Argentina's exportable surplus as a new workforce consumed beef and wheat. Import substitution worked in one sense: Argentina made more at home. But it had an adverse effect on commerce. Argentina failed to meet her quotas of beef for Britain from 1949 onwards, and the balance of trade got locked into adversity. The real impoverishment of the workers came in the postwar years, under a government elected in the labour interest: average real wages fell by 20 percent from 1948 to 1952.

Vainly trying to command the tide from the shore was one of the great charismatic politicians of the twentieth century, Juan Perón. He was born out of wedlock in 1895. His father was an evasive loser, a senator's disappointing son, who took refuge in small-time ranching, first in Lobos, then in Patagonia. Juan went into the army, but his career was desk-bound and dull as an instructor in the military academy, where he read much but thought little. He got political experience with the military regime that seized power in 1943, while building up a power-base of his own through a job which brought him into close touch with labour leaders. His biggest single asset was his mistress, tactfully transformed into a wife on the eve of the presidential election of 1946. Evita was a radio soap-star who had risen from poverty by talent abetted by physical allure. She was the darling of shirtless masses whose hopes and potential she was made to symbolize. After helping to mobilize a mass electorate in his favour, she became the power-broker of her husband's entourage and a secular Lady of Charity.

Perón, whose leadership style had much in common with European fascists and authoritarian dictators of the thirties, has been credited with a range of incompatible political philosophies. His own characterization of what he called "Justicialism" was typically self-contradictory: "Christian and humanist with the best attributes of collectivism and individualism, idealism and materialism." He was a working-class hero but seems to have been sincere when he promised employers that through "workers organized by the state . . . revolutionary currents endangering capitalist society can be neutralized." His emphasis on the catholic origins of his collectivism, with his genuine distaste for violent methods, seems to exonerate him from the charge of fascism. But as the policies of import-substitution failed, he relied increasingly on techniques of demagogy and personality cults to keep his hold on popularity. In 1950 he became "the Liberator" as well as "the leader;" in 1952 the dying Evita was proclaimed the nation's "Spiritual Chief," just in time to become the "Martyr of the Shirtless."

LEAL INTERPRETE
DE LOS "DESCAMISADOS"

Eva Perón and the Buenos Aires she helped to make. The poster, with braided hair and shining visage, presents the well-scrubbed image of a holy Magdalen, an icon with an unwanted past. The slogan, "The Faithful Voice of the 'Shirtless' Masses" encloses a pun. *Intérprete* means both "interpreter" and "actress"—an allusion to Evita's soap-opera career. The photograph of the busy Calle Corrientes was taken in 1958—about the last time, until the closing years of the Millennium, when Buenos Aires projected a really up-to-date look by European or North American standards, with tramlines, smart cars, modernist architecture, and the meretricious billboards.

Though his rhetoric and constituency were his own, Perón followed, in essence, his predecessors' policies of industrialization and import-substitution. Attempts to exonerate him by arraigning his conservative precursors, or vice versa, were equally flawed. Peronists liked to blame a mythical alliance of foreign exploiters and quisling capitalists: beef barons who mortgaged the people's food to British imperialists. To escape, Argentina had to unprise the tentacles of the British "octopus." The analysis dominated some of the toughest work of Argentine intellectuals in the late thirties. Raúl Scalabrini published scathing exposés of collaborationism in Britain's informal empire, and Mario Scofficio's film, *Kilómetro III*, depicted British railroad-monopolists frustrating a road-building programme to enforce low farm prices: the stationmaster who helps the farmers get their wheat to market loses his job.

Others looked for longer-term trends. Some of the most popular explanations have diffused the blame among Argentines of every class and over long aeons of history. Count Keyserling (1880–1946), the Nordic Swami, repudiated by Argentine followers of his mystical philosophy for daring to criticize their country, had even blamed the "telluric spirit" of Argentina—something in the soil which made failure inevitable. This was an analysis worthy of, and perhaps indebted to, Buffon and De Pauw (see Chapter 8). In what Carlos Gálvez called "the new Babel," even a bad "national character" flattered a people who were unsure of their ability to forge a common identity among immigrants: Ortega y Gasset found Argentines disqualified from greatness by "ferocious appetite," indiscipline, narcissism, and incompetence. One of the first native analysts of failure was the "radiographer of the pampa," Ezequiel Martínez Estrada, who, in an influential work of 1933, pronounced his country condemned by defects of birth: a combination of accursed geography and hereditary Spanish vices.

Other popular culprits have included the church—blamed for everything from terrorism to military coups—and an unstable political culture, traced, according to the prejudices of the investigator, to an anti-constitutional colonial legacy or to the effects of "revolutionary illegitimacy." A sententious thread runs through most explanations: Argentines blame themselves; their moral inadequacies are responsible; failure is a sort of divine scourge. "Argentina offered limitless wealth and countless opportunities," according to a characteristic exposition. "The future did not require any personal sacrifice or responsibility on the part of each Argentine." Sometimes a particular defect was blamed: gaucho *machismo*, for instance, or the personal anarchy allegedly inherited from Spanish forebears, or the racial degeneracy supposedly introduced by immigrants.

In this, as in many other ways, Argentina's modern history is a minatory lesson to the world. Among the countries of recent settlement, such as Australia, New Zealand, and the North American midwest, with their advantages of soil and climate, she seemed shamefully to have squandered her opportunities. To peoples classifiable in popular, late twentieth-century categories, like "the third world" and "the south," she appears as an admonitory case of arrested development, never able to mature into a fully developed nation or great power. In the context of other countries around the edge of the Atlantic, she looks like a victim of the decline of Atlantic civilization— over-dependent on a fragile transatlantic link, in this case principally with Britain. In all three contexts, the tendency to see failure as a moral issue is equally dangerous: it draws attention away from adjustable problems of politics and economics and starts self-fulfilling prophecies of doom. In Argentina, intellectual apprehension of failure preceded and perhaps precipitated the event. Her vital partner, Britain, with whose problems her own were so closely bound, is another case of a country which talked itself into decline.

John Bull's Second Childhood

One source of evidence is on my drawing-room wall: a series of cartoons drawn by the "Tory anarchist" Max Beerbohm in 1901, when, stuck in an uncongenial job as a drama critic, he was feeling bitterly disgusted with his fellow-countrymen. Max was an aesthetic boulevardier who hated vulgarity and philistinism. The hatred showed in his depictions of John Bull, the epitome of England, staring uncomprehendingly at paintings, sneering at the Muses, and condescending to Kipling.

England is shown as unpleasantly ageing, gouty, tipsy, somnolent. John Bull has worse traits than philistinism: he turns a fat behind on suffering Ireland. He chuckles maliciously at the battles of high and low churchmen. But he is, even more than contemptible, pathetic. With cobwebs in his hat, he reminisces inaccurately about the Elizabethan age and the American War of Independence. In his role as the new sick man of Europe he pretends only to be visiting hospital. He fawns on Germany and clings—prophetically, for 1901—to America's coat-tails. He yields to a pervasive feeling that he is done for. The Muse of memory is seen "pressing the English Rose between the pages of History." In a cartoon captioned "Saint George and the Dragon—Revised Version," a pair of spurred and armoured legs disappears down the dragon's maw.

By the time the caricatures were published in 1911, Max regretted their savagery. They expressed, however, a widely shared anxiety. In the last three decades of the nineteenth century, frustration or anger at Britain's perceived decline became a persistent tic in writers who compared her measurable strengths with those of competitors—especially with Germany and the United States. This was precisely the period in which British domi-

Max Beerbohm's St. George and the Dragon (Revised Version), drawn in 1901 but not published until 1911. St. George was the chosen image, in popular art, of English virtues, who wielded the sword and lance of the British Empire against the dragon of barbarism. Beerbohm's new version expresses the undermined self-confidence of a people who had talked themselves into decline.

nation of world trade was at its height and British imperialism at its most successful. This very success seemed to feed the pessimists with their cues and to incense the oracles to pronouncements of doom. British supremacy had been recognized as fragile almost from the moment of its emergence. In 1851, when the world was gaping at the first great universal exhibition at the Crystal Palace, which displayed the dominance of British industry and invention, *The Economist* announced the forthcoming superiority of the United States, "ultimately as certain as the next eclipse." The habit of dating the decline of Britain from the days of her most conspicuous greatness, begun by contemporaries, has been continued by historians.

The blight was in the eyes of the beholders. Almost every measurable indicator cited to demonstrate decline was misread or, at best, exaggerated. National income continued to rise during the late nineteenth century and up to the First World War. Though all Britain's competitors tended to catch up in relative terms, they still lagged behind in absolute terms. Output per head in Britain fell in the early years of the twentieth century but recovered spectacularly in the immediate pre-war period. The disproportionate scale

of British investment abroad was indicted for impoverishing domestic industry but was also evidence of enormous surplus wealth and a means of
nurturing new markets for the future. Free trade was a policy bitterly contested, not least because among its consequences was an adverse balance
of trade for Britain—a bleakly unique distinction among industrialized
countries on the eve of the world war. On the other hand, it was the basis
of British prosperity and the essential context of Britain's earnings from
shipping and financial services, which more than made up the deficit.
Judged by scale of public investment and measured results, German education seemed to dwarf Britain's for much of the period, with ominous implications for the future fitness of the workforce and the future progress of
research. But the strengths of British education, often informal or privately
funded, tended to slip out of the statistics, and even in the measured sectors there was an amazing recovery to levels close to Germany's in the
years preceding the war.

Not only did English education get measurably better, it rallied for practical ends. The value system taught in English schools in the late nineteenth
century has been condemned for producing "a race of innocents, dedicated
to romantic ideals" and incapable of enforcing and defending its power.
"Fair play"—that untranslatably English virtue—is said to have condemned
Britain to defeat by those who played only to win. Yet, considered from a
different angle, the ethos of team games suitably toughened an imperial
master-class. The reeling, rolling road of English history led from Plymouth
Ho through the playing-fields of Eton to Clifton Close. When "the regi-
ment's blind with dust and smoke . . . the voice of a schoolboy rallies the
ranks." The lessons learned by heroes of school stories really did play a
part in winning British victories or sustaining British effort in defeat: the
conviction of effortless superiority over foreigners; the cults of "pluck" and
of coolness in a crisis; confidence in the underdog's chances of triumph;
the deification of the gifted amateur. The English talent for inculcating altruism without emasculation was brilliantly demonstrated by the foundation of
the Boy Scout movement in 1907. While eschewing militarism as a nastily
foreign kind of "beastliness" and making a sort of religion of fair play, the
Boy Scouts practised woodcraft and fought off anaemia in spartan biv-
ouacs. They united gang spirit and team spirit, becoming the "janissaries of
the empire" and, in the prime minister's opinion, potentially "the greatest
moral force the world has ever known."

Prophets of decline, however, are not easily comforted and its historians
are hard to dissuade. Statistics can be infinitely reinterpreted and challenged; convictions of moral corrosion, of some rotten wormwood in the
state, are beyond the reach of reason. The founder of the Boy Scout movement, Robert Baden-Powell—a Peter Pan case of perpetuated boyhood
who became the youngest general in the British Army—was driven by a

"The greatest moral force the world has ever known." A Boy Scout troop photographed in 1910, two years after Baden-Powell had inaugurated the continuous history of the movement with the publication of *Scouting for Boys* and a camp in Northumbria where boys were set on a "Quest for King Arthur," who, according to Baden-Powell, "lies asleep in some hidden cave in the neighbourhood." The Boy Scouts were no mere militaristic youth movement: there was a subversive individualism about Baden-Powell's values and an emphasis—reflecting the founder's South African experiences—on the inspirational tactics of the guerrilla and the guide. It was also intended to transcend social barriers—mixing the classes in camps and making "gentlemen," defined as "anyone who carries out the rules of chivalry," of disadvantaged boys.

fear of incipient British degeneracy, signposted by welfare doles, class barriers, luxury, crime, and strikes. Even before it happened, English failure was ascribed to the enfeebling effects of empire, the snobbery of the élite, and the idleness of the proletariat. A series of unverifiable propositions was advanced then and repeated to this day: the empire encouraged a parasitical bureaucracy and smothered competitiveness in "soft" markets; anticommercial values starved industry of competent managers; workers responded in kind to the selfishness or indifference of other classes, or refined extremes of "bloody-mindedness" of their own.

These moral explanations of the English predicament derived not from the observed realities of the time but rather from the received conventions

of a literary tradition. The Bible was one source which predisposed its readers to expect to pay a political price for their moral shortcomings. Renaissance humanism had associated the decline of politics—and, in particular,
the fall of that exemplary empire, the Roman state—with enfeebling vices:
prowess enervated by despotism, virtue corrupted by ease. The British in
the late nineteenth and early twentieth centuries, conscious of their roles as
the Rome and Israel of the modern age, naturally expected the same sort of
change of fortune to befall them. Arnold White, explaining to himself and
other Englishmen their inefficiency in fighting the Boers, blamed the selfishness and irreligion of the élite, which, he claimed, spread its impropri-
eties through society: "the influence of a bad smart society," idleness,
dishonour, and untruthfulness were the pimples of this highly contagious
moral pox.

Objective evidence of the particular failings attributed to Englishmen by
historians of Britain's decline is hard to find, but history is moulded more
by the falsehoods men believe than by the facts that can be verified. Aware,
at one level, that by every measurable criterion Britain was the most heavily
industrialized state in the world—and always had been since the start of the
industrial revolution—the designers of the British pavilion at the Paris exposition of 1937 regaled visitors with a cardboard cut-out of the prime minister in fishing waders against a bucolic landscape with "not a single factory
chimney." The most famous speech of the preceding premier equated England with "the countryside," resonant with "the tinkle of the anvil in the
country smithy." These were a grown industrial giant's dreams of rural infancy, but the self-image British opinion-makers projected became the reality others perceived. Britons' own assumptions about the depths of their
decline were repeated at home and echoed abroad. A decline is equally un-
nerving, whether it is objectively real or only perceived. During and after
the Second World War, Britain was the victim of a self-evaluation which incited her enemies and depressed her own people.

Her lumberings and flailings in distress were those of a "troubled giant."
There were genuine problems for a country of limited manpower defending a vast and vulnerable empire, for "the first industrial nation" keeping up
with the need to innovate, for a commercial world-leader adjusting from
absolute supremacy to relative superiority. Early industrialization had bequeathed upriver shipyards, with steelyards over expiring ores. Commitment to heavy industries of the "heroic age" could not easily be reversed
nor the extemporized working practices of an experimental era revised.
Weakness in key fields of relatively late development, like electrical engineering and chemicals, was only slowly and imperfectly overcome. Oil—an
increasingly important source of energy—was in short supply from dangerously exposed sources. Yet British industry's recuperative and adaptive
powers were amply demonstrated in the crises of the 1930s and 1940s. The

collapse of world-power status and the precipitate imperial retreat were not the result of a long decline—except in self-esteem—but the sudden consequence of the peculiar circumstances of the Second World War, which overtaxed the resources of a still-mighty power.

Even in the second half of the twentieth century the relative decline of Britain was only made absolute in places ill-favoured by history, where outmoded industries could not be replaced, or on the Atlantic edge, where slicks from the ocean's spilled fortunes were washed ashore. Both kinds of predicament were concentrated in Liverpool, a once-great city which became, in the 1980s, a byword for urban disaster in Britain, a British Buenos Aires, the enemy of its own promise. In the mid-nineteenth century, that promise seemed irresistibly great; the eighteenth-century city, made by transatlantic trades in slaves and wine, had disappeared under layers of newer prosperity, provided by cotton and timber. Rebuilt according to the values of "busy, noisy, smoky, money-getting merchants," Liverpool had "no monument of antiquity, no mark of decay." A popular novelist in 1851, summarizing the growth he had witnessed in his day, proclaimed that thanks to "commerce guided by a wise and liberal policy" Liverpool "vies with some of the proudest cities in the world." The tonnage handled by its port almost equalled London's. It acquired slums to match its splendours—breeding-grounds of typhus, cholera, relapsing fever, and smallpox, where, according to a tenant of the 1860s, "the stench would raise the roof of your skull." The intimacy with which the crammed, cluttered magnificence of Victorian Liverpool was connected with Atlantic shipping and imperial communications can be sampled today in the saloon bar of the Philharmonic public house on Hope Street, built by ships' carpenters of tropical hardwood and surrounded by images of exotic flora and fauna in gilt and copper.

The first half of the twentieth century was a period of climacteric but not of decline. The centripetal city was fragmented by railways and tramways and motor buses, by suburban sprawl and by the incorporation of outlying towns. The representative new buildings of the era were the dazzling cinemas, the hundred "dream palaces" built between the First and Second World wars, scattered to be within walking distance for dwellers in suburbs and inner city alike. With their lavish décors—debased empire or glitzy art déco—and their glittering windows onto exotic celluloid worlds, the cinemas offered ordinary people a cheap share of some of the spectacular rewards of material progress.

After 1945, Liverpool lost an empire without finding a role. Some means of recourse were home-grown, like the Mersey Sound developed by the Beatles in the early 1960s which helped to make Liverpool, briefly, a worldrenowned breeding ground of popular bands, recruited from among underemployed young men who had plenty of time to practise. Other

The exotica and tableaux of colonial produce which decorated the Philharmonic in Liverpool appeared in public house décor more generally. This painted mirror is part of a rich scheme, vaguely imitated from French and Dutch rococo prototypes, in The Tottenham, Oxford Street, London, designed in 1890.

"Grass between the cobbles": the desolation of Liverpool, photographed for the French press in December 1985. "Is there still hope for Liverpool?" the original caption asked.

sources of relief came from outside, like the "inner city renewal" programme financed by central government to tackle the causes or mask the
effects of riots by the slum-bound unemployed in the 1980s. Others were
collaborative, like the local education policy which made Liverpool Britain's
"most computer-literate city" in 1990. But even these impressive activities
were consequences of or concessions to decline. Between the mid-fifties
and the mid-seventies, the population fell by a third. In 1981 the slum-
dwellers rioted. In 1985 the treasury was bankrupt, with a socialist council
reduced to distributing redundancy notices by taxi; local government had
to be suspended to get the graves dug and the streets swept. A returnee to
emptied docklands in 1987 found "no people about, no children playing,
just silence like a desert . . . and grass between the cobbles."

THE MATURE YEARS OF MARIANNE

Over much the same period as Britain, France was the home of a society in
self-styled "decline" with plenty of internal critics who were quick to condemn national morale. During the Third Republic, nationalists accused their
fellow-countrymen of "an almost Muslim fatalism" and "willingness to be
raped," while psychiatrists "related nervous exhaustion to a decadent civilisation." Hard-earned victory in the First World War silenced or muted these
reproaches; until well into the 1930s France seemed, on paper, again to be
easily the greatest military power in western Europe. But as that superiority
crumbled and Hitler rearmed, jittery morale was exhibited in the "naked
panic" of queues outside the banks in 1938. Prostration under the tracks of
German tanks in 1940 was attributed at the time, by observers of unchallengeable integrity and intelligence, to the "moral decadence" of the nation,
the "lost fraternity" of wartime, and the "lack of heroism" of the élite.

With even greater precision for France than for Britain, the year 1870 was
the starting-point of the sense of decline. Though chastened in the Franco-
Prussian War by defeat at the hands of an army less numerous and worse-
equipped than her own, France was still a great power, with military
potential unlimited by treaty and an overseas empire intact; but the political
consequences of her defeat included the unification under Prussian leadership of a German state with a population which soon exceeded her own.
This was a case of relative decline, dramatically concentrated in time. As an
artist, Emile Zola needed the defeat. It inspired the culminating volume in a
twenty-volume cycle of novels, which took twenty-two years to write and
in which are portrayed, through the fortunes of a family, the social history
and morbid anatomy of France. *La Débâcle* was intended as "a document
on the psychology of France" as well as a novel of *vérité humaine,* depicting "battlefields without chauvinism" and "the real sufferings of the soldier."

Zola, who was turned down for a place in the National Guard because of his short-sightedness, brought to a tale of vicarious experience the heartfelt pain of personal guilt. He attacked the research with battlefield élan and produced an outstanding work of oral history.

His most vivid material was supplied by a field surgeon. This was the source of the realism Zola deployed in the service of symbolism, in horrible hospital scenes and sickening evocations of decaying dead, gangrenous wounded, and frenzied amputations. The most explicitly symbolic moment is revealed to two characters who stumble on a party of French soldiers, apparently picnicking in the open air. Seen closer up,

> Les deux zouaves, raidis, les mains tordues, n'avaient plus de visage, le nez arraché, les yeux sautés des orbites. Le rire de celui qui se tenait le ventre venait de ce qu'une balle lui avait fendu les lèvres, en lui cassant les dents. . . . S'étaient-ils traînés à cette place, vivants encore, pour mourir ensemble? Etaient-ce plutôt les prussiens qui avaient fait la farce de les ramasser, puis de les asseoir, en rond, par une moquerie de la vieille gaieté française?

> [The two zouaves had gone stiff. Their hands were awkwardly cocked. They had no faces left—noses were blown away, eyes had dropped from their sockets. The smile on the face of the one who was clutching his stomach was the result of getting a bullet between his lips, smashing his teeth. . . . Had they dragged themselves to this place, while still not quite dead, in order to die together? Or had the Prussians done it for a burlesque: picking them up and sitting them round the table in mockery of the famous old conviviality of the French?]

Already celebrated for the realism of his description of suppurating cheese, Zola was unbeatable in the depiction of the wounds or the evocation of the horrors of war. Unbeatable, that is, in fiction; true stories of atrocities and cannibalism generated by the war were even more horrible.

By the time the book appeared in 1892 it was no longer solely or, in effect, chiefly an indictment of the decadence of the regime which had ended in 1870 but of the republic which succeeded it. Readers such as Anatole France—then in his forties and still at an early stage of his own fame—read that message in it or into it. Nervous self-doubt in the recollection of the defeat was betrayed by nationalists who denounced it for its frank portrayal of French failure or praised it for its brutal record of German atrocities. The historical accuracy of Zola's backgrounds was meticulously debated by critics with unpleasantly jolted memories. His Italian ancestry was blamed for the lack of a patriotic tone. The nation had been caught out in the collective practice of escape, like Napoleon III, in one of the most controversial images of La Débâcle, rouging his cheeks to mask his pallor.

Considered from one point of view, French self-doubt appears as the consequence of a very long history. Since the mid-fifteenth century, France had been western Europe's largest, most populous and—for most of the time—best-unified state, with an enviable concentration of natural resources and access to both the Atlantic and the Mediterranean. Yet she had been beaten to the rewards of imperial expansion, first by Spain and Portugal, then by Holland and England. All attempts to win continental hegemony had been buried: their epitaphs were written in the treaties of Câteau-Cambrésis (1558), Utrecht (1714), and Vienna (1815). The cultural hegemony established in the eighteenth century, which was an abiding source of solace to French pride whenever economic and political fortunes were low, was already being challenged from Germany even before German political unification. After 1870, however, France seemed to have lost for ever the chance to fulfil the elusive destiny which geography had proposed and history denied. United Germany, with a population equal to France's at the creation of the Reich, grew to a superiority of nearly 50 per cent by 1914.

Under this alarming shadow, the French succumbed to the same paradox as their British neighbours: anxiety about decline in a period of unparalleled material success and imperial expansion. Under-industrialization was the peculiarly French form of the disease of perceived failure (see Chapter 12). French industry collectively seemed to reflect a lack of seriousness or commitment, typified by Jules Siegfried, the enormously successful and innovative textiles manufacturer who engraved "To work is to act" on his cuff-links but retired in 1880, at the age of forty-four, to practise public service in politics and charity. In fact, by standards of measurement in vogue today, industrialization was just about as fast and thorough after 1896 in France as anywhere. Thereafter, until the First World War, steel production nearly trebled and that of textiles nearly doubled. But, as in Britain, real achievements did little to abate the anxieties induced by the success of competitors.

A traveller in France can map the incidence of relative decline as he travels from west to east. From the great ports of the early-modern period, such as Nantes, Saint-Malo, and Bordeaux, to the industrial cities of the interior, such as Clermont-Ferrand, Lille, and Metz, one seems to travel in time between the eighteenth and nineteenth centuries. Sometimes this is the result of development which stopped altogether in declining Atlantic ports—as in Saint-Malo. More normally, as in Nantes and Bordeaux, development continued in the nineteenth century at a diminished level, and earlier streets and buildings were unobliterated by change.

Lille, most perhaps of all French cities, was remodelled by the nineteenth century. The old Bourse, a surviving wing of the town hall, and the citadel built by Vauban show that it had a distinguished eighteenth century, of

French cityscapes from contrasting vantage-points. Lille is photographed along the Boulevard de la Liberté, looking away from the monumental centre towards the grimy industrial rim of factory-stacks beyond the spires. The Place de la Carrière in Nancy shelters behind eighteenth-century elegance in a picture which cuts out the huge industrial wen all around.

which, however, little more remains. Beyond the gardens, under the citadel, is a quarter rebuilt after the war of 1870. It laps the Palais Rameau, a "people's palace" of leisure and culture, and envelops the Collège de Saint-Joseph, the Eglise du Sacré-Coeur, and the Catholic University with its steep, Flemish skyline. From here the Boulevard de la Liberté was thrust south-west through the old town like a precisely machined piston, towards the massive Palais des Beaux-Arts of the late 1880s, at the centre, and the ponderous main square and the railway stations beyond. This rebuilding reflected a concentrated boom in Lille's fortunes: in the middle of the century, it was a town of 75,000 people; by the outbreak of the war in 1870 it had grown and incorporated its own growing satellites to number nearly a quarter of a million inhabitants.

Whether to rebuild in such a thorough and expansive fashion was of course a matter of aesthetic judgement and civic spirit as well as economic opportunity. Nancy is another *enfant prodige* of the nineteenth century, essentially created in its present form by the aftermath of the Franco-Prussian War, when refugees doubled the size of this one Lotharingian city which remained French. But its eighteenth-century heart of elegant plazas was too ethereally beautiful and too intimately connected with civic memories of the sovereign past of Lorraine to be expunged by new development. So Nancy today has an eighteenth-century kernel in a nineteenth-century husk, and the legacy of her pre-industrial artisanate—the elegant iron railings of the Place de la Carrière—are tipped with gold leaf. For most cities on the Atlantic coast, however, the choice available in the industrial northeast did not arise.

Brest is the exception; her role as a naval base set her apart. She had little to conserve, nothing to lose, and no civic character to assert, and so was rebuilt in an ugly, disorderly manner. The most representative case is that of Bordeaux, for no French city has had a history so intimately linked with that of Atlantic trade, since the 1730s, when she took the lead from Nantes in all colonial traffic except slaves. In about fifty years the tonnage through her port doubled and its value quintupled. She linked the world's most productive centres of coffee- and sugar-cultivation in the French Antilles with the world's most buoyant markets in western Europe. She had the large and diverse immigrant population that is the hallmark of a boom town, comprising examples of every type of fortune from Charles Kunckel, a Dutch Protestant who arrived in 1786 with 25,000 *livres* of capital, to the pair of Parisian pickpockets who were foolish enough to steal a constable's watch on 6 January 1785.

Against this background it was possible for Aubert de Tourny in 1746 to proclaim his plan to transform the city he governed "into the most beautiful in the kingdom in four or five years." All such ambitions are overoptimistic, and in 1754, Tourny had Bordeaux engraved in the image of his

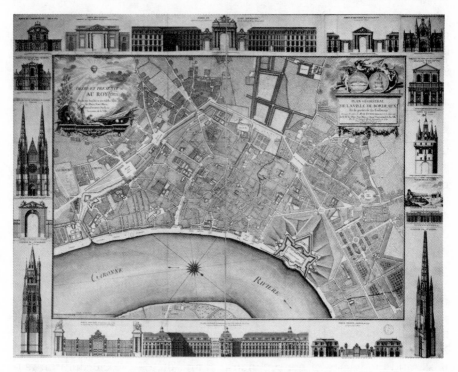

The Plan de Lattrè. Bordeaux as Aubert Tourny wanted it to be in 1754. The Place Royale is shown in elevation along the bottom. Notice the hint of nascent romanticism in the middle of the margin on the right: the effect of a ruined cloister adorning the public gardens.

plans in case he should die before finishing the job. He did have time, however, to reslice the city along enlightened lines. He replaced the old walls with spacious promenades, began a delicately baroque oval piazza, and extended into adjoining spaces the symmetry and equipoise of the Place Royale, which he had inherited from his predecessor. The taste of the next generation was more severely neoclassical, but the reshaping of the city continued in the same spirit. The building which is always said to sum up the character of enlightened Bordeaux is the Grand Théâtre of the 1770s, which set a new fashion for theatre buildings, reverting to an ancient and Renaissance type: a temple rather than a palace, behind a dense and elaborate colonnade.

Bordeaux's prosperity was a casualty of the revolutionary and Napoleonic wars of 1792–1815. Successive ill winds blew the ships out of the Gironde: the slave revolution and independence of Haiti; the French retreat from New World empire; the continental system; the British blockades; the loss of more colonies in the peace settlement. In the 1820s the last phase of the great urban reforms inaugurated by Tourny was completed in the Place de Quinconces, where pillars dedicated to Navigation and Commerce stared forlornly over the sluggish river.

The Bordelais thalassocracy scoured the world for new outlets. In 1819 the emperor of Annam inspected a cargo at Hue; places in the China Seas acquired the names of Bordelais families and vessels. Senegal and New Caledonia became common destinations. It is hard to assign a date to the recovery of Bordeaux's fortunes, in part because new projects never stopped, they simply took longer to mature and yielded less spectacular rewards than in the previous century. By comparison, the entire nineteenth century is commonly characterized as a *"temps de l'immobilisme."* From 1860, however, three circumstances combined to restore conspicuous growth to the city: the long, cumulative growth of the wine trade; the eventual fulfilment in that year of a long-frustrated project to bring the railway to Bordeaux; and the choice of the port to be the terminus of the South American packet-boat route.

The last generation of the nineteenth century was disfigured by slumps and blighted by phylloxera, but the character of Bordeaux was transformed in an almost continuous process of economic diversification, which filled its crevices with new industries and coated its crust with suburbs. By 1912, old Bordeaux faced, across the Gironde, a second city of chemical factories, food-processing plants, and builders' yards. "A swamp of low houses" surrounded its monumental centre. Its development was never fast or furious enough to hustle away the eighteenth-century urban heritage, but it set a sustainable pace of enrichment and growth. Although Bordeaux's history is remarkably similar to Liverpool's, there is no reflection here of the urban dereliction, economic stagnation, and social catastrophe that Liverpool reaped from Atlantic decline.

Walking in Bordeaux between the railway buffers and the Atlantic shore, you can sense how the railways tugged at Atlantic commerce—creating new opportunities and broadening the range of markets and suppliers, of course, but also setting up rival routes which diminished the relative importance of the seaways. Until railways came, except in the selective areas favoured by navigable rivers and canals, there was no long-range alternative to the sea for bulk goods. The system which reached Bordeaux in 1860 was dense in the quadrilateral bounded by Paris, Lille, Mulhouse, and Clermont-Ferrand, but it stretched only tentative limbs towards the Atlantic at Cherbourg, Rennes, and Saint-Nazaire. The distribution of the railheads was determined as much by strategic as economic considerations, but their effect was in part to draw business away from the ocean. The abiding effects show in a map of French Railways' plans for electrification in the mid-1950s: almost all the high-voltage lines are in the north-east. Observable, as it were, in miniature in France, the same phenomenon, on a vaster scale, dragged the centres of gravity of Europe and North America respectively east and west as the great transcontinental railways took shape.

THE MAGGOT IN THE APPLE

For a long time they called it the "Empty State Building." The skyscraper which came to symbolize New York was begun at the end of the city's most self-indulgent era. The twenties were a decade of unrestrained consumption, typified by the flamboyant life of Mayor Jimmy Walker, whose motto was "Never go to bed on the same day you wake up" and who was ousted in 1932 for graft. The start of work on the Empire State Building coincided with the abrupt end of the holiday decade in the Wall Street Crash of 1929 (see Chapter 16). The slump saved the contractors $20 million—nearly a third of the projected construction costs. Glutted with cheap labour and ready materials, the building rocketed up at an average rate of one storey every four and a half days.

The only shortage was of tenants. The building did not reach full occupancy until 1942. The projectors' hope of bringing workers in by daily airships, moored to the roof, was dispelled by lightning and high winds. Shame and oblivion threatened, but in 1933 the building suddenly became a *succès d'estime* when its summit was made the refuge of a fictional giant gorilla in the film *King Kong*. Like its fellow–New Yorker, the Statue of Liberty (see Chapter 13), it represents a triumph of hope over experience. It has only two floors' depth of foundations, but Manhattan's solid rock base has held up its 102 stories. Even when it was overtaken as the world's tallest building, it retained its grip on the affections of tourists and the imaginations of beholders. The World Trade Center at the south end of the island rises higher but is less conspicuous and has never rivalled the Empire State Building in the impression it makes. A 1976 remake of *King Kong* which used the WTC for its climax was a flop.

Like its most representative building, New York has shown astonishing resilience in disaster. Like Liverpool, its early fortunes depended on transatlantic trade but it also had privileged access to a huge continental hinterland. Between a deep ocean and a broad land, a big threshold was required, and during the first half of the nineteenth century New York became incomparably the biggest city in the United States. The population topped a million during the 1850s, when New York handled over a third of the country's exports and nearly two-thirds of her imports. Though lack of space and water power limited the growth and range of industries inside the city, the environs filled with enterprises dependent on New York's unrivalled harbour, which became the centre of "a symbiotic network of specialised communities."

Civilization at the mercy of savagery. The poster for the RKO cinema production of King Kong (1933), which dwarfed New York to chillingly vulnerable proportions, should be compared with Goya's vision of the peril of war, p. 489.

In the last third of the nineteenth century, New Yorkers evinced some of the same unease as their French and British partners in Atlantic prosperity; the city's leading paper in 1874 felt "haunted by the spectre of decline." One objective measure seemed to support these fears: from 1869 to 1900, New York's share of U.S. external trade, and even her share of the Atlantic trade of the north-east, fell year by year, cut by a structure of rail freight charges which favoured Philadelphia and Baltimore. But the overall expansion of trade, the immigrant traffic (see Chapter 13), and the unchallenged role of New York in supplying what would later be called corporate services to America created the New York of the new century: an image of beauty and terror, of urban dynamism and diversity thrust to their limits. H. G. Wells, who saw it in 1906, was staggered by "the unprecedented multitudinousness, the inhuman force of the thing" and thought it was "more beautiful than Rome." But he also sensed its fragility and in a novel of 1908 imagined it exploding under aerial bombardment in a futuristic war.

"Aerial Attack on New York," an illustration to H. G. Wells's *The War in the Air* (1908): "as the airships sailed along," reads the text at this point, "they smashed up the city as a child will shatter its cities of brick and card."

After the Second World War, New York might have escaped the relative decline which befell Atlantic-side centres, thanks to the city's elevation as a sort of world capital, housing in Manhattan the headquarters of the General Assembly and Security Council of the United Nations. Fortified with the financial institutions of Wall Street, New York seemed proof against the fates of a Liverpool or a Buenos Aires. Yet the marks of decline soon began to show. Between 1950 and 1970, in what became known as "the Great White flight," a million families moved out of New York. Though most of the loss was replaced by Blacks and migrants from East Asia, the effect on municipal income was calamitous. Population stabilized, then fell. By 1975 the city's debts had accumulated to $13 billion. Though private consortia intervened under the state government to mitigate the effects of civic bankruptcy, decaying public works and ill-kempt streets became part of the city's popular image.

The momentum of a glorious past seemed to carry New York through the crisis; in the 1970s and 1980s it was possible for Donald Trump and Leona Helmsley, property speculators of bad taste, to earn millions from selective bets on urban renewal. While manufacturing withered, banking, corporate services, and computer-borne industries surged in a worldwide boom. Ed Koch (mayor, 1977–86) balanced the books and could claim convincingly that "the future comes here to rehearse," before his administration collapsed amid the ruined lives, prison sentences, nervous breakdowns, and suicides of corrupt members of his entourage.

At a lower social level, measurable evidence of deprivation—poverty, welfare claims, the despairing clamour of public charities, violence, sickness, and mortality—all got relentlessly worse. During the Koch administration, the lowest 20 per cent of citizens' incomes fell substantially in real terms, while the uppermost 10 per cent increased by more than a fifth. New York became the schizoid city depicted in Tom Wolfe's *Bonfire of the Vanities,* riven by poor ghettos where the well-to-do dared not go. Cheap cocaine was the fuel of an unprecedented, jump-jet take-off of violent street crime from 1986. In 1990, when one New Yorker in four was officially classified as poor by national standards, the city was running an annual budget deficit of $1.3 billion.

Liverpool and New York rose together, and it would not be surprising if they were to fall together. But Metropolis is the home of Superman and is used to being saved against the odds. New York has every hope of long outlasting Atlantic civilization. Its information-intensive industries equip it for the post-industrial era. Even at its least lively moments, it is full of carrion for culture-vultures—libraries, museums, galleries, theatres, music-venues, studios, publishing houses, and élite schools. It could no more be allowed to crumble than Venice to sink. Its banking and corporate service sectors are tied by reins to the economy of the world: It is one of the three or four eyes of the sleepless monster of commerce—the others stare from sockets in London, Tokyo, and perhaps Los Angeles, "spanning and scanning the world in a twenty-four-hour sequence of shifts." It needs to stay where it is: in a complementary time zone. The Atlantic-side position, however, which made and sustained New York's greatness, has become an irrelevancy.

Chapter 18

LIFE AFTER EMPIRES:
DECOLONIZATION AND
COUNTER-COLONIZATION

The Hives of Aladdin—The Roots of the Mikongoe Tree—The Feasts of Monsters—The Monument to Our Struggle—The Shade of the Banyan—The Fate of the New Europes—The European Reflex

THE HIVES OF ALADDIN

Under rainy skies in a run-down suburb, a pair of squat, broad towers of Mughal flavour, hooped with folds of mouldings, crown a hilltop parapet. Opposite, across a low-slung concrete walkway, the Eastern Kayam Carpet Company exhibits its wares in a man-made cavern, where rugs hang in shy colours—industrial or antiqued—showering weaves over tightly knotted matting. The firm's vast exhibition hall is embellished outside with a heavy, angular colonnade and a frieze of lions' head-masks.

As the gaze broadens, then lingers to focus on details, the illusion of stepping into an oddly placed oriental Disneyland is dispelled by scenes of scruffy dereliction. There are piles of rubbish under the formidable, scowling porticoes of the neighbouring buildings, held up by girders and lengths of patio-wall. Behind a yellowing pediment, a once-huge basilica has been demolished but not cleared. Danger signs and crepitus doors lead across a cracked car park, past a rusting bus, to a chapel's pitted shell, sketchily painted inside with slicks of sickly green. The lions' heads, of which there are dozens, perhaps scores, are eroded into pantomime masks—growling maws worn into toothless smiles.

No emblem could be more apt. For this is Wembley, and these buildings are almost all that is left of the 220-acre site of the great Empire Exhibition of 1924, which celebrated, for 27 million visitors, the British Empire at its height. Here the King-Emperor George V—in a Palace of Engineering "six and a half times the size of Trafalgar Square," beside a statue of his son made life-size of Canadian butter—demonstrated the reach and range of his people's power with a gesture almost as economical as a twitch of Jove's eyebrow: he sent a cable message to himself, which circled the world along British wires, laid overland exclusively on imperial territory, before arriving back at its starting-point twenty-eight seconds later.

Today no barefoot friars sing in these ruins, but a new Gibbon would see new barbarians, mufflered and bobble-hatted or hobnailed and drunk, whenever a major football match brings shouting crowds to the stadium. The Eastern Kayam company, wholesaling industrial copies of tribal products from some of the vanished empire's remotest subjects, is an ironically fitting tenant of the space. For decolonization has been followed by counter-colonization. The heartlands of Europe's former world empires have been invaded by their erstwhile victims, and the ecological consequences of the imperial age—the effects of migration and disease and of the rededication of soils—are being reversed or redirected.

The "ecological imperialism" of a former age spread the "biological expansion of Europe" into regions remote from the imperialists' homelands, as European biota transformed environments, European microbes destroyed peoples, European tools flattened landscapes, and European settlers extended the range of their conformable habitats. White faces became dominant where they had never before been seen (see Chapter 14). Some of these changes are irreversible, and some of the processes are still going on. You can see them in a concentrated instance in the Senegalese breakfast—once a mixture of millet couscous and vegetables, now a slice of wheaten bread dipped in a solution of powdered milk and powdered coffee. Yams, millet, sorghum, cassava, white maize, beans, and plantains are dropping out of a regional ecosystem where they were formerly the most important foods. On the opposite shore of the Atlantic, rain forest continues to be felled, hectares for hamburgers. Yet, at the same time, taste for tropical dishes and for exotic and creole cuisines is colonizing western palates. Demand for fibrous, starchy, and protein-rich plants, unhonoured in their own countries, is generated by notions of healthy eating fashionable in Europe and America.

Again, in the earlier age of world expansion, the export of killer diseases was all one way—out of Europe into environments where the natives had no resistance; syphilis, which was once thought to have been the great exception, is now known to have existed in pre-Columbian Europe, and its appearance in venereal form seems more likely to have been the result of

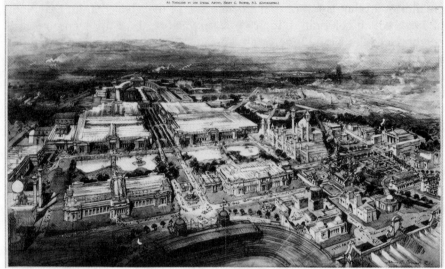

The eclectic empire. In the plan of the British Empire Exhibition of 1924, symmetrical order predominates and an absurd mixture of inspiration is disclosed. Canada's pavilion is described as "in a *néogrec* style," South Africa's (in the bottom right-hand corner) is "late seventeenth-century Dutch . . . New Zealand has an imposing façade in a simple type of English classic Renaissance and near it will be erected a beautifully carved Maori house." The Nigerian pavilion is surrounded with mud walls. The idea of exhibiting the Prince of Wales carved life-size in Canadian butter seems consistent with the spirit of the exhibition.

an evolutionary adaptation than of a transmission from the New World. To-day, AIDS has burst new out of Africa, via the bathhouses of San Francisco and the brothels of Bangkok, to threaten North America and Europe. Though its effects remain most virulent and apparently least containable in its home continent, it does represent—considered from one point of view—a grim form of retribution, showing that ecological traffic can carry a fatal virus to, as well as from, the White world.

Man tends to dominate any ecosystem of which he forms part, and colonists are the decisive warriors in any biological conquest. Foodstuffs and disease have contributed to the reversed direction of ecological ex-change, but human migrants are its principal vectors. And because, as Aris-totle said, man is, "by nature, a political and social animal," the counter-colonization which is eroding the White world today is inseparable from the decolonization—the retreat of imperial powers, the subversion of old élites, the withdrawal of intruded rulers—which has preceded and ac-companied it. The empires have decayed, while their former victims swarmed, and like the ruined halls of Wembley, the hollows of empire have filled with hives of exotic drones.

THE ROOTS OF THE MIKONGOE TREE

The White men's empires of the late nineteenth and early twentieth cen-turies played their tunes of glory mainly in Africa and south Asia—parts of the world protected by hostile environments where, for technical reasons, earlier White imperialisms could not reach. In these two zones, the imperial bandstands were dismantled, breath squeezed from the brass, the strings unplucked, at different rhythms by different destructive forces: Japanese conquest in Asia, in Africa "winds of change." In a terrible concentration of energy between 1941 and 1945, self-interested Japanese aggression drove White rulers out of British Burma and Malaya, French Indo-China, Dutch Indonesia, and the American Philippines. The United States, ruled by a Democratic Party that was always reluctant to undertake or support imperi-alism outside its own hemisphere, wanted Japanese power to be replaced by "independence," in a future imagined, through a nostalgic filter, as a reprise of America's own history. She set an example in the Philippines, handing power to an élite of ex-guerrilla leaders who had, at least, learned to talk the language of democracy with an American accent.

In other parts of the region the colonialists returned to abandon power gradually, with varying degrees of ill grace; the British stayed in Malaya long enough to impose a post-colonial regime to their taste; the French in Indo-China long enough to bury in defeat at nationalist hands the prestige they had returned to restore. The Dutch were too weak to hold on to Indonesia but kept western New Guinea detached from the new state as "a great and noble task" which "will help keep alive the spiritual urge without which no people can survive." That was still the common rhetoric of imperialism in its twilight: burden and sacrifice, spirituality and survival. Victims and masters might not do much for each other but were mutually improving sources of discipline, like a sound caning or a penitential fast.

In south Asia, India was a special case, imperilled but unconquered by Japan, consciously groomed for independence by an imperial administration anxious to escape from increasingly intractable problems of economic management, famine-fending, and inter-ethnic, inter-credal unrest. The agile solution contrived in 1947—partition between Hindu-dominated and Muslim states, both of which remained on terms of amity with the retiring power—was applauded by an astonished world, despite inter-communal blood-letting that claimed half a million lives before the borders were stabilized. In this misleading instance, the ingredients of the British formula partly worked: parliamentary democracy; a "national" myth instantly infused, like coffee powder, into a steaming brew; "rule of law" monitored by an independent judiciary, whiggish and wigged. The formerly autonomous Maharajahs, blackmailed, bullied, or bought by the British, abandoned their territories to the new India. The national rhetoric was maintained and apparently believed. Most impressively of all, democracy was never discarded, even in the India of nearly half a billion ill-assorted and conflictive people. Over a medium term, Pakistan's example was less encouraging. After about a generation of independence, the country was defeated in war by India, repartitioned by its own secessionists, and remarshalled by military rulers. Yet initial success encouraged the British in a series of more or less dignified retreats from other parts of the empire.

Compared with south Asia, Africa looked unripe for freedom. Except in the marginal cases of Italian colonies, the distribution of imperial authority had not been seriously dislocated by the ebb and flow of armies in the Second World War. Independence could be dismissed as impractical or denied by delay. In London a new Colonial Office, neo-Georgian in style and eight floors high, planned to fill an empty bomb-site, was projected in confidence before being abandoned in embarrassment. The common assumption of the imperial master-class—that natives could not be trusted to govern each other—became a self-fulfilling prophecy, justified, when independence eventually came, by bloodshed and mismanagement and "that African rage, the wish to destroy."

In the end, Africa had its equivalent of the Japanese conquests in Asia to prod or panic the imperialists into retreat. The two main colonial powers were humiliated together by a military and diplomatic débâcle in 1956: when Gamal Abdel Nasser, the nationalist leader of Egypt, appropriated the Suez Canal Company, Britain and France sent in troops "to teach him a les-

The new design for the British Colonial Office attracted objections because it was too big on aesthetic grounds: the projected eight stories would have obscured a view of Westminster Abbey obligingly exposed by German bombs. By 1953, it seemed too big for a shrinking empire. Cummings added a subtler level of satire. For the original style—Georgian, with its connotations of gentlemanly equipoise and aristocratic taste—the cartoonist substituted a cottage ornè with a suburban door, suitable perhaps for the dwelling of a gentleman's gardener.

son." Port Said Casino became a field hospital—symbol of the violent obliteration of an *ancien régime*. Nasser told the capitalists to "choke on their rage" and "drink the Mediterranean." Liberal British opinion "thought Nasser was right"; the government of the United States, keen to demonstrate anti-imperialist credentials, reproved their intemperate allies, who shambled out of the crisis, blinking uncertainly as if with sand-stung eyes. In every rout, impedimenta are dropped, stragglers abandoned. In the flight of the colonial powers from Africa, government responsibilities were discarded like deserters' backpacks, while settlers, ethnic minorities, and old native élites were left to what were often grisly fates.

Tunisia, Morocco, and the Sudan—"protected" territories never strictly under European sovereignty—were evacuated in the year of Suez. After that, the skirts of empire were lifted with indecent haste. France seemed unable either to stay or retreat in Algeria, trapped between the resistance of the natives and the fanaticism of the settlers. Realism settled the question in favour of withdrawal. All over British Africa, resistance heroes, mothballed in prison or disfavour, were spruced up by establishment valeting. The regalia of chieftaincy—the knob-headed canes, the fly-swatters, the leopard-skin caps—passed, in most cases, to adventitious leaders who came from bushland mission schools or the émigré middle class but rarely from the ranks of traditional rulers. Kwame Nkrumah, who led Ghana during a long transition to independence in 1957, had "PG" for "prison graduate" embroidered on his cap. Nineteen-sixty was the *annus mirabilis* of African independence, when fourteen new states—or "nations," as the fashionable jargon inappropriately said—came into being, including a vast swath of continuous territory from the northern Sahara to the River Zaire.

Most winds of change seemed to blow into Africa from the outside. Democracy in Europe—still patchy and imperfect until after the Second World War—enfranchised constituencies doubtful of or hostile to imperialism, such as the British working class who "did not know the empire exists." American pressure bore down on imperialist clients. A wind from the north blew out of the cold war, as western governments tried tactics of moral hijack in the face of Russian competition, empowering native opposition movements in order to detach them from Soviet influence or control.

In the generation or so before the empires collapsed, the colonial powers and indigenous élites had been jarred out of step by the world's "macroeconomic lurches," like runners in a three-legged race forced apart by a fall. The world depression of the early 1930s ended the illusion that colonialism would deliver unqualified prosperity. The economic consequences of world war included the relocation in Africa of some forms of production—especially rubber and food—with the consequent growth of an ambitious native middle class. There may have been, in the ranks of colonial decision-makers, a silent anxiety to escape from the consequences of the biggest single effect of imperialism: the demographic revolution wrought by western medicine. The uncontrollable growth in the numbers of needy people made empires obviously unprofitable. Rather than shoulder unmanageably escalating social costs, it was cheaper to grant independence and aid. Empires founded on collaboration between incomers and incumbents (see Chapter 14) crumbled when common interests changed or disappeared.

South of the Sahara, in the 1950s and early 1960s, native resistance, by comparison with these external influences, was generally feeble in its effects. Kenya became, for a time in the mid-1950s, a conspicuous exception because of the thrilling horror of the terrorists' outrages and the sinister bloodlust of the secret, orgiastic rituals with which they were credited. Mau Mau—the mysterious, incantatory name of their organization was never explained—arose among the Kikuyu people, agriculturists with no reputation for prowess, long oppressed by nomadic neighbours but now made equal by guns. It had characteristics of a totemic brotherhood traditional among some African peoples, but its purpose was to kill White men and their "loyalists." Because the Kikuyu were themselves divided and surrounded by enemies, security was enforced with sickening oaths, reputedly washed down with potations of human blood and milk, urine and sperm. A descriptive memo, according to the urbane colonial secretary Oliver Lyttleton, "got between me and my appetite." The secular minds that ran Kenya seemed incapable of referring to Mau Mau except in terms of "devilry" and "evil" or "sorcery." But it was the White response rather than the Mau Mau's methods that was irrational.

The alleged—and probably real—organizer was Jomo Kenyatta, a foundling who had come out of the bush in boyhood into a Scottish mission station and gave himself his name. Out of anonymity, he assumed ambiguity. The slipperiness of his slides in and out of identities, allegiances, and forms of marriage made him hard to track and, to the colonial authorities, hard to trust. Sent to England in 1929 by a society of Kikuyu squatters whose insecurity bred the earliest Kenyan nationalism, he earned some pocket money as an extra in the film version of *Sanders of the River* (see Chapter 14), bowing and scraping to the all-White supremacist and chanting, "Yes, Lord Sandy." A more useful part of his formation was acquired in Moscow, where he learnt to mobilize men and channel violence. But he was never suckered by Marxism. His nearest approach to an ideological credo was his tendentious anthropological study of his own people, *Facing Mount Kenya,* of 1938, in which Kikuyu virtues were extolled in terms closer to fascism than communism. "In the old order of African society, a man was a man," declared this advocate of female circumcision who was depicted in the frontispiece, in an unconventional portrait of the author, clad in a pelt while feeling the tip of a spear.

Under the pelt, Kenyatta's skin was a chameleon's. The well-travelled sophisticate, on friendly terms with Bronislaw Malinowski, Lady Cunard, and Prince Paul of Greece, never lost the common touch or forgot the folksy rhetoric that stirred the Kikuyu. He shared "the roots of the Mikongoe tree." When the ex-terrorist was released from detention to become prime minister of Kenya, he had no difficulty in projecting a new image as a bonhomous elder statesmen who kept a White man in his cabinet and appointed as chief justice, the judge who had turned down his own appeal. Nor did the nameless bush-boy look out of place in chiefly garb. These deft transformations provided role models which many subsequent African leaders copied.

"In the old order of African society, a man was a man." Jomo Kenyatta's image of himself in 1938, could at the time have been considered quaint but evinces, in retrospect, an air of menace.

THE FEASTS OF MONSTERS

All over the late-colonial world, native leaders were alienated into opposition or driven into resistance. Gandhi in India, despairing of British goodwill for his programme of self-government, gradually became an advocate of outright independence; unable to influence the colonial masters by collaboration, he switched to the tactics of "passive resistance." Ho Chi Minh progressed from socialism to communism and to unremitting militancy from hopes of uniting Vietnamese with Frenchmen in common citizenship. Bourguiba in Algeria was edged into increasingly violent resistance to a regime from which he would have been willing to accept independence by stages. Senghor, a Frenchified *fonctionnaire* who created in Senegal the most *étatiste* regime in independent Africa, had favoured a worldwide French federation, which his masters spurned. Ravoahangy in Madagascar, who wanted independence within some form of association with France, was unhelpfully condemned to death in 1948, though the sentence was left unexecuted. These disasters of colonial intransigence were usually the result of cultural reflexes rather than conscious policy.

In partial consequence, a legacy of resentment coloured the decolonized world. The continued involvement of former colonial masters in running independent states was a focus of suspicion; yet in most places it was inevitable: there were continuities of administrative personnel, of teachers, missionaries, businessmen, and technicians; there were relays of young White "voluntary service" workers who staffed social and educational projects cheaply. The leader of the Ivory Coast, Félix Houphouët-Boigny, had "no complexes" about continued dependence on France. The equivocal blessings of White capitalists, to nurture international business, or White mercenaries, to fight the new states' wars, were available if required. Aid was denounced as covert colonialism unless it was without strings; in practice, the strings were almost always there, often knotted into nooses.

France, Britain, and the Netherlands all tried to establish an institutional framework for cooperation with former colonies. The French idea of a union was too specific; common defence and foreign policies were its defining and impractical features. The British idea of a commonwealth of independent states, with a common focus of allegiance to the crown, had worked well in a community of White or White-led dominions which had rallied to Britain's side in the world wars but was changed unrecognizably after the Second World War by the divergent interests of the older member-states and the republican status of many new ones. The Dutch-Indonesian Union specified only token commitments: to "cooperation on foreign relations and defence and, as far as necessary, finance, as well as subjects of an economic or cultural nature"; but it was vitiated by the parties' obvious mutual hatred and lasted only a couple of years.

Colonialism persisted, in another sense, in the boundaries of the new states, which normally respected lines drawn on a map by colonial administrators without reference to the principle of self-determination or the dictates of common sense. In a typical photograph of a British Boundary Commission at work in 1903, a straggling line of porters wades aimlessly through swamp behind a limp Union flag. Ironically, these boundaries became enshrined in international law at the insistence of the newly independent states themselves, in an attempt to head off interminable and destructive border wars. The problems of demarcation were typified by the shifts of the eastern boundary of the Congo, which had been fixed in 1910 between British and Belgian colonialists in terms of a meridian which neither side could locate on the map; or by the disputes of Maghribi states over frontiers drawn amid the mirages and dunes of the Sahara, where nomads range and topography shifts in ignorance or defiance of the terms of treaties; or in the hospitality of borderland dwellers in Malawi, almost throughout the last third of the century, for kinfolk fleeing from Mozambique.

The curse of decolonization was the creation of states without history,

A British Boundary Commission at work, 1903. The boundaries extemporized by expeditions like these, trailing surveying equipment along straight lines, often unheeding of the human and physical geography, became the only immutable part of the colonial legacy.

extemporized for convenience, bereft of traditional élites or colonial peace-keepers, partitioned precariously or federated whimsically. Hurried preparation for independence rarely created an educated or economically responsible electorate but rather fools' democracies exploitable by demagogues, gangsters, and frauds. An extreme but suggestive case of unsophisticated voters was that of Papua New Guinea, where an early presidential candidate was nominated by cargo-cultists who believed—among other bizarre improbables—that "Agatha Christie would rule the country." Elsewhere, the results of under-preparation by departing colonial masters included territorial conflicts; struggles for identity in unconvincing nations; civil wars—uncontainable rages in once-big countries made small by cars and planes; and the rise of charismatic tyrants.

The cover of this edition had little to do with the plot of the book, but it inspired an odd form of cargo-cult in Papua New Guinea. Followers of the 1972 presidential candidate, Mathias Yaliwan, believed that under the messianic rule of Agatha Christie treasure locked inside the volcano of Mount Turu would be released.

Even the British success in containing inter-communal violence in India proved delusive. India and Pakistan were condemned to mutual hostility and periodic conflicts, while facing long secessionist struggles of their own. The wars of Turks and Greeks in Cyprus or Jews and Muslims in Palestine began confrontations which continued for the rest of the century. Projected federations had to be discarded in Central Africa and the West Indies during the 1960s. In the same decade, first in the Congo and then in Nigeria, in the name of the sanctity of colonial boundaries, secessions were bloodily suppressed. The principle of self-determination was seen to matter less than the inviolability of imperial frontiers and of the old colonialists' invented states. At intervals throughout the second half of the century, wars involving ethnic hatreds, ideological enmities, and secessionist movements, in different combinations, generated harrowing histories of destruction and atrocities in Indo-China, Sri Lanka, the edges of Indonesia and the Philippines, Somalia, Ethiopia, Sudan, Chad, Western Sahara, Zimbabwe, Burundi, Rwanda, Angola, and Mozambique. In none of these areas has the instability been eradicated, well into the last decade of the millennium. It was "very nice" in Mozambique, represented as a land of happiness, freedom, and dancing in an incongruously European "cheek-to-cheek" style: the lyrics of Bob Dylan—the most eloquent of the anti-imperialist "protest singers" who became popular in the west in the sixties and seventies—have not yet lost their irony.

Rootless states were artificially dignified with ancient names. Nkrumah called his state "Ghana" though it included virtually none of the territory of the medieval empire of that name (see Chapter 3). "Zaire" was adopted in place of the Congo with even less justification; it had probably never been a proper name but was based on a Portuguese corruption of an indigenous word for "river." Modern "Benin" does not include the site of the historic city-state of Benin. Extemporized identities like these were hard, perhaps impossible, to communicate to citizenries of diverse provenance who had never before been encouraged to revise traditional group feelings. Some leaders were trapped in internationalist rhetoric—communist or pan-African, which represented, in the circumstances, the worst kind of unattainable ideal, for it was an imperialist's perception of Africa seen as a whole from the outside, in a way barely intelligible to a vision from within.

Many states were linguistically riven and had to borrow the outgoing imperialists' tongue as a national language, though the Philippines invented a native alternative to maintain alongside English by renaming a dominant Malay dialect "Pilipino." In other areas, local patois was elevated to a similar status by a form of cultural compromise—Pidgin in Papua New Guinea, for instance, Krio in Sierra Leone, and in Surinam the lingo called Talkie-talkie or Negerengels. In Zaire, a synthesis of riverbank tongues was concocted by Joseph Mobutu (president, 1965–).

The problems of identity were most concentrated, perhaps, for the colonial minorities left stranded by the receding tides of empire. Their stories included heroic examples of survival by adaptation, such as those of White Jamaicans, Zimbabweans, and Namibians. There were tragic tales of rejection, like the Eurasians driven from Indonesia or the orientals expelled, expropriated, or massacred in much of the new Africa. Poignant cases occurred of disappearance by assimilation, like the Anglo-Indians brilliantly depicted in the transition to independence in John Masters' *Bhowani Junction,* whose heroine swaps English, Indian, and Anglo-Indian lovers according to the lurches of her own identity crises. By the late 1980s, her people seemed reconciled to their own extinction.

Leader-cults tended to fill the gaps vacated by traditional loyalties. In the

The basilica of Our Lady of Peace, endowed by Félix Houphouët-Boigny in his home village of Yamoussoukro, is bigger than St. Peter's in Rome, which it seems consciously designed to rival: the dominant dome and the curling arcade which frames the piazza are surely allusions.

decolonized world, Africa produced the grossest examples: the messianic delusions of Nkrumah, whose troops sang, "Nkrumah never dies"; the *folie de grandeur* of Jean-Bedel Bokassa, who declared the Central African Republic an "empire" and crowned himself amid reputed cannibal orgies; the sanguinary madness of Idi Amin in Uganda, who bought adulation with terror; the eccentric paternalism of Dr. Hastings Banda in Malawi, who flicked away opposition with a chieftainly fly-whisk; the presumption of the Zairean dictator who coined a name but no substance for "Mobutuism" and called himself by a title which means "the cock that leaves no hen alone"; the egotism of Felix Houphouët-Boigny, long admired as an exemplar for Africa—politically moderate, economically pragmatic, socially benign—who commemorated himself at breathtaking expense in the transformation of his home town. Now golden rams guard the entrance to Yamoussoukro, which encloses a pit of sacred crocodiles, a personal mausoleum in the style of Saint-Denis, and the world's biggest cathedral. Even the most rational, mentally temperate leaders seemed prone to develop obsessive tics—like the fanatical austerity of Julius Nyerere of Tanzania or the preoccupation with theoretical polygamy of Siaka Stevens of Sierra Leone.

Ghana, Africa's first independent Black state, became a "melancholy prototype for what was to become a widespread pattern": diminishing returns on resources, military rule, unserviceable debts. Real consumption per head fell by about a third during the 1960s and 1970s. When Nkrumah was ejected from power in 1966, crowds correcting a widespread misconception displayed placards which read, "Nkrumah Is Not Our Messiah"; but his policies, which had a certain nobility of ambition about them—damming the Volta, creating a tropical industrial revolution—were replaced by another form of gamble, borrowing against the surplus produce of peasants.

Here, as in most of the decolonized continent, "governments made most of the errors." Yet bad government at its worst was a contributory cause. The economic environment in which African development was arrested and reversed was in part the result of what looked to its victims like economic colonialism: a world price revolution which saw the value of primary products collapse, in the late 1970s and early 1980s, in relation to the goods of the industrialized world. The oil-led inflation of the early 1970s wrecked the old economic regime that favoured primary producers; the recession of 1979–82 came to seem a definitive turning-point. An abyss opened where there had been a gap before: in the neutral language of geography, between north and south or, rather, between the ex-imperialists and their former subjects. In 1982 cocoa commanded a tenth of its real value of 1977 on the world market. Between the early 1960s and the early 1980s, Africa's share of the world's ground nut exports fell from 85 to 18 per cent and of food oils from 55 to 3 per cent.

Unsurprisingly, against this background, misery and mismanagement be-

When Kwame Nkrumah fell from power in Ghana in 1966, ousted by the National Liberation Council, through streets which a few months before had echoed to the slogan, "Nkrumah Never Dies," a coffin painted with the skull and cross bones was borne by demonstrators anxious to bury him.

"The worst of the worst": Equatorial Guinea, the setting for Frederick Forsyth's *The Dogs of War*, inherited the beauties and burdens of Spanish imperialism—the lovely episcopal palace, shown here in the foreground, the huge spires of the cathedral, and "a society prey to the gang rule of clan bosses."

came twinned. The effects can be appreciated, even better than in Ghana, in the state reputed as "the worst of the worst," the "gulag" and "armpit" of Africa—the cocoa land which was the setting for Frederick Forsyth's block-busting tale of mercenary rampage, *The Dogs of War*. The Spaniards scuttled out of Equatorial Guinea in 1968, leaving a pretty colonial capital city, per capita exports that were the highest in west Africa, and cocoa output of 30,000 tons a year. They seem also to have bequeathed a dangerous legacy of Hispanic-style *caciquismo*—a society prey to the gang rule of clan bosses. Ten years later, cocoa production was a sixth and coffee and timber production a tenth of their pre-independence levels; foreigners had been expelled, and—by plausible estimates—a quarter of the native population was in exile.

The ravages had been inflicted by a mad dictator, Francisco Macías Nguema, who had impressed the electorate by keeping the roads in repair as Minister of Works. He was backed for the presidency by a coalition of disaffected politicians outside the named parties—in all of which he had served in turn. His campaign was funded by anti-Francoists in Spain with connections to potentially exploitative international business. Once elected, he turned on his backers, called in Russian "advisers," and began massacring potential enemies in "a country bled to death." His paranoia showed in the policy of razing the environs of the presidential palace. He was overthrown by a family coup in 1979, but only the worst excesses of his regime abated. When the economist Robert Klitgaard made his first visit to the country in 1985, he found no cinemas or bookshops in the streets, no blackboards in the schools; measles was a fatal disease; cholera seeped from the untreated water system; and the proportion of liquor to wholesome food in the market was nearly one to one. Not even cocoa production had recovered, as the forced labour formerly employed had run for home.

THE MONUMENT TO OUR STRUGGLE

It stands outside the main hospital of Addis Ababa, topped by a Red Star and an eternal flame. The huge bronze friezes depict a condensed version of African history: menacingly veiled, a man on horseback rejects the pleas of starving families—faint adults support sick children, with emaciated limbs and bellies distended by emptiness; in the background, bulldozers crunch traditional dwellings while a line of tanks crosses the horizon. It is meant to show the evils of the pre-revolutionary past, but it is just as accurate a summary of the post-revolutionary present. Though Ethiopia had only the briefest experience of colonial domination, her "biblical famine" of 1984 made her seem the sump of decolonized Africa's insoluble problems.

Africa became, in the eyes of the rest of the world, a continent of ill repute. Black Africa, in particular, seemed a nightmare of reason asleep, a synonym for economic atrophy as well as unsavoury politics, where, over vast areas, the responsibilities of governments for the welfare of the people seemed to be overwhelmed by growing numbers and abandoned to Malthusian checks. Decolonization left booming populations almost everywhere. It was a problem and opportunity which the newly decolonized world shared with other "underdeveloped" areas in Latin America and Asia—wherever improved medicine and hygiene impacted on societies unprepared to control the birth rate. It was particularly in parts of Black Africa, however, in the last third of the twentieth century, that apocalypse seemed to take the place of policy in managing the effects. In the late 1970s the Organisation of African Unity was warned by one of its top officials that the continent was "sinking into the dark night," bereft of "the smiles, the joys of life." In 1983 a UN agency forecast poverty of "unimaginable dimensions" by the year 2000.

From 1980 the rate of population growth, at over 3 per cent per annum, was about a third as high again in sub-Saharan Africa as in Latin America or

Asia. War, famine, and plague rode three abreast. Though food production fell in most of independent Africa, it was not overall shortages that inflicted hunger but breakdowns of distribution and the erosion of what food economists call "entitlement"—access and purchasing power, in effect. Economic mismanagement usually contributes to these effects, but the biggest dislocator is war and the worst famines have struck in war zones, in Ethiopia, Sudan, and Mozambique. The dead are claimed by starvation but more often by diseases rampant in enfeebled bodies. First, the body consumes its own fat, then the proteins in heart and muscles; pulse rate, blood pressure, and body temperature fall; sperm stops pumping, menstrual blood ceases to drip. Stooping and wrecked, the famine victims are recycled by nature's economy to host vile little parasites before they die. Sometimes they survive by grace of media attention, like the family whom journalist Peter Gill met on their way to Korem in 1984—above the "spectacular bends" which challenged relief vehicles—who were "not quite starving enough" to be filmed.

African failures in the face of these enemies are real enough, but the successes have been obscured by the first law of the news media: bad news drives out good. In the year of the Ethiopian famine, Botswana, Cape Verde, Kenya, and Zimbabwe were all ravaged by drought conditions of similarly exceptional severity, but all avoided famine by management. The Cape Verdean case is the most spectacular, for this is a country with the worst climate in the whole Sahelian region, an antiquated agronomy and a crippling dearth of natural resources; but sensible use of aid has kept famine at bay and, in 1984, protected the population through a drought of unprecedented magnitude. Every indicator of social progress has improved steadily since independence, and in some areas it has been startling: measured infant malnutrition was at around 8 per cent in the 1980s, whereas levels in the 30s and 40s had been reported in the 1970s.

Most of Africa's successes, however, have been qualified or vitiated: Burkina Faso revolutionized food production and significantly improved life expectancy and school enrolment in the 1980s by a remarkable "self-adjustment" programme, ahead of intervention by the International Monetary Fund; but the improvements seem unsustainable under the impact of world recession. Most "adjustment"—which in effect means substituting economic liberalism for state controls—has had to be imposed in Africa by outside agencies, with, so far, modest effects, of which "perseverance" is said to be "the ultimate test." Zimbabwe, once exemplary for its "food production miracle" became a victim of dearth in 1992. Houphouët-Boigny, once praised by the World Bank for presiding over an "unique record of real growth," boasted brazenly of his billions in Swiss banks. Tanzanophilia collapsed with the failure of Nyerere's policies of forced resettlement of labour in 1974. For every democratic success—like Kenneth Kaunda's submission to the electorate's will in Zambia in 1992—there seem to be countervailing betrayals, such as the resumption of civil war in Angola and the sad slide of Kenya into malign authoritarianism. And all optimism in Black Africa is overshadowed by a debt service outflow of over $10 billion a year, absorbing nearly half the region's export revenues.

THE SHADE OF THE BANYAN

The population boom in colonial and ex-colonial territories reversed the demographic trend of the second half of the millennium. The ecology of imperialism, filling vacant niches in the ecosystems of conquered lands, had covered underpopulated places with the descendants of European migrants. Now the balance of numbers was being redressed and the flow of migrants reversed.

In what might have been a prophetic instance, the direction of prevailing migration had been inverted, even before decolonization, between Ireland and mainland Britain. The settlement of English and Scotch at the expense of Irish victims in the seventeenth century was exceeded in numerical terms by the transfer of Irish labour in the opposite direction in the nineteenth. Like their more recent Pakistani successors, permanently uprooted Irish nourished their "myths of return," poignant in songs such as "Come Back to Erin." Religion and nostalgia fortified them against assimilation by mainland societies; thanks to dogged distinctiveness, they became a recognizable type in the human zoo of music-hall humour, docketed as safely stupid. When immigrants from the "New Commonwealth" arrived to join them, landladies added "No Coloureds" signs in their windows to those which read "Irish Not Required." This was the price of identity preserved.

After decolonization, this sort of contraflow between metropolis and empire would become normal. As birth rates in the former imperial powers dropped below reproduction rates, labour from the colonies was welcomed to take up the slack. It was perceived by those willing to acknowledge "racial" differences as a redress of racial balance: the White world shrank proportionately as Black and Brown worlds grew and spread.

It happened quickly, in pace with the dismembering of the empires. The first 500 Jamaicans arrived in Britain in fog on an old troop carrier in 1948, astounded at the sight of smoking chimneys and of White men doing menial work. There were 200,000 Algerians in France in 1958, four times as many twenty years later. In Britain immigration levels reached five figures annually from the West Indies in 1954, India in 1955, Pakistan in 1957. Between 1945 and 1971, when controls were tightened, the number of the identifiably Asian minority in England increased a hundredfold and was more conspicuous for being largely concentrated in a few urban areas. In the retina of White fear, "English culture" would be "swamped" and Britain would house "a coffee-coloured society" by the year 2000. There are now 4 million Muslims in France, more than 2 million in Britain, and a legislator of the party in government has declared "a threat to the British way of life." Inter-racial violence is common in France and Germany. By the end of the 1980s in the Netherlands, in the effort to accommodate nearly 800,000 Indonesians, Surinamese, Moluccans, and Antilleans, the multicultural consensus for which the country was renowned was being denounced as a myth.

Case studies of colonial immigrants in Britain have revealed what are probably typical histories of postwar long-range migration. Some resist "integration," like Tagore's banyan tree, which "sheds it beneficent shade away from its own birthplace." These are the counter-colonists in the fullest sense, who turn parts of the former mother countries into patches or parodies of their own worlds of home. Others become "helots," remoulded by the host societies and transformed over two or three generations into "belongers" who "go for walks in the park." The Maltese and Montserratian communities show the range of adaptive strategies.

The tiny island of Montserrat sent more people over in the 1950s and 1960s, proportionately speaking, than any other West Indian island, driven by the collapse of the island's sugar industry in 1952. There are fewer than 5,000 of them, but they stick together. They marry each other. They settle together in spots like Long Ground in Birmingham, named after a village in Montserrat, or worship together in Pentecostal churches in Stoke Newington. They share business, form rotating credit associations, exchange visits—called "passing"—at Christmas, and are tied to home by remittances and the fear of expulsion. By contrast, the Maltese—of whom there are 30,000 permanently in Britain by a common estimate—migrate singly and live dispersed. They blend into the British background—often in conscious flight from an identity besmirched by the "stereotype of the vicious ponce," the evil reputation of allegedly Maltese gang leaders who practised the "un-English crime" of pimping in the 1950s. The difference between the Montserratians and Maltese is not to be explained by the colour of their skins. Cypriots are keen to cocoon themselves in their own culture, "Uganda Asians" to forgo theirs.

For migrants seeking a new home, there is a lot of pull in old colonial bonds. When Ronnie Knox-Mawer returned from a magistracy in a South Sea island and was sent to a new branch of the British judiciary, he found his former Indian clerk installed ahead of him as his boss. In Salamanca in 1969, refugees from Nguema astonished a little girl who thought they must be "made of chocolate." In the 1980s uncensused Guinean and Angolan street vendors hawked beads to the milk-white tourists of the Algarve—the truck of the early colonial era, travelling in reverse; and the Inner London

"K.B.W." stood for Keep Britain White. The bleak wall under railway ridges, contemplated by Blacks of a highly respectable appearance in September 1952, is in Brixton, an area which now has a mainly Black population.

A man at the back seems close to a modified ecstasy; otherwise this Pentecostal gathering seems disappointingly tame. A boy is opening his mouth to yawn rather than prophesy. Boredom or distraction is on most of the faces. For Black communities, where it acts as a social coagulant, Pentecostalism functions more as an occasion for donning one's Sunday best and re-stoking one's sense of community, than as a spark for igniting tongues of fire.

Education Authority acquired an adviser on Bengali education. There are forty hours of broadcasts a week in Gujerati in Leicester, scores of Vietnamese restaurants in Paris, and dozens of Javanese eating establishments in Amsterdam.

The ocean of migrants, however, is full of cross-currents and countercurrents and, amid the increasingly restricted opportunities of the late twentieth century, "economic refugees" scoured the world for berths and work, without necessarily rewinding the threads of a special relationship with past colonial masters. The Philippines were an American colony, but they came to supply illegal labour for several European countries. Vietnamese "boat people"—before humanitarians lost patience with them—were spread all over a hospitable western world.

There are communities whose histories of migration have followed empires back and forth, from Africa to colonial slavery, then jobs in Europe; or from Asian homelands to Caribbean colonies or African main streets, as workers or merchants, before rejection or disillusionment sent them to new homes in the colonial metropolis. Exported overseas between 1830 and 1916 to replace abolished slavery, Indian communities form the "débris" of the departed British Empire. Sometimes the vagabonds of imperialism

A post-colonial world made vivid by V. S. Naipaul. A Hindu temple in Trinidad, guarded by a lion and tiger and superintended by the Lord Siva in his babyhood. The decorations were probably done by an expert brought specially from India, creating one of the odd visible effects of "cross-currents and counter-currents in the ocean of migration."

drifted between colonial destinations: the expulsees of Africa include Nigerians from Ghana and Ghanaians from Sierra Leone; there are ex-Algerian *colons* in Martinique, which has supplied Tamil road-sweepers to Trinidad, where paintings on a Hindu temple are renewed every year by an artist brought from India.

The unofficial spokesman of these richly experienced human flotsam is V. S. Naipaul, whose novels make vivid histories of decolonized worlds. He "had never wanted to stay in Trinidad." His removal to England was the fulfilment of a vow written "on the endpaper of my Kennedy's *Revised Latin Primer* . . . and for many years afterwards in England, falling asleep in bedsitters with the electric fire on, I had been awakened by the night-mare that I was back in tropical Trinidad." Yet even Naipaul, welcomed everywhere, was nowhere wholly at home, drawn, in his writings and travels, towards India by atavistic obligation, towards Africa by sympathetic curiosity, and back to the Caribbean by memories which clamoured for verification.

THE FATE OF THE NEW EUROPES

While old Europe changes under the impact of counter-colonization, the White character of the "new Europes"—established far from home, long ago, in the Americas and the southern hemisphere—is being eroded by comparable processes. The most dramatic case is the mental realignment of White South Africans, compelled by demographic logic to admit that their neo-Europe is really African; but the trend is ubiquitous in different degrees. At about the time European governments began to restrict inflows, Australia abandoned the "White Australia" policy. Since then the population has doubled in thirty years and in the 1990s is divided and contorted by an uncomfortable national debate about whether the country is really European or Asiatic (see Chapter 22). Former frontiers of imperialism have become frontiers again in the current repeopling of the world. To immigrants, Canada is one of the most hospitable of developed countries, the United States—because of its long border with northern Mexico, where the population is only lightly miscegenated—one of the most exposed. Aboriginals in Australia, "native Americans" in the United States, Mapuche in Chile, Maoris in New Zealand, and Inuit in Canada are all experiencing demographic revivals towards the end of the millennium.

Some migration, moreover, happens only in the mind but can still have a reforming impact. "Black consciousness" movements in North America, encouraging the rediscovery of African "roots" and even of African allegiances, have restored to parts of the United States and the Caribbean—in some perceptions, at least—the African character which briefly predominated during an earlier era of colonization (see Chapter 8). The racial pride of Blacks was awakened by Marcus Garvey, who came "screaming onto the American stage" from his native Jamaica in 1916; diverted from a promising start in American politics by a call to "Africa for the Black Peoples of the World," he tried to nurture this programme by distinctly Black business ventures. His "Negro" shipping line, for instance, collapsed amid fraud charges.

Garvey's enthusiasm for going back to Africa was replaced by a new state of mind which was both bolder and more realistic: a desire to Africanize America, in a mental recolonization of part of the White world. In a formula used in 1964 by the feared Black Muslim leader who called himself Malcolm X, "Philosophically and culturally, we Afro-Americans need to 'return' to Africa." This boiling Black Consciousness, bubbling on the home range with no outlet for the steam, was a powerful destructive force. It helped to produce the "New Ghetto Man" who inflicted repeated summer riots on American cities from 1964 to 1968.

Today, African awareness in the New World can take absurd but powerful forms, best exemplified perhaps by Rastafarianism, a movement which began in Jamaica in the early 1930s. Its rituals were dope-smoking and abstinence from washing; its tenets included the belief that Ethiopia was the homeland of New World Blacks, that the Ethiopian emperor was divine, and that Blacks were the true Israelites. Such silliness seemed beyond satire until an English comic novelist invented a White Rastafarian. The Black Muslim movement was only a little less illogical—Christianity has been a

Rasta Man: "It's not politic: it's really talkin' about roots." The Jamaican singer-songwriter Bob Marley became the voice of Rastafarianism from the late 1960s, when he became convinced of the divinity of the Emperor Haile Selassie, until his death from cancer in 1980. "I am one of the twelve tribes of Israel," he told an interviewer in February 1978, "and we are trying to unite the people so that we can move back to Africa . . . and Haile Selassie is the conquering lion." See *Bob Marley in His Own Words*, ed. I. McCann, p. 48.

Edward Asner and LeVar Burton in a scene from a TV movie version of *Roots* by Alex Haley. In a carefully posed shot, the hero, Kunta Kinte, is being chained in the hold of a slave-ship bound for America. The huge manacles thrust into the foreground, with the hoops and ropes behind, frame the visionary face of the young African. The captain, who is himself a prey to conscientious scruples, is made up in the mephistophelean tradition, with satanic eyebrows and goatee beard.

Black faith longer than Islam, while neither is essential to Black identity—but it was more dangerously militant.

It was founded in Detroit, at about the same time as Rastafarianism—in a period of prolific Black migration from southern farms to the industrial north of the United States—when Wallace D. Fard, a former pedlar of rain-coats, announced that he had come from Mecca to prepare "the Dead Nation of the West for Armageddon." His successor at the head of the movement, Elijah Muhammad, declared him a divine incarnation, echoing a common heresy of the Islamic fringe (see Chapters 3 and 7). He denounced all White men as devils, proclaimed a jihad against the White world, and demanded the handover of "one or more states" of the union in return for "over a century of free blood and sweat."

The acceptable face of the Black Muslim ideal was displayed in Alex Haley's book *Roots* in 1976, which enjoyed popular success and intellectual éclat as "an event of social importance," according to *Newsweek*'s review. Its achievement was to integrate Black Muslim doctrines with all-American

"I like to be in America!" Since Leonard Bernstein's *West Side Story* of 1957, the numbers of Hispanics in the United States have grown, their provenance widened, and their icons multiplied. The musical, however, which adapts the plot of *Romeo and Juliet* to the background of an inter–ethnic love affair, remains a classic depiction of *puertorriqueño* life and gang warfare in New York and a powerful indictment of the discrimination Hispanics have faced. In the number depicted here, women from Puerto Rico praise the rewards of being a migrant while their cynical menfolk remind them of its humiliations.

dreams, like a Black version of *How the West Was Won*. Instead of apple-cheeked settlers creating a great country in healthy open spaces, Haley's family of Black heroes survived the mephitic environment of slave plantations as, generation by generation, its members were tortured, brutalized, impregnated, bought, and sold by rapacious, cruel, or misguidedly well-intentioned owners. Eventually, they rose through emancipation to a dignified position in American society and produced Alex Haley himself, who traced his presumed ancestry back to an improbably fervent Muslim slave from Gambia in the mid-eighteenth century.

Though the intellectual credentials of Black movements in North America are patchy and their artistic achievements mixed, their importance in a counter-colonized world is enormous. The United States looks like becoming the most conspicuous arena of counter-colonization at the start of the new millennium, owing in part to the mental revolution that has extended a frontier of African awareness across the hemisphere, and in part to the demographic revolution represented by the Hispanic diaspora. This is a

movement of counter-colonization in the fullest sense: a repeopling of territories wrested by aggressors pursuing their "manifest destiny," a reversal
profoundly similar to the peaceful counter-invasion of European countries
by their empires' victim-peoples.

Most of North America's Hispanics are Mexicans—a "bronze people with
a bronze culture," who long ago completed their own mental realignment,
in rejection of the Spanish part of their ancestry, as guardians of an indigenous past (see Chapter 11). There are now 25 million Hispanics in the
United States. Los Angeles includes the second-largest Spanish-speaking
community in the world. There are so many holes in the border fence at
Chula Vista that the families of Tijuana use its barbed wire for barbecue
grills. The fantasy of a dusky, Catholic, Spanish-speaking U.S.A. in the
twenty-first century will never quite come true, because such predictions
are always thwarted by changing demographic trends. But when a Hispanic
crosses the border from Mexico—probably an illegal immigrant, in a vehicle bouncing across the desert night, as in a painting by Frank Romero—
"he sometimes asks," according to a revered Mexican intellectual, " 'Hasn't
this always been our land? Am I not coming back to it? Is it not in some
way ours?' He can taste it, hear its language, sing its songs, and pray to its
saints."

The European Reflex

One of my first ghost-writing jobs in the early 1970s involved supplying
speeches for an African politician who regarded the European Economic
Community as a conspiracy of ex-colonial powers, intent on perpetuating
their dominance and exploitation of a formally decolonized world. In reality, the community was born in a more defensive state of mind, in which
revulsion from the bloody internal divisions of the first half of the twentieth
century played a major part. Yet the influence of the background of dissolving world empires cannot be denied in coaxing the pace of European integration.

Today, cartographers are putting Europe back in its place in the world by
devising and promoting projections which centre on other areas and emphasize the paucity of Europe's dimensions. Other regions' claims to displace Europe in the centre of our world-picture are impressive: Africa,
despised and disordered, boasts antiquity of human settlement; Asia encloses mature civilizations; North America is commended by its economic
might, South America by its rapid development, the Pacific rim by economic promise and achievement alike. All this competition has shrunk Europe's share of the map but has also forced Europeans into an increased

dependence on one another and an enhanced European solidarity. They can no longer afford the internecine squabbles of the era of European world hegemony. The connection between European integration and imperial débâcle was made most explicit in Britain, where the debate about whether to join the Community was expressed in terms of the rival merits of a "common market" and "empire preference." The preferential trading links negotiated between the Community and some of its member-states' former colonies are, looked at from one perspective, the last practical ties of empire.

The era of decolonization has given European identity institutional vertebrae. The first creative steps in erecting supranational structures are usually credited to Jean Monnet, a former cognac salesman who had worked wonders in coordinating Anglo-French supply policy during the Second World War. He proposed a "High Authority" for coal and steel to overtrump Franco–German rivalry. Thus, at the start of the process of European integration, European identity was squeezed out like grout to smudge over the cracks between enemies. The European Coal and Steel Community was formed, with six countries participating, in 1951.

In its first years, this European initiative developed all the promise and all the limitations which have continued to characterize it. Member-states would not surrender "an iota of sovereignty." The High Authority gave way to a Council of Ministers which was in practice an international rather than a supranational body. A common approach to defence proved unattainable. The Messina Declaration of June 1955 proclaimed "work for a united Europe, by the development of common institutions, the progressive fusion of national economies, the creation of a common market, and the progressive harmonization of social policies," but the Treaty of Rome, which launched the drive—sometimes more of a drag—towards a common market in 1957 postponed almost everything else to a remote future.

Efforts in the 1960s to press towards a "United States of Europe" were frustrated by the strong nationalist susceptibilities of the French leader General Charles De Gaulle, then slowed in the 1980s by enlargement of the community to include twelve member-states by 1985. His role in pouring cold water on Euro-fever was taken up by the redoubtable British prime minister Margaret Thatcher, whose soubriquet of "Madame Non" was an echo of De Gaulle's diplomatic language. Her stress on the spread of parliamentary democracy and economic liberalism as preconditions for progress in European integration came to seem prophetic as Europe became increasingly homogenized and European institutions converged—not as a result of the efforts of the Community but because of two waves of political and economic realignment: first, in southern Europe from 1974 to 1978, when Greece, Spain, and Portugal all abandoned authoritarian systems; and again in 1989–92, when most of eastern Europe followed suit. Viewed from within or by the supplicants on its fringes, the European Community is a great internationalist crusade; looked at from far outside its rampart of tariffs and immigration controls, it is the last redoubt of retreating imperialists. Which characterization w.ill convince the galactic museum-keepers? It is impossible to be sure, but distance rarely flatters insiders' vision.

Chapter 19

THE MAZE OF GOD:
ISLAMIC RESURGENCE LATE IN
THE MILLENNIUM

*Face on the Moon—The Cycle of Revival—Signs Along the Road
—The Eye of Islam*

THE FACE ON THE MOON

Sattareh Farman Farmaian survived four revolutions, each more traumatic than the last. She was born among the roses of Shiraz, one of many daughters of a cadet prince of a fading dynasty. Though she claimed not to know the exact date, it must have been shortly before the coup of 1921, when power in Persia was seized by Colonel Reza Khan, an ex-ranker reputedly picked by the British to take over the country because of his commanding height in a culture where tall men inspire fear. Her mother's manservant, who blamed fate for the bad watermelons he brought home from market, was a symbol of the inhibitions which made Persia "backward"—impoverished, timid, and victimized by Britain, by Russia, and by a capricious, desiccating climate. Reza Khan held Islam responsible for the "fatalism and shiftlessness" which kept dung cooking-fires alight in central Tehran, in streets thronged with livestock, where filthy, hairy dervishes peddled cures for baldness.

The example of Atatürk's Turkey suggested that secularization would be a modernizing, progressive influence that would create cities of boulevards and streets of cars. Persian intellectuals had demanded "a clever doctor for a sick country," but Reza Khan's only life—man and boy—had been in

577

The Square of Maidané Aminés-Saltah, Tehran, awaiting the steamrollers of Reza Khan Pahlavi.

the army; he was better at giving orders than issuing prescriptions. He became a frenzied razer of medieval townscapes, a ferocious builder of gimcrack developments of western inspiration. He levelled the infant Sattareh's world, humbling the old dynasty and crowning himself shah. He destroyed her family's compound, the harem of many households where she lived, discarding the inmates "like maggots plucked from a carcass he was dismembering."

Revolutions are easy, reformations hard. Persia's secular institutions offered no resistance to Reza Shah; religion proved ineradicable, however, even though its formal power could be abolished and its outward symbols smothered or curbed. Persia was no different in this respect from other countries, or Islam from other faiths. It was a common mistake of twentieth-century intellectuals to suppose that God was dead and that religion must wither. The godly of every faith colluded in affirming the onset of a crisis by denouncing the growth and spread of unbelief, for nothing so stimulates religious reaction as the fear of pagan revanche.

Orthodox Christianity, for instance, was derided, tormented, and tamed even longer in twentieth-century Russia than Islam in Iran, but when the regime collapsed, the clergy, bent double under the blows on their way to the communist Calvary, sprang up, fully armed with spiritual powers, after more than seventy years of assiduous secularization. Soviet failure to promote secular culture in the Union's Islamic republics was reflected in the increasing desperation with which works of propaganda and scholarship lampooned the Koran and denounced Islam as bourgeois. The subtler, more insidious pressure on religion from materialism, consumerism, and humanism in the United States was followed by a religious revival strong enough to help "born-again" presidents to the White House and restore "three little letters, G-O-D," to political discourse.

Islam is as hard to suppress as other religions and perhaps harder to fillet out of politics. It is a political religion; its name implies a way of life as well as a system of faith; in Islamic usage, civil society and the congregation of the faithful are conterminous; the precepts of Muhammad were intended to be a sufficient code of civil law in their day and in some Islamic countries are treated as if they still are. In almost every Muslim polity, at every period of history, governments have sought a form of religious legitimation, even in some cases where non-Muslim rulers have intruded from outside. In Sudan—where the Mahdi's grandson served as prime minister as recently as 1989—the British, who supplanted the Mahdist theocracy, were proud of having "brought the holy places close" and "subsidized and assisted the men of religion." Though ostracized from political life since the 1920s, Islam has remained a potent moral force in Turkey, while elsewhere in the Muslim world, wherever secularization has been tried, it has been abandoned.

At first, in the Persia of Sattareh Farman Farmaian's childhood, Reza Shah needed the support of the mullahs. Once they had helped him get established, he turned on them and tried to drive them out of their privileged place of political and social influence. He banned self-flagellation and imposed headgear which made it hard to prostrate oneself in prayer. The name "Iran," or "Land of the Aryans," which he enforced in place of "Persia," was itself a proclamation of an identity shared with non-Islamic peoples in India and Europe. But the Koranic sense of transcendence, which every Muslim learns in childhood, survived and, with it, the reverence traditionally inspired by holy men. Sattareh's mother, who always put more meat and butter on the rice when a mullah ate in her house, warned that God would curse the Shah for impiety.

By the time secularization was reversed, after about fifty years of fairly consistent efforts by successive governments to marginalize Islam, Iran had experienced two more political revolutions at British behest. The first supplanted Reza Shah in 1941. The second, lubricated by the CIA, ousted Sattareh Farman Farmaian's hero, the nationalist premier Dr. Mossadeq in 1953. The net effect was to concentrate power by the early 1960s in the hands of a new despot, Reza Shah's son, Mohammed Reza Shah. His self-image was projected by a book of official photographs, called *Majesty in Power.* Glinting from glossy pages, emotion masked behind a mirthless rictus, with iron-grey hair and steel-blue eyes, he posed on thickly gilded chairs, uncomfortably upright, in his buttoned suit. His family, clustered round like the outline of a magnetic field, provided a human touch, instantly corrected by hieratic stances, coutured looks, and emotionless expressions. The lavish décor, too gaudy for good taste, was repudiated in his disingenuous claim that "although the furnishings in my palaces might suggest otherwise, I really wish I could sleep on the floor."

An apologist's account of life at his court shows what kind of man he really was: an opportunist determined to maximize oil revenues; a bully delighted to victimize interviewees; a misogynist who liked expensive prostitutes and recommended sexual therapy for his fourteen-year-old heir; an autocrat corrupted by vanity and isolated by sycophancy. He established a gratifying routine of ritually summoning the British and American ambassadors. This convinced him that his dynasty had ended Iran's era of dependence, while flattering the ambassadors' sense of self-importance. He drooled like a schoolboy over arms catalogues and spent the income from a world energy boom (or, more precisely, a boom in oil income largely driven by the Shah's own antic choice to quadruple its price in 1974) to indulge his taste for military hardware.

He continued the policy of secularization but with a disdain worse, from the mullahs' point of view, than the anxious hostility of his predecessors. He thought he was ruling a people who "resembled Americans" in "the France of Asia." He claimed to "believe fervently" in Islam and to have experienced childhood visions of the messianic "Hidden Imam" of Shiite prophetic tradition. This did more for his pride than his piety and gave him a snob's route to God, around the flanks of the Muslim clergy. "I felt," he declared, "a Supreme Being guiding me." He shared the antique monarch's dream "to ride in triumph through Persepolis" and reputedly spent $100 million celebrating the glories of the empire of Cyrus the Great, revivified—he believed—in his own times and person, in 1971. Without sense of contradiction, he also saw himself as a revolutionary leader, enforcing profit-sharing, enfranchising women, promoting rural education, and turning large estates into peasant smallholdings in what he called the "White revolution." Though this sounded like a project of land reform in the tradition of the French Revolution or Sun Yat-sen, it amounted in practice to an expropriation of religious endowments. Soon after the proclamation of the White revolution in 1963, demonstrating seminarians were shot by police in the shrine-city of Qom. A small but unremitting faction of mullahs from the holy city began—hardly heeded at first—to preach and plot for the overthrow of the Shah.

The oil boom of the sixties and early seventies could pay for enough social progress to allay unrest and enough men and arms to repress it. When the boom ended and economic difficulties piled up, the Shah's insulation from bad news protected him from knowledge of the problems and prevented him from finding solutions. The most dangerous opposition—the

"Is it not passing brave to be a king and ride in triumph through Persepolis?" The camp behind the ruins was built to house the Shah's guests for the celebration of 2,500 years of the Persian monarchy: a parvenu dynasty buying into the respectability of ancient origins. The ruins in the foreground became the set of an extravaganza out of the Hollywood of Cecil B. de Mille, with thousands of soldiers parading in pastiche uniforms of the bronze age.

most convincing alternative government—seemed to come from the nationalist tradition bequeathed by Mossadeq. But from the perspective of Islamic revolutionaries the nationalist leaders were infected with disfiguring heresies, like modernism, westernism, and secularism. With no means of their own of mobilizing a revolution, the nationalists could only come to power by collaborating with the Shah or by throwing in their lot with successful insurgents. An army coup would have suited them, but there was no one to carry it out; the clandestine Communist Party was credited with impressive menace, but its reputation was exaggerated, its help distasteful, and its reliability unsound. The only potentially revolutionary initiative lay with the mullahs from Qom.

The gradually accumulating success of their leading propagandist, Ayatollah Khomeini, was the reward of persistence. Though he hated other forms of modernization, he had grasped the techniques of mass communication and absorbed one of the fundamental principles of advertising: a simple message gains credibility with repetition. Khomeini's message was that the Shah's regime was a work of the Devil—this was meant literally—

Ayatollah Khomeini in giant illumination, looming over a festival podium in Nice. The image is affectionate—with comfortable pot-belly, fatherly beard, generously out-stretched palms, a posture in the tradition of cartoon fun. But some of the self-image of the revolutionary leader is also captured: hieratic state, serious brows, words of fire, the world-conjuring political dexterity. Images of corrupting western influence are scattered at his approach. At bottom right, pornography and booze are magicked away on a Persian rug. The fun-making is obviously an antidote to real fear.

which it was a religious duty to destroy. Iranian culture is rich in anticlerical humour; in a country where it could be said that the best way to kill a mullah was to invite him to overeat, Khomeini's obvious incorruptibility gave him authority. It was enhanced by his almost insane conviction of self-righteousness. His broadcasts from exile excited some of his audience to expect the imminent advent of the Hidden Imam and to see Khomeini's image disclosed on the face of the moon as a sign of God's favour.

The radio talks combined the techniques of pulpit oratory with the power of the sound-bite. They were circulated by means of pirate cassettes and acquired cult followings, undetected by the Shah's secret police or the world's press. Khomeini packaged his message in a political programme of magnetic naïvety: he divided the world into "oppressors" and "dispossessed"; his Islamic Republic would be a welfare state which would enrich all its faithful and in which the necessities of life would be free. Ironically, this vision seems to have been influenced by models of social welfare in the oil states of the Arabian peninsula, which Khomeini professed to abhor as realms of darkness; in Saudi Arabia and the Gulf Emirates, where populations were small in relation to oil revenues, universal benefits could indeed be scattered with a lavish hand, but such indiscriminate generosity would never be possible in Iran. Khomeini was also able to overtrump the programme of nationalism. The prospective foreign policy of the Islamic Republic would be nakedly xenophobic. This recalled the old nationalist theory of "negative equilibrium"—even-handed resistance, that is, to all foreign influence—and echoed the mood of Iranians outraged by the wealth and exhibitionism of the Shah's expatriate American collaborators.

Thanks to the immediacy of the message and the mastery of the medium, Khomeini made the revolution of 1979 by means of his almost unaided oratory. His eloquence filled the streets with demonstrators keen to incur martyrdom. He paralysed the government and the economy by calling out strikers, and emasculated the armed forces by encouraging deserters. The fundamentalists' revolutionary rivals were neutralized or mesmerized. But deeds were needed as well as words, and when the revolutionary threshold was crossed, unshaven cadres, long trained in underground cells, were waiting to organize committees of public safety; Islamic "freedom fighters" occupied the rooftops. The source of the armed manpower was revealed in the dawn of revolutionary success, when Yassir Arafat, the leader of the Palestine Liberation Organisation, appeared on the balcony of the Alavi school to receive Khomeini's public embrace. Meanwhile, on a killing ground on the flat roof above, the victims of revolutionary justice were being shot.

Sattareh Farman Farmaian did not see Khomeini. When she was hauled in for interrogation as a collaborator in the old regime, there were "no facilities" for women in the headquarters, and she was kept on the threshold for a day and a night by guards affectedly blind to her sex. She had founded and directed the Tehran School of Social Work and was well known for befriending the dispossessed. The charges against her included "killing millions of babies" by advocating contraception, and supporting Zionism by attending a professional conference in Israel on the Shah's orders. She was exonerated, sitting on a rifle box in a tent, by a conscientious judge, within earshot of the executions. Ordered to return to her post, she—like most of the rest of the professional élite—preferred to flee the country.

THE CYCLE OF REVIVAL

Among the Batak of Angkola in the uplands of northern Sumatra, Muslims and Christians share fellow-feeling in common clans without sacrifice of piety. Christians oblige by keeping no pigs; Muslims have grace said at meals for their Christian guests. Muslim notables attend the induction of Christian pastors, and the children of both communities exchange cakes on their respective holy days. In today's world, this ideal of a multicultural society is looking increasingly unusual.

Muslim-Christian antipathy has helped to bury Beirut in rubble and turn the ruins into a snipers' nest. The death squads of the Iranian revolution concentrated on credally identified enemies—Baha'is, Zoroastrians, Christians, and Jews. The Muslims of the Patani region of South Thailand have fought back against "attempted ethnocide." Self-styled crusaders and mujahidin have waged wars of extermination in Mindanao and East Timor, Ngorno Karabakh and South Sudan. "Pakis" have been beaten up on English streets, mosques burned in German towns. Muslim rage and Christian incomprehension have met in riots and demonstrations, provoked by an arrogant *fatwah* of death against a novelist unreasonably accused of traducing Muhammad. In the dark days of the Second World War, the intellectuals of Travnik in Bosnia met in Lufti's Bar to console themselves that "'everything now will once again be as it used to be and by God's will always was." Not this time round. After the ethnic cleansers, Lufti's Bar will not be opening again.

Militancy and violence are as different from each other as bark from bite. In Christian perceptions, however, sharp fangs appear whenever resurgent Islam opens its maw to howl. Muslim orators use a symbolically violent imagery traditional from the savage and strenuous times of the Prophet. To suitably prejudiced readers, the Koran encourages a world-view easily confused with dualism, in which societies are divided between "the House of Islam" and "the House of Darkness," people between the "parties" of Satan and of God. The conflicts of conscience inside every man are extended into the struggle against heretics and unbelievers; like the concept of a crusade for Christians in former times, that of jihad is routinely exploited by Muslim leaders who want to justify their wars. In the 1980s the Iran-Iraq war was claimed to be sanctified on both sides by leaders who "turned war into a great blessing."

One man's holy war can be another man's terrorism: Islam's image is besmirched in the west by association with the work of hijackers, bombers, assassins, and kidnappers employed or emboldened by "Islamic-revolutionary" regimes or by Palestinian liberation cells and gangs. In Muslim eyes, Christendom is an equal but different ogre, blooded with the guilt of imperialism, inescapably tainted by an anti-Islamic history. Christian sympathy for Zionism is interpreted as crude hunger, snapping another bite out of a formerly Muslim land. The indifference of the western powers, as Muslim Bosnia was cleft and carved in 1993, was easy to characterize as evidence of Christian complicity or conspiracy.

The world of Angkola, against this alarming background, can only be reproduced in small patches where local realities exorcise atavistic phantoms. On a global scale, Islam and Christendom are doomed to go on feeling each other's menace. In the 1980s and early 1990s, western opinion-makers and decision-makers struggled to resist the fear that resurgent Islam was a threat to world peace. The rattle of this serpent sounded as loud in some ears as those of fascism and communism earlier in the century. In 1977 a coup in Pakistan replaced a pronouncedly secular government with a self-consciously Islamic one. In 1979, Islamic revolution in Iran detached a huge fief from uneasy allegiance to western values and turned it into a partisan-state of terrible power, ruled by a theocracy of frightening candour. As

May 1981. Tradition triumphs over technology, Islam over the devilry of secularism. In a photograph taken in May 1981 Afghan mujahidin display the burnt-out shell of a captured Soviet tank to the press. Under the ideology of holy war, however, their struggle had some of the flavour of a traditional tribal and regional war, from which western volunteers returned disillusioned, having been misled into thinking that spiritual values were paramount, or, at least, that the mujahidin perceived themselves as part of a worldwide struggle against communism.

the decade opened, the mujahidin of Afghanistan launched their holy war against communism. In 1981, President Anwar Sadat of Egypt was assassinated by Islamic fanatics. In 1983, Sudan joined the ranks of proclamatory Islamic republics with laws which subjected civil societies to religious values. Almost everywhere in the Islamic world, leaders sought to head off powerful fundamentalist movements by pre-empting their rhetoric and modifying the law in response to their demands.

Some Muslim wars in the period were, from an outsider's perspective, comfortingly internecine—with Libyan forces tied down in Chad, Syria fully committed to intervention in Lebanon, Algeria pitted against Morocco over Western Sahara, and Iraq turning her vast armies first against Iran, then Kuwait; but Muslim muscle-flexing still frightened the west. There were rumours of Pakistani, Iranian, and Iraqi nuclear weapons in the offing. The success against Soviet armies of scattered, ill-armed, but religiously committed insurgents in Afghanistan demonstrated the moral power of Islam as an ideology adapted for conflict. In 1985, Israeli invaders withdrew from Lebanon, and in 1988, Islamic revolutionaries played a part in igniting a Palestinian uprising against Israeli rule. When the Soviet Empire broke up in 1989, resentful, militant successor-states were added to the Muslim world, as breeding grounds for revolutionary fundamentalism and votes in the United Nations.

History responds as often to falsehoods as to facts, and the strength of credal antagonism may—despite the lack of justification for it—make the next world war a Muslim jihad. Such apprehensions dwindle reassuringly, however, if the reality of the Islamic resurgence of the late millennium is examined calmly, either with the detail of the close-up or the detachment of the long-term view. Islam is genuinely a single civilization, which makes a useful unit of study, for all Muslim societies are underpinned by common—or at least similar—concepts and structures of family, community, and polity as well as of religion strictly understood. It is one of the underlying assumptions of this book that it makes better sense to talk about Islam than, say, the Middle East. But a recognizable object of enquiry is not necessarily suited to be a coherent political force. "Islamic resurgence" can mean quite different things in different places, and at times has seemed as likely to bring the House of Islam down in division as to unite it in a common stand against the rest of the world.

Sunni radicals, for instance, before 1979 knew virtually nothing of the zealotry of Iranian revolutionaries, even though their critiques of worldly regimes were equally indignant and their prescription—the rule of religious law—identical. After 1979, the attraction of Iran's model of success was allayed by Sunni suspicion: Ayatollah Khomeini's messianic confidence, for instance, that the Hidden Imam of the Shiites would return "to bring about all that Muhammad did not have a chance to achieve" was repudiated by

Sunni fundamentalists who saw it as a typical heretic's disparagement of the Prophet. Libya and Pakistan were both self-consciously Islamic states, with orthodox majorities and laws based on the Sharia, but their leaders hated each other and their regimes were separated by contrasting valuations of capitalism—abhorred in Libya, ingrained in Pakistan.

Islam is too big for coherent political action, too diverse to turn into a single amalgam. To change the metaphor, no surge of revivalism could be big enough to lap all its shores; when the wave rolls, leaders sometimes ride its surf but rarely succeed in controlling its power. Even the most promising identity within Islam—that of speakers of Arabic as their first language—has never generated concerted political action for long, despite having a focus of common enmity in Israel. Arab unity, according to Hosni Mubarak of Egypt (president, 1981–), "changes with the weather." All the United Arab Republics of the second half of the century, which have included, in different combinations, Egypt, Syria, Libya, and Sudan, have quickly fallen apart.

From asceticism to opulence. The jihad gets stymied in the seraglio. Desert-born ascetics end by spreading their rugs on marble instead of sand. Algernon Asprey's glamorous designs for the interior of the Saudi royal palace have—unless perhaps in the absence of figural art—no obvious affinity with the Wahhabite origins of the kingdom.

Easily lost in the stretches of space, Islamic resurgences also have to be considered in the perspective of time. Islamic history is full of revivalist movements, all exhibiting similar characteristics, all checked in a stammering series. The most impressive reform of modern times was the violent and austere call to primitive purity launched by Muhammad bin 'Abd al-Wahhab (d. 1792), which arose from the emptiness of the Arabian desert and got lost in the superfluities of oil-wealth. The original movement emerged from an intellectual landscape as featureless as the Wahhabites' natural environment. The founder, in his eagerness to trace his revelation directly to God, affected ignorance of his precursors. The zeal which impelled his followers to campaigns of conquest in imitation of the earliest Muslims ultimately got deflected into a Wahhabite state in Saudi Arabia, in which, when drilling started in the 1930s, the hardihood of the founder's ideals became smothered in oil. The royal palace was decorated in purple by Algernon Asprey; a super-rich social welfare programme gave the king-dom—among poorer Arabs—a reputation for a soft-living citizenry, depen-

"Whatever happens, we have got, the Maxim gun and they have not." The contempo-rary commemorative panorama of the Battle of Omdurman revels in the slaughter wrought by irresistible technical superiority. The young Winston Churchill, awed by the unrepeatable spectacle of a clash between two eras, enjoyed "a race lunch before the big event," which left 10,800 Mahdist dead, and at least 16,000 wounded, at a cost of 48 British lives—half of which were lost when Colonel Martin of the 21st Lancers insisted on fighting anachronism with anachronism by launching a cavalry charge.

The veils remain in place. The black chador gained popularity among Shiite women in Lebanon in the 1980s, thanks to the atmosphere of civil war, which augmented people's sense of belonging to their traditional communities, and to the example of the Iranian revolution—an encouraging example of the effectiveness of Shiite tradition in fighting back against the world. The photograph, taken in September 1985, shows women in Nabatiyeh marching in commemoration of the martyrdom of the Shiite warrior Al-Hussein in ninth-century Iraq.

dom—among poorer Arabs—a reputation for a soft-living citizenry, dependent on immigrant labour for its dirty work.

Like monastic reform movements and outbursts of evangelism in the Christian west, no Islamic resurgence has lasted for long without getting deflected or debased. Sometimes Islamic revival was stopped by defeat, like the Mahdists of the Sudan, machine-gunned at Omdurman in 1898; sometimes it was glutted with victory, like the Fulani jihad in west Africa in the early nineteenth century, which was so glorious that the Fulani retain to this day the reputation of a master-race. More usually, however, it was self-defeating, stymied by success, corrupted by ease, diverted by the demands of administering conquests and apportioning revenues. As the cycle of revival and decline entered a downturn, reformers would share the disillusionment of Akbar of Allahabad, prostrated at the sight of women without veils. When he asked where their veils were, "They have fallen," came the reply, "on men's intelligence."

This short staying-power of Islamic revivals is illustrated by the Iranian revolution. Even before the death of the Ayatollah Khomeini, the ground was prepared for retreat from the purity of Islamic principles. Institutions were erected to overrule the power of the Council of Guardians, which kept the legislature leashed to the Sharia. Khomeini's legacy was uncertain. His autocratic habits and impressionistic theology divided the clergy; he left—perhaps deliberately—no successor of a legitimacy like his own; and the limits of his popularity were suggested by riots in 1990 and 1992, when his effigy was destroyed in the street. The clergy's role ebbed with every election. In 1980 mullahs filled almost half the legislature; by 1992 their representation was down to less than a fifth. Educational purges had characterized the revolution at its height—when the universities were closed for two years, the staff and students gutted and the syllabus reformed to concentrate on "Islamic perception" and criticism of the west. But after 1983 these excesses were checked and reversed to remedy the neglect of scientific and technical subjects. The impressively Islamized media were outwitted by a public switch-off and a clandestine video trade.

In retrospect, the Iranian revolution now begins to seem as much "nationalist" as "Islamic"—its violence inspired by ethnic jealousy as much as by jihad. Earlier generations of nationalists prized a unity "that speaks in different dialects and worships God in different ways." Today's proceed by amputating minorities, as if national unity depended on cultural uniformity. In Iran, nationalism and Islam have provided revolutionaries with broadly compatible ideologies; normally, however, their effects collide.

Iran's neighbour, Iraq, which is singularly ill-qualified to be a nation, is a striking example—a conglomeration of minorities crushed into a national mould. The dictator Saddam Hussein (president, 1979–   ), a former bravo and bouncer at political meetings, inculcated Iraqi nationalism in defiance

Saddam Hussein, the new Nebuchadnezzar, rebuilding Babylon with his own hands: the scenes depicted on the stamps are records of a ritual Saddam really carried out. His exploitation of Babylon was not as extravagantly antiquarian as the Shah's use of Persepolis: the original Nebuchadnezzar was the conqueror of Zion, who had carried the Jews into captivity.

of the Arab nationalism of his own party as well as of the Islamic revivalism of his opponents. More remarkably still, he managed to appropriate the rhetoric and imagery of the very movements he frustrated and betrayed.

He appealed beyond Islamic and Arab identities to the glories of ancient Mesopotamia, depicting himself in his postage stamps as a builder and in public performance as the new Nebuchadnezzar, raising Babylon and "stamping the bricks with his own name." He justified his accumulation of a vast army, bristling with missiles, by threatening to obliterate Israel, but he used his might almost exclusively against fellow-Muslims. He claimed to be a descendant of the Shiite culture-hero Ali, but started a bloody war against Iran in 1980; he compared himself to the legendary Kurdish serpent-tamer Kawa, but he bombed the Kurds with chemical weapons from 1988. He was glib with the language of Arab and Islamic solidarity, but his last foreign war was an attempt to annex Kuwait. War on neighbours and subjects was essential to his vision of Iraq. By giving Iraqis external enemies, he forced on them a common purpose; by harrying internal minorities to death or flight, he sliced out some of the diversity. The nature of his regime was summed up in the monument of brazen vulgarity and crass militarism erected to commemorate the bloody stalemate against Iran: a soaring, gleaming arch, framing the mouth of the Shatt al-Arab, formed of giant scimitars grasped in a pair of chunky, severed forearms.

Deflected by nationalism, Islamic revival can also be thwarted by the drive to "modernize." That Muslim fundamentalism is incompatible with technical and scientific progress is a common and, even in some discerning eyes, a respectable claim. By insisting on the sufficiency of ancient knowledge and the perfection of Koranic society, Islamic revolutionaries have appeared to supply the evidence. Rejection of capitalist values has sometimes been ill-targeted, and scientists and scientific institutions have been felled by the spatter of revolutionary shrapnel. To compete with Europe and America, without imitation, demands rare resources of imagination. The problems of carrying modernization along in an Islamic resurgence are illustrated by the confusions and contradictions of one of the great founding figures of the Muslim awakening of the late millennium, Jamal al-Din al-Afghani (1839–1897).

His life moved to the rhythm of exile and expulsion, as he fell out with his hosts in each asylum in turn. In Egypt he was a government pensioner who demanded subversion of the constitution from his spacious corner table in the Café de la Poste; to his British patrons in India he was both a foe and a consultant. His exile in Persia ended when he was accused of plotting with assassins, and by the time of his death he had alienated the authorities in his final home in Turkey. He founded the Egyptian freemasons but upheld religion as the only sound basis of society; he wanted his fellow-Muslims to be abreast of modern science but anathematized Darwin as an atheist and materialist. His talk entertained the brilliant café society of Cairo, and his sermons roused worshippers in Hyderabad and Calcutta. He advocated parliamentary democracy but would not admit the insufficiency of the political lessons of the Koran. His dilemmas have been shared by Muslim leaders ever since. It is probably true that traditional Islamic law and society can coexist with technical progress and scientific advance. Muslims often say so, yet the demon of modernization is forever twisting the "path of the Prophet" into a detour pointing west.

SIGNS ALONG THE ROAD

The critical test for Islamic Resurgence is not whether it is sustained in Iran but whether it can succeed in Turkey and Egypt. Turkey would be a great prize for the fundamentalists to seize: the heartland of the world's greatest-ever Islamic empire; the historic home of a caliphate of widely revered legitimacy; the crossroads of Europe and Asia; the only Muslim country in NATO; the showplace of economic modernization in the Islamic world, the aspiring "workshop and garden of the Middle East" where half the population lives in big towns, manning an industrial economy that can contend seriously for a place in the European Union.

Islamic revival has been girding and arming here for a long time. During Ramadan in 1908, a blind muezzin from a mosque in the Fatih district of Istanbul led a crowd to the sultan's palace to demand that "the flock be led by its shepherd," that taverns be shut, and that women be veiled. It was part of a reaction against a new, secular constitution that embodied modernizing principles and imitated the constitutional monarchies of Christendom.

The same mosque remains a centre of the same project, with muezzins who utter the same subtext, to this day. Islam continues to provide opposition voices with "rhetorical ammunition against secularization." In the meantime, Turkey has become a secular republic, wrenched into modernity by Kemal Atatürk—the general who proved himself for power when he "chained the strength" of western invaders at Gallipoli during the First World War. As the Ottoman Empire fell apart, he was left as the effective dictator of a Turkish national state, where he proclaimed a republic in 1923. During the next few years he banned the more declaratory forms of Islamic dress, imposed the Roman alphabet, and abolished the caliphate. It was the beginning of a slow-burning cultural revolution. And now a woman has just become prime minister.

Yet under modern strains, the Islamic counterpoint has never stopped sounding. Sections of the opposition have always used Islamic language.

28 May 1993: The police seem more formidable than the fundamentalist threat in Turkey during a demonstration against a left-wing newspaper which had serialized extracts from Salman Rushdie's novel, *The Satanic Verses*. Rushdie had used the example of Muhammad to point out the impossibility of testing for the difference between true and false claims to speak for God. On the grounds that he was an Islamic apostate, Ayatollah Khomeini decreed Rushdie's death. Indignation in much of the rest of the Islamic world was hardly less intense.

Religious fundamentalism lit back fires against secularization which the recent resurgence has fanned. International developments have enmeshed the country more tightly in the politics of the Middle East: since 1974, involvement in Cyprus, where Turkey maintains a Turkish-Cypriot breakaway state, has made the goodwill of Islamic neighbours seem vital; trade has confirmed this new mutual dependence—nearly half of Turkey's exports now go to the Islamic world. Islamic fundamentalists have failed to make an electoral breakthrough, but they have patrolled the margins of political life, daubing walls, inciting demonstrations, urging women students to wear headscarves, and pursuing the "Iranian strategy" of "struggle from the mosque": the attempt, that is, to change values by propaganda from the pulpit.

To the visitor in Cairo or Alexandria, Egypt, seems proof against Islamic revolution. These are among the world's most cosmopolitan cities, near the junction of three continents, with acres of enlightened streets, scores of communities of different religions, and dozens of permanently resident ethnicities. Here influences from across the Mediterranean are washed ashore or upriver. Only the "holy blessing of the saints" can keep short skirts out of even the most traditional quarter of Old Cairo, where the *jinn* still visit women's dreams. More than any other Arabic-speaking country, Egypt has shared in European historical experiences. She bore the stamp of French revolutionary armies and felt the lure of imperialism and industrialization (see Chapter 14). The Christian minority is large, rich, culturally influential, and legitimized by antiquity. The Copts have coexisted with the Muslims for thirteen hundred years; they owe nothing to western imperialists or missionaries; their Egyptian credentials are unchallengeable. Against this background, Egypt's tradition has been unsurprisingly hostile to Islamic militancy; the tone of the intellectual life of the Muslim clerical establishment was set in the late nineteenth century by Muhammad 'Abduh, a liberal reformer who became the presiding genius of the hierarchy. Influenced by scholarly German hermeneutics, he encouraged critical reading of the Koran and advocated the compatibility of Islam with science. For most of the twentieth century, the ideologies which vied for dominance in the state were Egyptian nationalism and Arab nationalism, with Islamic consciousness a poor third.

Still, the potentially revolutionary effects of Islamic resurgence were already visible before the Second World War. The most conspicuous sign was the transformation of the Muslim Brotherhood, which had been formed to combat secularism and westernization by awakening the Islamic inner man within every Egyptian Muslim. Its founder and "Supreme Guide," Hassan al-Banna, was a man of political proclivities, responsive to the increasingly violent and active mood of the 1930s. By the end of the decade the Brotherhood was a clandestine revolutionary movement; within a few years more it had become a terrorist army. Another sign of the same climate was the formation and fortune of the Young Egypt organization, a paramilitary camorra of student "Green Shirts" who sought to ape the successes scored by fascism against the western liberal tradition. At the same time they wanted to give their movement distinctively Islamic and Egyptian tints, advocating, for instance, a return to religious law, extolling the continuity of Egyptian history from pharaonic times, and changing their name in 1940 to "National Islamic Party." The new label displayed the two traditions represented by the movement and also the balance between them: nationalism came first, Islam second.

Though it seems odd, at first glance—almost reminiscent of an M. C. Escher engraving (see p. 469)—that the photographer should have chosen to photograph President Anwar Sadat of Egypt with prayer-rug spread at the foot of the stairs, the key to understanding the image lies in Sadat's conviction that he was a mystical visionary, who had been enlightened by extraordinary spiritual experiences in prison. The *"scala dei"* have always signified mystical ascent, in Islamic as in Christian literature. Sadat is pictured, in a simple sufi-like robe, with the depths of the stairwell behind him and an ascent like Yakub's (or Jacob's) at Bethel awaiting him on the other side of prayer.

The army officers who seized power in 1952 were influenced by Islamic rhetoric, but their politics were essentially secular: predominantly Arab nationalist and socialist in the fifties and sixties, shading into Egyptian nationalist and capitalist in the seventies and eighties. This left Islam as the obvious rallying point of opposition. Anwar Sadat (president, 1968–81) fancied himself a mystic—like his friend, the Shah of Iran, with whom he kept up a relationship of mutual admiration. During a spell of imprisonment in the Second World War, he felt "initiated into that new world of self-abnegation which enabled my soul to merge into all other beings, to establish communion with the Lord of all Being." A photograph he was fond of showed him enraptured, wrapped in a prayer shawl, with a prominent "prayer bump"—the presumed result of overzealous prostration—showing on his forehead. Unlike the Shah, however, he did not use his supposedly privileged access to God as a pretext for bypassing the Islamic establishment; nor did he ignore the evidence of Islamic resurgence but tried to ride it, wielding Islamic language freely and incorporating religious precepts into civil law. For a political leper, spotted in pious eyes by a series of horrendous sins—who had made peace with the Zionists, allied his country with the Great Satan of the United States, promoted the meretricious influence of consumerism, and, on a personal level, attended the immodest entertainments of western celebrities—these were ultimately self-destructive concessions. Too late, in the last months of his life, he realized his mistake, called for "the separation of religion from politics," and proposed to bring under government patronage the forty thousand private mosques where Islamic extremism was preached.

As in England before the Civil War of 1642, revolutionary fanaticism was encouraged by a class of imperfectly educated, under-rewarded preachers. Between 1960 and 1975, the number of mosques in Egypt increased by two-thirds, while the population rose by a little less than a half. The brighter professional clergy got jobs abroad, while the domestic boom was serviced by enthusiastic amateurs who despised the "wireless Islam" of the regime and operated outside "local turbaned officialdom." Their preaching struck sparks at two flashpoints of danger: popular sectarian violence and revolutionary cells.

The first of these was surrounded by the dry tinder of a Coptic minority whose wealth attracted envy and whose tradition esteemed martyrdom. Early in 1980 bombs shattered two Alexandrian churches; by August of the following year, seven churches had been bombed, nearly two thousand suspected terrorists had been arrested, hundreds of wounds had been inflicted in sectarian street battles, an extremist newspaper had been banned, Coptic Easter celebrations had been cancelled, and a cinema had been burned for showing a film about Christ.

The origins and nature of the terrorist cells were gradually revealed by scholars and journalists who interviewed imprisoned fanatics. All the groups had their roots or inspiration in the old Muslim Brotherhood. All were formed or revived in the mood of introspection and breast-beating that followed humiliation by Israel in the Six Days' War of 1967, when Sinai was lost to the Zionists. All shared a strongly corporatist ideology, stressing the values of the *umma*—the collective of the faithful—above those of individuals or families. All throve in places of further and higher education in the seventies. All benefited from the indulgence Sadat extended from 1970 to 1973, when he was still hoping to harness the Islamic revival for his own purposes. All were consciously part of a pan-Islamic militant tendency, sensing solidarity with the revolutionary Islamic regime in Libya, the Pales-

The assassination of Sadat happened at a huge military parade, under conditions of apparently maximum security, with press photographers and television cameras present to capture every moment of the event. The results included some of the most dramatic pictures ever filmed. In this one, the assassins, disguised as participants in the parade, are pumping bullets into the viewing stand. Bystanders—after being momentarily numbed—are abandoning adjoining areas in terror, but guards and officers are still trying to reach or protect the president and build up the flimsily extemporized barricade of chairs, behind which Sadat is already mortally wounded.

tinian liberation movement, and the Iranian uprising. All shared the perception of Sayyid Qtub, the intellectual progenitor of Muslim terrorism in Egypt, whose *Signs Along the Road* depicted an apostate nation, reverting to the sort of godless chaos which preceded the mission of Muhammad.

The pathology of terrorism in Sadat's last decade is represented by the organization known as Takfir wal-Higra. *Takfir* is the act of the curse: identifying and denouncing heretics and unbelievers; *higra* means withdrawing from society—the withdrawal, in particular, of the prophet Muhammad from the merchant communities among whom he grew up but who refused to acknowledge his message from God. Surprisingly numerous, reckoned in thousands, the members were recruited by the operations of kinship, friendship, and worship, drawn in gradually by recruiting cadres over a long acquaintance.

The seed-group was founded by Ahmad Shukri Mustapha, a middle-class graduate imprisoned for membership in the Muslim Brotherhood, whose work he wanted to renew in greater secrecy and militancy. Gaol was the ideal environment—itself a kind of shrine of *higra*. Most of his recruits were in their late teens or early twenties, tweeny terrorists with the explosive confidence of young idealism. The whole of society outside their ranks was included in their anathema, clergy and all. Like most political utopians, they looked ahead to a future with a blurred horizon, uncertain how to turn rage into policy. But they were organized—ineffectively, as it turned out—for revolution. When Sadat was gunned down by a suicide squad from a different organization—rising to meet his assassins in a gleaming uniform, on a podium sprayed with bullets, on 6 October 1981—Takfir members in stolen police clothes were ejected from public buildings.

THE EYE OF ISLAM

As the end of the millennium approaches, the Islamic revolution seems to be over and Islamic revival seems stymied. As in previous revivals, the paths of the Prophet turn inwards and get wound into an insoluble maze. Sadat was succeeded by his deputy without any great mutation in the state or modification of policy. Iran's revolutionary fervour spent itself in the war against Iraq. In the 1990s, the Libyan revolution has a comfortably ageing, threadbare look, offering to deliver its terrorists to international justice. Ayatollah Khomeini is dead; his followers' beards have grown, and his republic has become almost respectable. Despite electoral popularity, Islamic fundamentalists are still being thwarted by military power-brokers in the Maghribi states. The victory of the mujahidin in Afghanistan has not been followed by the installation of a fanatical regime. Islamic republics in Sudan and Pakistan wear an air of compromise, vaunting the legitimacy of laws religiously inspired but excluding extremists from a share of power. Parties of "Islamic perception" are contained by the electoral systems of Indonesia, Bangladesh, and Malaysia. The Turkish state looks safely profane. After more than a hundred years of pan-Islamism, Muslims remain awkward in collective action and impotent, for instance, to destroy Zionism or influence the fate of Bosnia.

It would be a mistake, however, to discount the resurgence of Islam. It has faltered but probably not failed. If its future can be predicted from its past, the cycle will spin round again and the momentum of recovery will be retrieved. Though Islam remains riven by schisms, there have been impressive examples of inter-confessional cooperation—in the Iranian revolution, for instance, and the opposition to Saddam Hussein. The waning of differences and the acceleration of communications will make it possible from now on for each successive movement of revival to be more coherent and more powerful than the last.

For all that has been said, in potential competition with other cultures Muslims have great advantages. Demographic change, after a long period of adversity (see Chapters 3 and 12), has come in the present century to favour Islam. In the context of the Soviet state, this adjustment was so dramatic that the increase in the numbers of the Muslim nationalities reversed the balance of the population in the third quarter of the century, turning the ethnic Russians into a minority within the union. In the world of Islam as a whole, most of these growing numbers replenish a relatively compact band of territory, extending almost continuously from the eastern edge of the Atlantic to the Pacific rim of the Indian Ocean. As the initiative in world affairs shifts, with the world's economic centre of gravity, from the Atlantic to the Pacific, the Muslim world may come to appear left out—a brown smear on the film as the camera of history swings between white and yellow foci. If so, the effect may enhance Muslim solidarity.

There is a place where the unity and vitality of Islam can be seen in action, but no infidel is allowed to visit Mecca. Outside the city to the east, on the slopes of the mount of Mercy or on the plain spread at the foot of its stocky, granite funnel, pilgrims gather in tents—scores of thousands at a time—at the mid-point of their pilgrimage, to honour the place where Adam pleaded to be reconciled, and where Muhammad preached his last sermon. There they stand in prayer from noon to sunset. They return to the shrine of the Ka'aba, at the centre of a mosque big enough to accommodate half a million worshippers: the pilgrims, however, are often too numerous to fit and spill out into the streets and squares around.

Different sects and schools have their own traditional meeting-points in the holy precincts, but all are united in the same experience, sharing the same rites. Seven times they circle the sacred rock which Muhammad kissed—a meteoric fragment, set in a silver socket like an eyeball in an eye.

Stirred and swirled together, mingled pell-mell, they rush up and down in high, mosaic-tiled corridors, between a channel left free for wheelchairs, in ritual mimicry of Hagar's frantic search for the blessed spring of Zemzem. When the pilgrimage is over, they return in planeloads to homes all over the world and take a sense of mutual belonging with them.

The Kaaba is never unthronged: if there were no people around it, it is said that 70,000 angels would be there, performing the traditional ritual circumambulation. For most pilgrims to Mecca, the culminating moment of the pilgrimage is this circling of the Kaaba, when those who can get close enough imitate the Prophet by kissing the Black Stone. But it is a survival of a pre-Islamic rite and, properly speaking, the essential stage of the pilgrimage only begins here—leading to the Mount of Mercy some miles to the east, where the pilgrims stand in assembly from noon to sunset.

PART FIVE

THE PACIFIC CHALLENGE

We live around a sea like frogs around a pond.

PLATO, *Phaedo*

Chapter 20

THE WATCHERS AT DAWN: MODERNIZATION IN JAPAN

The Eaters of Whales—The Revolution of the Samurai—The Floating Wharf—A Mark in the World—The Stump of the Golden Pavilion

THE EATERS OF WHALES

The romance of whaling is not much appreciated nowadays. The hunters are denounced on shirts and bumper stickers. Cuddly whales are sold in toyshops. Recordings of the noises whales make are played to comfort human babies in the womb. Leviathan has become a precious and friendly companion for man, chatty and petted, while his ancient connotations of monstrous terror have got transferred to the whalers. The heroes of the seascapes and stories which whaling formerly inspired—images of collective triumph, won by the discipline of dedicated men over a looming fate in deadly environments—have been turned into the villains of a modern saga of readjusted ecological values. As almost the world's last eaters of whales, Japanese have borne a lot of the opprobrium. Resentment of foreign reproaches has made a taste for whale meat a patriotic badge in Japan and turned the flaccid, insipid fillets into a reputed delicacy.

Revulsion from the romance of whaling probably started with the practice of the whalers themselves. Anxieties about conservation and sentimentality over the prey came later. When Herman Melville wrote *Moby-Dick,* the most gripping and moving of all whaling romances, in 1851, the whalers' battle with their quarry was still nicely poised between the primal beast and the primitive technology. To Melville the whale fishery was a calling of "imperial dignity," but the harpoonists aboard the *Pequod* were all "primitives" themselves, drawn into the story from a remote age: Queequeg, the ex-cannibal, "savage and hideously marred" with unearthly tattoos and idolatrous yearnings; Tashtego, an "unmixed Indian," "snuffing in the trail," a "son of the Prince of the Powers of the Air"; and Dagoo, "a gigantic negro-savage with a lionlike tread." They hunted the whale to within a harpoon's throw in open boats that could be crunched or flailed to splinters. When a monster was seized—worried and wearied and harried to death—the carcass, lashed to the side of the ship, would make her list. Then the whole crew would kneel between decks in blood and blubber to chop the fat for rendering before it turned putrid. In the year of *Moby-Dick,* when the castaway John Manjiro returned to Japan with accounts of his life aboard American whalers, a Japanese artist illustrated the process—emphasizing the lashed whale, his fierce teeth, an eye still lively in death and the fires raging in the kilns on deck.

Within a few years of Melville's book, the industrial revolution came to the world of whaling. The romance fled with the risk and the raw, coarse trauma. In 1865, Svend Foyn introduced the killer ship. From his steampowered ironclad, mounted with a hefty cannon on a pivot at the prow, a

Processing a whale on board the John Holandby Kawada Shoryo (1851): a woodblock print to illustrate John Manjiro's account of his adventures aboard the American whaler. His fishing-boat was lost on the small island of Torishima in 1841 but he was rescued by the American ship and, after serving on her voyage to Honolulu, accepted Captain Whitfield's invitation to accompany her home to New Bedford. See pp. 611–12.

five-foot harpoon of a hundred pounds' weight thudded into the target's hide at short range. The hollow iron cap was filled with blasting powder; a timed fuse exploded the bomb inside the whale's body. Using fast engines, the carcass could be towed into port for processing. Every kind of whale could now be hunted—none too big or too powerful—and every part of it used. The flesh, which had formerly been discarded, could be ground for fertilizer. When the Japanese joined in factory whaling after the Second World War, they refrigerated it aboard and ate it.

Thus the industrialization of whaling kept pace with the "modernization" of Japan; the place of the whale in the modern Japanese menu is a result of the coincidence of both processes. This is a reminder of the great paradox of modern Japan: shared experience with western peoples did not mean assimilation to western ways or tastes, or incorporation in western history. Judged by the origins of their movement, as well as by the results, it is misleading to characterize the modernizers as imitators of Europe or the U.S.A. Nor—contrary to western self-flattery—was it western initiatives that brought isolation to an end and got the modernizers started. Butterfly's wings were already flapping before Pinkerton fluttered them.

In the early nineteenth century, Japan was, in words Yukio Mishima coined in a very different context, a "sailor who fell from grace with the sea"—an island empire, afloat on a vast ocean which her citizens were forbidden to navigate (see Chapter 11). Her maritime traditions were beached on her own shores. A bird's eye view in a woodcut of 1820 showed clusters of tiny vessels, for shallow fishing and cabotage, huddled close to the coasts. A strong literary convention celebrated the comfort or complacency of short horizons—the limited ambitions, say, of the poet Onuna Chinzan, who, on the eve of Japan's opening to world trade, would "strive to buy a barrel of wine, hold it to my breast, open it with a laugh of triumph." A rival tendency, however, of growing strength, felt the fascination of the far-off and appreciated the need for a lookout from the crow's nest even when in dry dock. In 1771 enthusiastic beginners in Dutch Studies had started meeting six or seven times a month to puzzle over the meaning of western books; after about a year "we became capable of reading as much as ten or more lines of text per day if the particular passage was not too difficult."

Holland proved an imperfect window on the west, darkly glazed and partly shuttered. The Japanese government did not know about American independence until 1808 and was kept ignorant by its Dutch informants of the success of the French Revolution. News of the fate of Holland in the Napoleonic Wars was suppressed. "Dutch learning" was received in an equivocal spirit. The translator Sugita Seikei (1817–1859) developed the habit of crying "Vriheid!" when drunk, but most Japanese readers of western books absorbed the technical and scientific lessons while rejecting the philosophical messages. Aizawa Seishisai (1781–1863)—who derived plea-

A bird's-eye view of Japan by Kensai Joshin (1820) brings out the paradox of the Tokugawa era: the isolation of a maritime people. The land is depicted in terms of sailors' landmarks—conspicuous castles, temples, high peaks, and useful harbours. Edo, with the two towers of the Shogun's castle, is visible at bottom right and the gleaming cone of Mount Fuji is given a distinctive look. The expanse of the Japan Sea leads the eye to the Korean coast in the background.

sure as a boy of eleven from flaying a picture of a European explorer—warned, from study of the enemy, that foreign profanities would destroy the sacred nature of Japan. Takahashi Kageyasu, author of the coast-watch decree of 1825 which reinforced Japan's isolation, revelled in the nickname of "Johannes Globius" given him by Dutch friends in Nagasaki; he was put to death when he breached security by giving their physician a map of Japan as a parting gift.

In this era of opening minds and closed ports, political reforms anticipated some of the themes of future "modernization." The campaign of moral rearmament waged by the chief minister Matsudaira Sadanobu, simultaneously with the French Revolution, was backward-looking: a reversion to Confucian standards of official rectitude and an ancient samurai ethos of service. But his programme, if sustained, would have brought into being something like the centralized state of a hundred years thence. In the 1830s a succession of crop failures and riots made reform seem urgent again. Most solutions concentrated on traditional remedies—economy, frugality, and the search for men of talent; but a call for the centralization of power caught the imagination of the most powerful minister of the next decade, Mizuno Tadakuni.

He was an unlikely reformer, susceptible to bribes of salmon sushi; his avowed aim was "to become senior counsellor as quickly as possible and then relax." Yet he spattered the demi-monde with traditional bans on mixed bathing, female music teachers, gambling, tattoos, and novelettes. His political reforms shifted power from the provinces into ministers' hands. He abolished the commercial monopolies and domain currencies of provincial lords and demanded from them long-lapsed subventions in men and cash for the government. He even tampered with the distribution of land in the cause of administrative efficiency, consolidating, for instance, under government control, land around the fortress of Osaka, formerly divided among 165 authorities.

When he was forced to resign for good in 1845, the start he had made was left dangling by a successor under whom "all the lords were content." "Western barbarians" had already prised open the ports of China (see Chapter 11) and might at any moment do the same in Japan. Revolution, however, did not have to be imposed from above or intruded from outside. Within the empire, peasant millenarians, frustrated provincial bureaucrats, and jealous domain lords were already trying or training to challenge the government, or even to replace it.

The prospects of mass movements of unpredictable power in the countryside were demonstrated, for instance, by the appeal of the pietism of Kurozomi Manetada (1780–1850), spared from tuberculosis after mystical union with the sun goddess. The potential social impact was suggested by a new religion—still going strong today—founded by a peasant woman with a healing touch, Nakayama Miki (1798–1887), who proclaimed herself a divine incarnation, abandoned her family, and distributed her land. The political possibilities were made explicit in a magnificently amateurish rebellion launched in 1837 by Oshio Heihachiro, who was also a prime example of the frustrations of the provincial bureaucracy. He was a victim of the self-importance of low-level samurai: a hereditary police inspector who compiled his own genealogy. His sense of *noblesse oblige*—or its Japanese near-equivalent, *nasake,* compassion for the swordless—helped to inspire the "excessive integrity" which won him the commendation of inferiors and the enmity of equals. Visited by a vision of the sixteenth-century Confucian philosopher Wang Yang-ming, he obeyed Wang's call to "Knowledge transformed in action" by selling his library and buying arms. Advocating the "egalitarianism of the Absolute Spirit," he blamed the government for famine, discarding the usual pious and fatalistic evasions. Few peasants answered his call to rebellion, but a contemporary scroll shows those who did, destroying tax records. Against a background of crop failures and

Peasant rages—common throughout the Tokugawa period—grew increasingly frequent in the early nineteenth century. This scene of a "smashing," in which records of taxes or debts are destroyed along with the environment polluted by them, represents the terms in which such events were typically recorded: violent reactions against poverty and oppression. Oshio Heihachiro tried to harness rage for a utopian programme: "to save the people from the hell of the past and establish paradise before their eyes."

tax extortions, peasant rages went on erupting ineffectively, sometimes recorded by womenfolk, who clung to the rebels' sleeves.

If peasant movements could not ignite revolution on their own, they could help kindle it by rubbing at the points of friction among rivals for authority: the shogun—the hereditary vizir in his bloated courtly metropolis of Edo, to whom the emperor's nominal power was effectively devolved; and the daimyo lords or chiefs of the 260-odd domains. The shoguns had the most obvious interest in radical change—in centralization, in modernization, in an effective army, equipped through an industrial revolution— whereas the domains might have been expected to evince reactionary sloth. "National" unification seemed, for the shogunate of the early nineteenth century, a natural vocation and an easy aim, as target practice was suspended on grounds of expense in lordly domains, while skeleton households rattled in poverty around the lords' big mansions at the shogun's court. For a time, however, after the fall of Mizuno, it was the

Gessann Ogata, "Perry in Japan" (1950): a well-imagined scene, in a pastiche of a contemporary style, captures the mood of Perry's reception in Japan with convincing fidelity. A Manchu interpreter is at Perry's elbow.

shoguns who shied from action, while rebellious spirits in some of the most powerful and peripheral domains began to nurture ambitions of taking over the central government, rather than merely resisting its growth.

This interlude of reversed roles proved crucial. By about the middle of the nineteenth century, the strongest domain—Satsuma in the far south—had the most formidable and up-to-date army in Japan. A number of other domains—Choshu, Tosa, and Mito, in particular—housed schools of ideologues who could justify civil war by appealing to the phantasma of imperial sovereignty against the reality of the shogun's rule. They were encouraged by suspicion and hatred of the foreign ships that were beginning to prowl offshore, but the formative influences were all inside the country and the new ideas flashed from the clash of indigenous traditions. Fujita Toko, whose *Records of the Kodokan,* begun in 1837, fomented the new ideology in the Mito domain, aspired to be "a demon of loyalty,/Who will guard the imperial house/For ever." The oath sworn in 1861 by swordsmen of Tosa, outraged when their lord was punished for opposing the admission of foreign traders, expressed the same ambition with due force and, typically, combined it with old-fashioned feudal loyalty and newfangled populism: "we will go through fire and water to ease the emperor's mind, carry out the will of our former lord, and purge this evil from our people."

Commodore Matthew C. Perry, defying the guns of Edo harbour in 1853 to demand rights of access for his countrymen, was a catalyst, not a cause, of the revolution which followed. The shock of his arrival was real: it made the emperor's court at Kyoto break a silence of centuries to call for temple bells to be melted into guns. A retrospective painting of the American ashore shows how he looked to the Japanese—angular and unyielding, bolt upright in tight clothes, which contrast with the soft and flowing robes that swathe his hosts. His lips are correspondingly taut; his eyes frown and his chins are compressed in ridges by the effort to look stern. It was an image that both attracted and repelled. In the background of the painting, the Japanese turn the prows of their boats towards the American ships but hang back, hesitating to approach. Yoshida Shoin, the influential military and political theorist of Choshu domain, wanted to leave with Perry and see the world; but he also regarded the commercial treaties imposed on Japan as an "abjuration of heaven which has angered all the deities" and "bequeathed shame to future generations." Exiled to a village academy where he taught future revolutionaries, he called for "a rising of independent patriots" to "reinstate the saintly emperor and the wise lords."

THE REVOLUTION OF THE SAMURAI

After the trauma of the treaties, according to verses by a Buddhist monk who killed himself in disgust with the government, "only the cherry blossoms," free of "rank barbarian stench," breathed "to the morning sun the fragrance of a nation's soul." Modernization, westernization, and industrialization became policies identifiable with the shogunate, while the rebel armies from the domains—for all their western weaponry and translated drill books—looked like forces of reaction. In 1867 the shogun Tokugawa Yoshimobu celebrated the arrival of a French military mission with a reception in morning dress, catered by his French chef. Members of his family were in Paris and the Hague, gleaning ideas for imposing centralization on Japan.

His overthrow the following year is conventionally the event from which Japan's revolution in modernization is dated. At the time it seemed more like a reactionary putsch; yet the revolutionary paradox soon showed through. The new rulers of Japan were young samurai, representative members of an old élite, yet they legislated their own class out of existence. They came from the domains, especially from remote, restive Satsuma; yet they imposed on the country a centralization—and "national unification," as apologists called it—which the shoguns had never achieved. It was as if German union had been thrust on Prussia by Bavaria, or the *Risorgimento* initiated from Sicily.

These self-transformations of samurai revolutionaries—more dramatic, perhaps, even than the self-reform of the English ruling class in roughly the same period—are often explained as concessions to the inevitable, like the submission, in a reformist leader's haiku, of "the pines at Takashi beach, in spite of their renown," to "the surge of historic tidal waves." The first manifesto of the victors of the civil war promised "deliberative councils" attuned to "general opinion," the "cooperation of all classes" and a "search for knowledge throughout the world": in other words, constitutional government and westernization—easy enough to mistake for a "bourgeois revolution." The author of the haiku, Okubo Toshimichi of Satsuma, was also the author of some of the policies which came to characterize the revolutionary era. He devised its pragmatic programme, expressed in the four-character apophthegm, "Enrich the country and strengthen the army." He reasoned further that modernization would have to embrace customs and laws, social relationships and economic principles. Conscription would displace the concept of a military caste. In breathtaking acts of self-destruction by the hereditary warrior-class—a sort of collective *seppuku*—military obligation would be extended to commoners, to whom arms were formerly forbidden on pain of death. Militarization, to adapt a slogan of the Third French Republic, would transform peasants into Japanese. Meanwhile, cut off from their defining traditions and privileges, the samurai would blend into the rest of society. The leadership of their descendants—though it proved surprisingly tenacious under the new order—would have to be claimed on merit and shared with other talents.

The Japanese language has long cadenze of endings and special words to convey levels of politeness. In a culture where hierarchy is embedded in the language, the conceptual problems raised by social reform had a stirring effect on mentalities as well as relationships. The connection with the effects of foreign influence is illustrated by the contrasting attitudes to American egalitarianism evinced by early Japanese visitors to the United States. John Manjiro, an intelligent fisherman whose sights were raised by

The fascination of "a society without etiquette": Fukuzawa Yukichi's prized photograph of himself with an American girl, taken in San Francisco when he was in America with the first Japanese embassy in 1860. The deputy leader of the mission, Norimasa Muragaki, could not approve the freedom with which the sexes mixed or "the extraordinary sight of men and women hopping about on the floor, arm in arm. . . . We were not altogether wrong in calling them western barbarians."

his education in America, thought that country as different from Japan "as heaven from hell." He alarmed interrogators on his return home by telling them that in America a man was judged on ability rather than ancestry. A few years later, Fukuzawa Yukichi, an officer aboard the schooner that escorted the first Japanese embassy to the States, struggled to come to terms with the brashness of a society apparently "without etiquette." In a famous incident, "one day, on a sudden thought," he asked after the whereabouts of George Washington's descendants. The casual and indifferent response shocked him, because although "I knew of course that America was a republic with a new president every four years, I could not help feeling that the family of Washington would be revered above all other families." He proudly took back to Japan a photograph of himself with an American girl, which he considered outrageously flirtatious but which displays only solemn decorum to western eyes. In the new Japan, he adopted a "proud and independent way of life," telling his countrymen that "heaven did not create one man above or below another," while Manjiro, the ex-fisherman, became a high official with the right to wear two swords.

The achievement of all these changes, accompanied and succeeded by an industrial revolution of remarkable power and precocity, is best understood in the context of the slow mutation of the self-perception and ambitions of the samurai. There were too many of them to be accommodated in an *ancien régime* of restricted opportunities, reduced to menial occupations, exposed to the contempt of their social inferiors. In Satsuma, where 40 per cent of the population were samurai, they commonly doubled as agricultural labourers. Most members of this decayed estate were victims of the system under the shogunate—landless, powerless, and dependent on petty offices in domain bureaucracies or daimyo households. A group of young samurai who met to devise ways of helping their country after Perry's first visit was baffled by the question, "What can we do without office?"

Frozen out of the top layers of a rigid system of honours, they had no vested interest against change. Desperate to supplement meagre stipends, some of them led picaresque lives, on the margins of respectability, of a sort depicted in the autobiography of Katsu Kokichi, who died in 1850. He lived beyond his means in "imported silks and fine fabrics," obliged to obtain extra income by trading in swords at street fairs, reciting incantations, and organizing protection for bordellos. Ostensibly, his was a cautionary tale of self-reproach, belied—however—by his satisfaction at "birth under a lucky star, the way I did whatever I pleased."

Lives which hovered like this on the fringes of the samurai world of values were common in the early nineteenth century—like the leaders of the failed peasant insurrection of Oshio Heihachiro, martyrs to *nasake,* or like Takiwaza Bakin, who resigned his rank to become a professional writer of stories in "yellow covers" and made enough money to buy back samurai status for his grandson before his death in 1848. Models for this sort of equivocal role-playing could be found in the theatre and literature of a period in which, according to the proverb, the world was "like a kabuki performance." The work of Tsuruya Namboku, in the 1820s, was full of strange alliances between high birth and low breeding. More popular plays and stories exalted knights of the road above those of the sword and inverted the value systems of the old warrior-caste, replacing the court with the bathhouse and barbershop.

Even at high levels of power and status, the freedom of rogues and vagabonds could seem seductive: in 1837, a domain lord was ordered into retirement for having himself tattooed. Like the gamblers and adventurers invented by storytellers, the revolutionaries of 1868, in crafting their own lives, were drawn into reckless, irregular, and unconventional courses by undermined confidence in traditional identities and by need of a new role. The successful young samurai rebels who seized power in 1868 were a country party incensed against the court and a faction of the excluded, gambling for control of the institutions they denounced.

Their slogan was "Expel the Barbarians" but, once in power, they confirmed the treaties, wore unknotted hair, rode in horse-drawn carriages, and flourished "bat-like" umbrellas on visits to brothels. In 1871 fifty leading members of the new government decamped on a tour of Europe and America. Their attitudes to the west remained, however, rippled with suspicions, and their revolutionary commitment was tempered by nostalgia for an idealized past. Every borrowing was an adaptation. In a satire of 1880, the creation of a legislative assembly was likened to the hesitations of a respectable client allying himself with a geisha in the face of jealousy from a slavish former mistress. The project of creating a Japanese equivalent of the Code Napoléon was held up for years by conflicts of values old and new, evolved and imitated: partible inheritance could not be reconciled with traditions of lineage, nor equality and humanity with ethnic customs and claims of blood.

In the midst of their innovations, the men of 1868 were self-proclaimed defenders of an historic order. They had seized power in the emperor's name, and their revolution was disguised under the style of a "restoration." They moved the emperor to the real seat of power, the old shoguns' city of Edo which they renamed Tokyo so that "quite a few nobles"—said an old satirist—"no longer think of home." They really did restore the emperor as a cult object, whose portraits and rescripts were displayed for veneration in public buildings, and, as a mouthpiece of government, whose voice, "the voice of the crane," was again heard in the land after an interval of centuries. The names of the departments and offices of state they created were borrowed from originals a thousand years old, and the language of decrees was self-consciously archaizing. Though the education minister, Eto Shimpei, ultimately broke with his colleagues, who had his head chopped off for rebellion, most of them would have agreed with him that Japan's attitude should be one "not of receiving instruction from the westerners, but observing them in a spirit of critical enquiry."

The contradictions of the revolution were enfleshed in the person of Saigo Takamori: mountainously enfleshed, for he was a former sumo wrestler whose corpulence was uncontained even by his own ascetic severities. He revered traditional weapons and martial arts, but modernized the armies of his native Satsuma in preparation for the civil wars. He was fanatically loyal to clan and domain, but toured the country as a reluctant advocate of the revolutionaries' abolition of autonomy. He feared the erosion of samurai status and ethics, but would not oppose the military reforms. He detested the ostentation of his government colleagues but confined his counter-measures to symbolic gestures, such as doffing his clogs in the rain outside the palace and giving Okubo's jewelled sword to a gardener. He agreed with Eto's demands—war against Korea and perpetuation of samurai privileges—but would not join his insurrection. And when he finally felt

"Drive out the foreign barbarian": a woodblock print by Ipposai Hoto (1861) shows how Saigo Takamon upheld the principles of national purity that contributed so much to the origins of the Meiji revolution: indeed, he was an embodiment of the sumo wrestler in the picture: the hero of "mountainous flesh," overthrowing foreign influence.

compelled to attempt a rebellion of his own, he flung himself into it fatalistically, relishing the sense of imminence of a death he had long desired, "like the tinted leaves that fall in Tatsuta/Before they are spoiled by autumn rains." The site of his last stand at Kagoshima in Satsuma is scattered with odd tombstones and thousands of his followers' remains—the flower of the samurai, withered in the blast from the gun barrels of peasant conscripts.

THE FLOATING WHARF

After Saigo's death in 1877, the men of 1868 faced no further challenges to their rule. Some of their projects, however, were delayed by the inertia of the system; others were extemporized at intervals, in an effort to keep pace with other countries. Within a generation's span, western dress and décor went out of fashion as a new, "self-esteeming" Japan worked out an equilibrium of taste between tradition and innovation. To writers whose earliest memories were of the time of the revolution, the selective absorption of western lessons came naturally. Mori Ogai (1862–1922) wore "two pairs of sandals," combining western ideas of genre and Chinese conventions of discourse. A story of his of 1910 recounts the meeting of a German woman and her Japanese lover in a café which, like Japan, is under reconstruction. "May I kiss you?" asks the woman. "This is Japan," replies the man. Natsume Soseki (1867–1916), who described Japanese society with the techniques of western writers in novels that remain popular worldwide, composed haikus inspired by lines from Shakespeare.

The project of the new generation was to turn equilibrium into equality by creating an industrial economy, comparable with those taking shape in Europe and the United States. This would make Japan "the floating wharf of the Pacific." Like the constitutional modernization which preceded it, industrialization in Japan would be exceptional—attuned to Japanese priorities and national genius. The smoke from the Tomioka silk-reeling plant in 1872 seemed to a draughtsman to curl upwards in parallel with the steam from the funnel of Mount Fuji. Despite the popularity in Japan of Samuel Smiles's gospel-books from the laissez-faire religion of work, business was perceived not only as a means of self-discipline and a source of self-enrichment, but also as a form of service to the community and state. Though the economics of supply and demand were well understood, the Japanese—who remain the world's highest accumulators of savings—were amenable to a regime of consumption restricted in relation to income and deferred in favor of investment. From the early days, Japanese businesses tended to resemble vertical structures of society, in which a sense of corporate belonging unites contributors at different levels of responsibility and reward, like the worker and boss shown bound in a three-legged race in a workers' paper of 1920. Government and business had a symbiotic relationship in a system of "capitalism from above": business leaders collaborated with governments, throughout Japan's industrial revolution, in intensifying investment, restraining internal demand, and giving priority to strength for war. Governments, in turn, manipulated contracts and concessions to concentrate wealth in safe hands.

The success of industrialization in Japan can be measured by the intensity of reactions against it, usually uttered with an arcadian accent. Saigo Takamori chose for his last headquarters a place with a beautiful view. Sensibility in the face of natural beauty is a much older rhetorical convention in Japan than in the west (see Chapter 1)—enhanced, perhaps, by the very ugliness of the crude industrial cityscapes of Japan today. The idealization of rural life has not been left, in Japan, to exiles from court hurly-burly or refugees from modern life: it has a deeply hollowed place in collective awareness of what it means to be Japanese. It has to be understood in a long context of Japanese history and a virtually timeless context of Japanese geography. Japan is, over most of its extent, an infertile and inhospitable country. Population has always been crammed into narrow coastal crannies. Even before the industrial revolution, it was a land of teeming cities, with several that housed hundreds of thousands of people. Only the most intensive agriculture known—back-breaking, bone-aching labour in rice paddies—could keep the nation fed. Villages and secluded wastes provided images of noble suffering, sacrificial discipline, and consoling solitude.

Critics of industrialization could therefore draw on a tradition which had summoned men back—in a spiritual sense—to the countryside in earlier crises. In the early nineteenth century, the village spirit was commended and earth deities evoked by physiocratic experts and peasant populists alike. The hymns of Nakayama Miki and the treatises of Sato Nobuhiro (1769–1850) both celebrated the good fields. In the late nineteenth and early twentieth centuries, a tough arcady was again extolled by the Nohonshugi movement, which advocated farming as a way of life and the village as a model for the nation, and by officials who idealized the countryside as "free of the baneful influences of civilization."

The industrial revolution wrung tears from this tradition: unwiped tears, for instance, on the cheek of an old woman who showed Ishikawa Takuboku a handful of sand—a symbol of industrial desiccation; the same

Nagatsuka Takashi's *Earth* filmed in 1939: a story of harrowing rural misery which nevertheless echoes the utopian themes of traditional Japanese idealizations of country life: peasant virtues, "village spirit," the sanctity of a family's relationship with the soil.

young poet shed tears of his own for "the declining people of my old village,/Rice fields, dry fields sold." *Earth,* a novel by Nagatsuka Takashi published in parts at about the same time (1910–12), is a numbing, harrowing saga of the ruin of a peasant family so downtrodden that the demoralized hero cannot bring himself to go to the police station to register his denial of a withdrawn charge. "I could not help confessing," he explains. A few years previously, in the real-life background to Nagatsuka's fiction, the authorities had levelled a village and flooded its site to obliterate the last peasant resistance of the notorious "copper pollution revolt." The horrors inflicted by the Ashio copper mines had become a symbol of the costs of industrialization: rabid expansion, deforestation, floods, and the poisoning of downstream waters. In 1896, thirteen thousand households were flooded and the victims had rebelled.

As the triumphs of industrialization got more strident, its critics fled further into nostalgia, mysticism, and fantasy. Tachibana Kosaburo in 1932 lamented the loss of village Japan "torn apart by money and materialism"; in 1936, Gondo Seiki, striving to enshrine the image of the sacred village in his contemporaries' hearts, tried to invoke folk memories of the origins of agriculture in the sun-goddess's commands. In 1934, Tanizako Junichiro made the glare of the light-bulb a symbol of industrial cruelty: he pleaded for a lost world of undisturbed shadows, "lavatories fit for meditation" and "the shadowy colouring of foods, skin complexion, and lacquer ware." Okawa Shume (1886–1957), participating in a widespread search for "the native place of the Japanese soul," found it within himself in a moral tradition which had seeped into an unfrequented level of awareness, recoverable by a sort of conversion experience. After all this agony, the degree to which rural Japan survived industrialization is surprising. In the mid-twentieth century, when land reform turned occupiers into freeholders, the number of small farmers living in hamlets and growing rice in paddies was almost as high as ever, only now they were part-timers in communities from which traditional hierarchies had disappeared.

A MARK IN THE WORLD

Tall and broad-shouldered, wide-eyed with determined jaws, armed and smartly uniformed, from kepis to jackboots, with the products of the industrial revolution, the ranks of conquerors tower and trample over feeble, anemic orientals. Their victims cower and cringe, with slitty eyes and shifty looks, dangling pigtails and hugging their gaudy silk robes. The modern soldiers push them screaming over a cliff edge or pile them dead in heaps or watch triumphantly as they are flung from rigging or riverbanks into waters reddening with blood. These could be crude images of the superior

The seams are visible in this Japanese screenfold propaganda-piece from the war of 1894–95. The scene is not only of a national triumph over foreigners but also of modernization against reaction; see also p. 634. By this date, Japanese influence was being felt as keenly on western art as the other way round: see below, p. 693 and S. Wichmann, *Japonisme: the Japanese Influence on Western Art since 1858* (1981), but the modelling of the horses here, in particular, seems indebted to a western tradition: they should be compared with the horses of San Marco, p. 76.

rage of western barbarians, giving the east a lesson in "modernity." In fact they are pictures from Japanese propaganda screenfolds, and their subject is the Sino-Japanese war of 1894–95.

In their imperialist adventures, Japanese actually saw themselves clothed in western battledress and even masked with western faces. They were never so thoroughly westernized as when fighting to win an overseas empire. In late nineteenth- and early twentieth-century warfare, the tactics and strategies of attack were broadly international, for aggression is a great cultural leveller. Only in the last stages of their imperialist age, when Japan was thrown back on the defensive and fighting for survival in the Second World War, did the Japanese turn back to traditions of warfare of their own and rely on suicide squads of samurai sensibilities, "living gods without earthly desires."

Though imperialism was an old Japanese demon, its revival in the late nineteenth century, after a lapse of about a quarter of a millennium, is a feature of Japanese history that really does benefit from being considered in the context of Japan's "Dawn to the West." Overseas empires and "civilizing missions"—such as unified nationhood, parliamentary constitutions, codified laws, trousers, and industrial economies—were club colours of the circle to which Japan aspired. One way of achieving equality with the aggressors from the west who burst into the China Seas was to impose unequal treaties on victims of one's own. The era of Japanese adventures overseas—reconciliation by violence in "grace with the sea"—coincided almost exactly with the great ages of British, French, German, and U.S. imperialism.

Of course, there was more to it than that. Nothing in Japanese history is adequately explained as imitation, and there were plenty of reasons impelling imperialism from within Japan. The country had the resources at home to start industrializing, but not to continue it indefinitely. Mainland Asia had, among other attractions, coal and iron to replace Japan's dwindling supplies. Oil was the object of the fateful decision to invade Indonesia and therefore take on the United States in the Second World War. Imperialism was a route of escape from poverty and vulnerability—the poverty of the Japanese hinterland, vulnerability to the embargoes of enemies.

It was also an increasingly pressing drive for living space. From the end of the seventeenth century until well into the second half of the nineteenth, Japan's population was virtually stagnant. This was not the kind of stability inflicted by Malthusian checks; for most of the period Japan experienced neither dramatic interventions of disaster nor high rates of births and deaths. The era of restraint—for such it seems to have been—ended in the last third or quarter of the nineteenth century when a state which needed labour and manpower for industrialization and war encouraged citizens to breed. By the early twentieth century the drive for empire was commonly expressed as a response to a "population problem" as the Japanese approached the goal of "our hundred million." The carve-up of the world by White empires that banned or discouraged Japanese immigration heightened the growing urgency with which Japan staked her claim to a share.

A form of received wisdom links imperialism to industrialization on the presumption that producers have to acquire markets, by force if necessary; the suspicion that Japan's imperialism was the policy of a typically capitalist alliance of soldiers and businessmen has been aroused by the suggestive overlaps between big business and militant nationalism in the early twentieth century. This line of possible explanation seems tainted by association with doctrinaire Marxism and conspiracy theory—yet it remains true that the Black Dragon Society, formed in 1901 to prepare and lobby for war against Russia, was a secret forum for contacts among generals, ministers, and executives of the arachnoid Mitsui and Mitsubishi companies. In Japan, moreover, conspirators in the armed forces had an exceptionally promising frame in which to make conspiracy theory work: the army and navy top brass were directly and, in some respects, independently responsible to the emperor—with access to a level of decision-making which bypassed constitutional safeguards. In Japan, wars could happen at short notice when maverick *provocateurs* engineered incidents. Wars with China in 1894 and 1931 were jump-started by soldiers who anticipated or even forced the government's hand.

Empire was an emotional issue. War had been implicit in the ferociously nationalistic language of the revolution of 1868. In the first flush of self-assertion the new rulers had reclaimed the Ryukyu islands and raided Taiwan. Discarded heroes of 1868, including, most prominently, Saigo Takamori and Eto Shimpei, had clamoured in the 1870s for war against Korea—almost as if seeking to retrieve the baton dropped by Hideyoshi centuries before (see Chapter 7). The ostensible pretext was Korea's insulting diplomatic language and gestures, but other reasons ran deeper: historic enmity; rage at Japan's impotence under the "unequal treaties"; anxiety to forestall the further extension of European imperialism in east Asia; samurai nostalgia for warrior glory; the suitability of Korea—still vehemently isolationist herself—as the first victim of Japan's new bid for a world role. Soon after 1868, Ito Chutei, future industrialist, the first peasant's son from his village to go to school, took leave of his teachers with the assurance, "You will make your mark in the world." All his classmates received the same admonition, and it became, in a sense, a national ambition. Above all, perhaps, for cultural conservatives like Saigo and his followers, war was attractive as a means of rot-stopping discipline, a source of purifying ritual for a polluted society at home. Soon after his death, a group of Saigo's admirers in Satsuma—including businessmen, soldiers, and militant political activists—formed the Black Ocean Society to foment war in Korea and to prepare for it by training spies and assassins.

Though the war of 1894–95 demonstrated Japan's superiority over China, it seemed only to confirm her inferiority to the westerners. Under Russian and German threats, the conquerors gave up the mainland Asian empire the Chinese were willing to concede. Japan could flourish some of the bunting of prestige: an indemnity with which to build up an even mightier war machine; and "unequal treaty" in her own favour which gave her people privileged access to Chinese trade; a territorial possession in Taiwan which could be ruled like a regular colony of a pukka imperial power. Embedded henceforth in western minds was the distinction between China and Japan later encapsulated by Noel Coward: "the Japanese don't care to, the Chinese wouldn't dare to." In Britain, in particular, the Japanese established a claim to esteem for "pluck," which, since the Japanese navy was trained on British principles, overspilled into self-congratulation. Japan was recognized in Britain as "the most western of the nations of the east" and even "the Britain of Asia." But admission, on terms of equality with White powers, to admiration throughout the world demanded, as a precondition, victory over a European enemy.

Russia was such an enemy in the offing. Russian contempt for Japan had not abated with the Sino-Japanese War. On the contrary, the success of

Pushkin Street and the inner harbour of Port Arthur in 1904. The warships *Kazan* and *Anzara* are immobilized; much of the town is devastated by the Japanese shells. The prominent, undamaged building in the foreground is the Post Office.

Russian threats in dictating the terms of peace reinforced Russian convictions of the superiority of "the White race" over "monkeys" who, "as a military factor, did not exist." The eclipse of China only excited Russia's own eastward imperialism and encouraged the Russians to march into the Chinese territories they had obliged Japan to vacate. "The cross was planted on the Amur," and vodka cocktails were served at Saratov's on Pushkin Street in Port Arthur.

The war which broke out in 1904 repeated the pattern of 1894–95: Japan had an almost total military victory, followed by a diplomatic check. The moral outcome, however, was decisive. Russian troops died "like locusts crossing a river"; Russia's navies were sunk in battles that were over in hours. The effect, it is commonly said, was to explode the myth of White invincibility and spread hope through the world for the victims of imperialism. Filipino and Vietnamese nationalists set up home in Japan, while in India "remote villagers talked over the victories of Japan as they sat in their circles and passed around the huqqa at night." The more immediate consequence, however, was to add another imperialist power to the world's already excessive stock. Within a year of the end of the war, a Japanese staff officer was urging a new programme of expansion into China, south-east Asia, the Pacific, and on to Central and South America.

By the end of the First World War, in which she was an equal partner with Germany's other adversaries, Japan was a fully integrated member of the imperialist club. Her solidly established empire covered Taiwan, Korea, southern Sakhalin, and an area round Port Arthur, technically leased from China, in south-east Manchuria. Imperialism is like appetite: it comes with eating. The arrest of Japanese empire-building in the 1920s could only be temporary.

The postwar combination of democracy and recession proved favourable—in Japan as in parts of Europe—to increasingly authoritarian and militaristic government; the Japanese economy, however, continued to grow, albeit slowly and patchily, while constitutional proprieties were protected by the reverence commanded by the throne. For most of the 1920s, the armed forces bore their share of government economies and eyes dropped from imperial horizons.

In retrospect the decisive moment of shift into an imperialistic and militaristic high gear can be dated to 18 September 1931 when conspirators in the armed services staged an explosion on the Manchurian railway; blam-

The Japanese delegation walking out of the League of Nations, caricatured by Hergé in *Le Lotus bleu*. "The Manchurian Incident" helped to transform the image of Japan in the west for the worse. Near the start of Hergé's story, the dog, Milou—who is often a spokesman for naive wisdom—asks his master, *"Les japonais, ce sont les bons?"*

ing Chinese bandits, the army—making policy on the march—overran the whole of Manchuria by about the end of the year. The civil government had, it seems, no active part in the conspiracy; on the contrary, it was precisely because a policy of peace was favoured at the time in Tokyo that the controllers of the armed forces felt obliged to act to force the government's hand. When the duplicity behind the provocation was exposed, the Japanese delegation at the League of Nations walked out rather than endure reproofs from the rest of the world.

A state of war—which the Japanese persisted in calling "the Manchurian incident"—continued, blending from 1937 into an undisguised attempt to conquer China. Like the old woman who swallowed a fly, Japan was driven to take ever more ambitious bites in the search for secure frontiers and supplies, which eventually, in the terrible escalation of 1941–42, extended the theatre of war as far as north-east India, the Hawaiian Islands, the Solomons, and the Timor Sea.

It was a comprehensively destructive undertaking. Japanese expansion helped to destroy every empire it touched (see Chapter 18): French, Dutch, British, American—and Japanese. The Pacific war was undertaken by Japanese decision-makers who knew that they would be unable to sustain it for long: their grand strategy relied on blitzing and bluffing their adversaries into peacemaking within a year. After that, the admission that Japan "would not necessarily win"—the fatal code of certain defeat—began to seep first into Japanese secret memoranda, then into official pronouncements. Outgunned, overextended, and running out of ships and planes, the Japanese redefined their perceptions of victory. The reformulation of their war aims in spiritual terms, the affirmation of the superiority of Japanese spirit in the face of material disaster, is often said to have been a peculiarly Japanese mental strategy. Yet the Spanish navy at Santiago and Manila in 1898 and the British army at Dunkirk in 1940 both founded national myths on the basis of the moral superiority of defeat. The Japanese were unique only in the degree of enthusiasm with which they embraced the prospect of self-immolation.

An officer in a suicide unit in 1944 told a young recruit that defeat was inevitable.

I couldn't believe my ears, an officer talking like this! "What was that you said, sir?" I asked.

"Japan will be defeated, Yokota," he told me.

I was shocked. I didn't know what else to say at the moment, for I had never heard anyone in the military discuss this possibility before, so I came back with, "Then why do you volunteer to die?"

"A man must do what he can for his country," was his simple answer. . . . "Japan will be defeated, of that I am sure. But she will be born again, and become a greater nation than ever before." . . . Our land was now being bathed in fire, he said, and she would emerge all the better because of it.

Suicide missions, which began as a rational tactical device for restoring the balance of air power by eliminating enemy carriers, became, in the last months of the war, a strategy of conscious despair. In April 1945, when the last surviving capital ships of the Imperial Navy sailed to join the battle of Okinawa, orders of the day made it plain to the men that this was "a suicide mission pure and simple, with not the slightest chance of destroying an important enemy target."

THE STUMP OF THE GOLDEN PAVILION

Soldiers, it is said, always re-fight the last war. Politicians tend to refashion the last peace. The end of the Second World War was clouded with memories of the First, and peacemakers were determined to avoid the same mistakes: the harshness of Versailles, the heavy indemnities, the stockpiling of

The Tokyo earthquake in a woodblock print of 1855. The flames are depicted in the form of the manes of traditional monsters. They seem to crush the houses with physical force and gobble them with devouring jaws: considered from one point of view, Japanese history is a story of tidying up and starting again after natural disasters.

revenge for the future. Aid became an inverted image of indemnities, while the vanquished reconstructed their cities and economies at the victors' expense. The origins of the resurgence of Japan in the second half of the twentieth century could be expressed in an adapted version of a traditional four-character slogan as: Japanese Spirit, American Benevolence.

Destruction in Japan had not been as prolonged as in Europe, but in some ways it went deeper. Only Japan had choked on fallout from the A-bomb—the "cruel weapon" which denied them the luxury of self-extinction. Conventional bomb damage appalled the American commander who arrived to mastermind the occupation, looking out, as he drove, "at a pulverized moonscape inhabited by staring scarecrows who giggled hysterically and fled. 'It was just twenty-two miles from the New Grand Hotel in Yokohama to the American embassy, which was to be my home throughout the occupation, but they were twenty-two miles of devastation and vast piles of charred rubble.'"

Japan could cope with that. The Japanese, who live along seismic faults, in the paths of typhoons, are inured to reconstruction and used to clearing up. Even the human losses—nearly two million dead, the cascade of some of the best of a generation, "fallen like cherry blossom"—could be absorbed in a system of values that put spirit, service, and sacrifice above individual lives. Imperialism was a blip on the screen of Japanese history; unlike Europeans traumatized by the disappearance of older and more heartfelt empires, the Japanese did not feel the need to adjust their sets when it faded. The damage wrought by their defeat was of another kind: "not merely," said the American supremo Douglas MacArthur, "the overthrow of their military might—it was the collapse of a faith, it was the disintegration of everything they believed in and lived by and fought for. It left a complete vacuum, morally, mentally, and physically." Never before in recorded history had Japan submitted to a conqueror or been occupied by foreign invaders. As the emperor renounced his divinity, his people disclaimed their "superiority over other races." Postwar opinion surveys showed that a majority conceded "superiority" to "civilized peoples like the Americans and the British."

Postwar Japan was like the burned-out stump of the Temple of the Golden Pavilion—the symbolic edifice in a novel by Yukio Mishima, destroyed by a monk who loved its beauty unbearably. As some of the advocates of suicide tactics had foreseen, the stump proved to be a good nesting place for a phoenix. Douglas MacArthur foresaw it, too. Though he could be brutal and egotistical, small-minded and vengeful, he was a happy choice for Japan: a generally benevolent despot who got the recovery off to a good start. He was, by temperament and formal powers, an absolute ruler who unwittingly appropriated some of the traditional divine attributes of the emperor. Suppliants prostrated themselves in his presence. A carpenter

The immolation of the Golden Pavilion in the film version of Mishima Yukio's novel.

who shared his elevator became the hero of popular songs and stories. The admiration was mutual. MacArthur approached Japan with an enemy's respect, convinced that "the energy of the Japanese race, if properly directed, will enable expansion vertically, rather than horizontally." His policy was not "to keep Japan down, but to get her on her feet again." He encouraged the American forces to fraternize and forbade them to victimize. Thanks to a well-run occupation, the postwar turn-around from enmity to friendship in Japanese–American relations happened surprisingly quickly and lasted surprisingly long. In 1951, when Japanese sovereignty was restored almost intact, it was as if Japan had reverted contentedly to "unequal treaty status," which lasted until the Americans returned Okinawa in 1972.

Japan's biggest postwar "miracle" was slow; the psychological recovery was still incomplete in the 1990s when most of the Japanese public remained reluctant to have the country take part in United Nations peacekeeping forces in fear of compromising the constitution's exclusive commitment to "self-defence." This reticence was remunerative. It helped the miraculously fast economic recovery. Minuscule military budgets liberated funds for investment in commercial products. The markets Japan could not win by war she now gained in competition.

While industrial activity benefited from much richer diversification than in the pre-war period, the miracle was worked by a restored economic order. Big corporations, in which workers spent a lifetime cultivating a place in a vertical structure, returned to dominate the economy and re-establish links with the state. The Americans had abolished them in 1945–47 on grounds of their presumed complicity in militarism and imperialism, but Mitsubishi was resuscitated in 1954 and Mitsubishi Heavy Industries in 1964; the venerable names of Mitsui and Sumitomo were revived. Other similar enterprises, such as Toyota, Hitachi, and the New Japan Steel Corporation, recalled the spirit, without reviving the names, of corporations of Japan's heroic age of industrialization. Embedded in the firm, the "salariman" forwent an independent social life and even sacrificed part of his personal identity. Kobo Abe (1924–) wrote novels representative of the era, in which individuals were sucked into alienating organizations or blended into shapeless backgrounds, such as in his *Woman of the Dunes*. For most workers in an era of growing prosperity, this sort of anonymity was comforting rather than smothering. Labour disputes in the 1960s took the form of lovers' tiffs.

The achievements of this command-capitalism were spectacular—indeed, too fast and high to track with economists' antennae. By the mid-1950s Japan was experiencing the Jimmu boom, named after the mythical founder of Japan on the grounds that nothing like it had happened in between. The pace of industrialization could be measured in new pollution scandals; the worst was perhaps that of the strange disease of the Chioto aluminum plant of 1953 when the likely fate of human victims was dramatized by the dance of cats drunk on methyl mercury effluent, who "jumped about madly and threw themselves into the sea." In 1960 a prime minister who promised that incomes would double in ten years turned out to have underestimated: the target was passed in 1967. Despite disastrously high energy prices in the next decade, Japan, almost without native sources of fuel, caught up with and surpassed the European average gross product per capita. In 1985 it became the world's largest creditor nation.

Because of the peculiarities of Japanese capitalism, which would never meet the standards of an enterprise textbook written, say, in Chicago, outsiders have tended to doubt the staying power of Japanese economic success. At the end of the 1980s and early in the 1990s, when world recession made life hard for what was by then emphatically the world's major trader-nation, predictions rained down of Japan's coming collapse. The economy would be corroded from within, it was said, by inbuilt inefficiencies or attacked from without by energy atrophy and seismic catastrophe. The Japanese, however, are used to steering between sirens. A rational and superficially convincing study of their economy in 1937, for instance, concluded that its basis was "too weak to bear the great burdens placed upon it and threatens at any moment to bring the whole vast superstructure crashing to the ground." This language is reminiscent of current predictions. In 1957 one of the world's most respected Japan watchers thought the economy had already grown to its full potential.

There are no straight flight paths in economic history, and Japanese progress is bound to swoop, dip, and duck after half a century of barely interrupted soaring. The scale, however, of Japanese investment abroad—especially in the new industrializing economies of east Asia and those of the rest of the Pacific rim, which are the subjects of the next two chapters—is a hefty indemnity against local difficulties. The frustrations and destruction Japan has already survived and sprung back from during the twentieth century will not be exceeded by any disaster in the offing. In the shift of initiative that marks the last phase of our millennium, Japan continues to lead the Pacific challenge, watching the rest of the world, as each new dawn comes up, with its back to the sun.

Chapter 21

THE GIANT AWAKENING: MODERNIZATION ELSEWHERE IN EAST ASIA

The Confucian Kitchen—The Barrel of a Gun—The Hall of One Voice—The Clash of Jade Pendants—The Ocean View

THE CONFUCIAN KITCHEN

The other English had fled. Only this one old man, indigent and elegant, with long white hands and a long white beard, stayed on in Peking through the Second World War until his death in 1944. He lived in genteel poverty, in a bed-sitting room in the plundered shell of the British legation, under the domestic tyranny of a Chinese servant. Sir Edmund Backhouse did not want to go home, where he had ruined his character by a record of bad debts and fraudulent pretensions. Though he was weak-willed himself— with a history of every kind of vacillation, every extreme of evasion—he affected contempt for the gelatinous fibre of his countrymen and admiration for their iron-hard adversaries. As the war front moved outwards and southwards, he relished every Japanese success. For years he had avoided English company, dodging behind columns to elude acquaintances or covering his face with a handkerchief when he passed a compatriot in his palanquin. Now he could glut his reclusive appetite in isolation from all who knew him, immured in the ruins of the court where he had once been appreciated for his sinological scholarship and his connoisseurship in curios. He became like an enfleshed version of James Ensor's painting of 1885, *Skele-*

ton Studying Chinoiseries: decaying amid tattered treasures in a garret-fantasy.

His loneliness, however, was interrupted. He had a regular visitor who brought out the worst in him. Dr. Hoeppli, the Swiss consul, who was responsible for the protection of British interests for the duration of hostilities, was an amateur psychiatrist with a passion for pornography. Backhouse became his patient and his pensioner. The literary talent formerly expended on translating or forging Chinese historical documents was now employed in its element, spurting lubricious "memoirs." They were confessions invented for a therapist and confections sold to a pervert, reminiscent of the letters of Baron Corvo—which, by a suggestive coincidence, were written to titillate Backhouse's first cousin, Charles Masson Fox. The pretended memories brilliantly evoked a world of *fin de siècle* European aestheticism, through which Backhouse claimed to have moved with well-lubricated ease as the catamite of statesmen and artists. He pretended to have shared sexual experiences with Verlaine and Mallarmé and described himself as "a young man privileged to have had sexual intercourse with a prime minister." No detail, however intimate or revolting, was spared in lending verisimilitude to the fantastic record.

It was, however, in the volume dealing with China that Backhouse could really be said to have got into his stride. His European conquests were not confined to a single sex: ladies, if sufficiently high-born, could also claim his favours, and he had already, in his own imagination, been the lover of two empresses before he removed to Peking. His profound knowledge of Chinese history and literature enabled him to surround the lurid details of his second volume with a plausible context and to draw on the already prolific literature about what he called Manchu decadence—the moral degeneracy of the court life of the late Ch'ing. It seemed natural to Dr. Hoeppli that the young Backhouse, after so much relevant experience, should charm the eye of Dowager Empress T'zu-hsi, the virago who effectively ruled the empire for half a century, from the centre of her intersecting webs of scandal and intrigue.

At the time of the first amorous encounter Backhouse claimed with her, the Empress was already seventy years old, but she kept her appetites in a state of stimulation by voyeurism in homosexual brothels. "Was I sexually adequate for Her Majesty's overflowing carnality?" mused Backhouse over-modestly as he was carried in a palanquin to a secret tryst along water-logged country bypaths. Though the fantastic "hidden life" he described was incredibly grotesque, it was believed—and not only by Dr. Hoeppli, who had an interest in the copyright—because of the abysmal notoriety of the dowager's reign. Indeed, Backhouse made his account plausible by modelling his adventures on the best-documented of her reputed lovers. "The Old Buddha"—as courtiers called her—was infamous not only for sex-

The ruler behind the screen: T'zu-hsi, photographed in 1903 at the age of sixty-eight. The Ch'ing dynasty had never before been effectively headed by a woman, but the beginning of the imperial minority of her son in 1861 created an opportunity for the revival of the ancient practice of "rule from behind the screen," which enabled a woman to adopt a man's duties with no overt offence against decorum. The coup which empowered the ex-concubine was engineered by the former emperor's brother, but T'zu-hsi had performed informal secretarial duties for the previous ruler and knew how to play palace politics; by tenacious longevity, she eventually became the most practised player in the game.

ual excess but also for breathtaking realpolitik and refined cruelty. A woman credited with the murder of her own son could easily be incriminated by Backhouse in the murders of nephews. To prolong her own power, it was readily believed, she fed the dragons that bore emperors to heaven.

Even when judged by standards higher or more generous than those of her own convenience, T'zu-hsi's rule might be acclaimed as surprisingly successful. When her supremacy began on her husband's death in 1861, the end of the Ch'ing dynasty was widely anticipated, generally with relish. Chinese self-esteem was insulted by the presence of western barbarians in the concessions they exacted under the terms of unequal treaties. Political and spiritual crises came mutually disguised. Muslim invaders prowled on the borders of Sinkiang, threatening jihad, while a credally motivated Muslim rebellion dislocated Yunnan. Great swaths of the heartlands of China were in the hands of a millenarian peasant kingdom headed by a self-proclaimed "brother of Jesus." In the north, bandit-champions of the underprivileged mobilized armies of thousands by gathering every grumbler and galvanizing every grievance. These rebels included tax protesters, victims of corrupt justice, and renascent followers of the White Lotus (see Chapter 4). Nomadic bands who resented ethnic Chinese hegemony combined with Chinese nationalists who still saw the Ch'ing as foreigners after two hundred years on the throne.

In these circumstances mere survival was a triumph. For most of China's historic dynasties, decline had spelled doom; once it started, it was hard to reverse. The Ch'ing recovery from apparently terminal troubles was said by those who experienced it to have been unprecedented since the eighth century. The renewed durability of the dynasty must be admitted to have coincided with the preponderance of T'zu-hsi: it started more or less with her first regency and ended in 1911, with the sudden and dramatic extinction of the monarchy three years after her death. In part it was achieved by luck, for rebels did the regime's work as they spilled each other's blood, and in part by foreign help, for the western powers preferred to deal with the devil they knew rather than risk a revolution in the affairs of this fairly pliant empire. China became another of the world's "sick" states, like the old Spanish monarchy and Ottoman Turkey, kept alive through a long decline because the body snatchers could not agree on how to divide the corpse. In part, too, Ch'ing survival was the product of slowly crunching demographic changes, which multiplied the numbers of ethnic Chinese and spread their settlement at the expense of the peripheral and minority peoples of the empire. In a world threatened by foreign competitors and predators, the throne became ever more closely identified with China's national cause; this sinicization—churning the empire to a Chinese consistency—contributed to the discouragement of rebellions and the popularity of the dynasty.

Yet the prolongation of Ch'ing rule was also due to the impetus of an inert system, rolling under its own weight. The Ch'ing revival was achieved by an unreformed mandarin class, with unabated confidence in the redeemability of the traditional imperial order. Tseng Kuo-fan, the model scholar-administrator who organized the imperial armies for victory over the rebels, was a spokesman for values of eternal resonance and immediate application. He was a dawn-riser who wept in disappointment at the corruption of his own officers. He advocated Confucian order in a society arrayed like the contents of Mrs. Beeton's kitchen, with everyone in his place. He saw political decline as the result of moral degeneracy and looked to the goodness and wisdom of philosopher-rulers—men like himself—to retune the strings and restore harmony. While insisting on the perfection of imperial institutions and rites, he uttered in a Chinese milieu the language of that founding document of western conservatism, Sir Robert Peel's Tamworth Manifesto of 1834: "the mistakes inherited from the previous age can be corrected by us; that which the past ignored, we can inaugurate." And this practical conservatism had an immediate task to address, while tradition was suspended. Tseng's "tiny but staunchly loyal heart" crossed "mountains of skulls and bones and deep pools of blood in the hope of bringing back to our side Heaven's will, which is against disorder." Nevertheless, he and his colleagues in government were convinced of the fundamental sufficiency of the wisdom of the past. The essence of the policy of "self-strengthening," which remained dominant throughout the era of T'zu-hsi's supremacy, was that superficial technical lessons could be learned from the western barbarians without prejudice to the essential verities on which Chinese tradition was based.

It was a surprisingly serviceable policy. Until the mid-1890s it seemed to work. The first three decades of self-strengthening had been inglorious, with erosion at the extremities of the empire under Russian, French, and Japanese pressure; but at least the pace of collapse had been slowed, the internal rebels contained or crushed, and the appearances saved of a barely ruffled cosmic order centred on the mandate of heaven. Propriety and righteousness were put above expediency and ingenuity. New arsenals, shipyards, and technical schools teetered precariously on the edges of traditional society.

Though the difference was not appreciated at the time, Chinese self-strengthening and Japanese "restoration" (see Chapter 20) were thus contrasting movements. The Chinese added epicycles to the motion of the spheres in their egocentric universe; the Japanese discarded old cosmologies and remobilized their whole society to catch up with the west. The two systems clashed in the war of 1894–95. The Japanese victory was comprehensive, but it was the naval encounter between nominally modernized fleets which tested most dramatically the merits of the two approaches. On paper, the Chinese navy, which had cost more, looked more formidable—bigger and more heavily armed, with two ironclads of 7,000 tons; the Japanese had no vessel over 4,000. But before the conflict, when the best Chinese battleships paid a courtesy visit to Yokohama, a Japanese officer scoffed at the piles of rubbish on the decks and the wash hanging from the guns. He dismissed Chinese war-readiness as "an over-fired sword, no sharper than a rusty kitchen knife." Money for munitions had been diverted to the building of T'zu-hsi's palace, and when combat was joined, the Chinese guns had only three rounds apiece. Most of their ships avoided action; those engaged were captured or sunk.

The most likely prospect for China, after defeat by Japan, was partition by the powers. The breakup of China, forecast by British "China Hands," seemed to have the momentum of a self-fulfilling prophecy. In 1899 the American State Department proposed rules of conduct for each power in the other's prospective spheres. Only the scramblers' quarrels about the distribution of the pickings prevented dismemberment. Even in the face of extinction, with the example of Japan before their eyes, Ch'ing decision-makers baulked at the abandonment of self-strengthening in favour of more radical reform. A long power struggle began, waged across a generation gap, between revolutionaries who wanted to modernize along Japanese lines and reactionaries who, confident of the underlying continuity of history, hoped to outface change.

In this conflict the influence of T'zu-hsi was decisive on the reactionary side. Even when she was discharging the office of an emperor, her sex kept her confined to an eavesdropper's closet. She heard in whispers and saw the world through a veil, from behind the silk curtain that kept the sacred throne from profanation. Though according to Sir Edmund Backhouse she was curious about certain personal aspects of foreign affairs—the relationship between Queen Victoria and her gillie, for instance, or, later, the liaison between Edward VII and Mrs. Keppel—the perspectives of the young reformers, who read foreign languages and travelled the world, were neither available nor interesting to her. Her physical universe was bounded by the caverns and corridors of the Forbidden City; her social sphere was a narrow *gynaeceum,* emulous and manipulative, peopled by women and princelings, eunuchs and mystics, lovers and sycophants. She was almost unchallengeable in her control of access to successive emperors and, while incompetent in wider politics, was mistress of the arts of power. The last years of her supremacy, from the crisis of the 1890s until her death in 1908, opened a long history of frustration, which continued for the rest of the millennium, and in which China's modernization was frequently projected but never achieved—thwarted by self-interested élites, halted by wars, aborted by mad or misguided leaders, mired in the paddies of a vast and unmanageable country.

Her unequal adversary in the struggle for China's future was a compulsive young radical, K'ang Yu-wei, who flirted, in his prodigious adolescence, with lots of incompatible ideologies before becoming single-mindedly devoted, after visits to Hong Kong and Shanghai, to a project of modernization in imitation of Britain. To his enemies he showed "a Confucian face and the heart of a barbarian." He bypassed the usual route of ascent to power—the civil service examinations system—by bombarding authorities with impressive memoranda. He obtained a series of personal interviews with the Emperor, who appeared to share similar opinions, at least when he was in K'ang's company. Attracted by the idea of modernizing China, the Emperor felt constrained by fear of his aunt. She allowed him a hundred days of reform on symbolic conditions: that he refrain from burning the ancestral tablets or cutting his pigtail. K'ang planned a coup in this breathing-space, but his conspiracy was riddled with treachery. The dowager imprisoned her nephew and resumed personal rule while K'ang fled to Japan.

In the following years she saw reform off, first by confrontation, then temporization. Her initial recourse was to mobilize, as a private army against change, the militantly xenophobic Boxer movement—more properly, the Society of the Righteous Fists of Order. The Boxer militia resembled the street armies of later European fascism. Its manpower came from the traditional peasant flotsam of previous rebellions, supplemented by workers unemployed through foreign competition, with fairground gamblers whose activities raised the funds. Boxer propaganda represented the

Supernatural forces rend, disarm, and scare away foreigners in a Boxer poster. The blighted but still orderly garden of China, with a scholar's tower and elegant pavilions visible in the distance, is preserved.

"righteous army" as a dragon devouring hairy foreigners in contempt for their weapons. Battlefield morale was inflamed by the dangerous conviction that mumbo-jumbo could make warriors invulnerable. In preparation for battle they cast spells, burned incantations, and spurned firearms.

Their outrages against missionaries and diplomats provoked a new invasion by a punitive international force in 1900. T'zu-hsi had incited them recklessly but their defeat only seemed to confirm her authority: the invading powers had no agreed alternative. To lend a specious air of sincerity to her promises of institutional reform, she publicly took upon herself the responsibility for China's humiliation. Her real policy, however, did not go beyond the old "self-strengthening"; she proposed to imitate, at most, the "skin and hair" of western methods in order to avoid criticism. Her prejudice against change was visceral; her commitment to her own power was beyond compromise. Yet her stand was principled—an affirmation of faith in an ordered world, where imitation of hairy barbarians or, even worse, of the despised Japanese would have been an unbearable act of desecration.

T'zu-hsi wilfully obstructed modernization; but no subsequent government, however well disposed in theory, was able to accomplish much. By the standards of its rivals in the region and the world, China has continued to seem stuck in a sub-industrial phase of development—a "sleeping giant," as Napoleon had said, now aroused but unable to shake off drowsiness. Under any regime, China was unsuited by nature to industrialization, without which no modernization could seem complete (see Chapter 12). Despite the dense populations of its valleys and flood-plains, it has never had much manpower to spare for the job. The demands of its labour-intensive agriculture are illustrated by the experiences of Chinese journalists visiting America in 1972, recounted by Fox Butterfield:

> The single most striking sight to them was hundreds of acres of corn growing near Ottawa, Illinois, on a farm owned by a heavy-set, gregarious man named Adrian Pike. As we stood examining the ripening green stalks, higher than the heads of the Chinese, one of the reporters turned to Pike with a mystified expression.
> "How do you irrigate your fields?" he asked. Pike replied good-naturedly that he just depended on rainfall. I could see the look of incredulity on the Chinese faces. Irrigation ditches for rice, wheat, corn, and cotton are the lifeblood of Chinese peasantry.

The intricacies of careful cropping, repeated reploughing, puddling, harrowing, and nurturing seedlings can only be partly simplified by mechanization. East Asia's more precocious industrializers in Japan, South Korea, Taiwan, Hong Kong, and Singapore have been able to free most or all of their people from the land by importing food. For China, with its huge population, that has never been a viable policy on a sufficient scale. As the end of the millennium approaches, well over two-thirds of its workforce is still committed to agriculture.

THE BARREL OF A GUN

In 1925, Harold Acton—the well-known aesthete who, at that time, described himself as a poet—hired a Chinese cook whom he found in a basement club for labourers in an insalubrious part of London. His friends refused invitations to dinner. "They associated Chinese food with snakes and scorpions," whereas for Acton it was the beginning of a long period of uncritical adulation of Chinese culture—an idealization of China which only bitter experience could make him abandon. He adopted chopsticks, "read about Dr. Sun Yat-sen and his programme of national reconstruction" (see Chapter 16), subsided into serenity induced by draughts of green tea, and "wished to be wholly in China."

Even then, his avowals of enthusiasm for his new servant seemed unconvincing. Friends found the cook sinister and unsettling: "When they came to see me, they trod gingerly, sniffing the air." Acton, growing restive under subtle dominion of a sort exercised by every servant of excessive competence, fled to Florence to write *The Last Medici.* Yet the yearning for China remained, and when Acton got there at last, just after the start of the Manchurian Incident (see Chapter 20), he choked any misgivings under extravagant praise. The imperial palaces excelled anything he had seen except the Vatican. Installed in a house of his own, which had been selected by a geomancer as invulnerable to goblins, he felt he had "caught the express of happiness." Disenchantment—though he was reluctant to admit it—began even before the Japanese marched in and destroyed the "symmetrical calm" in which he was enveloped. He would have kissed the soil on arrival, but was choked by the rising dust. He frankly disliked the south of the country, where "there was no respect for the past, yet the curio shops were more expensive." He found that Chinese art had—with honourable exceptions—become polluted by "rococo" aberrations. Chinoiserie palled. Disillusionment grew.

Disillusionment was a common experience in twentieth-century China, where every dawn was false, every paradise mislaid, and no change was for the better. The first wave of revulsion followed the first revolution. In 1911 a rebellion broke out in Szechuan over unequal indemnities for cancelled railway stock—a tragicomic image of faltering modernization. It was an unromantic issue, but it toppled the dynasty by exposing the forfeited loyalty of the armed forces. In blighted soil, where traditional legitimacy had been uprooted, power "grew out of the barrel of a gun." The revolu-

Harold Acton at home in Peking, photographed with Anna May Wong in his "perfect Chinese mansion" inhabited successively by a series of western Sinophiles and where—in defiance of this humdrum fact—he "wandered through halls of mellow carving," musing "on the mutability that had brought me, an alien, to this entirely Chinese abode. I felt I had inherited it from benevolent ancestors, who must have wished me here for some inscrutable purpose of their own." It was decorated to display the antiquities he collected. His prize piece is in the background: the circular moon-door, carved with "dense tracery evocative of a bamboo grove."

tion proved instantly corruptible, denounced by Lu Hsün's picaresque novel, *The True Story of Ah Q,* which told "in the language of wagon-haulers and street-mongers" the betrayal of a village simpleton, tempted into theft, by revolutionaries who sided with the property owners.

Disillusionment is the price of idealism, and Sun Yat-sen was quickly disillusioned himself. He hoped that the leading general, Yüan Shih-k'ai, would guarantee a republic which would make its citizens virtuous. Instead, Yüan, whose history of self-seeking included betrayal of K'ang Yu-wei's conspiracy in 1898, and who believed that all men could be bought or intimidated, proclaimed his own installation as emperor. It was then his turn to be disappointed as his provincial governors seceded and "warlord-states" multiplied. "What is there left for me to say?" he cried when the news of Szechuan's secession was telegraphed. "Please reply and say that I will retire."

The dissolution of China brought no comfort for republican idealists, who turned on each other in a secessionist state of their own in the south. Sun Yat-sen died, murmuring, "Save China," in 1925. He had devoted his last year to tempering an alliance capable of reimposing unity by force: the Nationalist Party, or Kuomintang. But even when his effective successor, Chiang Kai-shek, reconquered China in 1926–28, imperial legitimacy proved impossible to replace. The cycle of secession and civil war began again. Although Japanese conquest, for those areas that experienced it between 1931 and 1945, brought a suspension of chaos, it inflicted instead the humiliation of ritual deference, demanded by despised barbarians who were now transformed by strength into instructors from "the elder-brother country." Japanese rule depended unashamedly on fear, inspired by cinema shows of gory reprisals, where Japanese "watched the eleven- and twelve-year-old schoolgirls to make sure they did not shut their eyes or try to stick a handkerchief in their mouths to stifle their screams."

Liberation by the Kuomintang again excited long-deferred hopes of better times, but in practice it brought, in many areas formerly ruled by Japanese or communists, only the privilege of oppression by fellow-countrymen. Officials from distant parts of China "mercilessly milked and contemptuously treated" the victims of Japanese occupation—"slaves who have no country of your own," suspected of collaboration, or assumed to need re-education in Chinese nationalism. Despite this history of shattered expectations, idealism survived. Indeed, the last of China's messianic peasant revolutions was already under way against the Kuomintang. The longest—and therefore, by one standard, the worst—tyranny was yet to come.

The new peasant messiah was Mao Tse-tung. He was a communist by inclination rather than education. Though he claimed to be the intellectual heir of Marx and Lenin, even his mature writings show only a patchy knowledge of their work; yet his revulsion from bourgeois values—or, rather, from those of his "rich peasant" background—was heartfelt and constant. From adolescence he was disinclined to brush his teeth and upbraided a beggar for having clean feet. His rebelliousness against authority and his sympathy for its victims were nourished in hatred of his father, which he later confessed with an unfilial frankness shocking to most Chinese. He formed an image of himself as a potential liberator, fed by obsessive reading in the pulp fiction "of the green woods," with their romantic bandit-heroes.

The start of a revolution, domesticated by traditional depiction: "a lake of dead water, but the red waves reach the sky itself." Mao's longtime but liberal friend, Siao Yu, absenting himself from the pleasure-boat trip on which the Chinese Communist Party was founded, painted the scene from onshore, "with my brush feeling as heavy as a log."

When he was twenty-four, the Russian revolution broke out. The Chinese revolution, meanwhile, seemed hopelessly arrested and perverted. Its failure was agonizing his generation; the particular circle of friends he had formed—through school and through his early jobs in teaching and journalism—dug in its rubble to exhume its ideals. At that time Mao saw the Russian example as a model for recovering and applying them. On a pleasure boat in Shanghai in July 1921, the Communist Party was formed by those who agreed with him, while a companion who held aloof, and watched from onshore, painted the scene in timeless Chinese style.

The limitations of his education, the deficiencies of his knowledge of Marxism, and his isolation in charge of recruitment among peasants in his native Hunan all worked to Mao's advantage in the internal politics of the party. Unlike colleagues better informed of Marxist orthodoxy, he was able to evolve a strategy of peasant revolution—independent of the Russian model, defiant of Russian advice—which best suited China's circumstances. It was, Stalin said, as if "he doesn't understand the most elementary Marxist truths—or maybe he doesn't want to understand them." When he achieved power, the giant posters in Peking's main square displayed stages of a "shaving lesson" in the form of pictures of Marx, Lenin, Stalin, and Mao, as though at each stage of the transmission of communism some part of the tradition had been shorn, like razored facial hair.

The start of the shaving lesson: tractors, absurdly fitted with white-walled tyres, parade before images of Marx and Engels in Peking in 1970.

In Hunan he was able to build up a personal following—a party within a party. He established his overall ascendancy during crises: in the mid-'thirties when the party's Red Army was encircled and almost wiped out by the Kuomintang, and in the Second World War when he juggled "millet and rifles against tanks and aeroplanes." This confirmed him in a taste for crises for the rest of his life; when none arose, he deliberately induced them.

On any rational calculation he would have given up against the vastly stronger nationalist forces, but he was, at least, a good enough Marxist to believe that communist victory was ultimately inevitable. He contributed to it more by dogged perseverance than military skill. He summed up his strategy in an apophthegm which became famous in a concisely edited version: "When the enemy advances, we retreat; when he halts, we harass; when he retreats, we pursue." The balance of material advantages induced in the Kuomintang a delusive confidence until their overstretched armies snapped. The Communist Party's seizure of power, complete on the mainland by 1949, was a triumph of superior morale over superior numbers, the victory, according to Mao, of a "poet inspired as never before."

THE HALL OF ONE VOICE

"This dog was like thousands of other village dogs," but he loved his master and his master loved him. Old Xing, with his "simple farmer's reasoning," would not believe that the government really wanted all dogs killed to conserve food. The proclamation was explicit: "Lack of compliance with this order will be equivalent to harbouring a class enemy." But Xing's dog hunted for his own food and, in any case, "in the old society even beggars had a dog with them." Yet city dwellers began to arrive on bicycles to buy dog meat. After ten days, Old Xing's was the only dog left alive. One winter in the early 1970s, Xing kept the promise he made the night before his dog was killed: "You go first; I'll come a little later."

Mao's China was a land of capricious mass campaigns of destruction, launched from time to time, with apparent indifference, against dogs and sparrows, rightists and leftists, bourgeois deviationists and class enemies— even, at one point, against grass and flowers. Official crime rates were low, but the country resembled Oscar Wilde's nightmare-society, where people were brutalized more by habitual punishment than occasional crime. Some campaigns—perhaps most—were the nationwide eddies of ogres wading in the pool: factional contests in the communist hierarchy where cliques and gangs were redefined under each other's bludgeons as heretics or schismatics, or reallocated by Mao between the "wrong in thought," who could be redeemed by correction, and the "politically wrong," who deserved extermination. More positive campaigns were interspersed, usually with disastrous effects. In the late 'fifties, the drive to communalize agriculture caused famine; at the same time an amateurish drive towards industrialization burned up resources in "backyard furnaces" and turned school kitchens into inefficient smelting shops.

Mao drove China to the sound of crashing gears. At one level he achieved the precious stability that had eluded the country in the first half of the century. In the rhetoric of communism, in the image of China as a beacon to the world, in the cult of his own virtual divinity, Mao found means—undiscovered by any regime since the fall of the Ch'ing—of legitimating government and mobilizing popular enthusiasm. The stability of a practical mandate might have been a basis for economic progress, but he threw away its advantages in favour of a febrile atmosphere of revolutionary tension. Though he wanted a modern China, strong enough to defy the already industrialized powers that were her enemies, he was more the heir of T'zu-hsi than of K'ang Yu-wei. Envious of foreign examples—western and Russian alike—but obstinately resolved to repudiate them, he condemned himself to the mistakes of a sorcerer's apprentice, flinging mutually incompatible economic policies into a crucible. He turned down the chance to study abroad in youth and remained ignorant of the world outside China. He shared the fatal assumptions of the "self-strengtheners" of the last century: the superiority of Chinese ways and the barbarism of foreigners. He turned increasingly to a policy reminiscent of Ch'ing seclusion: self-reliance behind the closed door.

Some of his "revolutionary" principles were dazzlingly reactionary in practice. In the mid 1960s, for instance, class enmity was held to be genetically transmitted, so that the descendants of pre-revolutionary élites became a hereditary underclass while families of communist cadres were turned into a mandarin caste. Romantic love was outlawed as bourgeois, so that arranged marriage was institutionalized. Agricultural policies were warped by an age-old notion of the state as a hoarder and distributor of grain. The licensed revenge of the people against class enemies in the 1960s buckled the mainstays of progress. It eliminated a generation of professionals detested for their authority or envied for their economic privileges, including people the country needed to nurture prosperity—teachers and technicians, as well as the party directorate.

Of all Mao's campaigns to galvanize the masses none retarded the economy more or inflicted deeper trauma than the Great Proletarian Cultural Revolution launched in 1964. It started as a manoeuvre against a faction in the government, became a movement against complacency in the party, and degenerated into mob power. It was like a gigantic, violent parody of a medieval ritual of misrule in which children denounced parents, students beat teachers, the educated were demoted to menial work, and the ignorant were encouraged in the slaughter of intellectuals. Antiquities were smashed, books burned, beauty despised, study subverted, work stopped. The outrages were inspired by Mao's intemperate rhetoric and executed by squads of juvenile Red Guards. At first, recruited from well-to-do bureaucrats' families, they sewed patches on their clothes to look more proletarian when they lined up to be photographed, with copies of Mao's *Thoughts* cradled in uniformly crooked arms. Before her father's disgrace and her own "re-education," the writer Jung Chang was obliged, as the daughter of a high official, to join the Red Guards of her locality and witnessed typical incidents: scenes of bullies salivating with hatred and victims defecating with fear. Degradation of teachers, wrecking of libraries, looting of homes, beatings with belt buckles and houndings to suicide became "lessons in class struggle." By 1967 these early excesses seemed tamed as Red Guard units and gangs of licensed Rebels turned on each other. "Singing fountains" meant splitting opponents' skulls; "landscape painting" was slashing their faces into patterns. In 1968 "cleaning up class ranks" was a euphemism for massacre.

The Cultural Revolution was as pervasive as the Spanish Inquisition. It

In December 1966, at the age of seventy-three, Mao was sick and unable to walk without two nurses to help him. This made it all the more urgent for him to carry out swiftly the coup he planned against his old comrade Liu Shao-chi and other "men nestling beside us," who were uneasy about the Cultural Revolution. They were made to accuse themselves, in retrospect, of having restrained Mao's leftward instincts for years. Red Guard rallies like this one in Tiananmen Square became almost continuous as a frenzy of indignation was worked up: notice the unconvincing proletarian uniform of aprons and the well rehearsed unison of the open mouths and clapped hands.

worked by the same means of secret denunciation, public vilification, and arbitrary justice. Everyone suffered or saw suffering close at hand. The main Communist Party newspaper calculated, in retrospect, that a hundred million people had been affected. It is almost impossible to find a Chinese

The poster which caught John Gittings's attention in 1978, near the Shengli oil field. Oil was to be the "secret weapon" of the government's "Four Modernizations" programme—earning the foreign currency that would transform agriculture, industry, science, and defence by the year 2000. The peasant, worker, and soldier in the poster are victims of one of the recurrent ironies of long-term economic planning in Maoist China: visions of the future repeatedly distracted policy-makers from the problems of the present.

to talk to who has no scar to show or conceal, no horror story of those years to tell or suppress.

The limbs of the economy got broken in the beatings of the Cultural Revolution. The economic gap between China and the western barbarians was probably greater by the time Mao died in 1976 than it had been when he came to power. Productivity had peaked in 1952. Every subsequent recovery was reversed by a new social or economic experiment. Despite all the talk of industrialization, China remained a land of poor peasants, where an allegedly popular song was "The Night Soil Collectors Are Coming down the Mountain." Two hundred million peasants—by a communist estimate—were "in a state of semi-starvation"; after a generation of socialist convulsions, the distribution of their produce—more than a third to the richest fifth—was less equitable than in Taiwan. The frustrations of economic planning were illustrated by a scene recorded by journalist John Gittings outside an oil field in 1978. Proclaiming the government's modernization plan, a poster showed young faces gazing eagerly into the future; the figure 2000 gleamed in a sky streaked with rockets above factory skylines, behind a foreground of steel weapons and a huge satellite dish. "The peasants' carts, piled high with winter fodder, shambled past the hoarding, their drivers wrapped in sacking against the cold."

Mao's successor said, "To get rich is no sin." Every observer in the late 1970s and 1980s selected his own evidence of a return to stability, normalcy, and prospective prosperity. For some, better times were symbolized by the clean-up of the wall posters in central Peking, which had become the revolutionary medium par excellence. For Jung Chang, hope was signified by the reopening in 1981 of Szechuan's traditional teashops, which she had helped to close down as a young Red Guard fifteen years before. Her happiness was restored by the waitress who infused her tea in the old-fashioned way, with a deft arc of water from a kettle held two feet from the cup. Meanwhile, a policy of Responsibility was breaking up collective agriculture and reviving a traditional, wealth-creating peasantry. Capitalism—now called "the primary phase of socialism"—was inaugurated in retailing and manufacture. Suddenly released economic instincts over-heated the economy and, as I write in 1993, the Chinese government is struggling to restrain growth to 10 per cent a year. If China can hold together politically, the sheer size of her economy will restore her to economic preponderance early in the next millennium.

Yet T'zu-hsi still seems to be smiling up from hell. Development is patchy, and recent growth has been concentrated disproportionately towards the Pacific coast. In public sentiment and in the divided counsels of decision-makers, modernization has a precarious tenure, as if constantly expecting notice to quit. Party and peasants are allies in today's China against the cities and the intellectuals. In Peking in 1989, thousands of worshippers of the Goddess of Democracy were dispersed by soldiers—and hundreds massacred—after declaring their determination "to live no longer under the barrel of a gun." Thus, outside the agrarian sector, free enterprise operates, at best, in an equivocal political environment. As population growth slips out of control, food production continually reasserts itself as the most urgent objective of economic policy. And though Kentucky Fried Chicken can be bought near the site of the 1989 massacre, the recently opened door to China is kept by intimidatingly supercilious janitors who remain finicky about taking lessons or cash from the barbarians on the threshold. "The present leadership" according to a persuasive interviewee of John Gittings, "is showing the same kind of psychology that has been demonstrated by

Pounding the Chongno Bell in its new pavilion in Seoul: traditionally struck at the opening of the city gates, it became a symbol of liberation during Japanese occupation. The inexpertise of the officials trying to swing the hammer and the indifference of the audience of children attest a degree of emotional disinvestment since Sim Hun promised to pound the bell with his head.

the Chinese ruling class for over a hundred years. They regard western capitalism as an attractive lady whom they want to kiss" but are quick to disengage from a demeaning embrace. The recent history of foreign investment in China is written between the lines of broken contracts.

THE CLASH OF JADE PENDANTS

At the end of Yi Kwangsu's novel *The Heartless,* written in Korea during the First World War, a character with a scholarship on his way to America holds up a train ticket "soaked," he says, "in the sweat of people trembling with hunger and cold." Having repudiated traditional values—and, with them, his childhood betrothed—he had found himself "cast out, guideless, in a world where there were no ideals for the Korean people to follow." A sense of obligation to his fellow-countrymen eventually restored purpose to his life, and he set off for the west with the intention of bringing back "power, knowledge, enlightenment . . . so that we may help our people build a stronger and firmer foundation."

At the time and for long afterwards this programme of modernization seemed as elusive in Korea as in China. The self-strengthening ideal had seeped in from across the border in the late nineteenth century, but the need for revitalizing reform was unacknowledged until 1907 when a new emperor swore before his ancestors' shrine to "abandon old habits and foster new principles." It was too late. Japan had already decided to turn Korea into a colony—indeed, virtually a military camp. When the Japanese marched in, Koreans had, in a poet's slight hyperbole, "nothing, neither sword nor pistol, dagger nor club" to fight back with. Korea became "a peacock chained by the neck."

Although collaboration was irresistibly practical and Korean children had to pledge to "endure hardships in order to become good citizens of great Japan," patriotism throve during the occupation. Independence, ineffectively claimed, was ecstatically anticipated. The poet Sim Hun typically promised "when that day comes" to "soar like a crow at night and pound the Chongno bell with my head." Korean historians, looking back on the period, have imitated this fevour and dismissed Japanese rule as an unrelieved disaster. It is true that Japanese imperialism was crudely exploitative; that few of the economic installations of the conquerors lasted; and that towards the end of the occupation, when Japan was straining to sustain her part in the world war, the country was ransacked and exhausted. Nevertheless, the answer to the poet's question, "Does Spring Come to Stolen Fields?" was, "Yes."

For, though Korea's modernization was long deferred, the experience of subjugation by Japan helped to make it possible in four ways. First, by beginning coal and steel production at an early stage of the occupation, the Japanese left an example and a memory. Second, by intensifying local industrialization in order to wage war, Japan left a little industrial infrastructure—largely dismantled by self-interested "liberators"—but a lot of implanted ambition. Third, because all educated Koreans knew Japanese, Korea could easily tap into information on Japan's economic miracle. Finally, though Koreans were suppressed and enslaved for demeaning work, large numbers inevitably acquired industrial skills. The last census under Japanese rule showed over 700,000 managers and 2.8 million craftsmen in the population.

Korea followed Japan's example to create her own idiosyncratic industrial revolution, but it was delayed by frustration and marred by imperfections. The Japanese occupiers were followed by Russians and Americans, who installed mutually hostile regimes in their respective spheres. The southern half was cut off from the sources of energy in the north, and the north barricaded against the capitalism of the south. Both halves endured repressive regimes which upheld the traditional Korean distinction: "the government is superior and the people inferior." In the north the communists made their usual mistake of wasting resources on top-heavy industrialization, while the south was "a republic with imperial trappings," ruled by "an autocrat with rich democratic rhetoric" who was related to the old dynasty.

The war of 1950–53 was destructive but indecisive as the armies of foreign sponsors rolled back and forth up and down the peninsula. After it, all

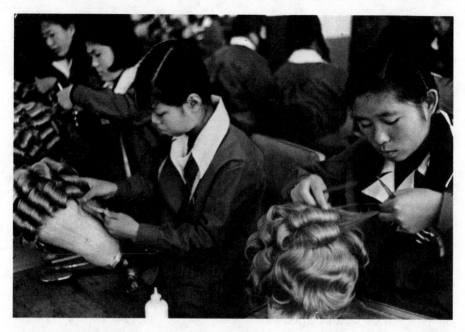

Scene in the Dana wig factory, Suwon, South Korea. The purposeful girls, uniformed in cramped rows on ergonomically designed seating, are one of the battle-lines of Korea's industrial "miracle"; the products they are making become part of the masking-equipment of westernization, as they crimp and curl the fake blond hairs into mockery of their own black, lank locks.

American aid to the south went on relief. War was only suspended, never officially terminated; defence soaked up funds, depriving Korea of one of Japan's big advantages during the years of reconstruction (see Chapter 20). The possibilities of progress had to be glimpsed in the gaps between intellectuals' visions of what Korea might become and the immobile realities of traditional society. The sexually liberated women, for instance, imagined by the novelist Chong Pi-sok in the mid-1950s, seemed like an adolescent fantasy in a country where smoking in public was a privilege reserved to venerable women who, at sixty, had exceeded the average life span of their sex by nearly eight years.

Thus the "miracle on the Han River" was delayed until the 1960s when a new president, the authoritarian technocrat Park Chung Hee, launched a far-sighted policy of buying national harmony with economic growth. Like Japan's (see Chapter 20)—and deliberately so—South Korea's industrialization was achieved by "guided capitalism" and close collaboration between government and huge conglomerates. In the three decades from 1962, the

A photograph taken by Arthur Miller's wife, Inge Morath, in Kweilin. A motor-bike has been transformed into a family vehicle by the same hand that made the bamboo stroller on the right.

economy grew at an average rate of 9 per cent a year; from 1962 to 1987 gross national product went up to $25 billion in real terms. Between 1961 and 1981 the proportions of GNP represented by agriculture and industry were reversed. By 1988, at a level of $5,000, GNP per capita in South Korea was approaching European levels. Thanks to exports of cars and electronic gadgets, as South Korea rose to eleventh in the rankings of nations by volume of trade, the names of Samsung and Hyundai became almost as familiar in the world as those of Toyota and Mitsubishi. As in Japan, governments strove with remarkable success to keep ownership in national hands. Social change kept pace. In So Kiwon's story of 1963, *The Heir,* a boy who found his ancestor's jade pendants—symbol of attainment in the old scholar-bureaucracy—used them only to make a clicking, jingling noise in his pocket.

For some economists' tastes, it all happened too fast: South Korea had to cover huge import bills for food and machinery; the export drive had to be subsidized by loans from abroad; the usual fatal enthusiasm for heavy industries in command economies dragged investment towards the relatively unremunerative heavy sector. In consequence, Koreans completed their in-

dustrialization with the biggest per capita debt burden in Asia. Still, growth
rates made the debts seem manageable and for other potential "new industrializing nations" around the world, Korea's was a dazzling example,
encouraging or intimidating according to taste. South Korea is a vivid
demonstration of the apparent special powers—or, at least, the exceptional
achievements—of Asia's Pacific rim: in no other part of the world have attempts to industrialize one's way out of third-world status been so successful.

China's failure to match this spectacular record is thrown into sharper relief against the background of expatriate Chinese success, over roughly the
same period, in Taiwan, Hong Kong, and Singapore. Chinese societies have
inherent virtues which ought to help them re-establish their old industrial
superiority over the west (see Chapter 12): a work ethic, rich in attributes of
self-discipline and social responsibility, inherited from Confucianism; and a
system of family values which keeps social welfare cheap. On the mainland, while the new industrializers were forging ahead offshore, Chinese industrial talent was evident but unsystematic, its character captured in a
Heath-Robinson photograph that Arthur Miller brought back from Kweilin
in 1979: a baby peeps from a motor bike modified for family transportation,
alongside a traditional bamboo stroller. In the three Chinese states outside
China this native aptitude and ingenuity, nursed by governments and rewarded by foreign investors and buyers, created industrial revolutions similar and in some ways superior to South Korea's. The little dragons learned
to fly before the mother-dragon.

The blast of war helped to put wind under their wings. Among the
clients and allies of the United States around the Pacific, the 1960s and early
1970s were bonanza years because massive American military involvement
in south-east Asia generated huge demand for manpower, supply, places of
rest and recuperation, and all the infrastructure of a wartime baseline. The
Americans came in increasing numbers from 1961 to defend "one of the
world's frontiers of freedom" in Vietnam, after French imperialism collapsed
(see Chapter 18) and partition between communist and anti-communist
regimes proved unstable. Their war of containment proved impracticable in
guerrilla-soaked ground. By "the politics of inadvertence" they got trapped
in what was called "escalation": ever higher costs, ever higher casualties,
ever lower morale. Public opinion at home would neither approve perseverance nor admit defeat.

The twelve-year agony of America and her allies dominated the world's
news media. Never before had a war been illuminated so brilliantly by the
flash bulb, approached so closely by the camera lens, and broadcast so
quickly by the television satellite. It was riveting entertainment, dramatic
and disturbing, made vivid by images of atrocities and ineptitude, played
nightly to hearthside audiences and rerun in the morning papers. At the

time it was thought to be important for its effects on the western world. It seemed to sap the American self-confidence on which the Atlantic world depended for defence. It stimulated peace movements and protest politics which spread a ripple of rebellion through Europe and America in 1968, toppling some governments and disturbing others. It inspired revulsion from the existing system in the west and impatience with the establishment decision-makers who seemed to have no antidote to their own poison. It encouraged the cults of flower power and drug-induced resignation in western youth, who now had a pretext for their generational vices of rebellion or indifference. The psychedelic fashions and didactic pop lyrics of the 1960s and early 1970s in the west are unintelligible except against the background of Vietnam. As a undergraduate freshman in 1970, receiving an unwonted visit from my father, I was embarrassed to explain why so many of my contemporaries affected unkempt hair and bare feet.

A Rambo poster proclaims the virtues of "a crudely mythical draftee." It will be hard for the galactic museum-keepers, if this image survives, to believe that Americans found this self-image flattering. The usual convention of war propaganda in the western tradition, in which a war is represented as a civilized defence against barbarous enemies, is here overturned. The American hero has become a naked savage, an instinctive killer, wielding a weapon like a gross phallus. The slogan, "No law can stop him," even discards the pretence of civilized constraint and implicitly defies the charge that American soldiers were guilty of war crimes. See illustrations pp. 489 and 543.

As the end of the millennium approaches, the effects of Vietnam seem to have got washed out of the west. The outcome of the war did not stimulate communist insurgency on the scale predicted by American strategists: most of the "dominoes" propped up by American policy stayed upright. In retrospect, the parties in the conflict soon came to look morally indifferent. My generation grew into "young fogies," repudiating radicalism. A taste for protest music became part of a syndrome of middle-aged respectability. Meanwhile, American popular culture recast the disasters of the war as a test of national virtue. The violence has been rehabilitated—indeed, glorified—by a series of Rambo movies dedicated to the celebration of a crudely mythical draftee whose heroism is measured in slaughter. Peace movements which once filled television screens and long highways with marchers, have dwindled to the dimensions of cranky affectations, while what is left of youthful idealism has got dissipated among other causes—religious revivalism, ecological awareness, ethnic self-assertion, feminism, neo-fascism, and campaigns for human rights. In Robert Stone's novel *Dog Soldiers,* the anti-hero Ray Hicks responds to Converse's statement that Vietnam is where Americans go to find out who they are with the comment, "What a bummer for the gooks."

The galactic museum-keepers of the future, however, will continue to assign importance to America's débâcle in Vietnam for its effects on eastern Asia: not the adverse effects which kept the whole of former French Indo-China economically backward or condemned Cambodia—a guerrilla corridor on the American flank—to a long, bloody, and destructive civil war, but the positive effects which spread American largesse among regional allies, pouring in technology for new ventures, investment for their development, and demand for their success.

American custom filled pockets of prosperity and, in some places, funded the take-off of industries or modern service sectors, including fast-food outlets in Manila and brothels in Bangkok. Today, for a sense of what Bangkok was like in the early 1960s, you have to go upstream to a part of Thailand which modernization has still hardly reached, like Damnoen Suduak, to see wooden bridges tacked over canals the colour of dung, between the low, curling roofs of rickety houses and temples. Though the Filipino economy—in some ways the most promising in south-east Asia in the 1950s—has underperformed consistently ever since, the Vietnam years masked its failures with the superficial prosperity of temporarily inflated growth rates. Much of Manila was reclothed in the era's architectural uniform of ferro-concrete and plate glass.

The biggest gainers from the spillage and seepage of rewards from the war were the already industrialized or industrializing economies of the region. Hong Kong and Taiwan had relevant experience, propelled towards industrialization by earlier wars. Hong Kong had benefited from China's

Traditional Thailand, now retreating upstream. A floating market off the main course of the Chao Phraya River, in 1966, with produce paddled in from up-river farms.

civil conflicts when exiled managers from Shanghai's old textiles factories opened up for business along the coast of the New Territories after 1949. Taiwan owed its start as an industrial power to the Korean War, which made Americans see it as "an unsinkable aircraft carrier" attractive to aid and investment. In these countries, as in Japan, the Vietnam conflict stimulated demand at a helpful stage of the cycle. For South Korea industrialization coincided with the American effort in Vietnam. Of the region's new industrializers of the late millennium, only Singapore started the process later, in the mid-1960s, and she was fully able to exploit the regional boom which accompanied the intensification of American involvement.

THE OCEAN VIEW

The cases of Hong Kong, Taiwan, and Singapore are tempting to generalizers, but they make a confusing mesh of differences and similarities. All are small by comparison with Japan and South Korea but all are densely packed with people, while Hong Kong is half as big again in population as Singapore, and Taiwan more than six times the size. Hong Kong and Taiwan are almost entirely Chinese, their Chinese-ness uncompromised by westernization: "Cousin Lee," the caricature-representative of the Taiwanese of the 1980s, had a slick western hairstyle and a "cool," brash swagger, but he wore a martial-arts suit and practised the traditional disciplines; Singapore, by contrast, has important Malay and Indian minorities but keeps a Chinese style in government and culture. Official campaigns to "Make Courtesy Our Way of Life" or "Start Mandarin Now" are like gentle travesties of Mao's way of animating the masses; unspoiled by prosperity, Singaporeans burn life-size paper effigies of Mercedes cars as offerings to their ancestors. All three countries have been accessible to multinationals, but Singapore has been particularly welcoming and Taiwan distinctly wary. All three postponed democracy until after industrialization, but all had different political backgrounds: Hong Kong was a British Crown Colony, whereas Singapore and Taiwan were sovereign states with, respectively, British and Japanese colonial experience.

Taiwan was big enough to have a shrinking agricultural hinterland of her own, which kept her industrial workforce fed, while Singapore and Hong Kong, where the lands of rural truck-farmers were smothered in housing in the 1970s and 1980s, were supplied from neighbouring countries. In Singapore, the Raffles Hotel, where a tiger was once shot under the billiard table, is now surrounded only by concrete jungle. Government in Hong Kong during industrialization was dominated by free-market thinking while Tai-

Slick hair, "cool" swagger, eastern martial arts: Taiwan in the 1980s personified in Cousin Lee, the popular cartoon character created by the American political caricaturist, Ranan R. Lurie, in 1985. The image is obviously equivocal, especially for western admirers of Chinese culture who are uneasy about its adulteration with imported values; but, officially at last, Taiwan liked it.

"Unspoiled by prosperity": after ritual blessing, a life-size paper Mercedes awaits immolation at a Singaporean undertaker's as an offering to the dead.

wan and Singapore were revolutionized by command capitalism similar to Korea's. Singapore, an emporium from her foundation in 1819, industrialized within her own traditions, handling and processing other people's products, while Taiwan and Hong Kong specialized in their own manufactures. Singapore's rise, after a deferred start, was more or less simultaneous with South Korea's; Taiwan and Hong Kong started early—not far behind the recovery of Japan in the 1950s when their businessmen began to play host to buyers from western chain stores. They belong to the China Seas, and both face the prospect of reunification with the rest of China: Hong Kong in 1997 at the expiry of Britain's lease of part of the colony, Taiwan at an indeterminate and probably far-off time which will have to await the agreement of both sides. Singapore is, by comparison, a long way from China, and her strongest political links are with her sometime federal partners in Malaysia.

From a more distant perspective, these differences disappear. The little dragons are examples, with Japan and some of the more industrially precocious areas of east and south-east Asia, of a single phenomenon, or, rather, of half a phenomenon, because development on the Pacific rim is connected across the ocean by exchanges of personnel, investment, expertise, and—increasingly—a Pacific consciousness: awareness of being linked and lapped by the ocean of the future, of living round the arena of exchange of some of the world's most promising regional and national economies, which between them account for half the world's gross product. The durability of that sense and the reliability of that promise can be judged by turning to the broader ocean view, from the perspective of the shores of the "White Pacific" in the Americas, Australia, and New Zealand.

Chapter 22

RIDERS OF THE SURF: THE WHITE PACIFIC

The Lost Caravels—The New Mediterranean—Under Open Skies—The Surf of History

THE LOST CARAVELS

Even rich Chinese were said to prefer steerage "so that they could eat Chinese food." This showed, if true, an odd sense of priorities. Unpleasantly, fetidly penned below decks, an ocean crossing with the Pacific Mail Steamship Company in the 1860s was tedious, wretched, and dispiriting. On the only established route, between Hong Kong and San Francisco, twelve hundred steerage passengers spent the thirty-three or thirty-four days' voyage with few or no breaks permitted on deck. They brought their own bedding, stretched on wooden boards which were cleared by day for sitting and eating; but for the poorer class of voyagers—the thousands of coolie labourers conscripted by kidnap or indentured for debt—even these conditions were comparatively luxurious. In the lethal environment of the clipper ships that carried Chinese peons to sugar plantations and cotton haciendas in Peru, death rates reached 40 per cent per voyage.

On the San Francisco run, twelve round trips were completed each year by four of the largest wooden-hulled, paddle-driven steamships ever made: each of 4,000 tons, they cost a million dollars to build. On average, on the transpacific route, each burned forty-five tons of coal a day. The company had started in 1848, plying with mail between the Atlantic and the Oregon coast around Cape Horn. From the 1860s, with the Chinese population and

659

business interests accumulating in California, Pacific crossings received federal subsidies; when the subsidies doubled in 1872, so did the frequency of the service.

The creation of this regular, reliable link across the ocean, for post and passengers, was a moment of concentrated achievement in a long process of enormous significance: the Pacific was being transformed into a single space, an arena of commercial and cultural exchange. The steamship liberated Pacific communications from the effects of two great limiting factors: inhibiting distance and unbiddable winds.

Today, the cultists who ride the surf on California's Malibu beach fall into cold water. The currents that chill them, even when the sands are shimmering with heat, helped to determine the direction and limit the range of Pacific traffic in the age of sail. Two powerful systems, forged by the most regular winds in the world, divide the ocean at the equator. In the southern half, sailing vessels can cross from east to west with the south-east trades and the south equatorial current, roughly between the Tropic of Capricorn and the equator. From Australia, New Zealand, or Melanesia, they can return with the east Australian current and the roaring forties. These routes were of limited usefulness, however, because until the nineteenth century they linked relatively unproductive and unfrequented coasts. Where reliable routes were needed, in the central Pacific, between the cash-rich Spanish American empire and the productive orient, nature was unhelpful. A direct crossing between Mexico and the Philippines was easy with the north-east trades and the north equatorial current. To get back, however, demanded a long detour to the north, through belts of stormy and unpre-

The first surfboard is said to have arrived in Australia in 1915. By the 1930s, the surfing lifesaver of indomitable muscularity had become a type of Australian manhood for others to emulate. Today, surfing is a national pastime, practised every day of the year, and a cult with its own heroes. In Hawaii and parts of California surfing has a similar status as a vital part of local or regional culture and identity.

dictable winds, before turning south again with the current that cools California's coasts. Timing was delicate; because the Philippines are clasped in a monsoonal wind system, ships in the season normally had to be turned around for the return trip—unloaded, loaded anew, and their business transacted—in a matter of days, or else six months would be lost.

It took a long time to explore and exploit these routes. The first recorded attempt was unencouraging: Magellan's pioneering crossing, made diagonally between Chile and Guam, with the trade winds for most of the way, between 28 November 1520 and 6 March 1521. By the end of the journey the explorers were starving, champing painfully—they claimed—on the leather covers from the yards with jaws weakened by scurvy, drinking putrid water, and eating wormy biscuit "which stank strongly of rats' urine." The voyage exposed the intimidating vastness of a one-way ocean which could be crossed, at terrible hazard and cost, but not recrossed.

The frustrating search began for a route that would link America and Asia in both directions. Expeditions from the Philippines combed south of the equator without success and ranged up to thirty degrees north in an unrewarded hunt for a westerly wind. Lost caravels roamed erratically, leaving mysterious bric-à-brac on remote islands—iron cannon on a Tuamotu atoll, a wooden cross on Anaa, east of Tahiti, Spanish helmets in Hawaii. The two-way route was not pieced together until 1565 when Andrés de Urdaneta, a retired navigator recalled from his friar's cloister, persevered with the longest voyage so far recorded without a landfall—11,600 miles in five months and eight days: a curling arc across the north Pacific, almost to forty degrees north. The chart he made became the basis for all Pacific sailing directions for the rest of the age of sail.

The discovery of the wind system made it possible to conceive of the Pacific as a potential whole but also showed how formidable were the practical obstacles to unification. Though the established routes became increasingly frequented—by pirates, scientists, missionaries, traders, whalers, and settlers—one effect of their creation was to withdraw shipping from the more inaccessible spots to which explorers had strayed in the era of route-finding. Hawaii is not known to have been visited again until Captain James Cook died there in 1779. The only regular transpacific traffic sailed in the Manila galleon, which made an annual round trip from Acapulco via the Philippines (see Chapter 11). The Pacific remained an almost intractable ocean for more than two hundred years after Urdaneta's achievement: a space on the map, stretched between myths: the "unknown continent" of Terra Australis in the south and the rumoured sea passage around America in the north.

Then, in ten years of revolutionary progress in Pacific exploration, investigation of those myths became the objective of Captain James Cook. After experience on coal-carriers out of his native Yorkshire, he had joined the

"A space on the map, stretched between myths." Hondius's map of Drake's and Cavendish's circumnavigations displays a typically seventeenth-century image of the Pacific: a much smaller ocean than it really is, with a north-west passage at the top and a "Great Southern Continent" at the bottom.

Royal Navy as an able seaman. Service in the north Atlantic in the Seven Years' War drew attention to his uncanny gifts as a coastal surveyor and chart-maker. In 1769 he was sent aboard an old Whitby collier to observe the transit of Venus from Tahiti, which astronomers in London advocated as the best scientific vantage point. He returned with an explorer's vocation as intense as any the Pacific had seen since the days of Queiros (see Chapter 8) and conceived the ambition to sail "not only farther than man has been before me but as far as I think it possible for man to go."

In three voyages of Pacific exploration he ranged the ocean with a freedom never before attained. He crossed the seventieth parallel north and the seventy-first south. By charting New Zealand, the west coast of Alaska, and the east coast of Australia, he delineated the extremities of the Pacific. He filled in most of its remaining gaps on the map, accurately locating the island groups of Polynesia, southern Melanesia, and the Hawaiian archipelago. He brought a new precision to cartography, using the latest longitude-finding technology, John Harrison's exquisitely accurate chronometer, as the "faithful guide" of his second and third voyages. He fairly exploded the myth of a Terra Australis or, at least, pushed its possible location into latitudes "doomed to lie for ever buried under everlasting snow and ice." His achievements overflowed the map of the Pacific; by rigorous standards, for instance, of hygiene and nutrition aboard ship, he contributed to the conquest of scurvy. He mooted the colonization of Australia and New Zealand. His ships brought back sketches and specimens of creation—human, botanical, and zoological—which helped to equip the science of the age of reason and stimulate the sensibilities of the age of romanticism (see Chapter 15). The possibilities seemed to be scented by the kangaroo George Stubbs painted—a reconstruction from a pelt which Cook brought home—sniffing quizzically over a hazily limitless landscape.

Cook was the spearhead of an enormous scientific invasion of the Pacific by late eighteenth- and early nineteenth-century expeditions from England, France, Spain, and Russia; between them, they acquainted the European public as never before with the dimensions and diversity of the ocean. It was now possible to conceive it as a geographical unit; but it could not begin to become an economic zone until the power of the steamship reduced it to manageable proportions.

Even then integration was slow, with most of the Pacific rim's long-range trade bound for destinations outside the region, overland by rail or into the Indian Ocean and the Atlantic. The Pacific was still a backwater compared with those other oceans—"the small change of Euroamerican empires"—until the spread of the industrial revolution to its shores. Relatively suddenly, in the second half of the twentieth century, with the impact of the events described in the last two chapters, the Pacific became an economic giant, supplying over half of the world's total product by the 1990s and carrying most of the world's trade. With particular intensity in the 1980s, a huge transfer of people and investment, originating chiefly in east Asia, gave patches of the White Pacific a colonized look, with conspicuous con-

George Stubbs's "Kangaroo," painted from a pelt brought back by Cook's first Pacific expedition in 1771, and from sketches made by the voyage's botanical illustrator, Sidney Parkinson. To Cook's eye the kangaroo resembled a greyhound, "but for its walking or running, in which it resembled a hare or a deer."

centrations of Asian settlers and a form of "business imperialism" directed mainly from Japan and Hong Kong.

The Pacific region became a reality because people who lived there believed in it; that the world was entering a Pacific Age became conventional wisdom in the early 1980s as dwellers on its shores exchanged admiring glances across "the ocean of the future." They gazed about them with a wild surmise and liked what they saw. Objectively, there was no reason for Pacific-side societies to share each other's company or hatch mutual projects in preference to collaboration with partners in other parts of the world. Modern technology has made geographical propinquity obsolete as a basis for economic cooperation or a shared sense of interest. But history rarely happens objectively; it starts in the mind. And the idea of a Pacific world seemed to appeal to many of those who lived in and around the ocean. "The inhabitants of the nations grouped by geographical accident around the Ocean's coasts," observed by Simon Winchester during a five-year odyssey around the Pacific, testing the depth of pan-Pacific sentiment, "had started to look inward, at themselves, rather than caring any longer for the views of those beyond, or behind. . . . They looked instead across the huge blue expanse of water, and they communed with each other—Shanghai with Santiago, Sydney with Hong Kong, Jakarta with Lima and . . . Roppongi with Hollywood—and by doing so perhaps they achieved a kind of Pacific identity."

The test of whether this is an enduring change, of the sort likely to be noticed by the galactic museum-keepers, has to be applied in the White Pacific, in communities such as Australia, California, British Columbia, and New Zealand, which have strong historic identities rooted far from the Pacific, emotional ties which tug them towards the Atlantic, Europe, and the American interior; they have ancient prejudices against "yellow" races traditionally branded as contemptible or "perilous." "Pacific civilization" will have come of age when the answer to the question, "Where is Vancouver?" or "Where is Los Angeles?" evokes the automatic answer, "On the Pacific" instead of "In Canada" or "In the United States"; or when San Francisco or Seattle seem on the brink of the east rather than the edge of the west; or when Australians complete their so-far tentative self-reclassification as an Asian people; or when White Californians or New Zealanders feel as united by common interest with Japanese and South Koreans as Netherlanders with north Italians or Alsatians with Luxembourgeois. It may never happen. But if the Pacific concept gets well anchored in the ocean, political storms will follow, drawn like the flash of Saint Elmo's fire around a mast; old enmities will sink and friendships founder, and the galactic museum-keepers will chronicle the breaking up of Canada and, later, of the United States and even, perhaps, of China as preludes to the rise of a Pacific confederation.

The New Mediterranean

When Ariel's victims were cast away on Prospero's island, their first disagreement was about the quality of the soil. Early colonizers of Australia reacted to their new environment with similar variance. Sir Joseph Banks, who was probably the single most important promoter of colonization, was so impressed with the fertility of the area he selected for settlement that he called it Botany Bay; Captain Cook, with his unerring eye, foresaw its productive future. Yet some members of the expedition which followed up the explorers' initiative in 1788 condemned "this solitary waste of the creation," where "there is not a single article in the whole country that in the nature of things could prove of the smallest use or value to the mother country or the commercial world." At first, the pessimists seemed justified. Almost all crops failed at Sydney and proved disappointing at Port Jackson, across the bay, where the soil was said to be better. George Worgan, the man who took the first piano to New South Wales, found "whether from any unfriendly, deleterious quality of the soil or the seas" that "nothing seems to flourish vigorously." Rations were reduced in September 1789. Famine threatened in 1790. The colony was still dependent on supplies from Britain in 1792.

Yet within a few years a "new Europe" (see Chapter 12) seemed to have taken root and blossomed. When the officers of a French fleet called at Sydney in 1802, they professed themselves "completely astonished at the flourishing state in which we found this singular and distant establishment." Sydney was already a solid and dignified town with stone buildings, dockyards producing vessels of up to 3,000 tons "entirely with native wood," and state ovens that could bake 1,800 pounds of hard tack daily. The environs included "pretty habitations" set in pastures of introduced grasses, where "no longer ago than 1794, the whole was covered with immense and useless forests of eucalyptus." The French commander confessed that he "could not regard without admiration the immense work the English have done. It is difficult to conceive how they have so speedily attained to the state of splendour and comfort in which they now find themselves."

This happy issue had not been procured without afflictions. The first four or five years of the colony were a time of feverish and often of failed experiments in matching introduced plants and livestock to particular spots and times of planting. The experimental era was captured in Worgan's reports of his efforts to tease a creditable performance from his peas and beans, or in the heart-wringing saga of James Ruse, a pardoned convict who had been a husbandman in Cornwall. In November 1789 he took a farm of thirty acres near Paramatta on "middling soil" which he thought

"A state of splendour and comfort": an engraving based on a view painted in the first few years of the nineteenth century shows the Sydney described by members of Baudin's visiting French fleet in 1802, with the neat town emerging from the wilderness and shipbuilding in progress in the dockyards.

bound to fail for want of manure. He burned the timber, dug in the ash, hoed it, clod-moulded it, dug in grass and weeds, and left it exposed to the sun for sowing; he proposed after reaping to plant turnip-seed "which will mellow and prepare it for next year." He made his own manure substitute from straw rotted in pits; and he did all this with only his own labour and his wife's.

Success in experimenting depended on willingness to try a diversity of products. From the earliest days, this was a strange "new Europe," made with yams, pumpkins, and Indian corn. On the warm coastal lowlands where the first settlers set up, maize proved much better suited than rye, barley, or wheat, which were the only grains brought by the founding ships from England. The woody plants Worgan grew from seed included the firs and oaks of home, but the rest were rather more exotic: Mediterranean oranges, lemons, and limes alongside indigo, coffee, ginger, and castor nut. On the voyage out to found the colony, the fleet acquired tropical specimens including bananas, cocoa, guava, ipecacuanha, jalap, sugar cane, and tamarind. In 1802 "the bamboo of Asia" was admired, growing alongside Government House. Most of the successful early livestock came not directly from Europe but from Calcutta and the Cape of Good Hope, which also supplied acclimatized fruit trees, originally of European provenance, robust enough to withstand the voyage.

This is not to say that the results of the experiment are inappropriately called a "new Europe." Indeed, the more exotic plants made at best only a marginal long-term contribution to the success of the colony. Their presence does show, however, how widely experimenters were prepared to range in the search for suitable species. They were not resolved to rebuild home, nor did they do so. The successful model in early colonial Australia, judged by the produce of its ecological frontier, was of a Europe generously conceived, which covered a very wide climatic band from the Mediterranean to unmitigated England. Overwhelmingly in practice—and even, to some extent, in conception—it was a Mediterranean rather than a northern Europe, in which predominated the biota of the south rather than of the colonists' homeland.

Sir Joseph Banks, who equipped the founding expedition with specimens from home, had established from observation, to his own satisfaction, that degree for degree over most of its extent the southern hemisphere was about ten degrees cooler at any given latitude than the northern. He therefore expected the climate of Botany Bay to resemble, as he said, that of Toulouse. His ladings included "all the fruits" of Europe, *largo sensu,* but alongside those common to Mediterranean and Atlantic climes he sent those peculiar to the Mediterranean, such as lemon, lime, pomegranate, orange, and shaddock, and stone fruits better suited to southern than northern Europe, such as the apricot, nectarine, and peach. Although "all the vegetables of Europe" fed convicts at Paramatta in the 1790s, early descriptions of the colony concur in depicting it in Mediterranean flavours and colours.

The first governor had in his own garden oranges and "many as fine figs as ever I tasted in Spain or Portugal" and "a thousand vines yielding three hundredweight of grapes." Watkin Tench, whose study of the soils in and around the area colonized in 1788 contributed to the success of agricultural experiments—his samples can still be seen, dried to powder, in a Sydney museum—commended the performance of "vines of every sort. . . . That their juice will probably hereafter furnish an indispensable article of luxury at European tables has already been predicted in the vehemence of speculation." He also spotted the potential for oranges, lemons, and figs. By the time of the French visit of 1802, peaches were so plentiful that they were used to fatten the hogs, and the French commander saw, in the garden of Government House, "the Portugal orange and the Canary fig ripening beneath the shade of the French apple tree."

The Mediterranean world also provided the colony with an exportable staple. In November 1790, Joseph Banks took delivery of a gift from a former Spanish ambassador of thirty-eight fine-wool merino sheep from one of the most famous flocks in Spain. Eight specimens from this source left for New South Wales in 1804. Only five rams and one old ewe survived the journey, but these were enough; the wool of the merino-cross sheep began to be exported in commercial quantities from 1811.

This early Australian experience set something of a pattern for new colonial worlds of the Pacific rim; "dumb continents" where "the roots are European but the tree grows to different pattern and design." The north American west, New Zealand, and, to a lesser extent, southern Chile were all settled in the nineteenth century, displacing isolated and underpopulated cultures with dynamic, outward-going, and relatively populous economies which greatly extended the range and frequency of transpacific contacts. All of them, in varying degrees, defied the intentions of their original projectors and colonizers and developed unpredicted characters—tricks worked by the alchemy that mingled settlers of diverse provenance in the crucibles of unexperienced environments.

Some of the effects took a long time to show. It is not, perhaps, surprising that colonists in Australia should have tried to match their cultigens to the climate; nor that Englishmen—especially in the late eighteenth and early nineteenth centuries when the esteem, indeed the Byronic passion for the Mediterranean, was so strong a fashion in England—should have sought to replicate in a warm south the seductive Mediterranean world rather than that of their own country. What is surprising is that this "new Europe," which flourished like a new Mediterranean and called itself New South Wales, should for more than a century have continued to behave, talk, play, dress, and cook like a new Britain (see Chapter 14). Even in the mid-twentieth century Australians still presented themselves to each other as members of a subset of "the British race," and in a sense—if Irish ancestry was included—the characterization was true. Until the last decade of the century a dwindling majority of Australians continued to count themselves as British by descent.

The crisis of identity which has left today's Australia stranded between European and Asian options was brought on by a series of events which made a British option impossible. The Second World War exposed the illusion of "imperial defence." The Suez affair (see Chapter 18) alienated liberals from British policy. Britain's overtures to the emerging European Economic Community (see Chapter 18) from 1959 induced a sense of *sauve qui peut;* common allegiance is always hard to contrive or maintain without common economic interest.

Above all, but little by little, through erosion rather than eruption, the provenance of the Australian people was transformed by liberalized immigration policies. The numbers of migrants from southern and eastern Europe grew—with fluctuations—from the late nineteenth century; but the attenuation of British Australia by this means was a very slow process. There were still only about sixty thousand Australians classifiable as south Europeans in 1947, when the numbers began to increase sharply. The United Kingdom remained—and still remains as I write—the biggest single

In May 1900, when the imperial parliament in London was debating the bill that established Australia as an independent federation, the people of Sydney were indulging in this rapturous display of British feeling and imperial solidarity, joining in the empire-wide celebrations of the relief of Mafeking. The photograph shows the illumination of the General Post Office with the royal monogram and the names of the commanders of the garrison and relief column. On Baden-Powell, see p. 531.

Mei Quong Tartan or He Would Be a Scotsman by Phil May. As Sydney's leading citizen of Chinese descent, Mei Quong Tart camouflaged himself in colonial society, until his death in 1903, by prominence in the Freemasons and a comic gift for self-westernization. His eagerness to perform Scottish airs in public was an extreme example, which led the true Scot, George Reid, to proclaim him "the only man living who has got the true original Gaelic accent."

source of immigrants. Not until the mid-1960s had Australia begun to acquire a significant population of Mediterranean origins, to match the character of the environment in which most Australians lived and which the experience of the first colonists had helped to create. The national anthem was edited to excise the lines: "Her sons in fair Australia's land/Shall keep a British soul."

By then a new, more prolific source of migrants was about to be tapped. In 1966 the "White Australia" policy was abandoned and Australia opened to "Asianization." The precedents—in a sense, the roots—of an Asiatic Australian community went back to the mid-nineteenth century when Edward Hammond, a failed California gold-digger, returned home to a tributary of the Macquarrie River where he felt "surrounded by gold." He called the place Ophir and swore that his old horse would be stuffed in a glass case in the British Museum. The subsequent gold rush needed coolie labour. By the time the White Australia policy closed in, about sixty thousand Chinese had entered the country. Race riots began in 1857. In 1884, when Cardinal

Moran suggested that oriental languages should be taught in Australian universities, he was dismissed as "the chow's friend." In the 1890s a typical newspaper editorial characterized hell as "a place full of Chinamen."

One Chinese who was accepted was Mei Quong Tart, a former gold-field worker who became a tea importer. Naturalized in 1871, he became a Freemason, volunteered for the Boer War, married an Englishwoman, and became renowned as Mei Quong Tartan for his spirited renditions of Scottish airs. Others kept the dwindling Chinese community alive during the years of White Australia, such as William Liu, Australian-born and Canton-educated, whose firm, based in Sydney, owned big department stores in Shanghai, Canton, and Hong Kong. The very paucity of the Chinese community was protection against the excesses of racism. While migrants were excluded, Australians, in their ignorance, were divided between rival Asiatic stereotypes. Until the second half of the twentieth century, when educational exchanges and tourism put flesh on their vague images, Asians were "either the Yellow Peril or Our Nearest Neighbours."

The relaxation of controls and the arrival of Asian immigrants revived an old debate about whether Australia was part of Asia. In 1968 the country's most distinguished historical geographer denied this proposition, "even in a geographical sense," and upheld the view that Australia was European by heritage. Relentless economic logic, however, was forcing Australian self-perceptions to change. In 1983, Barry Grant summed up the shift he was witnessing, with a sense of urgency:

> The Australian notion of isolation has always been ambiguous. It meant interfering in Asia in order to isolate "them" from "us," or withdrawing into a nuclear garrison, jumping into "Lifeboat Australia" ("Don't let on any more or we'll drown") or just passively opting out in the hope that if nothing were done, no one would notice. The situation is different now. Australian prosperity depends on Asia. The dependent prosperity of Australia has taken a new turn, northwards.

By the late 1980s, Vietnam, the Philippines, Malaysia, and Hong Kong together accounted for more than a fifth of settler arrivals, and the total they supplied outnumbered that from the United Kingdom. With bewildering rapidity, Australia became a multicultural society with streets full of oriental shops and restaurants and radio broadcasts in seventy-eight languages. The government boldly encouraged a debate about Australia's "place in the world," summoning citizens to face their future in a community of Asian countries. By 1991 the characterization of Australia as an Asian country was almost a Labor Party election plank. It provoked the retort that Australia was still "European by culture and heritage," offered, however, with surprisingly little indignation or vehemence. In 1993 the Australian prime minister advocated Sydney as Asia's best candidate to be the venue for the Olympic Games of the year 2000. The success of the city's bid was a sign of the times: three of the last five Olympiads of the millennium would be held in Pacific-rim cities.

Exchanges of population around and across the Pacific are among the most conspicuous signs of the increasing integration of the ocean. In practice this has meant a big shift of population out of Asia and the central Pacific into the White worlds on the southern and eastern edges. Australia—though it has caught up quickly—has joined in relatively late. Other parts of the White Pacific—such as California, effectively founded at about the same time as Australia, or British Columbia and the United States northwest, founded much later, or the much longer-established Mexico, Chile, and Peru—acquired big oriental minorities in the nineteenth century; though they all experienced violent racist reactions at about the same time in the 1880s, they have kept those minorities topped up at intervals ever since.

The case of New Zealand is *sui generis*. Even before White settlement began, unplanned change had transformed the country, thanks to adventitious organisms strewn casually or sewn speculatively by European visitors: wild cabbage, cow itch, potatoes, pigs, tuberculosis, and venereal disease. In 1839 there were only about 2,000 White people in the islands. In 1840, in order to contain change, Maori chiefs signed a treaty with Britain by daubing the paper with their personal facial tatoos; by 1854 the number of Whites had grown to 32,500. The Maori resistance this provoked was effectively over by 1875.

In the following quarter of a century the country leapt into maturity. The unformed, fragmented New Zealand of the start of that period was captured in an engraving of a coach crossing the Waimakariri in 1873: a mounted guide with a lifebelt showed the way, as the fords shifted with every flood. Everything else in the picture evoked the insecurities of frontiersmanship in an uncertain adventure—the driving rain, the coachman's anxious face, his flying whip, the straining horses, the jagged flotsam, and the shadowy mountains in the background. By 1901 the isolated settlements, formerly sundered by such indomitable barriers, had been drawn together by a penny post between seventeen hundred post offices handling seventy million articles and connecting a quarter of a million telephone calls annually. By then there were nearly as many women as men in New Zealand—a sure sign of emergence into post-colonial stability; and the New Zealand identity formerly dreamed of by self-styled New Zealand Natives' Associations had become a reality, as even the remotest rugby clubs joined the national union during the 1890s.

More willingly than their Australian counterparts, New Zealanders embraced their "Pacific destiny" and expected to exercise "natural mastery"

Defying the environment to create New Zealand. Beckoned through rain, current, and dangerous sands by a calm guide in a life-jacket on an imperturbable horse, the mail gets across the Waimakariri River aboard a Cobb & Co. coach in 1873. The coach has as slight a frame as possible, with curtained sides, to help make mountainous country negotiable. The illustration by Thomas S. Cousins was published in the *New Zealand Illustrated Herald*.

over distances which "seemed small to settlers from the other end of the world." Nervousness about accepting east Asian labour and traders surfaced only slowly, when the incoming communities were already established. A cartoon in the *Free Lance* of 1920 is typical: a White farmer and soldier, straphanging in a train, exchange scowls with comfortably seated orientals of sinister mien. New Zealanders, unable to share Australians' sense of propinquity to Asia, felt neither the threat nor the promise of the continent as intensely as their neighbours. But the Second World War made them feel more exposed than ever, and the collapse of the British Empire more isolated. Today, with a small and stagnant population, Asian immigration looks like a lifeline; and in a world market divided into blocs, the Pacific area has the comforting look of home. From 1985, Japan became the country's biggest trading partner and biggest source of foreign investment. New Zealand is being drawn into a world shared with other Pacific states that live around the sea like frogs around a pond.

Strap-hanging in New Zealand in 1920: Ellis's cartoon was inspired by industrial action among Auckland dockers, who refused "to handle ships landing Chinese or Hindus, as a protest against the numbers of aliens that have been allowed to come into the country."

UNDER OPEN SKIES

It never happened. Protestant evangelists of the mid-nineteenth century dreamed of a new New England of "thoroughgoing Yankees" in California, but something about the state wrenched its development out of the tracks they laid down. Anglo-Protestantism was displaced by radical, metaphysical sects such as the Christian Scientists and the Theosophists, more numerous here by the end of the century than in any other state of the union except Massachusetts. The graves of Adam, Eve, and the Serpent were pointed out to visitors to Los Angeles in 1882; and in the 1890s, when the Unitarian minister Benjamin Fray Mills arrived from Boston, he started quoting Buddha and Lao-tzu in his sermons.

California has long been in danger of dropping off the edge of the west and becoming an oriental country. Traditional American historiography ought to have been able to predict this effect. Almost exactly a hundred years ago as I write, Frederick Jackson Turner formulated the Frontier Theory of American history, according to which, as the U.S.A. was formed by the march of settlers from east to west, the frontier became a transmutative influence, not only on the environment it crossed but also on the people who bore it and on their relationships with one another. It opened discontinuities, as metropolitan society was left behind by rebellious spirits, social experimenters, and escapees from restrictive worlds. It made space for new forms and practices, for free and expansive gestures, for distinctive identities, and for what we now call generation gaps. Turner's frontier had a Darwinian touch: it changed societies, in part, by selecting the individuals of which they were composed. Thus—though not even Turner himself foresaw it—the frontier effect might have been expected to make California different. That California was ever an American state at all was the result of an accident, a revolt extemporized against Mexican rule, like the Bear Flag of the California Republic itself, painted hurriedly in 1846 with blackberry juice on a strip of unbleached cotton. California's failure to stay tied by the pioneers' trails and railroads to a culture made in the American east is an extreme case of frontier innovation.

Today, however, the Turner thesis seems to have been turned out of its own territory. Attacks on Turner—on parts of his thesis, on his particular mistakes—began in the 1920s when he was the incumbent genius of American historiography, and became prolific after his death in 1932. In the early 1960s his reputation still inspired deference, according to an opinion survey among American historians. Yet work since then on the American west is full of repudiations of Turner's influence. His long shadow, which once darkened the west, seems to have been cut short by a gunslinger's high noon, and there are storm clouds in the open skies of Turner's America.

His was a landward-looking America, but today's American historians feel their culture has been produced by odyssey as well as anabasis. Indeed, a colleague of mine at a summer institute of maritime history told me that he had only become interested in the sea when he moved to Kansas. Turner's America, moreover, was pioneer America, from which his frontiers excluded the Indians. Today's substitute is more ethno-sensitive and wears

warpaint under the racoon-skin cap. Turner's America was ecologically incorrect—destroying the "climax community" identified by the ecologists of
his day and regretted ever since. He died just before the dust bowls began
to blow out of the west over the rest of America. By implication, at least,
his America was unique; and although historians of the American west are
still in some cases resistant to comparative insights, the image of the frontier now informs and dominates the study of colonial histories all over the
world. Turner's has followed a trajectory familiar from the example of other
gospels, without honour in its own country but preached in all quarters of
the globe.

The rise of comparative colonial history has prolonged the life of the tradition Turner inaugurated but has also complicated its course. During the
period of growth of a comparative approach to the subject, roughly since
the end of the Second World War, without explicitly challenging Turner, a
rival view has been advocated of the way frontiers work, stressing and respecting the overarching continuities which link colonial beginnings to
their metropolitan backgrounds, joining apparent new departures to a past
in which changes accumulate slowly, before historians notice them. In the
work of the great Belgian historian Charles Verlinden and his followers, we
see new worlds shaped by old ones—Antillean economies, for example, in
the early-modern period prefigured by medieval slavery, administrative
methods in early European Americas influenced by so-called feudal precedents, debates about indigenous status foreshadowed in medieval ethnography, principles of imperial economic exploitation rooted in medieval
commercial and fiscal practices. In this tradition the frontiers extend the
reach and range of the societies whence the frontiersmen come. Clouds
apart, there is not much that is altogether new under those open skies (see
Chapters 8 and 14). Some of the specific challenges to Turner from the
ranks of historians of the north American west have been made from this
perspective: the view, for instance, that American democracy was made in
the east and transmitted west with the frontier rather than the other way
round; the characterization of the west, like earlier empires, as a plundered
land and the insistence of some scholars that the U.S. frontier, like those of
Latin America, was never immune from archaic social and economic forms.

These impassioning debates seem to have disqualified us from understanding the history of California. Shortly after the state joined the Union,
Richard Henry Dana—author of *Two Years Before the Mast,* which in previous generations every American schoolboy knew—paid his second visit
and was astonished at the evidence of rapid Americanization. What he remembered as a land of simpering *señoritas* and swaggering *señoritos* had
become a home of guys and dolls. Yet at the beginning of the twentieth
century, O. Henry confessed that "Californians are a distinct race," and the
conflict of perceptions has continued ever since. California's notorious idio-

syncrasies of culture are variously read as "leading where America follows" and pulling the Union apart. The state can be represented, with equal sincerity, as a vanguard of Americanization or a foreign country precariously perched on America's edge. It may look to a galactic museum-keeper as if California went from being Spanish to Asiatic with only a brief flash of American-ness in between.

The beginnings of the story can be glimpsed through the long, fluttering eyelashes of a romantic myth of California's Spanish origins. The myth is made palpable in the city of Santa Barbara, where even the Unitarian church is built in the Hispanic Revival style. Santa Barbara does have some claim to be a Spanish city, with a mission and garrison already in place in the 1780s; continuity of the Spanish heritage under American rule was guaranteed by the marriage of a daughter of the civic patricians, the De la Guerra clan, with Alfred Robinson, a Yankee factor, just before California joined the United States. Robinson, who converted to Catholicism for the occasion, was married in a tight Bostonian morning coat with a high stiff

Santa Barbara's self-image as a Spanish city is burnished to silly splendour in the annual fiesta of "Old Spanish Days" when a parade fills the streets with majorettes dressed in bull-fighting rig-out and floats of symbolically Hispanic flavour. Here the parade is joined by Mr. Dell T. Sepulveda, whose ancestors are said to have arrived in 1769. A supposed replica follows—wrong in almost every particular—of the ship in which Vizcaino first made a detailed survey of the coast in 1602.

Tyrone Power duels with Basil Rathbone in the 1940 production of *The Mark of Zorro*. The original film, with Douglas Fairbanks, Sr., portrayed a more realistically inchoate eighteenth-century California, but the remake smartened the Spanish colony up, according to a well established Hollywood convention. The elegantly posed duelling scene captures the tone. The celestial globe is a cunningly chosen prop: a reminder of the background of philosophical enlightenment which enables Zorro to wage his war of liberation—and of the global reach of the empire against which he waged it.

collar, looking to a fellow-countryman "as if he had been pinned and skewered with only his feet and hands left free." Thanks to this encouraging example, American immigrants who followed were happy to vote the De la Guerra family into office as mayor, judges, and senators. To this day their descendants are civic guests at the annual Old Spanish Days and Barbecue with which the city celebrates its supposed Spanish roots.

But Santa Barbara was never again so Spanish as in the 1920s when it became an embodiment of the Zorro fantasy—filmed at the time by Douglas Fairbanks, Sr., and again a generation later with Tyrone Power in the title role—from stories by Johnston McCulley in which old California was depicted as a place of twirling moustaches and clashing blades, the battleground of a struggle for social justice waged by an aristocratic bandito against the high-taxing forces of big government. The architect of the corresponding building style was Charles Fletcher Lummis, whose Hispanic Re-

One of Edward Doheny's gifts to the city of Los Angeles: the Church of St. Vincent de Paul, still conspicuous but overwhelmingly dominant in its surroundings when it was built in the 1920s. This was a suitable patron saint for the suddenly enriched oil prospector who was able to combine the conventional ostentation of the rich with varied and conspicuous charitable projects of his own.

vival plans had been rejected or outgrown by Los Angeles and who argued in his pamphlet of 1923, *Stand Fast, Santa Barbara*, that Spanish romance was "of greater economic benefit than oil, oranges, or even the climate."

Los Angeles, meanwhile, represented Americanization in an eastern image: a consciously "Anglo-Saxon experiment," where the children of the élite went to "the Harvard School" and only a few thousand Hispanics and Asians could be counted in a population approaching 1.5 million in the late 1920s. The possibility of a great metropolis backed by the Mojave Desert had been created by the diversion of water from Owens Valley. "There it is—take it," the engineer William Mulholland is said to have remarked to the mayor when the first aqueduct started flowing in 1913. In the 1920s the city became the "Oildorado" satirized in Upton Sinclair's novel *Oil*, where derricks—some of them phoney, installed to drive up real estate prices—appeared "right alongside Eli's new church and another by that holier of holies, the First National Bank." The White Anglo-Saxon Protestant dominion was threatened by the rise of outsiders like Edward Doheny, an oil prospector who built Saint Vincent de Paul Church—still a major city landmark under its obese, multicoloured dome—and whose house had a deer park, a conservatory for a hundred types of orchid, a dome of Tiffany glass, and a dining-room for a hundred guests supported on Sienese marble columns. The film industry came next, diffusing power to another parvenue élite of Jewish studio heads.

Meanwhile, however, if Santa Barbara represented California's mythical

San Francisco's "Little China"—the world's biggest Chinatown in the late nineteenth century. Here Kipling was surprised at "how deep . . . the pigtail has taken root." The huge concentration of his day was dispersed while immigration was banned. By 1927, when numbers began to recover, there were over 12,000 Chinese residents and by 1930 over 16,000.

Spanish past and Los Angeles its fleeting American present, to see California's future as an Asiatic land, bound to the orient by transpacific links, you could go to San Francisco, whose "Little China" was already the world's biggest Chinatown. Chinese had come, to begin with, to meet the labour demands of the gold rush and the railway age. There were perhaps twenty-five thousand in the 1850s; the Central Pacific Railroad employed ten thousand of them. By treaty with China in 1868, sixteen thousand were admitted annually—many to factory jobs in San Francisco, which had nearly fifty thousand Chinese residents by 1875. When Kipling landed at San Francisco in 1889, he could see "how deep down in the earth the pigtail had taken root." White tolerance was stretched tight, then snapped. After violence in the 1870s, Chinese immigration was banned.

Among the effects was a gradual increase in the number of arriving Japanese. Only sixty-eight Japanese were registered in the whole of California in 1880, but they were arriving at the rate of more than a thousand a year in the 1890s. Los Angeles had a Japanese Association in 1897 and a Japanese newspaper from 1903. From 1907, when thirty thousand Japanese entered the United States, a "gentlemen's agreement" with the Japanese government controlled numbers at the source; in 1913 a federal law prevented Japanese from acquiring land. As their defenders pointed out, they were adaptable and assimilable, with a convincing enthusiasm for self-

Americanization, but the Japanese of Los Angeles subscribed to an emotive demonstration of distinctive identity in 1931 when they offered a banquet to welcome Prince Takamatsu.

The Japanese-American Regimental Combat Teams, largely recruited in California—ironically, mostly from families incarcerated in wartime concentration camps by President Roosevelt's infamous Executive Order 1099—became famous as the most-decorated unit of the U.S. Army in the Second World War; it was thanks to the patriotic efforts of Senator Samuel I. Hayakawa in the 1970s that English was adopted as the state's sole official language. Yet today in California the Japanese presence is still ambivalent. The vast majority live in White neighbourhoods; a bare majority marry into White families; few transmit much knowledge of the Japanese language to their second generations. Like all other Asian immigrant communities in California, except those from Vietnam, they have been remarkably successful in achieving the middle-class goals that are inseparable from an ideally American way of life and have a measured standard of living much above the mean. Yet their "apparent 100 per cent American-ness'" is compromised in three ways: first, their acceptance in American society seems to depend on other Americans' image of Japan, which tends to fluctuate with the fortunes of economic competition. Second, ethnic identity persists in the businessmen's associations, civic clubs, and recreational organizations scattered throughout America's Pacific coast. For instance, at the Jan Ken Po Summer School in Sacramento, the Japanese language, religions, cooking, martial arts, and calligraphy are taught to children, while elderly Japanese Americans can revive the glutinous social habits of their homeland, warming sake around low tables at the Yu-ai Kai centre in San Jose.

Finally, the Japanese Americans are growing more conspicuous against the background of massive Japanese economic investment. Most of California's banking sector is in the hands of Japanese shareholders. Toyota, Toshiba, and Mitsubishi Chemicals all have major joint projects with American industries in the state. Economic and political involvement are inseparable. In the mid-1980s, Sony donated $29,000 to the political funds of Californian legislators in an attempt to get the state's tax laws modified, and other Japanese firms were said to have subscribed much more. In 1989 when the Sony Corporation bought Columbia Pictures, Senator Lloyd Bentsen's joke about Japanese infiltration had enough truth to be funny. On his way to dine with the prestigious Alfalfa Club, he told his wife he was going "'to meet with the great political and economic powers that hold America's future in their hands.' 'Oh,' she replied. 'You're going to Tokyo.'" Meanwhile, in the background, the pull of the Pacific continues. In 1990, 37 per cent of the freshman class at UCLA classified themselves as Asian. Japanese investors owned a third of the office space in Los Angeles; Hong Kong businessmen owned a tenth, by value, of downtown San Francisco.

In the late 1980s, California's top five trading partners were Japan, South Korea, Taiwan, Singapore, and Hong Kong.

Seas unite. Mountains divide. Like California, coastal British Columbia seems close to Pacific Asia and far from its continental heartlands. The Canadian Pacific Railway seems a narrow, feeble link compared with the broad shipping lanes, of an almost limitless capacity for freight, which cross the ocean from Vancouver Bay. Without oriental traders and labourers Vancouver would be—would always have been—unthinkable. As railway coolies in the late nineteenth century they worked for a third or a quarter of a White man's wages. As domestic servants they were sent by God, according to a housewife of the early twentieth century, "as all good things come from Him." They were so vital a part of the workforce of the canning factories that when a mechanical device was introduced for beheading the salmon, it was called "the iron chink." The leaders of the Chinese community in the late nineteenth and early twentieth centuries were genuine specimens of Pacific man: Yip Sang, the railway's agent whose own company was turning over $50,000 a year in international trade in 1907, had landed in San Francisco as a boy from Fukien; he panned for gold, washed dishes, and worked in a cigar factory on his way north. The trade of his rival, Sam

"A wen at the end of a wilderness": the Vancouver skyline at the beginning of the twentieth century.

Stage Driver Charlie Green and the enraged citizens of the town take drastic action to revise the voters' "list." By what one party considered an anomaly, Chinese workers qualified for the franchise in elections in Vancouver in 1886. One candidate mustered a crowd of them, whom supporters of his rival scattered by stampeding the stage team.

Kee, who, as one of Vancouver's richest citizens, spoke only Chinese, was an intra-Asian network of exchange: rice for salmon, dogfish, crabmeat, and herrings, caught and canned with Japanese fishermen and labourers, and exported to Hong Kong, Yokohama, and Chinese firms in Hawaii.

Vancouver in those days was a joke that Man and Nature had played on each other: a wen at the end of a wilderness. The irony is captured in a photograph of the crammed houses—the "neat frame cottage with a bit of lawn" erected after "battle against forest and stump"—bravely flying their flapping laundry, trapped among telegraph wires and dwarfed by warehouses. The economy depended on salmon, sawmills, and silos of grain. Most of the Chinese probably did not intend to stay and scorned integration "like raindrops rolling down new paint." Employers dishonoured promises of repatriation, and Chinese workers ended up in cemeteries where their bones waited to go home under unpainted headboards.

In 1885 immigration was restricted with the avowed aim of preventing it altogether. Chinese could now buy their way in only with an enormous ransom. Race riots became part of a way of life. In an election riot of 1886 a coachman became the hero of an engraving in the local newspaper when he scattered would-be Chinese voters by stampeding his team through the crowd. In the 1920s, when Chinese immigration was banned outright, the Japanese community increased by half to twenty-two thousand. An undifferentiated "yellow peril" obsessed alarmists, such as the author of *The Writing on the Wall,* a novel of 1923, illustrated with a prostrated White man, fallen amid stones under the sword of a bare-fanged samurai, while the complacent eyes of a Chinese onlooker smile through their slits.

As in the rest of the White Pacific, the Second World War set back the cause of Asian immigrants and their descendants. An oriental appearance chilled White spines and recalled predictions of the "yellow man elbowing his way in and taking possession." The rehabilitation of Asian citizens in Vancouver began slowly in the late 1940s and remained incomplete until the 1980s when a new wave of rich or skills-rich immigrants swept in from Hong Kong. In the first half of 1983, Hong Kong entrepreneurs invested $300 million in Canada, half of it in British Columbia. In 1985 the last discriminatory voting privileges in White electors' favour were abolished. By the end of the decade, a quarter of the population of Vancouver were officially listed as of Asian provenance or descent. Hong Kong businessmen own most of Vancouver's skyscrapers, the golf course, and the largest shopping centre in British Columbia. A quarter of children entering school for the first time speak Chinese as their first language, and a quarter more speak another language other than English.

THE SURF OF HISTORY

If Vancouver broke off from Canada and drifted into the Pacific, the rest of the world would react with surprise but not, perhaps, anxiety. California is different. Its rise to world prominence has been as rapid and spectacular as Japan's. From a population of only a million in the 1880s, it became the most populous state in the U.S.A. in 1962. If it were independent, it would be an economic super-power in its own right, figuring in the world's top seven or eight states by level of population or volume of trade. It gave the world the first supermarket (1912), the first motel (1925), the first fast-food outlet (1948), the first laser (1960), and the first microprocessor (1971). Long world-hegemony in films has given Hollywood more power over the transmission of cultural influence than any community of comparable size has ever exercised. The early Protestant evangelists may have been mistaken in their predictions about California's character, but in 1850, J. A. Benton, "the father of Californian Congregationalism," correctly foresaw its importance: "The world's centre will have changed . . . and no man will be thought to have seen the world till he has seen California."

California's power to challenge and subvert cultural traditions in widely separated parts of the world became apparent in the mid-1950s with the first impact of the "Beat generation." The Beat ethos was "dead beat"—exhausted at the materialism of the work ethic—and "beatified" by the emo-

Osbert Lancaster's 1967 cartoon described in the text: the hippie of a few years earlier has become complacently—where once he was artistically—scruffy, pot-bellied, and bad-tempered, shouting for the police to deal with the subversive irreverence of the establishment.

tionally liberating effects of self-indulgence, especially in drugs, sex, and poetry. "Dropping out" was a new form of effortless superiority. Beat art, produced by the "Great Ungifted," eschewed sense in favour of sensation. The roots of the cults of raucous self-expression, conventionless pandemonium, and sanctified ennui stretched a long way—across America to Greenwich Village and perhaps across the Atlantic to the Paris and Berlin of the 1920s; but California became the centre and leader of the Beat movement at about the time, in October 1955, when Alan Ginsberg read "Howl" to a meeting of drunken fellow-poets in Venice West. The title was faithfully descriptive of the poem's methods of evoking "drugs, buggery, devastated minds, slum alleys, 'angelheaded hipsters,' exultant madness, sexual anarchy."

The world responded devastatingly by classifying "beatniks" as containable eccentrics. The stereotype illustrated an article in *Reader's Digest* in 1960: underfed, droopy, sexually available girls in black, wastefully mated with weak, ill-kempt drips usually in spectacles. By 1967, in an Osbert Lancaster cartoon, the beatniks had become an inverted élite, invoking the police against a counter-demo by subversively old-fashioned gerontocrats.

A demonstration against the Vietnam War in Central Park, New York, in April 1967, attracts 100,000 marchers and corresponding numbers of balloons, placards, flowers, and media-microphones like the one at bottom left.

The movements' leaders disappointed revolutionary expectations. Jack Kerouac returned to Catholicism and conservatism, opining that communists had hijacked the Beat scene. Larry Lipton made and lost a fortune as an impresario exploiting the outside world's prurient interest in Beat misbehaviour. Ginsberg ended up attracting awards from the literary establishment. But California remained the drop-outs' Mecca, to which subsequent movements in the Beat tradition made obeisance. San Francisco was the home of the most powerful of such movements, the hippies in the 1960s.

Hippie values combined some of the seductive elements in Beat ethics, such as anti-materialism and revulsion from work, with some of the more addictive of Beat practices, such as sexual libertinism and the use of drugs alternately to intensify experience and escape its pains. Hippies' distinctive addition was an emphasis on pacifism and quietism, expressed in the representative graffito of the 1960s, Make Love Not War. In a world revolted by the Vietnam War (see Chapter 21) and frightened by the hydrogen bomb, this message was timely. Potent symbols of hippiedom spread, with the graffiti, all over the western world: the flowers, raided—or, as they preferred to say, liberated—by San Francisco hippies from public gardens, were adopted as symbols of peace by demonstrators against war and the bomb. The uniform of youth was worn between long hair tied with sweat-bands, at one end, and bare feet at the other. Amorphous, deliberately un-kempt clothing, which "freed" the wearer from conventional constraints, was affected even by people who could afford to look neat and tidy. "Psy-chedelic" fabrics and décor imitated the outbursts of colour exploded in the mind by doses of the chemical drug known as LSD. In the minds of the "dharma bums," hippie values got fused with powerfully mystical ideas from newly fashionable oriental philosophies (see Chapter 24).

Hippie influence was so strong on those who grew up in the western world in the 1960s that its vestiges are still around in the last decade of the millennium; personal indiscipline is still justified—especially by apologists of a certain age—in the language of hippiedom and sometimes clothed in its fashions. The original movement, discredited by its own heretics, was overwhelmed in the reaction of the 1970s and 1980s (see Chapter 21).

Since then, California has not produced a cultural movement of compara-ble power, but in the 1970s the gay writer Armistead Maupin could still have "a real feeling that what San Francisco does today the world will do tomorrow." The state's élites have stayed in the vanguards of radicalism of left and right, nurturing movements for feminism, gay rights, and ecological awareness, on the one hand, and libertarianism, low taxes, and free-market economics, on the other. The power of its studios and "stars" has been de-ployed to evangelize for those causes all over the world. In the context of an increasingly integrated Pacific, however, California's influence on the world has to be considered—where the galactic museum-keepers will probably put it—alongside the even more pervasive influences flowing from the ocean's opposite shore. If California's influence—so often meretri-cious or superficial—is an example of the flow of the surf of history, the subject of the next chapter is surely one of the tidal waves: a major reversal of the historic direction of cultural exchange, as oriental ideas take their re-venge on western tastes and values.

Chapter 23

THE REVENGE OF THE EAST: ORIENTAL RESILIENCE AND WESTERN CULTURE

The Seaside Xanadu—The Tao of Science—The Japaneseness of Japan—Silver Columbia

THE SEASIDE XANADU

In 1815 the "Prince of Pleasure" began the erection of an appropriate palace. The Prince Regent of the United Kingdom, who ascended the throne as George IV in 1820, two years before the palace was completed, was a man of implacable appetite and restless disposition. He was temperamentally incapable of contentment. His hyperactive imagination transformed everything he saw into rich, strange, and fantastic forms which he felt compelled to make palpable. In his transmutative touch, he was an embodiment of Midas; in his faddish extravagance, a pre-incarnation of Mr. Toad. His small and simple villa at Brighton, where he dallied with an unaffected mistress and dabbled in the fashion for sea air, was to be transformed, by the magic of vast expenditure and the alchemy of ostentatious taste, into a parody of the stately pleasure dome decreed by Kublai Khan at Xanadu.

The Brighton Pavilion was a wonder of its age in more ways than one. Gas-lit and supported on cast-iron pillars, it was loudly proclamatory of the early Industrial Revolution. In the fitted kitchen, under artificial palms, the genius of Marie Antoine Carême—inventor of caramel—was supported by

688

every convenience of the technology of the time. Yet this industrial monument was capped by a skyline of onion-domes and minarets, and the interior decoration, in the main rooms, was encrusted in exotic baubles. The banqueting room was lit by a blaze of dragons dangling lotus blossoms and surrounded by Chinese scenes. The music room was sustained by pillars lacquered in red and gold and entwined with dragons, more of whom flew up to a ceiling of gilded scales, from where a lamp was suspended in the shape of a Chinese water lily. These were carefully considered, not wholly capricious, designs.

The Prince had already experimented with Chinese rooms in his London palace of Carlton House, reputedly the finest in Europe. Linings of Chinese wallpapers in panels provided settings for hard-paste porcelain vases, crackle glazed and ox-blood, mounted with dragons of bronze gilt. There were candelabra hoisted by Chinese lady-percussionists in porcelain. A Chinese drummer boy with upthrust head kicked his legs in abandon as he waved a gilded clock, and clay figures of mandarins grinned at their ladies.

The Prince was in the avant-garde of taste. His objects were "defiance of the establishment" and *épater les bourgeois,* though neither term had yet been formulated. He made a virtue of self-indulgence. He regularly ordered more elaborate settings for the richest jewels and more sumptuous mounts for the rarest porcelain and ivory. In the Brighton Pavilion he extended the frontiers of extravagance beyond anything previously attempted. It was a theatrical setting for a calculated form of contrived decadence, in an atmosphere thick with music, perfumes, and liqueurs—"disgusting" and "effeminate," according to one guest. His admiration for oriental art in general, however, was highly characteristic of his time.

While the Ottoman Empire continued to provide a stock of exotic stereotypes, three new routes by which oriental taste invaded Europe became well travelled in the eighteenth and nineteenth centuries: from Egypt, from India, and from the Pacific-rim cultures of China and Japan. In a sense Egypt had the longest history of appreciation in the west, for in the sixteenth century Egyptian "wisdom" had been pursued by Renaissance magi in search of an alternative to the austere rationalism of classical learning. The pseudo-Egyptian mysticism of the text attributed to Hermes Trismegistos, which was actually the work of a Byzantine monk, was adopted by a generation of late Renaissance scholars who professed to see in it a fount of older and purer knowledge than could be had from the Greeks. They hoped to unlock through its magical formulae the secret of the mastery of nature. The Emperor Rudolf II, who patronized esoteric arts in his castle of Hradschin (see Chapter 15), was hailed as the new Hermes. Egyptian symbols proliferated in printers' pattern books and, after the cult of the pseudo-Hermes was dead, Egyptian imagery sustained a precarious life in western art in the traditions of the seventeenth- and eighteenth-century Rosicrucians

The "small and simple villa" in Brighton, transformed into an oriental fantasy by the extravagance of the "Prince of Pleasure." A section drawn by the prince's favoured architect, John Nash. Perhaps, like his admiration for his dynasty's Stuart predecessors, the design represented for the prince a hankering to be a despot, which the English constitution made it impossible ever to fulfill.

and Freemasons. These Egyptian affectations were all but dead, however, when Egyptian taste was suddenly and dramatically revived by Napoleon's expedition to Egypt in 1798.

It was oriental taste of a sort that took Napoleon to Egypt in the first place. The strategic pretext was that conquest would provide a base from which to strike at the British Empire and seize coals from the dying embers of the Ottoman world. Napoleon himself, however, who was instrumental in persuading the French government to attempt the conquest, was drawn by his own romantic notions of the east, where former world conquerors had arisen or gone, where "great reputations were made," and where lavish plunder could be garnered; his further, undeclared motive was, perhaps, to avoid inactivity.

Napoleon seems to have sensed that the most durable form of plunder was knowledge, and he launched a scientific expedition as well as a military campaign, with an ambitious programme of systematically recording Egypt's landscape, antiquities, flora, and fauna, as well as her needs and resources. A hundred and twenty-five savants accompanied him. In Cairo the house of a fugitive Mameluke was baptized the "Institut de l'Égypte," and in its former first-floor harem, behind screens of cedarwood fretwork, under a dome of eight-pointed stars, the institute's members debated the early fruits

of Egyptological research. Napoleon made himself its vice-president, inscribed among the twelve members of the mathematical section.

The scientific work of Napoleon's expedition provided western artists, craftsmen, and pattern-makers with an unprecedented new source of models and of inspiration. In particular, the potential range of taste was revolutionized by the drawings of the antiquities of upper Egypt, made on campaign by Vivant Denon, future director of the Louvre, balancing his drawing-board on the neck of his horse. There was instant appeal in decoration which achieved antique splendour beyond the familiar tyranny of the classical orders and in furniture patterns which were both novel and practical. The plates gathered in the *Description de l'Égypte* did not begin to appear until 1809, but Egyptian fashion was established by Napoleon's return in 1799 and the publication of Denon's report in 1802. The classicism of Napoleon's Malmaison, modified by Egyptian notions, became the characteristic style of the early nineteenth century throughout Europe. The sphinx-mask mount and the lion's-paw foot became cabinet-makers' commonplaces. Obelisks were sought again, as they had been in the sixteenth century, to enhance cities and salons.

The artistic influence of the more remote Orient in the west was exercized almost entirely through porcelain, lacquers, and textiles until the eighteenth century, when the delights of Chinese wallpaper became accessible to a rich élite and when the technique of "japanning" furniture came to embrace genuinely oriental motifs. Jean-Antoine Watteau's designs for Chinese and Tatar scenes to decorate an apartment for Louis XIV inaugurated a taste for schemes of decoration in Chinese style, which radiated from Bourbon courts. In the royal palace of Madrid, anemic, pigtailed fig-

"A blaze of dragons dangling lotus-blossoms" dominates the banqueting room of the Brighton Pavilion: "a theatrical setting for a calculated form of contrived decadence."

ures squint from the corners of a room entirely lined in porcelain. By the mid-eighteenth century, Jean Pillemont's engravings of Chinese scenes hung in bourgeois homes. In France the application of Chinese motifs remained purely decorative. Cabinet-makers of the late eighteenth century incongruously lacquered their bulky, bulging rococo products with delicate encounters of robed figures under parasols, which the Prince Regent, for one, would eagerly collect for his palaces.

In England, however, where the Duke of Cumberland faked a Chinese junk to sail on his artificial lake at Windsor, Chinese inspiration was made the basis of a new style, suggested by the garden-pavilion designs of

Chinese drummer boy clock, of French manufacture, probably imported into England between 1787 and 1790 to decorate the prince's first experiment in Chinese taste—the Chinese Room at the bottom of his London Palace, Carlton House. Like many of the prince's artefacts, it acquired embellishments as time went on: the cushion-like pedestal of bronze gilt was added in 1811, along with various plinths, stands, and domes for display.

William Halfpenny. His book of 1752, *Chinese and Gothic Architecture*, was the first of many to treat Chinese art as equivalent to the great styles of European tradition. Chippendale's designs for furniture in Chinese taste displayed extraordinary virtuosity, both in imbibing the principles of an alien tradition and in harmonizing them with the expectations of the English public of his day. The western decorator's vocabulary has been heavily laden with Chinese terms ever since.

Chinese and, with a time-lag, Japanese arts were able to capture western attention with their mastery of distinctive techniques: of hard-paste porcelain wares, of superior textile work, of fine lacquering, and, in the nineteenth century, of ukiyo-e Japanese prints. The arts of India were characterized by no such advantages, and their influence, long delayed, was always shallower than that of Egypt and the Pacific-rim civilizations. The domes of the Brighton Pavilion were probably more indebted to Turk-

Panckoucke engraved this composite image of the splendours of Egypt and their rediscovery by the French invaders for the frontispiece to the second edition of the *Description de l'Égypte* in 1820. Spoils in the foreground include a huge head of Rameses II, a painted relief from the tomb of Rameses III, and a capital from the temple of Dendera. Behind, on the left, the Great Pyramid is largely obscured; the centre ground is shared between a French bivouac and the ruins of Thebes. Napoleon could not be shown at such a sensitive time during the Bourbon restoration, but the commander of the expedition to Upper Egypt, General Desaix, appears in front of the obelisk and his farthest south, Philae, is visible in the background.

ish than to Mogul models. Indeed, the very notion of a pavilion, and the semblance, evinced from a distance, of a cluster of low, domed and arcaded buildings, evokes for the visitor to Brighton reminiscences of the inner courts of the Topkapi Saray Palace, with their tentlike throne-house and secluded kiosks. Despite the encroachments of Chinese taste, the Ottoman world was still the common home of oriental stereotypes, reached for by operatic librettists, political satirists, and designers of masquerade. Though Indian scenes were imagined, according to Alexander Pope, by ladies who took tea at Queen Anne's court, India remained largely unknown to the European public almost until the end of the eighteenth century. Returning English nabobs built themselves classical piles, such as John Carr's Basildon Park for the India-rich official resident, Sir Francis Sykes. Like other creations for such clients, this "most splendid Georgian mansion of Berkshire" was made as free as possible of references to the source of the wealth that paid for it.

Rooms entirely lined with an inner "skin" of Chinese porcelain, modelled in exotic and fantastic designs, are typical of Bourbon palaces. Gasparrini's bold designs for the royal palace in Madrid are startling for the way life-size figures loom from the upper corners. This is a light fitting.

Sykes's friend, Warren Hastings, was exceptional in making a collection of Indian art to adorn the walls of his country house at Daylesford, which became the focus of a limited artistic discovery of India in the last decade of the century. Hastings, the defendant in the most notorious show trial in British imperial history, was arraigned and exonerated for exploiting Bengal during his governorship. There can be no doubt, however, that India inspired him with disinterested curiosity and genuine affection. Like most Englishmen in the east, he went there to make money, but he was uncorrupted by crass imperialism's sense of its own superiority. His conviction that "every nation excels others in some particular art or science"—not a drive for wider dominion—underlay the policy of sending British missions into little-known parts of the subcontinent. When he got home, he cultivated Indian plants in his garden and encouraged the Indian tastes of the architect Samuel Pepys Cockerell, who adorned the house with a Mogul dome and helped to form the plans of his brother, Sir Charles Cockerell, for a country house inspired by Delhi and Agra. The journey to India of Cockerell's advisers, Thomas and William Daniell, yielded, in the late 1790s, the first detailed corpus of engravings of Indian buildings to be published in

Christophe Huet's decorative designs followed the lead in orientalizing taste given by Watteau and continued by Jean Bérain and Claude Audran. He used arabesques in the Hôtel Rohan (1749–52) and chinoiserie, as here, for the Duc de Bourbon at Chantilly in 1739, usually combining oriental figures with grotesque motifs and the impish absurdity of playful apes: these *singeries* reflected and perhaps lampooned some philosophers' anthropomorphic attitude to monkeys. See p. 473.

the west. Their influence, however, remained limited. Cockerell's "Cotswold Taj" at Sezincote was the only large structure they spawned in Europe. It was to remain unique for nearly a century after its construction in 1806.

Even the intimacy of British imperial penetration of India in the nineteenth century introduced Indian taste only to small patches of western society. British India was essentially a middle-class raj. Its memories were nurtured in England in suburbs and seaside bungalows. For a long time no

The Duke of Cumberland's "Mandarin Yacht"—a fake junk for his artificial lake of 120 acres at Virginia Water. The "bloody butcher" of the Jacobites at Culloden went on to a more decorous role as Ranger of Windsor Park and the opportunity to be an adventurous patron of landscape art. The éclat of the Mandarin Yacht helped to inspire the Chinese Garden made by Sir William Chambers at Kew in 1760, which in turn influenced taste and design in France, the Netherlands, and Germany.

arbiter elegantiae felt the call of Mandalay. "The gorgeous contributions of India" to the Great Exhibition of 1851 established Indian models as sources for textiles, and Owen Jones's *Grammar of Ornament* gave more space to Indian than to any other oriental designs. In other fields, India's impact remained sparse.

The grandest monument of the Anglo-Indian style in Victorian Britain was built—or at least begun—by an Indian when Prince Duleep Singh was expelled from the Punjab after the Indian mutiny. Pension-rich and prodigal, he smothered the interiors of his previously calm Georgian house at Elveden in Suffolk with gaudy, lacy plasterwork, painted in the warm, spicy colours of home. The experiment caught the imagination of Lord Iveagh, the millionaire manufacturer of bitter stout, who bought the estate in 1893 in order to have somewhere to win friends and shoot pheasant. On a visit to India, Iveagh had been touched with the exotic nostalgia that often afflicts travellers to the subcontinent—a taste for heat and dust in the pores of the skin, a trace of curry on the palate. Under scholarly advice, he worked on Duleep Singh's interiors to make them more "authentic" and enhanced them in a grandiose fashion by building a huge onion-domed central hall,

Moorish fantasies, English Alhambras: Leighton House, London, and Port Lympne, the former a characteristic work of George Aitchison of 1877–79, the latter an unusually flamboyant touch by the usually cozy architect, Philip Tilden: this fountain court with echoes of the Generalife was added as a "bachelor wing" just after the First World War to a house of Sir Philip Sassoon's in the "Cape Dutch" style (see p. 548). Honor Channon likened it to a Spanish brothel. See C. Aslet, *The Last Country Houses* (1982), pp. 80–81.

inspired by the Taj Mahal, to dwarf the existing house. The effect, though admired by Edward VII, who had *nouveau riche* tastes, was condemned by the cognoscenti. It was, as Augustus Hare said, "almost appallingly luxurious."

In the context of a celebration of the diversity of the British Empire, Queen Victoria's diamond jubilee procession projected a glamorous image of India, but even in the late Victorian and Edwardian eras decorators in search of exotic feel preferred a nearer east. The "arabesque" interior of Leighton House is a Nasrid fantasy. The inappropriate library of the Reform Club has the air of a Moorish seraglio. In Sledmere, Yorkshire, a Turkish bath was installed in 1913 with motifs from as far east as Iran but no farther. The fountain court of Port Lympne is copied from Granada. Music-halls were called after the Alhambra, not the Taj.

Only in two respects has Indian taste really gripped in the west, outside the east Asian immigrant communities which are particularly numerous in parts of England. From beginnings in Veeraswamy's, off London's Regent Street, which was once a haunt of Indian Army officers, Indian restaurants have become ubiquitous working-class favourites in England, from where they have spread to recover a certain chic in America and continental western Europe. Meanwhile, among western intellectuals, interest in Indian travel and culture—especially philosophy and, more selectively, music and poetry—became a cult in the 1960s and has retained unique status. Unlike Indian food, these are expensive and elusive tastes accessible, by their nature, only to a small minority, but they may be no less significant, culturally, for that.

That significance lies in a revulsion—especially among the *jeunesse dorée* of the culture of economic growth in the postwar west—against materialism and consumerism. From a comfortable but constricting world, the generation of the laid-back and the far-out sought to escape into alternative cultures that emphasized spiritual values and despised or derided the hard, angular realities of the material universe. At about the same time, the lure of the east was heightened by the popularity, as a catchword, of liberation—liberation from parental control, from repressive political systems, from the hag-ridden guilt of the west's history of colonialism. Indeed, under the force of bloody images from Vietnam (see Chapter 21), which bombarded the world's television screens throughout the 1960s, westerners seemed to need liberating from the effects of colonialism quite as much as its explicit victims.

Mystical practices such as Transcendental Meditation, which offered liberation of the soul from the body and the control of the physical environment through spiritual power, became popular in this atmosphere at certain levels of education and wealth. In 1978 the Maharishi Mahesh Yogi was able to buy Mentmore, the former Rothschild mansion, for £240,000 and

Japanese influence contributes to the kind of embarrassing pastiche favoured by western property developers: the advertisement appeared in *Country Life*, a forum of the expensive real estate market in Britain, in May 1991.

smother the walls with incongruous quotations from his works, inscribed on laminated signboards stuck onto stretched silk. The same guru proclaimed the "World government of the Age of Enlightenment" from a château on a Swiss mountaintop, on writing-paper embossed in gold. Escapees from parental tutelage and from unsatisfactory bodies were joined by those fleeing from the shadow of the bomb. The strain experienced by the first human generation to grow up under threat of nuclear immolation created a Peace Movement, many of whose sympathizers were drawn eastwards by the belief—belied by the facts of Indian history—that oriental philosophies could unlock the blessings of peace.

Underlying the eastward flow of fashion was a trend in the history of thought: in philosophy, against the crude pragmatism and positivism advocated by academics in the 1940s and 1950s; in science, against the brazen certainties of the mechanical universe which had been the dominant model from Newton to Einstein.

At what point in the history of a cultural movement does influence on taste become influence on thought? A West Coast physics professor who practises meditation weeps "one late summer afternoon, when I suddenly became aware of . . . the atoms of the elements and those of my body participating in . . . the dance of Shiva." In a street in Surbiton, a young stockbroker who cooks in a wok and sleeps on a futon maintains his motor cycle according to the precepts of Zen. In a villa near Florence, an old Etonian aesthete remembers his discovery of the delicacy of Chinese art and the superior simplicity of Chinese food, which led him to disillusioning experiments with a Chinese philosophy of life (see Chapter 21). In Coombe Hill, Surrey, a property developer announces Japanese-style apartments overlooking "idyllic Japanese watergardens" in an advertisement which sells not only a particular look but also an idealized oriental lifestyle. In the Bolivian bush a leader in a Mao suit dies, riddled with bullets, trying to apply the martial aphorisms of an old man in Peking. Within a stone's throw space in North Oxford, English children hang their haiku on the school wall, and in a college garden, a building is erected in imitation of a Japanese tea-house.

A plasterer in Birmingham and a professional golfer in Palm Beach share an interest in sumo wrestling and koipu carp, which gradually—even unconsciously—helps them shed inherited prejudices. A British judge is a Buddhist, a Harvard physicist a student of Tao. In New Zealand a potter has achieved world renown for his art by steeping himself, rigorously and exclusively, in Japanese traditions. In an alley near Trafalgar Square, a classicizing architect, punning on a patron called Ching, has remodelled a courtyard in Chinese Chippendale taste. Terrace gardeners in a flat above Madrid, following a fashion set by their prime minister, pot bonsai and practise ikebana. A gamelan orchestra decorates a foyer in the Royal Festival Hall. A Chinese classic on the art of war becomes a best-selling business book.

These are representative vignettes, most documented, all credible, of the reception of oriental influence in the western culture of the late twentieth century. Individually, they could be dismissed as idiosyncratic, eccentric, superficial, faddish, or short-lived. Taken together—and in alliance with the development, to which we must now turn, of eastern influence on the way western scientists think—they suggest that the world may be experiencing the reversal of the conventional direction of the flow of formative ideas. After two or three centuries of pummelling and kneading by western influences, the east is getting its intellectual revenge.

THE TAO OF SCIENCE

In 1947, Niels Bohr, who had revolutionized modern physics by formulating the concept of complementarity, was honoured in his native Denmark by the conferment of a coat of arms. Developing an insight of Einstein's, Bohr had resolved a dilemma over which physicists had agonized since the time of Newton: did light consist in particles or in waves? Or, rather, was the term "particles" or the term "waves" more applicable to the nature of light? Although the two descriptions are mutually exclusive, the behaviour of light, observed and measured experimentally, demands them both. Until Bohr entered the field, the scientific community recoiled from the absurdity of a single phenomenon with two mutually incompatible natures; such a cloud-borne beast was tolerable in a world imagined by Pan and peopled with centaurs. Theologians, whose constant study companion is a Being both human and divine, have no trouble with the concept. Scientists, however, require single, internally coherent explanations which cover all known results. Before Bohr, they blinked helplessly in the dazzle of a phenomenon which could not be accommodated by an explanation of this type.

Bohr's solution was to propose that the wavelike and particlelike properties of the light we experience are both contrary and complementary, like the poles of an axis. Neither description applies to the real nature of light but only to its observed nature; the result experimenters obtain depends on the nature of the experiment as well as on the nature of light.

Bohr fathered the "uncertainty principle," formulated by his pupil, Werner Heisenberg, which exposes the limitation of experimental science in an observed world where matter behaves in ways affected by the observer. He also inspired the Copenhagen Interpretation of the Fifth Solvay

Congress of 1927: its principles, which underlie all subsequent work in physics, effectively redefined the objectives of science. Henceforth, workers on the frontiers of subatomic physics would be aware of the inaccessibility of objective reality; they would seek to verify theories that explained changing relationships of which the observer was a part. Ever since, the traditional distinction between science and the humanities has faded until today the work of scientists such as Roger Penrose and Stephen Hawking can seem as subjective as literary criticism and as creative as monumental sculpture.

In choosing his knight's scutcheon, Bohr was as original minded as in his work on particle physics. His motto—*'Contraria Sunt Complementa'*—rings with the sententious timbre of a traditional heraldic device. His blazon, however, was unprecedented in heraldry: a circle, divided into light and dark moieties by a wavelike double-curve resembling a shallow, open-mouthed and inverted **S**, set slightly at an angle from bottom left to top right of the circle; two small circles, a light one set in the dark moiety and a

The coat of arms of Niels Bohr, conferred on him as a Knight of the Elephant in the Danish knightage, and incorporating his choice of a Taoist emblem.

dark one against the background of the light, were positioned along the diameter of the large circle, each at the mid-point of the radius, centred in relation to the jaws of the **S**.

He had chosen—and he clearly intended it as an illustration of his theory of complementarity—the ancient Chinese symbol of Tao, "the Way," a system of thought combining cosmogony and practical morality, commonly attributed to the philosopher Lao-tzu, of the early sixth century BCE. Taoism—which spawned a philosophical tradition and a popular religion that continue, vigorous and productive, to the present day—postulates a cosmic force of which all observable phenomena are effects. Like a number of other ancient philosophical characterizations of reality, it is reminiscent, to a modern mind, of the interpenetration—even the ultimate identity—of mass and energy implicit in the Theory of Relativity. The symmetry of the Taoist symbol evokes the harmony of the universe; its circularity emphasizes its unity and suggests its perfection; the wavelike separator alludes to the continuity of change, the ubiquity of flux; the light and dark moieties symbolize the flow of contrary principles—light and dark, masculine and feminine, negative and positive—which together complete the unity that encompasses them. The small circles represent the mingling of these opposites, each in the other's nature.

It seems extraordinary that a modern western scientist like Bohr should perceive in an oriental device 2,500 years old such exact prefiguration of discoveries revolutionary in his day. For three centuries before his time it was assumed, almost without exception, that oriental tradition had everything to learn from western science and nothing to teach. By a curious trick of the complementarity of history, the twentieth-century reception of oriental ideas by western science, instanced by Bohr's adoption of the Taoist symbol in his coat of arms, mirrored an episode of Chinese history of 1644 when Johann Adam Schall von Bell, of the Society of Jesus, was appointed director of the Imperial Board of Astronomy. Then began in earnest the transformation of Chinese science by western influence. A direction of exchange was inaugurated, which was long thought to be unchallengeable.

The Chinese Board of Astronomy existed not for the disinterested study of the heavens but for the computation and revision of a ritual calendar. The ceremonies of the court were attuned to the rhythms of the stars so that earthly order should reflect celestial harmony. For movable feasts and unique occasions, benign astral influences had to be secured. Like the context of Easter computation in the medieval west, the environment of a starstruck court stimulated the accumulation of scientific knowledge. Though the Board of Astronomy was young—created early in the seventeenth century—the Chinese tradition in the science was ancient, and it had been practised at court for centuries. The imperial observatory had a con-

In 1674 the Observatory at Peking was handed over to the Jesuits for reorganization: the results included this roofscape, which became the subject of popular eighteenth-century engraving, showing instruments built to European specifications on the roof of the imperial palace. Some of them have survived to this day and have only recently been removed to a museum.

tinuous history of some four hundred years behind it, and the number and quality of recorded observations available to Chinese astronomers had been unequalled anywhere in the west until well into the sixteenth century.

Yet when the Jesuits arrived—some of them were first drafted to help with calendrical problems in 1629—their superiority over the Muslim personnel who then ran the imperial observatory seemed so marked that the entire native tradition was abandoned and the whole practice of astronomy at court, on which the success of imperial enterprises and the life of the empire were believed to depend, were handed over to the foreigners. In 1669, after a brief interlude of resumed Chinese control, Ferdinand Verbiest took over the Board of Astronomy and completed systematic reform of the calendar. In 1674, at the emperor's request, the observatory was reequipped with instruments of Jesuit design. The rooftop scene, with the instruments erected like shrines on little platforms, protected by palisades, around a tiled yard, provided eighteenth-century European engravers with

The Yung-cheng emperor's affectation of western dress for his portrait inaugurated a fashion of which the most striking example is surely this portrait of Hsiang-Fei, the favourite concubine of the Ch'ien-lung emperor, in a western suit of armour. The artist, Giuseppe Castiglione, known in China as Lang Shih-Ning, was a member of the Jesuit mission from 1730 until 1768 who acquired a great reputation for landscapes which enhanced Chinese tradition with western techniques. He also designed the embellishments and—with other colleagues—the gardens of the summer palace, with the complicated series of fountains that constituted a feat of hydraulics.

one of their most popular scenes of Chinese life, enhanced and, in a sense, overawed by the apparatus of western ingenuity. The equinoctial and zodiacal spheres and the celestial globe were supported by curvaceous dragons; mythical Chinese beasts played around the azimuthal horizon; the deliciously rococo sextant, sprouting curlicues of brass, emerged from a dragon's mouth, and the quadrant was engraved with a griffin.

The Jesuit colonists of the court soon spread western influence from the roof of the palace to the living quarters. The Yung-cheng emperor (1722–1736) had himself painted in a western curled wig with a kerchief knotted at the neck over a waistcoat—an eighteenth-century version of an oriental emperor in a western outer crust, such as would not be seen again until the Meiji emperor donned military uniform on coming of age in late-nineteenth-century Japan. Yung-cheng was by no means an uncritical admirer of western ways. He checked the freedom of Christian missionaries to operate in the provinces because "the converts you make," he said, "recognize only you in time of trouble." Yet, while appreciating the dangers the foreigners posed, he was prepared to defer to barbarian taste and *savoir faire*.

His successor, the Ch'ien-lung emperor (1736–1796), was even more wary of western political and religious intervention, but he had the imperial summer palace near Peking embellished by the Jesuits with gardens, fountains, and pavilions in European style. One pair of fountains spurted from tall twin pagodas, which, with their slim, elongated forms and angular ornaments, contrived a classical feel within the broad conventions of a Chinese building type. Their bases were panelled with heroic designs and decorated with shell shapes in strapwork settings. The water jets which played about them were models of barbarian ingenuity, like the baubles constructed by Jesuit technicians in the previous century—the hydraulic pump offered by Father De Ursis or the long-playing clockwork soldier made by Father Magalhães. Between them stood a grotto in the Portuguese rococo manner, combining unearthly architectural forms—all ellipses and cusps and bulges—with heavy, naturalistic embellishment, reminiscent of the gardens of the Solar de Mateus, which were designed at about the same time.

These forms of western influence were precariously established and did not survive the dissolution of the Jesuits in China in 1773. By the end of his reign, Ch'ien-lung had grown contemptuous of barbarian technology, uttering in 1793 his famous rejection of Lord Macartney's proffered clocks: "I set no value on strange and ingenious gadgets." Yet the era of the Jesuit technicians marked a momentous reversal in the age-old relationship of supremacy of eastern over western science. Throughout the first half of our millennium, and for a thousand years before that, all fruitful initiatives in scientific ideas, all powerful innovations in technology, came from China. It is a commonplace irony that three inventions which helped to establish western world hegemony—the magnetic compass, gunpowder, and the printing press—had been known in China for centuries before they appeared in Europe.

The routes by which Chinese inventions reached the west cannot normally be reconstructed with any certainty, but the examples of probable or possible transmissions leave no scope to doubt the scale or fertility of Chinese superiority. Joseph Needham identified dozens of inventions the west got from China between the first and eighteenth centuries CE, including—apart from the three already highlighted—the efficient harness, the suspension bridge, the crossbow, water-powered metallurgical bowing engines, the stern-post rudder, canal lock-gates, cast iron, paper, porcelain, and the parachute. There were some transmissions in the opposite direction: the crankshaft, trepanning, clockwork, water clocks, and force-pumping for liquids. The balance of exchange, however, demonstrated the greater inventiveness and productiveness of Chinese technical prowess. The time-lag across which transmissions were made emphasized this difference. The Chinese were from one to thirteen centuries ahead with particular inventions. Scientific ideas were not traded along with technology, partly because of the language barrier and partly because Chinese tradition was stronger on practical technology than on what in the west would be recognized as scientific theory. Chinese speculations on the nature and behaviour of matter have tended to belong to what westerners classify as philosophical or religious texts, which only now, in the world of evanescent "quanta" and unglimpsed dimensions, laid bare by Einstein and Bohr, are recognized as kindred spirits by western scientists.

Today the supremacy of western science looks increasingly like a short interlude in a long history. The protracted dependence of western technology on Chinese inventions has been succeeded, after the interval of the last three hundred years, by western rediscovery of oriental "wisdom." Oriental philosophies, especially Tao and Zen, having been ransacked for "parallels" with developments in western science, are now providing models of explanation, means of discourse, and even agenda for research. In tracking the elusive particles of quantum mechanics, in imagining the "unactualized worlds" beyond the collapse of a wave-function, or in speculating about what lies on the other side of a black hole, the traditional language of western science—as its users often complain—is maddeningly inadequate.

The reception or re-entry of oriental ideas into the western scientific tradition is only part of a wider movement that is transforming our world as I write. We are experiencing a more thorough invasion of western society by oriental religion than at any time since the late Roman Empire. The sects encompass the foundations of respectable gurus, who attract the philosophically inclined, and also the followings of charlatans, who prey on weakness and insecurity. The "waste of Christian kisses on a heathen idol's foot" was never so profligate in Kipling's time.

In some still very small patches of western society—limited to particular age groups and classes—there is evidence of the modification of scales of values under Buddhist and Hindu influence and under the impact of increasingly popular martial disciplines and sports from the east. Oriental taste, long established in the west in the context of the decorative arts, is increasingly flavouring the food and selectively shaping the major arts in most western countries. The success of the Japanese economic miracle and the colonization of decayed centres of western industry by Japanese firms is introducing westerners to new models of economic and social organization, which could be as instructive for economic planners and political decision-makers as oriental philosophical traditions have been for western scientists. Those who once took the Road to Mandalay for nostalgia or greed are now drawn along the Narrow Road to the Deep North in search of enlightenment. History has not stopped with a world culture made in the west. The sun has come up again on the other side of the world, and the cultural imperialism of the present and the future emanates from the depths of Asia and—increasingly and decisively, I believe—from the shores of the Pacific.

The Japaneseness of Japan

Japan, despite her geographical position on the extreme rim of the habitable east, is often thought of as a late recruit to the western world. The modernization that was the subject of Chapter Twenty of this book is mistaken for westernization. News commentators commonly use the term "the west" to mean industrially developed nations of the G7 family or Organization for Economic Cooperation and Development, including Japan. Impressive examples conspire to convince us that cultural traits have been assimilated along with economic lessons: the fidelity and brilliance of Japanese interpreters of western music, for instance, contrasts with the typical experience of David Morley's hero Boon, who could not even detect the simplest melodies of Japanese popular tunes. The competence of Japanese architects in handling classical Mediterranean forms suggests a comfortable familiarity with the tradition, though the parties of Japanese tourists whom I observe from a library window in Oxford, as they blink, it seems to me uncomprehendingly at buildings they can neither value nor even distinguish, evince a less certain touch. While Japan has not so far produced any distinguished historians of the west, Japanese schoolchildren are on average at least as well versed, grade for grade, in the history of Europe and America as their counterparts from those parts of the world.

Yet the limitations of Japanese westernization are glaring, even in the midst of the most dense evidence of Japanese chameleonism. The reception of baseball—*baseboru,* as the Japanese call it—could, for instance, be seen as a typical case of adaptation. The game is played with every trivial trapping of its American prototype, down to the seventh-inning stretch. Yet in Japan baseball projects a cultural profile which is distinctively Japanese. Perhaps the most telling difference—evidence of the value Japanese place on social harmony—is their willing acceptance of tie games. The amateur teams which abound never appear sans uniforms, as would be normal in American neighbourhood games, because to be without a uniform in team colors would be *basho-gara wakimaezu*—not in keeping with the spirit of the occasion. The annual national schoolboy baseball final in Osaka is elevated to a celebration of "the beautiful and noble spirit of Japan"; more than just a game, according to the most authoritative coach and commentator, it is "an education of the heart" on "an exercise-ground of morality." The baseball craze first reached Japan in the early 1920s, so it had a long time to get "acculturated" as an ersatz national sport. Yet it seems odd that that most Yankee of games, deeply associated with Japan's only foreign conquerors, the occupation forces of the MacArthur era, should have been pressed so perfectly into the service of the traditional Japanese cults of youthful heroism and purity. Some nationalists want to exclude the name *baseboru* in favour of the indigenous term *yakyu.*

The Japanese, whose sense of national identity depends, like that of Spaniards in the west, on a conviction of their own uniqueness, are happier to avow affinities with their eastern neighbours than with their western partners. Even their former enemies or victims—and present rivals—the mainland Chinese, Koreans, and Taiwanese, are, in a peculiar and condescending sense, regarded as belonging to a racial confraternity. The Japanese are more conservative in their reverence for the Chinese writing system on which they still rely than, say, the Vietnamese or Koreans and even, in some respects, than the Chinese themselves, whose simplified modern characters are generally unintelligible to Japanese readers. Repugnance at the Roman alphabet is uncompromising in Japan, although objective experts realize that it would suit the language well. In Japan, as in the west, new religious movements are popular today, based on doctrines of social relevance and charismatic communal therapies, but in Japan they spring from Shinto or Buddhist traditions. Christianity—which made an impact in sixteenth- and seventeenth-century Japan as dramatic as it was short-lived—has no appeal now except as a source of fashionable marriage-ritual. Newly built skyscrapers are topped off with a shrine to Inari the fox-god. The ubiquitous spirits of Shinto even infest computers in a sort of high-tech animism.

Japanese attitudes towards the west are most paradoxical, perhaps, in their admiration for the aesthetics of western looks. "Outsiders" are rarely accepted in Japanese society, and the products of mixed marriages frequently take refuge abroad. The traditional Japanese images of western faces and bodies are repulsive—the "red barbarians" "stink of butter" and are long-nosed, florid-faced, clumsy, and gawky. The novelist Tanizaki admired western women from a distance; but "they are disappointing," he said, "when one gets too close and sees how coarse and hairy their skins are." Yet his fictional character who compensated for his personal inadequacy by procuring a bride with western looks exemplifies a widespread taste. Fashion models—whose main job is to display clothes designed in the west for western women—tend to have western blood. Chest wigs are affected by sunbathers. Cartoon heroes and heroines have big eyes, with no sign of a slit. On Spanish television—which buys its cartoons undiscriminatingly from all over the world for reasons of economy—it is astonishing to see the round-eyed appeal of the soccer and volleyball heroes and heroines of Japanese animation, cheered from the touchline by lesser mortals who look traditionally Japanese.

The epitome of cartoon heroes—Yamato Shinko, a boy-wonder who is a prodigy of prowess and courage as well as of good looks—is unembarrassed by his western appearance. His father was a kamikaze pilot. His education was a feat of endurance. His adversaries are not only vanquished—they are also converted to the cult of youthful purity. His exploits are full of conscious echoes of the careers of Japan's sixteenth-century Robin Hood, Musashi, and of the "road of trials" travelled by the fourth-century culture-hero Yamato Takeru. His very name evokes the ancient name of Japan. And despite his round eyes, like most Japanese who compare themselves with westerners, he is short.

The surface of the pool shimmers with western reflections, but the depths of Japan are unchanged beneath. The values disclosed by literature and popular culture demonstrate this. The Japanese adaptation of *Madame X, a Story of Mother-Love*, an English novel of 1910 transferred to the Japanese television screen in 1977, transforms a petulant adulteress into a matronly victim, driven out of the house by her wicked mother-in-law and forced into humiliating adventures by her determination to protect her son. The mother-son bond, in a society where children are nursed well beyond babyhood, is an essential element in a Japanese tear-jerker. The passivity of the heroine is demanded by Japanese notions of womanhood. The predatory female is recognizable as an incarnation of the devil-woman, but such a character could not engage audience sympathy.

The commonest theme in popular literature is that of *ninjo-giri*, the conflict of feelings and obligations or of personal and group loyalties. A society that sacralizes the group and idealizes feelings generates more than its fair share of dilemmas of this type. A similar dichotomy—between *tatenae* and

In the comic book, *I Am a Kamikaze*, Yamato Shinko, the boy-hero who personifies Japanese values, converts a baddie to the cult of youthful purity, with a touch of the knuckles. The young hero's prototype—indeed, the archetype of Japanese heroes generally—was the legendary Yamato Takeru, whose name means "Brave of Japan" and whose "road of trials" included numerous combats in which he reduced enemies to the emperor's obedience or slew them before his own heroic death.

bonne, appearance and reality, or *omote,* surface impression, and *ura,* inner reality, both of which have established but ill-defined places in Japanese scales of values—makes acceptable in Japan behaviour which would be denounced as sham or hypocritical in the west. It is part of the source of peculiarly Japanese paradoxes, such as the uncompromising censorship of displays of pubic hair in a land where sado-masochistic comics are a normal item of middle-class reading matter; it accounts for the ceremonial civility with which the girls of "no-pants coffee-shops" line up to take their leave of clients with a formal bow and a united chant of "Thank you for visiting our establishment." An increasing number of Japanese financial whiz-kids now go to business school in the United States, where business bestsellers in recent years have included *Leadership Secrets of Attila the Hun* and *The Marine Corps Manual,* as well as Sun-tzu's *The Art of War;* but only in Japan are military periodicals marketed under the slogan, "Businessmen, let's learn from the annals of war!"

The habit which most makes Japanese fit the western stereotype of the inscrutable oriental is *aimae*—the tentative, self-effacing, and ambiguous use of language, which is the only socially acceptable form of discourse. Like all linguistic habits, it is deeply ingrained. It makes politicians sound, to western ears, vague, shifty, and long-winded, while social relations seem strained; the object of any argument slips and ducks out of reach, abetted by Japanese abhorrence of explicit discord. The anecdotage of modern commerce is full of stories of western businessmen who mistakenly supposed they had clinched a deal in Japan because they took the term "yes" to mean, "I assent to your proposal" rather than "I am adopting a sympathetic attitude to your point of view."

At an even deeper level, perhaps, than *aimae,* the concept of *aimeru* informs Japanese behaviour: the primacy of sensibilities, of intuitive and affective values. The terms for *wet, soft,* and *gentle* have more evocative power in Japanese than in any western language, and any imagery that can conjure memories of mother-love has instant emotional force. Japanese children are suckled up to the age of five or six. In childhood they barely see their hard-working fathers save on brief holidays and snatched weekends. They live in households which are run on strictly matriarchal lines— in private, for in the public face of family life a dominant father scowls and a submissive mother smiles; this is the realm of *omote* and *ura.* Pampered and cocooned by smothering mother-love, the children are released at school age into a brutally competitive and rigidly disciplined premature adulthood. Against this background, western visitors' commonly expressed astonishment at the prevalence of infantile tastes and mawkish sentiments is understandable. From a western point of view, the Japanese are a nation of classic Freudian cases.

The catchphrase of the early Meiji reformers—*wakon yosai,* Japanese spirit and western knowledge—has been applied with extraordinary consistency in Japan. The absorption of western technical skills has left Japanese values uncompromised. Westerners, it seems, are beginning to recognize and even exaggerate this. In *The Rising Sun,* Michael Crichton's novel of skullduggery in a Japanese business empire in Los Angeles, the depiction of the Japanese seems indebted to the treatment of alien invaders from outer space in a traditional science-fiction story. The Japanese themselves, however, seem hardly able to share this assessment of the depth of western penetration, or, at least, to express it. Their media are full of complaints against what they call "the new humans," a younger generation allegedly corrupted by consumerism and selfishness that contrast with the austere and collective values of old Japan.

To an objective observer this looks like a generational "phase" rather than a "generation gap." In the interval between the merciless "examination hell" of adolescence and the acquisition of family responsibilities, with life-long immolation in a commercial or bureaucratic organization, young Japanese allow themselves a spasm of self-indulgence that seems to leave them no less well equipped to practise, in the late twenties onwards, the virtues of *aimeru* and to talk the language of *aimae.* A recent survey showed that girls at Japan's top universities claim to work on average only one hour a day. The market research of a distilling company claimed that students spend 20 per cent of their time drinking. In employment, however, people from similar samples behave with the efficiency and self-discipline of their parents. Even in their limited cultural rebellion, the new humans act as a cohort, conforming to an identikit look from Walkman top to cross-trainer toe. This is a clear sign that they have not renounced membership in a society where even gangsters are said to make themselves helpfully identifiable by their unofficial uniform of wide ties and lapels and where to be average is a term of praise. The anxiety aroused by the new humans has actually strengthened the peculiarities of Japanese culture by rallying those committed to its defence. Prime Minister Nakasone's education reforms were presented as a campaign to strip out the corrosive western influences implanted by the American occupation.

In Japan today the rhetoric of east Asian fraternity and east Asian cooperation is popular; the notion that Japanese resistance to westernization was a defence of "oriental" culture would, however, find no favour in Japan. To the Japanese, Japaneseness is unique. Only from a distance of 11,000 miles could a generalization as vague as "oriental culture" look other than laughable. Like "oriental despotism" or "eastern mysticism" or "oriental inscrutability," it is a term contrived as a refuge for those unwilling to examine the subject closely. Paradoxically, what makes Japan unique is precisely her accessibility to generalizations. The Japanese make generalizations about themselves, whereas it is usually from the inside that the diversity of a particular culture or family of cultures is most apparent. A north Briton, for instance, will be quick to correct an Italian host who introduces him as an "Englishman." A Catalan or Basque will hasten to qualify the sense in which he is "Spanish." Germany, which looks so formidably solid from a distance, is a genuine *Bund* of historic communities, riven by lingering fissures of *Kulturkampf* as well as by the effects of the recent political division of east from west. In Japan, however, which is comparable in size with any of these countries and which, because of its egregious length and mountainous terrain, encompasses a much greater range of climates and environments, you have to go as far north as the surviving Ainu or as far south as Okinawa to find people who resent the homogeneity of the nation or resist the identity embraced by the rest of their fellow-citizens.

Everywhere in the 1990s micro-identities are emerging from the woodwork of a world of "crooked timber," and it seems increasingly apparent that the unity of Japan has been exaggerated from the outside. Yet thanks to the geographical remoteness of an archipelago surrounded by wide expanses of stormy waters; thanks to the physical crowding that forces almost the whole population into narrow coastal strips, among the greatest population density in the world; thanks to an isolationist history that excluded foreigners and forbade travel for two hundred years in the early-modern period; thanks to all this the Japanese have become the world's most consistent people, the most thoroughly stirred of mankind's melting-pots. The most remarkable generalization about them is that so many generalizations hold true.

Cultures can borrow from each other without sacrifice of identity. The part-Japanese Harvard Nipponologist Edwin Reischauer nicely exposed the fallacy that equates or closely links industrialization with westernization in Japanese history:

> What the Japanese have taken over are the modern aspects of Western culture, which for the most part the west too has only recently developed in response to modern technology—things like railroads, factories, mass education, great newspapers, television and mass democracy. In this sense, Japan has more significantly become modernized, not westernized, and the process of modernization has taken place on the basis of Japan's own traditional culture, just as happened in the West, with the same sort of resulting contrasts and strains. A head start in the West of four decades in railroading and of a few years in television did not make these features of modern life distinctively Western as opposed to Japanese.

From the perspective of the galactic museum-keepers of the future, our millennium will not appear as a "triumph of the west," exemplified by the adscription of Japan to alien ways, but as a period of accelerating exchanges of influence back and forth across the east-west axis of the world that links the densely populated civilizations of the northern hemisphere. The time-lags involved in Japanese uptake of western innovations will seem trivial in comparison with the tardy western responses, earlier in the millennium, to Chinese inventions. Over the period as a whole, the east may well seem to have been more influential in the west than the other way around.

SILVER COLUMBIA

In 1935, Ishikawa Tatsuzo published *The Common People,* a novella about Japanese migrants in Brazil. They had begun to arrive in 1908—"swimmers like carp against the current"—to create farms in the forest. At Tomé Açu, which was opened for settlement in 1929, they fought malaria and black-water fever on twenty-five-hectare plots, with little backing from investors crippled or cautioned by the slump. By 1942 there were only forty-nine of the original households left, though a new wave of migrants saved the community from extinction in the 1950s. They kidded themselves that they had an imperial mission: they had "come overseas to extend Japanese influence for the good of the nation." More honestly, they admitted that they migrated because "there was no way of making it in Japan."

They belonged to an era of threatless colonization by fugitives from the Pacific rim (see Chapters 22 and 23), which posed no challenge to host societies and created no serious social problems, because the launderers, waiters, restaurateurs, and peons did low-status jobs and fulfilled useful functions. Brazil has recently had a Japanese senator and Peru a Japanese president, without arousing fears of Japanese imperial irredentism. Colonization does not become colonialism unless it embodies menace.

Now Pacific-rim settlers in the west are changing in both character and quantity. Formerly assimilable numbers, such as Europe and America were accustomed to accept, threatened to be succeeded in the 1980s by a form of mass migration: the outflow of Vietnamese "boat people," fleeing from communism for motives classified as political or economic according to the convenience of the potential host countries. The refugees whom the west was unwilling or unable to accept were sold out or bought off or accommodated in Hong Kong. The Vietnamese government was bribed to take them back and admonished to spare them from victimization. The wave ebbed. But a similar influx may be threatened when Hong Kong reverts to Chinese rule in 1997, or may be provoked by some subsequent confrontation between westernized and democratic elements in Hong Kong and an authoritarian Chinese regime. The United Kingdom has granted rights of abode to 250,000 Hong Kong residents; if violence or oppression should befall the former subjects of the crown, the moral pressure to admit mil-

Urban planners love to give Chinatowns Chinese-style street furniture: the pagoda-telephone kiosks are the identifying feature of the New York Chinatown. See pp. 16–17 and 680.

lions could become irresistible. The Hong Kong refugees will include a new class of immigrant to Britain, unprecedented except in the cases of a few of the richest Asian traders expelled from Uganda in the 1970s (see Chapter 18). The Hong Kong oligarchy could migrate *en masse,* with cash resources to make them an instant élite, a sudden new power group in the host community. To some extent this has already happened in Vancouver, which, as we have seen, is a favourite place for potential Hong Kong refugees to do preparatory nest-feathering (see Chapter 23).

Meanwhile, Japanese business interests have created a form of covert colonialism new to the west, which transfers real power over large numbers of westerners into Japanese hands. The sheer scale of Japanese investment in Europe and America represents an astonishing reversal of old-style White supremacy. In the middle of the twentieth century, Japan was America's defeated and dependent client; since 1985 it has held the bulk of America's debt. Furthermore, unlike the Arab money which has also been invested in western economies with a lavish hand, Japanese investment has led to takeovers of manufacturing industries and to the introduction of Japanese management over large groups of indigenous workers. In the United Kingdom, when Nissan established a car plant in Sunderland, hailed as a new lease on life for the moribund British car industry, the new relationship was brilliantly expressed by a television public-relations campaign in which an expression of satisfaction, uttered in a northern worker's unintelligible English dialect, was "translated" for viewers' benefit by a precisely suited, precisely spoken Japanese. The advertisement was engagingly funny, but local people in Sunderland found it so offensive that it had to be taken off the air.

Japan's need for overseas *Lebensraum* is even greater today than it was at the high point of Japanese imperialism. Japanese surplus cash and surplus population simply have nowhere to go but abroad. The growth of population, which has inspired heroic but only marginally helpful land reclamation schemes, and the narrowness of Japan's habitable coastal plains have crammed, in the most crowded zone, a population bigger than Spain's into a space no bigger than southern California. Japan's weak resource base at home is an irresistible incentive to use present wealth to buy a stake in supplier countries. Her shortage of food, which is bad enough to induce imperialist neurosis on its own, creates an urgent need to secure foreign sources of provisions. Japan produces little more than 50 per cent of her food needs, while her main rivals, the United States and the European Union, generate huge surpluses. World pressure to limit exports and increase imports obliges Japan to invest in manufacturing overseas; after a long period of insularist resistance, Japan began to buy foreign companies on a large scale in the late 1980s, while Japanese interests continued to combine to keep foreign raiders out of the Japanese stock markets.

Gleeful expectations of the reversal of the flow of Japanese capital are premature. The investment coups in foreign markets in the 1980s were made possible by a huge current account surplus; but at the end of the decade, when the surplus was cut back by modified exchange rates and international agreements, the investment went on, financed with short-term borrowing. The Japanese have gone on defying every manipulation of the exchange rate and every attempt to stack the terms of trade by working harder and restoring their trade balance. Their habit of personal saving cannot be broken and still generates cash for the rest of the world. The levels of the 1980s are almost being sustained in the 1990s, with new destinations—eastern Europe, Latin America, and the Pacific rim. Protection of Japan's home stock market has a daunting effect on the statistics. Partly because of the huge capitalization of Japanese companies, the six biggest Japanese corporations—in which foreign investors have little stake—control nearly 3 per cent of the world economy. Predictions of Japan's "coming collapse" (see Chapter 20) arise in part from the mistaken assumption that the Japanese are like everybody else and will demand the squandering of cash surpluses on welfare and housing subsidies.

Japan's irremediably favourable trade balance, which no increase in the value of the yen seems able seriously to dent, will probably continue to create vast disposable cash for investment abroad. The banks, because of competition from cash-rich businesses at home, are forced to put their money elsewhere. Japanese banks account for more than a third of international lending—controlling, for instance, about half the public sector market in Britain and America. Californian banking is becoming a Japanese offshore asset. Japan's importance as the world economy's top creditor makes the fragility of her home islands, exposed to hurricanes, undermined by seismic faults, and tortured by extremes of climate, imply unacceptable risks all around. An obvious response is to spread these by using worldwide locations for some of the nerve centres and personnel of Japanese decision-making, information-gathering, and business management.

The most serious problem, which makes the indefinite containment of Japan within Japan impossible, is the ageing of the Japanese population. Apart from Sweden, Japan has the world's fastest-growing proportion of over-seventies. People's lives, extended by the benefits of simple diet, last on average four to five years longer in Japan than in the United States. "Granny" has replaced the mother-in-law as the most topical source of friction in Japanese domestic comedy. Announced to coincide with the commemoration of the 500th anniversary of Columbus's inauguration of modern colonialism, the Japanese government's "Silver Columbia" programme proposed the settlement of aged Japanese in relatively cheap, sunny, "sheltered" developments, on a gigantic scale, in places such as Australia and Mediterranean Europe. Never before has there been colonialism without losers. The Japanese colonies of the future will be too old to breed, so there will be no racial problems; they will be too respectable for unrest, too frail for violence, too well nurtured for serious crime. They will give their hosts no trouble, while boosting demand and creating employment. The settlers will have none of the problems of Betjeman's British expatriates in Spain, with their borrowed *Telegraph* and scorpions in the bath, for they will be enfolded in a community of their kind, housed in a home where the language, food, entertainments, and domestic architecture will all be familiar. In this Uncle Tom's utopia there will, in theory, be neither exploited nor exploiters, neither master race nor victims. Is there anyone outside Japan who really believes it could work?

Just as the Japaneseness of Japan has survived long exposure to western influence, so—we can conjecture—the shoreline of western civilization will be only selectively changed by the reversal of the cultural tide. In a remote future, historians used to the world hegemony of Pacific-rim cultures will be able to write essays on "The Uniqueness of the West" and generalize about "the occident" as their predecessors did and do about the east. The force and importance of the changes we are experiencing as we enter the third millennium of our era should not, however, be underestimated. The cultural revenge of the east and the rise of a peaceful Japanese world empire are symptoms and signs of the shift of world resources and world leadership to the Pacific, which will play, in the early phases of the next millennium, the same unifying, shaping, and dominating role as the Nile in ancient Egypt or the Tigris and Euphrates in Mesopotamia or the Hwang Ho in old China or the Mediterranean in the civilization of antiquity and the Atlantic in that of the recent past. Civilizations are grouped around waterways, and, as they grow, world history proceeds by sea-changes, which produce rich and strange results.

Epilogue

ALICE'S UNVISITED

Yet all experience is an arch, where through
Gleams that untravelled world, whose margin fades
For ever and for ever when I move.

ALFRED, LORD TENNYSON, ULYSSES

There may always be another reality
To make fiction of the truth we think we've arrived at.

CHRISTOPHER FRY, A YARD OF SUN

Delightful though it be, as Kwai-lung said, "to wander through a garden of bright images, are we not enticing your mind from a subject of equal, if not greater, importance?" For some readers the past will be a refuge from the present; for others, a laboratory of the future. The end of a history book, near the end of a millennium, is not a bad place from which to try to look ahead.

Alice's Restaurant was the setting of a counter-culture song and a 1969 movie where "you can get anything you want." The freedom hobos seek in travelling, hippies in drugs, and creative artists in uninhibited imagination is hunted by historians—escaping from the disciplined contemplation of the past—in unlicensed speculation about the future. Historians' predictions are generally unwanted and usually wrong; but they may sometimes be worth hearing. The best argument against them cracks on the rack of paradox: the critic who shuts his ears to them, on the grounds that they have been wrong in the past, is himself making an inference on the basis of historical experience.

Neither I nor, I hope, most readers will have made any previous contributions to futurology; but, poised on the brink of the next thousand years, those of us who have got this far feel a natural impulse to peer ahead, which we may as well gratify together. Even after a hitchhike through a thousand years of history the restaurant at the end of the universe still seems a long way off. The panoptic vision of those galactic museum-keepers has been shared only in glimpses; nor has the right been earned to speculate without trammels. Still, without seeing what is cooking in the kitchen of the future, I propose to devote a few pages to trying to read the menu.

Disrespect for futurology can be happily liberating for the scholar tempted to dabble in predictions; the strain of preserving academic detachment and stifling moral judgements can be forgotten. In the predictions made here, I candidly confess my unscientific notion of the job and my abhorrence of the future I foresee. The museum-keepers may rescue their relics of our world from its burned-out shell; or from a moonscape crumpled and dusted by ecological disaster; or from an unpeopled planet reconquered by resurgent nature; or from a colony of space invaders; or, most surprisingly of all, from something recognizably similar to what we have got. But I propose in this epilogue to forgo their perspective and to envisage only the relatively short-term future prefigured in the trends of the last thousand years—to see how the next millennium might start to grow out of the last.

Futurology is a fashion. The approach of the end of the current millennium has stimulated it, but, judged over the length of a lifetime, it looks like a fashion in decline. It seems to my wife and me, as we gather, like citizens of Flatland, around the sort of hearthside evoked in the epigraph to Part One of this book, to have peaked in our own childhood and youth when public interest in the future was enlivened by debate between scientific perfectibilians and apocalyptic visionaries. The optimists predicted a world made easy by progress, lives prolonged by medical wizardry, wealth made universal by the alchemy of economic growth, society rectified by the egalitarianism of technologically prolonged leisure. The pessimists foresaw nuclear immolation or population explosion or a purgative world revolution—a cosmic struggle reminiscent of the millennium of Christian prophetic tradition—which would either save or enslave mankind.

No one gets excited by such visions today. Scientific progress has been, at best, disappointing—encumbering us with apparently insoluble social and moral problems; or else, at worst, alarming—threatening us with the mastery of artificially intelligent machines or genetically engineered human mutants. Economic growth has become the bogey of the ecologically anxious. Meanwhile, world revolution and the nuclear holocaust have been postponed, and apocalyptic prophecy has resorted to forebodings—variously unconvincing or uncompelling—about ecological cataclysms. Proliferation of nuclear weapons and the discovery that even peaceful nuclear installations can poison great parts of the world has, in some ways, made disaster impend more darkly; but lingering extinction and little local nuclear holocausts seem to lack, in public esteem, the glamour of a sudden and comprehensive armageddon. The future has become depressing rather than dramatic, and futurology has lost allure.

The first prediction we can safely make is that this trough will be a narrow one and that by the time the new millennium is upon us speculation will again have clambered out of it; the media will be as full of the future as of the news. For the rest, the predictions which follow are trenchantly asserted—but that is a rhetorical convention. By futurological standards they are meant to be few and tentative.

1. Population Growth Will Be Contained

Into the next millennium, futurologists will probably still be wasting their time on statistics. These are useless as a basis for long-range forecasting, partly because of the interventions of chaos and partly because we have no series big enough or reliable enough to constitute a guide. Early in the next millennium, we shall be disabused of two favourite predictions of gazers into these opaque crystals: first, that world population growth will outstrip food resources; second, that world peace will be threatened by imbalances in population between the demographically shrinking, developed "north" and the demographically expanding, impoverished "south."

Population trends have always provoked doom-fraught oracles, because their popular interpreters suppose that every new series will be infinitely sustained; yet, beyond the short term, expectations based on them are never fulfilled. The fact that two mutually contradictory trends are detectable, worldwide, at different levels of prosperity, is a clue to what will really happen: the areas of demographic decline will expand, and those of demographic growth will shrink. After what may be a convulsive period of transition, the overall pattern will be a gentle, containable rise.

The most reliable population check will be economic change. Birth rates fall as incomes rise: as manpower becomes less valuable in mechanizing societies, people produce fewer babies. First Latin America, then the middle east and Africa north of the Sahara will follow the industrialized world into the prosperity of high production per unit of energy and of time; the laggard parts of the far east will catch up with the "little dragons." As in the societies which developed ahead of them, potential parents in those parts of the world will gradually adjust their values to the new situation and breed less. The baby boom will sag. Like a string of balloons after a children's party, population bubbles will subside: there will be shocks and disturbances—the equivalents of the balloons' burpings and poppings—but the long-term trend will be towards a sustainable rise and, eventually, a return to demographic stability.

This will not have much to do with planned parenthood as it is conventionally understood. Overwhelmingly—today and throughout history—societies have regulated their birth rate by adjusting their conventions on courtship and marriage, postponing marriage until a part of the fertile period has passed. Compared with the effect of this sort of discipline, the technology of contraception, which is prescribed for the third world with such laughable solemnity by well-intentioned interferers, can make only an ancillary contribution; people have to adjust their values to include limited fertility before they take to contraception, which, whether slipped, slotted, or swallowed, is an intrusion naturally abhorred. Future fashions in contraception will include natural techniques and prescriptions from the pharmacopoeia of ethnobiology. Economic progress brings a further type of social change which has similarly depressant results on the birth rate: women's liberation encourages women to diversify from breeding into other productive occupations.

As the world's population planners confront their task, they feel little comfort in reassurance of this sort. Social values, they reason, take a long time to change, whereas the problem is urgent. Religion and tradition, they acknowledge, are terribly prolific midwives whose zeal must be countered. We can expect their panic to get worse before the situation gets better. Today's population trends are genuinely more threatening than ever before because the world has never been so protected from the effects of Malthusian checks—thanks to "medicine without frontiers," food surpluses in the developed world, and lumbering but life-saving international aid.

It is too early, however, to write Malthusian checks out of the script. Plagues, wars, and famines are still with us. The challenge of medicine seems to conjure ever more inventive and resourceful responses from disease, as destructive organisms adapt, as if with intelligence or even glee, to our efforts to check them. The speed and efficiency with which food surpluses can be redistributed encourages economic inefficiency in plague-prone areas, despite its containing effect on the mortality which ensues. Wars are waged with some of the most efficient killing machines ever devised—even when interrupted or confined by an international consensus which, for all its faults, is clearer and stronger than ever before. Above all, the current world population boom is happening because traditional societies are slow to adjust their habits of reproduction to the new environment of plummeting death rates and rising fertility suddenly created by western aid.

While we wait for those adjustments to happen, we shall probably have to endure a period of harrowing uncertainty in which Malthusian checks take their revenge: in which AIDS wipes out some of the people saved by aid; in which famine relief breeds structural famine; and in which the international aid system pays simultaneously for means to save lives and for wars to winnow them. AIDS, which is still uncontained in its reservoir of infection in Africa and which still has much havoc to wreak in the developed world, will surely not be the last mass raptor. In the volatile evolutionary world of micro-organisms, new or newly evolved diseases can emerge unpredictably and baffle science long enough to kill millions.

Eventually, however, our descendants will see population increase level off to a point where it can be handled by advances in agronomy, which—under the pressure of population growth and the need to exploit new or previously under-used environments—will replace medicine in the next century as the life-saving wonder-science of the world. "Miracle" yields are already within the compass of this science; only the enormous world surpluses in existing foods inhibit progress in application.

If needed, more relief on living space will come from colonization of new environments. Most of the world is still underpopulated, and despite losses to desiccation and erosion, more of it is becoming habitable all the time. Desert real estate already occupies some of the most expensive sites in the United States. A lot of this world remains to be converted to man's use before our descendants need to realize the sci-fi fantasies of colonies on the seabed and on other planets. On the other hand, it is of course possible—and, in some estimations, likely—that in the meantime man's habitat will be shrunk by climatic change or ecological mismanagement; the world has been forewarned of this but remains unarmed against it.

The whole world will gradually conform to the demographic pattern of the developed parts of it. Worldwide, we now have simultaneously the youngest and oldest populations, relatively speaking, in the history of the species. The third world today is blessed or encumbered with disproportionately vast cohorts of the under–twenty-fives, the developed world with a similar disparity in favour of the over-seventies. For sensationalists, this opens delightful prospects—of a world conflict exacerbated by hatred across a generation gap; of a west condemned to economic collapse by the imbalance of top weight. The realistic prospect is less exciting: once the disproportion in the third world has shifted to the other end of the age range, the world will be a more stable place as the natural conservatism of the elderly is asserted by unprecedented numbers.

When the world has become used to the new balance, no particular problems will be caused by the "shrinking workforce" predicted by some forecasters. The same improvements in health which prolong life will prolong working lives, and technical improvements in efficiency will continue to make work more productive. Of course—as in the transition to a period of contained population growth—the adjustments this implies in people's habits and expectations will take a long time and may need to be violently enforced. Comprehensive state welfare systems—viable only in a short period, now rapidly coming to a close, in only the richest of states—will collapse under the double strain of increased demand and unmanageable costs; but they may revive, later in the next century, as societies settle down to enjoy and exploit individuals' lengthening life-spans with, for example, targeted medicare and pensions at eighty-five or one-hundred-and-five years old. Contrary to recent trends in developed societies, the nuclear family—or the peri-nuclear family, taking in all surviving generations to one or two degrees of affinity—will survive and be strengthened in most of the world, simply because in the absence of workable universal welfare systems it will remain the most efficient way known of organizing mutual care.

2. Rival Totalitarianisms Will Return

There may be terrible conflicts and disasters on the road to this conservative nirvana, and there will almost certainly be a frightening political and moral price to pay. Fascism is flexing its jaws offshore just when people thought the world was at last safe for democracy. On the face of it, the triumph of democracy in the late twentieth century looks reassuring. It conquered southern Europe in the 1970s and eastern Europe in the next two decades. It survived terrible strains in India, Pakistan, and the Philippines, and has made patchy but promising progress in other parts of east Asia. In Latin America it lived through adverse conditions in Peru, Colombia, and Brazil, while Chile and Argentina were transformed in fluent strokes from sinister dictatorships to model democracies. In Africa the unsatisfactory pattern described above (see Chapter 18) is overshadowed, early in the last decade of the millennium, by democratization in the continent's richest state. The day of democracy looks as if it has arrived, but it will prove to be a false dawn or a short spell of wintry light.

A world which depends for survival on rapid revolutions in values and on a pace of change forced by breakneck technology is unsettling to most people and bewildering to many; in this state of mind, electors reach for "men of destiny" and prophets of order. In increasingly complex societies, struggling to cope with rising expectations, gigantic collective projects, baffling demographic imbalance, and terrifying external threats, order and social control will come to be more highly valued than freedom. The sanctity of life, a principle which is our best protection against the ultimate tyranny of the all-powerful state, will soon seem outmoded to most people, partly because of perceptions of population growth—for human life, like other commodities, is regulated by laws of supply and demand and is cheapened by glut; and partly because death will be the cheapest way of disposing of the criminal, the unconforming, and the otherwise unwanted.

In Europe and North America the authoritarian right is already prospering from public revulsion towards crime. In the autumn of 1993, a reputation as "tough on crime" has made a Republican—against all the historical form—mayor of New York; Alessandra Mussolini is widely expected to be mayor of Naples; and a British Conservative Party conference has cheered a barbarous programme for killing murderers and castrating rapists. As I write, the president of the United States is celebrating the fiftieth anniversary of the liberation of Rome in an Italy governed by a coalition that includes a post–Fascist Party.

Western liberalism, enfeebled by its inconsistencies, seems bound to be wishy-washed away by a new wave of fascism; it will be hard for my children's generation to find courage to fight for the sort of imperfect humanity which is willing to abort innocent lives while sanctifying those of criminals, or which undermines its own principles by banning moral absolutes as politically incorrect. Discouragement from striving "officiously to keep alive" will be followed by licence to kill. By historians looking back from a violent future, the massacre of undesirables will be seen to have started in our own times with the unborn and the elderly.

The authoritarian—and, hard behind, the totalitarian—right will start the new millennium in the strength of its near-monopoly of moral absolutism; it will have the advantage of the appeal of certainty in an uncertain world. The fascism of the past was essentially secular, with a crash programme to a worldly utopia. Some of the most threatening forms of quasi-fascism today are sanctified by the ayatollahs and the television presbyters of the "moral majority." Though the political threat of Islamic fundamentalism seems to be receding as I write (see Chapter 19), the movement remains strong and dangerously combustible.

Christian fundamentalism can be just as potent. So far it has affected only the rhetoric of politics in the developed world, but in parts of Latin America, protestant evangelists from rich North American sects have put their spiritually deracinated congregations at the service of right-wing politicians. In the next century, "Christian fundamentalism" could become a political term, just as "Islamic fundamentalism" has in recent times. The effect will be mitigated if the Catholic church—the world's biggest and most widespread communion—keeps up what may become a unique commitment to moral absolutism in defence of human dignity, individual freedom, social justice, and the sanctity of life. Yet the tempters who are always cajoling the pope to compromise will probably triumph—not when the present pontiff dies, because the long life in office of John Paul II has strengthened the moral fibre of the cardinalate, but in the next pontificate after that.

Although recrudescent fascism is the great political menace of the near future, we should also be wary of a rebirth of the authoritarian left. Communism and fascism have been dismissed as extinct dinosaurs, but they will be back, clawing at each other in the streets, like revivified clones out of Jurassic Park. The galactic museum-keepers will classify the Second World War as only the first round in a long, recurrent series of clashes between rival "final solutions."

Reports of the death of Marxism may be premature. Prophets' followers often grow in fervour while diminishing in number as their prophecies are proved false. The visions of Ellen Gould White, for instance, were inspired by her "disappointment" with the postponement of the Adventist millennium in 1846; in the Anabaptist kingdom of Münster in 1526, fanatics passed the "test" posed by the failed promises of Jan of Leyden; in the seventeenth and eighteenth centuries a dwindling band of Shabbateites found their faith reinforced when their messiah apostasized in his lifetime and omitted to rise from the dead. Two excuses have already been refined on the hard left. It is said, first, that the collapsed states and parties of the late twentieth century were not genuinely communist but rather examples of "state capitalism" or of some other perversion or heresy. And Marx's scheme of history is said to be unfulfilled only because it has not yet been given time. The class struggle goes on but is in a relatively quiescent phase; the revolutionary culmination is still coming, but with a muffled march. Marxism is a faith, impervious, like all the best religions, to rational argument; the pertinacity of its adherents is reminiscent of the survival of the church when the eschatological predictions of Christ, eagerly anticipated by the early apostles, receded into a remote time.

When hopes prove false of peace and plenty for the former subjects of communism in the post-communist world, when the fascist revanche creates new underclasses and mass victims of repression, the communist cause will arise again, proposed, in rivalry with fascism, as a solution to the problems of managing societies, of combating crime, of diluting inequalities, of containing humans' natural anarchy. This is not to say that in a shorter term Communist Party rule will survive in China and its few other remaining fiefs. The experience of the 1980s and early 1990s suggests that once economic liberalism starts, the political system has to change along with it because, if for no other reason, of the validity of the sound Marxist doctrine that power follows wealth; outside a system of rigid state monopolies, non-party members can grow rich.

3. Big States Will Continue to Fragment

Totalitarianism, which crushes individuality, obliterates diversity. Even those who do not fear a totalitarian revanche are alarmed or dispirited at the prospect of an increasingly uniform world. So many of today's trends seem to foreshadow it: a "global culture" has scattered the world with look-alike airport lounges and fast-food outlets and filled shops with the same products in Madras as in Miami. "Homogenization" and "convergence" are hallowed in western Europe like hard-to-please deities, to whom member-peoples of the European community have to sacrifice peculiar traditions and tastes. Instant communications spread shared images and a shadow, at least, of shared experience all over the world. In the global village, neigh-bours exercise pressure to conform.

Yet, as a matter of fact, mankind has never been so diverse, and, in suggestive ways, the divergences are actually increasing. Diversity covers a bigger range of material culture than ever before. In this time of unprece-dented change, much of the world has escaped its effects; there are still re-mote, "primitive" communities in tundras and ice-worlds, deserts and jungles that remained almost untouched by it, leading lives essentially un-modified, in their intimate interdependence with nature, for the whole of our millennium and, in some cases, several millennia more. The Brazilian government recently suspended its much-criticized programme of establish-ing "first contacts" with previously isolated Amazonian peoples.

Communities like these are unlikely to survive. They will be destroyed by exploiters or epidemics, or assimilated into neighbouring civilizations by at-traction or acculturation. Historians and anthropologists of the future will never again have at their disposal such a well-stocked laboratory of mankind, with societies frozen for their inspection at different stages of de-velopment. The diversity these represent will, however, be continued to some extent in other forms, by groups fleeing from the culture of con-formism—especially religious sects and good-life romantics. As in the past, such escapees are likely to be on the frontiers of new colonial ventures as new environments become exploitable to improved technology; but they will also thrive in anonymous modern cities and fill their decaying shells when and if cities become obsolete environments for the human societies of the future.

A concentrated form of diversity is characteristic of recent history. The growth of colonialism in our millennium and the counter-colonization that has replaced it (see Chapter 18) have created multi-cultural societies—where different ethnicities cram their contrasting looks, dress, customs, worship, and diet into small, shared spaces. This proximity can adulterate identity, but it can also refine it; for all human groups define themselves by means of self-differentiation from their neighbours. Immersion in multicul-tural states, which will continue to be a typical experience for increasing numbers of communities in the next century, may protect distinctive tradi-tions, mentalities, and values from erosion at long range in the global vil-lage.

A phenomenon closely related to the tenacity of particular minorities in multicultural societies is the durable self-awareness of historic communities in empires and super-states. Recent history has disclosed a startling example: the emergence of long-repressed peoples from the collapsed woodwork of the Soviet Union and the Yugoslav federation. As the European Community struggles shudderingly to transform itself into a European Union, something similar is happening in western Europe: the names of small peoples, formerly current only in the vocabularies of ethnographers and folklorists, have become key terms of political discourse. Suddenly, as at the fall of the Roman Empire, the map is scattered with the names of unfamiliar tribes. Forming regional associations which often cross the frontiers of long-established states, they are turning the old Europe of "nations" into a new Europe of peoples and regions. The agglutinative process masterminded from Brussels is compatible, it seems, with this fissiparous process encouraged from Pavia or Perpignan. The politics of the monster—engorgement in ever-bigger unions—coexists with the politics of the amoeba in which small entities multiply.

A trend towards bigger states, perhaps with a teleological destination in world government, has long been predicted or detected. In part, this has been a trick of the timing: the experience of the late nineteenth century seemed to establish a momentum of state growth, as the United States survived the threat of breakup and *risorgimenti* unified Germany, Italy, and Japan. The empires destroyed by the First World War—Habsburg, Tsarist, Ottoman—were so quickly replaced by others—Soviet and Yugoslav—that the trend was assumed to be unstoppable, and more irrationally big superstates were cobbled together by departing colonialists in Africa in the late twentieth century. Now all this looks like a brief clot in the flow of history.

The supposed trend to bigger states was supported, it was thought, by improvements in communications and in the methods and range of administrative coercion. Governments could make culture uniform in the areas they controlled through the schools they operated and the propaganda they broadcast; secessions could be repressed; separatists could be exterminated. The effects have belied the expectations. Communications seem to be unable to homogenize culture; the most surprising example is that of the English language, which, until recently, was widely hailed or feared as the world medium of the future; in fact, in defiance of the predicted effects of global broadcasting, the English of the English-speaking world is breaking up into mutually unintelligible tongues, as happened with Latin in the dark ages. Krio, Pidgin, and Negerengels are already unintelligible to speakers of other forms of post-English. The street patois of African-American communities has to be translated for residents of neighbouring streets. The specialized jargon of communication on the Internet is a hieratic code, professed to exclude outsiders. Copy editors and authors on either side of the Atlantic sometimes keenly feel the width of the ocean. As for political repression, wherever it has been tested, it seems not to have worked; short of extermination, it stimulates resistance and steels identities.

If recent history has a lesson, it is that whenever a big state is nestled, smaller-scale identities and political aspirations incubate under its shell until eventually they poke their beaks through the cracks and take flight. The latest mass hatchings in the Soviet Union and Yugoslavia happened in obviously fragile states, but other, tougher eggs are likely to crack sooner or later. The Russian Federation, Canada, Ukraine, and the optimistically named United Kingdom are already looking very fragile; Italy and Spain, a little less so. In the Africa of the next century, the recent enforced reunification of Nigeria and the Congo will be seen as only a papering over of spreading cracks; most of the states of the continent were jerry-built by colonial Heath Robinsons. It is surprising that some of them have lasted so long. It is incredible that many of them can last much longer. Even in Latin America, some of the larger states have worrying fault lines: the unity of Brazil is an anomaly which its historians have never explained; there is no reason why Yucatán or Chiapas should indefinitely remain part of Mexico; the historic divisions of Argentina might recur. Provincialisms, particularisms, and mini-nationalisms are surprisingly powerful political solvents. "Aberdonian Lost at Sea," a local newspaper is said to have proclaimed in allusion to the sinking of the *Titanic*. In a world where the bells toll for all, people prefer to listen for only part of the peal.

In the long run, there is no convincing reason why even the United States and China should be immune. America seems unbreakable only because its parts are still new. The old communities of which European states are composed, with their weathered shapes, have a gimcrack look when glued together by unconvincing political fixatives. The states of the U.S.A., by comparison, are smooth at the joins, slotted together with few rough edges. They were created, in most cases, by the spread of a single allegiance, not improvised, like the European Union, out of almost innumerable particularisms, long pickled in self-regard. The American states of the union are partners who married young and for love, not crotchety old bachelors and spinsters, set in their ways, making a late marriage of convenience like their European counterparts. Even love-matches, however, often end in divorce: the American union survived a spell of trial separation in the 1860s only by the forcible reassertion of marital rights. Paradoxically, the longer the union goes on, the more time is available for the formation of regional identities, particularist allegiances, and—ultimately—secessionist tendencies in the constituent states or groups of states. The Black and Hispanic "nations" within the U.S.A.—whose self-awareness and sense of

grievance are nurtured by well-meaning federal policies of positive discrimination—may anticipate these slow-moving historic forces in breaking up
the union.

   China also has a robust reputation—less, as we have seen, because of a
long history of unity than because her periods of disunity have always been
short. She has no better head for heights than Humpty Dumpty but has
proved easier to put back together again. China is still a uniquely big zone
of shared identity, but she encloses enough tensions to split her—across
the traditional divide between north and south, or the new economic divide
between the industrializing east and the underdeveloped centre. She may
fray at the edges: the conquest of Tibet, the recovery of Hong Kong, the
possible reabsorption of Taiwan are as likely to increase the centrifugal tug
of peripheral diversity as to affirm and strengthen unity. Muslim secessionists may grow stronger in other peripheral regions, especially if the worldwide Islamic resurgence—as forecast above (see Chapter 19)—recovers
impetus. Above all, China's unity is being undermined by ideological bur-
rowing. Han Chinese nationalism is the most likely successor-ideology to
discarded Maoism, but that will be divisive in itself and will send ethnic minorities scurrying for independence or for the protection of neighbours.

   Ethnic enmity is likely to continue to be a breaker of states. It would be
comforting to believe that people get more rational in their hatreds, but no
hopes that mankind would progress in wisdom or mature in morality have
ever been fulfilled. It seems inevitable that in the next century the world
will experience more rounds of ethnic cleansing. Some of it will be of a
sickeningly familiar type, wiping away colonies detached from their
mother-communities, or vacuuming up small groups outgunned or outnumbered by hostile neighbours. Most of eastern Europe's remaining minorities,
for instance, are probably doomed. The Russian diaspora fed from the Soviet Union will be wiped out, like the German diaspora after the Second
World War, in rage and revenge. There will be no long-term future for Magyar settlements outside Hungary or Ruman communities outside Romania
and Moldova. If the new multicultural societies, where distinct ethnicities
are mingled in intimate proximity, resolve their own tensions by violence,
the massacres will be bloodier and the conflicts more prolonged.

   The gravest dangers of this sort loom in India, where the survival of a
huge and broadly spread Muslim minority will come to seem like the unfinished business of previous wars; in the United States, where inter-communal violence is gradually becoming a major cause of crime; and in western
Europe, where the tide of empires has washed a lot of vulnerable life into
isolated pools. This does not mean that no multicultural society has a
chance of survival. At the cost of massacring many of its Indians, for instance, Brazil has established a remarkable degree of harmony among a ca-
cophonous collection of other ethnic minorities; and in Latin America

generally, societies show the kind of relaxed attitudes that reflect, perhaps, centuries of comfortable miscegenation.

South Africa's attempt to grow out of racism will be a heroic failure. The renunciation of apartheid has transformed the country's image in the world with astonishing suddenness; extreme odium has turned into extreme adulation. This is the measure of the hope invested by a world which desperately needs examples of successful multicultural democracies. Gradually, South Africa's history will be seen in a correspondingly glowing light. Instead of the moral leper-nation described in traditional liberal historiography, its will come to be seen, in the same tradition, as a colonial history which was, at least in one respect, uniquely virtuous. Most of the really successful and enduring colonies which Europeans founded outside Europe to be, like South Africa, new "home countries" of their own—in what became North America, Siberia, Australia, and the South American cone—succeeded by extruding or exterminating, massacring or marginalizing the indigenous peoples. South Africa's history of mastering and exploiting native and neighbouring sources of labour looks positively benevolent by comparison. There are and can be no Native American or Aboriginal or Samoyed equivalents of the African National Congress.

From the point of view of the colony's long-term survival, however, it has to be admitted that the most ruthless policies are the most effective. Where cultural minorities are small enough to be permanently pinioned or gradually absorbed, big states which are, in a limited sense, multicultural can last indefinitely. South Africa, to her credit and her misfortune, is a bundle of large minorities; the differences between Blacks and Whites, which are potentially violent enough to justify pessimism about the country's future, are less disruptive than the divisions between historic communities not defined by colour—especially between Zulu and Xhosa. With the best of intentions, the republic has been given the wrong kind of democratic constitution. Her only viable future is as a federation of cultures, not territories, each with a treasury and traditional institutions of its own, each represented in the legislature and government in proportion not only to its numbers but also to its importance to the state. By acknowledging this, today's decision-makers might have kept a hope of lasting peace alive. As it is, even a small error on the side of centralization will be seen by some communities as an intolerable threat and will blow the state apart.

4. Cities Will Wither

Without invoking Armageddon or uttering ecospeak, it is getting easier to imagine a time when London bridges are broken down and the grass is green on Ludgate Hill. An old debate among historians, which occasionally fizzles with a little life, is about which more affects the other: technology or social change. There are lots of instances in history—and several in this book—of technological novelties which have helped to reshape societies; generally, however, societies only get the technologies they want or need. If the ancient Romans had no steam locomotion, the Chinese no rifled guns, or the Aztecs no wheelbarrows, it was for want of a use for them, not of wit to invent them. We should not, therefore, expect the present pace of technological progress to be indefinitely sustained. At any moment, investors and customers may feel satiated and the world will revert to the sort of state of arrested technical development which—despite our recent experience in some parts of the world—has been the norm in most places for most of history.

In the developed economies on which the rest of the world depends for technical innovations, the signs of impatience or revulsion are already accumulating fast. The ecological movement—though it also has broader concerns—is in part a reaction against the high energy costs of some modern technologies, which actually consume the environment irreplaceably, or seem to threaten it alarmingly, in exploiting a short-term gain of food or power. Contrary to the predictions of a decade or two ago, fashions in dress, diet, and décor have got mired in nostalgia rather than racing at the pace of science into the aesthetics of high-tech. The confusion of values in contemporary architecture arises in part from the discovery that people prefer traditionally comforting buildings to technically advanced ones. The potential of medical progress to keep people alive into a dauntingly protracted "fourth age"—or to revive their freeze-dried tissue—is viewed as a threat rather than a promise. Research in human genetics—a nightmare science to imaginers of cloned dinosaurs and sons of Frankenstein—is already subject, in most developed countries, to statutory controls, which are likely to be tightened as the moral dilemmas multiply.

There are, however, obvious areas of technological progress where society shows no sign of wanting to throw the switch: information technology, energy efficiency, and labour-saving robotics. These can revolutionize the way space is arranged and lives organized, reversing one of the most pervasive trends of modern history: the growth of cities.

Today's cities are in part the products of functions which technological progress is gradually eliminating. They are, for example, places of collaborative work, commercial exchange, and high-level education; for all these purposes it is becoming pointless to gather people together. Already it is becoming apparent that the survival of workplaces, markets, and universities (except for the study of some sciences) is like that of the internal combustion engine (see Chapter 16): a matter of vested interests, ingrained habits, and insuperable inertia rather than relative efficiency. The technology exists, or nearly exists, to replace all of them or to transform them, unrecognizably, for the better; sometime early in the next millennium it will be developed and its effects applied with relish in undoing the monster-growth that has given the world São Paulo and Mexico City and inflicted increasingly intolerable lives on the citizens of Tokyo, Los Angeles, and New York.

The city will be left with the functions of the kind of monumental "ceremonial centre" which preceded it in some societies: as a place apart for kinds of cultural experience unattainable elsewhere, for forms of entertainment, worship, and secular ritual which demand large gatherings and monumental settings. For the sake of the informal intimacy which comes from having neighbours and meeting people, including new acquaintances, face to face, the survival of villages and modest towns can be assumed. What are now sites of big cities, however, will come to conform more to the model of Eurodisney than Paris: resorts for travellers making occasional short stays; churns for a turnover in their staffs of guardians; homes to little permanent population. Some specialized seats of government, such as Canberra or Brasilia, already foreshadow this character, to the annoyance of residents who want to make them more like traditional cities.

5. INITIATIVE WILL CONTINUE TO SHIFT

I did not write this book to draw lessons from it, but the experience has convinced me that as the impact of what I have called "initiative" has grown, the pace of its shifts has quickened. The period of "Atlantic supremacy" has been brief; if a period of Pacific-rim initiative does indeed succeed it, it will probably be briefer. There is scope for regional shifts within the global pattern. Just as in the early-modern civilization of western Christendom the sources of initiative shifted from the Mediterranean to the Atlantic, so in that of the Pacific today, leadership is likely to pass, after a while, from Japan and California. New areas will take over, of potential as yet unmobilized, like China's, or under-exploited, like Australia's or Siberia's. However fast the shifts, the galactic museum-keepers will retain their long-term perspective and see our millennium as continuous with the last and the next—characterized, say, by brief challenges from Islam and the west to an otherwise almost continuous history of Chinese preponderance. Though the pattern of shifts in the past has been between regionally definable civilizations, this need not be the case in the future. Collective self-perceptions can be shared by very widespread groups; and the shifts of initiative in the next millennium may be into the hands of worldwide élites or a few masters of cybernetics, moulding world culture from a specific location through millions of modems.

* * *

I have only one more prediction—one which reviewers, at least, will be tempted to single out for assent: these predictions will be ignored or dismissed. By the time this book appears, owing to the labours of many translators, in addition to the usual pains which delay the parturition of books, it will have spent nearly two years in the press. The very fact of its simultaneous first appearance in an unprecedented number of languages and countries will attract, I hope, a brief flurry of media attention. Much of it will get deflected, I fear, away from the history onto the predictions—if, indeed, they have not all been disproved in the interim. For a short time—unless these *verba sapientibus* deter—I shall have to dodge behind columns in the club and hide behind lecterns in the library to avoid friends and well-wishers who will buttonhole me to say that they disagree with this or that prediction.

After that, comfortable silence will resume. The curse of Cassandra lies on all would-be prophets. It was not imposed by the gods; it arises from the mind. Whenever we hear a prophecy, we first doubt its veracity; then we assert its familiarity; and we end by rejecting its importance. Every true prophecy rings some chord in the hearer's breast. Like a deaf egotist attributing something dimly heard to his own original thought, he therefore assumes that he was already thoroughly aware of it and armed against its effects. Every danger alerts the defences of the ostrich, and every bearer of ill news is blamed.

Well-meaning liberals will continue to advocate abortion and euthanasia, without realizing that these are forerunners of eugenics and death camps. Aid workers will still dole out condoms. Trendy theologians will go on urging the churches to slip their moral guard. Multicultural policies will go on banking the blood of future massacres. Ragged tacking of frontiers will still condemn minorities to ethnic hemming. Big states will go on ineffectively repressing the aspirations of small peoples until they explode with the pressure of their own policies. South Africa's new rulers will try to enforce a constitution that was born outmoded. Admonished decision-makers will go on winking at warnings, as they always have done, and the world, I feel tempted to conclude, will go on getting worse.

This is meant to be comforting glumness, which reduces prospective cataclysm to the dimensions of mere disaster. The joy of revelling in pessimism is that it indemnifies us against disappointment and arms us for the worst. A few pages ago I lampooned historians as escapees into futurology; more typically, perhaps, we tend to be temperamentally pessimistic—sheltering among problems of the past from anxieties about the future. But only the certainty of change makes the luxury of nostalgia enjoyable; the glories of the past, such as they are, would be boring commonplaces if we had not lost them. A sanguine reader of my menu from the kitchen of the future might prefer to emphasize the overall balance rather than blenching at the unfamiliar items.

If, for instance, we face a totalitarian revanche, at least we can hope it will happen in smaller states. If we have to acknowledge the unpredictability of the widely forecast ecological Armageddon, at least we can congratulate ourselves in advance on probably escaping a demographic meltdown. If our descendants blow one another up, at least they will probably do it a bit at a time rather than with the terrible economy of a global holocaust. If the future is likely to be conflictive, it should be as creative as former conflicts; if it is unlikely to be any better than the past, it may be just as good. One reward of living in it will be having an even longer—and, therefore, a fuller, richer—past to look back on. Earth has not anything to show more fair, *a fortiori*, because it has nothing else to show. And it would take a dull soul to be unmoved by a glimpse of history or unexcited at the prospect of having even more of it to study.

Today, Prunier's and Alice's restaurants have both closed down. The élite is fed on "New International" cuisine, which celebrates global culture by combining ocean-spanning flavours, or respects multiculturalism in menus that list dishes of clashing colours, from different continents, in neighbourly contiguity. The next fashion may be the "new soul" cooking favoured by Black graduates in Georgia, which has dumped the fat-rich food of southern tradition in favour of delicate confections of raw or marinaded vegetables. This diners' choice is more or less what—on a larger scale—faces the world. We can go on trying to combine the ingredients of a potential global culture in an attempt to create a single civilization of universal appeal; we can labour to preserve discrete cultures in the eclectic harmony of *The Worldwide Cookbook*; we can shrink back into the environment, admit our diminished status as small stakeholders in an all-embracing ecosystem, abandon our age-old relationship of conflict with nature, and defect to her side before she swamps us. We may not turn out to be good at adapting to any of these possible futures, but at least, after a thousand years' experience of fitfully growing interdependence, we can face them with a sense of shared prospects and therefore the possibility, at least, of pooled efforts. No earlier age had access to awareness of such comprehensive menace, or of such an awesome chance.

NOTES

These notes are intended to supply references for quotations and allusions in the text and to acknowledge the authorities on which particular passages, statements, or arguments rely. In a work of this scope, bibliographical notes on a generous scale would be an impractical indulgence, but I have included a few where I thought readers seemed most likely to want them. More sparingly still, I have indicated important sources of evidence or arguments against conclusions in the text. In order to keep down the total number of notes, some are grouped; this means that readers may sometimes have to look under a catch-phrase adjacent to the passage which particularly interests them, but I have tried to limit the practice to cases which would be easy to interpret and hope the results will not be too inconvenient.

PROLOGUE

PAGE

16   *earlier club:* A. Lejeune, *The Gentlemen's Clubs of London* (1984), pp. 59–60.

17   *frontier police:* J. L. Watson, ed., *Between Two Cultures* (1986), p. 195.

17   *other way round:* E. F. Vogel, *The Four Little Dragons* (1991), p. 68.

17   *figures of fun:* The *locus classicus* is T. Heyerdahl, *The Kon-Tiki Expedition* (1950), and the *reductio ad absurdum* the same author's *The Ra Expeditions* (1971). See the remarks of J. Ray, "Heroic Decipherment," *The Times Literary Supplement,* no. 4719, 10 September 1993, p. 26.

18   *no longer reconstruct:* J. Needham, *Science and Civilisation in China,* (1954), pp. 150–248.

18   *"portion of mankind":* E. Gibbon, *The History of the Decline and Fall of the Roman Empire,* 6 vols. (1910), i, p. 1.

18   *down the line:* J. H. Elliot, *Illusion and Disillusionment: Spain and the Indies* (1991), p. 9.

19   *in search of a method:* The most important attempts include those of J. M. Roberts, *The History of the World* (1992), H. Thomas, *An Unfinished History of the World* (1986), and G. Parker, ed., *The Times Atlas of World History* (1993). Also justly acclaimed for range, brilliance, or both have been W. MacNeil, *The Rise of the West* (1976), J. M. Roberts, *The Triumph of the West* (1985), F. Braudel, *Civilisation and Capitalism,* 3 vols. (1979–84) and I. Wallerstein, *The Modern World System,* 3 vols. (1974–89), but of these the first two have a teleological scheme, and the latter pair

also make deterministic assumptions and adopt what I think is a rather restrictive set of terms of reference. Braudel and Wallerstein cover only the second half of the millennium, but J. Abu-Luhgod, *Before European Hegemony: The World System, AD 1250–1350* (1989), may be regarded as a companion volume extending Wallerstein's approach back into the late middle ages. There have been many highly successful attempts to cover relatively short periods of world history; the most useful new methods for dealing with very large tranches include the comparative approach, pioneered, for example, by the series *Comparative Studies in World History*, published by Cambridge University Press, and the virtually inimitable ways devised by K. Chaudhuri in *Asia Before Europe* (1990). The virtues of tackling a long period by combining a thematic with a comparative approach have been demonstrated, for example, by P. D. Curtin, *Cross-cultural Trade in World History* (1984), G. Parker, *The Military Revolution: Military Innovation and the Rise of the West, 1500–1800* (1990), A. W. Crosby, *Ecological Imperialism: the Biological Expansion of Europe* (1986), and M. G. S. Hodgson, *Rethinking World History: Essays on Islam and World History* (1993).

19 *"in the universe":* J. L. Borges, *Obras completas* (1977), p. 625.

20 *set of sets:* K. Chaudhuri, *Asia Before Europe*, p. 14.

20 *bit parts and footnotes:* Since I shall not have to refer to it specifically, this is an appropriate point at which to pay tribute to the importance of E. Wolf, *Europe and the People Without History* (1982).

22 *states of mind:* J. L. Apostolou and M. H. Greenberg, eds. *Murder in Japan* (1987), pp. 85–96.

22 *"is, not was":* I. Wallerstein, op. cit., i (1974), p. 9.

22 *a current theory:* N. Eldredge, *Time Frames: The Rethinking of Darwinian Evolution and the Theory of Punctuated Equilibria* (1986), especially pp. 21–22, 77–78, 83, 93, 97, 115–22, 193–223.

23 *preceding its outbreak:* See for example C. Russell, *The Origins of the English Civil War* (1971), J. S. Morrill, *The Revolt of the Provinces* (1976); A. Fletcher, *The Outbreak of the English Civil War* (1981); J. C. D. Clark, *Revolution and Rebellion* (1986); and K. Sharpe, *The Personal Rule of Charles I* (1992).

23 *accumulating smoothly:* On the First World War, see chapter 13; on the French Revolution, S. Schama, *Citizens* (1989), especially pp. 254–60, which present the outbreak of the revolution in terms similar to those adopted by revisionists in describing the coming of the English Civil War. The same thesis underlies J. F. Bosher's *The French Revolution* (1989). On the Industrial Revolution, see chapter 12 and P. O'Brien and C. Keyder, *Economic Growth in Britain and France, 1780–1914: Two Paths to the Twentieth Century* (1978) and P. Mathias and J. A. Davis, eds., *The First Industrial Revolutions* (1989).

23 *"really alive":* quoted T. J. Cobble, *Black Testimony: The Voices of Britain's West Indians* (1978), p. 156.

CHAPTER ONE: DISCRETE WORLDS

PAGE

28 *"the whole world":* I. Morris, *The World of the Shining Prince* (1964), p. 250.

28 *all to themselves:* ibid., p. 261.

29 *"cry of the* kuina *bird"*: ibid., p. 63.

29 *"public domain"*: R. Bowring, *Murasaki Shikibu: The Tale of Genji* (1988), pp. 2–4; Morris, op. cit., p. 74.

30 *"upon the water's face"*: I. Morris, *The Nobility of Failure* (1975), p. 54.

31 *he belonged:* Morris, *Shining Prince,* p. 67.

31 *"as anyone"*: ibid., ed. E. Seidensticker, 2 vols. (1976), pp. 2, 23.

31 *"a high official"*: D. Keene, *Anthology of Japanese Literature* (1974), p. 165.

31 *public spectacle:* I. Morris, *World of the Shining Prince,* pp. 36–37.

31 *"leave-taking"*: ibid., p. 223; *The Pillow Book of Sei Shonagon,* tr. I. Morris, 2 vols. (1967), i, p. 30.

33 *pines of Amanohashidate:* I. Morris, *World of the Shining Prince,* pp. 30, 46.

34 *unstamped by passion:* R. T. Paine and A. Soper, *The Art and Architecture of Japan* (1955), pp. 44–45.

34 *out of the way:* A. Soper, "The Rise of Yamato-e," *Art Bulletin,* xxiv (1942), p. 374.

35 *summer irrigation:* A. M. Watson, "The Arab Agricultural Revolution and Its Diffusion, 700–1100," *Journal of Economic History,* xxxiv (1974), pp. 8–35; see the garden imagery of Sa'di, *Selections,* tr. F. Falconer (1838).

37 *ink than mould:* L. Bolens, *Agronomes andalous au moyen-age* (1981), pp. 21–33.

38 *"magnificence" and "fear"*: M. Acién Almansa, "Madinat al-Zahra en el urbanismo musulmán," *Cuadernos de Madinat al-Zahra',* i (1987), pp. 11–26.

39 *in his life:* E. Lévi-Provençal, *España musulmana* (1950), pp. 332–45.

39 *apocalyptic flames:* M. Brett, *The Moors* (1980), p. 114.

39 *obvious unease:* Ibn 'Idari, *La caída del califato de Córdoba,* ed. F. Maíllo Salgado (1993), pp. 67–68.

41 *"other lands"*: W. Barthold, *Turkestan down to the Mongol Invasions* (1968), p. 236.

41 *been complementary:* J. A. Bayle, ed., *Cambridge History of Iran,* v (1968), pp. 4–5.

41 *whole Islamic world:* W. Barthold, op. cit., pp. 235–37.

41 *"of the period"*: R. N. Frye, *Bukhara: The Medieval Achievement* (1965), p. 59.

41 *"human life"*: ibid., p. 93.

42 *twenty-six arches:* W. Barthold, *Historical Geography of Iran* (1984), p. 64.

42 *"lustful heart"*: M. Habib Sultan, *Mahmud of Ghazni* (1967), p. 67.

43 *India or Byzantium:* R. N. Frye, "The Samanids," *Moslem World,* xxxiv (1944), pp. 40–45.

45 *tomb of her husband:* R. Grousset, *The Empire of the Steppes* (1970), p. 129.

46 *"legitimate succession"*: Jung-shen Tao, *Two Sons of Heaven* (1988), pp. 26–29.

48 *baubles apart:* ibid., p. 37.

49 *"springs of avarice" of Szechuan:* R. von Glahn, *The Country of Streams and Grottoes* (1987), p. 85.

50 *official of the state:* ibid., pp. 12, 36, 89–90.

52 *"ancestral temple"*: D. Twitchett, "Clan Reform in the Sung" in D. S. Nivison and A. F. Wright, eds. *Confucianism in Action* (1959), pp. 97–132.

52 *"music reached everywhere"*: D. S. Nivison, "A Neo-Confucian Visionary: Ou-yang Hsiu," ibid., pp. 4–9; K. Smith, P. K. Bol, J. A. Adler, and D. J. Wyatt, *Sung Dynasty Uses of the I Ching* (1990), pp. 26–29.

52 *"old tippler's pavilion"*: Yu-shih Chen, *Images and Ideas in Chinese Classical Prose* (1968), pp. 109–32.

56   *wild, painted mime:* R. Grousset, op. cit., p. 134; E. Chavannes, "Voyageurs chinois chez les Khitan et les Joutchen," *Journal Asiatique,* i (1897), p. 378.

57   *professed monk:* R. d'Abdal i de Vinyals, *L'abat Oliba, bisbe de Vic, i la seva època* (1948), p. 55.

57   *"oblige you":* ibid., p. 265.

59   *"harlots of Venus":* E. Albert i Corp, *Les abadesses de Sant Joan* (1965), p. 48.

59   *of this world:* E. Junyent, *Catalunya romànica: l'arquitectura del segle XI* (1975), pp. 154–59.

59   *his duty:* K. Leyser, *Medieval Germany and Its Neighbours* (1982), p. 7.

62   *"clothes for the whole world":* K. Leyser, *The Ascent of Latin Europe* (1986), p. 5.

62   *"perspired at mathematics":* A. Murray, *Reason and Society in the Middle Ages* (1978), p. 158.

CHAPTER TWO: THE COCKPIT OF ORTHODOXY

PAGE

66   *"by Providence":* The Alexiad (1884), pp. 24 (I, x), 165 (VI, vii), 402 (XIII, x); G. Buckler, *Anna Comnena* (1929), pp. 441–78.

66   *"of the Romans":* F. A. Wright, ed. *The Works of Liutprand of Cremona* (1930), p. 264.

67   *as a captive:* M. Fuaino, "La battaglia di Civitate," *Archivio storico pugliese,* ii (1949), pp. 124–33.

68   *Christendom avenged:* Patrologia Latina, ed. J. P. Migne, 221 vols. (1844–55), clxiii, cols. 592–838.

69   *than a monastery:* S. Runciman, *The Eastern Schism* (1955), p. 47; *Patrologia Latina,* clxiii, cols. 973–83; C. Will, *Acta et Scripta quae de Controversiis Ecclesiae Grecae et Latinae Seculo Undecimo Composita Extant* (1861), pp. 136–37; G. Schlumberger, *L'Épopée byzantine à la fin du dixième siècle,* 3 vols. (1905), iii, p. 683.

71   *procession of triumph:* see M. McCormick, *Eternal Victory* (1986), p. 178.

72   *"nurtured and fostered":* The Alexiad (1884), p. 23 (I, x).

74   *"your own family":* Strategicon, chs. 2, 39, 51; C. Mango, *Byzantium* (1972), p. 82.

75   *before his feet:* see A. Friendly, *The Dreadful Day* (1981); J. C. Cheynet, "Manntzikert: un désastre militaire?", *Byzantion,* 1 (1980), pp. 410–38, underplays the result of the Turkish victory.

75   *capture the capital:* The Alexiad (1884), pp. 285 (X, v), 294 (X, ix).

75   *"Greek treachery":* Odo of Deuil, *De Profectione Ludovic VII,* ed. V. G. Berry (1948), pp. 40, 66, 76.

76   *"impure blood":* E. Gibbon, *The History of the Decline and Fall of the Roman Empire,* vi (1978), p. 174 (ch. 60).

78   *the crusaders' camp:* D. Queller, *The Fourth Crusade* (1978), p. 72.

79   *"knees before them":* Geoffrey of Villehardouin in *Joinville and Villehardouin: Chronicles of the Crusades,* ed. M. R. B. Shaw (1963), p. 56.

79   Blachernae Palace: T. Kirova, "Un palazzo ed una casa di età tardo-bizantina in Asia minore," *Felix Ravenna,* ciii–civ (1972), pp. 275–305.

83   *"function well":* I. Sevcenko, "Theodore Metochites" in P. A. Underwood, *The Kariye Djami,* 4 vols., iv (1975), pp. 17–92.

83　*"monk among bones":* ibid., i (1966), pp. 276–79.

86　*"against the Turks":* E. Denison and E. Power, eds., *Clavijo: Embassy to Tamerlane* (1928), pp. 61–93.

86　*foot-armour:* S. Runciman, *The Fall of Constantinople* (1965), p. 144.

87　*seen today:* G. H. Hamilton, *The Art and Architecture of Russia* (1954), pp. 121–26.

88　*"unheard of":* D. Obolensky, *The Byzantine Commonwealth* (1971), p. 196.

89　*"pride or arrogance":* ibid., p. 269; G. Vernadsky et al., eds., *A Source Book for Russian History from Early Times to 1917,* 3 vols. (1972), i, p. 127.

89　*in the papal archives: Monumenta Germaniae Historica: Epistulae Seculares,* xiii, I (1883), pp. 178–9.

90　*"wedding-feast or orgy":* E. Dulaurier, "Les Mongols d'après les historiens arméniens," *Journal asiatique,* 5th s., xi (1958), pp. 210–49.

90　*"reaches us": Monumenta Germaniae Historica: Scriptores,* xxii (1872), pp. 535–36.

90　*"other world":* A. van den Wyngaert, ed., *Sinica Franciscana,* i (1929), p. 171.

90　*"impious Khan":* J. Fennell, *The Crisis of Medieval Russia* (1983), p. 88.

92　*"sovereignty from God":* J. Fennell, *Ivan the Great of Moscow* (1961), p. 121.

92　*"new Constantinople:"* D. Obolensky, op. cit., pp. 246, 255.

94　*"among men":* G. Vernadsky et al., eds. op. cit., i. p. 25.

94　*"making merry:"* A. Kindersley, *The Mountains of Serbia* (1976), p. 50.

94　*"help of angels:"* S. Radojcic, *Frescoes of Sopoćani* (1953), n. p.

CHAPTER THREE: THE TOWER OF DARKNESS

PAGE

96　*"after ejaculation":* R. P. Blake and R. N. Frye, "Notes on the *Risala* of Ibn Fadlan," *Byzantina Metabyzantina,* i, part II (1947).

97　*"in the east":* Dede Korkut, ed. G. Lewis (1974), p. 56.

97　*"vomit blood":* ibid., pp. 74–161.

99　*resemble tents:* T. Talbot Rice, *The Seljuks in Asia Minor* (1961), pp. 110, 138, 141; A. H. Hourani and S. M. Stern, eds., *The Islamic City* (1970), pp. 195–206.

102　*"without interpretation":* B. Lewis, ed., *Islam,* 2 vols. (1974), i, pp. 46–59.

103　*"I saw there":* Nasir-b.-Khurau, *Sefer Nameh,* tr. C. H. A. Schefer (1881), p. 155.

103　*under Seljuk control:* K. Chaudhuri, *Asia Before Europe* (1990), pp. 51, 391.

104　*with the work:* G. Lewis, op. cit., i, p. 56.

104　*at their own whim:* Baha ad-Din, "La Vie du Sultan Youssef," *Recueuil des historiens des croisades: historiens orientaux* (1884), iii, pp. 361–66.

105　*"with the Franks": The Travels of Ibn Jubayr,* tr. R. J. C. Broadhurst (1952). Ibn Yûbair [Ibn Jubair], *A través del oriente,* ed. F. Maíllo Salgado (1988), pp. 335–37, but cf. pp. 357–68, 377–79, 395–98.

106　*in the rest:* Baha ad-Din, op. cit., pp. 18–20.

106　*Holy War:* ibid., pp. 23–26.

109　*"live in peace":* A. van den Wyngaert, ed., *Sinica Franciscana,* i (1929), p. 227.

110　*"cattle-pest":* W. Heissig, *The Religions of Mongolia* (1980), p. 105.

110　*an Armenian monk:* R. Grousset, *The Empire of the Steppes* (1970), pp. 355–58.

111　*seventeenth centuries:* W. Heissig, op. cit., pp. 24–35.

111　*"on the spot":* Rashid al-Din, *Histoire des Mongols de la Perse [Jami al-tawarikh],* tr. E. M. Quatremère (1830), p. 229.

113 *"of the Arabs":* R. Grousset, op. cit., p. 404.

113 *cult of dawn:* M. S. Ipsiroglu, *Painting and Culture of the Mongols* (1967), pp. 60–87.

115 *his conquests:* R. Grousset, op. cit., p. 415.

115 *"our power":* Sharaf al-Din 'Ali Yazdi, *Histoire de Timur-Bec* [Nizam al-Din Shami, *Zafarnama*], tr. F. Pétis de la Croix, 4 vols. (1722), i, pp. 8–11, 127–94, 224.

116 *"ugly objects":* G. Levi della Vida in *Orientalia,* n.s., iv (1935), p. 362.

116 *force of history:* Ibn Khaldun, *The Muqaddimah,* tr. F. Rosenthal, 3 vols. (1958), i, pp. 22, 59–64; C. Julien, *History of North Africa* (1970), pp. 138–209.

119 *middle ages:* Al-Idrisi, *Opus Geographicum,* A. Bombaci et al., eds., i (1970), pp. 22–26; N. Levtzion, *Ancient Ghana and Mali* (173), pp. 10–34.

121 *"of the people":* C. Sachau, *Alberuni's India* (1914), p. 23.

122 *"in his fury":* A. Chandra Banerjee, *A New History of Medieval India* (1986), p. 194.

123 *"the year itself":* M. W. Dols, *The Black Death in the Middle East* (1977), pp. 38, 67, 69, 102–9.

123 *"the call":* Ibn Khaldun, op. cit., i, pp. 64–65.

CHAPTER FOUR: THE WORLD BEHIND THE WIND

PAGE

128 *"be boundless": South China in the XIIth Century: A Translation of Lu Yu's Travel Diaries,* tr. and ed. Chun-shu Chang and J. Smythe (1977), pp. 39, 43, 56, 65, 120, 164–69.

128 *lower Yangtze:* E. Balazs, "Une Carte des centres commerciaux de la Chine á la fin du XIe siècle," *Études Song,* iii (1976), pp. 275–80.

129 *became Peking:* Jing-shen Tao, *The Jürchen in XIIth-century China* (1976), pp. 38–40.

129 *Chinese mentality:* Hok-Lam Chan, *Legitimation in Imperial China: Discussions under the Jürcen-Chin Dynasty* (1984), pp. 68–72.

129 *demonic assailants:* J. Mirsky, *Chinese Travellers in the Middle Ages* (1968), pp. 34–82.

130 *"my brothers":* R. Grousset, *The Empire of the Steppes* (1970), p. 249.

131 *"one family":* F. W. Cleaves, "The Biography of Bayan of the Barin in the Yuan Shih," *Harvard Journal of Asiatic Studies,* xix (1956), p. 256; M. Rossabi, *Kublai Khan* (1988), p. 90.

131 *tolerant Mongka Khan: The Book of Ser Marco Polo,* ed. H. Yule, 2 vols. (1903), i, p. 348.

132 *"the people":* J. Needham, *Science and Civilisation in China,* iv, part III (1971), p. 488.

133 *"white parasol":* G. Coedès, *The Indianised States of South-east Asia* (1968), p. 218.

133 *produced locally:* J. Mirsky, op. cit., pp. 203–4, 207, 214–15.

135 *"on the Veda":* G. Coedès, op. cit., p. 173.

137 *"mountain-folk":* Marco Polo, Yule, ed., op. cit., pp. 282–88.

137 *"in its rule":* E. L. Dreyer, *Early Ming China* (1982), p. 120.

138 *inland lakes:* W. Fuchs, "Was South Africa Already Known in the XIIIth Century?", *Imago Mundi,* x (1953), p. 50.

140　*conquistadores and colonists:* T. Pigeaud, *Java in the Fourteenth Century,* 5 vols. (1960), ii, pp. 9, 15, 18, 23, 97, 99, 110; iv, pp. 37, 547; A. Reid, *Southeast Asia in the Age of Commerce,* 2 vols. (1988–93), ii, pp. 10, 39, 45; K. R. Hall, "Trade and Statecraft in the Western Archipelagoes at the Dawn of the European Age," *Journal of the Malaysian Branch of the Royal Asiatic Society,* liv, part I (1981), pp. 28, 46.

141　*"myriad years":* J. Duyvendak, "The True Dates of the Chinese Maritime Expeditions in the Early XVth Century," *T'oung Pao,* xxxiv (1938), pp. 399–412.

142　*jade-green shards:* J. Needham, op. cit., iv, part III, p. 496.

144　*even stranger:* Ma Huan, *Ying-yai sheng-lan: "The Overall Survey of the Ocean's Shores,"* ed. J. V. G. Mills (1970), pp. 69, 179.

144　*port to Mecca:* K. Chaudhuri, *Asia Before Europe* (1990), p. 126.

144　*"may be calculated":* J. Duyvendak, op. cit., pp. 349–50.

147　*"as their sign":* E. L. Dreyer, *Early Ming China* (1982), p. 17.

148　*"it is nothing":* ibid., p. 67.

CHAPTER FIVE: A SMALL PROMONTORY OF ASIA

PAGE

151　*their wines:* J. Vieillard, ed., *Le guide du pèlerin* (1950), p. 32.

152　*shrinking forests:* R. Bechmann, *Les Racines des cathédrales: l'architecture gothique, expression des conditions du milieu* (1981), pp. 141–42.

152　*unkempt coiffures:* R. Bartlett, *Gerald of Wales* (1982), p. 165.

153　*"up to then":* ibid., pp. 19–20, 158–210.

158　*share of the tax:* G. Jehel, "Catalogue analytique et chronologique des actes du notaire Petrus Batifolius," *Cahiers de Tunisie,* xxv (1977), pp. 69–135; F. Fernández-Armesto, *Before Columbus* (1987), 109–11.

158　*only to breed:* Marco Polo, *The Description of the World,* ed. A. C. Moule and P. Pelliot (1938), i, pp. 86, 270–71, 328–29, 376, 378, 424.

158　*"way of the ocean":* F. Fernández-Armesto, op. cit., p. 157.

160　*coast in 1342:* G. Grosjean, ed., *Mapa Mundi: The Catalan Atlas of the Year 1375* (1978), sheet III.

161　*"in the world":* R. Muntaner, *Crònica,* ch. 8, in F. Soldevila, ed., *Les quatre grans cròniques* (1971), pp. 673–74.

162　*surplus wealth:* F. Fernández-Armesto, op. cit., p. 27.

162　*were missionaries:* A. Rumeu de Armas, *El obispado de Telde* (1986), pp. 23–124.

163　*with excrement:* P. Partner, *The Lands of St Peter* (1972), p. 394.

163　*"Braccio takes all":* ibid., p. 397.

164　*property and power:* see for example H. Kaminsky, *A History of the Hussite Revolution* (1967), pp. 32–55; R. R. Betts, *Essays on Czech History* (1969), pp. 269–73; M. Lambert, *Medieval Heresy* (1992), pp. 77–85.

164　*intentionally schismatic:* J. V. A. Fine, *The Bosnian Church: A New Interpretation* (1975); N. Malcolm, *Bosnia: A Short History* (1994), pp. 27–42.

165　*sermons of the time:* K. B. McFarlane, *Lancastrian Kings and Lollard Knights* (1972), pp. 148–221; J. Alexander and P. Binski, eds., *Age of Chivalry: Art in Plantagenet England* (1987), p. 220; R. Varty, *Renard the Fox* (1954).

166　*citizens' property:* F. Carsten, *The Origins of Prussia* (1954), pp. 137–40, 146.

166　*humanists, Cicero:* A. Murray, *Reason and Society in the Middle Ages* (1978), pp.

231–48; P. E. Russell, "Arms Versus Letters in Fifteenth-century Castile" in A. Lewis, ed., *The New World Looks at Its History* (1967); D. S. Chambers, *The Imperial Age of Venice* (1970), p. 75; A. Altamura, "Il concetto umanistico della nobiltà e il 'De Nobilitate' del Galateo," *Archivio storico pugliese*, i (1948), p. 82.

168   *right of blood:* R. R. Betts, *op. cit*, pp. 269–73. *Ctibor Tovačovsky of Cimburk, Hádani Pravdy a Lzi a Knezskí zbozi a Panováni Jich* (1539) [The Truth Disputing with Falsehood Concerning the Clergy's Property and Domination]. I owe this reference to the kindness of Professor R. J. W. Evans.

170   *Aragonese kings, too:* F. Yates, *Astraea* (1968), pp. 1–28.

170   *"sovereign and absolute":* P. S. Lewis, *Later Medieval France: The Polity* (1968), pp. 79–100; F. Fernández-Armesto, *Ferdinand and Isabella* (1976), ch. 7.

171   *new statutes:* G. R. Elton, "The Political Creed of Thomas Cromwell" in E. B. Fryde and E. Millar, eds. *Historical Studies of the English Parliament,* 2 vols. (1970), ii, p. 205.

171   *worldwide empires:* see E. Jones, *The European Miracle* (1987), pp. 104–49; M. N. Pearson, "Merchants and States" in J. D. Tracy, ed., *The Political Economy of Merchant Empires* (1991), pp. 41–116.

171   *Portuguese service:* C. Verlinden, *The Beginnings of Modern Colonization* (1970), pp. 181–95.

174   *"marble, and writing":* R. Feuer-Tóth, *Art and Humanism in Hungary in the Age of Matthias Corvinus* (1990), pp. 68–97.

176   *Christian story:* E. .Gombrich, *Norm and Form: Studies in the Art of the Renaissance* (1966), pp. 35–57.

176   *a myth:* see P. Burke, *Tradition and Innovation in Renaissance Italy* (1978); *The Italian Renaissance: Culture and Society in Italy* (1986), pp. 124–30.

176   *"Human Workmanship":* G. M. Rushforth, "Magister Gregorius De Mirabilibus Urbis Romae: A New Description of Rome in the Twelfth Century," *Journal of Roman Studies,* ix (1919), pp. 14–58.

176   *a classical building:* W. Oakeshott, *Classical Inspiration in Medieval Art* (1959), pp. 85–86, 92–93, plates 119–23; S. Ray, "L'Architettura di Brunelleschi e l'idea di 'antico' nella cultura fiorentina del primo quattrocento" in *Filippo Brunelleschi: la sua opera e il suo tempo,* 2 vols. (1980), ii, pp. 381–88.

177   *from Aristotle:* W. H. K. Guthrie, *A History of Greek Philosophy,* vi: *Aristotle, an Encounter* (1981), pp. 1–3.

177   *years before:* R. W. Southern, *The Making of the Middle Ages* (1967), pp. 166–77.

178   *plot by plot:* L. D. Reynolds and L. G. Wilson, *Scribes and Scholars* (1974), pp. 102–3.

178   *"age of iron":* H. Kamen, *The Iron Century* (1979), p. 1.

182   *to see it:* Fernández-Armesto, *Before Columbus,* pp. 148, 171–92; A. Navarro González, *El mar en la literatura medieval castellana* (1962), pp. 241–311.

182   *social origins:* M. Girouard, *The Return to Camelot* (1981), pp. 87–110; L. P. Fernández-Armesto, "The Experience of Officers in a New Service: The RAF between the Wars," London University M. A. dissertation, 1980.

Chapter Six: Shy and Retiring Empires

PAGE

185 *"the Great Cairo":* B. Díaz del Castillo, *Historia verdadera de la conquista de la Nueva España,* 2 vols. (1968), i, p. 45.

187 *the largest building:* C. Bruce Hunter, *A Guide to Ancient Maya Ruins* (1986), p. 309.

190 *of west Africa:* R. Oliver and A. Atmore, *The African Middle Ages* (London, 1982), p. 30.

190 *a generation later:* G. de Carvajal et al., *La aventura del Amazonas* (1986), pp. 59–94; D. Lathrop, *The Upper Amazon* (1968), pp. 43–57.

190 *world history:* except for those of the Aztecs and Incas, these societies are barely mentioned in this period in the works listed above (Prologue), though F. Braudel, *Civilisation and Capitalism,* 3 vols. (London, 1985), iii, pp. 404–5, deals with Mali and Mwene Mutapa only in connexion with European expansion.

191 *Europe nor Asia:* G. Grosjean, *Mapa Mundi: The Catalan Atlas of the Year 1375* (1978), sheet IV.

191 *at their height:* the account of the Saharan journey is based on *Ibn Battuta: Travels in Africa,* ed. H. A. R. Gibb (1929), pp. 317–19.

193 *he had borrowed:* N. Levtzion, *Ancient Ghana and Mali* (1973), pp. 108–9; E. W. R. Bovill, *The Golden Trade of the Moors* (1970), pp. 85–91.

194 *overthrow its oppressors:* D. T. Niane, *Sundjata* (Paris, 1991).

194 *outstretched arms:* D. T. Niane, ed., *UNESCO General History of Africa,* iv (1984), pp. 131, 162–63.

195 *"a black cow":* ibid., p. 150.

195 *sexual organs:* E. W. R. Bovill, op. cit., p. 91n.

196 *silver plate:* P. E. Russell, "White Kings on Black Kings," *Medieval and Renaissance Studies in Honour of Robert Brian Tate* (Oxford, 1986), pp. 151–63.

197 *"reason, like us":* M. Jiménez de la Espada, ed., *Libro de conoscimiento de todos los reinos, tierras y señoríos que son en el mundo* (1870), p. 14.

197 *linen stole:* A. Kammerer, *La Mer Rouge, l'Abyssinie et l'Arabie au XVIe et XVIe siècles,* iv (1947), Plate 23.

198 *Shoa and Gojam:* R. Oliver, ed., *Cambridge History of Africa,* iii (1977), pp. 159–60.

199 *"stars in the sky":* *The Prester John of the Indies,* ed. C. W. F. Beckingham and G. W. B. Huntingford, 2 vols. (Cambridge, 1961), i, pp. 266–307.

199 *exposure of royal infants:* Kammerer, op. cit., p. 10.

201 *"and their reliquaries":* ibid., p. 20.

201 *"moths at a lamp":* R. Oliver, ed., *Cambridge History,* p. 174.

201 *men could have made it:* J. de Barros, *Asia,* dec. X, bk. 1, ch. 1; W. G. Randles, *The Empire of Monomotapa* (Harare, 1981), pp. 188–89.

202 *centre of gravity:* P. S. Garlake, "Pastoralism and Zimbabwe," *Journal of African History,* xix (1978), pp. 479–93; R. Oliver and A. Atmore, op. cit., p. 170.

204 *oceanic trade:* W. G. Randles, op. cit., p. 3.

205 *collapse of the state:* R. B. Parker and R. Sabin, *A Practical Guide to Islamic Monuments in Cairo* (1981), pp. 16–93, esp. pp. 77, 80.

206 *sultan of Fez:* C. Julien, *History of North Africa* (1970), p. 225.

207 *Aztecs and Incas:* H. de Castries, "La conquête du Soudan par el Mansour," *Hespéris,* iii (1923), pp. 433–88; E. W. R. Bovill, op. cit., pp. 154–87.

207 *merchant in Marrakesh:* ibid., p. 190.

208 *own oracles:* J. Villagutierre Sotomayor, *Historia de la conquista de la provincia del Itza* (1933), pp. 303–11; N. M. Farriss, *Maya Society under Colonial Rule* (1984), p. 70.

211 *each of its corners:* Archivo General de Simancas, Mapas, Planos y Dibujos, II–14.E, leg. 7381–71.

211 *"Inca-king of Peru":* D. A. Brading, *The First America* (Cambridge, 1991), p. 489.

211 *"would betray me":* Hernán Cortés: *Letters from Mexico,* ed. A. R. Pagden (New York, 1971), p. 52.

211 *"he might be":* ibid., p. 50.

212 *three thousand citizens:* ibid., p. 73.

212 *to follow him:* J. Hemming, *The Conquest of the Incas* (1983), pp. 199–200.

213 *own nobility:* B. Díaz del Castillo, op. cit., i, pp. 260, 270–77.

213 *a crusade:* ibid., p. 115; F. López de Gómara, *Historia general de las Indias,* 2 vols. (Barcelona, 1966), ii, p. 40.

213 *"apostolic" church:* Hernán Cortés, op, cit., pp. 332–34.

213 *"dangerous it was":* ibid., p. 138.

214 *powdered foods: Codex Mendoza,* ed. J. Cooper Clark, 3 vols. (1931–32), i, ff. 19–55.

214 *"something else":* B. Díaz del Castillo, op. cit., i, pp. 271–73.

214 *tortillas:* F. Berdan, *The Aztecs of Central Mexico* (1982), p. 39.

214 *conversion of the Indians: Historia de los indios de la Nueva España,* ed. G. Baudot (1985), pp. 97–98.

216 *Duke of Plaza Toro:* "Lienzo de Tlaxcala" reproduced in A. Chavero, ed., *Antigüedades mexicanas* (Mexico, 1892).

216 *"we have been waiting":* Hernán Cortés, op. cit., p. 98.

216 *Bernardino de Sahagún:* A. Anderson and C. Dibble, eds., *Florentine Codex,* 13 vols. (1953–82), especially pp. ix, 17–19, xii, 1–3; *Historia general de las cosas de la Nueva España,* ed. A. M. Garibay (1939), especially pp. 722–26, 759–63.

218 *alien heritage:* F. Fernández-Armesto, 'Aztec' Auguries and Memories of the Conquest of Mexico," *Renaissance Studies,* vi (1992), pp. 287–305. H. Thomas, *The Conquest of Mexico* (1993), p. 43, points out that there really was a comet visible in 1506; but this was a long time before Cortés arrived, and the passing of a year of ill omen was celebrated in 1507; according to the usual cycle of fifty-two years, the next was a long way off when the Spaniards invaded.

219 *Aztec past:* F. Gómez de Orozco, "¿Quién fue el autor material del códice Mendocino?", *Revista mexicana de estudios antropológicos,* v (1941), pp. 43–52.

219 *position of fear: Codex Mendoza,* op. cit., f. 2r.

220 *kilometres of territory:* R. Hassig, *Aztec Warfare* (1988), pp. 201–20.

220 *"estate and majesty": Codex Mendoza,* op. cit., ff. 15–16.

224 *Lake Yahuar-Cocha:* P. Cieza de León, *The Incas,* ed. W. von Hagen (1959), p. 252.

224 *had been resettled:* N. Wachtel, "The *Mitimas* of the Cochabamba Valley: The colonisation policy of Huayna Capac" in G. A. Collier, R. I. Rosaldo and J. D. Wirth, eds., *The Inca and Aztec States, 1400–1800* (1982), pp. 199–235.

CHAPTER SEVEN: THE REACH OF CONQUEST

PAGE

226   *in the 1580s:* G. Sansom, *A History of Japan, 1334–1615* (1961), pp. 316–19.

228   *mastery of the world: Cambridge History of Japan,* iv, ed. J. W. Hall (1991), pp. 84–89, 263, 394.

229   *"prey of them all":* Park Yune-hee, *Admiral Yi Sun-shin and His Turtleboat Armada* (1973), pp. 72–73.

229   *self-aggrandizement: Nanjung Ilgi: War Diary of Admiral Yi Sun-sin,* tr. Ha Tae-hung and Sohn Pau-key (1977).

229   *"save the country:"* ibid., p. 203; A. L. Sadler, "The Naval Campaign in the Korean War of Hideyoshi, 1592–8; *Transactions of the Asiatic Society of Japan,* 2nd s., xiv (1937), pp. 177–208.

231   *"to be conveyed":* P. J. D'Orléans, *History of the Tartar Conquerors of China,* ed. the Earl of Ellesmere (1854), pp. 102–32.

232   *1,802 caravanserais:* R. Savory, *Iran under the Safavids* (1980), pp. 154–76.

232   *"Ismail remembered":* Venetians in Persia (1873), p. 206.

233   *"nothing like it":* K. Chaudhuri, *Asia Before Europe* (1990), p. 364.

235   *"like paradise":* S. P. Blake, *Shahjahanabad* (1991), pp. ii, 30.

235   *"melons and grapes":* M. Hasan, *Babur* (1985), pp. 47, 74, 126–27; S. F. Drake, "Steppe Humanism: the Autobiographical Writings of Zahir al-Din Muhammad Babur, 1483–1530," *International Journal of Middle East Studies,* xxi (1990), pp. 48–49.

235   *"intent on conquests":* S. M. Burke, *Akbar, the Great Mogul* (1989), pp. 1, 27, 31, 37.

236   *surface distances:* S. Gole, *Indian Maps* (1989), p. 47; *The Times Atlas of World Exploration* (1991), p. 28.

237   *oceanic highways:* F. C. Lane, "The Mediterranean Spice Trade: Its Revival in the Sixteenth Century" in *Venice and History* (1963), pp. 22–23; "The Mediterranean Spice Trade: Further Evidence for Its Revival in the Sixteenth Century" in B. Pullan, ed., *Crisis and Change in the Venetian Economy* (1971), pp. 52–53.

239   *"where they are":* N. Penzer, *The Harem* (1937), pp. 83, 112–17.

241   *"appearance of men":* S. von Herberstein, *Notes upon Russia,* ed. R. H. Major, 2 vols. (1852), ii, p. 42.

241   *to nourish them:* ibid., p. 58.

242   *"whereinto they entered":* R. Hakluyt, *The Principal Navigations, Voyages, Traffics and Discoveries of the English Nation,* 2 vols. (1959), i, p. 271.

242   *eye of Christ:* T. Armstrong, ed., *Yermak's Campaign in Siberia* (1975), pp. 88, 108.

243   *wrong colour:* I am grateful to Dr. Stuart Frank for this information. See S. M. Frank, *Inventory of Paintings and Drawings in the Kendall Whaling Museum* (forthcoming).

244   *wavering frontier:* C. Bickford O'Brien, *Russia under Two Tsars* (1952), pp. 105–22.

244   *"miles of property":* J. Bell, *A Journey from St. Petersburg to Pekin, 1719–22,* ed. J. L. Stephenson (Edinburgh, 1967), p. 110.

245   *archive in London:* Public Record Office, S. P. 94/4.

247   *Delagoa Bay:* C. R. Boxer, ed. *The Tragic History of the Sea* (1959), pp. 9, 25–26.

247   *royal arms:* D. Galvao, "Crónica de Dom Alfonso Henriques," Biblioteca Pública Municipal do Porto, f.1.

248 *even since then:* G. Schurhammer, *Francis Xavier,* 2 vols. (1977), ii, pp. 147–52.

252 *scientific proximity: Carlos III y la ilustración,* ed M. C. Iglesias et al., 2 vols. (1989), i, pp. 274, 295–301; ii, 712–21.

253 *"appears impossible": Cristóbal Colón: textos y documentos completos,* ed. C. V. Varela (1984), p. 146.

254 *out of steam:* E. Christiansen, *The Northern Crusades* (1980), pp. 109–17, 177–82.

255 *only one picture:* H. R. Trevor-Roper, *The Plunder of the Arts in the Seventeenth Century* (1970), pp. 39–40, 44–45.

257 *radical one:* H. R. Trevor-Roper, *Religion, the Reformation and Social Change* (1967), pp. 1–45.

257 *on the map:* O. H. K. Spate, *Monopolists and Freebooters* (1983), p. 180.

CHAPTER EIGHT: THE TOUCH OF EMPIRE

PAGE

258 *"your country is:"* Zhu Hong, ed., *The Chinese Western* (1988), p. 118.

259 *delicacies in 1788:* J. Waley-Cohen, *Exile in Mid-Qing China* (1991), pp. 105, 152–54.

259 *to the Chinese:* O. Lattimore, *Studies in Frontier History* (1962), p. 193.

260 *tenants of the natives:* J. Waley-Cohen, op. cit., pp. 15–18.

261 *Manchu language:* H. G. Lee, *The Manchurian Frontier in Ch'ing History* (1970), p. 22.

261 *keep Chinese in:* C. Blunden and M. Elvin, *Cultural Atlas of China* (1984), p. 33.

261 *"a younger brother":* R. H. G. Lee, op. cit., pp. 81–82.

262 *peasant migrants:* R. Grousset, *The Empire of the Steppes* (1970), pp. 538–39; Tu li-Sen, *Narrative of a Chinese Embassy to the Khan of the Torghuts* (1981).

262 *in search of it:* Lord Amherst of Hackney, *The Discovery of the Solomon Islands* (1901).

262 *colonization:* C. Sánchez-Albornoz, *España: un enigma histórico.* 2 vols. (1956), i, p. 15.

262 *return home:* P. J. D'Orléans, *History of the Tartar Conquerors of China,* ed. the Earl of Ellesmere (1854), pp. 102–32.

262 *"Tatars, and Russians":* T. Armstrong, ed. *Yermak's Campaign in Siberia* (1975), p. 42.

262 *moved on:* D. Rutman, *Winthrop's Boston* (1965), p. 23.

263 *official treaties:* G. D. Winius, "Portugal's Shadow Empire in the Bay of Bengal," in *Os Mares da Asia, 1500–1800: sociedades locais, portugueses e a expansão de Europa: Revista de cultura de Macau,* vol. v (1991), Part I, pp. 273–87.
"free spirits": F. Gorges, *A Briefe Narration of the Original Undertakings of the Advancement of Plantations into the Parts of America* (1658), p. 2.

263 *bigger than Saint Peter's:* F. Fernández-Armesto, *Before Columbus* (1987), p. 201.

264 *to be funny: Don Quixote,* ii, p. 53.

265 *"in anyone's service":* I. Altman, *Emigrants and Society: Extremadura and America in the Sixteenth Century* (1960), pp. 21–74.

265 *of Nova Scotia:* C. Nish, *Les bourgeois gentilshommes de la Nouvelle France, 1729–48* (1968).

265 *affectations of display:* N. Canny, *The Upstart Earl: A Study of the Social and Mental World of Richard Boyle, First Earl of Cork* (1982), pp. 9–19.

265 *"all merry":* A. L. Rowse, *The Expansion of Elizabethan England* (1981), pp. 136, 155.

265 *hostage towns:* J. Lorimer, *English and Irish Settlement on the Amazon* (1989), p. 164.

265 *of the Perizzites:* J. Parker, "Religion and the Virginia Company" in K. R. Andrews et al., *The Westward Enterprise* (1978), pp. 245–70.

266 *becoming heretics:* I. Mather, *A Brief Relation of the State of the New England* (1689), p. 3; J. Lorimer, op. cit., p. 303.

266 *"in my life":* J. Winthrop, *Journal*, ed. J. K. Hosmer, 2 vols. (1908), i, pp. 51–67; ii, 302–20.

266 *"God has given":* S. Urlsperger, *Der ausfürlichen Nachrichten von der Colonie Salzburgischer Emigranten erster Theil*, 3 vols. (1741–52), i, p. 52.

267 *hive of industry:* B. Edwards, *The History, Civil and Commercial, of the British Colonies in the West Indies* (1801).

269 *state of Georgia:* C. de Rochefort, *Histoire naturelle et morale des Iles Antilles de l'Amérique* (1681).

269 *those of Europe:* D. Brading, *The First America* (1991), pp. 428–62.

269 *also Black:* P. Gerhard, "A Black Conquistador in Mexico," *Hispanic American Historical Review*, lviii (1978), pp. 451–59.

271 *victim-societies:* See for example M. Aklein, "The Impact of the Atlantic Slave Trade on the Societies of Western Sudan" in J. E. Inikori et al., *The Atlantic Slave Trade* (1992), pp. 25–48.

271 *suit of armour:* I. A. Akimjogbin, *Dahomey and Its Neighbours, 1708–1818* (1967), p. 108.

272 *former kings:* A. Dalzel, *History of Dahomy* (1793), opp. p. viii, pp. xiv–xv.

272 *only when rustled:* J. F. A. Ajayi and M. Crowder, eds., *History of West Africa*, i (1985), pp. 39–40, 639–40; D. Henige and M. Johnson, "Agaja and the Slave Trade: Another Look at the Evidence," *History in Africa*, iii (1976), pp. 57–67.

273 *attendants on foot:* R. Law, "A West African Cavalry State: The Kingdom of Oyo," *Journal of African Studies*, xvi (1975), pp. 1–15.

273 *carry out abductions:* R. Oliver, *The African Experience* (1991), pp. 155–56; I. Wilks, *Asante in the Nineteenth Century* (1975), pp. 80–88.

273 *slaves who survived:* P. Hogg, *Slavery, The Afro-American Experience* (1979), pp. 20–30.

275 *slaves themselves:* H. G. Gutman, *The Black Family in Slavery and Freedom* (1976).

275 *African than European:* J. Thornton, *Africa and the Africans in the Making of the Atlantic World, 1400–1680* (1992), especially pp. 129–205.

275 *kept them repressed:* A. J. R. Russell-Wood, *The Black Man in Slavery and Freedom in Colonial Brazil* (1982), pp. 83–94.

275 *rum and tobacco:* ibid., pp. 104–27; W. Beckford, *Remarks upon the Situation of the Negroes in Jamaica* (1788).

276 *"invention into England":* R. Halsband, *The Life of Lady Mary Wortley Montague* (1986), pp. 71–72, 80–81, 104, 109–12.

276 *effective killers:* for an alternative view, based on the weakly infectious character of the modern smallpox virus, see F. Brooks, "The First Impact of Smallpox: What was the Impact of the Columbian Exchange?" in A. Disney, ed., *Columbus and the Consequences of 1492* (1994), pp. 33–44.

276 *seventeenth century:* D. B. Quinn, *New American World* (1979), p. 276.

277 *"skin with scissors":* J. Hemming, *Red Gold: The Conquest of the Brazilian Indians* (1978), pp. 140–45.

277 *leads them:* D. Vandiera, *Neuer Welt-Bot* (1733), p. 20.

277 *visitations of plague:* ibid., p. 274.

279 *edges of its empire:* Archivo General de Simancas, Mapas, Planos y Diseños, XXVII-7. S.G., leg. 6951; *Documentación indiana en Simancas* (1990), p. 254.

280 *image of the old:* H. Pérez de Oliva, *Obras* (1586), f. 133.

CHAPTER NINE: THE EMBRACE OF EVANGELIZATION

PAGE

284 *in the straits:* P. Wheatley, *The Golden Khersonese* (1961), p. 312.

285 *his hounds:* B. W. and L. Y. Andaya, *A History of Malaysia* (1982), pp. 32–35.

285 *the deceased:* D. G. E. Hall, *A History of South-East Asia* (1968), p. 213; C. H. Wake, "Melaka in the Fifteenth Century: Malay Historical Traditions and the Politics of Islamization" in K. Singh Sandhu and P. Wheatley, eds. *Melaka: The Transformation of a Malay Capital,* 2 vols. (1983), i, pp. 128–61.

285 *"one's neck":* R. Winstedt, *The Malays: A Cultural History* (1958), pp. 33–44.

288 *neighbouring states:* M. Hiskett, *The Development of Islam in West Africa* (1984), pp. 33–38.

289 *Islamic law:* ibid., p. 56.

290 *"in open country":* P. Burke, *Popular Culture in Early Modern Europe* (1979), p. 214.

293 *English Protestants:* D. Fenlon, *Heresy and Obedience in Tridentine Italy* (1972).

294 *"all was light":* W. M. Conway, *Literary Remains of Albrecht Dürer* (1889), p. 159; G. Strauss, *Nuremberg in the Sixteenth Century* (1966), p. 170.

295 *fiction of the day:* F. Fernández-Armesto, "Cardinal Cisneros as Patron of Printing," *God and Man in Medieval Spain: Essays in Honour of J. R. L. Highfield,* ed. D. W. Lomax and D. Mackenzie (1989), pp. 149–68.

295 *wholesome devotion:* D. de Estella, *A Method unto Mortification: Called Heretofore, The Contemt of the World and the Vanitie Thereof,* ed. J. Rogers (1608).

295 *saints' "merriment":* A. Pagden, *European Encounters with the New World* (1992), p. 119.

295 *meant Thunder:* A. Métraux, *La religion des Tupinambes* (1928), pp. 52–56.

295 *low-browed and unkempt:* O. Benesch, *The Art of the Renaissance in Northern Europe* (1965), pp. 38–39.

297 *unprompted by images:* K. K. S. Ch'en, *Buddhism in China* (1964), p. 448.

297 *latter days:* Masahara Anesaki, *History of Japanese Religion* (1963), pp. 307–8.

298 *farthest frontier:* V. Fraser, *The Architecture of Conquest* (1990), pp. 13–20, 160–67.

300 *left behind:* R. Gott, *Land Without Evil* (1993), pp. 150–51.

300 *"on their bodies":* I. Clendinnen, *Ambivalent Conquests* (1987), pp. 74–76.

301 *"guided the balls":* J. Hemming, *Red Gold* (1978), pp. 266–71.

301 *European colonists:* N. Salisbury, "Red Puritans: The 'Praying Indians' of Massachusetts Bay and John Eliot," *William and Mary Quarterly,* 3rd s., xxxi (1974), pp. 27–54.

301 *their temptations:* R. Ricard, *La conquista espiritual de México* (1947), pp. 187, 199.

303 *creole theocracy:* F. E. Marcos, *Tadhana,* ii, part II (1977), p. 183; M. Bataillon, *Études sur Bartolomé de Las Casas* (1965), pp. 309–24.

303 *years before:* F. Ximénez, *Historia de la provincia de San Vicente Chiapa y Guatemala,* 3 vols. (1929–30).

303 *pagan gods:* K. R. Mills, The Religious Encounter in Mid-colonial Peru, D.Phil. thesis, Oxford University, pp. 289–94.

304 *New Worlds alike:* B. Feijóo, *Treatro crítico-universal,* 3 vols. (1981), pp. i, 7–64; ii, 12–25, 35–44; O. Chadwick, *The Popes and European Revolution* (1981), p. 395.

304 *some penances:* F. E. Marcos, op. cit., pp. 138–64.

305 *unsurpassed thoroughness:* C. R. Boxer, *The Christian Century in Japan* (1993), pp. 308–62.

306 *client-states:* O. Lattimore, *Inner Asian Frontiers of China* (1951), pp. 84–86.

308 *"dog dung":* W. Heissig, *The Religions of Mongolia* (1980), pp. 24–38.

CHAPTER TEN: THE TANGLE OF TRADE

PAGE

310 *sterling in 1828:* D. Wilson, *Rothschild* (1988), pp. 35–99; E. Corti, *The Rise of the House of Rothschild* (1928), i, p. 458.

313 *towards the reparations:* H. F. MacNair, *Modern Chinese History: Select Readings* (1927), i, pp. 51–55; A. W. Hummel, *Eminent Persons of the Ch'ing Period,* 3 vols. (1943–44), s.v. Wu. I am grateful to Sebastian Fernández-Armesto for drawing my attention to the importance of Howqua.

313 *exported in exchange:* M. Wilson, ed., *Johnson: Poetry and Prose* (1950), pp. 333–47.

315 *his era lay:* L. Dermigny, *La Chine et l'occident: le commerce à Canton au XVIIIe siècle,* 4 vols. (1964), i, p. 23; F. Braudel, *Civilisation and Capitalism;* iii: *The Perspective of the World* (1984), p. 464; O. Aubry, *Napoléon* (1964), p. 43.

315 *native merchants:* J. C. van Leur, *Indonesian Trade and Society* (1955), pp. 226–45; see also M. A. P. Meilinck-Roelofsz, *Asian Trade and European Influence in the Indonesian Archipelago between 1500 and c. 1630* (1962); cf. above, p. 254.

316 *lost fortunes:* L. Blussé, *Strange Company: Chinese Settlers, Mestizo Women and the Dutch in Batavia* (1986), pp. 50–72.

317 *unhealthiness:* ibid., pp. 26–29.

317 *"drunk and dined":* ibid., p. 95.

319 *year of losses:* M. Guerrero et al., *The Chinese in the Philippines,* 2 vols. (1966), i, pp. 15–174.

320 *pairs of spectacles:* O. H. K. Spate, *The Pacific since Magellan; ii Monopolists and Freebooters* (1983), p. 59.

321 *Japan produced:* C. R. Boxer, *The Dutch Seaborne Empire* (1973), pp. 223–24.

321 *regional economy:* K. N. Chaudhuri, *Trade and Civilization in the Indian Ocean* (1985), pp. 105, 224–47; P. D. Curtin, *Cross-cultural Trade in World History* (1984), pp. 137–48, 158–60; A. Disney, *Twilight of the Pepper Empire: Portuguese Trade in South-west India in the Early Seventeenth Century* (1978), pp. 32–36; C. H. H. Wake, "The Changing Pattern of Europe's Pepper and Spice Imports, c. 1400–1700," *Journal of European Economic History,* viii (1979), pp. 361–403, with corrections on figures for the fifteenth century by the same author, "The Volume of

European Spice Trade at the Beginning and End of the Fifteenth Century," ibid., xv (1986), pp. 621–35; S. Subrahmanyam and L. F. F. R. Thomaz, "Evolution of Empire" in J. Tracy, ed., *Merchants and Empires* (1991), pp. 361–403.

321 *pledged to Armenians:* ibid., pp. 24–42. The cape route did contribute, however, to an abrupt decline of the overland caravan trade in the early seventeenth century. N. Steensgard, *The Asian Trade Revolution of the Seventeenth Century: The East India Companies and the Decline of the Caravan Trade* (1974), especially pp. 152–83.

322 *interlopers copied:* The Travels of Ludovico di Varthema, tr. and ed. J. Winter Jones and G. P. Badger (1863), pp. 65–73; *The Times Atlas of World Exploration* (1991), p. 212.

322 *their own junks:* M. A. P. Meilink-Roelofsz, *Asian Trade and European Influence in the Indonesian Archipelago between 1500 and c. 1630* (1962), p. 262.

322 *competitors of the Dutch:* C. F. G. Simkin, *The Traditional Trade of Asia* (1968), pp. 228–29.

322 *gunpoint in 1684:* H. Furber, *Rival Empires of Trade in the Orient* (1976), pp. 85–87.

323 *"better Malacca":* C. R. Boxer, *Francisco Vieira de Figueiredo: A Portuguese Merchant-Venturer in South-East Asia* (1967), p. 3.

323 *striking clock:* J. S. Cummins, ed., *Travels and Controversies of Friar Domingo Navarrete* (1962), pp. 113–25, 267–68.

323 *magnificently appointed yacht:* Boxer, op. cit., pp. 1–53.

324 *Dutch colony:* ibid., p. 26.

324 *make their land unattractive:* A. Reid, *Southeast Asia in the Age of Commerce*, 2 vols (1988–93), ii, pp. 277–81, 298–303.

327 *"into our bosom":* S. Schama, *The Embarrassment of Riches: An Interpretation of Dutch Culture in the Golden Age* (1987), p. 300.

327 *"superior in riches":* ibid., p. 293.

327 *Venetian counterparts:* P. Burke, *Venice and Amsterdam* (1974), p. 61.

328 *June and August:* ibid., pp. 70, 106.

328 *"in Amsterdam":* B. de Mandeville, *The Fable of the Bees*, ed. D. Garman (1934), p. 144, quoted in S. Schama, op. cit., p. 297.

329 *the same period:* P. Burke, op. cit., p. 93; S. Schama, op. cit., pp. 311–14.

329 *eighteenth century:* D. Howard, *The Architectural History of Venice* (1989), pp. 186–88.

329 *sixteenth and seventeenth centuries:* J. H. Elliott, *Europe Divided* (1968), pp. 43–69; F. Braudel, *El Mediterraneo y el mundo mediterraneo en la época de Felipe II*, 2 vols. (1953), i, pp. 389–547.

330 *early seventeenth century:* G. Parker, *The Dutch Revolt* (1977), pp. 249–50.

330 *in the world:* J. Israel, *Dutch Primacy in World Trade* (1989), p. 78.

331 *fed, and reassured:* J. Brown, *Images and Ideas in Seventeenth-century Spanish Painting* (1978), pp. 128–46.

332 *image of the city:* A. Domínguez Ortiz, *La Sevila del siglo XVII* (1984), pp. 13–82, 115–46, 175–248; P. Chaunu, *Conquête et exploitation des nouveaux mondes* (1969), pp. 271–314.

333 *surrogate empire:* H. Kamen, "The Decline of Spain: A Historical Myth?," *Past and Present*, no. 81 (1978), pp. 24–50.

334 *they were exported:* Cf. above, pp. 275–82; B. L. Solow, ed., *Slavery and the Rise of the Atlantic System* (1991).

334 *"an Atlantic economy"*: S. L. Engermann and P. K. O'Brien, in ibid., pp. 177–209.

336 *distant colonies:* A. Guimera Ravina, *Burguesía extranjera y comercio atlántico* (1985), pp. 58–93, 229–59, 317–35.

336 *seventeenth century:* H. Kamen, *La España de Carlos II* (1981).

Chapter Eleven: The Atlantic Chasm

PAGE

340 *in the old world:* The Rhode Island Historical Society, *A Most Magnificent Mansion* (1965).

342 *more than doubled:* B. Bailyn, *Voyagers to the West: Emigration from Britain to America on the Eve of the Revolution* (1987), pp. 8–20.

343 *democracy instead:* ibid., p. 23.

343 *European tradition:* J. G. Pococke, *Virtue, Commerce and History* (1985), pp. 73–88; J. G. Pococke, *The Machiavellian Moment* (1975), pp. 48–82, 156–219; B. Bailyn, *The Ideological Origins of the American Revolution* (1967), pp. 22–54; C. Robbins, *The Eighteenth-century Commonwealthman* (1960); J. C. D. Clark, *The Language of Liberty 1660–1832* (1994).

344 *"in our infancy":* J. McLaughlin, *Jefferson and Monticello* (1986), pp. 14, 36, 56, 102, 209, 229, 289, 357–59; S. R. Stein, *The Worlds of Thomas Jefferson at Monticello* (1993).

345 *"Gothic pedestal":* S. Bolivar, *Obras completas,* ed. V. Lecuna, 3 vols. (1964), i, p. 165.

346 *erect crosses:* J. Lafaye, *Quetzalcoatl y Guadalupe* (1985), pp. 264–65.

346 *the Tupinamba: Cristóbal Colón: textos y documentos completos,* ed. C. Varela (1984), p. 55; B. de Sahagún, *Historia general de las cosas de la Nueva España* (1989), p. 36; *The Maya: Diego de Landa's Account of the Affairs of Yucatán,* ed. A. Pagden (1975), p. 75; J. Hemming, *Red Gold: The Conquest of the Brazilian Indians* (1978), p. 47; J. Lafaye, op. cit., p. 233.

346 *victimization:* J. Muldoon, *Popes, Lawyers and Infidels* (1979).

347 *of the Eucharist:* B. de Las Casas, *Apologética historia sumaria,* ed. E. O'Gorman, 2 vols. (1967), ii, pp. 187–257; S. T. Mier, *Escritos inéditos,* ed. J. M. Miquiel and H. Díaz Thomé (1944), p. 141.

347 *province of Peru:* J. Lafaye, op. cit., pp. 267–69.

347 *"feathered serpent":* ibid., pp. 225–97.

348 *"the Feathered Serpent":* ibid., p. 283.

348 *"interests are distinct":* D. Brading, *The First America: The Spanish Monarchy, Creole Patriots and the Liberal State* (1991), pp. 583–602.

350 *travelling time:* F. Mauro, *Le Portugal et L'Atlantique* (1960), pp. 21–28, 71–74; A. J. R. Russell-Wood, *A World on the Move: The Portuguese in Africa, Asia and America* (1992), pp. 34–35.

350 *wealth of Brazil:* S. Schwarz, "The Formation of a Colonial Identity in Brazil," *Colonial Identity in the Atlantic World,* ed. N. Canny and A. Pagden (1987), pp. 15–50.

350 *boy-prince Pedro:* ibid., p. 15.

351 *until 1904:* M. Cunliffe, *In Search of America* (1991), pp. 22–38; T. J. Schlereth, "Columbia, Columbus and Columbianism," *Journal of American History,* lxxix

(1992), pp. 939–40; D. West and A. Kling, "Columbus and Columbia," *Studies in Popular Culture* (1989), pp. 45–60.

351   *intermarriage of sects:* J. Hector St. John de Crèvecoeur, *Letters from an American Farmer* (1963), pp. 61–70.

352   *mis-observation: The Works of Joel Barlow,* ed. W. K. Boltorff and A. L. Ford, 2 vols. (1970), i, p. xi; ii, pp. 138, 154–55, 245, 251.

353   *aborted with relief:* D. M. Clark, *British Opinion and the American Revolution* (1930), p. 273.

353   *"that rabble":* M. P. Costeloe, *Response to Revolution* (1986), p. 4.

353   *"rest of mankind":* E. Gibbon, *The Decline and Fall of the Roman Empire,* 6 vols. (1910), iv, p. 107.

355   *outsider's image:* S. Danforth, *Encountering the New World* (1991), p. 7; H. Honour, *The New Golden Land* (1975), plates 76–84.

356   *Tatars of the steppes:* D. Brading, op. cit., pp. 621–28.

358   *contrasting environments:* B. Keen, *La imagen azteca en el pensamiento occidental* (1984), pp. 310–14; A. del Río, *Description of the Ruins of an Ancient City Discovered near Palenque* (1822).

358   *membership in the church:* E. T. Morgan, "The Puritan Ethic and the Coming of the American Revolution," *William and Mary Quarterly,* 3rd s., xxiv (1967), pp. 3–8; C. Bonwick, *The American Revolution* (1991), p. 21.

358   *Providence plantations:* R. A. Billington et al., eds.; *The Making of American Democracy* (1950), p. 219.

359   *30 per cent:* C. M. Wiltse, *The New Nation* (1965), p. 173.

359   *moral factories:* A. de Tocqueville, *De la démocratie en Amérique,* 3 vols. (1864); C. Dickens, *American Notes and Pictures from Italy* (1957), p. 125.

359   *made perfect sense:* G. Wills, *Lincoln at Gettysburg* (1992), pp. 80, 123–33.

360   *his decision:* R. Rollins, *The Long Journey of Noah Webster* (1980), pp. 126–27.

362   *General Santa Anna:* F. Fernández-Armesto, Introduction to W. H. Prescott, *The History of the Conquest of Mexico* (1994).

362   *"rule of many":* Aristotle, *Politics,* IV, ii, p. 3; V, x, p. 30; ed. H. W. C. Davis (1905), pp. 148, 222.

362   *diminished freedom:* R. Blake, *Disraeli* (1966), p. 397.

363   *that period:* W. H. McNeill, *The Rise of the West* (1972); J. Roberts, *The Triumph of the West* (1985).

CHAPTER TWELVE: VOYAGES OF BOUNTY

PAGE

364   *had been right:* I owe this formulation of the problem, with thanks, to Professor Robert Finlay.

366   *European industries:* A. Smith, *The Wealth of Nations,* IV, vii, b. 61 (1937) p. 590; cf. L. Dermigny, *La Chine et l'occident: le commerce à Canton au XVIIIe siècle,* 3 vols. (1964), iii, p. 1442; W. P. Webb, *The Great Frontier* (1964).

366   *such treasures:* A. W. Crosby, *Ecological Imperialism* (1986), p. 215.

367   *"praised for ever":* *The Peregrination of Fernão Mendes Pinto,* tr. M. Lowery (1992), pp. 156–57.

367　*'the nightly entertainment':* F. Butterfield, *China: Alive in the Bitter Sea* (1982), pp. 39, 158–59.

368　*rate as Wales:* J. Crawford, "A Sketch of the Commercial Resources and Monetary and Mercantile System of British India" in K. N. Chaudhuri, ed., *The Economic Development of India under the East India Company, 1814–58* (1971), p. 222.

368　*hazardous to compute:* Ho Ping-Ti, *Studies on the Population of China, 1368–1953* (1959), pp. 281–82; I. C. Y. Hsiü, *The Rise of Modern China* (1990), pp. 64–65.

369　*in 1850:* F. Braudel, *Capitalism and Material Life* (1974), pp. 10–15.

369　*too glibly made:* C. Issawi, "Population and Resources in the Ottoman Empire and Iran," in T. Naff and R. Owen, eds., *Studies in Eighteenth-century Islamic History* (1977), pp. 156–57.

369　*over a quarter:* W. S. Thompson, *Population and Progress in the Far East* (1959), p. 12.

369　*in 1800:* C. Issawi, op. cit., p. 157.

369　*imported livestock:* A. W. Crosby, op. cit., pp. 146–70, 278.

371　*part of the walls:* M. Elvin, *The Pattern of the Chinese Past* (1973), pp. 242–54.

372　*earlier transmission:* M. Toussaint-Samat, *History of Food* (1992), pp. 65, 173.

372　*of Peking:* Ho Ping-Ti, op. cit., pp. 145–47, 183–87; "The Introduction of American Food Crops into China," *American Anthropologist,* lvii (1955), pp. 191–201; J. Lee, "Food Supply and Population Growth in South-west China, 1250–1850," *Journal of Asian Studies,* xli (1982); P. C. Perdue, *Exhausting the Earth: State and Peasant in Hunan, 1500–1800* (1987), pp. 114–26.

372　*of the region:* T. Naff and R. Owen, eds., *Studies in Eighteenth-century Islamic History* (1977), p. 146.

372　*Christendom's favour:* Crosby, op. cit., p. 180; W. H. McNeill, "American Food Crops in the Old World" in A. Viola and C. Margolis, eds., *Seeds of Change* (1991), p. 52; T. Stoianovich and G. C. Haupt, "Le maïs arrive dans les Balkans," *Annales,* xvii (1962), pp. 84–89; see also V. Magalhães Godinho, *Os descobrimentos e a economia mundial,* 4 vols. (1980–83), iv, pp. 23–50.

373　*rest of the world:* W. H. McNeill, op. cit., pp. 48, 50.

373　*late eighteenth century:* Ho Ping-Ti, op. cit., p. 185; "Introduction of American Food Crops," pp. 192, 196.

374　*natural tobacconist:* A. Grafton, *New Worlds, Ancient Texts: The Power of Tradition and the Shock of Discovery* (1992), p. 173.

374　*industrial processing:* H. Hobhouse, *Seeds of Change* (1985), pp. 18–29.

375　*"chocolate of Chiapa":* T. Gage, *The English-American His Travail by Sea and Land, or A New Survey of the West Indias* (1648), p. 107.

376　*hortus conclusus:* J. Amelang, *Honored Citizens of Barcelona* (1986), pp. 200–7.

378　*"whirr of wings":* M. Elvin, op. cit., pp. 271–87.

379　*"die of hunger":* T. Raychaudhuri and I. Habib, eds., *The Cambridge Economic History of India,* i (1982), pp. 262–96, 314, 460; K. Datta, *Survey of India's Social Life and Economic Conditions in the Eighteenth Century* (1978), p. 112.

379　*powdered stone:* T. Raychaudhuri and I. Habib, op. cit., p. 291; J. Fryer, *A New Account of India and Persia,* ed. W. Crooke, 2 vols. (1909–12), i, p. 284.

379　*"later invention":* C. Issawi, op. cit., p. 159.

380　*export lists:* T. Naff and R. Owen, op. cit., pp. 149, 225–29; C. Issawi, "Decline of Middle Eastern Trade" in D. S. Richards, ed., *Islam and the Trade of Asia* (1970), pp. 245–66.

381　*"ruin India completely":* K. N. Chaudhuri, op. cit., p. 235; K. Datta, op. cit., p. 154.

381 *jewels and pearls: The Writings and Speeches of Edmund Burke,* ed. P. J. Marshall, v (1981), p. 392; C. A. Bayly, ed., *The Raj* (1991), p. 28.

381 *water by hand:* M. Elvin, op. cit., pp. 298–319.

382 *products of Bengal:* C. Hamilton, *An Historical Relation of the Origins, Progress and Final Dissolution of the Government of the Rohilla Afghans in the Northern Provinces of Hindustan* (1787), p. 169; cited in C. A. Bayly, *Imperial Meridian* (1989), p. 39; cf. ibid., p. 188.

382 *"too large a share":* K. Datta, op. cit., pp. 146–48.

386 *British advance:* A. M. Davies, *Clive of India* (1939), pp. 148–231.

386 *115,000 men:* G. Parker, *The Military Revolution* (1988), p. 135.

387 *only for scrap:* ibid., pp. 128, 153.

389 *"against all":* T. Zeldin, *France, 1848–1945: Ambition and Love* (1979), pp. 63–76.

389 *industrial nation:* P. Gran, *The Islamic Roots of Capitalism* (1979).

392 *"effort and for merit": La corona de Aragón,* 7 February 1855; quoted J. Benet and C. Martí, *Barcelona a mitjan segle XIX,* 2 vols. (1976), i, p. 67.

392 *spiralling towers:* L. Lambton, *Vanishing Victoriana,* (1976), pp. 10–13, 32.

392 *Walt Disney:* P. Laslett, *The World We Have Lost* (1976), pp. 6, 161–65.

393 *in 1793:* P. Molas Ribalta, *Los gremios barceloneses del siglo XVIII* (1970), pp. 18, 83, 122–24, 392, 408; F. Fernández-Armesto, *Barcelona* (1992), pp. 132–41.

393 *company they keep:* D. Cannadine, "Cutting Classes," *New York Review of Books,* xxxix (1992), no. 21 (17 December), pp. 52–57.

CHAPTER THIRTEEN: THE CHASM SPANNED

PAGE

396 *"civil war":* P. Duignan and L. H. Gann, *The Rebirth of the West: The Americanisation of the Democratic World, 1945–58* (1992), pp. 181–82, 458–65, 644, 678–79, 707–11; E. Nolte, *Der europäische Burgerkrieg, 1917–45* (1989); the phrase "European Civil War" was coined by J. M. Keynes, *The Economic Consequences of the Peace* (1924), p. 3.

397 *eastern Europe: The Penguin Book of Twentieth-Century Speeches,* ed. B. Macarthur (1993), p. 91.

398 *deserved research:* C. Verlinden, *Les origines de la civilisation atlantique* (1966); M. Kraus, *The Atlantic Civilization: Eighteenth-century Origins* (1966).

400 *perfection of the sphere:* J. Juan and A. de Ulloa, *Voyage à l'Amérique méridionale,* 2 vols. (1753).

401 *impassable crevasse:* D. Botting, *Humboldt and the Cosmos* (1973), pp. 153–55.

403 *"go no further":* T. Cole, "Essay on American Scenery" in J. W. McCoubrey, *American Art, 1700–1960: Sources and Documents* (1965), pp. 98–110; "Correspondence between Thomas Cole and Robert Gilmor, Jnr," *Annual II: Studies on Thomas Cole, an American Romanticist* (1967), pp. 41–81; J. C. Herold, *Mistress to an Age: A Life of Madame de Staël* (1959), p. 339.

405 *of the vessel:* Charles Dickens, *American Notes and Pictures from Italy* (1957), pp. 2–3, 12.

406 *put customers off:* G. R. Taylor, *The Transportation Revolution, 1815–1860* (1951), pp. 113–14.

407　*in the 1880s:* T. J. Archdeacon, *Becoming American: An Ethnic History* (1983), pp. 33–37.

408　*"Latin, and Greek":* K. N. Conzen, *Immigrant Milwaukee, 1836–60* (1976), pp. 17–19, 45–54, 172–73.

408　*sizzling in seventeen:* T. Coleman, *Passage to America* (1972), pp. 32, 42.

408　*unpersuaded by socialism:* G. Fitzhugh, *Cannibals All or Slaves without Masters,* ed. C. Vann Woodward (1960).

408　*a Jesuit plot:* S. B. Morse, *Imminent Dangers to the Free Institutions of the United States through Foreign Immigration* (1835).

409　*"German Accent":* Coleman, op. cit., p. 228.

410　*half were Poles:* Archdeacon, op. cit., p. 113.

410　*30 per cent:* T. E. Skidmore and P. H. Smith, *Modern Latin America* (1989), p. 71.

411　*trades and professions:* D. J. Guy, *Sex and Danger in Buenos Aires* (1991), p. 16; V. Mirelman, *Jewish Buenos Aires* (1990), pp. 183–96.

411　*in a new way:* New Cambridge Modern History, xi, ed. F. H. Hinsley (1976), pp. 3–8.

411　*decades of the century:* ibid., p. 520.

412　*foreign loans:* Skidmore and Smith, op. cit., pp. 40–45.

412　*make a profit:* D. C. M. Platt, ed., *Business Imperialism, 1840–1930* (1977), pp. 93–94.

412　*covert resistance:* F. Richards, *Billy Bunter in Brazil* (1960).

412　*in foreign hands:* Platt, ed., op. cit., pp. 198–230.

413　*Porfirio Díaz:* R. Atkin, *Revolution: Mexico 1910–20* (1969), pp. 19–20.

414　*British Empire:* H.B.C. Pollard, *A Busy Time in Mexico* (1913), pp. 4, 56–61, 65–66, 140–42, 119–39, 238.

415　*shot out:* E. C. Corti, *Maximilian and Charlotte of Mexico,* 2 vols. (1928), ii, 823–24.

416　*First World War:* M. Eksteins, *Rites of Spring* (1990), pp. 326–63. I am grateful to Jim Cochrane for telling me about the reception of Lindbergh.

417　*little better:* A.J.P. Taylor, *How Wars Begin* (1979), pp. 120–22; L. Albertini, *The Origins of the War of 1914,* 3 vols. (1967), ii, 336–37, 512–13, 632–34, iii, 412–37; Z. S. Steiner, *Britain and the Origins of the First World War* (1977), p. 237.

417　*planners who conspired:* Taylor, *How Wars Begin,* pp. 100–20; L. Namier, *Vanished Supremacies* (1962), p. 99.

417　*"a crisis in industrial society":* M. Howard, *The Causes of Wars* (1984), p. 9.

419　*"our way of thinking":* A.J.P. Taylor, *The Struggle for Mastery in Europe* (1965), pp. 557–58.

419　*against Britain and France:* D. Dimbleby and D. Reynolds, *An Ocean Apart* (1988), pp. 78–79.

422　*"power among the powers":* A. E. Campbell in Hinsley, ed., op. cit., p. 693.

Chapter Fourteen: The Mirrors of Imperialism

PAGE

424　*in the background:* K. Sinclair, ed., *Oxford Illustrated History of New Zealand* (1990), p. 133.

424　*"from the bay":* T. Bracken, *Musings in Maoriland* (1890), p. 259.

425 *a seventeenth-century experiment:* W. D. McIntyre and W. J. Gardner, eds., *Speeches and Documents on New Zealand History* (1971), pp. 24–26.

425 *typhoid epidemic:* A. H. McLintock, *The History of Otago* (1949), pp. 210–49, 422–25, 473–76; *An Encyclopaedia of New Zealand,* 3 vols. (1966), i, 503–7.

425 *"a great omnibus":* H. Kingsley, *Recollections of Geoffry Hamlyn* (1910), pp. 221–22.

426 *London and Glasgow:* A. Briggs, *Victorian Cities* (1968), p. 278.

426 *anything back home:* ibid., pp. 300, 302.

427 *"growing for me":* Kingsley, op. cit., p. 439.

429 *age of imperialism:* J. M. Roberts. *The Triumph of the West* (1985), pp. 13–46, 412–31.

430 *the other with nails:* G. Prins, *The Hidden Hippopotamus* (1980), pp. 117–18.

430 *"like an elephant's trunk":* J. Harrison, *A. M. Mackay* (1896), p. 228.

430 *bloodily enough:* D. R. Headrick, *Tools of Empire* (1986), pp. 12–61.

431 *with their husbands:* E. A. Ritter, *Shaka Zulu* (1955), pp. 311–23; G. M. Theal, *History of South Africa Since 1795,* 5 vols. (1908), i, pp. 377–78.

431 *round his kraal:* D. R. Morris, *The Washing of the Spears* (1966), pp. 44, 47, 98–99, 106, 192.

431 *350 escaped:* S. Clarke, *Zululand at War* (1984), p. 122.

431 *Portuguese in 1895:* T. O. Ranger, "African Initiatives and Resistance in the Face of Partition and Conquest," *UNESCO History of Africa,* vi, ed. A. Adu Boahen (1985), p. 51.

432 *at bay for long:* J. Belich, *The New Zealand Wars* (1986), pp. 234–57.

432 *Africa in 1951:* See, for example, A.H.M. Kirk-Greene, *Principles of Native Administration in Nigeria: Select Documents, 1900–47* (1965).

432 *take the beatings:* P. Rigby, "Politics and Leadership in Ugogo," in V. Turner, ed., *Colonialism in Africa,* iii (1971), p. 401.

433 *such as Victor Hugo:* A. Arblaster, *Viva la Libertia: Politics in Opera* (1992), pp. 91–146.

436 *mountaintops:* M. B. Akpan, "Liberia and Ethiopia, 1888–1914: The Survival of Two African States," *UNESCO History of Africa,* vii, ed. A. Adu Boahen (1985), pp. 270–82; *Cambridge History of Africa,* vi, eds. R. Oliver and G. N. Sanderson (1985), pp. 645–65; H. G. Marcus, "Imperialism and Expansion in Ethiopia," in P. Duignan and L. Gann, eds., *Colonialism in Africa,* i (1969), pp. 449–53.

437 *"stock-jobbers' war":* G. M. Trevelyan, *The Life of John Bright* (1925), p. 434.

437 *"in their prayers":* P.R.O. F.O. 99/215 (12 November 1881).

437 *by his breath:* J. Mercer, *Spanish Sahara* (1976), p. 109.

439 *Britain and Germany:* N. R. Bennett, *Arab versus European: Diplomacy and War in Nineteenth-century East Central Africa* (1986), pp. 53–67, 116–84.

439 *as well as dangerous:* Ranger, loc. cit., p. 55.

439 *eventually reversed:* R. Robinson, "European Imperialism and Indigenous Reactions in British West Africa," in H. Wesseling, ed., *Expansion and Reaction* (1978), p. 146.

439 *licence trade:* J. D. Hargreaves, *Prelude to the Partition of Africa* (1963), p. 11.

439 *"keep him company":* H. M. Stanley, *The Congo and the Founding of the Free State,* 2 vols. (1885), i, 292–93; quoted T. Pakenham, *The Scramble for Africa* (1991), pp. 150–51.

440 the Perfect Lady: L. Spitzer, *The Creoles of Sierra Leone: Their Responses to Colonialism* (1975), pp. 13–25.

441 *"peace between them"*: Robinson, loc. cit., p. 153.
441 *"absurd" and "laughable"*: H. Brunschwig, "French Expansion and Local Reactions in Black Africa" in Wesseling, ed., op. cit., p. 138; T. O. Ranger, "African Reactions to the Imposition of Colonial Rule in East and Central Africa" in Duignan and Gann, eds., op. cit., i, pp. 293–321.
442 *"dusky Disraeli"*: Prins, op. cit., pp. 120, 199, 221, 235.
442 *a few huts*: H. Brunschwig, *L'Afrique noire au temps de l'empire français* (1988), pp. 120–23.
443 *and a drink*: Pakenham, op. cit., pp. 520–21.
443 *only very slowly*: M. Kilson, "The Emergent Elites of Black Africa, 1900–60," in Duignan and Gann, eds., op. cit., ii, pp. 351–98; P. C. Lloyd, *The New Elites of Tropical Africa* (1966).
445 *"old mother"*: Pakenham, op. cit., p. 464; L. H. Gan and P. Duignan, eds., *Colonialism in Africa*, i (1970), pp. 402–7.
445 *alien coffee*: E. Huxley, *The Flame Trees of Thika* (1959).
445 *"colonial towns"*: Philip Mitchell quoted in J. F. Ade Adayi, "The Continuity of African Institutions under Colonialism" in *Emerging Themes of African History*, ed. T. O. Ranger (1968), p. 191.
447 *railway in their country*: J. H. Patterson, *The Man-eaters of Tsavo and Other African Adventures* (1908), p. 21.
447 *tribal scar*: C. Miller, *The Lunatic Express* (1971), pp. 315–16.
449 *oranges, and pigs*: E. Huxley, *White Man's Country* (1968).
449 *6 feet tall*: C. Eliot, *The East Africa Protectorate* (1903), pp. 155, 160, 165–66.
449 *"anew in this land"*: F. de Janzé, quoted in J. Fox, *White Mischief* (1984), p. 33.
451 *"about the business"*: Brunschwig, "French Expansion," p. 121.

CHAPTER FIFTEEN: GRAVEYARDS OF CERTAINTY

PAGE
456 *place in nature*: A. Desmond and J. Moore, *Darwin* (1991), pp. 105, 495.
458 *British superiority*: ibid., pp. 266–67, 521–22, 652–53.
459 *conquered men*: this was the subject of A.R.D. Pagden's Carlyle Lectures of 1993 (forthcoming in print).
459 *"purity of blood"*: C. Lévi-Strauss, *The Elementary Structures of Kinship* (1969), p. 46.
459 *the Spanish crown*: A. Pagden, *The Fall of Natural Man: the American Indian and the Origins of Comparative Ethnology* (1982), pp. 58–118.
459 *inferior creation*: Desmond and Moore, op. cit., pp. 521, 535, 673.
462 *nature's power*: R.J.W. Evans, *Rudolf II and His World: A Study in Intellectual History, 1576–1612* (1984), pp. 196–274; F. Yates, *The Art of Memory* (1966), pp. 105–28.
463 *receding horizons*: D. Goodman, *Power and Penury: Government, Technology and Science in Philip II's Spain* (1988), pp. 50–65; F. Fernández-Armesto, ed., *The Times Atlas of World Exploration* (1992), pp. 162–69; J. H. Elliott, *Illusion and Disillusionment: Spain and the Indies* (1992), p. 7.
464 *sacred chronology*: R. S. Westfall, "Newton and Alchemy" in B. R. Vickers, ed., *Occult and Scientific Mentalities in the Renaissance* (1984), pp. 315–35; *The Life of Isaac Newton* (1993), pp. 110–32, 299–304.

465   *basis of matter:* R. Fox, "The Rise and Fall of Laplacian Physics," *Historical Studies in the Physical Sciences,* iv (1974), pp. 89–136.

465   *"the same bases":* C. J. Schneer, *The Search for Order* (1960), p. 293.

465   *"rest are details":* R. W. Clark, *Einstein* (1979), pp. 30–35.

467   *immobile brother:* ibid., p. 314.

468   *self-referential paradox:* D. R. Hofstadter, *Gödel, Escher, Bach* (1981), p. 17; P. I. Davis and R. Hersh, *The Mathematical Experience* (1981), pp. 162, 228.

470   *monstrous races and apes:* H. W. Janson, *Apes and Ape Lore in the Middle Ages and Renaissance* (1952), pp. 94–99; M.T. Hodgen, *Early Anthropology in the Sixteenth and Seventeenth Centuries* (1971), pp. 154–246.

471   *"mankind are human":* B. de Las Casas, *Apologética historia sumaria,* ed. E. O'Gorman, 2 vols. (1967), i, pp. 257–58.

472   *inclusive side:* W.D. Jordan, *White over Black* (1968), pp. 179–265; H. E. Pagliero, ed., *Racism in the Eighteenth Century* (1973); R. Horsman, *Race and Manifest Destiny* (1981), pp. 45–52; Janson, op. cit., p. 352.

472   *"and of man":* J. Michelet, *Histoire de France,* 17 vols. (1852–67), vii, pp. ii–iii; J. H. Elliott, "The Discovery of America and the Discovery of Man," *Proceedings of the British Academy,* lviii (1972), pp. 101–25. The next few paragraphs are adapted from F. Fernández-Armesto, *Before Columbus* (1987), pp. 223–45.

474   *"the nether world":* G. Eannes de Zurara, *Crónica de Guiné,* ed. T. de Sousa Soares, 2 vols. (1978), i, p. 107.

474   *satisfy more women:* T. Gasparrini Leporace, ed., *Le navigazioni atlantiche del veneziano Alvise da Mosto* (1966), pp. 50–54.

475   *trees and mountains: Monumenta henricina,* 15 vols. (1960–75), i, pp. 201–6; E. Armstrong, *Ronsard and the Age of Gold* (1968), plate II.

476   *almost forgotten:* F. Fernández-Armesto, *Before Columbus* (1987), p. 241.

476   *literary stereotype:* ibid., p. 245; A. de Espinosa, *Del origen y milagros de Nuestra Señora de la Candelaria,* ed. A. Cioranescu (1980), p. 35; M. R. Alonso, *El poema de Viana* (1952), pp. 311–13, 339–42; Lope de Vega, *Obras,* 15 vols. (1890–1913), xi, pp. 301ff.

477   *reverence and contempt:* F. Fernández-Armesto, *Columbus* (1991), p. 82.

477   *reports of Tenochtitlan:* E. W. Palm, "Tenochtitlán y la ciudad ideal de Dürer," *Journal de la Société des Américanistes,* n.s., xi (1951), pp. 59–66.

477   *with a past:* Pagden, Fall of Natural Man, pp. 151–200.

479   *in the New World:* A Grafton, *New Worlds, Ancient Texts* (1992), pp. 249–52.

479   *elements of civilization:* A. Pagden, *European Encounters with the New World* (1993), pp. 17–49.

481   *"what Nature taught":* H. C. Porter, *The Ignoble Savage* (1979), pp. 137–46.

481   *"we find today":* Pagden, *European Encounters,* pp. 120–26.

481   *out the light:* J. F. Bernard, *Cérémonies et coutumes religieuses des peuples idolatres,* 8 vols. (1723), vi; D. Channing Landis, *The Literature of the Encounter* (1991), pp. 54–55.

482   *"and their differences":* J. Rousseau, *The First and Second Discourses,* ed. R. D. Masters (1964), p. 211.

482   *"bury'd here":* E. S. Dodge, *Islands and Empires: Western Impact on the Pacific and East Asia* (1976), pp. 44–49; O.H.K. Spate, *The Pacific Since Magellan,* iii: *Paradise Found and Lost* (1988), pp. 237–63.

483   *or subjection:* G. W. Stocking, "Paradigmatic Traditions in the History of Anthropology," in R. C. Colby et al., eds. *Companion to the History of Modern Science*

(1990), p. 717; Horsman, op. cit., pp. 141–45; M. D. Biddis, ed., *Images of Race* (1979); C. Bolt, *Victorian Attitudes to Race* (1971).

484   *nineteenth century:* G. Stocking, ed., *The Shaping of American Anthropology, 1883–1911: A Franz Boas Reader* (1974).

CHAPTER SIXTEEN: THE STUMBLERS' ALIBIS

PAGE

486   *"Nature was silent":* E. Gibbon, *Memoirs of My Life,* ed. G. A. Bonnard (1966), p. 180.

486   *dimensions of a walk: The Letters of Edward Gibbon,* ed. J. E. Norton, 3 vols. (1956), iii, pp. 43, 295.

487   *rest of mankind:* E. Gibbon, *The Decline and Fall of the Roman Empire,* 6 vols. (1977), iv, pp. 107.

487   *ladies and gentlemen:* N. Sanson, *Atlas nouveau* (1730), title page.

487   *"original barbarism":* Gibbon, *Decline and Fall,* iv, p. 111.

488   *hallow massacres:* T. B. Macaulay, *The History of England from the Accession of James II,* 3 vols. (1867), ii, pp. 224–55, is the classic statement of such fears.

488   *Napoleonic battlefields:* H. Lachouque, *Napoléon: vingt ans de campagne* (1964), p. 140; D. J. de Larrey, *Mémoires de la chirurgie militaire,* 4 vols. (1812–17), esp. iii, pp. 39, 285–90, 419–69; iv, pp. 32–33.

490   *"imbecility and vileness":* T. L. Peacock, *The Complete Novels,* ed. D. Garnett, 2 vols. (1963), i, pp. 11–12.

490   *co-ruler of the mind:* V. Blasco Ibañez, *Los cuatro jinetes del apocalipsis* (1916); S. Freud, *Beyond the Pleasure Principle* (1920).

490   *"its arrival":* K. R. Popper, *The Open Society and Its Enemies,* 2 vols. (1947), ii, p. 72.

491   *befits a pessimist:* G. Merlio, *Oswald Spengler: témoin de son temps,* 2 vols. (1982), i, pp. 4–9.

492   *dismembering its empires:* J. M. Keynes, *The Economic Consequences of the Peace* (1924), pp. 194, 209–35; N. Coward, "Cavalcade: Portrait of the Generation" in *Plays: Three* (1990); E. M. Forster, *A Passage to India* (1957), pp. 280–82.

492   *"great alibis":* A. Césaire, *Cahiers d'un retour au pays natal* (1956), pp. 72–73; quoted G. Barraclough, *An Introduction to Contemporary History* (1967), p. 267.

495   *excretions of fear: The Complete Poems of Thomas Hardy,* ed. J. Gibson (1979), p. 538; D. Jones, *In Parenthesis* (1963), p. 54.

495   *a mental home:* P. Fussell, *The Great War and Modern Memory* (1977), pp. 64, 110, 169–70; A. Prost, *Les anciens combattants et la société française* (1990); T. Zeldin, *France, 1848–1914: Ambition and Love* (1979), p. 351; *France, 1848–1945,* 2 vols. (1977), ii, p. 836.

497   *in 1929:* F. Allen, *The Lords of Creation* (1935), pp. 350–51.

497   *investment advice:* ibid., p. 359; E. R. Ellis, *A Nation in Torment: The Great American Depression* (1970), pp. 24, 45.

498   *nervous disorder:* ibid., pp. 61, 96–97.

501   *slow and pounding:* A. Scotti, *Giuseppe Pellizza da Volpedo: il Quarto Stato* (1976).

503 *"it was building"*: W. A. Hinds, *American Communities and Co-operative Colonies* (1908), pp. 16–24; C. Wittke, *We Who Built America* (1946), pp. 339–61.

503 *real life:* D. D. Egbert, *Socialism and American Art* (1967), pp. 12–18.

504 *"not liquidating"*: A. Knight, *The Mexican Revolution,* 2 vols. (1986), i, p. 244; Ching Ping and D. Bloodworth, *The Chinese Machiavelli* (1976), p. 284.

505 *the cold war:* E. Noltke, *Geschichtsdenken in 20 Jahrhundert* (1991), pp. 143–68.

505 *Chamber of Deputies:* R. Low, *La Pasionaria* (1992), pp. 35, 46, 54, 58, 72, 91–92, 123, 148, 183.

507 *Saint Bartholomew:* G. Orwell, *Homage to Catalonia* (1938), p. 199.

509 *Spanish agenda:* V. Cunningham, ed., *The Penguin Book of Spanish Civil War Verse* (1980), p. 100.

509 *nationalistic paper:* Paul de Cassagnac, quoted in A. Cobban, *A History of Modern France,* 3 vols. (1967), iii, p. 90.

510 *"masters of the country"*: ibid., p. 54.

510 *"filthy loos"*: quoted in *The Times Magazine,* 19 March 1994.

511 *eagle-eyed:* D. A. Shannon, *The Socialist Party of America* (1975), pp. 4, 182, 264.

512 *thought so himself:* See the summary of newly released documents from the "Churchill Archive" in *The Times,* 25 November 1993.

512 *peace with Hitler:* W. Averell Harriman and E. Abel, *Special Envoy to Churchill and Stalin* (1976), p. 247.

512 *across Europe: Keesing's Contemporary Archives* (1946), p. 7770A. On the evolution of the phrase see H. Thomas, *Armed Truce: The Beginnings of the Cold War, 1945–46* (1986), pp. 504–7.

515 *level of the Nazis:* M. Bryant, ed., *The Complete Colonel Blimp* (1991), pp. 74, 173–80.

516 trahison des clercs: See also A. Bloom, *The Closing of the American Mind* (1987), pp. 69, 73–81.

518 *long survival:* G. Ionescu, *The Break-up of the Soviet Empire in Eastern Europe* (1965); A. Amalrik, *Will the Soviet Union Survive to 1984?* (1970).

518 *democratic "dissidents"*: T. Garton Ash. *We the People* (1990).

519 *back from Russia:* P. Longworth, *The Making of Eastern Europe* (1992), pp. 1–2.

CHAPTER SEVENTEEN: THE CASEBOOK OF FAILURE

PAGE

521 *"without a triumph"*: J. R. Scobie, *Buenos Aires: Plaza to Suburb, 1870–1910* (1970), pp. 186–87, 234, 244; J. Ortega y Gasset, *Obras completas* (1954), ii, p. 639.

522 *self-critical and agonized:* M. Falcoff, "Intellectual Currents" in M. Falcoff and R. H. Dolkart, eds., *Prologue to Perón* (1975), pp. 110–11.

523 *anguish of frustration:* J. E. Miguens, "Cultura de masas: un análisis del fenómeno," *Argentina, 1930–60* (1961), p. 331; M. Falcoff and A. P. Whitaker in ibid., pp. 28, 113.

524 *"face of hunger"*: G. Sosa-Pujato, "Popular Culture," ibid., pp. 141–50.

524 *value of output:* B. Sarlo, *Una modernidad periférica: Buenos Aires, 1920 y 1930* (1988), p. 13; D. Rock, *Argentina* (1987), p. 231; C. H. Waisman, *Reversal of Devel-*

opment in Argentina (1987), pp. 6–7. See M. Deas, "Argentine Adam," *London Review of Books,* viii, no. 20 (20 November 1986), pp. 17–21.

525 *Argentine produce:* C. Lewis, "Anglo-Argentine Trade, 1945–65" in D. Rock, ed., *Argentina in the Twentieth Century* (1975), p. 115; J. Fodor, "Perón's Policies for Agricultural Exports, 1946–48," ibid., pp. 149–61.

525 *1948 to 1952:* Rock, op. cit., pp. 292–301.

525 *"of the Shirtless":* J. A. Page, *Perón* (1983); Rock, op. cit., pp. 257–87, 304.

527 *loses his job:* Y. F. Rennie, *The Argentine Republic* (1945), p. 230; Falcoff and Dolkart, eds., op. cit., pp. 25, 155.

527 *Spanish vices:* ibid., pp. 27–28.

527 *by immigrants:* J. L. Maiz, *Los que mandan* (1970), p. 250; S. and P. Calvert, *Argentina: Political Culture and Instability* (1985), pp. 36, 134–67.

528 *dragon's maw:* D. Cecil, *Max* (1964), pp. 178–79; M. Beerbohm, *The Second Childhood of John Bull* (1911).

529 *by historians:* C. Barnett, *The Collapse of British Power* (1972), p. 95; A. Gamble, *Britain's Decline* (1981); M. Wiener, *English Culture and the Decline of the Industrial Spirit* (1981).

530 *preceding the war:* S. Pollard, *Britain's Prime and Britain's Decline: The British Economy, 1870–1914* (1991), pp. 194–213, 262–64.

530 *"ever known":* C. Barnett, *The Collapse of British Power* (1972), pp. 38, 95–106; P. Brendan, *Eminent Edwardians* (1979), pp. 238–48; S. de Madariaga, *Ingleses, franceses y españoles* (1946), pp. 23–33.

532 *corrupted by ease:* J.G.A. Pocock, *The Machiavellian Moment* (1975).

532 *moral pox:* A. White, *Efficiency and Empire* (1901, new ed. 1973), quoted in J. Morris, *Farewell the Trumpets* (1978), p. 100.

532 *"factory chimney":* Barnett, op. cit., p. 237.

532 *"country smithy":* *The Penguin Book of Twentieth-Century Speeches,* ed. B. Macarthur (1993), p. 337.

533 *gilt and copper:* D. M. Williams, "Bulk Trades and Development of the Port of Liverpool in the First Half of the Nineteenth Century" in V. Burton, ed., *Liverpool Shipping, Trade and Industry* (1989), pp. 10–11; T. Lane, *Liverpool: Gateway of Empire* (1987), p. 13; P. J. Waller, *Democracy and Sectarianism: A Political and Social History of Liverpool, 1868–1939* (1981), pp. 1–2, 84; W. H. Kingston, *Peter the Whaler* (1906), p. 21; L. Lambton, *Vanishing Victoriana* (1976), plates XXVII–XXXI; M. Girouard, *Victorian Pubs* (1984), pp. 231–36.

533 *material progress:* H. Ackroyd, *The Dream Palaces of Liverpool* (1987).

535 *"between the cobbles":* P. Taafe and T. Mulhearn, *Liverpool: The City that Dared to Fight* (1988), pp. 51, 82, 105–56, 203–41, 299; P. Ayers, *The Liverpool Docklands: Life and Work in Athol Street,* n.d., p. 1.

535 *of the élite:* T. Zeldin, *France, 1848–1945,* 2 vols. (1977), ii, pp. 843; R. Cobb, *A Second Identity* (1969), p. 21; E. J. Bois, *Truth on the Tragedy of France* (1940), p. 26; M. Bloch, *Strange Defeat* (1949), pp. 132–34.

536 *oral history:* H. La Rue Rufener, *Biography of a Novel: Zola's La Débacle* (1946), pp. 1–5, 26, 42–55.

536 *"gaieté française":* E. Zola, *La Débacle* (1984), pp. 338–39, 390.

536 *more horrible:* A. Corbin, *Le Village des cannibales* (1990).

537 *nearly doubled:* M. Lévy-Leboyer and F. Bourguignon, *L'Économie française au XIXe siècle* (1990), pp. 203–32; T. Zeldin, *France 1848–1945: Ambition and Love* (1979), pp. 63–76.

540 *elaborate colonnade:* F.-G. Pariset, ed., *Bordeaux au XVIIIe siècle* (1968), pp. 193–95, 201–202, 222, 332–46, 554–78, 592–616; C. Higounet, *Histoire de Bordeaux* (1980), pp. 224–25.

541 *Atlantic decline:* ibid., pp. 255–326; L. Desgraves, ed., *Bordeaux au XIXe siècle* (1969), pp. 46–48, 101, 173, 193, 204–8, 375–95; P. Butel, ed., *Histoire de la Chambre de Commerce et d'Industrie de Bordeaux* (1988), pp. 157–58, 167.

541 *north-east:* J. Boussard, *Atlas historique et culturel de la France* (1957), pp. 138–39; M. Howard, *The Franco-Prussian War* (1962), pp. 2–4.

542 *"specialised communities":* R. Stott, "Hinterland Development and Differences in Work Settings: The New York City Region, 1820–70" in W. Penack and C. E. Wright, eds., *New York and the Rise of American Capitalism* (1989), pp. 45–72.

543 *futuristic war:* J. Heffer, *Le Port de New York et le commerce extérieur américain, 1860–1900* (1986), pp. 1–3, 13–18, 355–83; M. Pachter and F. Wein, eds., *Abroad in America* (1976), p. 299.

544 *his entourage:* J. H. Mollonkopf and M. Castells, eds., *Dual City: Restructuring New York* (1991), pp. 7, 129; J. Newfield and W. Barrett, *City for Sale: Ed Koch and the Betrayal of New York* (1988), p. 20.

545 *$1.3 billion:* Mollonkopf and Castells, eds., op. cit., pp. 12, 27–28, 226, 238–39, 319.

545 *"sequence of shifts":* E. W. Soja, "Poles Apart: Urban Restructuring in New York and Los Angeles," ibid., p. 367.

CHAPTER EIGHTEEN: LIFE AFTER EMPIRES

PAGE

547 *hectares for hamburgers:* A. W. Crosby, *Ecological Imperialism* (1986); J.-P. Platteau, "The Food Crisis in Africa: A Comparative Structural Analysis" in J. Drèze and A. Sen, eds., *The Political Economy of Hunger,* 3 vols. (1990), ii, pp. 283–89.

549 *from the New World:* D. Brothwell, "The Ecological Impact of the Columbian Exchanges," forthcoming in *Proceedings of the British Academy.*

549 *America's own history:* W. R. Louis, *Imperialism at Bay: The United States and the Decolonisation of the Empire* (1976).

550 *"can survive":* P. Gerbrandy, *Indonesia* (1950), pp. 190–91, quoted in H. Grimal, *Decolonisation* (1978), p. 213.

550 *in embarrassment:* J. Morris, *Farewell the Trumpets* (1978), pp. 506–7.

550 *"wish to destroy":* V. S. Naipaul, *A Bend in the River* (1979), p. 33.

551 *"Nasser was right":* K. Kyle, *Suez* (1992), pp. 404–9; A. Nutting, *No End of a Lesson* (1967). *The Observer,* 4 November 1956.

552 *"empire exists":* G. Orwell, *England, Your England* (1953), p. 17.

552 *native middle class:* R. F. Holland, *European Decolonisation, 1918–81: An Introductory Survey* (1985), pp. 12, 48; G. Kitching, *Class and Economic Change in Kenya* (1980), p. 49.

553 *that was irrational:* R. B. Edgerton, *Mau-mau* (1990); C. R. Rosberg and J. Nottingham, *The Myth of "Mau Mau": Nationalism in Kenya* (1966), pp. 320–48.

553 *Kenyan nationalism:* F. Furedi, *The Mau Mau War in Perspective* (1989), pp. 13, 22–102.

553 *"Mikongoe tree":* J. Kenyatta, *Facing Mount Kenya* (1953), p. 323.

555 *on France:* M. Meredith, *The First Dance of Freedom* (1989), p. 371.

556 *"cultural nature":* H. Grimal, *Decolonisation* (1978), p. 256.

557 *"rule the country":* R. Trumbull, *Tin Roofs and Palm Trees: A Report on the New South Seas* (1978), pp. 27–28.

559 *own extinction:* C. Younger, *Anglo-Indians: Neglected Children of the Raj* (1987), pp. 21, 161.

560 *biggest cathedral:* Meredith, op. cit., p. 375.

560 *Sierra Leone:* S. Stevens, *What Life Has Taught Me* (1984), pp. 26–27.

560 *unserviceable debts:* J. Pickett and H. Singer, *Towards Economic Recovery in Sub-Saharan Africa* (1990), p. 13.

560 *"most of the errors":* D. K. Fieldhouse, *Black Africa, 1945–80* (1986), p. 236.

560 *per cent:* F. Idachaba, "Political Options for African Agriculture" in J. Drèze and A. Sen, eds., op. cit., ii, 197.

562 Dogs of War: R. Klitgaard, *Tropical Gangsters* (1990), pp. 7–11; M. Liniger-Goumaz, *Small Is Not Always Beautiful: The Story of Equatorial Guinea* (1988), pp. ix, 57.

563 *"bled to death":* ibid., p. 164.

563 *run for home:* Klitgaard, op. cit., pp. 19–21, 28–34, 43.

563 *post-revolutionary present:* P. Gill, *A Year in the Death of Africa: Politics, Bureaucracy and the Famine* (1986), p. 14.

563 *insoluble problems:* The phrase was used by Michael Buerk in a BBC Television News report on 23 October 1984.

563 *the year 2000:* Meredith, op. cit., p. 377.

564 *to be filmed:* Gill, op. cit., p. 1; N. Ram, "An Independent Press and Anti-Hunger Strategies: The Indian Experience" in J. Drèze and A. Sen, eds., op. cit., i, 146–89.

564 *in the 1970s:* J. Drèze, "Famine Prevention in Africa: Some Experiences and Lessons" in J. Drèze and A. Sen, eds., op. cit., ii, 129–36.

564 *Monetary Fund:* K. Savadogo and C. Wetta, "The Impact of Self-imposed Adjustment" in G. A. Cornia et al., eds., *Africa's Recovery in the 1990s* (1992).

564 *"ultimate test":* J.L.S. Abbey, "Ghana's Experience with Structural Adjustment" in J. Pickett and H. Singer, eds., *Towards Economic Recovery in Sub-Saharan Africa* (1990), p. 41.

564 *labour in 1974:* Meredith, op. cit., pp. 363–69, 370, 374.

565 *menial work:* E. Pilkington, *Beyond the Mother Country* (1988), pp. 10–11, 23.

566 *as a myth:* A. Bhat et al., eds., *Britain's Black Population* (1988), pp. 14–15; H. Tinker, *The Banyan Tree: Overseas Emigrants from India, Pakistan and Bangladesh* (1977), p. 167; *The Times,* 3 June 1993; F. Dieleman, "Multicultural Holland: Myth or Reality?" in R. King, ed., *Mass Migration in Europe: The Legacy and the Future* (1993), pp. 118–33.

566 *"in the park":* Tinker, op. cit., pp. ix, 5, 189.

566 *fear of expulsion:* S. B. Philpott, "The Monserratians" in J. L. Watson, ed., *Between Two Cultures* (1984), pp. 90–119. E. Pilkington, op. cit., pp. 10–11, 23.

566 *in the 1950s:* G. Dench, *Maltese in London: A Case-Study of the Erosion of Ethnic Consciousness* (1975), pp. 36, 47, 95, 203.

566 *as his boss:* R. Knox-Mawer, *A Case of Bananas* (1992), p. 173.

568 *departed British Empire:* H. Tinker, *A New System of Slavery* (1974), pp. 19, 367–83.

569 *from India:* J. Newel Lewis, "East Indian Influence in Caribbean Architecture" in I. I. Bahadur Singh, ed., *Indians in the Caribbean* (1987), p. 133.

570 *"in tropical Trinidad":* V. S. Naipaul, *The Middle Passage* (1962), p. 41.

570 *fraud charges:* J. S. Redding, *They Came in Chains* (1950), p. 259; E. Cronon, *Black Moses* (1948), p. 65.

571 "*'return' to Africa":* I. Duffield, "Pan-Africanism since 1940" in *Cambridge History of Africa,* viii, ed. M. Crowder (1984), 104–8.

571 *1964 to 1968:* N. Caplan, "The Consolidation of Black Consciousness" in D. Boesel and P. H. Rossi, eds., *Cities under Siege* (1971), p. 343.

571 *White Rastafarian:* S. Townsend, *The Secret Diary of Adrian Mole* (1984), p. 100.

572 "*blood and sweat":* C. E. Lincoln, *The Black Muslims in America* (1973), pp. xxiii–xxv, 14, 75–79; A. Haley, *The Autobiography of Malcolm X* (1968), p. 72.

574 *barbecue grills: A Day in the Life of California* (1988), p. 112.

574 "*pray to its saints":* C. Fuentes, *The Buried Mirror* (1992), p. 343; E. Shorris, *Latinos: A Biography of the People* (1993).

575 *and "empire preference":* A.J.P. Taylor, *Beaverbrook* (1972), pp. 826–27.

CHAPTER NINETEEN: THE MAZE OF GOD

PAGE

577 "*a sick country":* B. Alavi, "Critical Writings on the Renewal of Islam," in E. Bosworth and C. Hillebrand, eds., *Qajar Iran* (1983), p. 245.

578 "*was dismembering":* S. Farman Farmaian, *Daughter of Persia* (1992), pp. 53, 99.

578 "*Islam as bourgeois":* J. M. Landau, "Books on Islam in Russian," *Middle Eastern Studies,* xxix (1993), p. 150.

579 *political discourse:* the phrase was used by George Bush in the American presidential campaign of 1992.

579 "*men of religion":* F. Mading Deng, "War of Visions for the Nation," *Middle East Journal,* xliv (1990), p. 605.

579 *social influence:* M. H. Faghfoory, "The Ulama-State Relations in Iran, 1921–41," *International Journal of Middle Eastern Studies,* xix (1987), pp. 413–22.

579 *Shah for impiety:* Farman Farmaian, op. cit., p. 55.

580 "*on the floor":* M. Reza Pahlavi, *Mission for My Country* (1961), p. 46.

580 *he really was:* Asadollah Alam, *The Shah and I: The Confidential Diary of Iran's Royal Court* (1991).

580 "*guiding me":* Pahlavi, op. cit., pp. 29, 55.

583 *flee the country:* Farman Farmaian, op. cit., pp. 343–70.

584 *holy days:* R. V. Weekes, ed., *Muslim Peoples: a World Ethnographic Survey* (1978), p. 84.

584 *opening again:* Basil Davidson in *London Review of Books,* xv, no. 1 (7 January 1993), p. 7.

584 "*a great blessing":* H. Ram, "Islamic 'Newspeak': Language and Change in Revolutionary Iran," *Middle Eastern Studies,* xxix (1993), p. 212.

586 *strictly understood:* I. M. Lapidus, *A History of Islamic Societies* (1988).

587 *of the Prophet:* E. Siran, "Sunni Radicalism in the Middle East and the Iranian Revolution," *International Journal of Middle East Studies,* xxi (1989), pp. 1–30.

588 *his precursors:* M. Cook, "On the Origins of Wahhabism," *Journal of the Royal Asiatic Society,* 2nd s., ii (1992), pp. 191–202.

590 "*men's intelligence":* F. Rahman, "Revival and Reform in Islam," *Cambridge History of Islam,* ii, eds. P. M. Holt, A.S.K. Lambton, and B. Lewis (1970), pp. 649.

590 *video trade:* M. Haghayeghi, "Politics and Ideology in the Islamic Republic of Iran," Middle Eastern Studies, xxix (1993), pp. 36–52.

590 *as by jihad:* A. Parsons, "The Iranian Revolution," Middle East Review, xx (1988), pp. 3–8; S. T. Hunter, *Iran after Khomeini* (1992), pp. 92–100.

590 *"different ways":* M. Tarakoli-Targhi, "Refashioning Iran," *Iranian Studies,* xxiii (1990), p. 99.

591 *"with his own name":* A. Baram, *Culture, History and Ideology in the Formation of Bachtist Iran* (1991); D. M. Reid, "The Postage Stamp: A Window on Saddam Hussein's Iraq," *Middle East Journal,* xlvii (1993), p. 84.

591 *severed forearms:* A. al-Khalil, *The Monument: Art, Vulgarity and Responsibility in Iraq* (1991).

591 *respectable claim:* W. Montgomery Watt, *Islamic Fundamentalism and Modernity* (1988).

592 *lessons of the Koran:* N. Keddie, *Sayyid Jamāl al-Din 'al-Afghāni'* (1972).

594 *Islamic world:* J.-P. von Gastow, "Turquie, pays musulmans et Islam," *Revue du monde musulman et de la méditerranée,* 1 (1988), pp. 171–82.

594 *from the pulpit:* F. Ahmad, "Politics and Islam in Modern Turkey," *Middle Eastern Studies,* xxvii (1941), pp. 3–21.

594 *women's dreams:* el-Messiri, "Self-Images of Traditional Urban Women in Cairo," in *Women in the Muslim World,* ed. L. Beck and N. Keddie (1978), pp. 528, 532.

596 *"all Being":* A. El-Sadat, *In Search of Identity* (1978), p. 85.

596 *"turbaned officialdom":* P. D. Gaffney, "The Changing Voices of Islam: The Emergence of Professional Preachers in Contemporary Egypt," *The Muslim World,* lxxxi (1991), pp. 40–41.

598 *public buildings:* S. Ibrahim, "Anatomy of Egypt's Militant Islamic Groups," *International Journal of Middle East Studies,* xii (1980), pp. 423–53; "Egypt's Islamic Militants," MERIP Reports, no. 103 (February 1982), pp. 5–14; Al-Liwa al-Islami, June 1982.

Chapter Twenty: The Watchers at Dawn

PAGE

604 *kilns on deck:* M. Pachter and F. Wein, eds., *Abroad in America: Visitors to the New Nation* (1976), p. 99.

605 *"laugh of triumph":* Shuichi Kato, *A History of Japanese Literature,* 3 vols., iii (1983), p. 6.

605 *"not too difficult":* M. Jansen, ed., *Cambridge History of Japan,* v (1989), p. 438.

606 *parting gift:* ibid., pp. 13, 98, 103–6, 113; B. Tasdashi Wakabayashi, ed., *Anti-Foreignism and Western Learning in Japan* (1986).

606 *hundred years thence:* H. Ooms, *Charismatic Bureaucrat: a Political Biography of Matsudaira Sadanobu* (1975).

607 *165 authorities:* M. Jansen, op. cit., pp. 132, 144–5, 150, 156.

607 *her land:* H. Hardacre, *Kurozumikyo and the New Religions of Japan* (1986); C. Blacker, "Millenarian Aspects of New Religions" in D. Shively, ed., *Tradition and Modernisation in Japanese Culture* (1971), pp. 574–76.

608 *rebels' sleeves:* I. Morris, *The Nobility of Failure: Tragic Heroes in the History of*

Japan (1975), pp. 188–204; A. Walsall, ed., *Peasant Uprisings in Japan* (1991), pp. 202–3.

610 *"our people"*: S. Kato, op. cit., pp. 16–19; M. Jansen, op. cit., p. 322.

610 *"wise lords"*: ibid., pp. 194, 319.

610 *"nation's soul"*: B. Watson, ed., *Japanese Literature in Chinese*, 2 vols., ii (1976), p. 67.

610 *French chef*: M. Jansen, op. cit., p. 352.

611 *"tidal waves"*: P. Duus, "Whig History, Japanese Style," *Journal of Asian Studies*, xxxiii (1974), pp. 415–36.

612 *two swords*: M. Pachter and F. Wein, eds., op. cit., pp. 92–103, 134–44.

613 *"without office"*: T. C. Smith, *Native Sources of Japanese Industrialization* (1988), pp. 134, 139, 142.

613 *"whatever I pleased"*: Katsu Kokichi, *Musui's Story*, trans. and ed., T. Craig (1988), pp. xv–xvii; E. O. Reischauer, *The Japanese* (1977), p. 158.

613 *death in 1848*: L. M. Zolbrud, *Takizawa Bakin* (1967).

613 *barbershop*: M. Jansen, op. cit., pp. 10, 69–71, 124, 128, 177; D. Keene, *World Within Walls* (1976), pp. 456–69.

614 *visits to brothels*: D. Keene, *Some Japanese Portraits* (1978), p. 159.

614 *former mistress*: ibid., p. 180; D. Keene, *Dawn to the West: Fiction* (1984), pp. 77–78.

614 *claims of blood*: M. Jansen, op. cit., pp. 474–75.

614 *"think of home"*: D. Keene, *Portraits*, p. 156.

614 *"critical enquiry"*: M. Jansen, op. cit., pp. 477, 645.

615 *peasant conscripts*: I. Morris, op. cit., pp. 217–75.

616 *innovation*: K. Pyle, *The New Generation in Meiji Japan: Problems of Cultural Identity* (1969), p. 188; C.M.E. Guth, *Art, Tea and Industry: Masuda Takashi and the Mitsui Circle* (1993).

616 *lines from Shakespeare*: S. Kato, op. cit., iii, p. 113; D. Keene, *Dawn: Fiction*, p. 360.

616 *in safe hands*: B. K. Marshall, *Capitalism and Nation in Pre-war Japan: The Ideology of the Business Élite, 1860–1941* (1967); M. Jansen, op. cit., p. 39; T. C. Smith, op. cit., p. 264.

617 *"of civilization"*: M. Jansen, op. cit., p. 226; P. Duus, ed., *Cambridge History of Japan*, vi (1991), pp. 555, 570.

618 *had rebelled*: Kato, op. cit., iii, pp. 194, 208; *Journal of Japanese Studies*, i (1975); Jansen, op. cit., p. 709.

618 *conversion experience*: ibid., pp. 723, 727, 730, 753–54.

618 *had disappeared*: P. Duus, ed., op. cit., pp. 541–42.

619 *war of 1894–95*: D. and P. Warner, *The Tide at Sunrise* (1974), p. 53.

620 *births and deaths*: T. C. Smith, *Nakahara* (1977), p. 8; *Native Sources*, pp. 103–32.

620 *a share*: E. O. Reischauer, op. cit., p. 98.

621 *government's hand*: R. Storry, *The Double Patriots* (1957); S. N. Ogatai, *Defiance in Manchuria: The Making of Japanese Foreign Policy, 1931–32* (1964), pp. 3–4, 42–45, 58–73.

621 *"in the world"*: T. C. Smith, *Native Sources*, p. 144.

621 *spies and assassins*: E. H. Norman, "The Genyosha: Origins of Japanese Imperialism," *Pacific Affairs*, xvii (1944), pp. 261–84.

621 *"Britain of Asia"*: D. Sladen, *Queer Things about Japan* (1904), p. vii.

622   *South America:* Warner and Warner, op. cit., pp. 8, 74, 159, 175–76, 541; P. Duus, ed., op. cit., p. 275.

625   *"because of it":* I. Morris, op. cit., pp. 312–14.

625   *"enemy target":* ibid., p. 304.

626   *"charred rubble":* W. Manchester, *American Caesar: Douglas MacArthur* (1979), p. 465.

626   *"and the British":* ibid., pp. 464–66; E. Reischauer, op. cit., p. 105.

627   *to victimize:* W. Manchester, op. cit., pp. 454, 475–76.

628   *"into the sea":* W. Horsley and R. Buckley, *Nippon New Superpower* (1990), p. 87.

628   *seismic catastrophe:* J. Woronoff, *Japan as Anything but Number One* (1990); *The Japanese Economic Crisis* (1992); P. Hadfield, *Sixty Seconds That Will Change the World* (1991); B. Reading, *Japan: The Coming Collapse* (1992); C. Wood, *The Bubble Economy* (1992).

629   *"to the ground":* F. Utley, *Japan's Feet of Clay* (1937), p. 201.

629   *full potential:* E. O. Reischauer, *The United States and Japan* (1957); cf. the same author's *Japan Past and Present* (1964), p. 292.

Chapter Twenty-one: The Giant Awakening

PAGE

632   *emperors to heaven:* H. Trevor-Roper, *Hermit of Peking: The Hidden Life of Sir Edmund Backhouse* (1977), pp. 228–33, 243–59.

633   *eighth century:* J. K. Fairbank, ed., *The Cambridge History of China,* x (1978), p. 409.

634   *tradition was based:* ibid., pp. 410–15, 435–43; M. C. Wright, *The Last Stand of Chinese Conservatism: The T'ung-chih Restoration,* 1862–74 (1957), p. 13; Hao Chang, "The Anti-foreignist role of Wo-jen," *Papers on China,* xiv (1960), pp. 1–29.

635   *captured or sunk:* D. and P. Warner, *The Tide at Sunrise* (1975), p. 51; I.C.Y. Hsü, *The Rise of Modern China* (1990), p. 340.

635   *arts of power:* H. Trevor-Roper, op. cit., p. 255; P. S. Buck, *Imperial Woman: Story of the Last Empress of China* (1955); M. Warner, *The Dragon Empress* (1972).

636   *fled to Japan:* W. F. Hummel, "K'ang Yu-Wei," *Pacific Historical Review,* iv (1935), pp. 343–55; I.F.Y. Hsü, op. cit., pp. 361–84.

637   *spurned firearms:* ibid., p. 391.

637   *avoid criticism:* ibid., p. 411.

637   *"Chinese peasantry":* F. Butterfield, *China: Alive in the Bitter Sea* (1988), p. 331.

637   *simplified by mechanization:* H. T. Oshima, *Economic Growth in Monsoon Asia: A Comparative Survey* (1987), pp. 38–44.

638   *Disillusionment grew:* H. Acton, *Memoirs of an Aesthete* (1985), pp. 195–96, 198–99, 275, 299, 350–51.

639   *"street-mongers":* A. Miller, *Chinese Encounters* (1979), p. 199.

640   *"I will retire":* I.C.Y. Hsü, op. cit., p. 482; J. Ch'en, *Yüan Shih-kai* (1961), p. 232.

640   *"stifle their screams":* Jung Chang, *Wild Swans: Three Daughters of China* (1991), pp. 69–70.

640   *Chinese nationalism:* ibid., p. 80; I.C.Y. Hsü, op. cit., p. 641; S. I. Levine, *Anvil of Victory: The Communist Victory in Manchuria,* 1945–48 (New York, 1987), pp. 12–28.

640 *clean feet:* Siao-yu, *Mao Tse-tung and I Were Beggars* (1961), p. 122.

640 *bandit-heroes:* ibid., pp. 22–26; D. Wilson, *Mao: The People's Emperor* (1979), pp. 36, 54, 70.

641 *Chinese style:* Siao-yu, op. cit., p. 199.

641 *"understand them":* N. Khrushchev, *Khrushchev Remembers* (1971), p. 101; D. Wilson, op. cit., p. 265.

642 *"we pursue":* M. Elliott-Bateman, *Defeat in the East: The Mark of Mao Tse-tung on War* (1967), pp. 121–61; D. Wilson, op. cit., p. 132.

642 *"as never before":* ibid., p. 268.

643 *"a little later":* Zhang Xianlang, "The Story of an Old Man and a Dog" in Zhu Hong, ed., *The Chinese Western: Short Fiction from Today's China* (1988), pp. 75–99.

643 *smelting shops:* S. R. Schram, "Mao Tse-tung and the Theory of Permanent Revolution, 1958–69," *The China Quarterly,* xlvi (1971), pp. 221–44; L. T. White, *Careers in Shanghai: The Social Guidance of Personal Energies in a Developing Chinese City, 1949–66* (1978); F. C. Teiwes, *Politics and Purges in China* (1980); S. Karnow, *Mao and China: From Revolution to Revolution* (1972), p. 117; R. MacFarquhar, *The Origins of the Cultural Revolution: The Great Leap Forward* (1984).

644 *euphemism for massacre:* Jung Chang, op. cit., pp. 278–331, 371–76; J. Chen, *Inside the Cultural Revolution* (1975).

646 *tell or suppress:* A. Chan, *Children of Mao* (1985); Butterfield, op. cit., pp. 471–72.

646 *"down the Mountain":* ibid., pp. 262–63; cf. D. Bonavia, *The Chinese* (1989), pp. 40–41.

647 *"against the cold":* J. Gittings, *China Changes Face* (1990), p. 105.

647 *"no sin":* Deng Xiaoping, *Building Socialism with Chinese Characteristics* (1985), p. 62; J. Gittings, op. cit., pp. 109, 148.

647 *par excellence:* D. Bonavia, op. cit., pp. 260–71.

647 *from the cup:* Jung Chang, op. cit., p. 291.

647 *next millennium:* N. D. Krstof, "The Rise of China," *Foreign Affairs,* lxxii (1993), no. 5, pp. 59–74.

648 *broken contracts:* D. Gittings, op. cit., p. 250.

648 *"firmer foundation":* P. H. Lee, ed., *Modern Korean Literature: An Anthology* (1990), p. 15.

648 *"new principles":* A. C. Nahm, *Korea: Tradition and Transformation* (1988), p. 215.

649 *"by the neck":* ibid., pp. 218, 292.

649 *"Yes":* ibid., pp. 258, 305; P. H. Lee, ed., op. cit., pp. 80–81; C. Eckert, *Offspring of Empire* (1989)

649 *2.8 million craftsmen in the population:* H. T. Oshima, op. cit., p. 139; E. F. Vogel, *The Four Little Dragons* (1991), pp. 48–50.

649 *old dynasty:* A. C. Nahm, op. cit., pp. 476–77.

650 *eight years:* ibid., p. 511; J. Hoare and S. Pares, *Korea: An Introduction* (1988), p. 124.

651 *in his pocket:* A. C. Nahm, op. cit., pp. 485–514; Byung Nak-song, *The Rise of the Korean Economy* (1990); P. M. Kennedy, "Preparing for the Twenty-first Century: Winners and Losers," *New York Review of Books,* xl, no. 4 (11 February 1993), pp. 32, 35; P. H. Lee, ed., op. cit., pp. 169–83.

652 *burden in Asia:* H. T. Oshima, op. cit., pp. 9, 137–76.

652 *bamboo stroller:* A. Miller, op. cit., p. 249.

652   *"escalation"*: A. M. Schlesinger, Jr., *The Bitter Heritage* (1967), p. 31.

652   *admit defeat*: W. Scott Thompson and D. D. Frizell, eds., *The Lessons of Vietnam* (1977), pp. 85–93, 211–31, 263–77; M. Maclear, *The Ten Thousand Day War* (1981), pp. 224–39; T. Gitlin, "The Achievements of the War-Protest Movement" in W. Capps, ed., *The Vietnam Reader* (1991), pp. 157–67.

655   *and similarities*: E. F. Vogel, op. cit., pp. 83–112; H. T. Oshima, op. cit., pp. 3–9; R. Hofheinz and K. E. Calder, *The Eastasia Edge* (1982).

656   *traditional disciplines*: I.C.Y. Hsü, op. cit., p. 910.

656   *their ancestors*: H. Hofer, ed., *Singapore* (1991), pp. 29, 68, 76–77.

656   *neighbouring countries*: E. F. Vogel, op. cit., p. 67.

CHAPTER TWENTY-TWO: RIDERS OF THE SURF

PAGE

659   *"eat Chinese food"*: Sucheng Chan, *This Bittersweet Soil: The Chinese in Californian Agriculture, 1860–1910* (1986), p. 27.

659   *per voyage*: L. Pann, *Sons of the Yellow Emperor* (1990).

661   *"rats' urine"*: O. H. K. Spate, *The Spanish Lake* (1979), p. 47.

661   *helmets in Hawaii*: R. Langdon, *The Lost Caravel* (1975), pp. 11–23, 129, 273–77.

662   *"snow and ice"*: J. C. Beaglehole, *The Life of Captain James Cook* (1974), p. 366.

663   *"Euroamerican empires"*: O. H. K. Spate, *Paradise Found and Lost* (1988), p. 323.

664   *sense of interest*: see G. Segal, *Rethinking the Pacific* (1990). For a summary of the debate see *The Economist*, 14 September 1991, pp. 43–44. I am grateful to Ian Castello-Cortes for pointing this out.

664   *"Pacific identity"*: S. Winchester, *The Pacific* (1992), pp. 3, 5, 446.

665   *"or the commercial world"*: F. Crowley, *A Documentary History of Australia*, i (1980), pp. 10, 24.

665   *"flourish vigorously"*: G. Worgan, *Journal of a First Fleet Surgeon* (1978), p. 12. For factual information and references to sources for the next few paragraphs I am greatly indebted to Alan Frost for the use of his paper "The Planting of New South Wales: Sir Joseph Banks and the Creation of an Antipodean Europe," presented to a conference on Sir Joseph Banks at the Royal Society in April 1993.

665   *"find themselves"*: A. Frost, op. cit., p. 19.

666   *and his wife's*: F. Crowley, op. cit., p. 32.

667   *"French apple tree"*: A. Frost, op. cit., pp. 8–12, 20–22.

667   *from 1811*: H. Carter, *Sir Joseph Banks* (1988), pp. 263–64, 429.

668   *"pattern and design"*: A. D. Hope, "A Letter from Rome" quoted as the epigraph to N. Meaney, ed., *Under New Heavens: Cultural Transmissions in the Making of Australia* (1989).

668   *increase sharply*: C. A. Price, *South Europeans in Australia* (1963), p. 11.

670   *opened to "Asianization"*: A. T. Yarwood and M. J. Knowling, *Race Relations in Australia: A History* (1982), p. 290.

670   *British Museum*: R. Hughes, *The Fatal Shore: A History of the Transportation of Convicts to Australia, 1787–1868* (1987), p. 561.

671   *"full of Chinamen"*: D. Walker and J. Ingleson, "The Impact of Asia" in N. Meaney, ed., op. cit., pp. 289–92.

671 *"Our Nearest Neighbours"*: ibid., pp. 297–319, 400–401.

671 *European by heritage*: O. H. K. Spate, *Australia* (1968), pp. 292–98.

671 *"northwards"*: B. Grant, *The Australian Dilemma* (1983), p. 292.

671 *from the United Kingdom*: I. Castles, *Year Book Australia 1991* (1991), p. 274.

671 *indignation or vehemence*: see for example G. Blainey, *Reflections on the Current State of the Nation* (1991).

672 *grown to 32,500*: A. W. Crosby, *Ecological Imperialism: The Biological Expansion of Europe* (1986), pp. 228–41, 252.

672 *during the 1890s*: K. Sinclair, *A Destiny Apart: New Zealand's Search for National Identity* (1986), pp. 62–92.

673 *"end of the world"*: A. Ross, *New Zealand Aspirations in the Pacific in the Nineteenth Century* (1964), pp. 1–8.

675 *Lao-tzu in his sermons*: S. S. Frankiel, *California's Spiritual Frontiers: Religious Alternatives in Anglo-Protestantism, 1850–1900* (1988), pp. 3–17, 59–78, 92, 120.

675 *with one another*: See F. J. Turner, *The Frontier in American History* (1962).

675 *death in 1932*: J. M. Faragher, "The Frontier Trail: Rethinking Turner and Reimagining the American West," *American Historical Review*, xcviii (1993), pp. 106–17.

676 *rest of America*: D. Worster, *Nature's Economy: A History of Ecological Ideas* (1977), pp. 215–19.

676 *the frontiersmen come*: see for example C. Verlinden, *Les origines de la civilisation atlantique* (1966); *The Beginnings of Modern Colonization* (1970); A. Stella, "L'Esclavage en Andalousie à l'époque moderne," *Annales, économies, sociétés, civilisations*, xlvii (1992), pp. 35–63.

676 *guys and dolls*: R. H. Dana, *Two Years Before the Mast* (1859), appendix.

678 *"hands left free"*: R. H. Dana, *Two Years Before the Mast,* ed. J. Haskell Kemble (1964), p. 239.

679 *"even the climate"*: K. Starr, *Material Dreams* (1990), pp. 276–77.

679 *marble columns*: ibid., pp. 59, 87, 120–26; J. Walton, *Western Times and Water Wars* (1992), p. 152.

680 *"taken root"*: T. Pinney, ed., *Kipling in California* (1989), p. 50.

680 *adaptable and assimilable*: H. B. Johnson, *Discrimination against the Japanese in California: A Review of the Real Situation* (1905), p. 28; T. Iyenaga and Kenoske Sato, *Japan and the California Problem* (1921).

681 *above the mean*: H. T. Trueba et al., *Myth or Reality: Adaptive Strategies of Asian Americans in California* (1993), p. 41.

681 *in San Jose*: B. Hosokawa, *Nisei: the Quiet Americans* (1969), pp. 473–97; D. J. O'Brien and S. S. Fugita, *The Japanese American Experience* (1992), pp. 2, 102, 115–16; *A Day in the Life of California* (1988), p. 53.

681 *"going to Tokyo"*: P. Choate, *Agents of Influence* (1990), pp. xv, 109.

682 *Singapore, and Hong Kong*: K. Starr, op. cit., p. 146; J. H. Culver and J. C. Syer, *Power and Politics in California* (1988), p. 9; D. J. O'Brien and S. S. Fugita, op. cit., p. 130; S. Winchester, op. cit., p. 419.

682 *"come from Him"*: J. Barman, *The World beyond the West: A History of British Columbia* (1991), pp. 133–35.

682 *"iron chink"*: P. Yee, *Saltwater City: An Illustrated History of the Chinese in Vancouver* (1988), p. 19.

683 *firms in Hawaii*: P. Yee, "A Chinese Business in Early Vancouver" in R.A.J. McDonald and J. Barman, eds., *Vancouver Past: Essays in Social History* (1986), p. 77.

683 *dwarfed by warehouses:* J. Barman, op. cit., pp. 296–98; D. W. Holdsworth, "Cottages and Castles for Vancouver Home-seeker" in R.A.J. McDonald and J. Barman, eds., op. cit., p. 12.

683 *"new paint":* E. Carr, *The Book of Small* (1942), p. 107.

683 *unpainted headboards:* J. Barman, op. cit., p. 136.

684 *through their slits:* P. Yee, *Saltwater City,* p. 50.

684 *"taking possession":* Irene Baird, quoted in J. Barman, op. cit., p. 254.

684 *other than English:* P. Yee, *Saltwater City,* p. 141; J. Barman, op. cit., p. 334; D.

684 *first microprocessor (1971):* J. H. Culver and J. C. Syer, op. cit., p. 1.

684 *"seen California":* S. S. Frankiel, op. cit., p. 2.

685 *"sexual anarchy":* J. A. Maynard, *Venice West: The Beat Generation in California* (1991), p. 56.

687 *"will do tomorrow":* quoted in *Radio Times,* 25 September–1 October 1993, p. 42.

CHAPTER TWENTY-THREE: THE REVENGE OF THE EAST

PAGE

689 *capricious, designs:* H. D. Roberts, *A History of the Royal Pavilion, Brighton* (1939), pp. 45–53, 94–107.

689 *their ladies: Carlton House: the Past Glories of George IV's Palace* (1991), pp. 96–105.

689 *"disgusting" and "effeminate":* H. D. Roberts, op. cit., p. 110.

689 *mastery of nature:* F. Yates, *Giordano Bruno and the Hermetic Tradition in the Renaissance* (1964), pp. 27–74.

689 *new Hermes:* R. J. W. Evans, *Rudolf II and His World* (1984), pp. 212, 230.

690 *to avoid inactivity:* J. C. Herold, *Bonaparte in Egypt* (1963), pp. 2–4.

691 *mathematical section:* R. Anderson and I. Fawazy, *Egypt in 1800* (1987), p. 7.

691 *report in 1802:* V. Denon, *Voyage dans la Basse et la Haute Égypte pendant les campagnes du général Bonaparte* (Paris, 1802).

693 *public of his day:* W. and J. Halfpenny, *Chinese and Gothic Architecture Properly Ornamented* (1752); *New Designs for Chinese Temples, etc.,* 4 vols. (1750–52).

694 *"Berkshire":* N. Pevsner, *The Buildings of England: Berkshire* (1966), p. 76.

695 *parts of the subcontinent:* M. Aris, *Views of Medieval Bhutan* (1982), p. 18.

696 *spawned in Europe:* N. Edwardes, *The Nabobs at Home* (1991), pp. 34–43; T. and W. Daniell, *Oriental Scenery,* 8 vols. (1795–1808).

699 *existing house:* C. Aslet, *The Last Country Houses* (1982), p. 62.

699 *"appallingly luxurious":* M. Girouard, *The Victorian Country House* (1979), p. 27.

699 *explicit victims:* W. Scott Thompson and D. Frizell, eds., *The Lessons of Vietnam* (1977), p. 123.

701 *"dance of Shiva":* F. Capra, *The Tao of Physics* (1983), p. 11.

701 *philosophy of life:* H. Acton, *Memoirs of an Aesthete* (1970); see Chapter 21.

701 *oriental lifestyle: Country Life,* clxxxv (1991), no. 22, p. 90.

702 *coat of arms:* F. Capra, op. cit., pp. 173–75.

702 *nature of light:* A. Pais, *Niels Bohr's Times* (1991), pp. 22–23, 87–88, 230–32, 287.

707 *"ingenious gadgets":* J. L. Crammer-Byng, ed. *An Embassy to China* (1962), p. 340.

708 *particular inventions:* J. Needham. *Science and Civilisation in China* (1954– in progress), iii, pp. 448ff.

708 *maddeningly inadequate:* G. Zukav, *The Dancing Wu-Li Masters* (1979).

709 *Japanese popular tunes:* J. D. Morley, *Pictures from the Water-Trade* (1985), p. 85.

710 *spirit of the occasion:* ibid., p. 54.

710 *heroism and purity:* I. Buruma, *A Japanese Mirror* (1984), p. 147.

710 yakyu: E. Reischauer, *The Japanese* (1977), p. 395.

710 *their own uniqueness:* P. N. Dale, *The Myth of Japanese Uniqueness* (1986), p. 25.

710 *language well:* ibid., pp. 391–93.

710 *fox-god:* I. Buruma, op. cit., p. 17.

711 *refuge abroad:* J. D. Morley, op. cit., p. 244.

711 *"skins are":* I. Buruma, op. cit., p. 51.

711 *sunbathers:* P. Tasker, *Inside Japan* (1987), p. 41.

711 *Yamato Takeru:* I. Morris, *The Nobility of Failure* (1975), pp. 1–13.

711 *he is short:* I. Buruma, op. cit., pp. 143–45.

711 *notions of womanhood:* ibid., pp. 29–31.

713 *"annals of war!":* P. Tasker, op. cit., pp. 59–60.

713 *Freudian cases:* T. Doi, *The Anatomy of Dependence* (1980); P. N. Dale, op. cit., pp. 121–42, is harshly critical, but the evidence he presents is similar.

714 *American occupation:* P. Tasker, op. cit., pp. 101, 114.

715 *"opposed to Japanese":* E. Reischauer, op. cit., p. 228.

716 *"making it in Japan":* P. Staniford, *Pioneers in the Tropics: The Political Organisation of Japanese in an Immigrant Community in Brazil* (1973), pp. 12–13, 16–17, 19.

718 *stock markets:* Takatoshi Ito, *The Japanese Economy* (1992), pp. 316–21, 330–33.

719 *Mediterranean Europe:* P. Tasker, op. cit., pp. 127–28.

720 *the east:* cf. C. Wickham, "The Uniqueness of the East," *Journal of Peasant Studies,* xii (1985), pp. 166–96.

INDEX

Page numbers in *italics* refer to illustrations.

777

PICTURE CREDITS

The publishers have made every effort to contact the owners of illustrations reproduced in this book. In the few cases where they have been unsuccessful, they invite copyright holders to contact them direct.

814

Ffotograff/Lion Publishing: 292B
Foto Biblioteca Vaticana: 36
Fox/The Kobal Collection: 491
Fratelli Alinari: 159, 177
Geffreye Museum: 514
Stanley Gibbons: 591
Giraudon/Musée Condé, Chantilly: 696
John Gittings: 646
Frans Halsmuseum/Rijksdienst Beeldende
  Kunst: 400
Robert Harding Picture Library: 717
HarperCollins Publishers: 557
Illustration by R. J. Macdonald from *Billy
  Bunter in Brazil* by Frank Richards.
  Originally published 1949 by Charles
  Skilton. Facsimile edition published
  1992 by Hawk Books, London. Repro-
  duced by permission. ©1992 Una
  Hamilton-Wright: 413
Hulton Deutsch Collection: 71, 73, 87, 98,
  102, 134, 174, 175, 205, 260, 278, 284,
  292T, 426, 434, 463, 498, 501T, 502,
  520, 526T, 531, 567, 582, 589, 645, 662
The Illustrated London News Picture Li-
  brary: 548T, 548B
Image Bank/Don King: 660
Imma Julian: 508
Kean Archives, Philadelphia: 500T
The Kendall Whaling Museum, Sharon,
  Mass., USA: 244
David King Collection: 496
The Kobal Collection: 653
Kobe City Museum, Japan: 227
Korea Trade Center: 648
Kunsthistorisches Museum, Wien: 461
Kupferstichkabinett, Staatliche Museen zu
  Berlin/Preussischer Kulturbesitz: 296
The Late Chris Langlands: 450
La Trobe Collection, State Library of Victo-
  ria: 428
Robert C. Lautman: 345
Lebrecht Collection: 326
Leighton House Museum and Art Gallery:
  698T
London Express News and Feature Ser-
  vices: 551, 685
Los Angeles Times Photo: 677
Magnum Photos/Inge Morath: 651
Magnum Photos/Marilyn Silverstone: 650
The Mansell Collection: 76, 436, 438, 462,
  632
MAS: 37, 58, 264, 332, 376, 391
MAS/Biblioteca Nacional: 40
MAS/Museo Arqueológico: 38

MAS/Museo Maritimo: 179
MAS/Museo Palma de Mallorca: 161
MAS/Palacio Real: 695
The Methuen Collection, Corsham Court,
  Corsham, Wilts: 253
The Metropolitan Museum of Art, Gift of
  George Blumenthal, 1941 (41.100.157):
  61
The Metropolitan Museum of Art, The
  Cloisters Collection, 1953 (53.20.2): 180
Mirror Syndication International: 138, 140,
  370T, 395, 420
Mitchell Library, State Library of New
  South Wales/Image Library: 666
Musée Ingres de Montauban/Roumagnac
  photographie: 354
Museo Correr/Osvaldo Böhm: 167
Museo de América, Madrid: 274
Museo del Prado: 489
Special Japanese Fund Courtesy, Museum
  of Fine Arts, Boston: 32
Gift of Mrs. Maxim Karolik for the Karolik
  Collection of American Paintings,
  1815–1865. Courtesy, Museum of Fine
  Arts, Boston: 403
Museum of the History of Science: 237
Courtesy of the Director, National Army
  Museum, London: 588
National Maritime Museum, London: 483,
  697
The National Museum of Denmark, De-
  partment of Ethnography. Photogra-
  pher: Lennart Larsen: 307
National Museum Tokyo, by permission
  of the Imperial Household: 136
Courtesy National Palace Museum, Bei-
  jing: 54–55
National Palace Museum, Taiwan: 46, 47,
  706T
©1937 James Thurber. © 1965 Helen
  Thurber and Rosemary A. Thurber.
  Originally published in *The New
  Yorker:* 511
Novosti: 91, 501B
Octagon Developments: 700
Oxford County Libraries/Royal Commis-
  sion on the Historical Monuments of
  England: 466
By kind permission of the Trustees of the
  Parham Estate, West Sussex, England:
  663
Courtesy, Peabody Essex Museum, Salem,
  Mass.: 312, 405
Peabody Museum, Harvard University,